SECRETS OF THE MYSTERIOUS VALLEY

Christopher O'Brien

Other Books by Christopher O'Brien:

THE MYSTERIOUS VALLEY
ENTER THE VALLEY

SECRETS OF THE MYSTERIOUS VALLEY

Adventures Unlimited Press
Kempton, Illinois
Amsterdam, Netherlands

Secrets of the Mysterious Valley

Foreword copyright 2007
by David Perkins

First Printing
June 2007

ISBN: 1-931882-66-5
ISBN 13: 978-1-931882-66-8

Published by:
Adventures Unlimited Press
One Adventure Place
Kempton, Illinois 60946 USA
auphq@frontiernet.net

www.adventuresunlimitedpress.com
www.adventuresunlimited.nl

10 9 8 7 6 5 4 3 2

SECRETS
OF THE
MYSTERIOUS
VALLEY

Christopher O'Brien

Thanks to: David Perkins for his unsung herohood, humor, editorial savy and creative thinking, Brendon for all the journeys outside the box, Naia and Isadora for their patience, Kizzen for the *Eagle* flights, Tom and Iz for the initial data, Berle, Coshi, Don and Nellie's family, Thomas and the current SLV watchers, Pricilla, Jonnie and Van, Lynn Weldon, Jennifer for her editorial expertise and David H. Childress for suggesting we publish this book.

Dedicated to: Brendon, Eva, Frankie, Mitch, Sean, Molly, Phyllis, Laurie and the rest of my rediscovered family.

TABLE OF CONTENTS

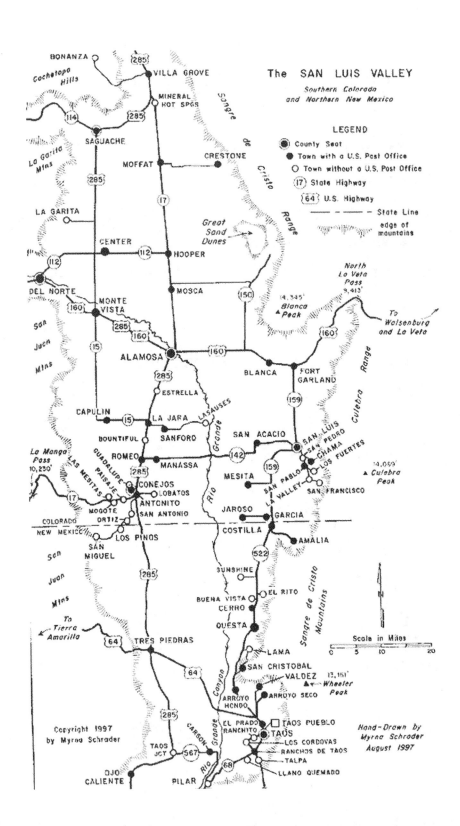

FOREWORD
by David Perkins

When we left our humble "amateur gumshoe detective," Christopher O'Brien, at the conclusion of his last book, *Enter The Valley*, he was suffering from his own personal version of shock and awe. The skies of his beloved San Luis Valley were filled with a blitzkrieg of UFOs, "military-esque" craft and anomalous lights of all shapes and sizes. Mutilated cows were literally raining from the sky and Bigfoot was running through the woods. Now a well-seasoned Chris returns to the figurative scene of the crime and, armed with "20/15 hindsight," attempts to make some sense of the quintessential nonsense.

I must admit that when I first met Chris in 1993, I was starting to get a little frustrated after spending 18 years attempting to solve the cattle mutilation mystery. Who or what was killing and carving up these thousands of animals? Mutilation, the word most frequently used by the media, never seemed to be the accurate term for what appeared to be the clean surgical removal of the animals' various organs.

And then, in my darkest hour, Chris popped into my life all bright-tailed and bushy-eyed, exuding boundless energy and enthusiasm "We can *do* this! We can solve it" he exhorted me. "Who *is* this guy?" I privately wondered, "and why is he so damned optimistic?" Chris reminds me that soon after meeting him, I said, "We will never figure this thing out." I did say that, but it was only to assess his resolve. I knew I was in it for the long haul and I'd seen plenty of flash in the pan "investigators" come and go. Too many of them had drained my time and resources.

I can now say that any doubts I had about Chris' determination and tenacity have long ago been put to rest. What strikes me first after reading this book is the prodigious effort Chris has made over the course of 15 years to document what is, without question, one of the most sustained outbreaks of pure weirdness in American history. With his steely Terminator-like relentlessness, this "naturally curious guy" has ventured into the vast uncharted waters marked "Here Be Dragons" and, whistling a tune brought us back a veritable treasure trove of precious information. He seems to have taken to heart the advice of the great philosopher Yogi Berra: "If you come to a fork in the road, take it."

As Chris brilliantly elucidates in this book, oh what a long, strange and fork-filled road it's been! Paranormal research is clearly not for everyone. The roadside is strewn with the smoldering burned out hulks of those who thought it would be easy. Some researchers we know have become permanently "destabilized." Others have sold off their libraries and moved on to more rewarding pursuits. Still others have destroyed their files in fits of frustration and/or paranoia. Many have simply faded into the woodwork, never to be heard from again. Armed with good intentions and a wicked sense of humor, Chris has managed to keep his sense of childlike wonder and avoid the obvious pitfalls of the trade. Admirably, he has not allowed himself to be crippled by paranoia although you'll see that, at times, he had good reason to be afraid, very afraid.

But let's not dwell on the hard times. There were lots of laughs, too. I still chuckle when I think of Chris, a man with no qualms about getting his hands dirty, with Vicks VapoRub-soaked tissues hanging out of his nostrils, hunched over yet another sun-baked godawful smelling carcass. The image brings back fond memories of me, standing naked on my porch after my wife Cari refused to let me in the house until I had removed my cow cadaverine-soaked clothes.

In this book, Chris mentions the stigma that goes with discussing such bizarre subjects as cattle mutilations, much less investigating them. Paranormal research is an instant one-way ticket to lowered social status. Bring up mutilations in "polite" company and you'll hear the nervous laughs and see peoples' eyes begin to roll. In small, conservative ranching communities the social stigma of having your cow mutilated can be both humiliating and frightening. Chris relates the story of an Hispanic rancher who quickly buried his mutilated cow before he arrived to investigate and then ducked his meeting with Chris. Later on the phone the nervous rancher told Chris that "the government" had hold him to bury it because it was an "environmental hazard." Chris notes that ranchers rarely bury their dead animals. In the case of another Hispanic family whose cow had been mutilated I arrived after dark, as arranged, for my interview. I found the rancher furiously at work burying the carcass with a backhoe, working by the lights of his truck. His wife intercepted me and demanded that I leave immediately. "My husband thinks this is the work of the Devil," she told me in a hushed whisper as I got into my car.

Another one of the joys of mutilation research is dealing with the skeptics. When they let fly their slings and arrows, writing books and articles detailing what a deluded fool you are, it can be somewhat demoralizing. Bashing paranormal research is easy. There is certainly no shortage of foolishness, credulity and uncritical thinking. Chris and I both know that healthy, informed skepticism is a vital part of the discovery process, but that is rarely what we get. At this juncture, Chris admits to being "more skeptical than ever" about claims of the paranormal.

For nearly 40 years, the mantra of the skeptics has been: The "mutilated" animals are the result of misidentified routine scavenger action. The ranchers who report these incidents are caught in a "delusionary spiral" brought on by hard economic times. The resulting "mass hysteria" is then fanned by the sensationalist media. For the life of me, I can't understand why these salt of the earth, no-nonsense cowmen would wake up one morning, go out into their pastures and conclude that one of their animals had been the victim of something "unnatural." These peoples' livelihood depends on their astute awareness of what goes on in the natural world.

From the comfort of their armchairs, the skeptics rely on "research by proclamation" (as ufologist Stan Friedman calls it) combined with *ad hominem* attacks and good old-fashioned ridicule. Rarely do they publish the results of any scientific investigation of so-called paranormal events. To do so they feel would only give credence to the nonsense.

An example of the skeptics' intellectual sleight of hand is arch-skeptic Joe Nickell's "investigation" of the recent mutilation wave in Argentina. Nickell is the big kahuna Senior Research Fellow for the nation's most prominent skeptical organization, the Committee for the Scientific Investigation of Claims of the Paranormal (CSICOP). Nickell's idea of scientific research was to spend a day with the local gentry on a horse ranch in the pampas. After an open-pit barbecue lunch, horseback riding and "experiencing other entertainments," Nickell talked with the head gaucho who told him that the reports of chupacabras mutilating animals in the area were nonsense. Case closed! The chupacabra is apparently a phantasmagorical animal that has been reported in primarily Latin countries for many years. According to some accounts, there have been as many as 3000 livestock mutilations since 2002 in Argentina and Chile. What is especially disingenuous about Nickell's "report" is that virtually nobody in Argentina thinks chupacabras have anything to do with the mutilations. The chupa was mentioned in a few tongue-in-cheek newspaper articles as a possible culprit. Nickell neglects to mention that a blistering UFO flap has coincided with the mutilation reports.

Sometimes the mudslinging between the skeptics and the "true believers" (as we're called) can get out of hand. In 1980 I publicly impugned the motives of an ex-FBI agent who was vociferously debunking the mutilations. I rather injudiciously told the press that I thought he was "a big moron" or something to that effect. The ex-agent blasted back that I was not to be believed about anything because I was a "known intoxicant." I was flattered. Who wouldn't want to have an intoxicating effect on those around them? This kind of stuff is just silly, but sometimes the attacks are more vicious and hurtful. Describing what he saw as the pathetic outcast status of many abductees, one skeptical commentator said: "They couldn't get the family dog to play with them even if they wore a pork chop necklace."

Another tactic of the skeptics and their running dogs in the media is to label someone "one of the black helicopter crowd." This is not a not-too-subtle code for "kooky conspiracy nut." I suppose Chris and I would both resemble that statement. The elusive and ubiquitous mystery choppers have been a part of mutilation lore since the early 1970s. Chris and I have both seen these beasties several times in the most suspicious circumstances. In this book, Chris does a meticulous job of documenting the activities of these stealthy craft, if indeed they are craft. I've heard some ranch families refer to them as "Hell copters."

As an investigator in this nervous post 9/11 world, I've noticed that it has become increasingly difficult to get witnesses to unusual events to go on record. Recently I watched a TV interview with a witness to a relatively mundane UFO sighting in the Midwest. The man didn't want his name used. His face was blurred out and this voice was modulated. Since when do UFO witnesses have to be treated like members of the Witness Protection Program? One would think the Mob was after them. Oh for the good old days when witnesses would stand outside, point at the sky and say, "I'm Dick Johnson and I seen it right over there!" It is a testament to Chris' resourcefulness and powers of persuasion that he was able to get so many witnesses, including law enforcement, to go on record for this book.

The hostility of the skeptics toward the mutilation phenomenon is understandable. What is perplexing is the attitude of the mainstream UFO research community toward the mutes and their proponents. For the most part, they have beaten us like red-headed stepchildren. Ironically, the skeptics have maintained that the UFO nuts cooked up the idea of a UFO/mutilation connection to bolster their belief in space aliens. In actuality, the major UFO organizations held the mutilations at arms length for as long as humanly possible. In their never-ending and futile search for "scientific respectability," these groups felt that the grotesque mutilations bloodied the waters of "pure" UFO research.

Recently, ufology has taken on many of the characteristics of a beleaguered cult, waiting for the fire-bombing siege to begin. Researchers with anything other to say than "UFOs are nuts-and-bolts craft manned by aliens" are subtly and systematically excluded from the most important conferences and publications. Ufologists have formed a kind of circular firing squad, engaged in continuous sniping between warring factions over points of orthodoxy.

One prominent ufologist with a cultish following once accused me of being a government agent for promoting the idea that mutilations were *not* the work of the government. According to his line of reasoning, the mutilations were being done by the government to give the kindly Space Brother aliens a bad name. In the lull between the end of the Cold War and the hostilities in the Middle East, the military was facing a dramatic decrease in funding. Public talk of a "peace dividend" was starting to make defense contractors nervous. Consequently, the military-industrial complex needed a new menace to keep fear and funding levels high. That the military might engineer a bogus alien threat is not totally implausible, but I'll need a little more evidence for the Space Brother part. Supposedly the ufologist knew all this because he had "been on the ships." End of discussion. What could I say other than "You're a big fat liar" and that seemed unproductive.

Although Chris and I have our differences, we agree on one basic point, The Extraterrestrial Hypothesis (ETH) is inadequate to explain the cattle mutilations and their attendant baffling phenomena. As Chris says, "I admit that at the beginning of my investigation… I automatically suspended my disbelief and leapt toward the extraterrestrial hypothesis." According to Chris, it only took "one whirlwind month" of investigation before "My ET-tinged thinking performed a screeching about face… the scenario was far more complex and convoluted than I had ever imagined."

In my case, it took perhaps a year. I had gone into the investigation fully believing that the government was behind the mutilations. After several months of interviewing ranchers, examining mutilated animals and reading sheriffs' reports, many of which said "a cow was mutilated and a UFO was spotted in the vicinity," I began to get an awful sinking feeling. Holy Cow! How could this possibly be??? I gradually turned the corner on the extraterrestrial idea after a series of puzzling events started my thinking in another direction. While I was researching reports of "hooded figures" near mutilation sites in several states, a cow was mutilated and hooded figures were seen cruising around my neighborhood. After finishing a long paper linking mutilations with nuclear sites, the next cow I was called out to examine had its head in a small stream which flowed down the mountain from nearby Los Alamos. Returning home from a mutilation conference, I was shocked to see a mutilated cow upside down in a shallow pond about a mile from my house. It was as if somebody was saying,

"Welcome home! Did you find what you were looking for out there?" This kind of thing continues to this day and has even come to be expected.

At the time I was forced to conclude that either I was losing my marbles, or that aliens were monitoring my every move and thought, or that I was dealing with a *reflective* phenomenon. It became evident that these events were *way* beyond meaningful coincidences. Could my own consciousness somehow be triggering these incidents? Why would space aliens travel millions of miles through the universe just to mess with my mind? It seemed clear that I was dealing with an "ideoplastic" phenomenon, something that conforms to the beliefs, needs, expectations and circumstances of the observer. Chris chronicles several cases where "alien" entities peep through peoples' windows, walk through their walls and stand around their beds watching them sleep. Have these Lords of the Universe got nothing better to do? Maybe when you get really smart you get really bored. Perhaps watching humans sleep or grass grow is comforting to them. The notion that these highly evolved space people have the time and inclination to insinuate themselves into every detail of human lives seems, shall we say, unlikely.

One of the primary reasons the UFO community has been so spectacularly unsuccessful in solving the UFO enigma is its propensity for self-censorship and intellectual dishonesty. "High strange" cases are treated as statistical anomalies. Data that doesn't fit the ETH is suppressed and neatly swept under the rug. With its emphasis on preserving the True Faith and stamping out heretical insurgencies, ufology is more akin to religion than science.

A group that briefly threatened to break this mold was the National Institute for Discovery Science (NIDS). This secretive and well-financed group boasted a roster of world-class scientific hired guns. In 2001, NIDS published a professional and thorough report on the wave of UFO/helicopters and animal mutilations which occurred in the Great Falls, Montana area between 1974 and 1977. The report carefully listed the correlations between the 192 UFO and helicopter sightings and 67 reports of animal mutilations. As a brief aside, the report mentions that NIDS files contained "over 60 other anomalies that are not presented in this report." When I saw that, I knew NIDS was cooked. They were not going to solve this mystery.

Having looked into the Montana wave extensively, I knew that these "anomalies" included reports of "a tall, hairy creature" carrying an object about the size of bale of hay with what appeared to be a piece of dark plastic flopping from the ends. In another case, two young women reported an encounter with a seven-foot tall "creature" with a face that was "dark and awful, not like a human's."

One of the young women fired a .22 rifle into the air in an attempt to frighten the critter. The beast fell down, theatrically pulled itself along the ground and then stood erect again. The women fled in a blind panic.

Since the UFO/helicopter incidents happened amid the missile silos surrounding Malmstrom Air Force Base, several documents were generated by the military due to national security concerns. I received a bundle of these documents after filing a Freedom of Information Act request in 1981. A reexamination of the Air Force and NORAD documents corroborated that "helicopters" and brightly lighted fast-moving "entities" were zipping around the area on the dates and times mentioned by NIDS. But on the other side of the NIDS coin, the government documents never once mentioned the 67 animal mutilations! Maybe *nobody* can handle The Truth.

As Chris has remarked to me many times, it's almost as if whoever or whatever is behind these phenomena purposely inserts the "giggle factor" into the mix to insure that few investigators or scientists will give them serious consideration. With no disrespect to large, hairy creatures, Bigfoot is an instant giggle factor. Chris and I both suspect that this factor may lie at the heart of the mystery rather than on it periphery. The beauty of Chris' documentation is that he records everything that happens, no matter how bizarre, frivolous or seemingly unrelated. If one of his witnesses reports "marching groups of two-foot high beings wearing keystone cop hats," I want to know about those hats. If another witness claims she was abducted by aliens, one of whom was dressed in "something like Elvis would've worn," I want to know about that cape and the gold lamé.

Chris and I agree that the animal mutilations represent something exceedingly strange and potentially of *major* importance. For both of us, the mutes remain our main focus. Lights in the sky are lights in the sky, but as far as evidence goes, a steaming thousand pound carcass is hard to ignore. We now have boatloads of data, a true embarrassment of riches, but what does it mean? Perhaps by examining a few of our differences, the reader might gain more insight and perspective into some of the issues Chris explores in this book.

After all these years, we still can't agree whether the animal deaths should be called UADs (unusual animal deaths) as Chris prefers, or animal mutilations, my preference. Chris argues that the word mutilation is a shocking and off-putting term which discourages interest by the scientific community and the public at large. I feel that the word and the act of mutilation are *meant* to be shocking. I see the mutilations, in large part, as staged or theatrical events, maybe even a form of communication. If "something" went around pulling up our rose bushes in the middle of the night, we would merely be annoyed. Apparently, "the mutilators" feel that we need to have the living bejesus scared out of us to get our attention.

It is Chris' opinion that at least some mutilation cases are perpetrated by hoaxers, vandals and copycats. Some of Chris's law enforcement sources described a few cases they had seen as "unprofessional" and "very sloppy" like "somebody tried to imitate the mutilators." It stands to reason that whoever/whatever is capable of doing the mutilations is also capable of making them appear any way they want, if confusing the investigators is an objective. From my point of view, the percentage of cases in this category approaches zero. OK, who hasn't gotten a little liquored up on a Saturday night and gone out into the local pastures to find some standing, sleeping cows and see if they could tip them over? But mutilating a cow? Risking serious prosecution, you would first have to kill the large animal (ideally) without using a gun. Then, leaving no tracks, you would have to perform a fairly delicate surgery on it in the dark without getting gored by a crazy bull, shot by an irate rancher or eaten by his dogs. It would be a bit more complex and dangerous than "tagging" a mailbox.

Another "bone of contention" for me and Chris is the percentage of cases that are the result of misidentified scavenger action. Chris puts the number at "30 maybe 40 percent." I would put the number at about 10 percent. Of course many cases are highly equivocal, making it devilishly hard to judge. I am not trying to pump up the magnitude of the true phenomenon. I base this opinion not as much on the evidence as the fact that the naturally reclusive and recalcitrant ranchers would be unlikely to call in the law and media unless they were pretty darn sure that it was "two-legged varmints" on the prowl. The ranchers see the carcasses when they are freshest. This is not "the first rodeo" for most of these folks and I tend to trust their initial observations.

A more significant difference in our viewpoints is the extent of military involvement in the mutilation scenario. Chris documents an astounding number of what are apparently military craft doing any number of unconventional maneuvers around the San Luis Valley. He feels that the likelihood of military involvement (on some level) with the mutilations is high. I admit to finding this evidence quite puzzling. Is the military doing the mutilations? Are they monitoring the situation? Are they trying to apprehend the mutilators? Are they covering for them? At one time or another, it appears that all of these options are true.

In 1997, a previously classified document was released by the CIA which might shed some light on the issue. Entitled "CIA's Role in the Study of UFOs, 1947-90," the document was compiled and written by Gerald K. Haines, a historian for the National Reconnaissance Office for an internal CIA study. Haines said that from the late 1950s, and throughout the 60s, 70s and 80s, the Air Force subtly and systematically misled the public into thinking that the "UFOs" they were reporting might be of unearthly origin. This was done to cover up the fact that the UFOs that were being reported were actually super-secret aircraft like the SR-71 Blackbird and the F-117A stealth fighter. Haines also maintained that "over half of all the UFO reports from the late 1950s through the 1960s were accounted for by manned reconnaissance flights." The Air Force refused to back up Haines' assertions. At a terse press conference, Brigadier General Ronald Sconyers said: " I cannot confirm or deny that we lied."

Besides showing how the military uses UFOs to hide its top secret projects, the report also mentions a curious fact: "During the late 1970s and 1980s... some in the Agency and in the Intelligence Community shifted their interest to studying parapsychology and psychic phenomena associated with UFO sightings." Huh? This gives credence to Chris' speculation that the military has been using the San Luis Valley as a "perfect laboratory" for testing mind control technologies, psychotronic weapons and other exotic technologies.

Knowing all of this, it is still my hunch that the military is *not* doing the mutilations and, in fact, doesn't know any more about what's behind them than we do. It is my tentative conclusion that the mutilations are beyond the capability of *any* human agency. Does the U.S. military have the capability of conducting 3000 successful missions in Argentina without a flaw? Could they pull it off for 40 years in the U.S. without a single crash or calamitous event that would lead to their apprehension? I don't think so...

The aforementioned Montana flap might provide a clue. Reports from both the government and law enforcement noted that the mystery craft were described as both UFOs and helicopters. What were described as helicopters hovered over missile silos and munitions storage areas in one of the most sensitive air spaces in North America. It's hard to believe that these lumbering helicopters could not be intercepted by state-of-the-art jet fighters based nearby. Unless... they weren't really helicopters. Chris also raises the possibility that many of the apparent military craft reported in the San Luis Valley might be "something else" cloaking itself in military garb.

So, no matter what government documents are doled out to the public, we are still mired in the same swamp of lies, cover-ups, misinformation and denials. Chris wonders if there are rogue elements in the government that have their own agendas. Maybe the right hand doesn't know what the left hand is doing. I was struck by a tidbit in the Haines report. When the *New York Times* published an article claiming the CIA was secretly involved in the study of UFOs, enraged Director Stansfield Turner harangued his senior officers: "Are we in UFOs?" You're the head of the freakin' CIA and you don't know if your agency is "in UFOs?" The general level of public mistrust in the government is summed up in a bumpersticker I've seen recently: "Don't believe anything until it has been officially denied."

While Chris feels that there may be multiple perpetrators with multiple agendas behind the mutilations, I tend to see the phenomenon as whole cloth...one "force" with one basic agenda. In his final chapter, he makes the assertion that, at its core, the mutilations are a "blood-based phenomenon." He ponders whether some ancient and elusive "predatory presence" could be at work "mocking our attempts at proving its very existence and agenda." Tracking blood-based belief systems into prehistory, he wonders if some modern version of God (or the gods) is still demanding blood. As he says, "Perhaps the power elite, the hidden control structure on our planet, has made a Faustian bargain with this ancient presence and is placating it and/or holding it at bay by conducting ritual blood sacrifice." Comparing the San Luis Valley, which sits like an altar at the apex of the continent, with the altars atop the Meso-American pyramids, Chris asks: "Could the San Luis Valley be called America's sacrificial altar?"

The history of humanity has been inextricably intertwined with blood sacrifice both animal and human. It seems the gods are always thirsty and their beverage of choice is that rich red elixir. Perhaps what was once given freely by humanity is now being forcefully taken by the blood-thirsty "deities." And you thought this stuff couldn't get any weirder.

To paraphrase biologist Lyall Watson, blood carries a greater psychic load and is richer in symbolism than any other substance. If you are what you eat, one might expect a great deal of both psychic and cellular resonance between humans and cattle. On some level this would seem to make them more vulnerable to projections from the human conscious or unconscious mind. In his summation, Chris toys with the idea of consciously created projections or "thought forms." In what he admits is a highly improbable scenario, he hypothesizes that perhaps a thought form(s) has been created by ritual adepts which somehow "got out of hand." The hypothetical thought form became too powerful to control and began demanding life essence and blood sacrifice. Chris continues, "Perhaps this theoretical thought form(s) has always existed and has been worshipped and appeased with the sacrificial offerings of warm-blooded animals...for millennia." To take this scenario to its logical conclusion in terms of the mutilations, Chris says: "It is not beyond the realm of reason that a modern form of ritualized blood sacrifice could continue today, perpetrated by a hidden group with access to military equipment and high-technology."

The concept of the thought form has long been associated with various forms of magical practice. In most descriptions of these practices, the thought form is brought into being through the focused intent of a group or individual. The thought form can then be willed to perform a specific function. According to the lore, the entity can either be malevolent or benevolent and even take on a life of its own, independent of its creator(s). Thought forms are generally thought to be complexes of energy or consciousness manifested from a combination of willpower and bioenergy. They are akin to the concept of the tulpa in the Tibetan Buddhist tradition. In Tibetan thought tulpas can also be manifested *unconsciously* and spontaneously. For obvious reasons, I have long been intrigued by the idea of something that could arise spontaneously from the individual or collective unconsciousness and have "real" effects on the physical world i.e., mutilations. Carl Jung surmised that UFOs were "materialized psychisims" emanating from the collective unconscious. In my encounters with Tibetan Buddhists I have found them to be quite sophisticated in their understanding of both the human psyche and the natural world. I began to wonder if tulpas were more than charming folklore. But why would these coherent bioenergetic aggregations wreak such sustained havoc on our cattle?

The answer might lie with the trickster, a character found in mythology world-wide. For many years, Chris and I have commented on the parallels between trickster antics in various cultures and the trickster-esque nature of the mutilations. Trickster lore is replete with tales of animal and human eviscerations, including the coring of rectums (which is frequently reported with animal mutilations.) Jung called the trickster: "God, man and animal all at once. He is both subhuman and superhuman, a bestial and divine being both superior and inferior to man." Mythology scholar, Karl Kerényi, has called the trickster "a powerful life spirit." In Jungian terms the trickster is a "root archetype," a universal image shared by all humanity. Root archetypes have been described as "amorphous concentrations of psychic energy" which can assume an endless variety of forms. This would make them at least cousins to tulpas and thought forms.

In trickster myths, the trickster (usually male) is always a vigorous force for deconstruction whose primary mission seems to be turning established hierarchies upside down. In his final chapter, Chris comments on the deconstructive and "antistructual" nature of post-modern manifestations of paranormal events, calling them "the bane of academia and bureaucratic control systems." He notes that phenomena like the mutilations create a sense of "societal impotence" in law enforcement, as if something is "toying with our social protective structure." This is what tricksters do, taunt humanity's authoritarian hierarchies and even mock our methods of investigation. Referring to both crop circles and animal mutilations, researcher Patrick Harpur has observed that they seem "tailor-made to discredit the very notion of causation itself."

In a review of George Hansen's excellent book, *The Trickster and the Paranormal* (2002) [*Magonia*, January 2003], I make the case that the shape-shifting trickster is an unrecognized force of nature, a personified (but veiled) *biological* mechanism whose function is to keep human society in "homeostasis," a vital and robust state of equilibrium. Although his actions brought cultural deconstruction, he also brought some benefit to humankind, including new skills and technologies. The trickster's "social inversions" only temporarily subvert established hierarchies. During these reversals of normal patterns, novelty and new forms of thought arise. The social order is reinvigorated, revitalized, enlivened and made more flexible. Although some scholars argue that there are no modern tricksters because they can only come to life in polytheist societies, George Hansen and I agree: "The trickster is a living thing!"

In this book Chris mentions the UFO and unusual animal death "memes." The new science of memetics offers us an extraordinarily useful tool for understanding unexplained phenomena. Biologist Richard Dawkins coined the term in his seminal book *The Selfish Gene* (1976) to describe "units of cultural information" that are passed on from person to person by imitation. As examples, Dawkins mentioned: tunes, catch phrases, beliefs, clothing fashions, ways of making pots or of building arches. Memes were thought to drive cultural evolution analogous to the way genes drive biological evolution.

The extraterrestrial (ET) meme probably originated in Greece during the fifth century BC with the idea of "the plurality of inhabited worlds." According to this democratic concept, people like us were thought to inhabit worlds like ours in other parts of the universe. The ET meme is not to be confused with the God (or gods) meme which originated much further back in humanity's archaic past. The ET meme simmered along for over 2000 years passing from brain to brain. The advent of science fiction in the late 1800s served to reinforce the ET meme. H.G. Wells' 1898 novel *War of the Worlds* introduced the alien meme which quickly latched onto the ET meme to form a meme complex or memeplex. A memeplex is a cooperative or symbiotic set of memes which increases the replication chances of the individual memes.

During the 20th century, the voracious fledgling ET/alien memeplex gradually incorporated the memes for flying saucers, alien abductions, animal mutilations and crop circles (as well as such "mini-memes" as alien implants, missing time and UFO healings.) The resulting super memeplex, one of the most successful in human cultural history, has unprecedented vitality considering that there is not one shred of unequivocal evidence that *any* form of life exists elsewhere in the universe.

In her book *The Meme Machine* (1999), Susan Blackmore argues that the dramatic increase in human brain size which began in our ancestors about two and a half million years ago took place to make us better meme carriers. Blackmore is one of the researchers I mentioned previously who threw away her paranormal files in disgust. According to Blackmore, the modern human brain has a volume of about 1350 cubic centimeters, which is roughly three times the size of contemporary apes of comparable body size. The question of why we have a brain "surplus to requirements and adaptive needs" has vexed evolutionists since the time of Darwin and Alfred Russel Wallace. Darwin's contemporary, Wallace, independently discovered the principle of natural selection and reasoned that supernatural intervention was responsible for our oversized brain. Some modern ufologists speculate that the brain's Big Bang was the result of interventionist tinkering by aliens, presumably to make humans more amenable to their purposes.

Blackmore's most interesting assertion in considering gene-meme coevolution is that, besides driving cultural evolution, the memes have now gained the upper hand, and have begun to drive physical evolution. The memetic pressure for larger brain size was but the first example of this major turning point. If the memes are now driving both cultural and biological evolution, what does that tell us about the role of the new engorged ET memeplex?

Chris' detailed examination of how reports of paranormal events are disseminated through the culture is a textbook example of how memes propagate. He comments that "something" seems to be engaged in "mythologic engineering" in the San Luis Valley and elsewhere. I propose that the ET memeplex is molding and conditioning the culture to become a space-faring civilization. The memes have created a belief system and, indeed, have engineered a new mythology which gives the idea of spreading our memes *and* genes throughout the universe an aura of inevitability.

Programs like SETI (the Search for Extraterrestrial Intelligence) and NASA's space program have drawn enormous vision and energy from the new mythology even if they don't fully recognize it. The ET meme has thrived for 2500 years because, somewhere in our biological unconscious, we have known that we must spread out the gene/meme pool or risk losing it all to a single life-ending event. In Darwinistic terms, this process is called a "species survival strategy," but one that works on an *unconscious* level. It makes Chris squirm when I say this, but in a sense, it doesn't matter if animal mutilations are "real" or not as long as the ET memeplex has the desired effect on cultural evolution, and therefore on biological survival strategies.

Now that we have unleashed the thought forms, tulpas, tricksters and super memplexes, we should add one last piece to The Big Picture — Gaia itself. The Gaia Hypothesis was formulated in the 1960s by independent research scientist Dr. James Lovelock. Named after the Greek goddess of the Earth, Gaia theory, in its strongest form, asserts that the entire Earth is a single unified organism with a biosphere that consciously manipulates the climate to create the most optimal conditions for life. This life-sustaining planetary homeostasis has been maintained within very narrow margins since the "life era" began some two and a half billion years ago. Even though the sun's luminosity has increased roughly 30 percent during this period, such important factors as average temperature, ocean salinity and oxygen levels have remained remarkably stable.

After Lovelock's theory was published in the 1970s, the scientific community spent a great deal of time skirmishing over whether Gaia was "conscious" or "aware" or "purposeful" or "sentient." Mainstream scientists attacked the theory on the grounds that it smacked of mysticism and "teleology" (the belief that all things have a predetermined purpose or goals of self-realization.) While New Age "tree-huggers" heartily supported the theory, the Christian right blasted it as "non-Christian ecological Satanism." In hopes of gaining scientific acceptance for his theory, Lovelock has been forced to tone down some of his earlier rhetoric. In recent years he has stressed the "provisional" nature of the theory and has said: "In no way do I see Gaia as a sentient being, a surrogate God."

Under the rubric of philosophical naturalism, the scientific community spent a great deal of the 20th century systematically denying the existence of purpose in nature, so it was predictably enraged by a theory that seemed "anti-human" and hinted at the possibility of "design," "intention" or divine guidance. Hard-core evolutionists argued that evolution was a strictly random process with no "goals" involved. The prevailing scientific consensus might best be illustrated by Nobel Prize-winning physicist Steven Weinberg's statement that "the more the universe seems comprehensible, the more it also seems pointless." Steve baby, you're a great physicist, but you really should get out more often.

The battle over Gaian terminology is significant. Taking a step back, how is "nature" defined? According to the *New Oxford American Dictionary*, nature is "the phenomena of the physical world collectively, including plants, animals, the landscape, and other features and products of the earth, as opposed to humans or human creations." Aha! Here's the root of the problem, codified into the language. In my opinion mankind has now *become* a force of nature. The idea that we are somehow apart or "opposed" to nature is perhaps the primary cause of our current ecological crisis. Our lofty "above nature" attitude is exemplified by the fact that we have the hubris to call our species *Homo sapiens sapiens* (man, the wise, the wise.) We're so smart that we found it necessary to say it twice, just in case somebody missed the first wise.

For most scientists the idea of a sentient Gaia is like the elephant in the room, there is a tacit agreement to not mention it. Gaia theory has otherwise proven to be a sturdy, viable and accurate model for earth system science. The situation is similar to that in quantum physics where the standard interpretation is that consciousness literally creates reality. "Nothing exists until it is measured," as Niels Bohr put it. Yet most physicists think it's preposterous to believe that a spoon could be bent with mental energy. Again, scientists are willing to overlook the elephant because quantum physics has become such a consistent and reliable model of the sub-atomic world.

Understandably, discussing "manifestations" in relationship to phenomena like animal mutilations and UFOs makes some people uneasy with its connotations of supernaturalism or spooky voodoo. The idea of "materialized psychisms" also left Jung with a case of philosophical vertigo. As he said, entertaining the notion "opens a bottomless void under our feet." In his fascinating book *The Secret Life of Inanimate Objects* (1990) Lyall Watson relates the details of his visit to CERN, the nuclear research facility in Switzerland. One scientist actually used the term "manifestations" to describe the new particles they were discovering and wondered if some of them could be "made manifest only in retrospect, like the memory of a dream." Another scientist pondered whether "we may be creating precisely that which we seek to find." Clearly, reality isn't what it used to be.

In this book Chris takes a hard look at the environmental damage caused both directly and indirectly by the ranching industry. According to Lovelock, the biggest threats to Gaia are "the three Cs—cows, cars and chainsaws." Besides nudging us out of the nest to fly into space, perhaps Gaia is focusing our unconscious hostilities toward the destructive beasts into a symbolic act which expresses her distaste for hamburgers. If Gaia encompasses all aspects of all life on the planet, this would by definition include both the conscious and unconscious minds of humans. That would give her a pretty big toolbox. It's elementary my dear Watson. It is Gaia that has the means, motive and opportunity to commit the "crime."

I intuitively feel that Gaia *is* a sentient being! There I've said it and wrecked my career. Gaia's teleological goal and purpose might be as modest as that of a human being who wakes up in the morning with the goal of staying alive another day. As for those "neo-pagan cultists" who the scientists love to disparage for enthusiastically embracing the Gaia concept; just because someone loves and respects their nurturing mother, does that make them a member of a "mother cult?"

I predict we'll be hearing a lot more about Gaia theory in the coming years. As the clock ticks on the global warming issue, we will be forced to take a much closer look at Gaia's finely tuned control mechanisms. Biologist Lynn Margulis, the co-author of the Gaia Hypothesis, has said that we must carry the knowledge and lessons of Gaia with us into space if we are to become part of the future "supercosm," the "hypothetical continued expansion of life from Earth into the solar system and beyond." Maybe there *is* a teleological reason for existence besides simply staying alive. Perhaps the universe will not be complete until it is conscious of itself. As physicist Eric Chaisson puts it in his book *The Life Era* (1987): "life's purpose and meaning, its *raison d'être* [is] to act as an animated conduit for the Universe's self-reflection." Whatever.

I am not the first researcher to propose a biology-based approach to so-called paranormal phenomena. In 1931, the great Charles Fort, the chronicler of all things weird and the father of "Fortean Studies," predicted that "someday there may be organic science or the interpretation of all phenomenal things in terms of an organism that comprises all." Writer/researcher Jacques Vallee has speculated that UFOs are somehow intended to lead human consciousness to new concepts of reality. "[UFOs] are part of the environment, part of the control system for human evolution." Even the physics community may be wandering off the reservation in regard to these matters. Charles Townes, Nobel-winning physicist and co-inventor of the laser, has said that discoveries of physics "seem to reflect intelligence at work in natural law."

Dr. J. Allen Hynek, arguably the most preeminent figure in the history of ufology, once confided to protégé Jerry Clark, that after decades of UFO research, he had come to the conclusion that "elementals" were behind the UFO phenomenon. Elementals are a type of life force or nature spirit who are generally viewed as benevolent creatures who maintain the harmony of nature. Like many old-school "scientific ufologists'" Hynek was uneasy with the advent of the abductees and their fantastic stories. It should be noted that the most prevalent theme in alleged alien/human interactions is the boiler-plate scolding lecture from the aliens that humans are destroying the earth.

Psychotropic research pioneer, Terence McKenna once said that "the transformation of humanity into a space-faring, perhaps time-faring, race is on a biological scale, the great goal of history." Not long before he died, Terence told me: "I'm so resistant to anything paranormal. I just hate it. I will crush it." This rather out of character comment surely reflected his frustration that his research had been largely shunned by the scientific community. In his mind, combining paranormal research with psychedelic studies "would be like adding an albatross to an anchor." This stuff does take its toll.

In the early 1990s I traveled to England to look into the crop circle phenomenon. Oddly enough, the crop circles are about the only "paranormal" phenomena that *don't* show up in Chris' beleaguered San Luis Valley. When I arrived in England, my British counterparts were positively aglow with the latest wave of crop formations. The most common descriptions used terms like awe-inspiring, artistically and aesthetically pleasing and spiritually uplifting. When I mentioned my mutilation research, I was told in serene tones: "Why do you chose to dwell on the dark side? Step into the light. We [the British] are a spiritually evolved people with a highly developed appreciation for art and beauty. You Americans are a mean, violent and bloody people. You get the phenomena you deserve." As the Roman poet Virgil said: "We make our destinies by our choice of gods." For me and Chris, perhaps "the gods" made our destinies by their choice of us. It's still too soon to tell.

There is more than one way to skin a cow, as they say. What I've tried to do here by presenting the "unrecognized forces of nature" approach is to establish another theoretical framework within which to view these unexplained phenomena. At least my theory incorporates *all* the evidence. Although I may have colored outside the lines a wee bit, I have not resorted to magical thinking, mysticism, metaphysics, conspiracy theory or the possibility of intervention by divine, supernatural or extraterrestrial forces. I've been accused of "reductionism" and criticized both for driving magic out of the world and injecting magic into the world. So maybe I've cancelled myself out and my magic quotient is now zero. No matter, for me the bottom line is still—biology.

Well, Alllllllrighty then! I've solved the mystery. Where do I pick up the reward money and my Nobel prize? What's next?

As Chris said recently, hopefully this foreword will encourage the reader to approach this tricky material without excessively "front-loaded preconceptions." I've tried to give you a feel for the mine-filled terrain of paranormal events that Chris tiptoes through in the following pages. I've spent enough time in these surreal fields to know that what he has accomplished here is not that easy.

This has been a long and whining road for us, complete with circling buzzards and a lot of cattle blood under the bridge. I've come to regard Chris as more than a friend, maybe something more like a "person of interest," or an "unindicted co-conspirator." After these many years, I can truthfully say that, of all the paranormal researchers I have known, Christopher O'Brien is one of them. Don't worry, I know he can take a joke because he told me he could. Don't let the jolly Zen exterior fool you. After reading this book you will see that this guy means business. He has a mind like a steel whatchamacallit. With his calm and reassuring investigative bedside manner, he could have played a doctor on TV. But he's not all Mr. Nice Guy. He knows how to play bad cop and worse cop when necessary. No matter what form of adversity is thrown at him, he shrugs his shoulders and says: "It goes with the territory." I think Chris has more than a little trickster blood in his veins. Why else would he seem to thrive on chaos?

For the skeptics who might accuse Chris of being a "mystery monger," I say balderdash! You don't get rich in this business. It's more like black hole that will hoover in any amount of resources that you throw at it. As he has said, "You can't be a faker or poser or it [the phenomena] will kick your butt and you won't last long." Although he says in this book, "I never hoped to solve these riddles," I think some small part of us feels that we can do what's never been done. There's got to be something to keep you going when pure personal curiosity falters.

Secrets of the Mysterious Valley is a monument to one man's perseverance or maybe just sheer stubborn orneriness. At any rate, I am eternally grateful for Chris' informed insights and strenuous data mining. He has certainly earned the right to have an opinion and the reader would be well advised to listen closely to what he has to say.

So…that's my story, your honor, and I'm sticking to it. If anyone has a better idea, let me know. Otherwise, enjoy this brain-rattling book (if enjoy is the right word.) I do hope that you all find what *you* are looking for.

David Perkins
Santa Fe,
New Mexico
April 1, 2007

CHAPTER ZERO:
Author's Notes

In nineteen ninety-three, I began investigating real-time reports of unexplained San Luis Valley (SLV), Colorado reports and researching the rich, impressive history of weird events that have been reported in this unique, remote region of the American Southwest. In the process of investigating these hundreds of claims of the unusual, at the risk of sounding presumptuous, I have amassed a potentially-important database of weirdness that suggests that the SLV may be an important, possibly pivotal, petri dish of the inexplicable, the unknown.

Secrets of the Mysterious Valley is a blow-by-blow account of my 1992 to 2006 investigative process, and although a dramatic decrease in reports in 2002 (and other pursuits) drew me away from the SLV, I have maintained a network of skywatchers, contacts and law-enforcement sources keeping me up-to-speed when unusual events are reported. As you will see, as I write this in late 2006, the activity in the SLV appears to be on the upswing.

Prior to my arrival in this mysterious valley on the roof of North America, knowledge of past activity had not traveled out into the mainstream of the culture. In this modern age of instant communication, local knowledge of inexplicable events echo around the San Luis Valley and, as in other "Hot-spot" regions, word of these events seldom ventures outside local communities' that experience unexplained activity. Experiencer's and witnesses' quiet descriptions to friends and family slowly filter into the local population with the details subtly shaded or lost as the stories are told and re-told. Small town papers occasionally hint that these unexplained events are occurring if reporters are assigned to the story. Mostly accounts are recounted at family-gatherings, picnics, the post-office over the back-yard fence and out in the grocery-store parking lot as knowledge of these events are slowly disseminated around the community.

Rumors of isolated high-strange events are generally ignored by the mainstream American media. Without confirmation from at least two additional sources, the events dissolve into history's trash bin and western culture-at-large is kept unaware of what the small-town papers suggest is occurring. Local knowledge of these unexplained events percolates within the region's population, but only if the events reach flap levels over a short period of time will regional media outlets become aware of the apparent activity. Occasionally, they dispatch reporters to investigate and begin to communicate word of these events to the culture at-large. At first these news stories mock the accounts but, if the events continue, photographs or video have been taken, a more serious tone is adopted and instead of the disingenuous, end-of-the-broadcast "little green men", or feeble "alien" jokes, witnesses are interviewed and local investigators are featured.

As a result of my investigations documenting the relentless, six-year wave of unexplained activity between 1993 and 1999 and the resulting coverage by mainstream media, the San Luis Valley is now considered to be America's #1 per capita UFO Hot-spot. The scientific community, whether they like it or not, are slowly becoming aware that the San Luis Valley and other Hot-spot regions are worthy of careful scientific study. Of course, professing a professional interest in these subjects is still considered to be a bad career decision but, finally, these questions surrounding the validity and reality of paranormal events are beginning to attract world-class, mainstream scientific scrutiny. Hot-spot areas of the world appear to feature unusual geophysical properties that may somehow be connected to the higher than normal incidence of unusual events and this could potentially provide a viable scientific rationale for investigating these regions' unexplained activity.

These remote regions are also a sociologist's gold-mine yet little work has been done to study those who live in these locations and experience these events. I sometimes wonder if the experiencers are more important than the details of what they experience. Although some publicly acknowledged efforts by scientists have been mounted in an effort to investigate location-specific "paranormal" events, mainstream science's apparent lack of interest is more than puzzling to me, and their continuing public indifference studying these intriguing mysteries is disingenuous at best—at worst, it may be indicate a cover-up.

Is it possible that the government/military industrial complex has already forged ahead, decades ago, in an effort to define and study the enigmatic physical properties that appear to be a work in these locales? Is it possible that they have solved these scientific riddles and are actively utilizing these region's properties for unknown agendas? This is a question that has not been adequately addressed by the paranormal research and investigation crowd too busy with Roswell and other red-herring cases.

There may also be a connection between these current unexplained events occurring in Hot-spot areas and the ageless indigenous tradition of sacredness, or a tradition of special-ness that may extend back hundreds, if not thousands, of years in time. Proto-scientific and sub-cultural examination of these traditions may help explain the true nature of what is manifesting today in these remote areas, but how does one investigate and explore something so timeless and inexplicable? When I began my amateur investigation, I didn't have a clue, but over time (and with the help of several experts and a lot of research) I was able to devise a fairly effective approach to documenting these events.

Complicating our recipe and my suspicions further, most, if not all, of these forgotten Hot-spot corners of North America (mostly found in the Southwest) have a nearby governmental/military presence that appears to be interested in expanding its presence further into the areas that experience these "paranormal" events. I have strongly contended for years that many reports of unusual aerial phenomena are misidentified military activity and this apparent military presence in and around the San Luis Valley muddies the investigative waters, rendering the job of investigating more difficult.

Hot-spot regions are unique in that they seem to be magnets for reports of paranormal events, but unfortunately, any attempt to define what constitutes a truly "paranormal" event is wrought with perilous philosophic and scientific challenges, lack of hard-data and is beyond the scope of my (admittedly) amateur investigation and research project in the San Luis Valley, Colorado. I have done my best to document and corroborate these claims and I will attempt to analyze the trends that these events suggest are occurring.

At the risk of sounding location-centric, after years of extensive research and investigation I suspect that the SLV may be America's most anomalous region. This is a rather bold statement, but to my knowledge, no other locale has a comparable variety and intensity of documented unusual phenomena. Of course, having spent almost fifteen years investigating this magical place, I might be a bit prejudiced, but as my "Event Log" of documented activity attests, I do have the ammunition to back-up this arguable conclusion.

At the beginning my investigation, in the early nineteen-nineties, I admit, like many closet "buffs" interested in these types of phenomenal events, I automatically suspended my disbelief and leapt toward the "extraterrestrial hypothesis" (ETH). I very quickly realized this approach was untenable. Today, in the twenty-first century, we continue to be programmed by culture to assume that these reports are due to "ETs" flitting around our airspace in high-tech aerial vehicles. Isn't it interesting that western culture has become bombarded with images of aliens? To some, these are of angelic beings fighting evil reptoids, to others, this activity is a hoped-for salvation dressed as a new messiah; ET space-brothers here to solve all our problems and save us from ourselves. I can understand this emotional, pop-culture rationale and wishful thinking but I don't support either of these premises. There appears to be something infinitely more complex at work.

A case in point: I suspect that the disturbing phenomenon referred to by the media as "cattle mutilations" could be an important clue to the nature and reality of so-called paranormal phenomena. Public awareness of this scourge began in September 1967 with the "Snippy the Horse" case that occurred here in the San Luis and this mystery, if truly involving "ETs", has proven most perplexing, throwing a monkey-wrench into the benevolent space-brother scenario. Interviewing baffled county sheriffs and the angry ranchers whose livestock continue to be targeted by the shadowy cattle surgeons, a pattern has begun to emerge. Most believe these cattle deaths were being perpetrated "by the government" but when you examine the Snippy case, the horses' owner, Nelly Lewis' assertion that "Flying saucers killed my horse" still fascinates a segment of ufology. When I initially began investigating mutilation cases it was a no-brainer, these events were probably due to extra-terrestrial intelligences and I figured that people need to know what is going on. But after a whirlwind month of investigation and research, my thinking performed a screeching about face. The scenario was more complex and convoluted than I imagined. I realized other players may also be involved.

My first two mysterious valley books are filled with hundreds of investigative and journalistic reports of the unexplained and hundreds of witnesses (including law-enforcement, ex-military, scientists and trained observers) have been quoted on-the-record. Over the years, I have researched and compiled San Luis Valley data from every qualified source I could uncover. This is not an easy process and I realize today in 2006 that the further I venture back into the history of this magical region, the more enigmatic and compelling the data, facts, stories, legends and tradiions I have uncovered about the region become. After a love/loathe relationship with this process that spans back to 1989, today in Sedona, I have begun to interpret this mountain of data I have amassed. Where appropriate, I've attempted to put this compilation of my investigative process into some sort of context, but ten years later, twenty/twenty hindsight can only provide us with a distorted veneer of insight into the events myself and others experienced. I now realize that the qualitative insights of true understanding combine the unfolding "now" with this compilation of data from the "past".

How does one reconcile what could be described as witnesses' front-loading? Many witnesses were convinced their experiences were due to aliens, some, the military, others said their experiences were due to witches or other paranormal phantasmal characters. A few predictably descended into the closet of complete denial. How does an investigator differentiate between all these possible explanations? The simple answer is: you don't. I feel we owe it to ourselves to use our powers of observation as best we can and make informed decisions. Unfortunately, this sounds good on paper, but when you are experiencing the unusual in real-time, objective analysis tends to be difficult. A few frustrated readers pointed out that my books were short on analysis attempting to define and explain the true nature of these bewildering events. I take this criticism as a compliment. It made sense to me at the time to present the facts as pristinely as possible, let the phenomena speak for themselves, through the witnesses' perspective, but write everything down, keep my opinions to a minimum and present unadorned primary data. I felt I owed it to my readers to stick as close to the facts as possible and let the events and accounts define themselves.

Over the years, I have attempted to put these events into some sort of rudimentary cultural sub-context, but truthfully, at the time, I was so overwhelmed by the waves of apparent activity it was all I could do to simply log the events and attempt to interview as many witnesses as possible. So, as an aspiring "proto-scientist", I chose this *laisse' fare* approach: I understand that garbage in/garbage out data alone can't overwhelm the mystery, but in its purest form, these facts can provide what is necessary for others more knowledgeable than I to conduct a detailed analysis at a later date.

After fifteen long years of investigation and research into these perplexing events I can assure you I am no closer to definitive answers than I was back when I started, however, my thinking has subtly changed in regards to the causal elements hidden inside, above, alongside the witnesses to events I've investigated and researched. I may not have any firm answers but I do have my suspicions—many of which I will share with you in this book.

Much of my thinking today revolves around the importance of focused investigation of so-called Hot-spot areas and whether modern science agrees with me, or not, is unimportant; I will continue to believe that these magical regions may be our lynch-pin of discovery and my work in the San Luis Valley is a small contribution toward a time in the future when data may finally solve these wondrous, last remaining mysteries of the twenty-first century.

—Christopher O'Brien

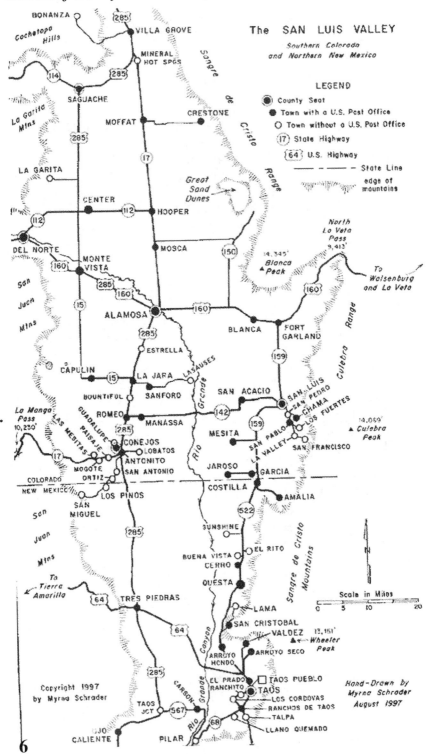

CHAPTER ONE:
Discovering the Mysterious Valley

The Fall of the Summer of Love

Imagine the excitement of a bright-eyed, inquisitive ten-year-old – fidgeting while standing in line with his mom at Safeway—when his eyes behold something fantastically beyond belief staring out from a magazine rack, something beyond mundane human understanding. I remember thinking back then in the Fall of 1967, as that bug-eyed ten-year-old, I have to convince my mom to buy this World News-type rag with the lurid headline, "Fly-saucers Killed My Horse"! The headline adorned a cover photograph of three people inspecting the remains of the horribly mutilated corpse of a horse named "Snippy," located somewhere in the high-mountain wilds of south-central Colorado. Sometimes, even a motivated ten-year-old can move mountains and I was able to convince my mom to buy the paper trumpeting the sensational claim. Even as a little kid, I recognized that in the after-glow of the summer of love, the events of the Snippy case potentially cast a foreboding shadow over the cultural glow and boy, was I ready to read all about it! The article was fairly well-researched and I remember thinking, it *must* be true, only aliens could possibly have done something so horrific to that poor animal.

This was my introduction to the mysterious San Luis Valley (SLV) in October 1967 and the death of Snippy, forty-years later, remains one of the most enigmatic and controversial so-called paranormal events in modern history.

In 1989, before moving to Crestone, in the south-central Colorado mountains surrounding the SLV, I wasn't aware that hundreds of unexplained phenomenal events had been reported in the region. I knew about the area's most celebrated incident; the "Snippy the Horse" controversy, considered to be the world's first unusual animal death (UAD). As a result of this case, the SLV is considered to be the publicized birthplace of the unusual livestock mutilation phenomenon. In the twenty-first century, Snippy the Horse has become an icon, a thing of legend. After years of official denial and thousands of alleged reports world-wide, the livestock "mutilation" phenomenon, at its core, still defies explanation. I will cover the highly complex and confusing mutilation phenomenon in detail later.

So why should the Snippy Case be considered important? This is a justifiable question. There are a handful of key, paradigm-shifting occurrences that recalibrate cultural perception of unexplained, "paranormal" events and introduce new ufological memes into the equation. Snippy joins Fatima, Kenneth Arnold's sighting, Roswell, the abductions of Betty and Barney Hill, Travis Walton's missing time and 1997's Phoenix Lights as a pivotal event in culture. What sets the Snippy Case apart is that for the first time, a disturbing blood-based element was introduced into the equation.

Could it be that beef-eating humans have developed a cultural blind spot? In what could be described as one of the more intriguing examples of what could be called cultural denial, is the subject of humankind's ancient, incestuous relationship with cattle and how it is connected to the unidentified flying object (UFO) mystery. Whether we care to admit it or not, bovines— worshipped and utilized as a food source for thousands of years—are the most detrimental life-form on the planet besides humans and beef will probably be outlawed as a source of food protein in the not-too-distant future.

Are there deep-rooted, ancient forces and agendas at work warning us about cattle; the second-most detrimental life-form on planet Earth, beside humans? The Snippy Case introduced the UFO into the "cattle mutilation" equation and could be into Western Culture and I sense that this pivotal event performed on the altar of North America, should be interpreted as a shot across the bow of beef-eating humans. I will cover this theory in depth later in the book. Global warming, land-use, desertification, water pollution

Peripheral to the Snippy case were the hundreds of UFO sightings that allegedly occurred during that eventful fall of 1967 through 1969 in the SLV, which inexorably linked the Appaloosa's mysterious death with the UFO phenomenon. This link between these unexplained livestock deaths and UFOs, whether accurate or not, has existed ever since.

Snippy the Horse

First some background on the Snippy Case and the principals involved: The Urraca pioneers settled the western slope of the San Luis Valley's Blanca Massif in the late 1870s, and one of those hardy Morman pioneer families were the Kings. The King family owned a two-thousand-acre cattle ranch and homestead that extended down from the foot of the Sangres out onto the valley floor. The upper portion of the ranch contained a small cabin at the original homestead site and the main ranch house, corral and pasture land was located three miles away in the valley. A windswept, arid area nicknamed Rancho Chico, the lower King Ranch sat on the drainage of Zapata and Urraca Creek on some of the meadows visited by prehistoric man in the Americas. Ten miles to the north sits the world's highest sand dune desert, the mysterious Great Sand Dunes National Park.

Eighty-five-year-old widow Agnes King was the King Family matriarch and she lived at the ranch with her two sons, Harry and Ben, and a daughter named Nellie. Ben King was a self-styled mountain man who could identify every animal and plant in the San Luis Valley and name every creek that flowed down the western slope of the Sangres. Ben's older brother Harry was the King Ranch boss, running the livestock and tending to the ranch's daily affairs. Nellie, married to Iowa native Berle Lewis, lived with her husband in the cabin on the upper ranch property. The Kings were a hard-working cattle family, putting in long hours, sun up to sun down in one of the valley's most breathtakingly picturesque areas.

This much is known about the filly named Lady dubbed by the press as "Snippy the Horse." It was a blustery morning, September 8, 1967, and Harry noticed that only two of their three horses were outside waiting for water. Thinking this was unusual, he headed out into the morning glow to find her. He immediately sensed something was wrong for Lady, Nellie's Appaloosa filly, was nowhere to be found.

After waiting until the following morning for her to show up, a concerned Harry went searching for the missing horse. After an hour, he spotted something lying in a meadow a quarter-mile north of the main ranch house which raised the hair on his neck. Lady's corpse was missing all the tissue from her shoulders to the tip of her nose, the exposed bones glistening, bleached white, like they had "been in the sun for thirty years."

The fated animal lay on its left side, facing east in a damp meadow; it had rained several days before and the ground was still soft and muddy in places. Harry determined that the three horses had been running full speed and Lady had been "cut from the herd" then veered away from the other two, who continued on toward the house. Lady's tracks continued for several hundred yards, by King's estimate, where they inexplicably stopped in full gallop.

The "official" story diverges at this point into two distinct versions. Version one is supported by several newspaper articles, Coral Lorenzen's *Fate* magazine article and Berle Lewis' account. It says the tracks ended at full gallop and the carcass was found

9

over one-hundred feet farther along the meadow. Version two, supported by several other articles and Don Richmond's original Aerial Phenomenon Research Organization (APRO) investigation, stated that the tracks went in a tight circle several times, like something was circling around the horse, and that the corpse was found twenty-to-thirty feet away from Lady's circling tracks.

A careful examination of the area, on September 16, 1967, by Nellie, Harry, Berle and friends found what appeared to be four burned areas in the ground at four, nine, thirteen and twenty-one feet away from the carcass to the northwest. Like an upside-down question-mark, eight burned areas in the ground were found to the southeast ranging forty to fifty feet from the body. Five "giant horse tracks" measuring eighteen inch wide by eight inches deep were found in the chico bushes near the body.

A University of Colorado investigation was included in the now-famous "Condon Report," undertaken for the Air Force's Project Blue Book in October. The report claimed the burnt areas were probably a black fungus called black alkali that is found in highly alkaline areas such as the San Luis Valley and that the "giant horse tracks" were more than likely old horse tracks made in the mud, which had hardened.

After a week or so had passed, Nellie finally called Alamosa County Sheriff Ben Phillips to report the strange demise of her three-year-old horse. Phillips branded the horse's death a "lightning strike" and didn't bother to drive out to the scene to investigate. He later admitted that it was odd that the horse had no evidence of burn marks usually associated with a lightning strike.

Nellie, however, was convinced that something highly irregular had happened to her horse. She was aware of the several UFO sightings in the weeks prior to her horse's demise and she and Berle, and close friends, had experienced sightings that previous spring. She was convinced there was a connection.

On September 23, 1967, two weeks after the horse was discovered, Nellie was aided by US Forest Service employee Duane Martin. Martin borrowed a Geiger-counter from a local civil defense unit, and checked the area for increased levels of radiation. He received, in his determination, heightened radiation readings near the flattened chico bushes and burn marks. The readings decreased as he approached the carcass. Increased levels of radiation were also detected on Berle's boots.

Later, questions were raised of Martin's proficiency with the Geiger counter and he admitted that he had only operated the equipment in an indoor training session. He had never operated the detection equipment in the field and there is no reference, in any of the numerous articles about the Snippy incident, of Martin taking any control readings away from the mutilation site. Without a control reading, determining accurate radiation levels at a site is impossible.

The Lewis' were initially reluctant to go public with the story. Inevitably, during the first three weeks after the discovery, word spread locally about the truly mysterious and unusual animal death. Curious locals began showing up at the site and, initially, Harry tried to confine the visitors to a small area near the body to maintain the integrity of the scene, but as word got out, the crowds of visitors become more and more difficult to corral.

At the end of the first week of October, Nellie's longtime friend Pearl Mellon Nicholas, society editor for the *Valley Courier*, let word of the strange death of the horse out of the proverbial barn. During the following four weeks, the Snippy the Horse story spread from the local to the regional, national and international newspaper press. As an inquisitive ten-year-old, I was always on the look-out for claims of unusual events and this was the time period when I first became aware of the case.

It is important to remember that a curious element of modern ufological mythos was created (or miss-created) as the facts of the Snippy Case subtly twisted in the wind of dissemination. The San Luis Valley's apparent corresponding UFO activity lent a 'guilt by association' scenario and the inexorable linking of UADs with UFOs that October of 1967. This link, whether accurate or not, has endured ever since.

People of the press, by their very nature, can be careless and lazy. Even Coral Lorenzen of the well-respected Aerial Phenomenon Research Organization (APRO) mixed up several important facts in her May 1968 *Fate* magazine article. Crucial elements, like the horse's gender and name got mixed up, jumbled up and turned around. During my research, I wondered how basic facts could become so screwed up. The process of discerning reality from any subtle form of chaos is daunting and I had to continually check and cross-check each article against the others. As the discrepancies piled up, I wondered if anyone could ever weed out the misinformation in the controversy.

The facts were so irregular, maybe they were altered by design? It appears to this investigator/researcher that a blatant process of creating misinformation may have been at work that October, which continues today, forty years later. As a result, whether you like it or not, Snippy has become a part of our cultural mythos. Maybe the stranger events that occur through time, and subsequently become a part of the mythic tradition, are somehow impacted by a veil of unconscious cultural uncertainty around the events. One thing I can tell you with confidence: this case changed my life forever.

Secrets of the Mysterious Valley

The research community is so gun-shy that they swept the crucial misnaming of the horse under the rug and have tried over the years to discredit the whole subject.

The times, they were a-changin' back in late 1967, I was a young Beatles fan with Peter Max posters on the wall, but that brooding fall day reminded my young, impressionable mind that the times weren't all flower power and groovy. I devoured the Snippy article in the back seat of the 1948 Volkswagon camper van before we arrived home and I wondered what it would be like to visit the San Luis Valley, the site of Snippy the Horse and the killer UFOs.

Dreams of a Child

Looking back at my childhood, there are several more strange events that forever altered my view of our consensus reality. One incident that occurred while I was very young still puzzles me after all these years. It was around 1964, I had just turned seven and Ann, one of my older sisters had moved out of the house. I had just moved up into her vacated upstairs bedroom with my six-year-old brother Brendon. We shared a built in bunk-bed on the east wall of the room. Which had a four by five foot window on the northern side that overlooked the backyard. I had the top bunk. I remember awaking one night to an intermittent rattling noise. I opened my eyes and immediately noticed a fluorescent light-green glow faintly bathing the room from a light source that seemed to be coming from outside, toward the front of the house. I still heard the rattling noises, and looking down, I was amazed to see the two drawers in the bed stand next to the bottom bunk bed, floating in and out of the drawer openings. For some reason, this didn't seem strange to me. The green-colored glow seemed to be coming from the downstairs windows in the living room, which were magnificent sixteen foot high picture windows presenting a breathtaking view of the entire downtown Seattle skyline, out across Lake Washington.

I tip toed down the upstairs hallway, and then down the four steps into the front door entrance foyer and peered out toward the front of the house. I will never forget the image. I saw to the southwest, there was a uniform overcast sky as far as I could see, about ten to twelve miles. The Seattle skyline was bathed in its customary incandescent glow, but I noticed the cloud cover about halfway across the lake pulsing the weird green color. Suddenly, like magic, first one, then two perfect discs mushroomed down through the cloud layer and began to head directly toward the water, curving to the east, directly in my direction. Disturbed clouds even trailed after them as they broke through the cloud layer and headed down toward the water. I remember being transfixed—then nothing!

12

It was instantly morning. The experience stands alone, out of context, in my childhood. I don't even remember much of what happened around that particular time period in my life as a first-grader at Medina Elementary.

I told my brother about this "dream" experience in 1988 and the hair stood up on his arms as I described the green saucer-shapes bursting down through the clouds and heading across the lake. He broke out in a visible shiver and said, "Of course that was YOU!" I asked him what he meant. He told me, he had the exact same dream as a kid, but he thought he was watching himself looking out the window. "I thought it was me standing there. Remember, we had those blue and white striped pajamas when we were little? That was YOU!" I still don't know what to make of this apparent shared "dream" experience. This particular lucid dream, if that's what it was, is also etched deeply in my memory.

Brendon and I have talked at length about other shared dreams and episodes we didn't know we both experienced as kids. Childhood and the formation of the important building blocks of experience is a magical time. A child's wonder, every breathing second. The thrill of discovery. The elongation of time. That relaxed moment in the summer sun with the radio on that seemed to last forever...

Certain 'magical" childhood experiences may be examples of what author Colin Wilson called, ". . . a kind of three dimensional consciousness, contrasting with the ordinary two-dimensional humdrum consciousness."

Western culture seems to be devolving out of this three-dimensional consciousness. As we grow, and inevitably acquire layer upon layer of experience, we seem to lose this childlike innocence. Wilson suspects this fresh, child-like three-dimensional perception of reality may be an important key to understanding our vast potential as sentient beings.

Wilson's interviewer stated in an *Atlantis Rising* magazine article: "Wilson believes that we are on the threshold of a time when we will be able to find the kind of balance between modern rational thought and the ancient intuitive knowledge that will enable us 'to become masters of peak experience.'

He intuits that this imprinted innocence may be a clue to help us understand legendary megalithic cultures that lived tens of thousands of years ago in harmony with themselves and their environment; until entropy and/or a cataclysm destroyed their "golden age."

I'm not sure about golden ages, but I am unwilling to simply discount my magical, unexplainable childhood experiences as the wanderings of a young, impressionable mind in the sixties. I was a very bright child and during several memorable, unexplained events I instantly realized that these experiences were outside of the cultural norm. The memory of these experiences still provide me with an important, personal context against which I bounce all of my subsequent experiences. But, having said this, as I become older (and hopefully wiser), I feel compelled not to react to any experience in a way that compromises, or adversely affects, my objectivity. I could try, like many people, to convince myself that these events never happen, or that these events aren't important, but I choose to be as fully present as possible.

Back Home for a Visit

After growing up in Medina, Washington, during the wild and wooly 1960sand early 1970s, right out of high-school, I moved to New York City in the spring of 1975 after high-school graduation to attend Lehman College and I spent fourteen years back east before moving out to the semi-arid San Luis Valley in 1989.

Several incidents from my twelve years in New York stand out as peculiar and were instrumental in the development of my deeper interest in the "paranormal." I experienced key events that I cannot explain away as simple mundane experiences. Two in particular, come to mind. They occurred three months after I left Washington State for NYC. I had relocated to Riverdale, NY to attend Lehman College and moved in with my sister Molly and brother-in-law, Joe Cody.

In August, 1975, me, Molly, Joe and my new three-month-old nephew, Kevin, took off in Joe's Volkswagon van to head across the country to introduce their new arrival to our family. We spent several days on Whidbey Island at my parents' summer house in the San Juan Islands. One of the first things I did upon arriving back in Washington was look up my high school sweetheart who pleaded with me to stay and not return to NYC. It was hard to tell her I was returning back east — I hadn't even thought about staying behind. Moving to the Big Apple hadn't been easy; returning proved to be just as difficult.

I also reconnected with several of my high school buddies who also expressed a wish that I stay on the West Coast and not return to New York. The day after we arrived on Whidbey, I remember getting the flu and being sequestered in a guest bedroom —fighting a chill I couldn't shake, bundled under a pile of blankets. My mother (who was quite an amazing, insightful woman —way ahead of her time) suggested with a smile that I read a book she had recently finished. I forget the title, but it was a scientific examination of what would happen to Western Washington if a nine-point or larger sized earthquake should impact the region. The book presented a detailed projection that suggested an event of this kind would be catastrophic to the area and I read several sobering chapters before falling into a fitful sleep. An hour or so later, I was shaken awake by an earthquake! The synchronicity was impressive and my mother just smiled her secret, knowing smile and I pondered my decision to return to the East Coast.

Several days later, I had firmly resolved to leave the temperate rainforest environment where I was raised and return back east to school. In late August 1975, I found myself negotiating a crucial intersection in my life process. We loaded up the van and headed south to Aberdeen, WA to visit our grandfather, who had recently suffered a debilitating stroke, and was in a nursing home living out his final days. On one side of his bed were stacks of books he was getting ready to read, and on the other side was the impressive stack of books he'd already finished. The young, nubile nurse, with a very short skirt, turned the pages while Pappy devoured page after page after page. It was the last time Molly and I ever saw him.

The four of us spent a couple of hours with him before saying our goodbyes and heading south toward Portland, OR, where I made a left turn and drove the van east along the Columbia River. I made it about one hundred miles upriver before stopping for the night at a KOA Campground, tired from the long, eventful day. We unpacked, I pitched my little square-roofed pup tent, grabbed a snack and then climbed into the tent only to toss and turn while I tried to go to sleep.

The difficult decision to return to New York weighed heavily on my eighteen-year-old mind and, fully awake, I began to imagine instead of heading back east, what would have happened if I had made the choice to stay in Washington State. I had left my girlfriend behind and she had pleaded for me to stay. The unfolding what-if events that swirled through my mind quickly took on a life of their own. In the quiet, meditative state I had descended into, I remember being absolutely amazed at the lucidity of the events as they unfolded. Whole chains of events ebbed and flowed on a strange kind of auto pilot. I met new people, got married, changed careers, raised children and at one point, I found my middle-aged self walking slowly alone down a beautiful Puget Sound beach. I saw something laying up ahead on the beach. I walked over and it was a children's sand bucket, sitting at the water's edge. I walked over and stood over the little pail and slowly looked down into the bucket.

I'll never forget the sensation that I next experienced. It was as if my eyes had fallen out of my head and landed in the bottom of the bucket that had a thin layer of sand on the bottom. My eyes saw the regular pattern of square-ish sand particles, but something about the pattern appeared to be too uniform. I can't fully describe the sensation when I realized I wasn't looking at grains of sand, my eyes were somehow pressed against the square weave of the tent fabric three feet above my head on the pillow! Some part of my awareness was pressed up against the ceiling of the tent. As I slowly melted upward through the tent I could see the glorious sky as it opened up above me. I felt like I had astral-projected outside of my body. The shock of this realization slammed me back into my body with an audible whoosh that literally forced all the air out of my lungs. I evidently had made a noise that was loud enough that it woke my sister. She called out to me to see if I was alright. Molly and Joe were about twenty-five or thirty feet away in their own tent and she said later the next morning I made had a sound like I had been slammed onto the ground. I found this passage from *Hunt for the Skinwalker* by Colm Kelleher and George Knapp that sums up my existential angst at the time:

> Have you ever wondered what your life would be like if you had gone to a different school, accepted a different job, married a different person? In the multiverse, all of those other things have happened, or are happening, and each of those individual alternatives has millions of its own parallel realities, different from the others by nearly the immeasurable factor of a single atom or quantum.

What had I experienced? Had I truly "astral-projected"? Or had I somehow gained access to a parallel me, in some other quantum reality that a part of me was experiencing in some other quantum multiverse? I remember, during the movie-like part of the experience, hearing nearby cars on the highway and my brother-in-law snoring in their tent nearby. I also remember being absolutely convinced I hadn't been asleep and dreaming.

My First UFO Sighting

In 1979, I lived in a basement apartment in the Bronx, a few blocks away from Lehman College, with a roommate, a philosophy major named Gustavo. Gus and I and the gang of students we hung-out with, were '70s seekers interested in all kinds of esoteric subject matter and pursuits. My fascination with the paranormal and the occult found me devouring countless books on many hidden subjects and checking out various schools of so-called secret knowledge. One day in early spring, while reading a hard-to-find

16

book called *Weird America* by Jim Brandon, I was reminded of the strange death of Snippy the Horse and the many UFO sightings reported in the SLV during the mid-to-late 1960s. This book, a county-by-county, state-by-state listing of anomalous areas in the United States, led me on a 26,000 mile expedition around North America with trickster buddy photographer Fritz Kleiner. We made a point of placing the SLV on our meandering journey out west and we almost made it to the SLV, but a fierce spring snowstorm dissuaded us from heading up to the 7.500-foot high valley, as I found out later was the world's largest alpine valley.

September 21, 1979, New Paltz, New York. College town, Upstate. Six after returning to NYC, Brendon, myself and our girlfriends headed north from the Big Apple to visit several friends at the college and attended a Gentle Giant concert. Since the mid-1970s, English Art-Rock had fascinated me. Bands like Genesis, Pink Floyd, Yes and Emerson, Lake and Palmer constantly graced my turntable. Gentle Giant, one of the more "out there" bands, even by progressive standards, was one of my favorites. What other band could go from a heavy-metal band, to an a cappella group, to a chamber ensemble all in the space of one song? Then, switch instruments with each other for the next song?

What a show! The crowd was mesmerized by the band's kaleidoscopic performance and I remember being a bit puzzled by the drummer's questionable stand-up comic routine, featuring off-the-wall "hemorrhoid" jokes. The show ended with a rousing finale, and our group of six friends, ranging in age between eighteen through twenty-two, headed rambunctiously down the hill to sky-watch in the center of the New Paltz athletic field, before car-pooling to a party outside of town.

Always a country boy at heart it was nice to get out of the city, with its gross light pollution, breathe the fresh air and really see the glorious sky. I laid down on my back with my hands behind my head and basked in the starlight, picking out constellations and planets. I was the one who noticed the group of objects first. Five orange points of light, high up, straight overhead, seemed to drift in the sky pretending to be stars. They were definitely 1+ magnitude in brightness and about the size of Mars. I watched for several seconds to make sure my eyes weren't playing tricks on me. Sure enough, they were moving. As soon as I realized this, they stopped, then dimmed slightly. They were hiding. I felt sure for some reason, they had responded to my awareness of them.

Without taking my eyes off them, I casually mentioned the objects to the group, who initially paid no attention. They were too busy horsing around. Finally, my brother Brendon looked up long enough to confirm what I was describing, and the rest of the group began to watch.

The lights just milled around for several minutes with no discernible pattern to their movement. Brendon suggested we attempt to communicate with them. At first, everyone laughed, but we were able to convince the group to lay on the field while Brendon traced out geometric shapes out of our line of sight behind us. We watched the objects closely. First, he traced out a square. I stood in the middle to verify. Sure enough, the lights quickly arranged themselves into a square. I gave a running monologue. "Yep, now the one on the right is moving closer to the one on the left, while Mr. Lower left is heading toward Mrs. Lower right—we have a square." You get the picture.

Next, Brendon traced out a circle. The objects obliged him and formed a circle high in the sky. I was watching, when someone asked rhetorically, "I wonder why they don't come closer." Someone exclaimed "LOOK!" The objects appeared to rush downward towards us as they became larger and brighter. Someone else said "No, not that close," and they slowly appeared to stop and then slowly regain altitude. This brought out oohs and aahhs from the group. Brendon quickly traced out a triangle. Again, the lights responded in kind. It seemed we were communicating with these unidentified lights in the sky. I suggested that Brendon try tracing out three wavy lines, a play on the parapsychology test-card. A sixth light approached and joined the original five and we stayed on the field for a while longer watching the objects drift around and, like typical kids, I'm embarrassed to say, *we got bored and went to the party!* I quizzed everyone the following day about our shared experience, and no one thought it had been a big deal. "Yeah, that was kinda cool man, playing with the UFOs…" Years later, I found out that it was during that same Fall 1979 time period that Whitley Strieber claimed he had amazing alien visitation experiences at his nearby New Paltz cabin – just a few miles from the college where we had our group experience.

A Night in the Desert

After twelve years in New York City, I was ready to move on to greener, more serene pastures. I had been the director of visual merchandizing for the oldest electronics retailer in the world for seven years, while I negotiated the soft, white underbelly of the New York music scene. I had immersed myself into the music business after re-learning the keyboard and acquiring an rudimentary expertise in analog synthesizer programming. But the hectic lifestyle and mindless entertainment industry hacks left me wanting something more spiritually-connected to my higher purpose in life than pop-music hooks, gratuitous name-dropping and calculating who you knew that owed you a favor. Oh well. I had a small rock combo in the late sixties as a kid and I loved playing with other musicians, so I immersed myself in the "music biz" all through the eighties.

By 1987, Brendon had moved from New York State to Somerville, Massachusetts, where he had started a house-painting company. In May 1987, I called and mentioned to him that I was feeling the itch to leave NYC. He suggested I move to Beantown and help out with his new business, so, that's what I did. I moved to Porter Square – just over the Cambridge, MA line—and began exploring the realm of the cutting brush and painter's ladders. I also began instruction in sound healing and high-magickal studies, and I rediscovered the hidden world of Western esoterica. The move also found me unable to completely shake the pop-music bug and I auditioned for and was enlisted by Boston's top club band, The Lines. Being in a hard-working New-Wave band further reminded me that I needed something much more fulfilling from life than the fast lane, so, after recording an EP and touring all over the countryside for a year, I quit – concentrating on my new solo, more esoteric musical pursuits that involved sound healing and indigenous music. I also met Debra Floyd, a gifted empath, and together we immersed ourselves into the world of ritual training.

In 1988, while living in Boston, a friend of Debra's, a psychic councellor asked me to assist in the possible healing of a six year-old girl who had injured herself in a fall off the back of a pickup truck, and had lain comatose for six months. I was humbled by her request but agreed to help. The little girl's family had given up hope—they were all set to pull the plug—but my friend had been visiting working with the girl for almost three months and was convinced Carrie Ann could, and would, return to consciousness. A compassionate nurse at the hospital, who had taken a personal interest in the case, had asked my friend to seek help for one final attempt; this was it for the six year old.

Debra's friend, an occult healing practitioner, trained in Salem, MA, immediately contacted another healer (a Native American) and another friend who was considered to be a "psychic healer," to come in and do round-the-clock healing work. She came over to my house and asked me to record a copy of a meditation soundtrack I had recorded.

I had recently been given the music while asleep and in a dream state, and upon awaking I discovered that I had written down detailed recording instructions which resulted in my recording. She had heard the piece and thought it was worth a shot and said it couldn't make a bad situation worse, so I went ahead and made a copy of the tape on an endless loop cassette. Hidden just below the audible sonic level I subliminally recorded the following words. "Wa-a-a-ke up. It's a beautiful day, there's friends to play with and fun to have, wake up, wa-a-ke up. You have your whole life to live and people who love you, wa-a-ke up, wa-a-a-a-ke up Carrie Ann!" This repeated over and over again.

The twelve minute endless-loop tape was put in a walkman and the headphones placed on her head as the six-year-old laid in her hospital bed. The healers came and worked with her and one final marathon attempt was made to bring her out of coma. The sessions ended after two days.

The following day, inexplicably, after six months in a coma, the little girl awoke. There was no apparent physical or psychological damage and she thought she had just been asleep. It seemed miraculous to everyone and I don't know how, or why she awoke. I would like to think that my dream-inspired piece on the tape had a little something to do with the healing, but several accomplished healers had worked many hours and perhaps the concentration of concerted healing work managed to break through to her.

What is it about that non-linear processing lump of gray matter between our ears? This marvel of nature is not completely understood. Coma, for one, is not completely understood. Or how do you explain a person suffering little or no physical damage after losing substantial portions of the brain? The more I learn about this wonderful biologic computer, the more I am humbled by the realization that we have only scratched the surface of understanding this enigmatic higher organ.

Life in Boston went on and I managed to land a job at Capron, the largest special events company in New England. As an audio/video technician at Boston's World Trade Center, I worked Michael Dukakis' election night headquarters. The following day, after the Bush landslide, I mentioned to Debra it was time to think about leaving Massachusetts.

During this time period, Roland (a friend of ours from Boston) and his wife, Laura, moved to the Baca Grande Development Subdivision, next to Crestone, Colorado, in the SLV. I remembered the valley where the horse that wouldn't go away, Snippy, was slain. "You'll move here eventually," Roland told us in whispered, almost reverential tones, and he insisted that we should "get off the East Coast and move out here." The two offered us a place to stay if and when we moved out west. At the time I remember thinking: we have got to get out to big sky country and do a bit of exploring, and, *voilà* an opportunity presented itself. Fritz Kleiner, my photographer friend had acquired a new hobby: fossil hunting. He had spent several months in Hanksville, UT which sits in the middle of the only region on the planet that features gem-quality vertebrae fossils.

He suggested we accompany him on a fossil-hunting trip to Utah. Sounded good to me!

In April 1989, Debra and I and a friend of ours, Peter, headed west to go fossil hunting and for some much-needed R and R. Roland and Laura, in the Baca, were on the way, so, naturally we planned a visit on our return trip to Beantown. I had blanked out what happened that first night in Utah until three years later my brother reminded me that I had told him of the experience.

Ten miles north of Hanksville on Highway 24, the nearest house over twenty-miles away, we turned right and headed out into the desert over a bumpy dirt-road. We made camp in an the otherworldly Utah landscape in the middle of nowhere, just east of Capital Reef, between Factory Butte and the Factory Bench. This ancient Upper Jurassic portion of the Morrison Formation, that extends north toward the San Rafael Swell, contains the gem-quality vertebrae fossils. Fritz drove deeper into the desert and located his solo camp a quarter-mile away from our camp.

Around one-thirty a.m., my professional empathic girlfriend and our other friend, Peter became extremely nervous. They both sensed something lurking around outside our four-man tent in the middle nowhere.

Comfortable with the surreal Utah desert and not feeling afraid, I grabbed a flashlight and volunteered to stand guard in the car. I made light of their fear, but I too felt the peculiar sensation of a presence quietly scurrying around in the dark. I carefully scanned the entire campsite area with a powerful flashlight and found nothing unusual. I climbed into Peter's Monte Carlo, kicked back in the front seat, and listened to tunes while I marveled at the magnificent Utah sky.

After about five or ten minutes, movement in the rearview mirror caught my attention. I stared into the mirror and I remember saying to myself, "you are just seeing things." Then it happened again and strange pale shapes began darting around coyly behind the back of the car. They seemed to be about four feet tall and played with my peripheral vision, jumping from one rearview mirror to the other as my eyes raced to follow. I turned off the tape deck, rolled down the window and pointed my flashlight toward the rear of the car. I looked and listened carefully. Nothing. I turned to face the front, blinked, and it was morning! The sun was five degrees above the horizon and the flashlight was still in my hand. I had absolutely no sense of ever falling asleep. I am normally a very restless sleeper and wake up numerous times each night, but that night felt like hours had passed in mere seconds! The flashlight was turned off and the batteries were un-drained.

The incident, at the time, was puzzling and the memory of

that night faded. Two days later we found ourselves driving down Saguache County Road "T," the twelve-mile access road that heads east from Highway 17 toward the 14,000 feet high Sangre de Cristo Mountains glowering over the tiny village of Crestone. Upon realizing where Crestone was located, I remember commenting out loud to my companions, "This place is carnivorous. It'll eat you up and spit you out if you're not careful." Little did I know the valley would spend the next thirteen years masticating me before spitting me out.

Three years later, I was reminded of the Utah missing-time experience by my brother. I had completely forgotten about it and was puzzled as to why I had put the strange incident out of my mind. I asked my ex-girlfriend Debra if she remembered anything about the experience. She matter-of-factly recalled the incident but was puzzled why she couldn't remember anything that took place after I had left the tent to sit in the car.

Follow Your Bliss

Driving through the little ex-mining town for the first time, it was apparent to me that the proud, independent residents of Crestone and the Baca Grande Subdivision reflected the relaxed urbanized rural lifestyle of a high-mountain desert paradise. Everyone I met during my short, day-long visit was open, friendly, reflective, yet extremely present. People looked you in the eye. How refreshing. I immediately felt entranced by these intelligent, spiritual people who seemed so relaxed. Surrounded by the pristine mountain splendor of this forgotten region of southern Colorado, I felt right at home. But I doubted I could stand living sixty-miles from the nearest stoplight so I put the fleeting thought of relocating there out of my mind.

Midway through my one-day visit, while having lunch at the Bistro, the only restaurant in town at the time, I met Robert Troutman, a master plasterer, and cabinet maker. We talked at length about Crestone and the SLV, and at one point I told him that I was tired of living on the East Coast and needed to make a change. His Joseph Campbell-inspired response was simple and direct, "Follow your bliss, Chris" The next day while gliding along a lonely stretch of I-70—through Kansas, with Boston on the distant horizon—I smelled change in the air.

Three months later, Debra and I moved to Crestone. Initially we thought Santa Fe was where we'd move. But two days in Sante Fe turned out to be enough to know this wasn't meant to be. I witnessed the aftermath of three fatal car accidents and it was apparent that Santa Fe was actually a smaller, western version of New York City. We decided to call Roland and Laura (150 miles north in the Baca) to see if they were up for guests, and they re-extended their offer.

While in Santa Fe, we stayed with Debra's friends, Tony and Annie Adomitus. Shortly after arriving at their home (trailer in tow), I noticed that Tony seemed fidgety—nervous, but excited. After sitting around talking for awhile, Tony asked me to step out into the backyard to tell me something important. I asked him why outside? He told me he it was best for us to talk outside. OK. We went out into the backyard and he proceeded to tell me, in a furtive, matter-of-fact manner, all about an obscure, self-published manuscript called *The Matrix*, written by Valdamar Valarian. It was a strange compilation of subjects: aliens, underground bases, cutting-edge technology, government conspiracies and beyond. This was my innocent introduction into the shadowy world of UFO-fueled conspiracy. Tony presented a scenario that was disturbingly resonant. He claimed there was information to suggest that the government had already signed a treaty with an alien race and that the humans and aliens were working together under a mesa outside of Dulce, New Mexico, among other places… Hmm, I'd be surprised, but maybe not… He mentioned the work of William Cooper, John Lear, Linda Moulton Howe and other supposed "insiders" who had gathered evidence of an alleged vast alien-based conspiracy underground and over our heads. I remember, at the time, thinking that I should quash the urge to guffaw and look up and around, for fear of insulting him, but he seemed very insistent that all this information was possible. Looking around the alien New Mexico landscape, who was I to disbelieve the rationale?

At the time, I obviously didn't buy into any of it, but for the first time, I had become exposed to the conspiracy-tinged side of ufology, and, whether I liked it or not, these unbelievable-sounding scenarios would surface again years later.

The Brothers: Easter 1965

1967 Sixth-grade class photo about the time
of the Snippy, Case , Bellevue WA

New Paltz, NY 1979

The Snippy Headline Photo, October 1967

Playing with Kosme at Magique, NYC January 1983.

First modeling job for Gilla-Roos Agency NYC. 1982

With the Lines in Malibu, CA
West Coast Tour 1988.

Yardena: We played together in NYC from 1981 to 1987.

25

Bone hunting with Peter Meadows: missing time at Factory Butte, west of Cainesville UT April 1989.

With Debra Floyd headed to Santa Fe, NM.

Crestone, CO
"This place is carnivorous, It'll eat you up and spit you out if you aren't careful."

26

CHAPTER TWO:
Welcome to the San Luis Valley

The San Luis Valley (SLV) is located in south-central Colorado and north-central New Mexico. It is the largest alpine valley in the world. Zebulon Pike was the first white American to cross into the valley that humans have been visiting for over ten-thousand years. The four thousand square mile, semi-arid desert valley floor sits at an average elevation of seven thousand, six hundred feet, over a mile-and-a-half above sea level. The valley floor averages less than five inches of rainfall per year. Its entire wish bone shape is ringed by majestic forested mountains on all sides. Along the eastern side of the valley stands a solid wall of rock soaring to heights of over 14,000 feet, the imposing Sangre de Cristo Mountains. The southern end of the SLV is dominated, on its eastern Sangre de Cristo side, by Wheeler Peak, the highest mountain in New Mexico. The western side of the valley is bordered by the older San Juan Mountains rising above a labyrinth of deep valleys and roaring rivers.

The famous Rio Grande River originates in the San Juans, near Creede, CO, before snaking its way from the valley's midpoint — southward to the Gulf of Mexico. The Sangres mark the second largest rift valley on the planet. (Only the Great Rift Valley in Africa is longer.)

The San Juan and Sangre de Cristo Mountains merge at the extreme northern end of the valley in Saguache County after emptying over one hundred creeks into the largest freshwater aquifer in the United States. The second youngest mountain range in the continental United States, they owe their jagged appearance to their age of less than a million years.

One cluster of promontories, which I'll call the Blanca Massif for convenience contains the Valley's highest mountains. Situated mid-point in the Sangres, this twenty-five square-mile jumble of peaks stands like a host of brooding sentinels. For thousands of years, Blanca Peak and its neighbors have been the focus of Native American myth and tradition.

Aside from the southern end of the valley that opens from Colorado into New Mexico, there are only four main entry points into the valley. These Colorado mountain passes, Poncha in the north, Cochetopa in the northwest, Wolf Creek to the west and La Veta to the east, all cross above 9,000 feet and are often temporarily closed in the winter during the long winter months due to snowfall amounts of over 150 inches. Wolf Creek

Pass, astride the Continental Divide, can receive as much as 350 inches of snow in a single season!

Three main highways bisect the SLV. State Highway 160 travels east and west the valley at the center, entering and exiting over La Veta and Wolf Creek Passes. It serves as "Main Street" of the valley's largest towns Alamosa and Monte Vista. Alamosa, with a population of just over 10,000 sits at an elevation of 7,500 feet in the valley's center. State Highways 285 and 17 travel the length of the valley north and south like twin shotgun barrels, meeting to exit over Poncha Pass to the north. The incredible view of the surrounding mountains from Highway 17 prompted a group of visiting Tibetan monks to call the area "America's Tibet."

The southern and middle portion of the valley was the first settled region of Colorado, and over the border in New Mexico, along the Rio Grande are some of the oldest European settlements in the country. San Luis, in Costilla County Colorado, founded in 1851, is the oldest town in Colorado. As a result of the sixteenth and seventeenth-century influx of settlers from New Mexico, the southern part of the geographic valley has a rich cultural tradition, with Spanish-speaking residents making up half of the population.

Physically and metaphorically isolated from the outside world, this Spanish-American culture has developed its own unique character, combining elements of indigenous Native American beliefs with an Old World style of fundamentalist Catholic piety. This close knit Hispanic subculture is very superstitious and generally wary of outsiders, creating an effective roadblock for outsider researchers and investigators who've come here over the years attempting to uncover the many secrets of this valley.

The Baca Grande Development

The enigmatic Baca Grande Subdivision could be called ground-zero in this book. The "Baca" is where I lived for thirteen years and was a base from which I conducted hundreds of investigations. I admit, mysteries attract me like a moth, to the glare of a flickering incandescent bulb and I was curious why there were over a dozen of the world's great religious and spiritual traditions concentrated in Crestone's Baca Grande Development.

The following is a brief history of the Baca Ranch and the northeast corner of the ranch that was subdivided to create the Baca Grande Subdivision/Development. The Baca Ranch is one of the oldest established ranches in Colorado and has a colorful past. The following, is from the official Baca Grande Property Owner's Association website, and was written by long-time resident Mary Abdoo:

In 1823, King Ferdinand VII of Spain expressed his

appreciation of his loyal subject, Cabeza de Vaca, by a land grant of five hundred thousand acres. This grant was known as the Baca Grant and was originally in New Mexico for Vaca's seventeen sons and six hundred head of horses and mules.

The Vaca family (anglicized to Baca) can be traced in Spanish history to 1235 when the Spaniards were victorious over the Moors in battle. A man, using the head of a cow as a symbol was given the title "cabeza de vaca", meaning "head of a cow". The Luis Maria Cabeza de Baca family made their home on the Grant until a roving band of Navajo Indians drove them from their home to the village of Pena Blanca. One of Don Luis' sons became employed by American trappers and stored illegally trapped furs in the Baca home. Mexican soldiers came in search of the illegal furs in 1827 and when Don Luis refused to admit them, they shot him. After his death, the family began to disintegrate and nothing was heard from them for several years.

The family returned to the grant in 1835 to find that a second grant was being petitioned to obtain the area for the present town of Las Vegas New Mexico. The land was now under U.S. jurisdiction. In 1860 Congress declared that the land should be granted to the town of Las Vegas. and gave Luis Maria Cabeza de Baca five new grants in exchange. No. 1 and 2 were in New Mexico and No. 3 and 5 in Arizona with No. 4 in the San Luis Valley in Colorado.

In 1859, John S. Watts, the family lawyer, led the family to claim their Baca Grant land which consisted of twelve and a half square miles, composed of one hundred thousand acres, approximately eighteen thousand being mountainous. Watts was deeded the Baca Grant #4 for the sum of three thousand dollars in 1864 to cover his legal services. The first structure, which was built at the ranch, however, was a small three-room adobe house with a huge fireplace including the date of 1823. Lily and Coberly of the L.& C. Rough and Ready Flour Mills of Littleton, Colorado held a lease on the grant and purchased it in 1869. Reportedly Joe Coberly had a racetrack at the grant and raced with the Ute and Jicarella Apache Indians for their blankets. In 1870 it was sold to Alexander C. Hunt, who had been a US Marshal, a Judge, Territorial Treasurer, and the fourth Territorial Governor of Colorado.

In 1877, William Gilpin, a former Governor bought the Grant from Hunt for non-payment of taxes. Gilpin and his associates secured the services of a prominent mining expert, Professor James Aborn, to explore the mineral potential of the Sangre de Cristo Mountains that surrounded the Grant. Gilpin then tried to sell the Baca Grant to European investors, however, was unsuccessful.

George Adams had been leasing the land from Gilpin and raising Hereford Cattle imported from England and in 1885, bought the Grant for two hundred and fifty thousand dollars. In November 1880, E. A. Reser and George Adams also purchased a tract of land at the foot of the mountains on the northern boundary of the Grant, platted a town site, sold lots and called the town, Crestone. Crestone became the headquarters for the miners who were beginning to roam the district in search of mining sites. In 1900, Adams sold [it] to the San Luis Valley Land and Mining Company for $1,400,000. It was a subsidiary of the United Gas Improvement Company of Philadelphia, PA.

The San Luis Valley Land and Mining Company stockholders, wealthy Philadelphia Industrialists, were lured to purchase the land for the potential wealth of the Independence Gold Mine located near Spanish Creek. They put in the largest stamp mill of its kind in the world, a 100 stamp mill. The San Luis Valley Land and Mining Company built a railroad spur from Moffat to Crestone and on to the mine under the title of the "Rio Grande and Sangre de Cristo Railroad." The Independence Gold Mine became the richest mine in the district for actual production because it could handle thirty tons of ore in ten hours. An estimated fifty million dollars worth of precious metals have been produced from the district of the Baca Grant and several men have become millionaires from their good fortune here. The company changed its name to the San Luis Valley Land and Cattle Company.

In 1930, Alfred M. Collins, a major stockholder of the San Luis Valley Land and Cattle Company, visited the Grant and took over management of the one-hundred-thousand-acre ranch. While he was a fifty-four year-old polo player and horse enthusiast, he was unprepared to take over management, however, decided he needed to keep a close watch on his investment during the low ebb of those depression days. He improved the land over the next ten years and it began to pay off, and by 1940, there became an increasing demand for registered bulls from his herd. In 1949, Alfred Collins was named "Cattlemen of the Year"and had created one of the finest spreads in the United States. He retired at seventy years of age. The cattle herd was sold following Alfred's death and set a world record for a cattle dispersal sale.

In 1950, he sold the ranch to Newhall Land and Farming Company of Arizona and California. In 1962, the Arizona-Colorado Land and Cattle Company acquired the Baca Grant.

30

They had kept up the tradition of fine cattle and were leaders in the breeding and the raising of famed French Limousin Cattle. The Luis Maria de Baca Grande Grant #4 is the only one of the five original Grants to remain intact for over one-hundred years.

Arizona-Colorado Land and Cattle Company formed the Baca Grande Corporation, in 1971 and sales began. A choice portion of the ranch was to become The Baca Grande, a recreation and leisure living community. It was set aside and master planned by another subsidiary, Coe & Van Loo Consulting Engineers, Inc. In their master plan, twenty-eight percent of the land was reserved for green belts and common areas so that property owners and guests could enjoy the beauty and tranquility of the San Luis Valley without destroying the environment. Land was sold in phases with areas designated as Mobile Home Estates, Chalet Units, I and II, the Grants, and later, Ranchettes. Along the main county road T was developed a commercial strip with the Inn, a lake (Lago del Oro), a nine hole golf course, administration/maintenance building, library and camper village. Other amenities were added. On May 12, 1971 the Baca Grande Corporation recorded the Declaration of Protective Covenants and Restrictions for the Baca Grande in Saguache County. The Baca Grande Property Owners Association Articles of Incorporation were dated December 18, 1972. Marketing areas included sales offices in Colorado, New Mexico, Texas, Oklahoma and in Korea, Hawaii and Guam.

In promotion of land sales in the Baca Grande, you might have arrived on the airfield, been taxied to a night at the Inn with its swimming pool and lake, played golf, toured the historic Independence Gold Mine or experienced the Rodeo. As the Baca Corporation changed to the Baca Grande Property Owners Association, the Inn was sold to the private sector, the airfield returned to the ranch and the gold mine became Manitou property. The rodeo grounds became a baseball diamond. The ranch was managed independently as The Baca Ranch and in 1998 was sold to Gary Boyce.

Beginning in 1979, Hanne Marstrand Strong, wife of Maurice Strong, Chairman of AZL Resources, Inc. invited several organizations to locate in the Baca after a visit from prophet, Glen Anderson in 1978. These included the Lindisfarne Association; the Aspen Institute of Humanistic Studies; the Carmelite Order (Spiritual Life Institute); two-hundred acres to the Tibetan Monastery, a Tibetan Order of Buddhists; the Village Group (an alternative community); and Rediscovery-Four Corners (a camp for American Indians). More religious centers have been added.

The real story behind somnambulist prophet Glen Anderson, Hanne Strong and the establishment of an eclectic representation of human spirituality has never been disclosed. For several years before I left the valley, when area residents would ask me what my next book was about, I'd tell them: "The real inside story of the Baca and I'm going to move two weeks before it's published."

Hanne and Maurice Strong

The two most prominent residents of the Baca are Hanne and Maurice Strong. Although Maurice spends little time in the SLV, his wife, Hanne, is a full-time·resident and their involvement here in this mysterious valley may be revealing when examining the various players and agendas that seem to be operating below the radar. The following are brief biographies on Hanne and Maurice Strong taken from Wikipedia. com. and a variety of sources.

Maurice F. Strong, was born April 29,1929, in Oak Lake Manitoba is an industrialist and public servant who was the Secretary-General of the 1992 United Nations Conference on Environment and Development (UNCED), better known as the Earth Summit. He was senior advisor toUN Secretary-GeneraKofi Annan although he suspended his involvement two years ago while being investigated for financial ties toTongson Park, a lobbyist involved with the Iraq Oil for food scandal.

Working in the background as an advisor to powerful world figures, Strong has been featured in a number of conspiracy theories. CBC reporterAnn-Marie McDonald described him as 'a cross between Rasputin and Machiavelli.'

Strong became wealthy during his career in the [Canadian] oil and utilities industry. He was President of Power Corporation until 1966. As such he was a mentor to Paul Martin giving him his first job and putting him in a position to become a powerful corporate executive.

Strong left Power Corporation to become head of what became the Canadian International Development Agency. In the early 1970s he was Secretary-General of the United Nations Conference on the Human Environment. He then became the first Executive Director of the United Nations Environment Program.

He returned to Canada to become Chief Executive Officer of Petro-Canada from 1976 to 1978. In the early 1990s he was Chief Executive Officer of Ontario Hydro.

Strong was the UN's envoy to North Korea until July 2005. According to Associated Press his contract was not renewed "amid questions about his connection to a suspect in the UN oil-for-food scandal", Tongsun Park, as well as due to criticism that he gave his step-daughter a job at the UN contrary to UN staff regulations against hiring immediate family.

Maurice Strong is associated with the town of Crestone, Colorado, having briefly held a controlling interest in AZL, a land owning company which laid out the Baca Grande, a large land development south of the town. Together with his wife Hanne Strong, who remains a local resident, the couple made a number of grants of land to the small spiritual communities which give the Crestone-Baca community its distinctive flavor. He was also one of the principals in the abortive American Water Development, Inc. (AWDI) scheme to pump and export underground water from the San Luis Valley.

It is interesting to note, readers, that this agenda may have been connected to a grander vision nicknamed the "Grand Canal" which proposed the creation of a natural desalinization operation at the tip of Hudsons' Bay and a monumental project to supply water for the Southwest U.S and as far south as Northern Mexico. The Grand Canal, if constructed, would be the single largest works project undertaken by man—dwarfing the pyramids and the Great Wall of China. In the proposed design, five river systems would be manipulated, and with the aid of nuclear reactors, fresh water would be pumped up to the San Luis Valley to refill the aquifer after it was pumped out. At 7,500 feet, the SLV could be called America's water tank. The water from the re-charged aquifer would then have been sold and distributed downhill to the arid American Southwest and Mexico. The details of this little-known proposal were revealed in an *Atzlan Journal* article in 1990.

Maurice Strong is [was] the President of the Council of the United Nations University for Peace. UPEACE is the only university in the UN system able to grant degrees at the master's and doctoral levels.

An article written by James Hirsen, Ph.D. attempted to define the complex behind-the-scenes influence of Maurice Strong's globalist, "sustainable-development" activities.

Strong has emerged as one of the most powerful and enigmatic figures on the international scene. He wields considerable influence in the areas of business and politics. Twenty years ago, The New Yorker magazine described

Maurice Strong as the man upon whom "the survival of civilization in something like its present form might depend.

Strong has supported New Age movements in the U.S. and once helped finance a second ark in preparation for the next great flood. [Does Maurice Strong know something we don't know?] His many global activities are orchestrated with the philosophical bent of a long time believer in the establishment of a new world religion.

Strong has instituted what is ostensibly the global headquarters for the New Age movement at the foot of the Sangre de Cristo Mountains near Crestone, Colorado. He and his wife run the Manitou Foundation and call this center the "Baca." It is an international collection of alternative religious beliefs. Located at this New Age mecca are a subterranean Zen Buddhist center, the Haidakhandi Universal Ashram, a facility for Native American shamans and a Vedic temple where devotees worship the Vedic mother goddess.

The Manitou Foundation's agenda at the "Baca" appears to be the cauldron within which this one-world/one-religion vision is being forged and there are many powerful players that appear to be involved.

From the official Manitou Foundation website:

Hanne Strong is President of the Manitou Foundation, a non-profit organization founded in 1988 to assist Mrs. Strong in her philanthropic interests, chiefly to establish the most complete ecumenical and sustainable community in North America, set in the Rocky Mountains of Colorado. Over the past twenty years, she has traveled to over ninety countries where she has frequently been an invited speaker at seminars and conferences on the subject of sustainable communities and spiritually based environmental education. In 1992, during the United Nations Conference on Environment and Development (UNCED), Mrs. Strong organized and sponsored two conferences attended by spiritual leaders from around the world.

In 1977, she organized three conferences for children, youth and the handicapped that paralleled HABITAT, the UN Conference on Human Settlements in Vancouver, B.C. It was the first time ever that children addressed the world in the United Nations Plenary with their views and recommendations

"Mrs. Strong has founded numerous non-profit organizations for Native Americans, handicapped and homeless children. She has worked extensively with Native Americans and other indigenous peoples in their struggle for the preservation of their spiritual and cultural values, and she has received spiritual training from North and South American Shamans, Tibetan Buddhist Lamas, Hindu masters and other indigenous Shamans from around the world.

As a result of the Strongs' philanthropic work in the Baca, this little subdivision has quietly evolved into one of America's most intriguing and unusual near-towns. Where else can you find as many esteemed religious groups in one location? Some have called the Baca, "The Spiritual United Nations." This tag is fairly revealing and, in my estimation, is accurate, to some extent. There are many things about this remote enclave that don't make sense. People have asked me how is it that people from so many different belief systems can peacefully co-exist in such a small town? Good question. My stock answer has always been, it's everyone else that seems to get into contentious fights and disagreements, the spiritual adherents are generally the folks who do not get involved in local politics and controversy.

Crestone

I was intrigued that many of the Baca residents I met felt that everyone who moved here and stayed in this historic part of Colorado was "called." Were they being called? By whom, or more accurately, by what?

"This is where the teachers are taught," a resident told me shortly after my move. "You'll know very soon if it's your destiny to be here. The mountains will let you know." Now, I consider myself a pretty open-minded individual with more than a few experiences in my life that defied rational explanation but I still had to swallow a rather cynical, knee-jerk NYC response when I heard this. As I soon discovered, living way out here in the boonies of southern Colorado can be tough. *Real* tough.

The official visitor's guide sums up the mundane history of Crestone:

> The western slope of the northern Sangre de Cristo Mountains and the San Luis Valley have drawn people since Neolithic times. Arrowheads and spear points, lost between fifteen-thousand and ten thousand years ago by ancient hunters tracking migrating herds of mammoth bison that loved to graze on the rich grasslands of the Valley, have been unearthed near the San Luis Lakes State Park, between the town of Mosca and the Great Sand Dunes. The people of the Taos Pueblo, which is located at the southern end of the Valley, claim one of these lakes as the Sipapu, or point of emergence into this world. And Blanca Peak, just down the range south of the Dunes, is sacred

to the Navajo people.

Rich hunting grounds drew many Native American peoples to the Valley. Comanche, Ute, Kiowa and Navajo people have all hunted and camped in the Crestone area. An ancient quarry was discovered near Pole Creek, where various tribes quarried rock and chipped points and tools.

The first Europeans to enter the northern end of the Valley were Spanish settlers. In 1822 the King of Spain awarded a huge grant of land to Don Luis Maria Cabeza de Vaca (Baca). The original land grant, which ran from Las Vegas, New Mexico to Crestone or Kit Carson Peak, included 496,446.96 acres of land on both sides of the Sangres. The grant shrank considerably in size, following the Mexican Revolution and the war with the USA, which, made the grant a part of this country under the Treaty of Guadalupe Hidalgo in 1846.

Settlers were encouraged to bring their families and herds to colonize the area. Remnants of these early settlers can been found in crumbling adobe buildings. An ancient Spanish arraste, used to crush stone, possibly to extract minerals like gold, was found near Cottonwood Creek. The grant was one of five land grants in the southwest to remain intact for over a hundred years.

The end of the American Civil War brought an influx of Anglo settlers to the northern Valley. Harry Hopkins, a Confederate veteran, built the first frame house in 1868 in the area just outside the current Crestone city limits.

In the 1870's the first big gold strikes were made in Burnt Gulch, east and a bit north of Crestone. Around 1874, a rich "float," a deposit of gold "floating" free of a vein in the earth, was discovered in the gulch amid the rock and aspen. Burnt Gulch buzzed for a while with gold fever. Mining cabins clung to the steep sides of the gulch. But the big load was never unearthed in Burnt Gulch, and by 1880 most of the miners had abandoned their claims there and moved down to the newly platted Town of Crestone.

The year of 1886 saw the first in a series of great gold strikes of high-grade ore. Many of these strikes were made in the southern part of Crestone District in the Baca Grande Grant. In 1859 the Vaca (Baca) family had sold the grant to their attorney. The grant had changed owners several times since.

Every now and then the owner of the grant would evict all the miners from the grant. Miners and owners of the Baca Grande were often in litigation. The owners of the grant won and miners would be evicted from their claims and homes. While violence was generally avoided, miners were forcibly evicted from the Baca Grande Grant more than once.

At its peak around 1900, the Town of Crestone boasted a population of two-thousand, and the entire district had a population of ten-thousand residents. Businesses thriving in Crestone in January 1901 included: five general stores, two lumber yards, seven saloons, one assay office, two butchers, one bakery, one barber, one bank, three doctors, one sign painter, four pool halls, two livery stables, four restaurants, two drug stores, one dry goods, one feed store, one printer, one laundry, two lawyers, two real estate offices, and two blacksmiths. The spacious, two story Hotel Crestone was erected in February of 1901, on the corner of Cottonwood Street and Silver Avenue.

A local festival was held in 1901 to attract residents to the new boomtown of Crestone. According to a local newspaper account from the time, a local cowboy, Juan Fernandez, took full and perhaps unfair advantage of the free food and libations. He ate three cans of pig's feet, three cans of baked beans, two cans of salmon and topped this off with liberal consumption of liquor.

Well it turned out to be Juan's last supper! He died that very night of indigestion. His epitaph, written on a board and nailed to a tree near his grave read, "Here lies the body of Juan the Glutton, who could eat a beef and a couple of mutton, to fame and fortune quite unknown, he brought a famine to Crestone."

The momentous year of 1901, marked the coming of the railroad, as a spur line was laid for the Sangre de Cristo Railroad from Moffat to Crestone, and from there to the settlements of Cottonwood and Duncan on the Baca. It took ten hours then by rail to go from Denver to Crestone. During the heyday of the Independence mine, eighty-thousand dollars worth of gold bullion was shipped by rail monthly to the Denver Mint.

By 1910 many of the smaller mining camps and towns in the Crestone District had become ghost towns. Crestone was down to one doctor and one minister. The town revived again in the early 1930s when the mines on the Baca Grande were reopened briefly. Crestone remained quiet again until the development of the Baca Grande Subdivision in the 1970s.

What Mary Lowers' visitor's guide article fails to mention is the world-class eighteen-hole golf course that was built in the early twentieth century. The original golf-course was abandoned in the twenties, however, a nine-hole course was built in the seventies in an attempt to lure retirees to the newly-created subdivision. The current management spends over ten thousand dollars per month to water one of the most scenic golf-courses in America and, during my time there, I played as many rounds of golf as possible.

One thing that I should mention comes from my own hard experience in Crestone this windswept valley is one of the poorest regions in the United States, with an average per capita income in 1990 of under nine thousand dollars per year. Upon moving to the area, it was immediately clear to me that if I wished to create a niché in this mountain paradise I would have to creatively multi task and generate enough outside income to pay for it, or spend my savings.

Miraculously, I was immediately able to land a job on a local Baca-based construction crew. I hadn't worked for only six dollars per hour since high school but I was extremely lucky to find a job at all. Coming up from sea level, I quickly discovered how hard physical labor is at 8,000 feet (it takes six weeks to acclimate, if you are lucky). I had never worked so hard and made so little in my life. However, I did get back into shape.

One of the first things I did after working at my new job that first hot, dusty week in July, 1989, was spend some casual time in "Olde Town." This simple cluster of historic buildings, built at the end of the nineteenth century and now owned by the Snider family, at the time, could have been called the Crestone Business District. A three story building that, in the town's hey-day, had housed a bank, then the assayer's office, then had evolved into a small boutique and liquor store. The Sniders are a hardy, down-to-earth family. Katie and her husband Frank were self-professed bikers both pushing sixty in the 1950s and true free spirits.

My first foray into the Snider's "Twenty-first Amendment Liquors" was revealing. A hitching post adorned the porch where a large mule had decided to hang out next to the door. I guessed that the sign on the store door summed up life in a small mountain town.

> Open most days we open about 9 or 10, occasionally as early as 7, but SOME DAYS as late as 12 or 1. We close about 5:30-6, occasionally about 4, or 5, but sometimes as late as 11 or 12. SOME DAYS, or afternoons, we aren't here at all and lately I've been here just about all the time, except when I'm someplace else, but I should be here then too.

After three or so minutes of being seriously sniffed by the Snider's several friendly, but wary dogs, Katie Snider appeared at the door. "Howdy" she said, unlatching the rickety screen door that had captured a couple of feeble mosquitoes inside. I paused before entering and then introduced myself, telling her as I entered the dimly-lit store of my decision to move to Crestone. I took everything in, all the antique mementos of a bygone era: a huge safe, shovels, picks, scales, ancient bottles, old calendars, and numerous elk, deer and pronghorn trophies. It had been a hard, short-of-breath, day on my new job carrying one-hundred pound bundles of asphalt roofing tiles up three floors in thin mountain air and I was thirsty.

Katie was coy, yet informative. In a scant twenty minutes, she took me on a crash course through her recent personal history in Crestone. "See that guy in the old beat-up truck, he's the local plumber. We used to be best friends, but we don't talk now!" I squashed the urge to ask "why?" The big old mule was still standing on the porch outside, but now blocking the door, it's long tail impatiently swishing flies in the dry, lazy air. Déjà vu—leaning on the weathered counter, I felt completely at home.

Our conversation went on for a spell, with Katie answering my various queries about the town with apparent honesty and humor. Out of nowhere I suddenly blurted out, "I've heard there are a lot of UFO sightings around here." Katie's eyes flashed and she quickly responded, looking down "Oh that's a lot of nonsense. Don't believe those stories!" I noticed she seemed nervous as she hurriedly bagged my selection. End of conversation. I was disappointed that she didn't confirm my casual suspicion that the area I had just moved to did have the occasional UFO sighting but I knew I shouldn't press her. Little did I know at the time, ten years later I would complete a $600,000 dollar building project for Katie and her family.

My first month in Crestone was exhausting. "Half the O2 and twice the UV," I've often told out-of-breath, sunburned visitors to the area. After years of cushy jobs and a rock and roll NYC lifestyle, exhausting physical labor was an eye-opening, back-breaker. I regained a athletic lean meanness that goes with the rural territory and working construction. I worked hard and looked for opportunities to play hard and to relax, I concentrated on writing and recording the meditation and healing music I'd begun experimenting with in Boston.

August 13, 1989, 10:00 p.m., the Baca,
I was sitting on the front porch after a rewarding solo recording session. I had been working on a piece from a collection of "indigenous music" recordings I had written that are musical approximations of tribal music that I imagined would be played in 2100 AD. The album was called "Dancing on Mountains."

The star-spangled Colorado sky shimmered above me as I powered down the synthesizers and went outside to the west-facing front porch. I looked up at the dazzling Milky Way that stretched from horizon to horizon. The area had experienced a spell of unusual heat during the end of July and early August and the A-frame house baked from the blistering ninety five-degree day. I sat blissfully enjoying the cool breeze flowing off the 14,000 feet peaks glowing in the moonlight two-miles away, with the last mix bouncing in my head.

Suddenly, something bright above me moved and caught my attention. A brilliant point of light was headed across the valley from the west—right toward our location in the Baca. "Wow, you guys, come here...QUICK!" I called to Roland and Laura. They rushed out to the porch just in time to see the bright descending orb of light silently explode into pieces over town, two miles north of our vantage point. There were streamers blown out from the central orb as it disintegrated and they sprayed downwards in the direction of travel. A faint trail of smoke streamed behind the object as the trail was momentarily illuminated by the explosion's flash.

"What in the world was that?" Roland asked as the event faded.

"That was no shooting star," Laura replied.

"It almost looked like a giant bottle rocket!" I said. "Like a giant cheap firework."

It had appeared to be less than two miles away when it had popped with a flash right over town, and knowing a bit about meteors, I knew that if we saw smoke, this was not a meteor. The object was completely silent! And there was absolutely no sonic indication of the visual event we had witnessed. The duration of the object's flight was at least seven to eight seconds, time enough for my friends, to run outside from the kitchen, two rooms away, and witness the object. We talked about it for a while and agreed that whatever it was, it was unusual. We went about our evening as if nothing had happened.

This was my first sighting of a type of apparition I have dubbed "cheap fireworks." I witnessed dozens of these puzzling objects over my thirteen years of skywatching in the valley—some as close as twenty-five feet away. I and others have seen three or four "cheap fireworks" events in one evening! I am absolutely convinced that these phenomenon are not meteors or defined celestial objects, and their occasional close proximity to the observer may be highly revealing of their true nature. One sighting of a bright bluish-white orb, about the size of a quarter, prompted a witness to describe the event as it flashed less than twenty feet away as being "...like watching Tinkerbelle crash."

I will examine this apparently location-specific phenomenon later in the book. I suspect that this is one of several examples of rare natural phenomenon that occur in the San Luis Valley, and these manifestations of energy may be a clue as to the energies at play above the spine of America. But there are more familiar phenomena to be found here as well. Prior to my arrival, I was only mildly interested in ghosts and hauntings. This changed when I moved into a house that featured some peculiar properties. This was my first exposure to the phenomenon, and it sparked an interest in me that continues today.

Mr. Douglas

Late August, 1989, Baca Grande Development.

The west-facing house located in the Baca Chalets that we shared with our friends Roland and Laura was a three bedroom, two story A-frame that faced serene San Luis Valley. A large porch afforded us a two hundred degree vista that extended from the top of Wheeler Peak, to the south all the way to the top of Mount Shavano, a distance of over 150 miles. Originally built in the early 1970s, the chalet-style home sitting on rail-road ties was a land-scam developer's idea of that "perfect little summer getaway." No foundation, no insulation and a tongue and groove ceiling that leaked like a vegetable strainer. Debra and I had one of the two bottom bedrooms, Roland and Laura had the other. There was an open-story living room with a peaked eighteen foot high ceiling. An open staircase ascended to the upstairs. The entire upstairs loft area, which consisted of a fifteen by eight foot office/landing at the top of the staircase, opened up into a large, steeply-peaked bedroom with a half-bath. At the time, the upstairs was empty due to the unbearable heat that turned the space into a furnace during the late summer afternoon.

One night in late September, I was awakened by strange thumping noises. A martial stomp-stomp-stomp paced back and forth upstairs in the empty bedroom. I lay there and listened for a minute trying to figure out what it could have been. The first thing that came to mind was Roland. Being quite the nature-boy, he could be found pacing downstairs in the living room, stark naked but for his army boots when he was perturbed by one of life's little curve-balls. An ayurvedic healer who was a gun buff (go figure) he was quite marshal. I got up and quietly tip toed out the bedroom door, down the short hall, through the kitchen and into the living room. Something didn't seem right. I could plainly hear the stomping as it paced the five or so steps from one end of the room to the other. What was Roland doing pacing back and forth in his army boots at 3:00 in the morning? I stepped on the first of ten steps that led to the second floor. The sound stopped. So did I. I listened carefully, starting to wonder if it really was Roland. I quickly ran up the remaining stairs as quietly as possible and burst into the dark room, flicking the light on immediately as I entered.

Nothing.

I scratched my head. How could this be? There was only one way in or out of the upstairs. I checked around in the closet, in the bathroom and out on the small porch that faced the magnificent Sangres, two miles away. I sprouted a serious set of goose bumps because I knew something was very wrong with the scenario.

I went back downstairs a bit bewildered and laid back down in bed. The instant my head hit the pillow, THUMP-THUMP-THUMP. Thinking back, I chuckle when I remember how I covered my head with the pillow and tried the best I could to go back to sleep.

The next morning I mentioned the incident to my house mates, and Roland mentioned that he had heard the sound too, but hadn't gotten up to see what it was, figuring it was probably me. This was my introduction to a presence I now call "Mr. Douglas."

Secrets of the Mysterious Valley

A few weeks passed and in late October I experienced another inexplicable event. Roland and Laura had moved back to their other house in California, and Debra and I assumed the rental and continued living in the A-frame in the Baca Chalet 1. One Fall night, I was alone in the house, well not quite; my girlfriend's cat and our two blue-heeler puppies were keeping me company. I was quickly settling in to the routine of heating an poorly-insulated house located on an eight-thousand foot mountain chain. We had a bundle of "slab"— twelve foot long strips of skinned bark from the mill — and I lopped off a two day supply of firewood with my chainsaw. I laid down on the couch after stoking up the wood stove. The couch was located against the wall where the stairs ascend to the upstairs. All of a sudden, all three animals who had been hanging out in the living room with me became quite agitated. The two puppies started whining and running from room to room. Their was behavior highly out of character. Elric, the cat, was a rather sensitive Persian; I could understand him zorching around, but why were the young dogs acting out? I hardly had time to sit up when I heard the first of seven large, footsteps start to slowly descend the stairs. Each step produced an unmistakable groan from the stair tread. I froze staring up the empty open backed stair risers. The stairs descended right past the back of the couch, and as the last audible step occurred — right at eye level — I saw the step flex as if a considerable weight was being placed on it. When whatever-it-was stopped next to me, I'm not sure what happened next, because I evidently had raced outside on the porch, my chest heaving, and I'm sure, my eyes bugging out! The animals had run into one of the back bedrooms and wouldn't come out for the rest of the night. Upon her return, I excitedly told Debra what had occurred. She looked at me with a strange expression and then shook her head and smiled.

A couple of months later, in the dead of winter, a third strange event occurred. I don't know if any of these events were related, however, my gut told me we had company in the house. During the winter months, naturally, the upstairs becomes the bedroom of choice. Hot air does rise, and although we had no insulation in the house, we did have the roaring wood stove. On a couple of occasions, much to our horror, it turned to a glowing, semi-transparent white from too much of our freshly acquired hot piñon firewood.

One frigid night in early January 1990, I awoke with a start. My eyes were focused on a basketball sized glittering mass of faintly-glowing orange light the hung near the ceiling, just to the right of the hanging chandelier-style lamp that extended down from the twelve-foot cathedral ceiling. Panicked, my first thought was that we had started a chimney fire. I immediately threw on my shoes and grabbed a robe, ran downstairs and dashed out the door thinking I had seen the reflection of the fire's glow on the snow outside. It was extremely cold, with three-feet of snow on the ground around the east and north side of the house. I ran around the house, looked up and, nothing! There was a thin stream of smoke coming out of the twelve inch wide stovepipe. Puzzled, I ran back inside shivering from the frigid mountain night air, headed back upstairs and lay back down under the warm covers. As my eyes slowly became re-accustomed to the darkness, I could plainly make out a glow still hovering next to the ceiling. I woke Debra and asked her if she saw anything peculiar. She could see what I described, but I seemed to be able to see it more intensely. We lay there wondering what on earth it could be and after a few minutes it seemed to slowly fade out and we so did we.

First, the phantom marching sentry upstairs in the empty bedroom, then after moving up into the bedroom for the winter, this strange light phenomenon above our bed indicated something strange was afoot in the house. These events somehow seemed important so I casually began to research the house and the town's history. I also joined the crack Baca Grande volunteer fire-department. The Baca Grande and the history of the development alone could be the subject of a very compelling book, but at the time I immediately found out an interesting fact about the house where we had been living.

In the early 1980's, a retired couple named Douglas had built and then lived in the house. "Mr. Douglas," as I have dubbed what may be his continued presence, was a three-hundred-pound-plus behemoth of a man, and I found out he had died unceremoniously of a heart attack while naked on the toilet in the upstairs bathroom. He evidently lingered for awhile before dying and his horrified wife had found him the following morning. She called for the local volunteer EMT crew, and the groundskeeper at the Baca Townhouses was one of the first-responders that dashed over to the house, sirens howling. The rookie (it was his first emergency response case) vividly remembered the call. He and his senior EMT partner had to spend a considerable amount of time and energy to extract the dead man who had become tightly wedged between the toilet and the sink. Moving the corpse down the stairs and out to the ambulance was not an easy task.

Hearing the EMT's account of the demise of "Mr Douglas" I immediately could see how this man's demise might explain the weird things that had been going on in our rental home's upstairs bedroom. This seemed like a classic case of a ghost. I'm curious but not particularly drawn to the subject of ghosts or haunted houses, but I was familiar with stories of hauntings and the theory that troubled souls may linger where they met an unfortunate end of mortal life. I thought this may be a classic haunted site. I was on high alert – ready for the next event, but although I did see the glittering orange light on one other occasion, we never had a blatant example of a ghost-like encounter the rest of the time we lived at the house off north Baca Grant Way.

Secrets of the Mysterious Valley

Life continued and after four years the hardship of landing in one of the poorest counties in America impacted our relationship, and Debra and I parted ways in August 1991 after moving out of the Douglas house. But there is a post-script to the saga of "Mr. Douglas." The house then had a number of renters over the next two years, and to my knowledge, no one ever experienced strange events while living there, but on July 4, 1993, my new partner Isadora and I were attending the Crestone/Baca Fourth of July dance, when we were introduced to new arrivals Ed and Nancy Valko. Turns out, they had just bought the old Douglas house. I jokingly asked them if they had met Mr. Douglas yet. They asked me what I was talking about. I told them about the various experiences I had had with something unusual in the house. They seemed genuinely interested; maybe because they had just moved in the day before. I ended by telling them about the events surrounding the unfortunate demise of Mr. Douglas on the toilet upstairs, and both the Valko's faces went white. Nancy began to stammer.

"When we moved in yesterday, we replaced the toilet seat upstairs with a new one. Nobody had even used it yet! When we went upstairs this morning, it was cracked!" They hadn't even cut the paper strip that circled the lid and the base.

The Valkos didn't stay long. I haven't been told of any additional events that one would deem strange, but almost fifteen-years after moving in, I'm convinced, a three-hundred-pound ghost at one point lurked about the place. An uneasy soul, cursed by its unceremonious demise, that can't bring itself to pass on to the other side. Or something like spooky like that… This year and a half experience living in what may be a "haunted house" sparked a long-term interest in the subject of ghosts and hauntings.

Ace Inn George

Back to the San Luis Valley and the beginning of my haunted site research. Today, I am convinced that location-specific portal type areas may offer investigators the most direct route to the investigating the paranormal and unknown.

In 1993, I began inquiring around the SLV about possible haunted sites. I suspected that there are other allegedly haunted houses and buildings in the San Luis Valley and I was right. One location, the Ace Inn, now called Trujillos, in Alamosa, has experienced a string of unexplained occurrences that have been witnessed by female workers at the quaint little restaurant and bar. The "Ace" was owned by my former Crestone Post Master, Monte Collins, and the location has a history of occurrences that go back into its original heyday. One day, while picking up my mail, he told about several weird occurrences workers at his restaurant had experienced recently while cleaning up after a long day.

Life in a small town, like Crestone, can be an interesting experience. It might be hard to believe, but months can go by without seeing, or running into many of our reclusive residents that in the early nineties, numbered around one-hundred and seventy.

One gentleman is hard for any local resident to avoid. We all saw him almost every week-day. It's our postmaster, Monte Collins. Monte is an efficient, cheerful, hard-working man who tends to the post-office Monday-through Friday, then goes south to his home sixty-miles on his ranch just outside of Alamosa. That's a one-hundred-plus mile commute every day!

I couldn't imagine how he and his wife Peg did it, but they managed to not only operate their farm/ranch, but in addition, for four years they successfully operated a restaurant and lounge in Alamosa called the Ace Inn.

One afternoon in 1997, I picked up my mail and Monte mentioned several very strange events that his restaurant help had claimed they had experienced over the course of the four years the Collins' had owned the "Ace." With the release of my first book he knew I was interested in mysterious happenings, and we both had a few minutes to talk. After listening; spellbound to several occurrences, I knew I had to sit down and "officially" interview him.

We finally made a lunch appointment to talk at length and met at the Mountain View Cafe in Crestone. Over lunch, Monte started right in. "Chris, I don't know how much you know about the history of the Ace, but the Ace Inn restaurant was originally built in the early to late 1930's. Who lived in it before, I have no idea. Early on, some people who were living in the original house, evidently turned it into a restaurant. Prior to owning the restaurant, this lady ran a brothel in Texas, and her husband was a bare-fisted boxer, you know, they didn't use boxing gloves back then."

"A pugilist. With Jack Dempsey growing up near here, that's not surprising." I commented. He continued. "Stories that I've been told about the early days, well, let's say…I guess they had some pretty bloody boxing matches back in those days."

"Right there in the Ace?" I was surprised at this bit of information. "No, they had boxing matches around the place?"

"You mean outside?"

"Yes, the 'boxer' passed away in the mid-1970's and she (his wife) just passed away in a nursing-home in Pueblo just last year. That's just a little of the history. The building has been added onto four, or five times. It started out as a very small one-bedroom house with a small kitchen and a very small living-room. Now it's about a thirty-five hundred, to four-thousand-square foot building."

"As far as this 'ghost-thing' I've told you about, I personally have not seen it; nor have I ever felt it, but there has been, I'd say, over the four-years we've had the restaurant, probably ten people in the restaurant have felt a presence; seen a shadow; have heard noises and even heard their names called. One time, a coal bucket was totally thrown from the hearth of the fireplace that's in the lounge to the floor. Peg has experienced a shadow passing by her like a gust of air swishing her hair.

The latest incident that happened....we have a foyer that comes into our east entrance. Theresa, our bartender was in the process of locking the exterior doors. She had her back to the other two doors. She closed the two doors, and the other doors behind her slammed by themselves and locked. She couldn't get out!"

"She was locked in?"

"She was locked in. She was locked in the foyer. She was yelling for the kitchen help to come get her out. This only happened three weeks ago. She's a pretty rugged type girl and not easily spooked."

"We had another bartender named Sheila, and she experienced a lot of this 'passing by' stuff. Feeling a shadow and turning around and seeing the shadow go by. She'd turn around and there was nobody there. " Monte thought for a minute then mentioned, "You know, this has never been done to a male. All females. These gals have experienced hearing their names called, seeing shadows pass by, feeling coldness pass by. . . ."

I wanted to know what Monte thought was behind these unexplained experiences his workers had reported to him. "What does your gut tell you? What do you think is responsible for these occurrences? Has anyone who has had these experiences received any impressions at all about who, or what might be behind these events?"

"Well, I can only speculate in my mind as to what might be possibly going on. You know, as I mentioned, this lady ran a brothel. I don't know how many ladies she had, her husband was the boxer. My feeling is that it's George (the boxer). I feel George is still in the restaurant."

Monte also mentioned another oddity that he feels may, or may not, be related to the apparent haunting activity at the Ace Inn.

"When we bought the restaurant, there was this picture-frame that had a royal flush, with the last card down encased behind the glass. It was going across the corner of the wall, in the lounge and it sat on a shelf. Well, it could have been a coincidence, but behind this picture-frame on the shelf we found an actual human skull, in the corner behind this picture. How long it had been there, I have no idea, but it was real old and brown. I don't know if it has anything to do with it (what was going on), but I thought I should mention it."

Monte finally sold the place in 2000. The new owners began to remodel the Ace Inn to create a top-shelf gourmet Mexican restaurant named "Trujillos." New owner Pamela Trujillo experienced a number of strange events during their first two-years of operation as did several workers at the restaurant. It seems "George" may still be lurking about the place. Pamela mentioned that the several occurrences seemed to be similar to events Monte's waitresses had experienced.

The House on River Road

The most enigmatic story I uncovered, of an alleged "haunted" site in the San Luis Valley, involved an old house that had burned down near the Rio Grande River, just north of Alamosa, CO. Early on in my investigation I was told by a couple of sources that the property, located on North River Road—near the present day location of the Cattails country club and golf-course, was worthy of research. I was so taken by the several stories I was told, that I actually drove around the area in 1994 searching for the old spooky-sounding building. I never was able to locate it as the house had burnt to the ground the prior year. Then I received another call that mentioned the same house on River Road and I was told about an article published in the Valley *Courier* in the early eighties that documented the location's history.

I located the article easily. I simply looked at all articles published on Halloween, There it was, October 31, 1983. The Valley *Courier* article, written by two Alamosa High School students named Hayley Martin and Cindy Peck. It was reprinted with permission from their school paper, *The Alamosan:*

> Most stories of haunted houses have little basis in fact. However, there is ample evidence to support claims that a real haunted house exists outside Alamosa. …The house itself stands on 160 acres, and stables still exist where horses were kept during the days when it was used by the Pony Express when it ran from Denver to Santa Fé. According to evidence found on microfilm at the Adams State College and the Alamosa County Courthouse, each of the first five families who owned and lived in the house from its origin until 1951 experienced some sort of violent death within the family. The first of the deaths happened soon after the house was completed in 1872. The owner, Jerry H. Kent, killed his wife, and then committed suicide. Jeannie Craig, the next owner of the house, committed suicide. On December 14, 1915, she was found hanging from the stairway light. In 1934, Edward King,…lost a son under mysterious circumstances when the boy was found poisoned. The next victim was Edna May Herriman, who hanged herself from the front room chandelier. The last deaths within the house occurred when the owner killed his wife and then committed suicide…when the sheriff arrived to investigate, breakfast eggs were still on the stove. Eight small children were upstairs in the home when the murder occurred.

After another Valley *Courier* article published the first week of August,

Secrets of the Mysterious Valley

1997, written by editor Mark Hunter, requested people with strange experiences to call your amateur San Luis Valley gum-shoe investigator, I received a call from a Kay Thompson. She was a cordial, sober-sounding individual, and she immediately launched into a flurry of stories about a "haunted house" that she and her family lived in from 1982 to 1989. She was talking about the same house I'd heard all the stories about! I really like when the synchronicity crackles and raises its timely head. I didn't need to ask many questions. Kay immediately began her account. "When we moved in, we had heard about the stories relating to the house, but my boyfriend, at the time, was a non-believer. Well, 'they' got him. He believes now!

"The house was real old, and the Valley *Courier* wrote an article about it in 1981, or 1982. Another place to look is the Alamosa library, they have information about the house too. The place was definitely haunted, and a lot of very strange things happened there."

"How much do you know about the house's history?" I asked, noting her comment corroborating the potential documentation at the newspaper and the local library.

"Well, quite a bit, in the [19]60s, a man named Munoz lived in the house. He was a drinker. I guess one time he got real drunk and flipped out. He killed his wife, then he killed himself. When whoever found them came into the house, it was strange, there were still eggs frying on the stove, but they had obviously been dead awhile. A lot of people were killed in that old house, nine, I think, all together. Every tenant except maybe two or three tried to commit suicide in the house."

"Really, that's incredible! Do you know if there was another house at that location before this one was built?"

"No, but there are huge 'matrimony' vines on the property that are an indication that an Indian camp site was located there. There's also an actual 'hanging tree' on the property. It's a big Navaho willow. We tried to hang a swing on it three or four times, but the rope would always break. A twenty-two-year old kid tried to commit suicide in [19]92, or [19]93, and again the rope broke. I guess a little nine-year old boy was poisoned there as well."

"Did the previous tenants tell you anything?" I asked.

"Yes, the people who lived there before us, Jerry and Paula, told us they tried to clean the blood stains off the old inlaid linoleum floor. They couldn't get the stains out. They finally ended up sanding them out. "

"From Munoz killing his wife?"

"Yes. They told us before we moved in, that they had experienced lights flashing on and off in the house and one time, when their parents called the house, the phone was answered by a little boy. We weren't home and the house was all locked up, and for some reason, they didn't think this was strange, and I guess they talked with him for quite awhile. But, at the time, there was no one home! The boy told them where Jerry and

48

the other renters had gone, and, like I said, Jerry's parents didn't think anything of the conversation. Until they found out no one had been home. Kind of sounds like it could have been the nine-year old boy who was killed."

"So what happened when you and your family moved in?"

" Well, we noticed right off, there were some pretty weird smells. Sometimes there was a horrible smell in the house. Like something rotten. Often times at night we noticed the smell of blood out in the yard. I actually became afraid to go outside in the yard at night," she continued, ". . . One night, right after we moved in, my kids had a slumber party. I remember it was Friday the Thirteenth. At the stroke of midnight, all their posters fell off their wall. Other strange thing happened to the boys. There was something in there. The boys would be on the stairs, and something would throw them back down the stairs. This happened three different times. "

"Another time my oldest boy Bill was in the front room with his girlfriend. He heard a noise at the front door and yelled for who-ever-it was to 'come in.' He heard the door open, and something came in and grabbed his girlfriend around the wrist. It grabbed her so hard, it turned black and blue. Then, the next morning something tore Bill's cross earring right out of his ear."

"He had a pierced ear?" I asked, hating to interrupt Kay's accounts of the strange happenings.

"Yes. . . but not anymore " She continued right in with another strange account.

"There was a strange door in the house, it used to be between the living room and the dining room. But you couldn't keep it closed. Paula and Jerry even put a hasp lock on it, and it would still bang open when they were out of the room! They finally just took the door off the hinges."

I located another ex-tenant of the house. The thirty year-old woman also had numerous accounts of the weird goings-on in the North River Road "haunted house." But first she related hearing about another strange Alamosa house. "Do you know about that old house on First Street? There's a house there that's been moved three or four times, and every time they move it, it causes all kinds of weird problems. They had to move it back and put it back on its foundation. I've known about it every since I was a little kid. I've heard that the house is haunted. It's been moved to La Jara, and Manassa, (Colorado) and within two months, they had to bring it back and put it back on its original foundation! "

"That's interesting," More material to research. "How long did you live in the North River Road house?"

"Almost two years."

"When was this?"

"In [19]86 and [19]87. I lived with Kay Thompson for a while, and when she moved out, we took over. All kinds of weird things happened in that house. . . There were occasions when I called over there and Kay wasn't home, I'd call, and this seven or eight year-old little boy would answer the phone. He'd say, 'No, no one's here.' I'd ask him. 'Well, do you know when they'll be back?' He'd say, 'No. No one's here. I'm all by myself.' I got to thinking about it a time or two, and I think we figured it out. It seemed he'd only answer if the phone was left in a certain place in the house. After I called, I even went over there a time or two. I thought, maybe someone dropped him off because they thought Kay was home. I'd go out there and I couldn't find anybody! The second time it happened, I asked Kay, 'What is going on? Who's the little boy that answers the phone?' She said, 'Oh, he's a ghost. He answers the phone every now and then.' Evidently a little boy was poisoned by his father, and died in the house."

"What are some of the other things that happened while you were there?"

"Kay's son, Billy, and I were watching TV one night in the front room. I was dating him at the time. We were sitting there and we heard this light tap at the door. Billy got up, and looked out the door, and no one was there. He just kind of blew it off. We finished the program we were watching and heard it again; this time it was a little heavier. Billy thought it was his brother messing around and went over and yanked the door thinking he was going to catch somebody. Nobody was there. The third time, well he got sassy and yelled, 'Well come ON in, the party's in here!' Whatever it was came in. We were sitting there on the couch and I looked at my hand, and it was turning blue. It felt like somebody had their hand wrapped around my wrist! They were cutting the circulation off! We kept saying, 'this ain't right, this ain't right!'

"The next morning after this had all happened, I was in the back room, and I heard Billy yell out, 'let me go!' Kay and I kinda looked at each other and went over to where he was. He had had a pierced earring in his ear. Well, the earring had been completely ripped out of his ear! He had marks on him that he couldn't have put there himself! I had fingerprints from a hand bigger than Billy's around my wrist. You could see the bruises where fingers had squeezed. Kay saw it. We've never been able to find somebody that could explain these things.

"Other little things happened. We'd move the furniture in the house, and the next morning it was all back were it had been. Nobody ever heard a sound. This was strange. Nothing ever physically attacked me, but you would get a real cold, cold sensation. . . I had a horse there and that horse was well trained: You could lead it anywhere you wanted to take him. But he absolutely would not go near the house." She related another story of seeing a black-wagon with somebody driving, coming up the road, then it turned around and went off. She continued with accounts of sonic apparitions.

"There were nights where you could sit outside and hear the Pony

Express and the stage change. We could hear the chains that were on the stage coach and people yelling. It was only certain nights of the year, or maybe during particular weather conditions, but you could hear the chains on the stage coach. We'd hear them come in, but we would never hear them leave! It was the darndest thing! It was extremely weird.

"There was one window upstairs that you could not close. If you closed it and went back downstairs, you went back upstairs, the window was open! This window, we even nailed it shut, and in a half-hour, the window was open and broke. You couldn't leave it open two, or three inches, it would always end up open all the way. We even put plastic on it, and the plastic was ripped off and we never heard anything."

The house was burned down when partying kids threw a bottle of whiskey into the stove and the place caught on fire. The fire department let it burn to the ground. As it burned, orange flame-filled holes in the roof were aligned like a "giant smiling face," then the roof fell into oblivion amidst a rising shower of sparks.

I ended up talking with five former renters who lived in the place, and their stories were related with honest and earnest conviction. I heard rumors that teenagers would go out to the house after the last tenant moved out and when the house burned down. They may have performed rituals and tried to raise the spirits said to dwell there. The many stories I uncovered relating strange occurrences in the old house on River Road are too numerous to fully cover here, and I think it's safe to say that no one shed a tear when the old place was finally destroyed.

Dead Whisper Trends

I am firmly convinced that location-specific sites of unusual, so-called paranormal activity; portal areas [small, defined locations where unexplained activity seems to be centered], haunted sites and other concentrated areas of activity, may be our most direct investigative path studying the mechanics of paranormal manifestation. And today in 2007, mainstream America has embraced "ghosts" as their latest paranormal fascination *de jour*. It seems like every month there is a new "ghost" television show and there may be good reason for this. Perhaps investigators should be closely following polls that track public interest in various aspects of the paranormal and adjust their focus accordingly.

An entire book could be written simply looking at the hypothetical affect of pop-cultural trends and their relationship to flaps of unexplained event reports. For instance: perusal of UFO flaps from 1950 to the present suggests to me that there appears to be a correlation between North American UFO flaps and the year preceding a political party change in the US executive branch, i.e., he years proceeding Eisenhower, Johnson, Nixon, Reagan, Clinton first terms were flap years. Looking at my database I notice a sizeable percentage of UADs in the SLV occur within two days of a full moon and so appears to be a moon-phase correlation within the unusual livestock death phenomenon.

Haunted sites and "ghosts" are fertile ground for aspiring paranormal investigators. Is Life Imitating Art? Or is Art Imitating Life?

I refer interested readers to deadwhisper.com. I am helping spearhead an effort to educate aspiring ghost-hunters and portal site investigators. And (with DVD sales) fund future scientific "haunting site" investigations by the Dead Whisper Project.

Filming Dead Whisper, Manteno State Hospital, 2006 with RJTV and the Indiana Ghost Trackers.

Juan Bautista de Anza

Juan de Onate

Kit Carson and John Fremont

Zebulon Pike

The Sniders. "Ol Town" Crestone, 1990.

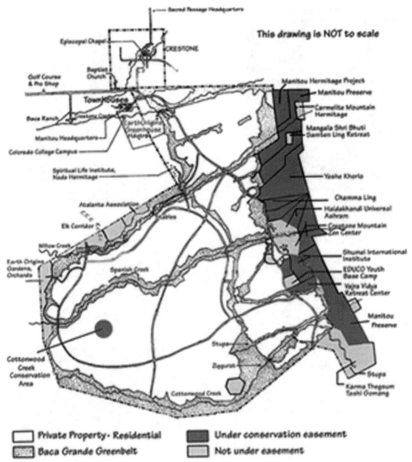

Baca Grande Subdivision map wih the Manitou Foundations' grants to the unbroken spiritual lineages

Hanne and Maurice Strong. Have they created the spiritual UN?

Crestone Peak, Challenger Point and Kit Carson. The Chalets extends out from the base of these mountains.

Hopi Elder Martin Gashweseoma and the Venerable Adzom Rinpoche, Crestone 2006

Sierra Blanca circa 1889 Fourth Highest in CO

By 1901 the Crestone/Moffat region had a population of over ten-thousand — mostly miners.

The haunted Ace Inn in Alamosa, CO

Haunted house on North River Road

CHAPTER THREE:
There's GOLD in Them Hills

In June 1993 I heard a rumor of unusual activity at the mouth of remote San Creek Canyon. I met the source, an outfitter who had led a small group on horseback down Sand Creek Canyon. He claimed his group of riders observed military-garbed personnel, wearing "chrome helmets" buzzing around on ATVs. I researched ownership and found that there is a small privately-held parcel that sits between the Baca and the Federally-owned Great Sand Dunes National Monument (now a National Park). By early summer 1993, I had zeroed in on this southeastern corner of the Baca Ranch as a key investigative region and I strove to uncover as much documentation about this remote region as possible.

This ten mile portion of the Sangre de Cristo Mountains stretches from the northern border of the Great Sand Dunes north to the southern edge of the Baca Development. A black hole on any map, this is one of America's most remote areas and one of the least (publicly) visited areas of the Rio Grande National Forest. In 1988, a good friend of mine trespassed onto the Ranch and bushwacked his way up to the upper [Deadman] Lakes. The fifteen mile journey, with detours, took him two days. He camped up at the pristine, untouched lake; one of three, located at eleven thousand feet under the watchful glower of 13,414 foot high Cleveland Peak. He observed that the area was so pristine he was able to catch trout "…on a bare hook …they would hit anything that flashed. It was like an aquarium." The only public access to this part of the mountain range is made by crossing over the crest of the towering Sangre de Cristos, from the Wet Mountain Valley, through National Forest, a difficult proposition. Few individuals are granted permission to travel the easiest route through the very private Baca Ranch to access this part of the National Forest on Sand and Deadman's Creeks.

Buddy & Gary

After moving to the San Luis Valley one of my part-time, extra jobs was bi-weekly mowing the lawn of Buddy Whitlock's, lawn down at Ranch Headquarters. It had been years since I had mowed a lawn, but just like riding a bike, right? When I first met him, Buddy was an amiable, good 'ol boy; riding herd on the three-hundred thousand acre spread. At one point during my second visit, Buddy took me aside and during the conversation he told me an interesting story concerning his support role on horseback with a pack train, hauling out all the "trash" left behind by special forces (training?) up at the extremely remote Sand Creek Lakes area. On his way out, he was caught by an early season blizzard and "barely made it" back out alive. Whitlock was former supervisor of the Rio Grande National Forest, a huge expanse that extends the length of the Sangres behind the Baca Ranch.

I'm not much in the lawn boy department, so I only lasted a month, or so, as Buddy's lawn mower, but I was able to pump Whitlock for some background history about the Ranch area. Later that fall, Buddy recommended me to Speartex Ranch manager Bob Lamm, who needed help feeding the company's Moffit, Colorado-based herd during the winter of 1989-1990. Each dawn during my first winter in the Valley, along with ranch-hand Bob Pickle, I fed a hungry herd of impatient Texas Longhorns. At times I had to beat back the herd with a pitchfork when they stormed the hay trailer. A couple of the young bulls were particularly fearless and I quickly grew eyes in the back of my head, gave their impressive horns a wide-berth, and learned how to quickly wield my pitchfork.

After Boyce's Baca Ranch purchase intent was announced, in early 1993, I applied after seeing a help-wanted notice for ranch-hand employment on Boyce's future expanded holdings. I called to set-up an appointment not thinking I'd hear back from Boyces' business headquarters. Gary and his wife Joanna (a heir to a Hollywood fortune) had met me as they had become casual fans of a couple of bands I played for—they enjoyed getting out, flashing their chic cowboy garb and dancing. Much to my surprise, Gary responded within a couple of days and he suggested I join him on a jeep-tour of his property. OK, I figured working on the ranch was better than working construction for six bucks an hour. We met at his Rancho Rosado headquarters—just east of Crestone—off Road T, and he suggested we take a ride. We climbed into his Jeep and headed up onto the Sangres to visit a bear-hunter's blind between Dimick Gulch and San Isabel Creek. This is a little-known elk corridor utilized by a sizeable herd during elk season (wink). I bounced along with the strikingly handsome cowboy (with his huge, wide-brimmed Mexican cowboy hat and Colt-45, on his hip. As we headed down past the San Isabelle gravel pit, he told me about a very low-key multi-million dollar treasure search that had been launched out onto the Baca Ranch prior to his offer on the three hundred-thousand acre ranch to embattled American

Water and Development Inc (AWDI)

AWDI, and the Baca Ranch connection to the United Nations, "globalist" Maurice Strong, the nature Conservancy and Uncle Sam will undoubtedly someday be the subject of an in-depth journalistic investigation. Resource allocation and the emerging "one-world" mindset of the cultural/political elite will be an important subject in the early part of the twentieth-century and this scenario involving water and the SLV is liquid gold for a savy proponent of "sustainable development," a term often used by Strong. Strong's connection to the before-mentioned, little-known "Grand Canal" scheme to de-salinize water at the tip of Hudson's Bay and send it to the SLV is not well-known. After diverting five river systems, with the aid of several nuclear power plants, the water would be shipped uphill to continually refill America's water-tank—located at seventy-five hundred feet in the SLV The water would then be sold, distributing this precious commodity downstream to the parched southwest and northern Mexico. Maurice and Hanne Strong are key-players in the San Luis Valley saga. Google 'em for yourself …

Apparently. the treasure-hunters that Boyce mentioned, out on the Baca Ranch in 1990-1991, left quietly. However, two years later, a jet-powered Bell helicopter was seen crisscrossing the Baca Grande Development with a magnetometer suspended below on a long cable like a sinister torpedo. (see photo section) Later, we surmised they were probably attempting to locate the Deadman's Cave treasure mentioned later in this chapter. Locate the hidden Spanish canon made out of iron and you may find gold nearby?

Keeping Your Ear to the Ground

The San Luis Valley features a variety and intensity of anomalous phenomena found in few locales, but there are also mundane mysteries. The history of this relatively unknown region of North America is extremely interesting and the more I dig into the past, the more dirt I seem to uncover. Occasionally, if a prospector digs hard enough, they may strike the mother lode. During my first two years in the SLV, I was fascinated when I was exposed to beliefs that link real-time UFO sightings to gold and the discovery of hidden treasure. On the surface this attribution may seem inconsequential, but it is compelling and it may be crucial to an anthropological analysis of the San Luis Valley. This peculiar linkage between two very divergent phenomena is found predominantly in the southern portions of the Spanish-American San Luis Valley. You could summarize the local tradition as follows: if a UFO is observed in fairly close proximity to a witness, they immediately contacts his/her family and they watch the object closely, hoping it will linger over an identifiable spot, for underneath "treasure" is to be found. If and when a site is identified, the family converges on the spot with picks and shovels, and the digging begins.

Fifteen years after first being exposed to this peculiar version of attributional thinking, I still have no concrete documentation that this technique has proven successful, but it sure sounds good on paper. I've also met another local resident who has supposedly seen "a Spanish gold-piece" found underneath a hovering UFO, but I personally have never seen it. Obviously, lacking simple, verifiable proof, my left-brain jury continues to scratch its right-brain enthusiasm regarding the effectiveness of this UFO-inspired treasure-hunting technique.

But what would you make of the following prospecting technique? In the late seventies and early eighties, a SLV treasure hunter, armed with a dog and a broom, would allegedly wait for fireballs to appear over Blanca. According to a prospector who knew him, the man would camp at a specific observation point he had identified, located on the southwestern side of the Blanca Massif. When a fiery orb descended from the sky and then bounced down the mountainside, he would allegedly be able to identify the exact spots where the fire ball touched down. In the morning, he would brush off the circular burn marks on the ground and underneath, he allegedly found "ashtray-sized" solid gold discs, a little "larger and thicker than a sand dollar." According to his prospector friend (whom I interviewed extensively for a chapter in *Enter the Valley)* the prospector collected quite a number of these gold discs, and by the mid-eighties, he was able to buy a large farm in the Midwest. According to his prospector friend, he died under mysterious circumstances from a gunshot wound while prospecting in the SLV before moving to his new spread.

Dig Here!

As I began researching and gathering the myths, legends and stories, I learned that the Greater San Luis Valley region is one the oldest settled areas in Colorado/Northern New Mexico and that the region features literally dozens of Spanish treasure legends, numerous lost mines and lost treasure accounts. When you include several notorious lost robbery hordes and sub-cultural beliefs linking UFOs to treasure, you have an area with many potentially lucrative secrets to investigate—maybe more than any specific location in the great Southwest. Stories have evidently circulated around this section of the Sangres and the southwest in general since the early seventeenth century and I discovered historical documentation concerning claims of gold and treasure. I discovered many more additional "legends" and stories than I could possibly include in the brief, two-thousand word article I was asked to write for upstart vanity publisher Gary Boyce. I turned in my piece, but he folded the *Needles* just before my article was to be published.

Nonetheless, it was a good experience and it inspired me to look into the area's history. My curiosity had been tweaked and during the course of the next several years, I had my ears and eyes open for any conclusive data firmly establishing a Spanish treasure-hunter presence in the San Luis Valley prior to the acknowledged 1692 de Vargas Expedition. I have always been fascinated by history, and I wondered, why didn't the Spanish "officially" venture north from the Taos area for over one hundred years? When the conquistadors and the ever-present Catholic missionaries first established a presence in Taos, at the extreme southern end of the Valley, during the mid 1600s, the vast area north of Taos was a place of mystery and awe.

> The Utes traditional homeland encompassed most of the state of Colorado, including the San Luis Valley and Elbert County, both of which, as we've noted, are areas of high strangeness. In the San Luis Valley, the warlike Utes drove the Navaho out. In the early 1800s, the Utes allied themselves with the Jicarilla Apaches (the same tribe that now occupies the paranormal hot spot of Dulce) in a bloody war against the Navaho, all at the behest of the Spanish ..."It could be argued that the Utes have historical ties to nearly all of the areas that are now regarded as paranormal hit spots. And there is no question that they, along with most of the other tribes in the American West and Southwest, consider the subject of witchcraft to be very serious business." *Hunt for the Skinwalker*

The Utes maintained a presence during the warmer months, but other visiting tribes mostly came to visit in small bands, or individually. Some Plains Indian tribes considered the SLV to be where "dead souls" go. The *Dine'* considered the Blanca area to be "where all thought originates," or the sacred "Mountain of the East," Sisnajiini. Taos, NM, geographically, is located at what is considered the extreme northern reach of initial Spanish power. The Spanish didn't extend military power north of the Taos Pueblo until the Don Diego de Vargas expedition which was mounted to subjugate the Pueblo peoples, twelve years after the 1680 Taos uprising, when the Pueblo Indians revolted. Although the De Vargas expedition

61

is considered the first Spanish major incursion into south-central Colorado, others must have ventured north. It is known that de Vargas, accompanied by one hundred soldiers, seventy settlers with families, eighteen Franciscan, and Indian allies, marched up the Rio Grande into what is now Conejos and Costilla Counties, but decided to return to Sante Fé. A long improbable time period passed before the next official expedition north into Colorado. The 1779 "Campaign" of New Mexico Governor Juan Bautista de Anza against Comanche Chief, Cuerno Verde, or Greenhorn is considered the next Spanish push into the region.

Dr. Marilyn Childs, an eminent archaeoastronomer, recalls an aside mentioned by a college professor while she was a student:

> One of my professors at the University of Washington, who taught classes in archaeology, was Dr. Alex Kreiger. He was one of the scholars that did lots of research on the different Spanish expeditions. He knew I was interested in ufology, so he looked up some of the information in the chronicles for me. Apparently the Spanish were seeing lights around Mount Blanca (sic), in the Sangre de Cristo Range; even back in the 1500's, and they also heard some kind of sounds they said were coming from the ground.

I found it curious that one of the oldest continuously inhabited dwellings (some three-stories tall) in North America were located at the south end of the Valley at the Taos Pueblo, and yet officially, the Spanish never expanded north, into the rest of the San Luis Valley, for over two hundred years.

As human nature would dictate, there were undoubtedly many secret mercenary forays up to *del Norte* into the San Luis Valley. Over the years, the discovery of Spanish canon barrels, conquistador helmets, arrastas, smelters, and enigmatic carvings, such as the Maltese Cross at the mouth of the Upper Spanish Caves, have always fueled the colorful legends of lost "Spanish Treasure." These same stories were heard by the original Colorado gold-rush prospectors as they arrived in Colorado in the late 1850s and early 1860s.

> The first legend of the Southwest begins for Europeans when Alvar Nunez Cabeza de Vaca saw an Indian give a *cascabel de cobre*, a copper rattle, to one of his companions. This simple happening combined with the tales he had heard about gold-paved cities created the legend of Quivira .... Stories continued to circulate and accumulate, not only of cities paved with gold but of mountains of solid ore

and lakes shimmering with quicksilver in 1692, however, the story of this fabulous mountain not only reached the ears of Diego de Vargas but also those of the Viceroy who sent for specimens of a substance thought to be quicksilver. Some historians go as far as to suggest that the legend of Cerro Azul was the primary reason for the re-conquest of New Mexico by Don Diego de Vargas.

One shiny thing above all motivated the Spanish. Huerfano County resident, investigative journalist David Perkins, who has researched our area's treasure legends for many years, wrote an insightful history of *Caverna de Oro,* and the various area gold legends in *Western Spirit* Magazine*:*

> Capt. Elisha Horn, who is credited with discovering the Cavern of Gold in 1869, supposedly found a skeleton clad in Spanish armor that was pierced with an arrow. He also found a 'Maltese cross' which marked the cave's entrance. The cross is still visible. Although several intriguing artifacts have been found in the cave, and nearby, there is no direct evidence that it was ever a gold producing mine or treasure cache. Numerous spelunking ventures have attempted to map the 'seemingly infinite catacombs,' but experts will venture no guess as to how extensive the cave system will turn out to be. It is now estimated to be one of the five or six deepest caves in the U.S.

This labyrinth of caves and passageways sits just to the east of The Great Sand Dunes. The largest cavern system in Colorado, the Marble Caves are one of several enigmatic entrances to a netherworld beneath the San Luis Valley and the surrounding mountains that figure prominently in many of this area's myths and legends.

Over the course of the late seventeenth and into the eighteenth century, the Spanish combed the West for gold, silver, and mercury. Although Don Diego de Vargas was acknowledged to be the leader of the first officially sanctioned expedition into the San Luis Valley in 1692, rumors persist, to this day, of earlier clandestine forays into the area by gold-seeking Spanish mercenaries. Other legends persisted from the early days of the Spanish exploration of Northern New Mexico. From Perkins' article:

> There is a story in Taos about a Mexican by the name of Vigil who found a document in a church on Guadalajara, Mexico, stating that in 1680 the Spaniards

covered up fourteen million peso's worth of gold in a shaft in the mountains near the pueblo of Taos. This treasure has been hunted by many who believe that the Indians know much more than they are willing to tell. Some of the early prospectors who came to Taos have explored all the likely spots in the area as far (north) as the Red River and into the Moreno Valley, but aside from small locations like the one of a Swede named Gus Lawson, nothing like a Spanish gold horde has been discovered ...

Finding the Final Clue

After much data mining, and a bit of coincidental luck, I've met several knowledgeable "treasure hunters." I have uncovered many stories describing actual "treasure maps" that had failed to lead to fabulous hordes of SLV treasure. For hundreds of years, people have taken these stories very seriously, and some have inspired their descendents to keep the search alive.

During gigs around the Valley, one of our biggest fans was an amiable, unassuming man I'll call Tomas Ortiz (not his real name)., A world-class mechanic and professional drag-racer he is an in-law to a multi-generational treasure hunting family. Tomas' wife is the daughter of the family patriarch. At one point in our initial conversation about "treasure", Tomas casually told me that his brother-in-law has an authentic "treasure map" written in French," and that his in-laws are "direct descendents of Le Blanc." "For three generations" the family has been quietly searching for the fabled lost French Gold Treasure. The family's claim is backed up with what appears to be, a genuine map, supposedly drawn by the harried second expedition before they unsuccessfully tried to escape the Ute Indians with their lives.

After painstakingly searching for decades, by the 1990s, family members had allegedly located seven out of eight landmarks and clues carved in rock that are shown in the map. The most important eighth and final clue has eluded their efforts for two generations. In 1993, their luck apparently turned.

In 1993, on an overcast late fall morning, thirty-year-old Tomas was stalking an solitary elk bull, in the mountains southeast of Del Norte, Colorado. The clouds were building threateningly, and a cold hard rain spat down. The pale pre-dawn gloom cast faint detail to the surrounding vegetation and Ortiz looked around for shelter from the rain keeping a vigilant look out for his elusive prey. He spotted a small three-foot opening in the ground; hidden by some underbrush, and after removing some loose rocks, he squeezed through the opening to get out of the brooding weather. He peered back into the darkness that extended down the path of the low tunnel into the hillside. He clicked on his flashlight and was surprised to find he had entered a five-foot high, four-foot wide tunnel that led back into the dark. It was obviously man-made. Ortiz cautiously squirmed down the gentle-sloping narrow passageway, and after wriggling about twenty feet into the hillside, his way was blocked by an apparent cave-in. Exploring the dim narrow passageway, he spied a carving on the exposed rock wall next to where the blockage closed access deeper into the hill. Quite aware of his in-law's long, multi-generational quest, he was understandably elated by what he saw. It was the long-lost eighth clue that (according to the treasure map) indicated the hidden location of the fabled lost French Treasure.

Completely forgetting the wily elk he had been stalking, Tomas excitedly rushed back to town to tell his in-laws of his find. The following day, he led an expedition back to the tunnel. You can imagine the excitement. Members of the party, consisting of twenty family members of various ages, began eagerly excavating the cave-in, and after several grueling hours of hard work, they extended the tunnel an additional twelve feet into the mountainside. Thirty-two feet in, they encountered a large boulder that that appeared to have been purposely rolled into place to seal the rest of the passageway. By this time, the sun had set and the elated high-fiving group gathered at the entrance and took a break as twilight approached from the east. Undaunted by the approaching gloom, Tomas lined the length of the passageway with a dozen equally spaced unlit candles.

According to Tomas (and his brother-in-law,) the ensuing events allegedly occurred "in a matter of minutes." As Ortiz placed the last candle at the far end of the tunnel, a "large rattlesnake" lunged out of the gloom and narrowly missed striking him. He frantically scrambled backwards out to the entrance followed by a boiling swarm of bats that began pouring out of the hillside. Uncharacteristically, and much to their dismay, the small mammals began squeaking and diving aggressively at the surprised party-members. What they claim happened seconds later quickly erased the elation and excitement of the expedition.

As Tomas knelt down to light the first candle at the entrance to the tunnel, the "candle at the far end" of the passageway inexplicably flared on by itself! The stunned group, knowing no one was back in the tunnel, stared at each other in horror. "At that instant," out of the dark, a "huge owl" dive-bombed the shocked party within inches of their heads.

That was evidently the last straw. As if chased by a ghost the terrified group grabbed their kids, raced down the hillside, piled into their cars and, as Tomas put it, they all "got the hell outta there!"

Tomas told me later, "the French and Spanish placed curses on their [hidden] gold" caches. In light of the strange sequence of events, the family of treasure hunters is understandably wary and they are planning to proceed with caution. Several members now flatly refuse to even venture back to the site.

The story of the lost French gold does not end here. Further research has uncovered tantalizing information suggesting that the attacking Ute Indians may have acquired a substantial portion of the French gold during the running battle, and I've encountered stories that the Utes may have hidden it down near the mouth of the Rio Grande Canyon—near the Colorado/New Mexico border.

The Skulls in Dead Man's Cave

Another fascinating account of treasure is one of the very few SLV discoveries that have officially produced documented gold. This one comes fromthree creeks over from where I lived for almost thirteen years,

The lucky discoverer only brought out a small portion of the alleged treasure. However, as it goes with the territory, the location was lost and the piles of gold bars are probably still there, at the southern end of the Baca Ranch, where Gary Boyce claimed the multi-million dollar treasure hunting expedition concentrated their efforts in the early 1990s.

The Fairplay Flume, 1880; *Empire Magazine*; and *The Denver Post*, have all published articles about this particular gold-treasure story about three prospectors, E.J. Oliver, S.J. Harkman and H.A. Melton. Back in the fall of 1880, the three men had been prospecting two-miles north of what became known as Dead Man Camp, (about eight miles south of where I lived for thirteen years) The sky threatened, and before long the three men found themselves caught in a furious early blizzard. Knowing under ideal weather conditions travel is difficult, at best, in the rugged Sangres, they found shelter underneath a convenient ledge near the mouth of a canyon. Looking across the canyon, one of the men noticed what appeared to be a small opening in the canyon's shear rock wall. They made their way across to the opening and made several crude torches before venturing inside. The opening was very narrow and less than four feet high, and extended into the cliff about ten-feet. It then opened up into a large twenty-foot long vault. Shining their torches around, EJ found the first of five skeletons scattered around the dusty, dark cavern.

After exploring the cavern further, they found several tight passageways extending into the gloom of the mountain, and chose one to explore. It to led into the mountain for some distance and opened up into a larger vault-like chamber. Toward the far end, Melton noticed what appeared to be shelves carved into the side of the western wall. He lit the area and observed some peculiar-looking stones stacked on the shelf. He picked one up; surprised at its heavy weight, and brought it back to his partners to look at. Imagine their delight when the "stones" under the torches glare turned out to be crude bars of smelted gold!

In their excitement, thinking the opening would be easy to mark and find again, the men gathered up five of the bars from the pile, and headed over the pass to Silver Cliff, in the Wet Mountain Valley. The bars, etched with what appeared to be Spanish engravings, proved to be worth nine-hundred dollars apiece, and the men became instant celebrities. Although asked by many, the men steadfastly refused to divulge the actual location and secretly made plans to return to Dead Man's Cave. An article in the Denver *Post* noted:

> The men slipped off in the spring. But they never found the Dead Man Cave. They had thought it would be easy, but on their return they found so many places that looked like the area in which the caves were found. In fact, practically the entire area seemed strange to them. They went back frequently. Many others went back frequently. Nobody found anything.

Colorado has treasure rights which can be obtained for the right to look, find and keep treasure found at specific, deeded locations. I wondered who owned the treasure rights for the area around the Dead Man's Treasure. AWDI? Gary Boyce? Maurice Strong? What defines "treasure"? Instinctively, I have sensed that the Deadman Creek and Sand Creek area—just over the northern edge of the Great Sand Dunes could be a treasure trove of knowledge and discovery. Headed south on Highway 17 to rehearsal, I witnessed an immense glow of arc-welding type light phenomenon reflecting off the western face of Sand Creek Canyon from over twenty mils away. The prolonged flashes of light appeared to out of my direct line-of-sight up and around the east facing canyon. I remember thinking it was like 'Thor' using his arc-welder. The amount of energy it must have taken to produce the effect would be like two or three Superbowls. Could this event be connected to the behind-the-scenes maneuvers to gain control of today's treasure under the Baca Ranch region's trillion's of gallons of water, billions of dollars of methane and possibly oil? Now that the Deadman/Sand Creek area is under Federal "management" environmentalists beware, all bets are off. As in the past, the modern version of age-old traditions of hidden treasure in the San Luis Valley holds the promise of incredible riches, but the odds of hitting the jackpot are doubly difficult, even for Uncle Sam and his globalist bunch.

Treasure maps, stories and legends of lost gold and death-bed confessions concerning a secret goldmine are endlessly fascinating to me. Maybe, as a kid, watching Greg Peck and Omar Sharif in *McKenna's Gold*, or maybe Bogey pondering after the *Treasure of the Sierra Madres*, "we don't need no stinking badg-eez" sparked my interest. My second book, *Enter the Valley*, has an entire chapter devoted to these many compelling treasure legends from the greater SLV region. The more you dig the more dirt you uncover. I highly recommendThomas Penfield's book *Dig Here!*—a meticulously-researched listing of notable southwestern United States treasure legends.

The simple listing of the San Luis Valley and Huerfano's lost mines and treasures in *Enter the Valley* is, to say the least, impressive: Accounts from the seminal works, *Lost Mines and Buried Treasures of the West*, by Thomas Probert, (the University of California Press, 1977); *Treasure of the Sangre De Cristos*, by Arthur Campa, (The University of Oklahoma Press, 1963); the volumous *Directory of Buried or Sunken Treasures and Lost Mines of the United States*; (True Treasure Publications, 1971) the compelling *Treasure Tales of the Rockies*, by Thomas Penfield, (Sage Books, 1961); the northern SLV's *Post Marks and Places*, by Jack Harlan (Golden Bell Press), *Colorado's Lost Mines and Buried Treasure*, by Caroline Bancroft (Bancroft Booklets, 1961) and various other sources were used.

Of course, right when you think you have zeroed in on historical treasures, life throws you a screwball. I still don't know what to make of the following claim...

Michael's Strange Adventure

By far, the most unusual claim in my investigation of treasure legends involved the linking of gold to UFOs and the claim arrived in late 1997. My September 1997 *Enter The Valley* deadline had blown by like a literary freight car, and I congratulated myself for having completed my second book on time after havingto trim it down from its bloated one hundred and twenty thousand words. Three weeks after delivering the final seventy thousand word manuscript, I received a phone call from the father of a recently-arrived Crestone resident (a hardworking twenty-something year old woman with an eight year old daughter who I had met while on a construction project.) Her boyfriend had recently relocated to the valley and she had worked with the my brother Brendon's AdobeWorks crew on the Sanctuary House project. One day after work the woman hinted that her boyfriend's dad (who was in town researching high-tech gold detection equipment) had experienced an otherworldly encounter involving treasure and that we should talk. She and her boyfriend were both aware of my various interests and they wondered if I might be able to help dad in some way. Hey, sure, wow. I told them, tell him to give a call, and that I'd be back at the house later that afternoon. I didn't promise I'd meet with him at such short notice. There was a lull in our local sighting activity and I welcomed some downtime, but the vibe behind the lead tweaked my curiosity and my intuitive sense had been well-triggered. I was really making a push with my crack band of hot players, Laffing Buddha and this lead became a diversion.

An intelligent voice called later that afternoon, identified himself as "Michael" (not his real name) and the mercurial, jittery voice on the phone quickly briefed me on the mundane aspects of his treasure-hunting project. He hinted around that he had be "given" information. I was on high alert from the beginning of our conversation. I played it low-key and I don't think he had a clue about my process, but in less than five minutes he managed to trigger a couple of my closely-held red-flag indicators that I look for to remind me when to perk up and take notice. (I could write an entire chapter alone on these indicators buried inside witnesses' anecdotal accounts, but later …)

Michael cut to the chase and confided in me. I appreciated his matter-of-fact summary to the extent that I rearranged the following morning's schedule to meet with him. We met in downtown Crestone at the Peristroika Café. Over coffee, surrounded by the exuberance of town kids running about with dogs barking, we took each other's measure. As Michael's unique story unfolded, I remember wondering to myself if he could be some sort of set-up; some sort of disinformation agenda. His claim combined several high-strange elements that I have studied and the coincidence was suspect. In a short half-hour I received his cut-to-the-chase overview and I suggested we meet to record an in-depth interview at his home down in northern New Mexico, at his convenience.

He left town and I mulled over my meeting for several days and re-visited my database of events generated from the area of the Sangres that directly straddle the Colorado/New Mexico border. This region extends south of "Wild Horse Mesa" down across the border to Amalia, NM, and up Costilla Canyon. Note: This geographic area hides in a curious black-hole inside my database. There are few, if any, reports that I have found documented in this border region of CO/NM. There is a curious parallel with Archuleta Mesa that straddles the CO/NM border less than one-hundred miles west. The border area between north-central New Mexico and south-central Colorado should receive maximum public scrutiny.

A couple of weeks after our coffee-house meeting, we set-up an interview date. The day arrived and Isadora and I headed out into a wild and windy early spring day and headed south to meet with Michael. It was a spooky day. We bucked a forty-mile-an-hour headwind the entire way south. Turning off Highway 522 and driving east, high up the foothills toward his house, Isadora and I noticed the nearby Sangres had recently been scorched by a massive forest fire, leaving a ghostly landscape of dead shuddering trees that whistled in the wind around Michael's house. Climbing out of the Jeep, I noticed the outside of his house was adorned with black scorch-marks from the raging fire that had bypassed his home. The clouds boiled a greenish welcome above our arrival. Later we learned that the day's strange weather spawned three tornadoes, just east over the Sangres about the time we first sat down at Michael's crow's nest home.

We were welcomed by a warm fire and a tale worthy of the fiendishly-windy day. Michael wasted little time on small talk and formalities; he immediately began telling his matter-of-fact story into the tape recorder. It is obvious; the man is brilliant, has a laser quick, comfortably nervous, enthusiastic style and earnestly believes he had a truly remarkable experience from out of the blue. He was sometimes prone to head off on lightning-quick tangents, but, for the most part, I was able to keep the conversation on point. Isadora and I listened to his intriguing account while Michael's wife slept in the next room.

Michael cut to the meat, "I approached Chris because I had an experience that seemed to indicate something fantastic had happened to me, and I was looking for a machine with the technology with which one could find gold." We all chuckled.

Michael then nervously lit the first of many cigarettes. He looked at me closely, thoughtfully, before shaking his head and blurting out, "I don't believe in 'flying saucers.' If there's one in my front yard, well, there's one in my front yard. If there isn't, there isn't." We all chuckle again. He took a drag and looked down, and rattled off a series of claims, "Well, I don't know ... everyone around me, and around here, have found emasculated cows. I found one that had been done within two, or three hours of my finding i¹ ... We've seen flying saucers go right over with colors underneath. We've seen the beams of light going down where they found the cows later. And lights going around in a circle, through binoculars at night; about three thousand feet above the ground"

This was too good to be true, but I was rolling tape and willing to have a listen. I still don't know what to think. You decide, was it worth the trip through a tornadic storm? I think so…

What The Locals Are Seeing Around the Border

Michael's revelations concerning the intensity of activity around the Colorado-New Mexico border area where he lives further validated suspicions I'd had since the early stages of my amateur investigation. This forgotten border area of the SLV has produced no credible documented reports. This is one of several curious locales of the "greater" SLV that has a complete lack of concrete data; rumors yes, but nothing documented. I've heard stories of everything from UFO craft in dogfights with the Air Force— just north of the Taylor Ranch/ Culebra Peak, area in the mid-seventies, to recent 2006 Bigfoot encounter claims. I suspect that this is a key "hot-spot" locale that deserve 24/7 monitoring

I noticed the careful languaging Michael employed when he described his supposed experiences …"One time, when we were lying in a field at night, we saw arrow-shaped black [craft] coming in gray and black waves. Four at a time, then whoosh. Off …you know? We've seen your globes …. There was one that was maybe a kilometer-sized gold ball. A guy in town and his wife saw this thing, it was huge. It was lighting up every sagebrush for a distance of six miles. Another time, this fellow was camped way out at night, and a sheepherder ran down the mountain and stumbled into his camp. He was just terrified. His fifty-five sheep had been 'sucked-up.'"

"About three months before my [abduction] incident [summer 1995], I was lying in bed and a light came through the window. It was coming from up in the air, and came through at a slant. This beam of light was so bright, it made the inside of this cabin look like I was on the moon. Black versus the light beams. I did not get in it [the beam of light] because it wasn't moving, it was immobile, slanting into the room. I was scared. It lasted for about three minutes, then it went away.

Six years after my visit with Michael, there was a strange incident over the 2003 Fourth of July weekend that involved a number of his neighbors who claimed to have watched hundreds of small craft entering and leaving a huge lenticular cloud that was hanging just south of Ute Mountain, which straddles the Colorado/ New Mexico border. Over the course of an hour, the objects were seen, through binoculars, to enter and exit the cloud. One witness estimated that "at least four hundred" separate objects were seen during the mid-day sighting. A couple of days later, a photograph of the cloud was featured on the Jeff Rense web-site, although no mention was made by the photographer of any similar UFO sightings associated with the cloud formation.

Finding Gold With The Aliens

Michael paused an hour into our interview and lit another cigarette and nervously poked the fire before he launched into an alleged "abduction" account. I checked the recorder to make sure I had enough tape. He continued ...

"About three months later, [fall 1995], I suddenly woke up in a flying saucer. I know this sounds as absurd as I felt at that moment. I was in the forward part [of the ship] and looking down through a large window. To the right was a panel of raised buttons. They were shaped like diamonds and squares and they were in primary colors.

"I kept looking around and I saw these three beings standing there toward the back with dome-heads and slanted eyes. They were wearing white robes and they were different heights. But I could tell they didn't want me to look at them. When I first turned and looked at them, I got this felling [from the beings] 'No, no, no.' It's real difficult to make logical assumptions, but I was real sensitive to this; they didn't want me to look at them.

Michael's sense that "the beings" didn't want him to look at them is a bit unusual. I can think of few cases were this type of alien-reaction has been observed. He continued ..."So, I looked around and thought, 'what am I going to do? How interesting I can think about what I'm doing.' I thought, hey, 'I can look at the controls, maybe I can decipher how this whole thing works.'

"As I looked over to my right at the bank of controls, it was almost as though, hidden to my left behind the wall, there was a white plastic covering in the shape of the control panel. It went around [covering the control panel] just slightly faster than my eyes, so, I was looking a shiny white, [smooth] curved panel. I imagine they covered the controls as a containment procedure. I thought, boy, 'this is interesting! They're either handling my mind, or this is really a real phenomenon. So what am I going to do now?'

"In this experience, speaking and thought would have been the same thing. It felt as though I was speaking. It felt as though I was in my body. It felt as though I was standing there, and so forth. I said, 'can this window do anything?' And in a FLASH—it was very fast—in half a second, the window was covered in not only letters and numbers, but also hieroglyphics. In orange . . ." he chuckled, " ...then the letters and numbers went away real fast. I said, 'Ohh-kay, What am I going to do now? They don't want me to look at them, they don't want me to see the controls, I'm looking out this stupid window ...What am I supposed to do?'

"In hindsight, I would've asked 'what's the cure for Alzheimer's', or 'how does your technology work? Can we interact?' I seemed to be interacting with something that made physical changes. Well, I looked at this window, and I asked, 'Can it show gold?' It took about a half a second to go approximately thirty to forty miles north. I deduced that flying saucers can go about sixty miles per second. Two seconds to Albuquerque is pretty cool! They're so fast you can't even see the 'friggin things! It seemed to me that the machinery was reacting as fast as I could think. It could pick up what my brain patterns were going to do before I cognized [sic] the fact. Their techniques are absolutely fantastic, not to mention their machinery. I have a photographic memory, and I've spent a lot of time thinking and looking at this experience."

"So, anyway, I'm up in the air, about two miles out, up in the air about three thousand feet. I'm looking down at an angle at some mountains. There's this ray of light going down, and it lights up this huge gold aura at the base of the ray. I remember thinking, 'I know where this place is!' Anyway, to fully explain, I need to digress for a moment."

Historical Evidence

"There are stories coming down from the Crestone area concerning the loss of two wagon-loads of gold south of the [Great] sand dunes [National Park]. A lot of people have looked in some of the nearby canyons trying to find them, but nobody has, that I know of. Well, I was out fire-fighting in Southern Arizona in the early '70's, and this Indian 'fella walked up to me and said, 'I've never told this story to anybody else this ...' and he told me this incredible story. Out of the blue. Evidently, one time he was in a sleeping bag, sleeping on the porch in a ruined house, in the middle of the prairie and about thirty Indian elders showed up. Then, a whole pile of youngsters showed up who were going to go through some kind of initiation. Anyway, they all sat around and told stories, and one of the stories this Indian fella told me about. He said he'd never told the story before, because he thought they'd kill him because he overheard their initiation ritual.

"So, I'm not sure exactly when this happened, but this wagon train was coming down from up north and was ambushed near Wild Horse Mesa [just southeast of San Luis, Colorado]. The

Indian scouts accompanying the two loads ran into an Apache war-party. Then some soldiers took the Indian scouts about a mile south to where there was water. Then the remaining soldiers started digging a ways back up the trail, and it was assumed by the Indian scouts accompanying the wagon train, they were burying the gold. The Indian scouts thought this was funny, because they could hear the troops digging the hole all night. In the morning, it was confirmed, because here came the wagons, loaded with rocks. The impression the wheels made in the ground were less [than when they were loaded with gold]. The Indians thought this was funny too. Probably when they were laughing, they were jumped by the Apaches, and they [the Apaches] killed everyone except a small boy, who hid, and the story came from him, and turned into this Indian legend.

"I suspect the first place I was shown [while aboard the saucer], was the location of these two wagon-loads of gold and I suspect that the first place I was taken was where this gold was cached …" There are countless stories and accounts of lost treasure and knowing about these stories, I took Michael's claim of being shown an actual treasure location seriously. Michael continued with his account and described the rest of his alleged encounter:

"The ship was interacting with my mind. I asked the beings, 'So, are there any more [locations of lost gold]? And z-z-zip, there I was, another six or eight miles north, and I was being shown another one. In this case, I was about a mile above it. I memorized this particular hill and again I photographed it in my mind. I asked, 'Can we go closer?' This was odd, for all of a sudden, we were right over it tilted at an extreme angle, so that I was looking down from about forty feet up. I even started putting my arms out [in front of me] because I was afraid I was going to fall. I was reassured that it was OK. The ship was tilted at an extreme angle over this particular location, and I was looking down at this rather large amount of 'something', in the ground that showed this gold aura. It was about a third as large as first one, but it was sizeable. I seemed to be looking at actual objects *in* the ground. I saw this one thing …Did the Indians make things like spears, out of gold? Because one object looked like a spear sticking out from all this mass of stuff.

"Afterwards, I drove up and down the road [Colorado State Highway 159] six times looking for it, [where he suspected this particular mountain is located] and didn't find it. Then, one day I happened to be on a back road approximately under where I had been hovering in the flying saucer, and I was looking forward at just the right angle, and 'blow my mind,' there was the mountain! Now, when I see things *after* the event, I think maybe this really

74

happened and something 'went down.'

"So, they [the beings] let me get a look at that location, and I got an urge to ask about one of the major canyon [treasures] in this area. I was over this third location. Again, it was very fast. I was suddenly looking down at this mountain full of gold! I noted where it came up close to the surface, where a crevice might be located for a person to find something. The aura around this gold was about a quarter mile out. Remember, there was a ray going down, and at the end, was this aura of what I assumed was gold. The aura seemed relative to the amount of gold I was seeing. It was weird, three miles away there was a ray of light going down illuminating the gold. One would assume I was watching a pictographic display of some kind.

"Then, there was this kind of voice, or thought, coming from the back [of the ship], which was kind of gravelly. Kind of commanding. Short. Not what I expected. It said, 'That's enough.' I said, 'Thank you,' and I woke up in my bed...Most people interacting with a being, say, one without a mouth, or something like that ...would freak. Why me? I have no idea," he let out a short chuckle. "In my circumstance, my motivation isn't the same as someone else's. I have a teacher ...This is really difficult. I don't like making assumptive statements, but I would help my teacher. My teacher deals with the inner experience, life itself. In other words, don't go into belief [about] something that 'isn't.' Why gold? There's an outside possibility, that not being greedily involved makes a different set of conditions for these 'beings' than one would otherwise suspect...

So Many Roads, So Little Time

After such a fantastic experience, Michael naturally began the task of identifying the exact locations of the treasures he had been shown. This endeavor proved difficult because of the birds-eye perspective at "one-thousand feet" in altitude he had experienced while aboard the craft. Everything looked different when he began searching on the ground.

"This was two years ago [Fall 1995] and I've spent a lot of time thinking about it. I've probably made twelve field-trips to different areas. I am as skeptical as anyone else ...with a scientific bent in me that doesn't unbend. Until I found this signatory mountain that indicated this one location ...let's say, ...I was very surprised. It blew my mind! At that point, I had to think, 'well, there could be some veracity to the rest of my experience.'"

The area from Culabra Peak's drainage; Chama Canyon—south to Costilla Canyon is fertile, virgin investigative territory, And check east over to the other side of the Sangres, in Alamosa Canyon—south of Stonewall, CO, where all the earthquakes, one mile underground, have been occurring since 2002, or west across the SLV above Cat Creek, south of Greenie Mountain where the large metal doors were discovered. The area north of Michael's location produced rumors of portal-type activity and several interesting sightings since the early 2000s. Just below the border, west of Amalia, NM, in late 2006, a Bigfoot encounter was published in the *Taos News*. These stories are all centered west of the mouth of Costilla Canyon. Go further west from there, out into the valley. On the horizon, about twenty-five miles away is the solitary shadow of glowering Ute Mountain. Head south on 522, east of the Rio Grande Gorge. You will pass the Tres Ritos Ranch about ten miles north of Questa, and just south of town is the intentional community where Michael lives. His house sits one-thousand feet above the valley floor and has a ringside seat overlooking the entire border area of the central San Luis Valley where several strange events have been reported.

I can state in confidence that this is one of a number of locations where serious attention should be bought to bear by the well-heeled, unfettered public sector. Aspiring investigators, fearlessly motivated; with a relentless sense of destiny, dialed into truth with a budget ....

It should be noted that Michael's highly unusual assertion, is not unprecedented. Although extremely rare, there are a number of UFO cases where gold has proved to be involved. In the 1970s, ufologist/ scientist Jacques Vallee investigated the puzzling case of Spaniard Jacques Borda, an alleged contactee who lived in Castile, Spain. Borda claimed to have repeated interactions from beings that claimed they were from "Titan." He also claimed the entities paid him with gold nuggets for the food he obtained for them while they were visiting earth. Vallee stated in his book, *Messengers of Deception*:

> Jacques Borda .... is one of the most remarkable European contactees. He claims to have received gold from a strange being whom he met repeatedly in the Pyrenees [Mountains] in 1951.

I admire Jacques Vallee. Although his theories and opinions fly in the face of ufological convention, he steadfastly maintins a healthy, out-of-yhe-box perspective. For almost fifty years, has investigated UFOs; and is understandebly skeptical of encounter claims. But Vallee is still puzzled by the unique Borda case.

> The story of Borda is much more substantive than the tale of the ordinary contactee... not only does the jeweler remember the gold nuggets that Borda brought for his assessment, but several people in Casteil do recall *'l'etre estrange,'*

the strange being that came everyday to speak with him.

Michael plans to continue the process of acquiring Colorado State treasure rights to the four locations he has been able to identify. He is firmly convinced that his experience was real, and that the information he was awarded will lead to the discovery of the fabulous caches he was allowed by the ETs to see. Your San Luis Valley gum-shoe has put him in touch with two knowledgeable treasure hunters and I've offered any additional assistance I can provide. This saga is still developing...

The Taos Pueblo: Oldest continuously inhabited dwellings in North America.

Twelve different tribes visited the San Luis Valley

There is treasure to be found in the San Luis Valley.

The disappearing cloud witnessed over the Great Sand Dunes

CHAPTER FOUR:
The More You Dig...

The Green Fireball

January 1991, 3:30 a.m., Road T, Saguache County:

My new band, Expedition, had just ended a weekend in Salida at the venerable Lamplighter lounge. I played keyboards and kept the audience and my band-mates entertained with my questionable brand of humor. The band was an enthusiastic well-rehearsed group, by local standards, but playing for a bunch of hard-drinking locals yelling "country" frustrated this urban rock and roller. Nevertheless, folks around the valley loved the band's unpretentious mix of old-rock and country and, hey, we did get paid! The extra gig money sure came in handy.

I remember that bitterly-cold moonless night and the ride home vividly. I was proceeding east toward Crestone on Road T, just before the first S-turn, my ears still ringing from that night's performance, when I noticed a crackling, static sound in my ears. The strange sound reminded me of white noise between AM radio stations. I slowed the truck. Movement over the Sangre de Cristo Mountains near the Great Sand Dunes drew my attention and from the southeast, I beheld a huge, brilliant-green, full-moon-sized glittering ball of light gliding up the range!

Behind it streamed a short tail. It remained at a constant altitude parallel to the mountain tops and the distance it traveled, from the moment I first spotted it, until it disappeared from view to the north, must have been seventy-five to eighty miles. It covered the distance in less than five seconds! As the object sailed north toward Salida, the high-frequency crackling sound in my ears faded. I was so tired from playing, and driving the eighty-miles home, that the sighting didn't really register fully until the following day, when I mentioned the experience to a couple of friends. This was the second time I had witnessed something out-of-the ordinary in the night sky over the mysterious San Luis Valley.

As I've mentioned during my first three and one-half years here, from 1989 to 1993, I had been hearing occasional off-hand comments concerning strange lights, aerial objects, animal

79

"mutilations," ghosts, witches and treasure legends. Being a naturally curious person, I began to casually make note of the more colorful events featured in the history of this forgotten area at the top of the Rockies. Now having now seen a couple of pretty strange aerial phenomena myself, these stories piqued my curiosity. I figured, if even a newcomer like myself had seen something weird, I was willing to bet other locals had seen unusual things in the sky. But I felt I'd better keep my inquiries extremely low-key as I began researching the rich history of unusual events in the SLV.

As time went on, my casual historical research took a definite back seat to the task of making a living and putting together the best local band featuring the best rock and roll players that this remote area had to offer.

The 1893 Aereolite

The aerial phenomenon I witnessed that hot August night after moving to the Baca was compelling. Could my eyes have deceived me and had I misinterpreted mundane celestial phenomena as unusual? I started digging. One account I uncovered was a curious article from The American Museum of Natural History (AMNH) magazine in 1941, noting an event that occurred on the Baca Ranch in 1893.

> An outstanding event was the discovery of what is believed to be a meteorite crater - the first within the boundaries of our state (Colorado). The find was the culmination of a search which began in 1931 and has continued through the years. After hearing from former residents of the San Luis Valley of a great (meteorite) fall which occurred in the year 1893, Dr. (AMNH Department of Meteorites, curator) and Mrs. Nininger devoted a portion of the summer of 1937 to search for meteorites in that part of the state . . .
>
> The immediate result was the discovery of a new stone known as the Alamosa aereolite (weight four pounds) ... During the sojourn in the valley that summer, Dr. Nininger called at the ranch home of C. M. King of Blanca (CO) to hear the account of the great fall of 1893. Mr. King had seen the phenomenon from a distance of only a few miles, for he declared that it had reached the earth between where he stood and the nearby range of the high Sangre De Cristo Mountains ...
>
> The crater is situated on the western, lower, unforested slope of the Sangre de Cristo Range, between Cottonwood

Creek and Dead Man's Creek, where the terrain consists of deep sand deposit on top of a typical boulder-gravel out wash from the mountains. It is about six miles northwest from the boundary of the Great Sand Dunes National Monument. The dimensions of the crater are three-hundred and fifty by two hundred and fifty feet measured rim to rim.

The lowest part lies twenty-nine feet below the highest point on the rim, which rises conspicuously above the surrounding terrain. A magnetic survey was made of the crater by Harry Aurand of Denver. His results indicated two magnetic masses which seemed to warrant investigation. A well driller was employed and both these locations were drilled. At depths of sixty-nine feet and seventy-eight and one-half feet respectively, objects were encountered through which it was impossible to drill. Six other exploratory holes were placed to ascertain the internal structure of the crater. These clearly revealed a disturbed condition in the boulder deposit under the sand. Plans have been made for further investigation of the masses encountered.

Although plans were made by the AMNH to come back to the site, no evidence exists that they ever returned. The original dig still adorns the western rim of the crater and the old gray boards left behind by the drillers, half-covered in sand, are the only visible indication of man's casual interest in the site, fifty years ago. The two large magnetic masses still lie undisturbed, seventy feet below the shifting sands of the Baca Ranch. Incidentally C.M. King, the only witness to the event, was the father of Nellie, the owner of the notorious "Snippy" the horse!

I sense that this interesting, possibly revealing synchronicity may be important. Nellie's father was the primary witness to a spectacular and rare celestial event and this must have impressed his daughter, hearing the story while growing up twenty-miles south of the impact site. Perhaps as a child, this event took on great significance to her and the event may have instilled a sense of celestial awe that manifested in her famous comment in 1967, "Flying saucers killed my horse." This valley is a sociologist's gold-mine.

Light On The Mountain

Sightings of unexplained orbs or "cheap fireworks" as I call them, may have a natural explanation. They appear to be plasma energies and as I began to track occurrences of the celestial objects I noticed that they seemed to occur during time-periods prior to and at the close of outbreaks of more conventional UFO sightings.

July 18, 1992, 4:30 a.m. Sand Dunes Road, Alamosa County:
Brendon O'Brien, my younger brother, and investigator/ videographer Bill McIntyre had taken a trip to Cuchara, CO. While there on business, they were introduced to an alleged "abductee" being shielded from publicity by the local townspeople. They also met an individual who, along with three other families, had witnessed a large diamond-shaped object extending a telescoping shaft into an abandoned mine, in broad daylight the prior year. Several of the witnesses had evidently studied the strange object through binoculars. Brendon and Bill found that no one they interviewed would go on-the-record concerning the event but they all insisted the events they experienced happened. Brendon and Bill took care of their business and started back toward Crestone late that night.

Returning to Crestone, Brendon was driving while Bill snoozed in the passenger seat of the small Ford Ranger truck. In the predawn, eight miles southeast of the Dunes, a brilliant-white explosion lit up on the high mountainside. McIntyre was awakened by the impact of the light. "Whoa, stop. There's no moon out. You can see the trees ... That's way above tree-line, there's no road anywhere near there! Pull over!" McIntyre told Brendon. They stopped one hundred feet up a dirt road and parked with the light framed in the truck's windshield.

Brendon switched off the headlights but left on the large orange parking lights. The distant light changed to orange. "Wow!" Brendon exclaimed, "Did you see that?!" McIntyre sat quietly, staring at the light that he estimated was three to four miles up Pioneer Canyon, at about eleven thousand five hundred feet.

Brendon turned his headlights back on and the light instantly changed back to white and appeared to start revolving in place. The two sat dumbfounded until Bill finally stammered, "Should I get the camera?" Bill had an S-VHS camera in the back of the truck but one of them would have to get out and walk behind the truck to grab it.

"I don't know if it would be a good idea to tape it yet, let's get closer," Brendon suggested. Experimenting, he flipped his headlights back off, leaving his parking lights on. The object again matched the color. "What the hell IS that?" He switched the headlights back on, he put the truck in gear and started up the mountain.

"Wait a minute, wait a minute," Bill yelled as the light mirrored their actions, and hurtled down the mountainside directly at them! The tops of the trees illuminated as it fell below tree-line. Brendon panicked, making a quick U-turn, racing back toward the pavement. Reaching the Highway 159, he hit the brakes for a quick right turn. McIntyre, never taking his eyes off the light, watched it turn red. "Hold it!" he yelled to Brendon. "It stopped."

The sat silently for an undetermined time as the light gradually grew smaller and more intense, reminding them of a "ruby-red laser-light." It then "floated across the valley" to the south, shot straight up and out at a forty-five degree angle, and according to both witnesses, "turned into a star."

The next morning they told me of their experience, and I remembered my own strange sightings of the green fireball and the 'cheap firework." One element that surprised me was the two witnesses' wildly different estimation of how long the event lasted. Brendon thought the experience had only lasted about five minutes, however Bill thought they had sat and watched for almost an hour.

Landing Site

July 20, 1992, Mineral Hot Springs, Saguache County:
Seventy miles north of Blanca, the black cloudless sky was punctured by a flash. A chorus of crickets were silenced as a heavy stillness enveloped the dim moonlit terrain. A vivid orange glow pulsed behind a series of low hills that surrounded a natural hot spring, four hundred yards east of a cluster of small dwellings.

Sally Sloban stirred in her sleep as her two small dogs barked furiously in the lush greenhouse that faced the main hot spring. As she awoke, she noticed an orange glow reflecting off the wall in her room. She slipped on her sandals, and wrapped a cloak around her lithe dancer's frame and peered out through the steamy greenhouse glass at the dark terrain, intermittently punctuated by the eerie pulsing light. Then, a sudden bright flash and the orange light source extinguished.

Sally climbed back into bed and fell into a fitful sleep. The following morning, two visiting friends walked with her out to the area where the glowing light appeared to be emanating the night before.

Behind a low hill, one of her friends knelt beside a strange circular mark in the ground. A thirty-foot diameter impression was clearly visible. Crushed chico bushes and prairie grass were whirled flat around a three-foot-deep hole at the center of the depression. The hole was a foot-and-a-half across and appeared to have been caused by intense heat from a powerful, concentrated, downward blast. After looking around, they wandered back to the house for breakfast, enthralled by the obvious landing site so close to the house.

Word of the landing circle quietly circulated for several days through Crestone. Brendon and Bill heard the story and, because of their unexplained sighting of the strange light the week before, drove the thirty miles north from Crestone to visit Sally at the hot springs.

Sally led them out to the location, and related her experience the night the mark appeared. Several other curious locals have already come out to see it. They walked closer and Brendon looks down the "blast-hole."

"Bill, look at this!" Standing perfectly straight "on the last three inches of it's tail" at the bottom of the hole, is a two-and-a-half-foot bullsnake, its tongue occasionally flicking out to sniff the air.

"No!" exclaimed McIntyre, as he quickly unpacks his video camera. "Get back, don't scare it. I want to video tape it."

He shot several minutes of tape and they wondered aloud what the heck a bullsnake is doing standing on its tail in an apparent UFO landing circle blast hole. They returned two days later with a visiting NBC videographer and visited the site. Sure enough, the same bullsnake (or one just like it) was standing there on its tail! The circular impression remained visible until the following summer.

The Tar Baby

December 31, 1992, Crestone-Baca Grande, Saguache County:

Isadora Storey and I had met and began dating in the Fall of 1991 and we hosted a New Year's Eve party at Isadora's recently remodeled Baca house. As the party wound down and folks began to leave, I overheard a friend recalling UFO sightings she had experienced recently with her boyfriend out over the Baca Ranch. She told the small captivated group gathered around her of unusual lights and "glowing" objects. I listened in captivated by her descriptions.

She appeared calm, yet excited, as she described the experience almost poetically. I started asking questions, trying to find out as much as I could about these occurrences. She named other witnesses who had apparently seen what appeared to be the same unknown lights the next three nights. Some of these witnesses, including her boyfriend, were at the party. As the conversation progressed, first one, then another "witness" walked in from the other room and joined the animated conversation describing sightings over the Baca Ranch on November 25th and December 9—12, 1992. I found it disconcerting to hear people talking so casually about these events. One couple had taken their kids up to the Independence Gold-mine, with its stunning view out over the Valley. The lights were back. They sat in their car and munched popcorn and watched the "dancing lights" that had re-appeared over the ranch.

Then came the clincher. Another party-goer, Charlotte Heir, a local closet-UFO buff, mentioned she had seen a short article in the regional newspaper, Alamosa's Valley *Courier*, reporting a "mutilation" on a small ranch in Costilla County. The event took place the very same night that Baca area witnesses had seen unexplained lights. Unbeknownst to me at the time, I had firmly grabbed hold of a Tar-Baby!

My official, full time investigation literally began as a result of those testimonials that New Year's night. I look back and view my naive excitement at the time with a smile. Had I realized the consequences of my efforts my excitement would have undoubtedly been tempered with the realization that years of expensive, frustrating and unrewarding hard work lay ahead with no promise of any firm answers. I felt motivated to investigate the extent of these elusive events. I would be shunned by some for my public involvement but also sought out by many who hoped for answers to their questions. At no time did I make any promises to anyone about anything. I never actually hoped to solve these riddles, let alone provide advice to those who sought answers, but fifteen years later I am still motivated. It's ok with me that I am more confused than ever and none the wiser, at least I haven't established foregone conclusions that I'll go to the ends of the earth to prove. One thing I can say in all confidence; I have gained a real respect for witnesses of these events who are grounded enough to report their experiences.

I have always been curious how unusual events affect people; what was their thinking before the event and how was their view of reality changed after their experience(s)? How did their experience impact them emotionally? I look for an identifiable shine in their eyes when they attempt to describe the indescribable. I have learned when to perk up and take notice and conversely, when to turn off the tape. After fifteen years at this work, I am harder to impress, more jaded and skeptical due to the unavoidable element of front-loading. Of course, there is no substitute for a well-honed BS meter without the bells and whistles that come with the inexplicable.

Obviously, reality-shattering phenomena are touchy subjects in western culture. In early 1993, when I began my public investigation, I quickly experienced subtle ridicule from some people and overt respect from others. This prompted me to examine closely the social implications of the investigative process I had elected myself to perform. I realized right away it would be prudent to define my aspiring "paranormal investigator" learning curve in some form. I devised Thirteen "Rules of Investigation," inspired by James Redfield's "Insights" from the *Celestine Prophesies*. Readers of my first two books should recall these axioms of my investigative process. They will be re-explained in the time-line where they were realized.

Investigative Rule #1
Controversial subjects generate polarized responses in the average person.

Seems kind of obvious on the surface, but the morning after the party, January 1st, 1993, I was oblivious to the social implications of starting a murky investigation into the potential of the locally bizarre. This was unexplored social territory. I thought most evolved folks had a curiosity about the true nature of reality, but this isn't exactly true. Many people have a hard enough time dealing with the consensus reality within which we all find ourselves immersed. Growing up, most of my friends only professed a casual interest in the so-called paranormal. Back in college, I was the one whom would bring these subjects up in conversation and I would invariably be the one who was most knowledgeable. I learned to keep my fascination with strange phenomena to myself. During my twenties in NYC, in the late 1970s, I remember a number of spirited conversations with college buddies about our shared New Paltz UFO sighting, the on-going cattle mutilation mystery, the Travis Walton abduction, the nearby Hudson Valley sightings and other topics of the inexplicable that ranged from pyramid power and astral-projection to ritual magick and bigfoot.

I've always had this fascination and my inclination was casually supported by my adopted mother, Catherine O'Brien. Leaving behind my emotional baggage surrounding my rather troubled childhood, I remember her as an amazing, gifted woman—years ahead of her time. I like to tell folks "she was either born a thousand years too late or a hundred years too soon." She introduced me to the piano (a black-lacquer Steinway baby-grand, that she spent three-years stripping down to it's natural blonde color), Eastern thought, various forms of divination—including her specialty, pendulum magic (she successfully 'water-witched' Brendon's Crestone house site in 1992) and other subjects and individuals (including Edgar Cayce) that went against the grain of conventional thought. Since the 1940s, she had recycled her organic compost into an amazing vegetable garden, that one year produced a fifteen-pound zucchini that had escaped our detection over our neighbor's backyard fence. She made her own mayonnaise, canned home-grown vegetables, she pickled, she baked, she grafted, hybridized and she boiled the hell out of everything—the Irish school of cooking. The whole inside of our kitchen covered by grape ivy that on one occasion went up in a short, furious flash fire. I have yet to taste anything close to her apple-butter recipe. Unlike most people, I grew up with an apple tree that had several different types of apples. Catherine, in the late 1950s had grafted branches from other varieties of apple trees onto the apple tree in our backyard. I loved being able to go out and pick the particular variety of apple that suited my palette at the moment and, as a child, was disappointed that other peoples apple trees only featured one variety of fruit …

I again remind you that I feel it is important to qualify my investigative process with information about my upbringing, my front-loading, so to speak. This information will hopefully provide you with some perspective and give you insight into my process. We all can only respond to reality based on our own, personal process, so I am attempting to bring you up-to-speed so you will have sufficient context with which to bounce your understanding of my "official" investigative process.

Big Cow Training

Arriving in the Baca and establishing a foothold in the austere quasi-spiritual environment was not easy, but I had already had preparation for the roaring silence of the mysterious valley. In 1976, my sister and brother-in-law became interested in Transcendental Meditation (TM) and suggested I attend a series of instruction in the technique with the both of them. Initially a little cynical—I was only eighteen —we attended the introductory talk, and I was surprised by the TM system. It made sense. I continued with the classes and during the final class I was then "given" my own personal mantra for my practice. On the way home, I couldn't wait to try it out! Within a week I had learned to descend into my wonderful space of complete, total stillness. It was exhilarating in an understated way and one meditation session, in particular, stands out from that first week. For several years I faithfully meditated twenty-minutes everyday and although I have fallen out of this daily TM-style practice, for over thirty years I have formulated a personal meditative mindset that I strive to maintain in my everyday life.

Perhaps another reason I was able to assimilate myself into the select Baca community is my life-long fascination with what some call "The Divine." I will always honor the width and breath of the interpretation of that which is "Divine." I could quote from the 'spiritual bill-of-rights' if one existed yet I have always questioned everything that they teach you growing up. I suppose its fate, or something akin to a predisposition toward curiosity.

I was raised by a progressive Irish Catholic family and watched Pop drift off asleep during the sermon every Sunday morning after my Evergreen Point, Medina, WA paper-route. The Sunday papers were too large to deliver by bicycle so he would drive me around on my route once a week. I guess this was supposed to be our time together.

I was in and out of Catholic School through my childhood and attended Sacred Heart Parish school in 1967, 1969, 1970 and Seattle Prep in 1971. In 1968 I left Sacred Heart for sixth-grade at Ardmore Montessori. The educational set-up was very loose and made no sense to me. I became quickly bored. I was busted for selling racing decals and stickers to other students. I was isolated for individualized instruction in a bare room away from the other students—monitored by Ardmore principle Dr. Abenhaus. I was allowed to work on projects that I wanted to work on, and reject others. Anything having to do with art, history, space, science or sports was fine with me, so I made use of my isolation and devised my own curriculum. I had just completed a course of fine-art training at the Museum of History and Industry and was developing a rather unique artistic interpretation of reality. I remember Dr. Abenhaus was quite taken by my elaborate painting that depicted the death of Narcissus.

While in eighth grade—back at the Sacred Heart school I found myself head altar boy. But, as the nuns would have told you, I was no angel. We were never busted, but my friends and I gambled in the sacristy, munching the losing hosts of Frisbee contests while sipping the sweet wine from the safe that paid the cash we made during funerals and weddings. I remember one time being called out in front of the entire student body by stern, foreboding Pastor Moore, during school mass, for tapping a friend's Adam's Apple with my communion plate as he received the host only to gawk it back up onto the plate.

I've jokingly mentioned on a number of occasions that "I'm one of the few people you'll ever meet that was given up on by the Jesuits." I was expelled from Seattle Prep in May 1972 after being caught mimicking the cleft-pallet vocal stylings of the school's vice-principle who was my first-period, advanced algebra teacher. The late-arriving Brother Loren caught me, with my version of his cleft-pallet in my mouth, in the middle of a stand-up routine in front of the class. That was the last straw, I suppose as I was expelled from school. I knew I was in big trouble back home and I was terrified.

Instead of taking the twenty minute bus-ride to Medina, across the Three-Points floating bridge, I walked the long way around Lake Washington, a distance of fifteen miles, before facing my parents with the news of my prep-school disgrace. It went downhill at home after that and the following August I was convinced by my two adopted sisters, Molly and Ann O'Brien to leave home and remand myself back into Washington State Care. I won't bore you with the details of high-school years as a ranch-hand—struggling to maintain an athletic career while experimenting with fast cars, wild girls and wilder substances during the turbulent early-to-mid-1970s.

While in college (1975 through 1978) I knuckled down and studied broadcast media, history, philosophy, anthropology, geology and explored many divergent belief systems on my own time. By 1980 I had studied many of the world's great religions and more esoteric schools of philosophic thought. I was drawn toward Gurdjeif and Ouspensky, Blavatsky and Levi, Crowley, Mathers and Regardi. The great alchemists and occultists, like Crowley, Dee, Bacon and Levi held a particular fascination. During my first trip to Europe in 1971, seeing the famous platter half transmuted from silver to gold by St. Germaine at the palace of Versailles impressed my curious mind.

I remember being asked at an upscale Manhattan party in 1978, "what religion do you practice?" I remember I responded carefully, "Practice? I'm into spirit, I'm not into religion. Religion is the 'colonization of spirit,' religions are societal control mechanisms ...I'm on a spiritual path." Perhaps that was a rather precocious response from a long-haired, twenty-something dressed in jeans hiking boots and a flannel shirt to make, but when asked this question I still reply with this response. The questioner was the owner of a up-and-coming student travel company. I didn't know at the time but evidently he and his wife had been tripped out on mushrooms at the party. Evidently my interaction with them hit a chord as they recruited me as a student travel marketer/coordinator for their company.

My many years back east probably doesn't seem like preparation for my move to the San Luis Valley and the Baca Grande Subdivision, but those years in New York, and later, Boston were crucial to my process. Evidently, I was sufficiently front-loaded for my move into America's most anomalous region.

"Write me an article, but please don't make it too long"

The Crestone/Baca is located in a region literally decades behind the times. The Baca residents are opened-minded but caught up in their own little dramas. I instinctually knew I would need to tread carefully if I wanted to maintain any respect from friends, skeptics and local law enforcement officials when it came to asking about so-called paranormal events. Professing an interest in UFOs and dead cows can severely impact your social standing in a small community

My natural reporter's instinct took hold after the New Year's party and the next day, January 1, 1993, I made my first phone-call to find out more about the cattle "mutilation" or Unusual Animal Death (UAD) that had allegedly occurred in Costilla County in late November.

Long-time local resident and *Crestone Eagle* newspaper publisher, Kizzen Dennett, not a person to shy away from controversy, suggested I do some research, conduct a couple of interviews and write a short article for her eclectic small-town monthly newspaper. She laughed when I asked her how much she'd pay me for writing an article. It was apparent that I wasn't going to make much money writing for the *Eagle* or, as I later learned, any "fringe subject" publication. But, money wasn't the motivation, and ascertaining "the truth" drove me to begin my "official" investigation.

Luckily, Kizzen still had a copy of the *Valley Courier* article concerning the Costilla UAD. She found the potential story and the apparent correlation compelling and urged me to contact reporter Ruth Heide to obtain rancher Manuel Sanchez's phone number. "Give him a call, let me know what he says. Write me an article but, please, don't make it too long."

Ruth Heide still had her interview notes. I called the ranch and asked Mrs. Sanchez if I might speak with her husband. She put him on and he sounded scared and angry. I then called Billy Maestas, the Costilla County sheriff who investigated the case, and found out that neighboring Los Animas County had logged a UAD report that same day. I was getting somewhere fast!

I called Los Animas Sheriff Lou Girodo's Trinidad, CO, office. "They're back!" he exclaimed when I related descriptions of the lights that had been seen over the Baca Ranch by over a dozen witnesses the night the cattle surgeons resumed their work. Back? Who was back?

The apparent synchronicity between the Baca lights and the unusual cattle deaths really intrigued me. What was going on? Was there a connection? I was going to find out.

At the time, like most people with a minimal knowledge of the unusual animal death phenomenon, I was under the false impression that these animal deaths had ceased since their media hey-days in the mid-to-late 1970s. I hadn't seen a single reference to current cattle "mutilations" for years and when I thought about it, it seemed strange that I never saw a single reference to them in the news during my first four years in the valley. At the time I had a suspicion that the Snippy case may hold key clues to possibly help explain the area's unusual activity. The San Luis Valley's supposed role in the phenomenon is well-documented in ufology. I wondered if "Snippy's" owners were still around. Perhaps they could shed some light on these recent southern Colorado events.

Nellie's Diary

During the first week of January 1993, one of my neighbors, Pam LaBorde, had mentioned a "diary" that her husband Roger and a group of friends from the Universal Educational Foundation (UEF) had discovered while cleaning out a newly-purchased old cabin in the foothills of the Blanca Massiff. Pam mentioned that the cabin sat on the old King Ranch homestead and that the diary had evidently belonged to Nellie Lewis, "Snippy the Horse's" owner. I called Roger to inquire further. The "diary" turned out to be a handful of loose-leaf pages that the couple insisted had contained peculiar descriptions and drawings of UFO-type craft, dates, times and accounts of visitations, even sketches of "strange beings in robes ... There was a drawing of a triangle and snake emblem the beings had on their robes."

'Snake?' I thought. 'As in bullsnake?' or 'evil reptoid?' Roger was convinced that the pages belonged to Nellie Lewis. "It had her name right on it." Then Roger told me the fascinating account of the discovery. He had been on a work party at the cabin in 1988, with ten members of the UEF who had just bought the old upper King Ranch cabin from Mr. Berle Lewis, Nellie Lewis' husband. They were cleaning up the yard and outbuildings when Roger found the curious pages in a pile of old paper and refuse. He called the rest of the work party over to read them. Hosca Harrison, who had organized the clean-up, put the pile of pages inside the cabin on the kitchen counter and everyone went back to work cleaning up the property.

Roger remembered: "A few minutes later, two men in the work party that I didn't know, left. I thought they were friends of someone else and didn't think much of it," Roger said. "Later we discovered that the pages were gone, somebody had taken them!" The UEF work crew had a real mystery on their hands. "Everyone there swore they hadn't taken the notes, and no one seemed to know who the two men were. I remember thinking they looked out of place—one of them was dressed in an undershirt and had on dress shoes and slacks ...Neither of them [were] dressed in work clothes."

Roger LaBorde is a world-famous coma specialist. He has been instrumental in healing some very high-profile coma cases and is a spiritual, down-to-earth individual. A full length interview with Roger can be found at the end of my second book, *Enter The Valley.* This being said, with all respect to the account, Roger and Pam's story was perplexing. Later, I checked with four others who were in the work party that day. All four related to me the same basic account. This put the alleged diary discovery and theft event into the realm of corroborated testimony.

Now, the obvious question should be, why would two well-dressed strangers crash a work party in the mountains? And what would they want with a handful of pages describing UFO sightings and alien visitations? What's up with this? I should have asked the UEF'ers if they were wearing Ray-Bans and drove a brand new 1957 black Cadillac.

During my interview, I asked Roger if Berle Lewis, who lived in the cabin for years, was still alive. Nellie had died mysteriously in 1976, an apparent suicide, but yes, Berle was right down the hill at the Great Sand Dunes Country Club where he was the maintenance man.

Feeling as if I had become a gum-shoe private detective, I called Berle, who was in the phonebook. The high-pitched, raspy voice on the line related the strange events surrounding Snippy's death so colorfully, I knew I had to arrange a full-length video interview and put him on-the-record. I asked him whom I should call to learn more about the strange animal deaths I thought had ceased years ago. "Call them Paris, Texas boys," he suggested.

"Who?" I asked.

"Tom Adams and Gary Massey. They know more about these things than anyone, 'cept maybe that TV lady." ("mutilation" investigator, author and film producer, Linda Moulton Howe.) Boy, was he right—they were extremely knowledgeable.

Tom Adams

My investigation was getting really interesting. Three days after the New Year's Eve party, I called and left a message for Adams, hoping he would call back. That evening, January 3, 1993, he did. At first, he was understandably suspicious of who I was and what my agenda might be, and it took a little convincing that I wasn't just another time-waster, or debunker. Much to my delight, Adams gave me a whole hour of his time. 'What an incredible fountain of information,' I remember thinking to myself during our first conversation. Once he felt a little more comfortable with me, he provided names, dates and phone numbers of witnesses from the past thirty years plus dates and descriptions of many bizarre, little-known accounts of sightings and UAD reports in the San Luis Valley. With no apparent notes, he pulled dates, names and facts right off the top of his head. I was impressed with his semi-photographic memory.

I scribbled four pages of notes during our conversation, realizing that he was saving me weeks of research. The information I obtained from him during that first conversation was, and still is, invaluable to my investigation and research. Before hanging up, he promised to send along a dossier of information. I was elated upon its arrival. The package contained every *Valley Courier* article he had collected for fifteen years monitoring the San Luis Valley's many reports of UFOs, UADs and other weird events.

During those first two weeks of January 1993, I interviewed over a dozen witnesses in Saguache County who had seen the anomalous lights the prior November and December. Most of them didn't know that others had shared their sighting experiences. I was intrigued by the exact descriptions (three of the witnesses used the exact same words, "bouncing over the Baca Ranch"). This spurred me on to find out as much as possible about this apparent current upsurge in unexplained activity.

All of the incredible stories and reports of sightings from the 1960's that Adams had sent me now seemed immediate. Could these recent sightings be connected somehow to the historical reports? What about the reports of UADs? Was there a connection between the sightings and the unusual animal deaths then, and now? I followed a hunch that more activity had been recently witnessed than reported and spent the first two weeks of January following every lead I could uncover.

Slowly establishing and cultivating dialogues with law enforcement officials, witnesses, historians, ranchers and farmers, the pieces of a perplexing puzzle slowly began to fall into place during the first month of my investigation. Fortunately, because I was a local, I was been able to research specifics and follow-up leads pertaining to an amazing collection of events that had occurred. The locals refuse to talk to non-residents about such controversial subjects, and I had a feeling that I was lucky to get any of these reluctant witnesses to talk with me. This leads me to my second investigative realization:

Rule #2
Record or write everything down as soon as possible, no matter how inconsequential, or insignificant it might seem at the time.

Take notes readers: I cannot overstress the importance of writing everything down. No matter how insignificant, WRITE

IT DOWN! You will be amazed at how inconsequential appearing tidbits grow into amazing correlations later on down the road.

Waiting for the Eclipse

As I quickly gathered up relevant reports of high-strangeness, a compelling picture began to come into focus. Here is a overview of that Fall's activity . . .

December 9, 1992, 8:45 p.m., Denver, Colorado:
Astronomer Michael Robertson and a friend were scanning the heavens before the lunar eclipse when they spotted an orange object approaching from the northeast. As it reached eighty degrees above the horizon, a second object approached from the northwest. Both trained observers agreed, "The objects did not appear to have lights and were flying just under thirty thousand feet, reflecting the setting sun." The two objects crossed paths over downtown Denver and headed toward southern Colorado.

Robertson stated to Colorado Mutual UFO Network (MUFON) investigators, "In thirty years of watching the skies, I have never observed anything like those objects."

About thirty minutes later, 9:15 p.m., Crestone-Baca Grande, Saguache County:

Kirsten (not her real name) had recently moved to the Baca where her parents and grandparents lived. The single, thirty-something Chicago native was watching television in her rented Chalet home. A college graduate and gifted singer with a razor wit, Kirsten, like her parents, had little time for "new age knuckleheads and flying saucers." She was, however, an avid skywatcher anticipating that night's lunar eclipse.

As she left the couch to turn off the television, she saw two unusual golden-white orbs of light flash overhead. The sixteen-foot high A-frame window afforded her a spectacular view of the objects as they streaked over the house heading southwest down Spanish Creek, one of the many creeks that flow year round out of the Sangres, into the valley floor. Running out onto her porch, Kristi watched the objects follow the tree-lined path of the creek as they shot out across the valley at "fantastic" speed.

Also at 9:15 p.m., Baca Grande Development, Saguache County:

Luna Bontempe and Lucas Price were outside enjoying the crisp December night. They were house-sitting for Richard Enzer, a friend whose impressive hogan-style home sits beside Spanish Creek in the Baca Grants, anticipating that night's impending

94

eclipse.

Luna was the first to notice the unusual lights, low to the ground and south of their location. The small glimmering lights appeared to be over the southern end of the Baca Ranch and were "bouncing around, creating geometric shapes." First they formed a square and hung motionless like stars in the late fall sky. "Check that out!" she exclaimed, drawing Lucas' attention as the lights formed a triangle. Lucas then spotted two brilliant orbs of light that streaked down the western slope of the Sangres over the Chalet section of the development, off to their left. They followed Spanish Creek at treetop level out over the valley, turned toward them silently at incredible speed. The "large laser-like ovals" zipped directly over their heads, continued past them and hovered behind a grove of cottonwood trees, about "two hundred yards" due south of the house. The objects started "shooting off milky beams of light," so bright the two of them saw "owl nests lit up in the tops of the trees!" As they watched in amazement, the bright beams simultaneously vanished. They completely forgot about that night's eclipse. The small glimmering lights reappeared and danced like clockwork over the Baca Ranch on the following three nights.

Holiday Visitors

I learned of this following event when John Browning called a National Public Radio program (NPR) as I was being interviewed.

November 1, 1992, 3:00 a.m., Saguache County:

John Browning, his son and two friends were camped about twenty miles north of Saguache, during a Halloween hunting trip. The four Denver residents were dog-tired after spending all day in the mountains tracking an elusive elk herd. After making camp and cooking dinner, the weary group bundled up to ward off the cold mountain air and quickly fell asleep.

At 3:00 a.m., Browning was awakened with a start. A strange stillness permeated the forest campsite and an unusual glow bathed his camper. As his eyes grew accustomed to the dark, his eyes were drawn to an array of lights traveling slowly above, headed south toward the western side of the SLV. He could make out the outline of an enormous triangular-shaped craft that blocked out a sizeable portion of the night sky. He was so intrigued that he left his warm sleeping bag and ventured out into the cold to investigate.

"There must have been fifteen or sixteen lights in a semi-circle with four of them flashing around the center," he told me during a phone interview, "There wasn't a sound!" Browning said he felt "mesmerized" by the lighting array which flashed hypnotically overhead. "I'm telling you, this thing was huge! It must have been at least a quarter-mile long!"

He hurried to wake his son to witness the incredible sight before it disappeared but by the time he was able to roust his son, it was too late. "Whatever that thing was, it wasn't from this world" he concluded.

I wasn't so sure. The immense craft certainly sounded impressive but as a aspiring investigator, I had to remain skeptical. Going with the sincere-sounding veracity of John Browning, I was sure he had seen something but was it truly extraterrestrial? I had heard rumors of secret government craft and wondered if the fantastic sighting could have actually been top secret, and very terrestrial.

That same night, ninety miles southeast of Browning and his party, forty miles west of Trinidad, CO, rancher John Torres' herd of cattle had a deadly Halloween visitor. The following morning Torres discovered a three-year-old dead cow in a remote area of his ranch. The animal's tongue, genitalia and eyes were missing. Torres had "never seen anything like it" in his years as a cattle rancher. "That was no predator. They were real, real sharp cuts with no ridges. There were no tracks, no blood, no nothin'!"

Later, when Greg Barman, NPR reporter, asked him who he thought was responsible for the "mutilation" of his cow, Torres answered with a nervous laugh, "Well, as far as I'm concerned, it was aliens. Seriously, I really think it was something from out of this world, to do something like that without leaving any evidence whatsoever."

The Camino Real Encounter

November 25, 1992, 8:30 p.m., Baca Grande, Saguache County:

Michael and Andrea Nisbit enjoyed a quiet evening at home. The Nisbits, expert mineral and crystal wholesalers, were relaxing after preparing for a trip to South America to finalize the transfer of two lucrative amber mines to their wholesale business.

He and his wife had seen strange lights and "ships" near their house (at the extreme southwestern end of the Baca Grants) on several occasions but not up close.

At nine o'clock p.m. a powerful beam of light blasted down, from outside and above the house, turning night into day. They scrambled off the couch, running to a window that faced the Baca Ranch. A bright reflection hit their cars parked outside. Above them an orange-white light traveled silently across their yard toward the end of Camino Real, a street that dead ends less than a half-mile away. Around the bright beam they could faintly make out pulsing lights.

Suddenly, as if a switch had been flipped, the lights disappeared. The Nisbits held each other in the eerie darkness while the moonless sky pulled slowly back into focus. Later, in that Thanksgiving morning, a double-propped military helicopter thundered less than fifty feet over the Nisbit's house, heading south toward the Great Sand Dunes National Monument. Michael and Andrea agree, "Every time we see lights or ships or something we can't explain here out on the Baca, the next morning we see helicopters headed in the same direction." That previous night, at 8:30, they were the lucky ones.

Barbara, (not her real name) weaver and forty-year-old mother of four, suddenly realized she was behind the wheel of her truck, seven miles from her home and her children. A strange force compelled her forward. That "something" was in complete control of her free-will and she couldn't fight the fact that she was driving out into the Grants. Barbara was pulled as if by a magnet to the remote southwestern corner of the Baca development which borders the Baca Ranch. She parked less than a half-mile from the Nisbit's home.

"What am I doing here?" she remembers asking herself as she numbly sat in her small truck at the end of Camino Real, overlooking the ranch, two-hundred yards away. In a sweat, she loosened her coat and turned off the heater. "What's gotten into me? Who's looking after my children?" Her watch read eight-thirty p.m. The silence roared in her ears.

Barbara, now shivering, pulled her light coat around her, wiping her nose with the back of her hand. It was now freezing inside her truck. She looked at her hand. It was streaked with blood. "Oh my God!" Her nosebleed could only mean one thing. Her watch revealed it was 10:30 p.m. She shuddered. "They" had taken her again.

It had been five years since the last time Barbara awoke with a nosebleed and "that peculiar feeling." They had come to her many times in the preceding twenty-eight years. They always came at night. She knew it was them because of the bloody nose. At first, when she was seven, their visits frightened her. She could never quite remember the details of what happened when they came but she remembered a voice. The voice comforted her and kept her from being afraid. As she grew older, she "learned to trust the voice."

"My children!" She wiped her face clean, turned the ignition, jammed the truck in gear and rushed back to her house. Her children slept undisturbed.

The next morning, Barbara felt exhausted but elated, reminding her of one morning after an unbelievable night in 1978 when the visitors actually revealed themselves to her. It was her first, fully-conscious encounter with the beings she now calls "the little brothers." A week before she had been diagnosed with ovarian cancer.

She had felt their presence that night in 1978 and hadn't been able to sleep. A tremendous lightning storm had swept through the area. They often arrived during lightning storms. She didn't remember falling asleep but evidently she did. Upon waking:

"I was lying on a soft table in a white, circular room. I could only move my head. I don't recall how long I lay there but I felt peaceful. Then I heard the voice. It told me that I needed their help. I asked the voice if I could see them." They appeared in front of her, around the foot of the table. "There were four of them, all identical. They were three-to-four-feet tall, ivory-white, and had large almond-shaped eyes." A fifth being appeared in front of the four. This one was a little taller. "Its eyes were intense! I couldn't stop staring into them!" The taller being communicated directly with her mind and told her to not be afraid. She recognized the familiar voice.

"I don't remember how I got there but somehow I found myself immersed in an L-shaped tank. A long segmented arm came out of a console next to the tank and inserted itself into me. It wasn't painful but it didn't feel comfortable. I had to relax and trust the voice that kept telling me not to be afraid." The next thing she knew it was morning and she felt extremely tired and didn't have a nosebleed.

Four days after this alleged encounter, Barbara says she returned to her doctor who, at her insistence, performed the same tests he'd used to determine the status of her cancer. The tests came up negative. "They cured me of ovarian cancer," Barbara says proudly. She is puzzled why they had her drive so far from her home that Thanksgiving Eve after not visiting for five years.

"I don't remember anything during almost two hours in my truck but I know it was the little brothers," she assured me. Now, almost fifteen-years later, I ask myself should I include this account? After checking up on "Barbara" she is healthy and happy. Maybe the "little brothers" did aid her healing process.

Barbara's unbelievable-sounding story was one of the first requests for anonymity I had received from witnesses of unusual SLV events. I realized right away that some people would be OK with me using their names, officially, on-the-record. Others would not be comfortable allowing their names to be used. This fact leads me on to Rule #3.

Rule #3
Always credit your sources and respect requests for anonymity.

Initially, it appeared that certain people were more prone to sighting experiences than others. But wanting the experience didn't necessarily mean an individual would have one. Some of the most ardent believers in UFOs and ETs have never had a sighting experience.

November 27, 1992, 2:30 a.m., eighty miles south in Costilla County:

Manuel Sanchez (the Costilla rancher from the *Courier* article) couldn't sleep. He peered out the window of his modest ranch house across the pitch-black pasture, seeing and hearing nothing unusual. He finally fell into a fitful sleep until just before dawn. As he left the house the following Thanksgiving morning to check on his herd, he stopped. Not fifty feet away from the house, one of his prize breeding cows lay motionless on her side, obviously dead. It's rear end, udder and tongue were cleanly removed with the mandible bleached a ghostly white. One of the twentieth century's most enigmatic phenomenon had returned to the place of it's publicized birth.

He ran toward the animal, He had seen it before. The carcass filled him with the same dread he'd felt after losing a cow in identical fashion eighteen years before.

An angry, worried Sanchez immediately called Costilla County Sheriff Billy Maestas who investigated the scene with deputy Roger Benson. "No predator could have done that," Maestas agreed. "I've seen a lot of dead livestock in my time and this really concerns me." Maestas immediately called Los Animas Sheriff Lou Girodo to ask the UAD expert for assistance and found out John Torres had lost a cow in the same manner.

Sanchez also called the *Valley Courier* and spoke with reporter Ruth Heide. "I called the paper to warn everybody to keep their eyes open for lights or anything. I mean, if they could do this to my cow, maybe they could do it to humans. A lot of people disappear in the mountains around here and are never seen again!"

Girodo, a longtime law enforcement official had puzzled over unusual animal deaths for almost twenty-years. He had been interviewed in Linda Moulton Howe's book, *Alien Harvest* and in her Emmy award-winning documentary, *A Strange Harvest*, about the UAD problem. He was convinced that the phenomenon was a true mystery, worthy of investigation.

The Yellow Whirlybird

During those first couple of weeks in January 1993, I was so intent on corroborating the unexplained activity rumored to have occurred during the preceding three months, it hadn't occurred to me that we were in the midst of an on-going flap. I thought I was just researching an intriguing fluff article for a small-town newspaper. Almost fifteen years later, I remember the following series of crucial events with a smile.

As the process of painting an accurate picture of the history of SLV UAD reports and UFO sightings unfolded, it became obvious that more cows had been mysteriously killed than the local media had reported. Initially, it appeared that Saguache County, where I lived, had no documentation, or official reports of UAD cases. Several ranchers told me that cases had been reported in the 1970s, but I could find no reference to them in newspaper archives. Even the acknowledged top researcher in the field, Tom Adams, was unaware of any official Saguache County cases, or even rumors of reports.

It turned out that the local *Saguache Crescent*, over the years, had never published a single article pertaining to the many UADs that allegedly occurred here. The editor patiently explained, "Oh, they happened but we only write about good news." I called Sheriff Dan Pacheco and he claimed there were no records of any "mutilations" or UFO sightings in his office. He sheepishly told me that most of the previous sheriffs had never kept accurate files. "We don't even have files on murders that took place in Saguache County back in the sixties and '70s."

Two days after my talk with Sheriff Pacheco, he called to tell me he had searched through old boxes in the basement and found a packet of pictures. I picked them up at the sheriff's office the next day. The packet contained twenty-four color photographs of eight cows and one horse that had been reportedly "mutilated" in the late summer of nineteen-seventy-five. Only two of the photographs had any writing on the back explaining who owned the animal and when the report was filed. But, here it was, proof in my hand that Saguache County had experienced reports of unusual animal deaths.

The photos haunted me. What, or who, could have done this to these poor animals? The horse appeared to have been cut with a laser. A strange tar-like substance ringed the incision areas, the horse's rear-end appeared burned-out and it looked like the animal had been there for days. I found out later, from the

100

owner of the once-beautiful palomino show horse, that the photo had been taken at the time of discovery, just a few hours after the horse's death. I figured that if Tom Adams, the "top" expert in the field, was unaware that reports had been filed in Saguache County, maybe this whole phenomenon was more pervasive than I had imagined.

Looking through the photos, I noticed that one picture was of a Hereford bull. Fortunately, I was able to contact the former Saguache County deputy that had taken the photos. With the former deputy's help, I was able to identify the ranches that had apparently been targeted by the cattle-surgeons. It took me a couple of days of sleuthing and phoning to establish that the bull in the photograph belonged to the Sutherland family, who had a large spread several miles west of Moffat, less than twenty miles from my house in the Baca.

I spoke with Mrs. Virginia Sutherland, featured in author Sam Bingham's best-selling book, the *Last Ranch*. She confirmed the case in a matter-of-fact manner: "Yes, we had a bull killed in June 1980." She described the incident in detail over the phone and invited me out to the ranch to interview her family the following day. I was impressed by Virginia and her no-nonsense, hard-working ranching family. They remembered the incident with dispassionate clarity and I interviewed them separately to cross-reference their personal accounts. They all agreed on the details of the events of that unusual day in 1980.

The seventeen-hundred pound Hereford seed-bull had been in a separate pasture about five-hundred yards directly south of the ranch house. At dusk, on the early evening of June 5, 1980, the family was sitting down to dinner when they heard the droning thrumming of a helicopter fly slowly over the ranch house, headed south. They often observe utility company choppers checking the power lines, located three miles west of the house, but that particular evening they found it unusual that a chopper should be flying so low over the ranch, so far from the power lines. Fifteen to twenty minutes later, they heard the sound of the chopper again but this time it seemed to be taking off from their seed-bull's pasture. The chopper, "an old-fashioned, two-man, whirlybird-type of helicopter, mustard-yellow in color," was rising from the pasture where their bull was located. "It didn't seem to have any markings whatsoever. I thought that strange," commented Mrs. Sutherland. "I also thought it was peculiar that it had evidently landed in our field." The chopper flew back to the north, right over their house. "We all got a real good look at it. It was one of those, like you see on M.A.S.H-type helicopters. It was only thirty or forty feet over our heads!"

101

The next morning, they discovered the dead bull, its penis and eyes gone, its rear end "deeply cored-out," and a "one-inch plug missing from the brisket." Inexplicably, the hordes of flies that had landed on one side the carcass were dead. Thirteen years later, with the help of the Saguache County Sheriff, I held a photograph of the bull in my hand while I listened to Virginia's story.

The Sutherlands, understandably angry at the death and disfiguration of their prize seed-bull, immediately called every aviation facility in southern and central Colorado and northern New Mexico, trying to determine where the old-fashioned helicopter was based. They came up empty, no one had ever seen a mustard-yellow, whirlybird-type and they were told that this type of craft was extremely rare and astronomically expensive to keep in the air because of its age, plus it had very limited range, due to fuel consumption. With standard tanks a UH-1 had a range of about ninety miles.

Thirteen years later, Virginia was still puzzled, "It was the strangest thing, that [dead] bull was never touched by scavengers. Flies wouldn't land on the upside [of the carcass] and it took years for the carcass to melt into the field!" Virginia remembered.

I asked her to take me out to the location. Upon arriving out in the pasture where the bull was found, I was amazed to see the bones and hide laying exactly where the animal had fallen. Thirteen years later, it was still remarkably intact. All the flesh had rotted away years ago, but the hide was intact. I asked her if I could have the skull. I later painted it yellow and hung it on my office wall. It is probably the world's only decorated cattle mutilation skull.

I thanked the family for their time and for the graciously-loaned second photo of their peculiarly-slain bull. I assured them I would give them a call if I unearthed anything that might shed some light on the untimely demise of their animal. As it turned out, I would make that call the very next day!

The following morning, as I sat over a cup of coffee in our dining room, reviewing and typing up the Sutherland interview notes, I heard the faint sound of a helicopter headed down the Sangres. I glanced out the north-facing window just in time to see a mustard-yellow, old-fashioned, "like you see on M.A.S.H-type helicopter." As it approached our house, less than two-hundred feet up, it wheeled sideways and I saw the glint of something pointing down, out the passenger's side. Isadora, her eight year-old daughter Brisa and several neighbors also saw the chopper as it sauntered low over the Baca. I was floored and I was so startled I forgot to grab my camera to visually document this weird coincidental chopper sighting. Years later I look back at that pivotal morning with a smile. Today, if I had to identify that specific moment when

I realized that Jung's theory of synchronicity was alive and well, the yellow-helicopter incident would be that moment. Something inside me was whispering, there is something bigger going on with my investigation of the "paranormal in the San Luis Valley," so go for it!

This event solidified the realization that the investigator needs to be prepared at all times. Video and audio is best, but taking notes (Rule #3) is absolutely imperative. Rule 4 is self-explanatory:

Rules #4
Always be ready for anything, anytime. Look for coincidences when investigating claims of the unusual. Often, there may be a synchronistic element at work.

I remember commenting on the phone to Paris, Texas researcher, Tom Adams, during that last week in January 1993, "It just can't get any weirder than this!" He quickly assured me that it could.

Y'ain't Gonna Print Ma Name, Are Ya?

My first *Crestone Eagle* article hit the newsstands February 1, 1993. Eagle publisher, Kizzen Dennett, (usually claiming space-limitations in her monthly paper for running extended fluff articles like mine) dedicated an entire page to the unusual events of the previous two months. This was the first of twenty *Crestone Eagle* articles over of the next three years in which I attempted to fully cover the San Luis Valley reports of unexplained activity to a local readership.

Crestone/Baca area residents, upon reading the first article, expressed either support or skepticism to me and each other about my investigation. The article created a buzz and appeared to polarize readers into scoffers or knowing believers. The few who were not polarized seemed quite indifferent. I noticed a subtle current of unease in several people who talked with me concerning the implications of what I'd written, mainly, the never-stated but inferred alien involvement in the cattle death phenomenon. I realized during these conversations that it was imperative to maintain as objective a view on what I was reporting as possible. I was treading on volatile terrain and it was obvious, I needed to choose my steps and words carefully. Thus, Rule #5:

Rule #5
It is impossible to be too objective when investigating claims of the unusual.

Objectivity is imperative when investigating claims of unusual events. Investigators would be well advised to not jump toward any conclusions until all the facts are in and the data has pointed toward a definitive conclusion. I cannot overstate this enough. Long-time investigator Gary Massey, a firm proponent of the extraterrestrial hypothesis (ETH) says, "If it looks like a duck and quacks like a duck, it must be a duck." I disagree with this observation for several reasons. These phenomena are fraught with subterfuge and misdirection. Over the years I have learned not to take any unexplained event, or description of inexplicable occurrences, at face value because chances are, the phenomenon in question often masquerades itself as something it is not. After factoring out all possible mundane explanations, I suspect there are strange forces at work with unfathomable as yet undefined agendas. There are also governmental agendas at work that are attempting to *create the appearance of* something otherworldly. I have learned to second guess everything and believe in nothing. My suggested approach flies in the face of the "true believer" mindset, but it makes scientific sense in that it forces the investigator to approach his/her work from a open-minded, healthily analytical perspective.

Over the previous three months, the regional media was largely unaware that anything peculiar was going on due to the absence of official reports to local law enforcement and local media concerning UADs and UFOs. The initial Sanchez cattle death story passed like a whisper and no follow-up story was published by the *Valley Courier.*

My first *Eagle* article did, however, have the effect of making folks around the Baca and Saguache County more aware of the night sky. It encouraged residents to keep their eyes open and report any anomalous objects to me, to the *Eagle* or local law enforcement.

Much to my surprise, reports immediately came in out of the woodwork. During sighting periods, I've received as many as seventeen calls per day from witnesses. Many are from complete strangers who hear about me through my articles or through friends; they describe their sightings in great detail, offering names and phone numbers of additional witnesses and they always ask if anyone else had reported what they claimed to have seen.

From the late-1970s until my arrival there hadn't been a local SLV paper or investigator encouraging valley residents to call and report mysterious events. As a direct result of my initial public request for any witnesses of unusual events to call, residents with sighting experiences had someone locally with whom they can talk about their experiences. There is a fine line, however, between creating recourse for witnesses and becoming too highly visible in the local population. I'll address this conundrum later. Then there is the anonymity factor.

During the first week of February 1993, after publication of my first article, a nervous rancher called me and hesitantly described three years of unidentified light activity on his remote Saguache County ranch. After over an hour of descriptions, dates and observations pertaining to unknown occurrences in his area, he asked me just as we were ending our conversation, "Ya ain't gonna print ma name, are ya?" This understandable reluctance of some witnesses to "go-on-the-record" suggested to me that this would be a major factor in the creation of credibility around my investigation of these inexplicable events. The anonymity factor is a major obstacle to investigating and documenting claims of genuine paranormal phenomena.

I quickly realized that a proper course of action would be to set-up a network of vigilant on-the-record skywatchers around the valley. Multiple pairs of eager eyes around an entire region would undoubtedly observe more than my single pair of eyes, no matter how much time I spent surveying the sky. And these reports would be on-the-record.

As the reports continued to filter into weirdness-central, I naturally found myself spending increasing amounts of time outdoors at night. I smoke tobacco. I dislike the smell of residual cigarette smoke, so I have elected to light-up outdoors for years. I've turned this habit to good use. A few times every evening I would step outside, light up and survey the wonderful panorama that extended from the foothills of the Sangres out across the SLV. On new moon nights during the summer, the Milky Way stretches from horizon-to-horizon. It became apparent to me that I needed to re-familiarize myself with the night sky. As a child, I developed a fascination with the heavens. Growing up, I studied star maps and learned the basics of astronomy. Brendon's "godfather" was family friend NASA top engineer and administrator Louis Mogavero and the Mercury, Gemini and Apollo space programs were enthusiastic topics of family conversation growing up at the O'Briens. But later, after living for so many years in midtown Manhattan, with its gross air and light pollution, I lost the opportunity to view an uncluttered horizon. Fortunately, Isadora had a planesphere star map which became instrumental in reacquainting me with the glorious high-altitude night sky.

The telltale vapor-trails of mundane commercial jet traffic gave me an accurate map of the various commercial flight routes in constant use over the valley. I noticed at once that these pathways were divided into north-south/south-north, east-west/west-east, with a few planes flying diagonally. Commercial flights travel at predictable altitudes and speeds, over defined lanes of travel. I acquired pilot maps for the Denver and Albuquerque flight control areas.

La Veta Military Operations Area (MOA)

Strange lights seen at night are one thing but close-proximity daylight sightings are optimal. A shared, unexplained daylight sighting experience that previous September 17, 1992, at 1:30 p.m., in the Huerfano Valley—to the east, over the other side of the Sangres should have alerted me that there were strange things flying around Southern Colorado. Today, looking back, I find it ironic that my first, really good daylight sighting of a anomalous aerial craft happened in the "not so mysterious" Huerfano Valley (as my mentor David Perkins refers to his stomping grounds over the hill).

We were headed southward on State Highway 69, seven miles north of Gardner, Colorado. Isadora was driving, I was riding shotgun in the front passenger seat, Brisa had the backseat all to herself. To our right, the backside of the Blanca Massif and the Sangres loomed twenty-miles away, to the west out across the Wet Mountain Valley. I glanced at a series of steep pinon-covered hills to our left when something silver flashed between two low hills, less than three-hundred yards away. "What was that? Did you see that?" I asked Isadora. She looked at me with a smile and a nod. My first impression was of an oversized radio-controlled airplane scooting along in our direction of travel.

"It looked like a model plane," she guessed. The craft emerged from behind the hill to our left, obviously having made a quick right hand turn and it zipped directly across the windshield from left to right, east-to-west. It was about seventy to eighty feet off the ground and just over three hundred feet away, directly in front of us. The sun glinted off its skin. I looked directly at it and it appeared larger than I had originally assumed it to be. "That's no model plane!" I exclaimed as it headed off over the valley that stretched to the Sangres—about seven miles away. I got a really good look at it as it headed west.

Isadora suggested it might be some sort of remote-piloted military drone. We were right in the middle of the La Veta low-level MOA and the craft we were watching certainly could have been military. I grabbed my binoculars off the seat and watched it speed across the valley toward Medano Pass.

The craft appeared to be about twelve-feet long with tiny stubby-wings, and I thought I might have seen a small clear cupola and a dark headrest and helmet. I'm not sure of this but that was my initial impression when it zipped across the highway. In a matter of seconds, it had traveled far enough across the valley for me to lose sight of it, because of its small size, against the silhouetted mountain backdrop. I thought it strange, the way it appeared to dart through the sky. It seemed to be pulled rather than propelled, as if it was attached to fishing line that was quickly being reeled in. I rolled my window down as it sailed out over the Huerfano but didn't hear anything over the low-pitched hum of the Buick's V-6 engine. The following March, Berle Lewis' description of the small Remote Piloted Vehicles (RPV)-type craft that were observed just over the range in 1966-67 sometimes flying directly into an opening on Middle Creek Hill reminded me of the small craft we had seen. Looking back fifteen years later I smile wondering what the lure and bait meant.

Since our sighting of this miniature craft, I have seen pictures of RPVs that our government publicly acknowledges using but the craft we saw didn't remotely resemble any of them. I thought at the time that there was something weird about the craft, but who really knows what the military is secretly flying around the country's Military Operations Areas (MOAs).

The La Veta Military Operations Area is a key component to our mysterious valley equation. Closely situated in close proximity to the SLV—just east over the mountains, this seventy square mile area is one of the Nation's most important, extensively used low-level flight training areas in the country.

An informative brochure from Open Space Alliance - Huerfano Valley Citizen's Alliance points out plans for this part of Colorado's airspace:

> What the Air Force and National Guard have in mind for Huerfano, Custer, Saguache and Alamosa Counties is to create a permanent "simulated war zone" in the skies above our region. Under the new Colorado Air Space Initiative (CAI), not only will the number of sorties be increased to at least 3,120 per year, but the majority of the missions will be authorized to fly as low as one hundred feet above the ground. The National Guard's rationalization for the proposed change is that modern warfare techniques require pilots to be skilled in low altitude, radar evasive techniques. (The guard also plans to release ten thousand flares per year on these maneuvers.)
>
> Another little-known provision is Project Shining Mountain in which, it is alleged, the government is flying prototype and secret military aircraft around the SLV

region. The press was never told about this secret provision. The brochure continues:

> If the National Guard's proposed plan is allowed to be implemented, the way of life that we have all worked so hard to create and sustain will be destroyed. We can either move elsewhere or spend the remainder of our days in the living nightmare of a simulated war zone.

A nightmare indeed! I experienced the fly-boys up-close and personal while working thirty feet above the ground on a two inch by twelve inch plank. I had moved to the Baca a couple of months earlier and was in awe of the view of my spectacular surroundings. painting from the top of a three-stage construction scaffolding. I momentarily heard a ripping sound and WHOOSH, an F-16 fighter hurtled past less than forty feet from me! I saw the pilot look back at me in that fraction of a second before I dove, belly-flopping to the plank. The sonic blast of the engine noise hit me with an ear-shattering explosion, rattling the entire scaffolding.

I jumped up cursing the hotshot pilot, but the SOB returned eight minutes later for another, even closer pass! It was episodes like this, and jets buzzing Moffat High-school, that sparked many in Saguache County to support the Open Space Alliance's efforts to stop the harassment.

There appears to be a parallel between the ebbing and flowing of low level aerial activity military planes in the Military Operations Area (MOA) and reports of unexplained aerial activity on the periphery of this low-level training area on the eastern side of the valley. If this is so, could this military usage of eastern SLV air-space also explain sightings on the western side of the valley, fifty miles from the edge of the MOA?

The twentieth-first century finds our Air Force ready to kick some tail feather with billions of dollars worth of aeronautical toys and almost unlimited funding. Granted, we've spent many billions of dollars on hardware and our pilots need to train, but who (or what) are we training our pilots to do battle with? The Iranians have no Air Force to speak of, the Chinese don't appear to have imperialistic designs on North America. The Russians ...well we know who won the Cold War. The only Air-Force equal to ours is the Israeli Air-force, one-tenth the size of ours, and supposedly, we're on the same team. But we've got 'em and we have to use 'em. Either we give our fighter pilots flight time, or we lose these valuably-trained professionals to the airlines. With thousands of sorties costing millions of dollars, the Air Force is conducting business as usual in the skies over the Middle East. Perhaps the

108

multi-national arms developers who supply the million dollar toys have their eyes on loftier skies. The F-22 has now officially joined our arsenal of state-of-the art aerial weapons systems as our most advanced "conventional" fighter plane and there are rumblings about a rapid deployment space-plane designed to carry US Marines anywhere on the planet within hours.

There are legitimate arguments questioning such intensive use of domestic flight training areas. Accidents do happen, for instance during a seven-day period in September 1997, six United States military aircraft crashed in the US, including an F-117A stealth fighter, which narrowly missed taking out spectators at an air show in Virginia. Except for "air show" appearances and other exhibition flying, our fly-boys are tasked to scream around designated flight training areas where training and simulated aerial war games are conducted, like over the Huerfano, next door to the SLV. Coincidentally, the son of a good friend of mine in Virginia is a Major in a prestigious military aeronautic demonstration team.

The La Veta MOA covers the low-level airspace over parts of Huerfano, Custer, Saguache, Alamosa, Costilla, Chaffee and Pueblo Counties. Air Force and National Guard flight operations are conducted daily. For reasons not clearly stated, the United States Government continues to attempt to expand our countries MOA's. Why? According to the Huerfano Valley Citizen's Alliance, a group dedicated in the late 1990s to stopping expansion of the local La Veta MOA;

> …The Colorado Airspace Initiative (CAI) is the tip of the iceberg in an alarming trend—the military's insatiable appetite for new land to disrupt for practical maneuvers. The Military already controls an estimated fifty percent of the airspace in the U.S., and owns many millions of acres. The proposed CAI is only one of multiple initiatives for Military Operations Areas in the United States…Huerfano County has already served as an aerial playground for the military since the late 1970's, when the La Veta MOA was approved. According to Air National Guard figures, the current utilization of the La Veta MOA is 2,929 sorties (individual jet missions) per year. Under the New Colorado Airspace Initiative (CAI) proposal, not only will the number of sorties be increased to at least 3,120 per year, but the majority of these missions will be authorized to fly as low as *one hundred feet above the ground.* An F-111 or F-16 flight directly overhead at six hundred miles per hour is a bone-rattling and brain-numbing experience…

The National Guard's rationalization for the proposed

change is that modern warfare techniques require pilots to be skilled in low-altitude, radar-evasive techniques. In addition to the low-altitude training, the new proposal will allow for every variety of air combat training, including 'dog-fights,' involving two to eight aircraft. The National Guard also anticipates releasing approximately ten thousand flares yearly as part of these maneuvers. Supposedly, the flares will 'largely disintegrate' before they hit the ground. The plan calls for revised military training routes (MTR). These training routes are meant to be 'aerial highways' for low-altitude flights at high speeds. The are *five major proposed air corridors*—all converge at a point near Gardner—then proceed north over Greenhorn Mountain to the Airburst Range near Ft. Carson where the pilots 'complete their weapons delivery mission.' This means that *Huerfano County will be the most heavily impacted area* under the new plan. (Their emphasis retained)

This proposed expansion of the La Veta MOA does not make sense. The United States is not planning to go to war with any other country besides Iraq, and Afghanistan, right? Our Air Force is considered the very best, and faces no perceived challenges anywhere else on the planet. Now that China has successfully deployed a satellite killing missile the stakes have been raised all the way up into space, so why greatly increase low-altitude military flight operational training areas like here in the Huerfano?

The following press release questioning the rationale was published by the Open Space Alliance (OSA), a coalition of regional citizen's groups opposing the mid-1990s expansion of the La Veta MOA.

"The Air National Guard's (ANG) proposal, which started as the Red Eye Complex and evolved into the Colorado Airspace Initiative, revamps more military airspace in Colorado and Kansas than any other ANG project in the country."

That means Southern Coloradans are among the most impacted from these proposed expansions. *Backpacker* Magazine stated in their April, 1994 issue,

"…There will also be no restrictions on the future use of Colorado's airspace by other branches of the military, leaving the skies permanently vulnerable."

110

Not only are "other branches of the military" interested in Colorado airspace, a new development, pointed out in an advertisement published by the Custer County Action Association, now concerns many area residents.

> "The people of Germany wouldn't tolerate low-altitude military over flights. Their property values, personal safety and quiet country-sides were all being destroyed. In peacetime. So the Luftwaffe had to leave. Guess where they went? Right here. The German Air Force will be flying out of New Mexico and over our mountains, valleys and national wilderness areas as part of the 'Colorado Airspace Initiative.' . . .They've sold our skies. . ."

What's wrong with this picture? The Front Range of Colorado reaps the rewards of billions of dollars every year and the citizens of the SLV and the Huerfano, who gain nothing, have to tolerate the many ear-splitting over-flights (and possible covert aerial activity). And some conventional flights are now conducted by foreign air force clients!

Another article published in the *Crestone Eagle,* in May 1997, written by OSA advocate Pat Richmond, addresses the probability that *un*-conventional, secret aircraft are being flown here.

> ...[In the April 5-11 1996 edition of] the Denver Business Journal (DBJ) has revealed in a cover to cover exposé that Pentagon 'black' dollars are being channeled into Colorado's Front Range communities. Labeled the 'hottest news story of the year,' the journal's investigation and analysis of 'Colorado's Stealth Economy' identified companies and agencies within Colorado that serve as a 'spy-hub' for the nation. Economic analyst Henry Dubroff wrote, 'make no mistake about it. The most important city in Colorado is Washington D.C.'...While the DJB report may seem like hot news to some, residents on both sides of the Sangres know there have been unusual aircraft in our airspace for quite some time. Sightings of Stealth bombers or F-117s or black helicopters repeatedly have been brought to the attention of COANG's Brig. Gen. Mason C. Whitney. He seemed to know nothing about military operations by 'secret aircraft' yet the DJB article makes it clear that the Colorado Air National Guard not only coordinates secret flights but also serves as landlord for the Pentagon's spy hub.

In this investigator's mind, without a doubt, the United States

111

military is conducting undisclosed sorties and other clandestine aerial maneuvers in and around Southern Colorado and Northern New Mexico. With the second-largest source of state income being utilized and spent by the intelligence agencies *vis-à-vis* the military in Colorado, it makes sense that the fly-boys would concentrate their activities in the remotest areas of the state. A perfect *petri* dish, no?

Pat Richmond wrote a follow-up article in the February 1997 *Crestone Eagle* which pointed out the possibility that many of our nocturnal anomalous light sightings are very terrestrial in nature. Makes sense to this investigator ...Richmond also uncovered undisclosed information concerning military air and ground operations conducted in the Rio Grande National Forest.

Open Space Alliance has discovered the existence of an Inter-Agency Agreement between the Department of Defense and the Rocky Mountain Regional Office of the National Forest Service. (Department of Agriculture) that could explain "strange lights" and other puzzling "phenomena" that periodically appear in the night skies of the San Luis Valley and surrounding areas.

Contrary to media coverage promoting speculation about UFOs, some residents in the SLV, including retired military personnel familiar with Pentagon activities and procedures, have long believed that most night sky "sightings" are connected to military operations such as experimental testing of prototype craft, routine training maneuvers, or special aircraft used to provide coordinates for tracking and/or retrieving missiles launched from Ft. Wingate or White Sands...'Is there an agreement between the military and the Forest Service that would allow night training activities within the Rio Grande National Forest?

Ron Jablonski—Rio Grande National Forest public relations officer... decided that he could not allow Richmond to see the document because it was 'just a Draft...' Jablonski stated the agreement between the military and the forest service would permit small groups such as the Green Berets to engage in special forces training within the forest. He emphasized that any activities involving helicopters or other aircraft over Wilderness Areas would have to go the National Environmental Protection Agency process and would require approval all the way to the top—the Regional Forest Supervisor...Although Jablonski denied knowing the specifics of a finalized document, he referred to training activities being limited to times outside hunting season. He also offered the comment that trainees would not use laser weapons, but lasers might be used for locating or targeting either aircraft or ground personnel.'

Let me remind the aspiring investigators out there: it's tough investigating the sensational unknown, people will automatically assume you are "a ufo crazy," running around claiming "the Martians have landed." Even if you attempt to utilize the power of objective realism and apply a new, actualized approach to the equation, you will be swimming upstream against a cultural current that would impress even the laziest salmon. I find it ironic that my assertions in the mid-1990s suggesting a high percentage of the San Luis Valley's current "so-called" nocturnal UFO sightings may be due to secret military activity was never acknowledged by the media and/or opponents of the MOA and its opposed expansion. There is a social stigma attached to the subject and you better be ready to deal with people questioning your motivations and your sanity.

Privately my hunch has always been that the government is utilizing San Luis Valley high-ground airspace (and the air space above other hot-spot regions) for covert, aerial projects designed to illicit a programmed response, and it stands to reason that certain cutting-edge military technologies may be so fantastic in appearance, witnesses of this technology might think they were witnessing something "other worldly." What a potential psychotronic weapon for warfare overseas! Utilizing exotic technologies, the boys-with-toys are probably examining the impact of their psychotronic war-games on unsuspecting witnesses of seemingly inexplicable events. When you think about it; if you were in charge of conducting new weapon systems' effectiveness studies, why not trot out your new, multi-gazillion dollar technologies for an innocent remote region of the country to witness and then gauge the resulting perceptions they filter back into culture-at-large? The designer/operators would want to know; what was reported and by whom? How was the "op" perceived? If reported, how does the media and law enforcement view these anomalous claims of the inexplicable? Do they take these calls seriously? If so, do they publicize these reports? Do they put a spin on them? Over the past few years, a handful of researcher/thinkers have asked these questions and this rationale that may explain some (but not all) "UFO sightings."

One underlying probability needs to always be remembered, regardless of any government involvement, something extraordinary has apparently been flying around the world's airspace for hundreds, perhaps thousands of years, and no matter how hard

113

the skeptic in me might try, the above hypothetical government/military scenario cannot explain away all UFO sightings.

My research would suggest that the government/military has conducted extensive operations in the greater San Luis Valley. Law enforcement rumors of the "C.I.A. training Tibetans Nationals" up on the Blanca Massif back in the mid-1960s, coincidentally around the time of the Snippy case and later in the early seventies, stories concerning secret Mars Lander mock-maneuvers on the Great Sand Dunes cannot be ignored. A local sheriff's deputy claim that "Aryan Groups" were suspected training in remote inaccessible areas in the Sangres is worthy of discussion as well.

There's no question in this investigator's mind that our government/military is utilizing this region's airspace as extensively and efficiently as possible. To compound the drama, it appears that they have made our sovereign airspace available for training to other countries as well, at a price.

Assume a Mundane Explanation?

When examining all the elements that may be at work and play, flitting above us in rarified air, we must keep in mind we are dealing with a highly complex scenario. This potential for misidentification tempers my reaction to all "anomalous light" reports from the eastern side of the Sangres, in the La Veta MOA, and for that matter, all of Southern Colorado and Northern New Mexico.

In January and February 1993, during my initial enthusiasm investigating witnesses' claims of UFO sightings in the valley, my natural inclination was to enthusiastically jump toward the fantastic, like most UFO enthusiasts. When I started my investigation I had no idea that the La Veta MOA even existed. Several pointed comments by area skeptics, whom I respected, helped temper this misinformed response. Without a healthy sense skepticism, I could have very easily fallen into a trap of thinking, if a witness thought it sounded, looked and/or felt unusual, it must have been "extraterrestrial".

Rule #6
Always assume there is a mundane explanation until proven extraordinary.

In light of the airspace allocations above southern Colorado, some of my first inquiries were made to local sheriffs and the Colorado Air National Guard. Six weeks into my investigation, on

February 12, 1993, I spoke with Saguache County Deputy Lynn Bogle. I asked him if the sheriff's office had fielded any recent cattle "mutilation" reports. He told me "no, not that he knew of," but that he had been on a ranch just north of Center, in May, 1978, when they found a "mutilated" three-year-old cow. "The rear end was gone, the eyes were gone, there was no blood, and the heart was gone!" Without asking him whom he thought was responsible, he volunteered that he thought "it was the military …our government does a lot of things they don't want us to know about."

Deputy Bogle told me that a highly visible clear cut area on the western slopes of the Blanca Massif was supposed to be used as an artillery range but the locals stopped it. He had also heard of an Aryan-base, near Mosca Pass. His fascinating accounts included a summer-long chase of "turbo Hughes and Bell choppers" in 1991, seen in the Bonanza and Hayden Pass areas. Choppers were reported regularly and sheriff's deputies raced around in an attempt to find out where they were going. "We saw them May to frost. The Denver Center FAA (who monitor SLV airspace) had no radar reports." (Eighteen thousand feet is the absolute lowest ceiling for radar detection in the SLV).

Then the former-marine surprised me with an interesting story from his teens. "Years ago in the sixties, my parents would take summer trips with the family up to the Platoro Reservoir area. There was an old miner, a hermit who lived in the Summitville area year-round. He was like the caretaker, he'd take the tourists on informal tours, that sort of thing. He told us several times that during the late fall and winter, the aliens visited him. They would land right outside. He said he even talked with them, said they were just like you and me!"

"When was that, do you remember what year?" I inquired.

"The early to mid sixties. One time we went up and he told us the military had run the aliens off. He said helicopters landed and some guy told him never to talk to them again." I asked Bogle what had happened to the old miner. He had died a few years before and Bogle couldn't remember his name, he thought it was maybe Carter. I made a note to call around to find out more about this colorful character.

Bogle then mentioned a man named Glenn Anderson. I remembered some vague stories I had already heard about this enigmatic character. He evidently had attracted a group of young followers in the late 1960's and, it's alleged by these followers that he "channeled" all kinds of interesting information and predictions. According to Bogle, "Frank Scott has tapes and transcripts." Scott was a local school teacher, so I called him about the transcripts

115

and tapes.

Frank Scott didn't have them anymore but told me some interesting things Anderson had said. "He told us, 'the whole universe is interested in us,' and that 'there would be a lot of ET activity.'" Scott told me of other friends' experiences, including a light from high-up on Blanca chasing a man in his car, reminiscent of Brendon and Bill's July 1991 experience. Scott also mentioned Bigfoot sightings north of Mosca Pass near the Marble Canyon - Marble Mine area.

He eventually asked me if I'd like to visit the 1893 Alamosa Aereolite meteor crater, on the Baca Ranch, with his class the following week. You bet I did. At the time the public was usually denied access to the ranch. The crater was unmistakable and I imagined those two magnetic masses deep in the sand below us. The kids dragged magnets on strings and collected impressive amounts of iron from the sand in the stony meteor site. Go figure, kids.

More Synchronicity

February 23, 1993, 8:30 a.m., the Baca:

Isadora and I were enjoying the bright cheery morning over a cup of coffee when Brisa bounded down the stairs. I was a little surprised, it usually took her a while to wake up. She seemed excited.

"I had a really neat dream last night," she announced.

"What did you dream about," her mother asked.

"There were these little men and they had a ship right outside. They came into my room play to with me. They were really cute! They had these funny hands that sort of looked like cactus." (She was referring to the prickly-pear cactus that dot the landscape around here.) Something about her matter-of-fact demeanor made me sit up and pay attention.

"So what happened?" I asked.

"I don't remember but I know I had fun!"

Paddle-shaped hands? Her dream was intriguing. "Brisa, could you draw me a picture of the little men and their ship?" I asked.

"Sure." I gave her a convenient manila envelope and a pen and set her up at the dining room table. She drew a hamburger-shaped ship and several tiny figures with strange little Ping Pong paddle-shaped hands with little spikes protruding like fingers. Isadora and I asked several more questions but didn't make a big deal out of her claim or put too much emphasis on her dream.

Later that afternoon, when I picked up our mail at the post office, there was a sizable package from Tom Adams, in Paris,

Texas. He had already sent along several invaluable sets of articles, reports and accounts of the mysterious, from the San Luis Valley, and I had been eagerly awaiting this next installment. Since I was catching up-to-speed on SLV history, I appreciated his packages more than anyone else's.

I opened the large, thickly-stuffed envelope and started perusing the various SLV articles and reports from a variety of sources Adams had tapped. I remember thinking how lucky I was; here was a guy in Texas sending me volumes of documented information about the magical place where I live.

One thirteen-page account caught my attention, entitled, "Another Unidentified Flying Object Story:

> My name is R. B. (Bud) Hooper, a newsreel cameraman since 1924, I have seen a lot of unusual events that took place in the news field as the years rolled by. During this time, several situations relative to UFOs that I was more or less involved with took place. In August 1959, I experienced the most unbelievable and mysterious event in my life.
>
> I was making pictures (sic) in Southern Colorado, I had a helper with me by the name of Guy, we were traveling east on Highway US 160, between Alamosa and Ft. Garland, I was driving and Guy was looking to the south as quite often one could see a mirage, usually a lake reflecting the mountains...
>
> I turned on an old road and drove in about a half mile and found a place to park...The next thing I remember I was standing in a large transparent cylinder about seven or eight feet high, and around four or five feet wide. The first thing that I noticed was that I was in a large room that looked to be around fifty feet across looking straight ahead.
>
> Next, I saw before me and slightly to my right were two objects that were moving. They were in armor that appeared to be made of the same material as the round construction. Straight ahead and past the two objects, from now on I will refer to them as men, a third man about thirty five feet down the room was seated in front of what seemed to be a panel. I noticed that these men had arms and legs. On the end of each arm was a highly polished and slightly curved disc three inches in diameter.

Three-inch disks for hands? Here was another one of those absolutely bizarre examples of synchronicity that had started to become commonplace in my investigation. Brisa had gone into great detail describing "little men with cactus-shaped hands," and here I was, less than an hour later, reading an account from over thirty-five years before, describing beings encountered in the SLV with three-inch curved discs for hands. I showed Bud Hooper's account to Isadora and we both marveled at the uncanny timing off its arrival. The story continued . . .

The eyes were also highly polished discs that looked like mirrors about four inches wide. The time consumed in sizing up this situation did not take over two or three minutes. At this time I had a feeling that they wanted me to convey to them what I wanted to know ...No voice, but by transfer of thought or telepathy. My first question was obvious, 'Where am I?' The nearest armored man pointed up to the round enclosure and conveyed to me that I was in a space vehicle or satellite from outer space.

At this point, the cylinder I was in made a short turn and raised above my head and I received a command, 'Come with us.' They led me to the man sitting in front of a panel containing what looked like many round shiny discs like those on the end of their arms. They were actuated by these magnetic discs.

It was conveyed to me that now the wheel inside was turning at the exact speed of light and that is what the earth people saw when reporting seeing UFOs or "flying saucers." The pilot raised his arm again to the large control and I sensed a feeling of rising for a second or two and the lights went out. The pilot conveyed to me that the wheel was now turning faster than the speed of light and therefore the earth people cannot see this space vehicle even though we are only a few feet above the ground. The pilot further explained that by controlling the speed of the wheel creates an anti-gravity function that makes it possible to raise and lower the craft. When we leave the earth's atmosphere to return to our planet, we speed the wheel to overcome Earth's gravitational pull.

I was led back to the position under the cylinder ...He conveyed to me that until earth people can discover or create a hard material that has very little weight that can be magnetized to attract or to repel, Earth people will not be able to travel to an outer galaxy or accomplish much in our own universe. 'Why was I contacted this way?'

'We were hovering just a short distance away when you drove up. It was decided to bring you aboard in a sort of trance, mainly to learn what reaction you would have when you became normal in the cylinder.' It was conveyed to me that I was one of the 'few Earth persons that did not panic, threaten us, act crazy, you showed no signs of being the least bit afraid. You are showing an interest in wanting to learn about us ...Furthermore we cannot accept the many descriptions as to what we look like ...some describe us as midgets, green blobs, big horrible looking objects with feelers and horns. Like Earth people, we do not all look alike, some of us are short, some tall, some handsome, some not so handsome. Having you as a visitor, we want you to pass along the things you have learned so that your people will understand that we have no desire to capture your world. We would like a landing area for a few of our satellites to use as a stopping off place to adjust our radios and antennas before we go beyond your sun and universe seeking to find other galaxies. Above all, tell your people we want to be friendly, when we land, generally on a farm we are usually greeted by the farmer waving a pitchfork or shot (sic) gun at us. . .'"

A voice conveyed to me, "We are returning you the same way we brought you here as the cylinder you are in must be lowered to your car and we do not want you to take the chance the transfer would frighten you and you would forget all the things you have learned."

Adams' latest package of information also contained other accounts from the 1950s in the SLV. In November 1956, then Alamosa resident John DeHerrera and his brother were delivering newspapers eastbound on State Highway 160. As the DeHerrera brothers approached town, a sudden glint of light caught their eyes.

We observed a strange object ahead on the left side of the highway. This object came toward us, moving slowly, approximately forty miles per hour and about five feet above the ground ...As the object turned and headed skyward, a long, colorful flame shot out the back. Then it turned and crossed the highway directly overhead, accelerated rapidly and vanished in the distance."

This daytime encounter, observed under ideal conditions, proved to be a pivotal one in John DeHerrera's life. So impressed with the unusual experience and the unmistakable reality of the object, he went on to become an eminent UFO researcher, currently living in southern California.

This letter written by Episcopal minister Robert Whiting, stated:

The first 'contact' I had with what might be a UFO was several weeks ago while driving at night from Monte Vista to Alamosa. At the right of the road as I was going east, there was an object about twice tree top height which I took for a low flying plane or helicopter. Since it was so low, I thought it might be an aircraft in trouble making a forced landing on the road, so I slowed down. As I recall the object, it displayed a large red and green light, the rest was dark and the light was not flashing as one would expect. This is all I can say about the object and the only visual sighting of the UFO, if indeed, that is what it was. All other contacts were mental.

At any event (sic) I was reassured that there was no danger to them or myself in resuming speed and for the next fifteen or 20 minutes as I drove along, a 'conversation' (I'll try to explain this later) took place. Those 'people' (I'll go into that later too) assured me they are friendly and will eventually make closer contact with us. Their purpose is to study our planet and they would like to trade with **us to** our mutual advantage. Some of the main obstacles thereto are that we are inclined to be violent when faced with the unknown and unusual and that our dealings with those who do not look like ourselves can be somewhat unfortunate - they seem to know all about our race problems. However, they feel confident that eventually these problems will be overcome and that we will one day join them in exploration of the universe and the peaceful and proper uses of its resources. They seem to feel we are more advanced then they are in some fields and they are far in advance of us in others, but specified only one technology - apparently a consuming interest (and maybe because it is one of my interests) photography. It seems the main difficulty lies in the effect of radiation, both in space and in their craft, on both films and their preservation whereas the protection of humanoids of almost any species, including ourselves, is no real obstacle.

I've had two other contacts. The one who contacted me said they look very much like us, though not sufficiently different to be commented upon. On structure, they would correspond to both ourselves and the insects, in that they are vertebrates with an interior skeletal structure, but also have a very thick 'skin' something like, but not quite similar, to the shell of an insect, but through which they had both protection from heat and cold along with considerable sensitivity in feeling and touch. However, both their crew and others came in all sizes and colors from many different 'worlds.' The little green men that have been reported, according to them are actually so. Some of them developed where the coloring of the environment was green and their color afforded them protection from enemies - though this is no longer necessary. Others came from worlds where food, as we know it, is scarce, and have developed a method of survival through a process akin to photosynthesis. For some reason, not explained, these are the humanoids who can land and explore our atmosphere with the smallest amount of equipment, but, and this was said with humor, they are well aware that none of us are green so they proceed with extreme caution.

The other contact was very brief, although interesting. I was driving, again at night thinking about a radio talk I was to give the next day, and right in the middle of it, I was told that my thoughts were very interesting and they knew I was busy and didn't want to interrupt, but there was a dead animal ahead and I should pull over a bit to the right. In about thirty seconds, or so, I came to a large dog which had been run over and lay partly in my lane. I might have hit it had I not been warned. After this I resumed my planning and felt they were still 'listening,' but there was no further conversation. Both of these latter 'contacts' I was told came from deep in space. There was no visual sighting. One last thing. I did bring up the local matter of Snippy the horse. They told me they knew nothing about it, and when I asked if they knew what a horse was they told me humorously and almost derisively that, of course, they knew what a horse was. . .

The reason I don't want publicity is two-fold - the obvious one is that I don't want to be considered a nut and the other is, as I have said before, this may all [be my] imagination even though I do hope I am in contact with friendly and very pleasant humanoids. If this is true, they are 'damned nice people.'

The Silver Derby

During the first part of January 1993, as I chased leads and researched accounts of the many valley UFO sightings that appeared to be occurring, I noticed that a vast majority of these reports were of anomalous lights at night. There had been some daytime sightings of craft (or objects) in the past but no documented cases from the last several years. Assuming a mundane explanation for a vast majority of these nocturnal sightings still leaves many that are potentially unexplained.

Several daylight reports that I've uncovered are puzzling. In April of 1992, a Monte Vista emergency medical technician and mother of three, had seen a "Bell-shaped object as big as a school bus" hovering over her neighbor's house in the late afternoon. "It was unbelievable! I've seen weird lights at night around here, but this was unmistakable. It looked like a big hat." She quickly called her neighbor who also saw the object out her kitchen window. "I don't want to talk about it," the neighbor told me after I obtained her phone number from a friend. "My kids say 'it chased them' when they went outside to look at it, and I'd rather not talk about it."

February 24, 1993, 10:30 a.m., Highway 17, between the towns of Mosca and Hooper:
A thirty-seven-year-old baker, Judy DeBon, and her artist mother, were driving south toward Alamosa, on Highway 17, on a cold February morning to do some shopping. As they approached Mosca, they noted a flash above them and to the east. A silent bell-shaped object, the color of brushed aluminum, flew over their car, headed toward the Blanca Massif. It was clear and still that day and they "got a real good look at it."

"My mother wouldn't let me stop to watch it," Judy told me a couple of hours later after they had returned from town. "My mother was pretty scared and thought it wouldn't be a good idea to stop. I'm sure the people in the car behind us saw it because they did stop. It flew over us about one-hundred feet above the road. Since I was driving, I couldn't watch where it went but it was heading toward Blanca."

This was not the first time Judy and her mother had seen a "bell-shaped object." She had related a previous sighting a couple of weeks after it happened, before the above description. On December 21, 1992, at 2:40 p.m., they were driving north from Alamosa, again on Highway 17, between Hooper and Moffat, when they observed "the same object" hovering against the mountains. "We drove along and watched it for a couple of minutes. It was in the vale over by San Isabelle Creek. I couldn't believe how fast it shot to the north when it disappeared!"

"What was that?"

My second *Crestone Eagle* article was released the first week of March, 1993. Kizzen again devoted an entire page to my investigation and research, the article attempted to give a quick overview of many of the more celebrated San Luis Valley cases that had been reported through the years. With a rare full page devoted to soft-news, I had a fraction of the space needed to barely scratch the surface of my findings and I knew there were more than enough facts to write the first of several books. However, although I knew there was enough information to justify a research project, at the time, I had no context; no idea how this abundance of treasure related to itself or to me!

After two solid months of investigative work, I confess, I was more confused about these many reports and the history of this type of activity reported in the SLV. The more data this neophyte investigator accumulated the more jumbled the overall picture appeared. It seemed inescapable to me; there was a complex, multi-layered scenario at work in the valley. Many of these events—both real-time and historical—were filled with inconsistencies and some of the data made no sense at all. There seemed to be government involvement along with an inexplicable "giggle factor" involved and I resolved to dig into the multifarious mystery as fully and completely as possible.

At the time, it was obvious to me that the sheer variety, number and scope of these occurrences was not fully known to knowledgeable local residents, local law enforcement and outside investigators. But, there were the primary facts and data these investigators had gathered over the years that needed to be correlated and coalesced. So, I created a set of rigid data points and began correlating the many hundreds of already documented events into a chronological, time-line formatted event-log of unusual SLV events. As of 2007 this "event log" has grown to over sixty-thousand words.

The "beehives." Who built these curious stone structures?

The Shaman's Cave 1991 What you banish you invoke?

Isadora, 1993: Behind every man is a woman with patience... How did she put up with all the years of investigative intensity.

Catherine O'Brien

Rainbow slips into the Spanish Creek "portal" with red-tail hawks.

125

The Sutherland Bull, June 1980

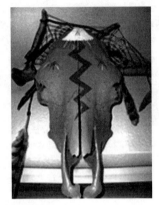

The little Toyota that could!
250K from 1992 to 1998.

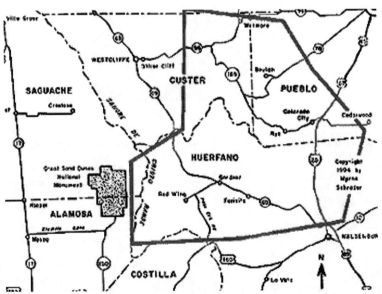

The La Veta Military (low level flight) Operations Area 1994.

CHAPTER FIVE:
Initial Analysis

Patterns of Dissemination -The Creation of Mythos

After a scant two months collecting and collating everything I could find concerning the "paranormal" events allegedly happening here, I found myself being touted as some sort of "expert" regarding current events occurring in he San Luis Valley. I began being pumped about the more obscure aspects of SLV history. My mailbox at the local post-office seemed to be a magnet for people seeking answers and I was increasingly amazed at the amount of mail that poured into my address. All these years later the "expert" tag still makes me laugh. In case you didn't know, there are no experts in this quicksand realm and if anybody says they are "an expert" slowly swim away; I find slow, rhythmic dolphin-like undulations work best. Today, in 2007, I admit, I'm really just another interested seeker taking it upon themselves to document what occurs in the neighborhood, in the Heart and elsewhere. It's OK that how confused you are is relative to your level of expertise. Like you — l am really being confused by phenomenal events so people call me 'expert'.

But back in late 1993 and early 1994 when I was looking down into a deep trench of intense investigation, it was exciting, but fifteen years later I feel tempered by irony and a slowly-fading sense of humor. The trickster in me knows there many areas of scrutiny and documentation that deserve yet escape publicly-acknowledged scientific attention. David Perkins and I kid each other about being "proto-scientists". I remember, early on in my investigation it appeared a sizable percentage of SLV witnesses had heard stories of various strange goings-on, but until they had a personal experience they could explain happen to them, they hadn't thought much about the 'stories'. Interestingly, many claimed they had no idea that this type of activity (or the specific event(s) they had witnessed) were being reported by others. I also noted that a majority of witnesses born after the sixties had no knowledge of the extent of the publicized activity from the fifties, sixties and early seventies,. Witnesses born in the sixties or earlier remembered Snippy and other unexplained disseminated into the community in the late sixties and early to mid seventies.

I began to suspect that it didn't seem particularly strange to most folks in the valley, just odd occasional events that occurred to others in their everyday reality.

Naturally, I began to examine the pattern of dissemination of these events within the community. What was communicated to the authorities, the media, neighbors and family? This subject appeared to be important, so I investigated this process of communication and dissemination. I theorized that the very realization, or experiencer-derived understanding of local events might be crucial to both the individual-experiencer and the culture-at-large. Could communication of individualized experience, introduced into the culture, influence how extensively understanding of these events permeate into culture as a whole? Is this the tip of an iceberg of mythological programming? For the sake of argument, who are these mythologic engineers, and what are they up to?

Look at the process of communicating, or disseminating perceptions of unusual occurrences. Are the disseminating groups either inadvertently or by design, altering third, fourth and fifth-hand accounts? Do they simply report the facts to us, or do they try to whitewash and hide them? Do they get all the facts straight, or just a portion of them? Does the media, for example, only concentrate on certain aspects of the phenomena but downplay others? I even began to wonder if the symbolic and emotional effect of the wording, "UFO" or "mutilation" for instance, has any impact on our cultures' perceptions of the phenomena. I found myself having to question everything, and to believe nothing. This approach has served me well all my life and I still adhere to this objective methodology

Looking back at my healthy naivety, one thing is firmly etched in my mind. Even if the events that allegedly occurred in hot-spot areas are merely misinterpreted mundane phenomena, the very fact that a belief-system exists attempting to explain these events may hold an important clue to the scientific and sociological causal elements behind these manifestations. Aspiring "ufologists," this systematic process of sub-cultural interpretation may be an important emerging area of study and I cannot stress enough how crucial this line of reasoning could become in the final analysis.

In this age of broken wheel, nuts and bolts ufology, certain inevitable questions are bound to arise when negotiating such uncharted waters. Case in point: there was just too much unexplained activity going in the San Luis Valley for the whole scenario to be simply due to mass-hysteria, sensationalism, or wishful thinking as the debunkers would want you to think. I wondered at the time if, at any time during the disclosure process, are there attempts by government, law enforcement, or even publishers, to whitewash and/or obscure knowledge (and the dissemination) of these events out to the public? And then I got to thinking: what was my role in this process of investigation and disclosure? Early on I was constantly reminded that, for the most part, locals apparently did not know the full scope of our mysterious phenomena being reported, past and present and I was providing a local network for like minded people to connect and network. But who was I to be in this position? How much did I really know? The more I dug and uncovered the more complex and bewildering the microcosmic picture appeared to be. I remember several times reminding myself that I 'better be careful what I wished for'!

Even back then in my neophyte role, because the whole picture appears so convoluted and complex, I began to suspect that multiple groups, or players, were behind not only our region's activity, but the phenomena as a whole. If by chance this conspiratorial scenario is true, how many subtle, or perhaps even blatant agendas were at work? And why? What was the motivation? Regardless of the implications of various players with an agenda, I sensed, intuitively in late 1993/early 1994, that something even larger lurked behind and underneath this multiple group agenda scenario. Possibly something ancient and obviously extremely elusive. I realized I had to remain open to the question: could a separate super-agenda exist alongside all the various mundane, and even possibly extra-mundane agendas? Not many researcher/investigators have had the courage to tackle this legitimate question that appears to bind together (on some level) all paranormal phenomena.

The reports I logged, themselves seemed to be subjugated by the media-induced perceptions of Western human culture. Initially I suspected that this was simply a cultural by-product, like the fodder for the inevitable creation of urban-legends. But this may be an overly simplistic explanation. Like the party game 'telephone.' I had a hunch that the truth behind the very appearance of these unusual experiences was somehow, through dissemination, being blurred, as accurate details of the experiences become altered with the telling and retelling of "the stories." The actual agenda behind the appearance, I am now convinced is something completely different. I wondered, how can the underlying truth behind the nature of unexplained events be found, when even the appearance of the events may be misleading? The probability that the phenomena may not reflect its true nature, possibly intentionally, is a major, almost insurmountable obstacle to anyone investigating unexplained events. This intuitive heaven can be a rationalist's hell.

Rule #7
Appearances can be deceiving. There is always a possibility of more happening than meets the eye.

This whole realization surrounding the idea of programmed deception was disheartening and I wondered at the time if, as someone investigating these phenomena, I could ever hope to identify the "players," let alone discover the essential core agenda behind these events. By early 1994, any faint hope of this was firmly dashed from my realistic self. I even began to wonder if it was possible for witnesses of bizarre events in the San Luis Valley, and elsewhere for that matter, to actually differentiate effectively between reality and imagination! I was no exception. It was during this time that I began to feel like cameras were documenting my every move. It is hard for me to describe the immediacy of that feeling of eyes watching my every move, but I distinctly felt something happening. I was cruising along, surfing real-time energy that was validated by synchronistic examples of validation. Today in 2007, after a six year absence from the valley, this feeling has returned. Is the experience truly more important than the experiencer? I don't think so.

Witness Bias and Chaos

Interviewing multiple witnesses of a single phenomenal event, I immediately noted subtle personal shading, slight differences of impressions from one witness to the next. Most of the individuals' general impressions of a shared event were similar, almost exact in most cases but there was always a slight variation or, perhaps a bias. Knowing a little bit about chaos theory and the significance of even the most minute causal variations at the beginning of any unfolding sequence of events, I wondered if these slight variations in perception of an extraordinary experience may be incredibly magnified at the other end of the dissemination process. The witness invariably subtly alters or shades recollections of the unusual phenomenal experience, and their interpretation of the event may not be accurate. This "front-loading," as I mentioned earlier, is unavoidable as the witness most often reverts to basic reality concepts and cultural archetypes when confronted with the wondrously inexplicable. The crucial pathway, or connecting point between experience and experiencer may be a major ignored element in ufology and all paranormal research and investigation as well. A few readers of my first two books pointed out that I

130

don't postulate many theories or attempt to define, or attempt to explain the process behind these conundrums. I may not have any answers, but the process of "front-loading" and the bias of multiple witnesses of single events may point us in the right direction.

It probably makes some ufologist's philosophic-heads hurt trying to integrate these and many other hypothetical factors into our paranormal equation. With few exceptions over the past fifty years the introduction of other inexplicable phenomena has overloaded the singular focus of ufology and this is the rut from which the broken wheel of ufology cannot extricate itself. The first year of my investigative process involved so many kaleidoscopic reports of weirdness, I knew all along it will always be a seemingly impossible quest, but a few of us or so intensely interested in these phenomenal events that we will forever quest after the grail of disclosure for this could well define the true nature of human perception and reality itself.

Remembering back to the early-to-mid seventies when I was reading Castenada, I am reminded of the concept of an "assemblage point." Hot-spot areas could be described as assemblage points on the continent. Areas that seem to have energy manifesting through it, in the form of paranormal events, seemingly from nowhere, that radiate out from the center. In late 1993-early 1994 I began to suspect that the very process of becoming involved in publicizing current and past paranormal events held some sort of key pertaining to possible first and second level players and agendas. But I had to ask myself, what was MY motivation?!

Choose Your Spin Carefully

When I began my investigation, I had no clue that my role as investigative, journalistic documentarian was a determining factor in how what I was reporting was occurring in the SLV was being received beyond the region. I slowly realized I had entered upon volatile ground should be extremely careful; keep my reporting as accurate as possible, keep my journalistic facts straight and not add spin to my reportage of these events. I realized it isn't easy to establish a healthy sense of objectivity and establish a perspective neutral centered-ness

Rule #8
If you publicize claims of the unusual, choose your words wisely for your "spin" may have tremendous influence.

What you say is important, but how you express it may is more important. At the time, I didn't realize how much of an integral factor I had become by publicizing these events out to the culture-at-large. Initially, I thought I was simply reporting locally-experienced unexplained events, happening virtually in my front yard, simply for the bemusement of interested Crestone-Baca and Saguache County residents. As above, so below, the macrocosm reflects the microcosm and I had stumbled onto something huge. Not only was I right in the middle of these occurrences, by publicizing these unexplained events and mythic traditions, public perception of UADs, UFOs and the other strange, unexplained phenomena that occur here in this SLV petrie dish I was setting into motion an aspect of cultural programming. In early 1994, I began to realize that I might inadvertently becoming part of the problem; I realized I was possibly contributing to the creation of cultural "mythos," and this thought was sobering. If this was so, whose agenda was being enacted? Something larger loomed underneath these events.

It was around this time that I felt like there were cameras constantly focused on me. I know this sounds crazy, but there were times when I felt like I was under 24/7 surveillance. I lived in a small town and (human intelligence assets) HUMIT would have a hard time observing anything or anyone without being noticed, bit the feeling I experienced was palpable. I didn't sense something covert, clandestine and spooky, but the feeling was more existential — more akin to Shakespeare's "we are but actors on the stage." I remember commenting to Isadora that I felt this feeling but I then joked, "I want to know what the name of the play was, who is the casting director, and who is paying for the play." I was kidding, of course... but only on the surface. I began to feel the unmistaken impression that I had suddenly attracted the attention of something more the local readers of my local newspaper articles..

I distinctly remember, in the spring of 1994, that the glimmering glow called truth seemed to emanate just below the distant horizon, but no matter how hard I tried, I wasn't getting any closer to any definitive answers. Not even close. The realization was disappointing but in a challenging sort of way. It felt like the events (both historic and current) were a strange challenge—a golden carrot dangled in front of a snippy horse, and someone else, namely me. I plodded forward, scratching my befuddled head while countless questions with questionable potential answers loomed like a bevy of humongous speedbumps before me. Three steps forward *bump,* three steps back *bump,* I guess terrain comes with the territory. Chasing rainbows that skirt away playfully toward a pot of gold, I resigned myself and chased reports in my four-wheel drive, replaced my shocks, licked my finger, pointed up to the sky and studied my topomaps in an uncertain breeze.

I was certain there were clues in the historic record, seek and you shall find, and my discovery of these next two "legends" may hold significant clues.

Be Careful What You Wish For

The gold-seeking Spanish, upon their arrival and travels up the Rio Grande River Valley, brought with them the current religious thinking of a turbulent sixteenth-century Roman Catholic Church. The Grand Inquisition was in full swing, and hard-core religious orders, like the Dominicans and Franciscans were making it happen. Christianity slouched toward a fundamentalist view of sin and repentance.

Another notable character on our journey is Sister Marie de Jesus Agreda, born April 2, 1602, in Agreda, Spain. Christened Maria Fernandez Coronel, she donned the blue habit and took her vows as a nun in the Franciscan order, and in 1627 she became abbess of the Agreda Franciscan monastery until her death in 1665. The Encyclopedia *Brittanica* states:

> Her virtues and holy life were universally acknowledged, but controversy arose over her mystical writings, her political influence, and her *missionary activities*. Her best known work is The Mystical City of God (1670), a life story of the Virgin Mary ostensibly based on divine revelations granted to Maria. It was placed on the Index Libroum Prohibitorum in 1681, but the ban was lifted in 1747. (my italics)

In 1620, teenaged Sister Maria of Agreda, began having unnerving visions, or 'raptures'. Cloistered in the convent, she would often meditate for hours, sometimes all day, and return and tell her fellow sisters wondrous stories of her "over five hundred" spiritual travels to a faraway land, meeting savages and telling them of the Word of Christ. She experienced so many of these episodes of rapturous meditation and alleged bi-location that word began to spread of the young nun in the Franciscan convent. Finally, convinced of the reality of her experiences, she wrote a book in which she described, in great detail, her missionary work bringing the Word of Christ to the savages of The New World.

In early Fifteenth-Century Spain, this was not a prudent claim to make during the height of the Holy Inquisition, whose members quickly put to death untold thousands found "guilty" of witchcraft and dealings with demonic forces. Before long the Inquisition took a pointed interest in the good Sister of Agreda, and she found herself at the center of a dangerous, whirling controversy. She insisted to the Father Inquisitor that she was indeed bi-locating and doing God's work, but to no avail. A very public trial ensued with the full brunt of the powerful Church bearing down on the poor nun from Agreda.

During the height of her trial, a newly returned expedition of conquistadors and friars arrived in Spain with a wondrous tale. It seems that the Spanish explorers, while in the unexplored region north of Mexico, had encountered numerous Native American tribes in New Mexico, Arizona and Texas who had already been converted to Christianity, and somehow knew of "Jesus Christ" the Savior. Even more fantastic were the Indian's claims of being visited by a white-skinned "Blue Lady" who appeared to many, drifting in a blue haze while she preached the word of the Lord in their native languages. She helped them to build crosses and places of worship, and even handed out rosaries and religious objects. Spanish journalist Javier Sierra spent a considerable amount researching this enigmatic nun for his 1991 article published in Anõ Cero magazine, issue number sixty-eight. His research states:

> From 1620 to approximately 1631 the Spanish nun flew from Spain to the North American State of New Mexico on more than five hundred occasions. Thus it was established in the open case of the Holy Inquisition against the nun in 1635, in which it was affirmed further that no one in the convent noticed her absence during those flights. On occasion they would happen twice during the same day...How then can we explain a woman of scarcely eighteen years of age that could bi-locate to New Mexico, and while there, she would dedicate herself to distribute among the natives rosaries and other liturgical objects as she instructed them about the truth of the Christian faith? Her trips occurred shortly before the diocese of Mexico decided to send evangelizers [north] towards those unexplored territories. Her visits made their efforts considerably easier.

These first Spanish explorers to the Southwest were amazed by the Natives knowledge of Christianity and were baffled by the rosaries they were shown and by their earnest descriptions of the "Blue Lady" that had come from afar and preached to them. Sierra notes:

> Finally, when the first Franciscans, led by Friar Benvenedes, arrived [at the Isleta Pueblo] they discovered a singular spectacle. Thousands of Indians approached the Franciscans and asked earnestly for baptism.

134

Benvenedes wrote later of the Spaniard's efforts to ascertain how the Indians had foreknowledge of Christianity:

> When those Indians were asked to tell us what was the reason for which, with so much affection, they asked for baptism and religious indoctrination, they answered that a woman had come and preached to each one of them in their own tongue.

Could the rapid Spanish conquest and control of New Mexico in the Fifteenth and Sixteenth Centuries may have partially been due to Sister Agreda's solo missionary efforts on behalf of a bewildered Catholic Church?

> Only in New Mexico did the Franciscans baptize more than fifty-thousand people in record time and rapidly install twenty-five missions and minister to more than ninety towns. The Indians remembered with special veneration the Blue Lady, the one whom they gave this name due to her blue mantle of celestial tones she wore on her back.

During the mid-sixteen-hundreds, the celebrated bi-locating nun from Agreda garnered national notoriety. King Philip of Spain may have enlisted her help in foreign affairs, and it is firmly documented that the king carried on a life-long correspondence with her. It is surmised by some that Sister Agreda may have even bi-located to foreign courts on covert foreign-policy missions on behalf of Spain.

Now one would think that this story alone is compelling, but the unbelievable saga of our talented nun and her doppleganger-twin does not end there. Even in death, Sister Agreda defies the rationalists and supplies non-believers and the faithful with evidence of her fantastic talents. In a secluded crypt on the grounds of the convent we find what proves to be the most dramatic chapter to her story. Sister Marie Jesus Agreda's body, it turns out, is incorruptible. Like eleven other deceased mystics and Catholic saints, the nun's body refuses to naturally decay, even after three hundred and thirty-five long years. The flush of her cheeks and her life-like features still baffle the Catholic Church and modern science. During an opening of her casket in 1909, a cursory scientific examination was conducted. Eighhty years later, in 1989, a Spanish physician named Andreas Medina participated in another examination of Sister Maria Jesus Agreda as she lay in repose at the convent of the Conceptionist nuns — the same monastery where she had lived in the 1600s. Dr. Medina told Javier Sierra in 1991:

> What most surprised me about that case is that

when we compared the state of the body, as it was described in the medical report from 1909, with how it appeared in 1989, we realized it had absolutely not deteriorated at all in the last eighty years.

Complete photographic and scientific evidence was obtained by investigators before the respectful closing of her glass-lidded casket. She is beatified by the Catholic Church and may someday become a saint in the Catholic tradition.

Although the Blue Lady is said to have visited the Rio Grande River Valley as far north as the pueblos around Sante Fé New Mexico, less than a hundred miles from the San Luis Valley, I can find no direct evidence that Sister Agreda ever bi-located here. But I would not be surprised if she did. I feel her compelling story may provide all of us with important clues pertaining to the understanding of unusual religious/belief-based phenomena.

Sister Agreda's story, as fantastic as it might appear, is almost believable when pondering supposed appearances of a demon I've dubbed "old scratch." He has been reported in the Rio Grande Valley all the way into the San Luis Valley for at least one hundred years. Maybe the nun from Agreda has competition?

Many thanks to Javier Sierra and Ana Cerro magazine for graciously granting permission to utilize Sierra's well-researched Agreda material, and for use of his rare 1991 photograph of Sister Agreda for this book. (see photo section at this chapter's end)

A Devilish Twist

May 8, 1993, the Baca:

I was tracking the mystery rancher who had reported a UAD to Costilla authorities the same morning of the mournful moo-o-o-o on Clarence Vigil's ranch. The reporting rancher lived near Questa, NM, and had (I assumed) called Costilla County Sheriff, Billy Maestas, to report that a helicopter that had flown out of his NM pasture, where his bull was "mutilated" the night before. I called the Sheriff and according to Maestas, the rancher had evidently watched the helicopter head north from his ranch into Colorado and altered Costilla County. The New Mexico State Police investigated the report but I could locate no one at State Police Headquarters who would acknowledge the report let alone comment on the status of their investigation.

I called the Questa chief-of-police to find out the status of his local investigation of the matter. He said his deputies had chased "red and white lights" flying down from the huge molybdenum mines that sprawl dramatically to the east along the mouth of Red

River Canyon, located to the east of town. They flew over town and headed out into the SLV. He told me, "My guys were chasing the lights all over. I guess they were helicopters. What else could they have been"?

I asked about other reports of the unusual. He hesitated, then out-of-the-blue he told me this peculiar red tinged tale. A close relative, an uncle, had been driving home late at night, north of Questa on Highway 522, Easter Weekend 1993. He was heading south about seven or eight miles north of Questa when he spotted a "'woman hitchhiker dressed up in red,'" walking along the side of the highway. Naturally he stopped to see if she needed help or a ride into town. He stopped, and without a word, she climbed into the pickup and sat next to him on the truck's bench seat, silently looking straight ahead. As he pulled back onto the road and turned to ask her why she was walking along the road alone so late at night, he noticed she had "'goat's legs and cloven hooves.'" Before the startled man could react to the sight, she dematerialized from his front seat!

Huh? I scratched my head. Here was a Police Chief sincerely telling me a story that sounded like a Twilight Zone rerun. "My uncle is a church-going man whom I, and everyone respect, and if it had been any other witness, I would have told him to stop drinking!" According to the police chief his uncle was extremely "honest and stable" and that "he wouldn't make up such an outrageous story for any reason… We tried to talk him out of making a report, but he insisted…"

I'd read about and heard stories about mystery hitchhikers and "shape-shifters" that are occasionally reported in the Four-Corners area, but this incident was alleged to have happened right here in my petre dish. I couldn't help but shake my head in wonder. First off, I was surprised he had confided such a story to a reporter he didn't know, but after thinking about it, the account sounded somehow familiar. Then I remembered. Two *Rio Grande Sun* newspaper articles had recently arrived in a package from Tom Adams just prior to the Questa, incident. I remembered dismissing them as another case of creative journalism. They had mentioned appearances of a "devil," so I dug them out.

Written by Gail Olson, excerpts from the first article suggested, tongue firmly planted-in-cheek, there were 1984 reports of the devil appearing to NM residents:

The story began when a dark, handsome stranger, a young man dressed in white, entered Red's Steak House in Ranchitos (NM) and began buying drinks for a covey of besmitten smiling maidens. One source said the stranger ordered a "Red Margarita." The Devil focused his attention on the table at which the four most attractive young ladies were seated, charming them with his urbane airs, compelling smile and dancing eyes. The young man attending the maidens glowered at the intruder, but left. The Devil, as yet unrecognized, danced with three of the maidens, saving his last dance for the youngest and prettiest of all, the Rose of Española. She blushed with delight, but felt a chill as he took her hand, an inexplicable shiver of fear. He smiled, removed his glove, and she screamed. His hand was a claw. The alarmed intruder made a hasty retreat, but his boot fell off as he ran, revealing a cloven hoof, according to reports. As he rushed through the door, a spiked tail trailed behind his impeccable tailored white sports coat. The maiden, in a dead faint, was rushed by ambulance to the hospital in a deep state of shock, the story goes. A photo taken at the bar that night of the mysterious gentleman showed no image of him when the film was developed, though the table and the girls were clearly visible in the photos.

As I discovered while researching my first book, stories of "old scratch," as I call him, the urbane devil are still circulating through northern New Mexico and southern Colorado. I wasn't surprised to learn that stories of this ilk are not exclusively found here in the SLV. I received a letter from a UFO investigator, who lives in Brussels, Belgium. he is very intrigued by the accounts of "old scratch" I mentioned in *The Mysterious Valley*. He noted:

> I was particularly interested in what you had to say about devil sightings among the Hispanic population of the SLV. I happen to be a Mexican-American myself and I grew up in San Antonio, Texas. Although my upbringing wasn't exactly steeped in Hispanic culture and tradition, I do remember hearing stories virtually identical to some of those you've reported. The suave dancing gentleman who woos young ladies in a nightclub and then turns out to be cloven-hoofed, for example, with variations, is an oft-repeated classic among Mexican-San Antonians…

Perhaps this traditional legend of an urbane devil has common roots that extend back into the dim reaches of pre-Hispanic lore and legend and is found throughout the entire American Southwest. It even resembles an ancient Aztec legend.

This is evidently an enduring legend, but as with a majority of these types of stories, the principle witnesses are never identified, and no corroboration is given. The most recent stories I've assembled are similar to the traditional historic versions, but contain new, modern twists. I was sent an Albuquerque *Tribune* article, by Harrison Fletcher spookily titled: "Something Evil is on the Prowl in our Casinos." The article relates several alleged 1995 New Mexico appearances of the devil, said to have occurred at the Indian-owned Isleta Gaming Palace near Espanola, New Mexico. (The same Isleta Pueblo where the Blue Lady, Sister Agreda supposedly converted hundreds of Pueblo Indians.)

It seems a woman was gambling the slots on "Good Friday," 1996, and, much to her dismay, she lost all her money to the one-armed bandits. As she was leaving, "a handsome old man, who had sat behind her, the entire time," gave her three dollars and urged her to try her luck one more time. The woman refused, but was talked into accepting the money and playing the slot machine a final time. She put in the money and won three thousand dollars! She quickly turned and looked for the man to thank him, but he had disappeared. She was awarded her winnings, and as she happily headed to her car in the parking lot, she happened to notice the elusive old-man in a parked car. She went over and knocked on his window to thank him. He turned and she was horrified to see, "He had burning red eyes and pointy horns. . . It was the devil!" She evidently donated her winnings to her local church. If that story is not enough, here's another one being told in the community as reported in Harrison Fletcher's article.

> ...Another woman was playing blackjack at Isleta Gaming Palace. She too had been gambling all day and losing her money. Just as she stood to leave, a tall, dark and handsome man in a black coat tapped her shoulder. 'Why don't you play the slots?' he said. 'The one in the corner will win.' At first, the woman refused, but she too relented. Two minutes later, a five thousand dollar jackpot! She wheeled around to thank the man, but he had begun walking away into the crowd. Just before he disappeared, she noticed something peculiar poking from the back of his coat: a pointed tail!

Although a spokesperson from the Isleta Gaming Palace downplayed the stories, I found out from a local that "they closed the whole place down" for the following entire weekend and performed an (Native American) ceremony to clean the place of evil spirits. Need I tell you, casinos normally don't close on weekends for any reason.

Predictably, stories of this ilk are impossible to pin down and corroborate, for obvious reasons. I have only investigated one alleged event in which the primary witness was named by a reliable source. Usually, the solemn story-teller attributes the event to a friend of a friend. You know...'There's a guy, whose sister's, neighbor's, cousin's brother was there, and he saw it all!' We could surmise that such stories may have some kernel of "truth" at their core, however there are loose ends that need to be melted away.

Although I can't prove it, I suspect there may be a real cause and effect event that initially creates a burgeoning of these stories. Of course, the probability exists that the primary, causal event differs from the resulting "stor[ies]" and disseminated accounts of the original story may not accurately portray the core account. However, the resulting "story" spreads like wildfire (through a largely superstitious community) and is invariably told and retold; blurring, even radically altering, the exact details of the original event.

There are prehistoric traditions that are associated with the San Luis Valley that are murkier than the unfathomable historic record and this research may provide us with potential insight into the deeper, more hidden nature of this remote area of what I sense is North America's altar. In the beginning of my research I found little, is any, published information examining the unique traditional knowledge of this magical region. I re-doubled my efforts to corroborate what many Hispanic locals already accept as truth. This is difficult territory for any Anglo to tread – even so-called 'local'.

Priscilla Wolf — Apache Storyteller

Priscilla Wolf is a self-professed "Apache storyteller." She was born in Del Norte Colorado and raised in Sanford. We first met during a booksigning in Alburquerque. She had sent me a letter as a way on introduction and I was taken by her intensity, knowledge of the old ways and her knowing smile.

We tried many times over the years to coordinate a meeting and in 2005, we spoke together in the SLV, but we weren't able to spend any quality time together. In December 2006 we were finally able to sit down for a recorded interview, when she traveled to Sedona:

> My grandmother was Apache and my Grandfather was from Madrid, Spain. My parents moved from Northern New Mexico in Southern Colorado and I was born in 1944. My grandmother was an orphan from Geronimo's tribe. She was also a medicine woman and a seer. She predicted quite a bit — everything in my life that would happen; my children born — everything that would come in my life until the day I would die.
> One day I was playing outside, I must have been about

two years old, I had my first contact with something that wasn't from this earth. We lived at the farm, between Del Norte and Monte Vista and I went outside to get a cup of water from pumping the water outside. It was a pink anteater and it just stayed there looking at me. He was pink, pink like the skin was raw…Later on in first grade I saw [a picture] in a magazine, it was identical [except for the color]. I think this was my first 'encounter.

I became very quiet and my parents gave me to my grandparents at [age] four because I stopped talking. [When I was little] I knew too much and nobody wanted to listen to what I had to say. I would ask who was there in the house with them…and there nobody yet I would see people. It turned out I was seeing the dead walking among the living…. I would say 'they talk to me' so they thought mentally there was something wrong with me. So I went to live with my grandparents.

My grandmother would take me out and teach me the 'Indian Way,' and grandpa would teach me the Catholic/Spanish Way. I was caught in between two worlds and I didn't know which world I wanted to follow. But the Indian Way was more interesting to me, because there is such a freedom in it and I didn't have to work so hard to it. It seemed like it was such a part of my life…we had statues all over the house and I couldn't see myself — why was I praying to a statue?

That statue couldn't do nothing for me but yet I could [have my answered] out on the river and fish with my grandmother. Watching the deer and the animals and the fish did more for me. I told grandmother, I could see other people, I could use things and it turned out she could see too. We had some great time together.

When I was four years old, I was playing with some antique dolls in my aunt's bedroom and I looked out east toward the [Pinon Hills]and saw a bright light. I couldn't understand where it was coming from. It was in the afternoon and grandfather was out feeding the horses and he cows. This light was nothing like the light of the day! All of a sudden it was a silver, uh like a saucer. It would flash…there were some men that came out of the inside …he had a rod. It looked like an Egyptian rod like a lot of them Egyptian people carried.

He was testing the ground and underneath, yet I could see this saucer just laying still with no sound, no nothing. I opened the window to look more at him, I was so fascinated,

141

I had never seen anything like that before. He had like an astronaut silver uniform around him with a mask around his face. He turned around all of a sudden and looked at me and he lifted that rod — it was a lightning that went straight into my head and into my eyes. He then vanished into this saucer and disappeared! So I ran in and my mother and my aunt were sitting in the kitchen having coffee and I was just screaming that I had just 'seen the devil.' Catholics teach you that everything you see bad is evil. So, to me, the only explanation was that I had seen 'the devil.'

Priscilla is a veritable treasure trove of indigenous stories and legends and we are planning on documenting as many of these accounts as possible.

For this book, I chose the above account as it provides us with a rare melding of native American, Catholic and San Luis Valley lore into one neat package. It is intriguing to me that her experience in 1948 occurred less than thirty miles from where another notable sighting experience took place. I will cover this account later in the book.

Native American Traditions in the San Luis Valley

In the process familiarizing myself with the valley and its prehistoric traditions, I cannot overlook the thirteen different tribes of Native Americans who are known to have visited here for hundreds, probably thousands of years. Many of these tribes still view the valley and its surrounding mountains with reverence. The Crestone-Navajo custodian of *Sisnaajini,* (or the Black Sash Medicine Belt Mountains), told me that the portion of the Sangre de Cristo Range that extends from the Blanca Massif, north to Crestone, plays an important role in the mythic tradition of many Southwestern, Great Basin and Plains Indian traditions. The Dine', or Navajo tradition, attaches particular significance to the valley in its creation myth. The following was excerpted from Peter Gold's groundbreaking 1990 book, *The Circle of the Spirit*:

Let's first consider the most important of the four sacred mountains, Blanca Peak (Sisnaajini), or East Mountain. East Mountain is a distinctive, snowcapped, pine and fir-clothed peak in the Southern Rockies of Colorado. It is considered the 'leader mountain,' because it stands as the holy mountain of the east, the place of beginnings, the dawn. It is associated with the guiding light of the day and the qualities that dawn universally signifies. As with all significant Navajo mountains, East Mountain was created and fastened firmly to the earth by the first people to emerge into the fifth world...by a bolt of lightning - a 'thunderbolt'-whose intense light and quality of energy is most appropriate to that of the dawn.

Existing within the four sacred mountains are their indwelling forms. The large size of the indwelling divinities of East Mountain -Rock Crystal Boy and Rock Crystal Girl - indicates their relative importance. . . Their bodies are constituted of rock crystal. This is only natural, since the mind is considered clear as crystal, and east is the direction of 'thought itself...'

Stalking the Indians

Hunt for the Skinwalker, written by biologist Colm Kelleher and Emmy-winning investigative journalist George Knapp, covers the National Institute of Discovery Sciences' (NIDS) eight-year investigation of the infamous Sherman Ranch Case, in the Uintah Basin of Utah. In my estimation, the Sherman Ranch case may be the most fantastic case of paranormal activity on record. Surrounded by the Mountain Ute Indian Reservation, the four-hundred and eighty acre ranch has an ancient Native American tradition of mysterious appearances of "skinwalkers," thus the name of the book chosen by its authors. This case was the only case that drew me outside of the Greater San Luis Valley during the first ten-years of my investigation. The subject of skinwalkers, sorcerers, *brujos* and *brujas* in the San Luis Valley is a current focus of my research into the mysterious valley.

In late June 1996, I was contacted by *Deseret News* investigative journalist Zack Van Eyck who broke the mind-bending story of paranormal occurrences alleged by the Sherman family to be occurring on their remote ranch, located just south of Ft. Duschene, UT. Van Eyck had conducted research into Hot-Spot regions and had encountered my work in the San Luis Valley and called to ask for my help with his article. He gave me a rather detailed overview of the Sherman Ranch case and asked me for my opinions as to what the beleaguered family was experiencing. He also suggested I call and talk with Terry Sherman who Zack said was having a very difficult time dealing with the weirdness occurring on his Fort Duschene ranch. Knapp and Kelleher noted:

Like many other tribes and bands, the Navaho visited, hunted in, and inhabited the San Luis Valley, off and on for hundreds of years. Historians believe that the Navaho were finally ousted from the valley by...the Utes. It is a development the Navaho people are not likely to forget, since they regard the valley as a special place and a fundamental cornerstone of their culture. Mount Blanca (sic), the fourteen-thousand-foot peak that towers over the valley, known to the Navaho as *Tsisnaasijini'*, the Sacred Mountain of the East, is revered as one of four mountains chosen by the Creator as a boundary for the Navaho world. It is considered to be an essential component in the Navaho quest to live in harmony and balance with both nature and the Creator. If the Navaho were Christians, Mount Blanca (sic) would be their Bethlehem. If they were Jewish, it might be their "Wailing Wall.

Some indigenous peoples have a sacred tradition relating to the location of the *Sipapu*, the place of emergence into the current world through a hole in the San Luis Valley. The exact location of the place of emergence may never be known but Dollar Lake and Head Lake are considered to be two of several possibilities.

Not surprisingly, the [San Luis Valley] region also oozes Native American mysticism and legend. The Yuma culture was in the valley five thousand years before the birth of Christ. The list of tribes, bands, and peoples that are known to have moved in and out since then is long. Among those indigenous groups that managed to survive into this century, the San Luis Valley is almost universally revered as a special, mystical place. The Tewa Indians, descended from the Pueblo people and now living in New Mexico, believe that the San Luis Valley is the equivalent of the Garden of Eden. The Tewas say the first humans to enter this world crawled up through hole in the ground to escape their previous plane of existence. Native Americans who live in the valley today say they were taught that the creator still lives in the mountains that surround San Luis and that He sometimes appears to humans in the form of a Sasquatch...

I thank God that I'm tenacious for, if I weren't, I would have given up this quixotic quest long ago. Today in 2007, I'm happy to report Pancho is still on the case and being asked to help outside of my stomping ground.

LEGEND

— Roads
··· Wildlife Area Trails
🅖 Entrance Station
❶ Needles Picnic Area
❷ Boat Ramp
❸ Mosca Campground
❹ Park Office
❺ Vehicle Fishing Access
❻ B.O.R. Pump House
❼ Conveyance Channel
❽ San Luis Lake Feeder Canal
❾ Day Use Parking

San Luis Lakes Wildlife Area

Head Lake

Wetlands Area

◄— Wildlife Area Boundary

—Trees

N↑

Elevation - 7525 ft.

Wildlife Nesting Area Closed to Boats

Buoy Line

San Luis Lake

Could this be the location of the fabled *Sipapu?*
Dollar Lake is at the upper left corner of map.

Apache Storyteller Priscilla Wolf

Colorado Petroglyphs

145

The Isleta Gaming Palace. Did the devil make an appearance?

Tales of an urbane devil are an enduring urban legend.

Pricilla Wolf took this picture of the Lobo Light, north of Taos.

Sister Marie Jesus Agreda in 1990— 330 years after her death.
photo c 1991 by Javier Sierra for *Ana Cero Magazine*

147

View from Mineral Hot Springs—site of the 1990 Landing.

Tom Adams, David Perkins, November 1993

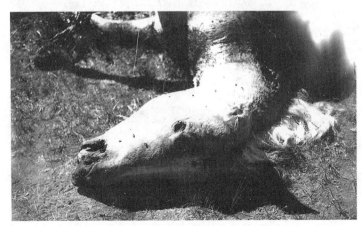

One of the 24 Saguache County Sheriff's photos.

CHAPTER SIX:
The Horse's Mouth and Primary Data

Texas researcher Tom Adams graciously sent me many Valley *Courier* articles he had saved reporting the "Snippy" case and Wyoming UFO researcher Tom Rouse added dozens of additional articles from the Denver Post, Rocky Mountain News and Valley Courier. The colorful cast of characters were perfect media fodder, and the press had a field-day with the story. I decided I needed to examine, not only the alleged events but the process of dissemination that unfolded that fall of 1967 to see if there were any parallels with the activity our area is currently experiencing.

I wanted to verify as many facts as I could about the incident. Newspaper accounts proved unreliable but the primary data, i.e. interviews with the principles; Nellie and Berle, notes by the original investigator, Don Richmond, and Nellie's friend, Valley *Courier* editor, Pearl Nicholas might fill in the blanks. By comparing the primary data against the press accounts, I hoped to reveal the true story behind the demise of "Snippy" the horse. I found out that ascertaining the truth behind the story was more difficult than I imagined, and for good reason:

Rule #9
Media coverage of the unusual, because of its sensational nature, is often inaccurate and cannot be accepted as totally accurate by the investigator.

When utilizing media accounts reporting high-strange events, the investigator is best advised NOT to rely exclusively on media-generated data. Linda Howe's first book on the mutilation phenomenon, *Alien Harvest* is a good example of the pitfalls of trusting the accuracy of media coverage of unusual livestock death reports from the seventies. Early on I realized the importance of the UAD phenomenon so I decided to go directly to a primary source of data for the pivotal Snippy Case, the oldest remaining living member of the extended King Family, Berle Lewis.

149

The Horse's Mouth

March 12, 1993, Great Sand Dunes Country Club:

After a couple of unsuccessful attempts, I was finally able to pin down Berle Lewis, Nellie Lewis' husband, for a video tape interview. He agreed to meet at the Great Sand Dunes Country Club in the maintenance shop where he worked.

My brother Brendon, friends Michael and Andrea Nisbit and a UFO investigator from Westcliffe, Colorado arrived at the Country Club. I asked were we could find Berle. And we were directed to a maintenance facility located just south of the main country club. Berle emerged from the building. The short, white-haired, stocky-man in his late sixties reflected a hard life of work in his slow but sure movements and he invited us inside his wood-shop. The place had the comfortable, busy look of projects-in-the-works. shop tools, wood, various worktables and workbenches provided the backdrop for my hour-and-a-half video interview.

Berle asked if I'd spoken to Tom Adams yet. I noted his high-pitched Coloradan drawl, a dead-ringer for the real McCoy, Walter Brennen. I was struck by his colorful, humorous demeanor that was offset by the honest and matter-of-fact way he described many unusual and some downright unbelievable stories from the late 1960s. I found him to be a very credible, down-to-earth and convincing man, certain to shed some light on this controversial episode. To my knowledge this is the only full-length interview ever conducted with Berle Lewis, who today at age ninety-one lives with his wife Barbara about fifteen miles from the original King Ranch.

"Berle, when did you first start hearing about UFOs and strange lights being seen around here?"

"In '67, in August."

"So all the sightings started just before the whole Snippy episode?"

"It all started right there. I never paid no attention to it 'till after the horse was killed."

"Until it happened right in your back yard?"

"You might say the backyard, it happened right out back of the house." Berle laughed.

"Ok, lets get in a little bit and talk about Snippy, or Lady, I mean. The press changed the horse's name, I guess Snippy was a more colorful name?"

"I never corrected them when it came out. I kinda smiled and said hell, Snippy's all right with me, Snippy was the horse I rode on, Lady was her colt, so it's kinda funny the way it turned out. They called the colt "Snippy," and the horse I had Lady, so I never corrected them."

[This important piece of ambiguous gender and name mis-identification could be extremely relevant and I will address this element later in the book.]

"What did you Nellie and Harry think when you found the horse?"

"We had no idea what caused it because I know nobody with a knife could cut that meat so smooth and nobody could ever take the meat off the bones where it was as white as that piece of paper over there. Now I don't give a darn who you are, there's not a butcher of any kind that can make that bone look like it's sat there for years! The eyeballs were gone, the tongue was gone, the esophagus was gone, and the windpipe was gone. All the hair, the mane hair and hide on the neck, clear down to where the collar fit. But that cut, completely around, was smooth! It's just impossible to cut it that way!"

I inquired about the medicinal smell that was reported around the carcass.

"Well, it just hung over the horse really it seemed to be floating in the area."

"Nellie was quoted as saying it smelled like embalming fluid."

"Naw, I wouldn't say it was embalming fluid, I've smelled plenty of that. It was like medicine. That's the way I'd put it but I don't know what kind of medicine."

"Do you have any idea how they removed the brain out of the skull?"

"Hell, I know how the skull got cut open, I was there and I held the light for the guy that cut it open."

"And there was no brain in there?"

"It was dry!"

"So there was no opening in the cranial cavity?"

"The was no opening of any kind."

"How about the green glob that looked like a chicken liver that Nellie found?"

"Well, I don't know what that was, I'll be darned if I do. It was like an acid burn, but there was no smell of acid or burnt hair."

"When you look back at the Snippy incident, and understand that Snippy was the first (publicized) mutilation from all over the world, what do you think about that?"

"Well, I never thought nothing about it." Berle lifted his hat and scratched his head quizzically. "I guess, with the whole deal, I

151

thought sooner or later I would learn what happened but hell, it's been thirty years."

"I read somewhere that Harry found a bull and calf he owned blinded right around the time of Snippy."

"He had a bull that was blind all right, it happened about a month or so before."

"A month before Snippy?"

"Yes, it just went blind. It was never tied to anything . . . but this one calf, his head looked like a basketball. His nose, off the end of a basketball, if you can figure out what that looked like. His hooves were about that long (he extended his hands about a foot apart) and they looked like sled runners. He had an awful time walking. The ears looked like they'd been frosted off, and his body didn't look like it had developed like it should have. We never tied the calf in with anything else."

"Did he ever have a vet look at it?"

"I don't think he ever did."

"Was it born that way?"

"Well, not really, I don't think so, nobody ever said anything about it. But as he got older, why he just got worse. So, that one time, he just shot the thing and I drug it off into the bushes."

I asked Berle to describe some of the various lights he'd seen.

"One time we saw, from the cabin porch down to the corner of mile eight, in that field back that way, it just looked like a switchboard! The old-time switchboard, you know, with the lights flipping on and off? Well that's what that whole field looked like. If it had been back in Missouri or Iowa, I would've swore it was fireflies. Ain't no lightning bugs around here, though."

"Did the lights move?"

"It was just like that, (he jabs all over in the air with his finger) the whole field was lit up!"

They chose to watch the lights from the porch through field glasses rather than go down to investigate. The phenomenon lasted around three hours. Berle related another sighting soon after.

"I come out of a town meeting in Blanca. They were getting ready to put water in the town of Blanca and they had a town meeting. Nellie covered it for the Chieftain and I went with her. So when we come out and walked across the street, where the cafe is now, and over on the mountainside, we saw this light. I knew it couldn't be a house, and it was stationary. So I went back to tell them, and they all came out, I interrupted the meeting, and this one guy said he'd seen it there just before."

"How far away was it?"

"Oh, it looked like probably two or three miles. This one light, we left the meeting after they went back inside, we started back to

Alamosa, and when we pulled in on (The Sand Dunes road) 150
. . . We parked there, and this light we had been watching back at
Blanca, sitting on the hillside; it moved across and went clear back
over to the Creede or Del Norte area. It went over the mountain,
clear out of sight. We were sitting there talking, wondering what
it could be and here it come! It got about 11:00 o'clock, and then
it exploded! One light went into five, or three, then it closed and
went into five, then went into six and seven, then it floated down
over the Brown (San Luis) Hills.

Berle contacted an Air Force investigator staying at the Alamosa
Sands Motel to report the incident. "He never did go down to
the Brown Hills to look, he just sat there in the bar a-drink'in.
He wasn't even interested. I can't remember his name, I wished I
could."

"How about the sounds everybody was hearing around here
for awhile?"

"Motors, deep motors, it seemed like a big diesel engine
running an air compressor and sounded like they was drill'in."
This mirrors numerous contemporary reports from the Taos, MN,
area, one hundred miles south, which have been dubbed 'The
Taos Hum.'

Berle remembered one night when he and friends heard the
sound. "Ken Wilson and Genevee, and Pearl Nicholas and Nellie
and I, we sat down there, Ken had the car. And Ken always smoked
a little cigar, about that long (He measured three-inches with his
thumb and forefinger) like a torpedo, small at both ends. Ya never
seen him without it. He was always chewing on that, and he had
it in his mouth all the time, with only that much sticking out of his
mouth. Odd way of smoking a cigar but that's the way he done
it.

"So anyhow, we were sitting there looking and that motor
started up on the hillside, about two miles or three miles away,
and boy, I mean it was loud." Ken excited dashed around the car
and, "All at once, he couldn't find his cigar." (We both break into
laughter.) "So, we sat there and I had a flashlight and I looked
around that whole area, I mean I really looked for it. We never did
find that cigar."

"He swallowed it?" I guessed.

"That's right."

Berle mentioned that he, Nellie and a friend had skywatched
almost every night for six to eight months after the horse was killed.
I asked who the friends were.

"That was Pearl Nicholas. And Father (Robert) Whiting used
to come up. He had an experience through Del Norte and Monte
Vista. He used to come up to the cabin quite often, he's the one

153

that Leo Sprinkle, he hypnotized Father Whitting up there one night.

"One time, a mile west of the intersection. (Of the Mosca and Sand Dunes Roads.) There's a dirt road there and a gate. I looked out in the field and there was a pinpoint of light. Hell, it wasn't even as big as a light bulb. It was just a pinpoint about two blocks off the highway." They knew there were no houses, nor even roads, in that area. "Then all at once, why, I could see an outline of what I call, a Quonset hut. Probably thirty five feet high; one hundred feet long. I was standing there looking at it, and all at once it come to me that something was moving toward us. Black. I described it as about six-feet-wide and about eight-or-nine-feet high. It was coming and, of course, Nellie got to feeling bad and got hysterical, so I came around and got in the car and we left. We got over to Harmony Lane and went north about a mile and a half and with a pair of field glasses. I could see this metallic building setting off the road in the pitch-black dark! You could still see that object!"

Just before dawn Berle took a co-worker back out to the site. "We walked that over and we didn't find nothin'! Not one mark, nothin' had sat down, but I know that building had to have been there!"

I had heard from Tom Adams that Berle and Nellie were missing a few hours that night.

"We don't know where we spent two-hours-and-a-half. We just drove back and it was 3:00 (a.m.) when we got in the house."

"And that's, what, about a twenty minute drive to your trailer?"

"It couldn't have been over twenty minutes," he assured me.

I was impressed by Berle's amazing recall of the events which had taken place thirty years before. I asked him why Nellie told reporters she was convinced that flying saucers had killed her horse.

"I don't think she was convinced it was UFOs or anything like that, but she knew it was something that we don't know about killed the horse. Now, I know it was something we, I don't know about, killed the horse. I figured after all these years I'd have the answers to it, but I don't have any answers. As far as I'm concerned, an unidentified object killed the horse! It wasn't anything natural. Couldn't be natural."

"Do you know Ron Jousma?"

"Yeah." (Jousma worked at the Great Sand Dunes for many years and lives just southeast of the Great Sand Dunes Oasis, which he built in the late seventies.)

"Ron said, that when he was working down at the dunes with Ben (King, Nellie's brother), he said that a government agent interviewed Ben. Ron wasn't sure what agency he was from."

"I don't know who it was either. I never did know."

I had previously talked to Ron Jousma who had told me, 'Ben was on his knees in front of the agent, with tears streaming down his face,' and the agent was telling Ben, 'too bad we weren't here, we have a special weapon that can bring them down.' The agent was talking about UFOs. Ben was begging him not to shoot them because they would come and hurt him.

Berle shook his head. "I never heard that part of it. Ben King knew every creek, every bird, every flower, every type of grass from Poncha Pass to La Veta Pass. I mean that guy was about as good a naturalist, I believe I've ever seen. And he only had an eighth-grade education. They asked him to name all the creeks from Poncha Pass to Blanca, and he only missed one."

"Do you know anybody that has photographs of some of the lights that were seen back then, or any accounts, anything written down?"

"Ken Wilson, over there in South Fork, he probably does. I don't have any."

"Did you ever have any photographs?"

"I had one picture that was taken on the sidewalk in Alamosa about the same time. I took the picture myself and it was of Nellie and her mother. They were on the sidewalk in front of her candy store. That picture turned out funnier than I ever saw! I can't find that picture, unless it's in that one box that I haven't looked in. Over the top of the head of each one of them was an object about that long (six inches) and that wide (two inches) torpedo-shaped with a little propeller turning in front of it, over both the top of them."

I tried to ask the next questions delicately. This was personal. "How about the day you buried Agnes, and Nellie didn't come down from the cemetery. That must have seemed kind of strange."

"We went to the funeral, everybody left and went back down. Don and Alice Richmond's car was in town (Alamosa) so they rode back with me. Nellie, she didn't want to go to town. She said she'd be all right at home. So I took them to town and come back. The other car we had was gone and that's when I found her up at the cemetery. She committed suicide."

"Do you have any theories, why she did that?"

"I had no idea, no indication. When I left she said she'd be all right. She went down to Harry's and when I got back from town Harry said she just went up to the cemetery, so I beat it up to the cemetery but it was too late. That was the day they buried Agnes."

"Did you ever suspect foul-play or anything unusual about that?"

"I never thought about there being foul-play."

"Well it would seem to me that if I was in your shoes and Nellie said she was going to be all right, and that she'd see you, and then you go up there to the cemetery and find her. . . She didn't give any hint?"

"No indication at all. She put the hose in the exhaust pipe and plugged up the windows."

"Did Nellie ever think that the things she witnessed in her life, the lights, the various things, had some kind of significance to her life? Did she have any feeling that she was special because she was getting to view these things?"

"No, not at all. She was just like anybody else. Just like we're sitting here talking now. She never had no misgivings about anything. I can't say that she had any other feelings. If she did, she never told me about them."

"How would you describe your feelings? You must have been very surprised when this happened."

"When I got up to that cemetery, I was damned surprised! I don't know why she done it." Berle stared at the floor. I noticed he was visibly shivering, probably a combination of the cold room and the intensity of the questions. We wound down and I thanked Berle for his cooperation, leaving him to the memories of his beloved wife.

Several rumors were heard by researchers concerning statements the mother and daughter had made to friends about passing on to the other side together. Nellie's friends claimed, "Beings would come for her and her mother on the same day."

Long-time friends Ken and Ginny Wilson remembered changes in her behavior after Snippy died. "Nellie became obsessed with the occult. She started using an ouiji-board and reading all kinds of books about UFOs." The Wilson's also recalled that Nellie was "particularly impressed with the Betty and Barney Hill story, and the (John Fuller's) book, *Interrupted Journey*."

So many nuances surrounded SLV events during the late 1960s. I often wonder about the timing. Was the death of Snippy on September 7, 1967 significant? One curious element surrounding the period concerns the turmoil in our culture during the late summer of 1967. Hundreds-of-thousands of "flower children" across the United States were becoming psychotropically aware through the use of mind-altering substances. I have wondered if this immense wave of expanding awareness could somehow be linked to the incredible upsurge of unexplained UFO activity, and the birth of the publicized phase of the UAD, during the end of the "summer of love." Could some sort of psychic door have been opened with a "key" called psychedelics? Did something slip through this door? The timing of the "Snippy" case, in culture, intrigued me.

One thing is certain. The extent of the "flap" of 1967 through 1969 in the valley has become unalterably blurred through time. The true nature of the many strange events have become lost in the inevitable process of dissemination, effectively beyond reach, in dusty newspaper articles, and word-of-mouth tales. Facts have been mixed-up, added, deleted, forgotten and altered. Even the eyewitnesses, who should be able to effectively clarify the events they witnessed, may be contributing to the creation of mythos, or folklore by their perceptions of unusual events. The fodder of new legend. Without question, Nellie Lewis' Appaloosa, Snippy, has joined the ranks of notable horses in history; Pegasus, Traveler, Man O' War, Trigger, Roy Rodgers stuffed companion and Pokey the ubiquitous "Trojan Horse."

Costilla County

Here is a quick overview of Costilla County's history and geography taken from the SLV Guide http://www.slvguide.com/Costilla/History.HTM.

Costilla County was inhabited by the ancestors of today's families well before Colorado became a state. Those first Hispano settlers brought with them a language and culture that still exists today, four hundred years after the Spanish first arrived in the Americas. Except for the Native Americans who were here first, this is the oldest community in Colorado.

Costilla County is located in south central Colorado, sharing its southern boundary with New Mexico (of which it was once a part). Costilla is part of the San Luis Valley, an eight-thousand square mile alpine valley nicknamed the American Tibet, with an average altitude of seven thousand-eight hundred feet above sea level. Costilla County is the home to Colorado's oldest town, San Luis, founded in 1851. Many villages of the County were the last to be established on a Spanish/Mexican land grant in this country. It is home to Colorado's oldest Christian structure (the San Acacio Mission) and the nation's newest shrine, the Stations of the Cross. California's gold rush was about gold. Colorado's gold is water, and the state's first water rights, the San Luis Peoples Ditch, is located right here in Costilla County. And to top all that, Costilla County has the last working Commons in America [formally the privately-owned Taylor Ranch, from 1963 to 2004] where local residents have grazed their sheep, cattle and horses on six hundred shared, unfenced acres for hundreds of years.

Note that the long running dispute over legal commons" access to the Taylor Ranch has been resolved, the Taylor Ranch has been re-opened for use by the community. This part of Colorado is over ninety-five percent Hispanic and the area is not well-known to outsiders. The county figures prominently in the cattle mutilation wave of the mid-seventies in the San Luis Valley.

April 28, 1993, 9:00 a.m., San Luis, Costilla County, CO:
I had made several calls on April 26, and confirmed interviews with ex-Costilla County Sheriff Ernest Sandoval and rancher Emilio Lobato, Jr. These two men may hold the dubious distinction of being the hardest hit sheriff and rancher in the publicized history of the UAD phenomenon. Sandoval and his deputies were run ragged from 1975 through 1978 chasing the mysterious cattle surgeons through the dark pastures of Costilla County. Lobato lost a whopping "forty-nine head" of cattle during a frenzied two-week period in
October 1975. Ten of the animals were reported as "mutilated" the rest were either "shot or stolen." It had taken Lobato many years to recover from his financial loss.

Before embarking on my journey to San Luis, I brushed up on the decades-long dispute over the Taylor Ranch properties. The one-million-acre Sangre de Cristo Land Grant was originally granted to Narciso Beaubien and Stephen Luis Lee by the Republic of Mexico in the 1840s. Both men were killed in the Taos Uprising of 1847 and Beaubien's father, Carlos, picked up the property for one hundred dollars. He granted tracts of land to various individuals and families in an effort of settle the territory, also putting aside common areas for local usage.

One seventy-seven thousand acre mountainous commons, known by the locals as La Sierra, remained in public use for firewood, hunting, fishing and other essential uses after the Mexican-American War under the 1848 Treaty of Guadalupe Hidalgo. The first governor of the Colorado Territory, William Gilpin, bought the grant (at the same time he bought the Baca Grande) under the stipulation that it would remain common land.

North Carolinian, John T. Taylor bought the property in 1960 for less than $7 per acre, setting off one of the great land debates of the west. Alan Prendergast wrote in Denver's Westword magazine in July of 1994:

"Taylor barricaded the access roads to the ranch and someone promptly shot up his bulldozer. . . On the night of October 15, 1975, he was shot in the left ankle. . . He offered locals twenty-five thousand dollars to testify in court, but no one would."

Wanting to hone my interviewing skills, I enlisted the help of former Valley *Courier* editor, John Hill, who graciously agreed to accompany me. The amateur investigator who had accompanied me to interview Berle Lewis tagged along to take still-photographs for me. I had heard disturbing stories about racial problems in Costilla County and was glad I would not be going alone.

The three of us found ourselves in a very spartan-looking coffee shop in San Luis planning that day's activities. A woman who was sipping a cup of coffee, came over and said, "I couldn't help but overhear you talking about 'mutilations.' When I was on my way into town this morning, I spotted two dead cows and a dead horse out in the middle of nowhere, east of Mesita, where I live." We thanked her for the tip and got detailed directions to find the location. Wow, another of those coincidences. There was not enough time to investigate immediately, so we agreed to go there later in the afternoon, after our interviews.

We wound our way out of San Luis toward San Acasio, a small hamlet several miles south, where Ernest Sandoval and his wife Marie live. A picturesque stream gurgled happily in the spring sunshine as we drove over a bridge. Cows grazed quietly in pastures where adobe shacks, some hundreds of years old, dotted the countryside. This was historic country, some of the earliest settled areas by Europeans in Colorado.

I was anxious to ask Sandoval about specific cases I had found in Adam's material, especially a nineteen hundred pound bull that was found inside an abandoned adobe shack, on a wooden table!

They Kept On Coming

We arrived at Sandoval's humble little ranch where a long metal gate barred our entrance to the property. Sandoval emerged from the house with a friendly wave. He had a slight limp and looked like a kindly grandfather in his early 70s. A small dog scampered friskily around him in the front yard.

I introduced the three of us and we were invited in. Sandoval sat us around the kitchen table while he rummaged through some boxes to locate files pertaining to "mutilation cases" he had investigated in the 1970s. He had taken the reports with him upon retiring as the Costilla County sheriff. With the video equipment running, Ernest began his story.

"When it first started (the first UADs), you know, we figured it was somebody pulling a stunt, doing the thing for the hell of it. But a couple of days after that we got another one and they kept on coming."

"Did the early reports have helicopter sightings associated with them, or was it just people finding their cows?" I asked.

"No, the early reports, what they sighted were lights. It was happening right around midnight, according to people who heard noises, or seen lights. But soon after that, when it started to get kind of heavy, the choppers would come in kind of early. They would come across the Rio Grande. It's isolated out there, nothing but prairie."

He gave us directions to the area where the initial chopper sightings (in the fall of 1975) occurred. This was the exact area where the woman at the coffee shop had seen the dead animals that very morning!

"People would come down and report what they described as choppers. As soon as they would see the cars, ZOOM, they'd take off. But, they never seen the chopper involved in the actual mutilation until later, when I happened to go out one time, right around 3:00 o'clock (a.m.) when I saw these choppers land right around the Wild Horse Mesa, just west of here. They were landing at the Wild Horse Mesa, and they were landing at the Taylor Ranch."

"You witnessed these helicopters yourself?"

"Oh, yes, I did see them quite a few times, we used to go out on patrol and we'd see them land. They would disappear right around Wild Horse Mesa. I would have a patrol car on this side of the mesa, and another one on the other side, on highway 159 that goes into New Mexico. We would keep in touch using the radios in both patrol cars and we would spot one and he'd go across the valley to the mesa, then it would disappear. It wouldn't come out either side. So, the only explanation is that they were landing at the Wild Horse Mesa. Right around that time there was a man that moved up on Wild Horse Mesa, and he was a former Army officer and he was an aircraft mechanic. Maybe that was the explanation."

"He was a resident up on the mesa?"

"Yeah, for a while. But after this happened, he took off and I never saw him again. I can't recall his name."

"Did you ever find any physical evidence like tracks or footprints around a mutilation site?"

"The Manzanares bull."

"That's the one they found inside the abandoned shack?" Aha, he had brought it up himself.

"Right, that's the only place we found where you could tell

160

that they used a wheelbarrow, I think it was like a wheelbarrow, you could see one track, a single tire, going in one door where they killed the bull, and out the other one. This is the only case where we found where a chopper had landed. They took the testicles, they took the rectum. I think what they did was kill the bull inside the house, then they took whatever machine they used . . . they did away with their tracks. That's the only explanation, we didn't find any tracks."

"Other than the wheelbarrow track."

"The grass was real tall around the spot where the chopper landed. Another time these people from Mesita came in and made a report. These people came in and told me they had seen this helicopter that had a cow hanging from an apparatus, they described a harness. They were taking it from one place to another.

"Then there was another time right there at Emilio's (Lobato) place. These two loggers were coming down from La Valley (CO). They seen the chopper, they seen the lights, and the helicopter was sitting by a cow in the center of the highway. There was a man on top of the cow, and they really got excited and went straight to the sheriff's office and when they came back, the cow was gone. They did find where the cow had urinated."

"Right there in the road?"

"Right in front of Emilio's place. That was right after he moved his cows from Chama Canyon to his residence."

"Chama Canyon is next to the Taylor spread?"

"Right."

Emilio had mentioned to me that he had leased some grazing land out there. "Now, to your knowledge, did Taylor ever lose any cows?"

"They never reported any that I know of. You know, (he laughs) Mr. Taylor singled me out as the 'godfather' of Costilla County in some paper back east. He passed away a few years back, five or six years ago."

"Did you ever wonder if, or have reason to believe that anybody else in the Taylor family might have been involved in all this, or was he the main guy?"

"He was the main guy at the time. But he had his foreman out here who was a very tough old-man. See, people used to go on the ranch looking for stray cattle, maybe go in and fish, or poach, or whatever. For whatever reason, people would go in there, if he'd find them there, he'd scare them away. If he could apprehend them, he'd take the law into his own hands and beat them up, even juveniles. There were so many incidents prior to me taking office involving the Taylor Ranch; it was kind of bad, you know. By the time I took it over, it simmered down a little bit. But it still went on. "

I asked when the Taylors had moved to the county.

"I don't think they ever moved here, they bought the place (in 1960) and built the headquarters. He used to have a guest house there and he used to have his own house, he used to come and go. He had tenants, people taking care of the place. They had over 50 or 60 cows and he never lost any."

"Yet Lobato was losing cows left and right during that time period. Who was the previous foreman?"

"His name was Barber."

"What part did Taylor have in all this?"

"Money can buy anything! I had to go before the Grand Jury on Taylor's word alone. The governor (Lamm) went along with it. The county commissioners, myself, and all the county officials went up there (to Denver) and I remember, I talked to the US Attorney, by the name of Smith, before I went in and he said, 'the only person who'll probably get indicted is you, because you're the chief law enforcement officer in Costilla County."

"Just what you wanted to hear."

"Thing is, I took with me a lot of reports as to what Taylor was doing. His foreman, his help, were beating up people. Believe me, I was prepared, notarized statements, signed. I presented them to the Grand Jury and they asked me about three questions and I was out of there! It didn't take ten minutes."

"Do you have any reason to believe that Taylor, or his foreman, were directly involved in the mutilations?"

"Well, I have reasons to believe the choppers were landing there on the Taylor Ranch. The hippies were going up to the Taylor Ranch. Believe me, I know all the people around here. They all tried to help me. Nobody liked what was going on. Nobody! A lot of them were losing, they probably had four or five head of cattle and you lose one, you lose $500, right? So, that's a lot of money in this part of the county. So, everybody was trying to help me. It was happening! "

"It's kind of hard to argue with all these photographs, " I commented, viewing the dozen photos he could find. "When did you notice that these animal deaths were not just a series of isolated events? When did it start picking up in intensity?"

"I believed that after the second or third one, naturally, there had to be something wrong. But it was happening and the things they were doing to these poor animals, each one was a little different. In some instances they would take the skin off the jaw bone, or the eye. I had so many pictures. I don't have them. I wish I knew what happened to them."

I asked about the helicopters. "At first they used to come in late at night. Later on, when it was happening here, and in Alamosa County, Conejos County, adjacent counties, even Trinidad and in Huerfano County. They were hitting everybody right around the same time."

"The helicopters?"

"Right, but I think there were other people involved beside the government. But the government is the only one that has vehicles such as this. They were pretty fast, you know."

We looked at the mutilation reports Sandoval had managed to save. "I noticed in some of the reports here that at various times the mutilations were sloppy."

"Yeah, I had reports where people had found a dead cow. They come back the next day and it was 'mutilated.' They didn't know if it was natural causes, it was probably done with a dart. They came down and killed the cow and came back the next day and 'mutilated' it. In Blanca we found evidence that somebody tried to imitate the mutilators, you know."

"Copycats?"

"Yeah, copycats, but they went in with a very sharp knife, and there was blood all over the place."

I cringed as my investigator associate began a series of rather leading questions. An investigator should refrain from supplying the answers and this was the last time I let him tag along on an interview.

"And in the 'classic mutilations' that you investigated there was no
blood?"

"Right."

"Ever?"

"That's it."

"And the incisions were made with high-heat?"

"Exactly."

"And there was no evidence that there was any blood left in the body of the cow?"

"Right."

"And there were no tracks of any kind, to or from the cow?"

"No."

I quickly took over the questioning in an effort to allow Sandoval to volunteer information rather than confirm pre-drawn conclusions from leading questions. I asked, "Do you have any theories about this? It is my understanding that this has gone on all around the country and not one person has ever been brought up on charges."

Sandoval began to tell us his suspicions. "These are the reports that I was hoping I would find. (Again he searches unsuccessfully through his paperwork.) These guys had an altercation with these hippies that were living over in La Valley and, according to them, these hippies were involved. They used to follow them going to the Taylor Ranch. The theory was that these guys were helping with the mutilations. When one of these guys moved out there by the Sanchez Reservoir, they found a big diagram on a piece of plywood. It described the full-moon. The testicles, the liver the heart, the whole thing was on that."

"You mean actual, physical cow parts, right there?"

"No, it was a painting. I used to have pictures of that too. That thing stayed in the office, that drawing was in the sheriff's office for a long time. I don't know what Pete (Espinoza) did with it, I doubt it's still there but I left it there. Emilio was the one who found it after this guy left. I think his relatives (Lobato's) own that property, so when he went out there and found it, he brought it to me."

"So you tie that in with these hippie types?"

"Devil worshipers, or whatever, Satanic. I think that's the proper wording. We started to bring these guys in, investigating these guys, asking them if they have any part of this, where they were at certain hours of the day. I used to keep a twenty four hour patrol on that (Chama Canyon) road every day. We suspected that these guys were helping. Gradually the hippies started taking off, and the mutilations stopped. According to a lot of the hippies that were here, their families had all kinds of money. A lot of them were richer than hell! It's weird, they were living a very miserable life. I guess they were living like that by choice."

"Do you have any theories?" I asked. "I mean, you don't have the hippies around here any more; you've had some mutilations."

"Funny thing, they'd find an empty house and they'd move in without the owner's permission. I had quite a few incidents like that."

"Squatters."

"Yes. The fact is, they were doing it at night. We could never catch anybody doing it in the daytime. I think it was happening after midnight. "

"Did anybody attempt to try and find where these helicopters were taking off from and landing?"

Sandoval started nervously rummaging through his paperwork again, "Um, one of these guys that wanted information on this, he told me . . . it's not in writing, but he told me that he had heard a report from somebody that one of those choppers barely made it back to base, which was Ft. Carson (in Colorado Springs). Later on, I found that my deputies could have fired at one of those. They never reported that to me (but) they used to do it [fire at choppers] all over the [six county] 12th Judicial District."

164

"So ranchers were shooting at the helicopters? As well as law enforcement personal?"

"I think so. I never did shoot at them and I used to tell my deputies not to shoot at the choppers unless they would catch them in-the-act, or defending themselves."

Glancing at my watch, I realized we were supposed to meet Emilio Lobato soon. We thanked Ernest and his wife, got directions and headed south two miles toward the Lobato's house. I was reluctant to accept all the information that Sandoval gave me at face value. I felt that there was definitely some misidentified scavenger at work in at least some of the cases he had investigated. But it did appear that there was a connection between the chopper and UAD reports.

We Were Threatened

Emilio Lobato, Jr., a shy, short swarthy man in his late forties or early 50s answered my knock. The former high school teacher invited us in and I set up the video equipment. I had spoken several times with Emilio and was anxious to get his first-hand account of that two-week period in October 1975.

Emilio needed no prompting. "You know, a lot of people here, when something like this (UADs) happens to them, they don't say anything. And this is what people told me, 'you shouldn't have said anything.'"

"Who told you that?"

"Different people. Because when this happened, a lot of people came to see me to offer their help, and they'd say 'I lost one.'"

"Do you think people are being threatened?" John Hill asked.

"At that time we were being threatened. They said they were going to drive us out of here. This is one of the fears a minority always has. You know what's going on in Bosnia. A minority is always afraid that there's going to be something like ethnic cleansing. There's always that fear, you know. You can't really do a lot, you've got to hold things down and not complain too much."

We talked for a while about the social implications of the UAD wave in Costilla County and Lobato recalled the 'mutilations' he had experienced in October, 1975.

"The first mutilation we had was the one that puzzled me the most. I had been there (to his Chama Canyon Ranch, next to the Taylor Ranch) late one evening. The cows seemed to be very calm. The first one they did in a ditch. They cut out the rectum, and the sexual organs. There was no blood at all! Not one drop of blood. They would cut the left lip, half of a hoof on one side. On a cow, they would cut out a portion of the udder, the tongue and one

165

eye."

"Which one?"

"I don't remember. I've tried to forget so many things," he said shaking his head. "But then we noticed a lot of activity on the Taylor Ranch. We noticed that 'so-called' hippies were going over there and pretty soon I started getting (threatening) calls. We called CBI (Colorado Bureau of Investigation) I don't know if the sheriff called the FBI at that time, or not. They told me, 'Whenever they call you, try to hold these people (on the line) to see if it's a local call, to see if they have any regional accents.' Of course, I'm not that acquainted with regional accents but I had been in Texas, and I had heard Texans, and these calls were by someone who had a southern drawl (possibly North Carolinian?). They were telling me they wanted to see me over there. It was me they were after. They wanted me to go to my ranch. I had my cattle right next to the Taylor Ranch."

"So they actually threatened your livestock?"

"They threatened me! They told me if they caught me by myself, they'd kill me. They would liquidate me. Taylor, I had had many problems with him and he had also threatened to kill me. I had never owned a gun, so I had to go and buy one, and I started shooting. Although I had been a member of the National Guard for a number of years, I wasn't that acquainted with pistols. I was a medic and I wasn't too interested in guns, so I had to get one to protect myself. I told them I was going to come to my property, whether you like it or not and if you try to stop me, you'll have to kill me. John T. Taylor bought the mountain over here. We are still fighting for that land. See, I was one of the leaders in the fight for that land because that land, according to the Treaty of Hidalgo, that land was given to the people as a common. It was sold several times illegally and we're still fighting for it."

"Why do you think he threatened your life?"

"He just wanted to scare me, I think."

"Because you own property adjacent to his?"

"Yes, and he said 'I want your property.' I told him my property was not for sale. He said, 'Everything is for sale, it's just a matter of price.' I said, 'I never will sell my place for anything.'"

"Was he actually offering you a great deal of money?"

"I told him, 'I wouldn't sell it for a million dollars.' (Taylor said) 'Just say so, and we'll pay it. Just say how much you want, and we'll pay for it.'"

"How many acres?"

"I just have a little over one-hundred acres and I said 'How come you want this place?' He said, 'As soon as I get rid of you, I'll get rid of everybody else.' He wanted the whole valley. He had

166

already threatened a lot of my neighbors. Here's what happened.

"When one of the first 'mutilations' happened to my neighbors, he sold out. In order to hurt people very badly, you hurt the pocket. I made the decision, I'm not going to sell, I told my family, my wife and my children, 'If something happens to me, don't sell, just keep up the payments, just pay the taxes.' He threatened me, and why he didn't shoot me, I don't know because I was there all the time."

Lobato lost forty-nine head in two weeks. "Seventeen we found dead at the ranch, ten were mutilated and at that time we already had people there twenty-four hours a day, and all they (the perpetrators) were doing was shooting them (cows). Prior to that time, they had already taken the rest. The reason why we found out they were taking them somewhere else because they'd call the sheriff, Sandoval, and they told him that they had found some cows over at the Rio Grande that were 'mutilated.' They called in the Brand Inspector and they found that they had my brand on them." (The Rio Grande River is over thirty miles west of his Chama Canyon ranch.)

"So who do you feel is doing the 'mutilations?'"

"I feel that the first 'mutilation,' I can't give you an explanation for it, because it wasn't the same people. But I think that Taylor had a lot of push with the government. He could call the governor (Lamm) over here, and the governor would run over here and bring the National Guard with him. When we started seeing all this activity over at the Taylor Ranch, the 'hippies' going over there, he had brought in, uh, I don't know how many people, I talked with one person who said that about five-hundred people, to hunt in the area at the time. This was during hunting season.

"There was a lot of activity on the Taylor Ranch. A lot of the people who were watching and helping me watch noticed that a lot of helicopters were landing on the Taylor Ranch. They were going from the Taylor Ranch to somewhere on the (Wild Horse) Mesa over here. They knew about my comings and goings. The 'hippies were informing him of my whereabouts, and I think that Taylor was involved in letting whoever was doing the mutilations to come in."

(This may be the first time anyone has been named publicly as aiding and abetting or conducting UAD activity.)

"When Jack Taylor was shot, this fella told me, 'I shot at a helicopter,' he said, 'and I'm quite sure that I . . . because he was hit on the heel."

"Taylor was?"

"Yes, and he said, 'I think that I hit him, because we were shooting at a helicopter. It stopped right there and turned right

167

back. It went back to the Taylor Ranch and he said, shortly thereafter, they came down because Taylor had been shot. He said, 'I think I was the one that shot him.'"

"Who was this person?"

"He was in jail, he had just been let off jail and he went with the deputies over there and he said, 'We shot at that helicopter.'"

"These are Costilla County deputies?"

"Yes, they said, 'We shot at 'em. I think I hit 'em."

"But as soon as he was shot, the 'mutilations' stopped dead?"

"The 'mutilations' stopped, yeah. I hadn't realized this until at a meeting in Alamosa, one time, this man told me, 'Did you know that when Jack Taylor was shot, that was the end of the 'mutilations?' We always figured that it was Taylor and the hippies."

I asked him who he thought was responsible for the UADs in neighboring Costilla County.

"One of my conclusions was that there was not one group involved. I think there was more than one group involved."

We again started talking about the mystery helicopters that had been reported almost nightly during the fall of 1975. Emilio shook his head. "Some people told me that they had seen those helicopters here and that they went extremely fast. Faster than a usual helicopter or even a plane!" At first he had thought it was the motion of his own car which caused the appearance of such velocity. "But then, when they went overhead, they were going extremely fast. Stopping very rapidly! That's what threw off a lot of people.

"We see jets flying through here every day. They saw lights that were going back and forth (across the valley) so fast it seemed just like a flash of light. Very few people said this light seemed to be like a helicopter. A lot of people were telling me these were UFOs. I don't know what to believe any more."

I was curious about the locals' response to the cattle deaths. "How about the local government, at the time, in '75. Did you ever get the impression that there was a real, legitimate desire by the local government to get to the bottom of why cows were being 'mutilated?' I mean you lost close to fifty!"

"They got people to watch my place twenty-four hours a day. They were constantly calling me to make sure things were okay. They, CBI, they called the FBI, and they came to talk to me."

"The FBI did?"

"I told them, if the government can't protect me, I have to protect myself."

Emilio's phone rang. It was his nephew, Dale Vigil. Vigil had called Ernest Sandoval to tell him he had just discovered a 'mutilated' cow that very morning, at his Chama Canyon ranch, two ranches from Emilio's ranch! Sandoval told him about our investigation. Dale agreed to take us to his ranch to investigate the downed cow.

Synchronicity crackled. I couldn't believe the timing. This trip was, without question, right out of a movie. We continued our conversation with Lobato as we waited for his nephew to show up and found out that there had been attempts on Lobato's life back in 1975! He claimed on three different occasions, there had been shots fired at him on his Chama Canyon Ranch.

I couldn't help but exclaim, "This is too weird, this is TOO weird!"

The Mournful Moo-oo

Vigil arrived in a pick-up and we followed him at breakneck speed over the windy back country roads to his small ranch. We drove around the back of the ranch house to see a knot of men standing over a dead cow less than one-hundred and fifty feet from the Vigil ranch house. My first "fresh one." We hopped out and, as we walked over toward the cow, I hoped feverishly that I had enough juice left in the video battery to document the scene.

Emilio introduced us to the seven or eight local ranchers and I set up the camera. The animal lay on its right side underneath a grove of scrub willow. The rear-end was missing, the udder had been removed, the upside eye looked like it had been sucked out, and a patch of hide, just above the left knee, was missing.

Vigil said the cow had given birth at "around 3:30 a.m., last night," and when he and his brother, Clarence, went out "at 5:30 a.m., they found the calf bawling over it's mother, who was dead." He immediately called Sheriff Billy Maestas, who came out with Undersheriff Roger Benson to investigate the scene a couple of hours before we arrived.

They found a small amount of oily, clear, yellowish matter on the animal's side, which they collected to have tested. We also found a small amount of strange material which we collected into a sealed film-container. We carefully cut off tissue samples from the incision areas and collected about twenty ccs. of uncoagulated blood from the body cavity. These samples would be sent, overnight air, to Denver hematologist, Dr. John Altshuler, for testing.

I asked Dale to show me where the calf had been born, and he took me one hundred yards to the east by the small creek that flows through his ranch. "She was born right there," he said, pointing to a fairly large spot of dried blood. By this time, my battery had died, and I carried the now-useless camera in my hand. As we started back to the dead cow, I noticed that a large red, Limousine bull had been slowly edging over toward the carcass. The rest of the small herd was grazing obliviously three hundred yards away, at the other end of the pasture. The bull cautiously walked up to the carcass, sniffed it, and let out the most heart-wrenching, mournful "MOOO-O-O-O-O!"

Instantly, the other thirty to forty head of cattle came thundering across the pasture to the dead cow. They gathered around, snorting and pawing at the carcass and the whole herd started slowly circling around it in a clock-wise motion. Damn, I sure wished I had some battery power left so I could have video taped this unusual spectacle. If only I could have panned the cow ritual, then zoomed in on the line of ten ranchers, watching with their mouths dropped open in amazement, I'd have captured a classic movie shot.

I asked the ranchers if they had ever seen cattle do this before. Several couldn't even answer, they just shook their heads NO! Lobato, said, "In all the years I've been a rancher, I've never seen cows do that before!" Although I felt blessed to have been an eyewitness to the day's activities, I might have (almost) "kissed" the Tar-Baby that day in Chama Canyon.

We left the Vigil Ranch, and headed south toward Mesita, to check on the three animals we'd heard of that morning. I spotted the faint outline of a dirt road exactly where the woman in the coffee shop had described it. I noted fresh tire-tracks heading off to the south. Sure enough there were three large carcasses about two-hundred yards down the road. We drove toward the site and parked.

Through our open windows came the powerful smell of cadaverine molecules. There are a lot of elements that are unsavory in UAD cases, and this is the worst of them. We were downwind and it really stunk, bad! I am often asked how I can stand it. My trick is to put Vick's Vapo-rub under my nose and hold my breath when I'm downwind. Unfortunately, I hadn't brought any Vick's but vowed I would never leave home without my trusty jar of vapo-rub again.

I took a deep breath, and ran to the upwind side of the animals. A bull and a cow lay back-to-back in the dirt road. Twenty yards away to the east was a horse skeleton. The horse carcass had apparently been devoured by scavengers but the cattle remained intact. There was a large rectal coring, genitalia and an upside eye were missing, and upon closer examination, (holding my breath, I might add) I found that several downside ribs and the downside horn had been snapped off! It looked as if the animal had been dropped from a great height.

We noted the location of the animals in the environment. We

were standing in a remote, unfenced area of sparse prairie that obviously was not used as grazing land. There were no signs at all of any other grazing animals for miles. Could the carcasses have been dropped there by a passing rancher? How about the snapped off ribs and horn? Something didn't make sense but I hesitated to jump to conclusions. John took some pictures and we started back toward home.

When Altshuler opened the film container, there was no trace of the strange yellow material! Tests on the container revealed only plastic and the traces of the film that had been in the container. Tests on the blood revealed that the animal may have been hit with an unusual dose of "carbon-monoxide."

"It seems enigmatic to even perceive in the wildest imaginations that animal mutilations, that are so pervasive and so common everywhere, continue to defy witnesses," mused Dr. Altshuler.

He Was Real Spooked

Thankfully, the following two weeks were pretty quiet in the SLV. I needed some time to digest that first trip to Costilla County. I also used this time to rehearse with my band, The Business, for a series of shows we would do throughout the region that spring. I worked feverishly on a financing proposal for a ninety-minute documentary concerning my amateur investigation.

I had approached several friends concerning leads on possible investors for the project and John Hill mentioned Hisa Ota, a well-to-do Japanese architect who owned the Zapata and Medano Ranch. Ota had recently put in a championship 18-hole golf-course at the Great Sand Dunes County Club. The two ranches he owns make-up the western border of the Great Sand Dunes National Monument and contain some of the earliest sites of human occupation in North America.

This rich archeological locale is important to its owner. He had been financing an on-going Smithsonian dig on the Medano and I thought, if anyone might be interested in the project, it would be him. After a couple of cancellations, we finally made plans to meet for dinner at his four-star Great Sand Dunes Country Club restaurant, May 3, 1993.

Coincidentally, I had spoken with Ota's Medano Ranch foreman on March 9. He had been "chasing lights" at night around sections of the ranch the previous summer. He told me of several fascinating encounters with what I have dubbed, "The Bigfoot truck" lights. Evidently, he and his ranch hands, and even Great Sand Dunes' personnel, had witnessed peculiar lights that seemed to travel mainly on the dirt roads, didn't open and close locked gates and left no tracks. The foreman, a "professional tracker for ten years," was understandably bewildered, and a little hesitant to talk to me. "Ya ain't gonna put me in the paper, are ya?" was his initial response to my call. I told him I wouldn't use his name in my articles and he proceeded to tell me about his experiences — sometimes for several nights in a row.

"They come out at night around nine - 9:30 in the late summer and in the fall. I've seen 'em, four and five nights in a row, and they coincide with helicopter activity. I've even chased 'em around on my motorcycle. The headlight doesn't work, and I try to sneak up on them to see who they are."

"What do the lights look like?" I asked.

"Well, there's two large white lights like headlights, about ten feet apart and about eight to ten feet off the ground. When they seem to turn around, there's two smaller red lights in back, like a big truck, or something. They're completely silent and don't leave any tracks. The last time we saw 'em, me and a ranch hand scoured the whole area for a whole day, all the way to the Baca Headquarters (almost ten miles) and didn't find a trace of them. No tracks, footprints, cigarette butts, anything! Last summer, we saw 'em a half a dozen times or so. The first couple a times it was kinda fun chasing them around. But then I hit a barb wire fence doin' thirty (mph) and messed myself up. It ain't no fun no more."

"How close have you been able to get to them?"

He thought for a second. "Oh, maybe three-hundred yards, or so. One time, one of them let me get real close, and then it blinked off. About four, or five minutes later, it flashed on just for a second, right behind me. Scared the hell outta me! It's almost like they're playin' with me!"

I asked him who or what he thought was prowling around Ota's ranch. "Well, the guys at the (Great Sand Dunes) Monument have seen 'em come right out of the dunes. I dunno, maybe they're military hovercraft, or something. They gotta be using night vision plus they don't open any gates, and don't leave tracks. I know that if there had been any tracks, I would have found 'em."

"Where do you usually see them?"

"We usually see 'em north on the Baca border, and east between the Medano - Monument border. We've seen 'em over just northeast of the (San Luis) Lakes, near Head Lake."

I remembered that this lake could be the actual location of the Tewa "place of emergence." "When did you see them there?" I asked.

"Last summer. We've seen 'em over there a few times."

As I left the foreman I was sure that his boss, Hisa Ota, would be interested in the strange activity that had historically been reported on his ranches in the mysterious valley. As the crow flies, the distance between the Baca and the Great Sand Dunes is less than twenty miles. The only paved route is fifty miles around the Baca Ranch, a trip of almost an hour.

I found Hisa to be gracious, curious and obviously extremely talented. He designed the Disney corporate headquarters in Florida and is a well-known and successful architect. The history of the Zapata Ranch and Urraca areas interest him a great deal, and having hired Berle Lewis as a handyman (who lives at the country-club), Ota was aware of some of the unusual occurrences that had been documented on his property. He had already marveled at some of Lewis' colorful stories and was acquainted with my articles. He seemed eager to hear more about my investigation.

For the next two-hours, over an excellent quinoa and trout dinner, I talked extensively with Ota about the area. He declined my proposal, explaining that the reason he doesn't live in the Baca was because "so many people would be asking me for money." Oh, well. After thanking him and saying goodbye, I started my hour-long journey back home.

At 10:30 p.m., halfway between Hooper and Moffat, I noticed a strange, refracted glow behind me in my rear-view mirror. It appeared to be a mile or so behind me as I headed up Highway 17. I ignored it. Then, off to the right, thirty feet off the road, I saw the outline of a car. I strained to see if the driver needed help but I saw no one.

The rest of the trip was uneventful but, two hours later, my brother Brendon called. He was out of breath. It was his car I had passed. He had just arrived home after being given a ride from a Saguache County deputy.

Brendon had recognized my truck, with its homemade camper shell, and tried to flag me down. "As I ran up to the road and watched your taillights, I heard a car coming right after you with its lights off! It was a brand-new, white sedan with two men in the front seat. They must have been wearing night vision, it was really dark out. It was scary. They were about a half-a-mile behind you and really flying, they must have been doing a one-hundred mph."

Brendon had watched me make the turn onto Road T and head east toward Crestone. The brake lights of the mystery sedan came on as the driver made a U-turn and started back on 17 toward him, its lights still off. "I was real spooked," he admitted. "I crouched down off the road behind a bush out of sight, thinking they might have seen me. I heard the car turn off 17 about two miles or so up the road. I ran up to the road and saw that the car had turned (east) on a dirt road and was headed out onto the Baca Ranch, with its lights on."

Still shaken, Brendon observed, "It's really weird the way my throttle cable had broken. It's almost like something wanted me to see that car following you."

On five different occasions the following week, military-style trucks were seen coming and going from the Baca Ranch on the same road the sedan had taken the night of May 3rd.

My mind whirled with supposition. Had I became a player in a potentially dangerous game? Was I getting close to something I wasn't supposed to see? Was someone monitoring me? I refused to allow fear to dictate my state of mind. However, I did go through my paces for a couple of days. Coming on the heels of my first trip to Costilla, this latest possible example of interest in my activities was a bit disconcerting.

During the first week of May 1993, I had set up a meeting with current Alamosa County sheriff, Jim Drury. Drury was midway through his fourth term as sheriff and I was surprised at his eagerness to talk with me. He suggested I come down to the sheriff's office the following day.

I was impressed by the brand-spanking-new sheriff's office and county jail. If he could swing the money to have this built, in the dirt-poor SLV, this guy was on the ball. I was "buzzed in" the reception area and directed to his office.

Drury, with a warm smile, extended his hand and told me to have a seat. An impeccably dressed, relaxed man, he surprised me with his candor and open mind. He told me that after I called, he went into his archives to find reports pertaining to UADs and UFOs that had occurred in the county. He also checked for any paperwork on the "Snippy" case.

"You know, it's funny, I couldn't find a single file on animal mutilations or UFO sightings," he said scratching his Irish-red hair.

"Hmmm, that's strange, I have a lot of *Courier* clippings that mention cases in Alamosa County in the seventies." I began looking through my files for exact dates.

Drury talked a bit about the UADs and he seemed genuinely interested in the phenomenon.

"When I moved down here and became sheriff, I had no idea this kind of thing went on here. I remember reading about some of the Front Range reports from the seventies, but I had no idea that it happened here."

"I think a lot more occurred here then is officially on-the-record." I said, showing him my documentation of unpublicized

174

cases from Saguache County.

He asked me if I had any theories concerning who, or what was behind these animal deaths, and we talked at length about the various attempts to explain the mystery. It turned out that Drury had a professional fascination with "non-traditional social, political and religious groups," better known in the media as cults. Not only did he have an interest, he was considered an expert. He'd taught college-level courses and trained law enforcement officials all across the country. A perfect person to help interpret the non-traditional phenomena I was stalking.

Drury seemed genuinely interested in helping with my investigation. I asked him about known cult activity in the valley and he told me about some investigations he'd conducted attempting to unmask a ritual-magic group. I casually mentioned that I was planning to go down to Costilla County to conduct some more interviews and he warned me to "tread lightly down there." When he heard I might be speaking to Jim Cockrum, an ex-Alamosa County Sheriff, he even offered to be my cameraman! I didn't quite know what to think of this. What was he intimating? I told him I'd welcome his company and we confirmed the trip for May 6, 1993. Unfortunately, duty called, and Drury couldn't make it. I wish now he had.

Return to San Luis

May 7, 1993, Highway 159, Costilla County, CO:

My initial video interviews with Berle Lewis, Ernest Sandoval and Emilio Lobato had gone well, and with confidence, I lined up interviews with current Costilla County Undersheriff Roger Benson and former Costilla County Sheriff, Pete Espinoza, who had served during the height of the UAD wave in the mid to late 1970s. My many unanswered phone calls attested to the fact that current Costilla County Sheriff Billy Maestas was not interested in talking to me.

I also scheduled an interview with former Alamosa Sheriff Jim Cockrum. He had reported UADs in the 1970s, on his ranch outside of Ft. Garland after his tenure as sheriff. He was now foreman of the controversial Taylor Ranch.

As John Hill and I drove toward San Luis, I was disappointed that Sheriff Drury wasn't able to be with us. "I've heard Costilla County is a pretty tough place for whites." I was trying to ignore the fact that, for some unknown reason, I was nervous.

"You'd be amazed at some of the things that go on down here," I then mentioned what Drury had told me.

"After that first trip, no I wouldn't ." We sat in silence, watching

the scenery sail by. "What can you tell me about Pete Espinoza?"
I asked after a minute.

"Well, he was pretty controversial during his term as sheriff.
They firebombed his house and his squad-car."

"Wow, you're kidding! Who did?"

"Some of the organized elements down here. A whole lot of
nasty stuff went down a few years back."

'No kidding,' I thought to myself as I remembered the story
of a white woman teacher, much loved by her students, her San
Luis house was shot up one night. It would seem that they were
responding to a fire up at the Taylor Ranch, our second scheduled
destination. From the sound of the call, it was pretty serious.
Evidently a ranch outbuilding had been burned down the night
before. We could simply drive up to the Taylor Ranch and talk
with both Benson and Cockrum. Two cops with one mic.

We buzzed, noticing a video camera gleaming down from the
corner. As the dispatcher finished her call with Benson, I asked her
to tell him that I was there for our scheduled appointment.

Benson told us to come up to the ranch. One of the ranch
hands would meet us at the gate and bring us up. A coincidental
fire, huh? Perfect timing. We obtained directions and made tracks.
We headed southeast, across the lush pasture land of an ancient
floodplain, excitedly hypothesizing what could be going on up at
the Taylor Ranch?

The Chama Canyon entrance of the mammoth Taylor Ranch
was located about ten miles southeast of San Luis, across the
valley at the base of fourteen thousand foot Culebra Peak. The
surrounding countryside looked innocent enough. Cows grazed
undisturbed in pastures. Ancient adobe houses appeared melted
into the ground next to modern ranch-style houses.

It was difficult for me to imagine this area as one of the hardest-
hit locales in the history of UADs. But I knew, from talking to
Sandoval and Lobato, that this surface appearance was misleading.
My instinctual unease didn't make sense and it made me even more
nervous, like an itch I couldn't scratch.

We wound our way through the small hamlets of San Acasio
and Chama and I smiled at several old broken-down adobe shacks
with high-tech satellite dishes outside. "Imagine living here!" I said
to John. We started winding up Chama Canyon, crossing a rickety
bridge.

As we headed higher toward the majestic mountains, I noticed
that the surrounding foothills effectively hid the canyon from the
outside world. A perfect little valley, lost in time. We turned onto
the dirt road that led to the Taylor Ranch.

As we approached the gate, I spotted our escorts, two ranch

hands repairing a section of fence next to the gate. It appeared to have been cut. We slowed down and one of the ranch hands, who was on a CB radio, motioned us to stop. He told us Jim Cockrum, the ranch foreman, was heading down to meet us. We thought this strange since we had been told by Benson to come up to the ranch house. John stuck his head out the window and asked him how far the headquarters was. "Not too far, about half-a-mile. But I told you, you can't go up! He should be down in a minute."

A brand-new, dark-purple Cadillac sedan raced down the dirt road toward us. The license plate read; YA#1. The driver cranked the wheel to the left and skidded sideways, spraying gravel, stopping thirty feet away, blocking our way up the hill. A thin, craggy man emerged from the car. Cockrum strode toward us, kicking up dust clouds, taking off his sunglasses. In his mid-sixties, he wore western clothing and cowboy boots.

"Sorry boys, ya just can't come up." He said, leaning on the car.

"Everything all right?" I extended my hand and introduced myself.

"I've got the DA and the sheriff up here investigating an arson fire," he told us nervously. "With the burning, and the investigation, we have to put the lid down tight."

"Can we meet with you later in town?" I asked hopefully.

"Well, I've got the (Taylor) family here, maybe in a couple of hours. But I can't talk about the fire. I'll talk about the mutilations, like I said but I won't talk about the fire!" Three dour, sunglass-clad, male passengers peered out the caddy's windows at us.

We thanked Cockrum and started back down the hill. "Boy, he was sure acting strange," John said. "Did you see the way he swerved the car in front of us to block the road?" You bet I had. My second trip to Costilla County was turning out to be another mystery. Why had Cockrum acted so nervous? Was it because we were the "press," or was it something else?

We reached the bottom of the hill where we were supposed to turn, and I told John to stop. "Let's park up on the hill there and see what happens. Let's shoot some video," I suggested. We started filming.

"Look who's here!" John said. The caddy was parked at the intersection where we should have turned to head back toward town. We puttered around for a few minutes and decided to head back into town and give Pete Espinoza a call. The caddy followed us. We stopped twice to tape, and each time, they halted a few hundred yards back, following us all the way to town.

"There's definitely something weird going on," John mused aloud. "Let's go over to the fire department and see what they know."

Several firemen were cleaning a big pumper-truck. "You guys hear anything about a fire last night up at the Taylor Ranch?" I asked.

One of the firemen looked up at us gringos. "Nope." He went back to washing the fire truck.

"None of you guy's heard anything about a fire?" I asked again.

"I didn't hear nothing. Any of you guys hear anything about a fire?" None of the other firemen answered.

I switched tactics. "If there was a fire up at the ranch, would they call the fire department here in town?"

"Depends. Depends on how big it was."

"We heard that at least one building was damaged."

"Hmmm. Yeah, you'd think they'd call us, we're the only fire department around." Maybe we did have another mystery on our hands.

"Does seem a little strange if they didn't call you guys," John chimed in.

"They try to keep everything quiet up there," the fireman said, feeling a little more comfortable with these two questioning strangers. "Who are you guys?"

"We're researching a story," John quickly interjected.

"Oh, reporters, huh." He turned away from us and resumed his scrubbing.

"Well, thanks for your help." We headed toward the phone at a nearby gas station to call Pete Espinoza.

"What's with this place anyway?" I asked John. "You can sure tell they don't like outsiders."

"Hey, there's Cockrum," John said. "It looks like they're going into Emma's restaurant."

I was tired of the runaround and being tailed. "Let's mess with them a little." I suggested that we follow them inside. We ordered lunch, sitting three tables away from Cockrum and the Taylors, hoping to overhear something. All four ignored us, and made a show of laughing and joking, appearing not to have a care in the world.

An imposing muscular Hispanic man, in his late twenties, who had been sitting with a buddy slowly stood up. The slick-haired scowling guy with the golden chains dangling over his sleeveless tee-shirt, gave a quick glance in our direction before sliding over to whisper in Cockrum's ear, then entered the bar. Cockrum excused himself and also entered the bar.

We had a scrumptious Mexican lunch and headed toward the pay phone to call Espinoza. The bruiser from the restaurant and his buddy followed us. They climbed into a late-model blue van and rolled in our direction.

"John, remember those two muscle-bound guys with the gold chains?" He nodded. "Well, here they come!"

They drove slowly by, watching us through wrap-around sunglasses, making a U-turn at the next block and parking.

The phone was broken and we headed three blocks north to another phone booth. I adjusted my passenger-side mirror to watch the van follow us. Again, they drove slowly by, checking us out. They turned at the next block, drove by us again, and parked across the street. The driver adjusted his mirror to keep an eye on us. "Do you have a feeling, like you're being watched?" I asked, to break the tension. The watchers certainly wanted us to know they were watching. The whole scene reminded me of a Ludlußm novel.

Pete Espinoza invited us out to his ranch. At that moment we would have accepted an invitation from almost anyone and we were grateful to have a friendly destination. Espinoza's two dogs met us, barking furiously. The blue van continued on by. Espinoza came outside and called off his dogs. He was a burly, no-nonsense Vietnam vet in his early forties, who obviously kept in good shape. He spoke with a rapid-fire Spanish-accent.

Even A Chopper Can't Do That

John Hill was familiar with Pete Espinoza after writing a couple of Valley *Courier* articles while Espinoza was sheriff. Pete seemed relaxed and eager to talk to us, on camera.

"Sure, I'd be happy to answer a few questions if I can," he said extending his hand for me to shake. His grip was firm. A tasteful array of plush furniture and art adorned his house. John and I sat down on a sofa, Espinoza took a seat at his desk across the room. The rays of sunlight knifed through a second-story window, illuminating his face. We related our aborted meeting at the Taylor Ranch and described the late-model Cadillac. Just then, the caddy drove by.

"So, Emilio told me you talked with him and Ernest," Espinoza said, as we watched the car pass, turn around and head back the other way.

"Yes, some of the things Sandoval told us were pretty amazing," I responded, as I unpacked the video camera. "You guys sure have a lot of weird things going on down here."

Espinoza asked what we wanted to talk about. I told him that a couple of the stranger cases might be a good place to start. I rolled tape.

He got right into it. "When I left the office of deputy sheriff, the whole (UAD) thing just died out. But, I had a few encounters that were very close. There was a thirteen thousand dollar reward (to catch a 'mutilator') at the time and, boy, I was after it bad! I'm not after any publicity but I'm the one who came the closest, and I know I am. I was pretty into it at the time.

"There were two or three cases that were unexplainable. Like the one time I found that bull the sheriff told you about. It was a humongous bull. It was on this wooden table in an old abandoned adobe shack. The most amazing thing to me was, how in the hell did anybody, or even ten guys for that matter, put a nineteen hundred pound bull on top of a table? It was there! And, hey, I'm not just telling you this! That's where we found it. For some people to go into a small shack, put a bull on top of a table and 'mutilate' it, that was amazing to me. To this day, I can't put that together. It was my case and I couldn't come up with anything solid. We had to just close the case."

Espanoza went right into the next case, in which he and other officers staked out Emilo Lobato's unfortunate herd one moonlit night. "We walked in (to the surveillance point) and I told my deputies, 'I'm not trying to brag about what I'm going to do, but we're gonna use some Vietnam tactics here, buddy. If we have to go crawl on our bellies for fifty feet, hey, we're gonna have to do that.'"

By this time Lobato's herd had dwindled to fifty or sixty head. "So we ended up in this little shack, out there on the hill, and we stayed there from, I would say, maybe 8:30 (p.m.). We were like whispering because I figured if it was anybody that might have real high-tech equipment, I didn't want nobody hearing us. I didn't let 'em smoke, or nothing. At one time, the cows would kind of stray, you know, ten would go this way and I would have one of the guys watching them. I'd watch the main body, and I have one of the other guys watch the other side and then once in a while, we'd move over to where each other was at and we'd say 'Hey, can you still see okay?' 'Yeah, we can see. There's nothing coming down or nothing.'

Around 1:30 a.m., they witnessed flashing lights appear to land at the Taylor Ranch. "They were like a reddish-gold. Not a real dark gold but like a light bulb, bright yellowish and red. They went down at the Taylor Ranch, and nothing came out of it, we never saw them leave, or nothing. So we just sat there. We sat there and then it was about 5:00 o'clock in the morning and behind the mountains I could already see the glow of the coming day."

Not wanting to be seen, Espanoza led his team down the road before dawn and called for a deputy to pick them up. "During this

180

time-span, maybe twenty five to thirty minutes, Mr. Lobato got up early and went up there to check and right in front of the shack that we had been in, watching all night, there's a downed cow, and it's 'mutilated.' So we missed it by twenty minutes!

"That's the closest anybody's ever got. It's amazing! This happened man, it actually happened! When we got to the office, Mr. Lobato came in and said, 'Hey guys, there's a cow and it's mutilated.' Where? 'Right in front of the shack,' No, Bullshit! It can't be. He said, 'There is!'" So we rushed back up there to check and, sure enough, forty to fifty yards in front of my face, exactly where I was, there's a downed cow, and it's mutilated."

He shrugged. "Some people said it was the government, and some people were talking about the aliens. Other people were talking about the government paying people to scare the Mexican people into running out, so they could buy the land for the minerals here, oil and gold, what have you, okay? I was pretty sick of it already. I was very sick of it because I couldn't reach a single conclusion.

"One night, Monica Sanchez had a bunch of teenagers in the car. They had gone to a movie that night, and they were coming back up to San Francisco (CO) to drop off some of the kids who lived up here. They were on Road 242, and right about fifty yards from Mr. Lobato's residence, where he had all his cattle at the time, according to them, there was a cow in the middle of the highway, blocking the road, and it had something silver sticking out from it's side. They saw a helicopter right next to the cow and some of the kids said it had a cable. They went to tell me right away, and I rushed over there. I didn't find nothing except for some kind of a . . . it wasn't oil, it wasn't blood, it some kind of liquid. A little puddle, eight inches in diameter, of some kind of fluid."

"Ernie thought it was where the cow had urinated," I interjected. "That was his guess."

"Naw, it wasn't urine. I got down to smell it. It wasn't urine."

"Did you touch it?"

"Yes, it was oily. But it wasn't like motor oil. It sure wasn't nothing like what a normal person would touch. There wasn't enough to have tested. It was right where they said the cow was at. To this day, you know, there's something else that always bugged me. I never got the help that I wanted. You can quote me on that. I never got the help that I really wanted! Maybe a search team that really knew what they were doing, infrared scopes, whatever, I never got it. No government help, state or otherwise."

Espanoza had tried to tie this case to the Manzanares bull case, but to no avail. "How do you bring a chopper down by an adobe shack, and take a nineteen hundred pound bull through a small opening that's supposed to be the door, take it from there, and put it on top of a table? Even a chopper can't help you do that! Ten guys couldn't do that! As far as the other 'mutilations,' there were a bunch that I investigated, some, I can't even remember what I did. There were so many." I pointed out that the sheriffs in Costilla, Alamosa and Saguache counties had no documentation pertaining to unusual animal deaths.

"Really?" he shook his head. "I sure wished I'd kept my pictures."

"Did you have the feeling, while you were doing your investigations, that the same people were doing it?"

"Oh yeah, definitely. Some people tried to tell me it was a cult. But, every cult comes to an end. For whatever reason, all cults come to an end. These (UADs) never came to an end. That's why nobody can convince me it was a cult. Call me crazy. I was after that thirteen-thousand dollar reward. Back in '75 and '76, thirteen thousand dollars was like a hundred thousand dollars today. I thought it was a case that anyone could solve. Then it got hard. It got really hard! Impossible. That's the word, it got impossible."

"Kind of hard to solve a case if they don't leave any clues," I said with mock sarcasm. "You know, the skeptics say, 'Oh, it's just scavengers.'"

"In every 'mutilation,' I ruled that out. I had a heck of an argument one day with another deputy. He said, 'Man, it has to be coyotes, it has to be a mountain lion.' I said, 'Fine, okay, fine. Let a mountain lion come and chew on a two-thousand pound bull but that mountain lion ain't gonna put him up on a table."

"What role did the Taylor Ranch play? We've been hearing a lot of opinions that the Taylor Ranch was somehow aiding and abetting whatever kind of craft that was flying around out here doing this."

"If you've got the time, buddy? I'll talk to you some more."

"That's why I'm here!"

"Understand, we claim this [Taylor] ranch is a Mexican land grant. How Jack Taylor acquired the mountains is beyond us. To this day. It's still being fought over in court. [In 2005, the county won their suit and locals are again allowed to utilize the Taylor Ranch area.] One day this man [Taylor] walks in, starts fencing, starts bulldozing the roads and we can't go up for a picnic, we cannot go up for firewood, we can't go hunting. Nothing. Zero! They started a land war. Shots were fired at him, shots were fired back. He used to take some of the locals, who were on horseback up there, beat 'em up almost to death with his ranch hands, take off their shoes, and take them high up into the mountains and make 'em walk! He did this to my cousin. I mean, this guy was brutal! But generations started growing older and older, and finally somebody shot him up real good."

He backtracked. "You know, at first, when Taylor arrived, people here were saying, 'Wait a minute. Maybe if we talk to him in a nice decent way, we can get a different attitude out of the man.' Now we heard later on, that this man was a lumber man from North Carolina, and that he had shot some, as he put it, 'niggers. I don't want niggers on my land,' so he shot 'em. We had documentation here, at that time, that he had shot a black man in the face.

"This man came up here with a hell of a prejudiced attitude, and at first, our fathers and grandfathers were intimidated. But believe me, buddy, this is not a place where you come in and do that. This place is ninety nine percent Hispanic and people here are known to kick butt. We're not going to roll over for anybody, we stick together," he said proudly.

"I myself did not hate the man. I think if he had been a little bit more cooperative, had different relations with the local people, they would have even helped him take care of the place. One man can't take care of seventy thousand acres. The only way we can survive here is with our land and our cattle. This is a motive. This is how they're trying to run us out. If they hit our cattle, we got to move out.

"A lot of people would come up to me and say, 'Mr. Espinoza, there ain't another place in the whole of Costilla County that we see so many lights landing, and taking off, as we do the Taylor Ranch.' That's when I started doing a side investigation. Why all of a sudden? The Taylor Ranch is not selling lumber. They aren't renting out pasture. Why are so many lights being seen at the Taylor Ranch? Lights, always lights." No sounds were associated with these reports.

"So we started hitting the Taylor Ranch. Me, and deputy Bernie Sanchez, who owns a ranch just north of the Taylors. Every time we saw lights coming over and landing at the Taylor Ranch, we take the back roads, as far as their gate, to see where they were landing. We never, never once got permission from Jack Taylor to go in and do any surveillance. When I tried to talk to him in a decent way and ask him if I could do surveillance, he never let me. As a matter of fact, he even got a restraining order against the sheriff (Sandoval). The only county in the United States where the sheriff of the county had a restraining order, and he can't go in! Can you imagine that? They shot him (Taylor) in 1977 and he died a few years later. Now, the family doesn't want anything to do with this place."

"They're here right now," I told him.

183

"No, they're not."

"They're in that car that drove by when we arrived. They drove right by the house."

"That fancy new one that went by?"

"You got it."

"Aw, man, I didn't know that. That was the Taylor people?"

"With Cockrum driving. How come he's got the number one plate in the county, "YA #1?"

"I don't know."

"That might say more about what's going on around here, then practically anything," I said. "That is the hardest plate to get in the entire county and he's got it."

"See, that's what I'm talking about Chris. This is Costilla County. Only in Costilla County, buddy. I'll tell you, when I left the office of sheriff, I got a lot of publicity. Like I said, I'm not one to look for publicity but I do like to talk about what goes on down here. People even came and fire-bombed my home. They burned my garage, they burned my firewood, they fire-bombed my cars. I made A Current Affair on television. They even want to make a movie about what happened to me. A modern day, Hispanic, *Walking Tall*. People found out about me and came, just like you did today. There's a lot going on here."

I asked if he was aware that the largest untapped gold deposit in Colorado is rumored to lie underneath the Taylor Ranch.

"Yes. That's what I've heard. And not only that, but we're supposed to have oil here, and we're supposed to have geothermal water here, too. They've been talking about that for years and years. We're 99% Spanish owners of the land around here, and that's why they can't get to it. People would rather will it, and deed it over to the next generation, than give it up. "

"Have you ever had occasion to draw your gun and shoot at anything you suspected that might have something to do with the 'mutilations?'"

"I haven't, no. I hope it doesn't get to that, because I will, believe me. Something's got to give. If something's real close to my corral, shining lights, or spinning lights, whatever, I'm going to shoot, believe me. Then, if I have to face the government, whoever the hell . . . because I shot a UFO, I shot a plane, I shot a cult-member, or something, I don't give a damn. I'm going to do it. This is my way of supporting my wife and kids. I've got an arsenal right here I'm pretty good with."

"Pete, we really do appreciate you sitting down talking with us. This place, I can't believe what's going on down here and nobody knows. You go up to Alamosa and they have no idea what's going on here!"

184

"Like I told you, only in Costilla County, buddy!"

We watched a Current Affair segment about Espinoza's experiences as Costilla County sheriff. Reporter Steve Dunlevy interviewed an Anglo witness about some of the criminal activity in the county and Espinoza chimed in, "For a long time, he was the only white guy living here, and a couple of weeks after they interviewed him, somebody murdered him!"

John and I looked at each other, aghast. Oh great, just what we wanted to hear. I think we were both stunned by the potential magnitude of this complex hidden story. This information, and the blue van, did nothing to assuage our nervousness. It still felt like we were in a Hollywood movie which was rapidly evolving into an action thriller. Perhaps central casting had sent the wrong color guys, us.

We headed north. No one followed but I didn't breath any easier until we hit Ft. Garland, sixteen miles north. What a day! I thanked John profusely for his help with the interviews. Without him, I would have been down there alone.

John and I both agreed that this amazing valley, Costilla County in particular, was a universe unto itself. My head reeled from the complicated scenario in which I was quickly becoming a major player. What really happened down in Costilla and Conejos Counties in the mid-to-late 1970s?

I realized I needed to look into the publicized history. I wanted to see how the information, from these credible witnesses I had interviewed, had been covered by the media. It was during the long drive home that I realized the need to put together a time-line listing of the hundreds of reports that had been separately filed in this mysterious valley. I had a veritable wealth of resource material from which to accomplish this, thanks to investigators like Tom Adams.

Initially, it was quite a daunting task but I slogged away, compiling my comprehensive listing of reported occurrences of the unexplained.

The SLV Flap: 1975 – 1978

Sandoval, Espinoza, and Lobato's incredible experiences from the seventies set me in high gear. I needed corroboration. Did the press (local, regional or national) fully cover these events? Was their coverage accurate? I suspected that aspects of the media coverage may have influenced perceptions of these events by the public.

Several elements of the local coverage stood out. Most importantly, only one person wrote the Valley *Courier* articles during the height of the "flap" period, a reporter named Miles

185

Porter IV. Porter's descriptions of the carcasses in his many articles all had a similar tone. Descriptions attributed to ranchers and law enforcement officials all shared a similar quality. Case upon case revealed identical descriptions of the UADs and the surrounding "crime scene." There were even identical verbatim quotes from one article to the next! Hmmm.

I had heard identical descriptions of unknown anomalous lights during the New Year's Eve party that previous January. I couldn't resist diving into the hypothetical realm of the Jungian "archetype." My gut told me it was no accident that these witnesses apparently perceived these unexplained UAD and UFO-type events in very similar ways from witness to witness, case to case.

Rule # 10
The human mind, when faced with the unknown, reverts to basic primal symbols, to rationalize its experience.

Computer scientist Dr. Jacques Valleé, considered one of our premier ufologists has long insisted that UFOs appear to be a conditioning or control mechanism in culture. I had read and re-read every Valleé book I could find and his theoretical concepts rang true for me. I could see his rationale applied to UADs as well.

One of my hunches concerning an outbreak of UAD reports in a given localized area suggests that the initial cases might be the most revealing. I had a feeling that these first UADs might have some kind of programmed symbolic impact that subtly impacts the way the general populous subsequently views the ensuing flap of activity.

An important companion to the many UAD reports from the fall of 1975, were the mystery helicopters. Reports of choppers sighted around UAD sites poured into local sheriff's offices all over Colorado and the western United States. Tom Adams had compiled an impressive listing of activity called, *The Choppers, and The Choppers*, which documented almost two-hundred sightings around UAD sites, many of which were reported here in the San Luis Valley.

I have utilized Adams' research to help compile the following activity. I include some pertinent regional and national UAD information for perspective. In 1975, in the valley, there was no context when it came to reports of what were perceived as "cattle mutilations." They became relentless and undeniable.

186

Initial Reports - August, 1975

The initial unusual animal deaths of the SLV flap period of 1975 through 1978, appears to have begun in northwestern Saguache County, at the foot of Cochetopa Pass, at the western edge of Saguache Park. There had been no publicized UAD reports since 1970 in the SLV, and these early unpublicized reports in August 1975 occurred during a two-week period when several others were filed from over the Continental Divide in Gunnison County.

Several Saguache and Gunnison County ranchers reported UADs during the first week of August and investigating Saguache County deputy, Gene Gray, was convinced there was "something unnatural" about the condition of the cows and steers reported as "mutilated." He took photographs and interviewed the owners but no one had noticed anything unusual. There was talk of unknown helicopters sighted but, initially, they weren't directly tied to the Cochetopa outbreak. Gray doesn't recall the exact dates of those initial reports but he remembers they were during the first week of August.

To my knowledge, SLV residents were never informed about these initial reports from the local press, although mutilation and mystery helicopter reports may have leaked out from the Gunnison and the Front Range areas through regional media. Here are some of those incident that never made the papers:

The Loman family has a secluded ranch just west of the town of La Garita, on the western side of the north-central portion of the SLV. The night of August 7, 1975 he remembered hearing his dogs barking around 3:00 a.m. The following morning he went out early to feed his horses and noticed his daughter's palomino show horse lying in the pasture several hundred yards from the house. The rear end appeared to have been "burned-off," the horse's lips and eyes had been removed and a thick, black, tar-like substance ringed the upper body incision areas.

Photographs of the horse, twenty-years later, appear to show a horse dead for many days, although Loman had seen it alive the night before. Gray investigated and took photographs that morning. "I knew after that one, that something really weird was going on," Gray recalls. "There's just no way that animal should have looked like that."

The following week, helicopters were spotted and reported near "mutilation" sites in Gunnison County. A rancher saw an unmarked helicopter hovering over a hog in Gunnison County, that he "chased off." A hog allegedly turned up missing from a neighboring ranch.

On August 21, 1975, Tom Adams (who happened to be visiting the San Luis Valley with research associate, Gary Massey) wrote of the following experience:

> "Leaving the [Gunnison County] sheriff's office after discussing mutilation investigations with Deputy David Ellis, Project Stigma investigators Tom Adams and Gary Massey drove south toward Saguache County *[Not knowing that between six or seven cases had been reported two weeks before on this exact stretch of) State Highway 114]*. Nearing the county line, they observed a small helicopter — of the Hughes 'Cayuse' type — flying west-southwest across the highway toward the Powderhorn — Los Pinos area, where a cattle mutilation had occurred earlier in the week. The helicopter was filmed on Super-8 movie film as it passed out of sight over a ridge. The distance was too great to discern details."
> (my italics)

Is it possible that rumors of "mutilations" in neighboring counties contributed to perceptions of ensuing SLV activity. The Saguache *Crescent* editors earlier assertion rang in my ears, "We only write about good news."

With much fanfare, during the last week of August 1975, all hell appeared to have broken loose in the valley. Or so the headlines read. The Friday, August 29, 1975 *Courier* screamed "Five More [SLV] Cattle Are Mutilated." I could find no reference to earlier cases but this much is known: two cows were discovered "mutilated" in the mountains west of Antonito, and an additional three animals were discovered near Fox Creek. All five animals were discovered on August 26.

A bull belonging to Max Brady from Manassa, had been shot and the tail and an ear had been removed. Another bull owned by rancher Farron Layton had been shot and the tongue reportedly removed with a "sharp instrument." The third animal "had been shot but was not mutilated."

According to the *Courier*, "vandals" were blamed. For me, this was the first instance of a "mutilation" involving a firearm!

The fourth and fifth were discovered west of La Jara. A steer, owned by Jim Braiden was "missing the tail, tongue, penis, and right ear," and the animal had reportedly been drained of blood before being "mutilated with a sharp instrument." These first reports during August were confined to the western side of the valley. I noted the words "sharp instrument" constantly appearing in Miles Porter's UAD articles of 1975.

188

Several days later, a calf was reported "mutilated" to Conejos County officials. They concluded that it occurred Tuesday night, September 2. A white-faced four-hundred pound calf owned by Ed Shawcroft was found missing it's "tongue, ear, genitals and tail."

To the east, in Costilla County, Deputy John Lobato and Sheriff Sandoval both told Miles Porter IV of seeing helicopters flying in the area where a "mutilated" cow was later found. Dr. Joseph Vigil reported a UAD on his ranch south of San Luis on September 3.

Helicopters were seen by Costilla County officers the next three nights. Sandoval said that early Thursday morning he saw what he believed to be a "helicopter with a red light fly south into New Mexico."

On September 5, rancher John Catalano reported to the Alamosa County Sheriff, the discovery of a dead calf on his ranch south of Alamosa. News sleuth Miles Porter was dispatched to the scene. To his untrained eye, "The black heifer calf had definitely been cut in the removal of its left ear, and some internal sexual organs. The calf had been dead about two weeks." He couldn't have surmised that the rotting animal "had definitely been cut," with no veterinarian pathology training, two-weeks after the animal's death.

Later that same Friday, Ted Carpenter, foreman of the Medano Ranch, found a yearling steer laying on its left side, missing its downside ear and tongue and a suspicious heel print was found near the carcass. The first thing I check is if any downside organs have been removed. Unlike many of reports from the fall of 1975 that noted only upside organs being removed, this report differed. These were the first known UAD reports in Alamosa County since the 1968 "mutilations" of two steers on the Zapata Ranch.

Saturday, September 6, unknown helicopters were reported near three UADs in Park County, forty-five miles north of the SLV.

During the next three weeks, the valley got a break as UAD reports suddenly hopped to the extreme northeast corner of Colorado, in Logan County. Reports were also filed in Texas and Wyoming during the second week of September. Apparently the cattle surgeons can cover an immense amount of geographic territory in a short amount of time.

On the night of Monday, September 22, helicopters were reported in Pueblo County by ranchers and a state patrol officer. One interesting incident from, *The Choppers, and The Choppers* states:

189

A man in a pickup truck was run off the road by a helicopter. He called for help on his CB radio and two auxiliary policemen responded to find the victim 'frantic.' One policeman fired a shot from a 30 - 30 rifle at the still-hovering helicopter and heard a ricochet. Deputies from three counties, guards from the Pueblo Army Depot and Colorado state patrolmen chased the helicopter west to the Pueblo airport before it turned to the north and disappeared. The chopper made a noise 'like the whistling of air coming from a tire.' Other area residents reported being chased by helicopters during this time period.

That same afternoon, a two-year old heifer was found "mutilated" on rented pasture several hundred yards from a house on the Taylor Ranch. "No tracks or blood was found around the calf," Undersheriff Levi Gallegos told Miles Porter. "The heart, right eye and sexual organs had been removed through skillful incisions. The eye was removed in a 'two-inch diameter hole around the eye, clean to the bone and then they pulled the eye out.'"

Porter stated a continually valid point, "The number of the cattle mutilations here in the valley is not known, due to the lack of reports and also the lack of any central clearinghouse recording of the incidents." I wondered how many of these "reports" were actually UADs, or just mundane deaths that were misidentified.

Three days later, a six-month-old calf belonging to Verl Holmes was discovered six miles north of Alamosa, missing its tongue and all the hide off its right mandible. Holmes said that he had seen the animal alive late Wednesday night. He was alerted to the dead calf when he noticed his herd of cows pressed against the opposite fence-line, "baw'lin." According to the *Courier* sub-headline, "Predators were ruled out by authorities." CBI was sent tissue samples which later revealed some evidence of tooth-marks attributed to "kangaroo rats."

"Another fresh carcass was found Thursday, near Hoehn, CO, in Los Animas County. An autopsy determined that "a toxic substance was present in the spleen, liver, and kidneys, all were badly decomposed. Other organs including the heart appeared to be healthy," the article concluded.

Six more reports were filed in Costilla County on Sunday, September 28th, by area ranchers. Sheriff Sandoval stated, "It is getting out of hand. There are no clues. This is what's really bugging me!" A bright light had been seen by locals Thursday night, near the Sanchez Reservoir but officers were unable to get close enough to identify the craft before it vanished. Five of the reports came from Chama Canyon on the Ernest Maestas Ranch. All were missing sexual organs and various other parts. A sixth was discovered six miles west.

The following day the "Manzanares bull," was discovered on the table in the abandoned adobe shack. Porter does not mention the table and the picture in the Valley *Courier* showed the bull on the ground. I wondered why. Wouldn't this crucial fact prove, without any doubt, that this animal could not have died of attrition? Why was this fact left out?

Another animal, "a large black Angus steer," owned by rancher Bonnie Lobato was found three-quarters of a mile away from the five Chama Canyon UADs the following day. It was tied to the other reports by law enforcement.

The following week was quiet, except for several mystery helicopter sightings, including one report of a landing "on the mountain, southeast of San Luis." (The Taylor Ranch?) Locals were alerted to keep a vigilant eye skyward.

On October 7, Emilio Lobato lost his first animals. It could not be determined if the initial animal had been "mutilated" because predators had already begun eating the carcass. Two other calves were discovered by Sandoval and his deputies while investigating the first report. "Sandoval said the one calf had probably been dead only one-half hour and the other for about an hour." I wondered how this time was estimated.

Helicopters were seen nightly that entire week in Alamosa and Costilla Counties. On October 10, San Luis rancher Pat Sanchez reported to the sheriff's office two UADs at his ranch two miles west of San Luis.

During the next two weeks there were no reports of UADs or mystery choppers covered in the local press. According to Espinoza, Sandoval and Lobato, it was during this two-week period that Lobato lost forty nine head. Why was this amazing crime-spree not publicized? This was probably the ranching story of the decade in the entire country, let alone the San Luis Valley. I believe Lobato, Sandoval, and Espinoza were telling me the truth but I wonder how this could have been kept quiet? The press had shown a willingness to cover UADs but looking back at how the fall of 1975 unfolded, I began to smell a cover-up.

During this two-week period, reports of "mutilation" activity appear to have moved out of the SLV, east into Baca and Routt Counties in Colorado, and to areas in Oklahoma, Wyoming, Montana, and New Mexico.

On October 27, Pat Sanchez again discovered a "mutilated" cow west of San Luis. Later that afternoon, he found yet another one. Josephine Maestas of San Pablo also reported a UAD on the

27th. Then, if the press coverage is accurate, the San Luis Valley flap temporarily ended for over fifteen months.

Debunkers have propounded the theory of "misidentification of scavenger action" to explain UADs. If these skeptics are right, and UADs are simply "media-induced hysteria," then why did the reports stop cold, following a flurry of activity? The sudden, complete, cessation of reports seems to overrule this explanation. What? Did predators decide to stop eating for a year? All of a sudden, cattle don't die and scavengers don't scavenge?

Those who examined the carcasses refused to believe a predator was involved. So what did happen? Did the mystery surgeons simply decide to move on to greener pastures? Or could it be that the ranchers stopped reporting UADs to officials because of all the publicity and the stigma of having their livestock targeted?

What Was Not Reported

After examining the publicized unusual animal deaths reports from the Fall of 1975, I continued my investigation into the unpublicized accounts. Counting only the unpublicized Cochetopa cases from August and the additional Lobato animals, the actual figure of twenty-three "mutilations" doubles. Adding the Lobato animals "shot or stolen," the amount is almost tripled. I knew the number was much higher than the publicized thirty-nine.

During the entire month of December, 1975, almost nightly, mystery helicopters were reported to Alamosa and Costilla authorities while the mystery cattle surgeons apparently turned their attention to northern New Mexico, Kansas, Texas, Wyoming and Montana. Government officials claimed no knowledge of nocturnal chopper flights in the valley during this time period.

Another potentially important aspect of the fall flap of 1975 was the abundance of unpublicized UFO sightings. The only aerial craft reported in Miles Porter's Valley Courier articles were described as "helicopters" but other objects were evidently flitting through the skies over the San Luis Valley that fall. According to Lobato and Sandoval, there were sightings of objects that appeared to defy the laws of physics. In addition, I uncovered several claims of "classic" UFO sightings during September and October and none of these accounts ever made the papers.

These claims were perfect media fodder so, again, why were these sightings by Costilla County locals and law enforcement officials unpublicized? Was it possible that Miles Porter had a reason for not reporting the full-extent of our aerial activity because of a personal agenda within his coverage?

Five months had passed in the San Luis Valley since the last (publicized) UAD on the Pat Sanchez ranch in Costilla County. After an exhaustive search, I found no articles reporting suspected UADs during this apparently quiet six-month period but several interesting cases did make the papers concerning the killing of livestock by "vandals."

On April 12, 1976, a single "mutilation" was reported to the Costilla County sheriff's office. Investigating deputy Levi Gallegos was at a predictable loss trying to explain the UAD.

A strange calm appears to have descended on the valley through the rest of the year. To my knowledge, no known UAD, UFO, or mystery helicopter reports were filed, or publicized. Reporter Miles Porter IV left the Courier and attempts have failed to locate him.

The ensuing coverage of UADs during 1977 and 1978, were relegated to small, non-sensational articles in several local papers. If the local press coverage alone determined the extent of the flap, I would be led to believe the "problem" had subsided or ceased altogether. Some reports were still being filed to local authorities but were not covered in-depth. I continued to ponder how Porter's style of coverage, during the fall of 1975, dictated the public's perception of the UAD claims. After his departure, the tone and substance of the coverage dramatically changed but had the local perception of UADs changed?

Ernest Sandoval brought home numerous UAD reports and files after leaving as Sheriff. All his reports are only from the 1976 through 1978 period, leaving him confused because much of the material he thought he had is now "missing." He was able to provide me with twelve complete reports and accompanying photographs but Sandoval claims these were a mere portion of the overall official documentation he actually brought home. Fortunately, these surviving reports cover the period between 1976 and 1978 when press coverage was scant.

As I documented more cases of UADs, both historical and contemporary, my personal life took a few zigs and zags. Even the way people viewed me, running this way and that with cameras and night vision devices, investigating missing organs and helicopters, changed. I began to receive birthday presents such as a plastic cow, with the rear end missing. David Perkins sent several postcards and birthday cards featuring a cow with punched out eyes and rear ends missing.

The Flap Returns: 1977

According to a small three-paragraph article in the Valley

Courier, May 27, 1977, a fourteen-month-old bull, belonging to San Pablo rancher Alfonso Manzanares, was reported to Costilla County authorities as "mutilated." The article stated, "The bull had been cut in a manner similar to mutilations in the area two-years ago."

Even law enforcement officials' cattle had been targeted by our fatal surgeons. On June 17, 1977, former Alamosa Sheriff Jim Cockrum (yes, the same foreman who prevented our entry to the Taylor Ranch) reported to the Costilla sheriff's office he found a six-hundred pound, white-face steer "mutilated" on rented pasture at the "Lobato property at Ventero." He estimated the time of death as being three or four days earlier. Ernest Sandoval's official report stated:

"Jim Cockrum reported to the sheriff that one of his white-faced steers was mutilated in the same fashion as prior mutilations done before. Tail was cut off, testicles were cut off. The right ear and tongue. Went to area described and verified the fact that this job was done by the same professionals as before. No tracks, no blood and no nothing."

My observation? Steers don't have testicles, they are steers. And how in the world could Sandoval tell that the animal was killed by the same professionals responsible for prior cases?

Here is a perfect illustration of how potential explanations of mysterious animal deaths can be misinterpreted by law enforcement and the public in general. Without the services of a qualified veterinarian pathologist, no one could accurately ascertain thantogenesis (cause of death) or establish the cause of damage to the carcass. It may look like a "mutilated" duck, it may smell like a "mutilated" duck but that doesn't necessarily make it a "mutilated" duck.

Rule # 11
When investigating claims of the unusual, one cannot reach conclusions based on intuition alone.

My skepticism grew immeasurably concerning the pervasiveness and validity of many (if not most) UAD claims. All claims need to be backed up with irrefutable, substantiating data, obtained by trained professionals. Otherwise these "mutilations" are just claims based solely on appearance. Specific cases might be mysterious to the untrained eye but it might be commonplace to a veterinarian pathologist, or diagnostic crime lab.

This realization, that it was impossible to accurately study the historical UAD phenomenon in the San Luis Valley — based only on research and hindsight, was a bit disheartening. I did not,

194

however, let this important fact dampen my enthusiasm. That people viewed these animal deaths as a "mystery" was compelling enough. The "garbage-in, garbage-out" scenario is hard to avoid (when utilizing pure hindsight), and impossible to overcome.

The following reports of UADs in 1977 and 1978 were centered around three ranches, just east of the town of San Luis. The Pat Sanchez, Mike Maldanado and the Eben Smith Ranches appear to have been singled-out and hit repeatedly throughout this next year-and-a-half period. Emilio Lobato, Jr., and these three ranchers may be the hardest-hit in the entire documented UAD phenomenon. The four together claim to have lost around eighty cattle. I looked for some common link between Maldanado, Sanchez and Lobato.

I called Mike Maldanado and asked him about a possible connection between himself and the other ranchers. "Do you belong to the same organizations? Do you go to the same church? Are you politically active in the same party or . . ."

He interrupted me. "Now that you mention it, we do share something in common, we're all teachers." Now this coincidence was to glaring to ignore. Teachers? A lesson was being sent but who were the instructors?

Costilla Sheriff's Reports

The following seven official reports are from the files of Ernest Sandoval.

After an apparent three-week lull, a report was filed with sheriff's deputy John Martinez, by Mike Maldanado on October 8, 1977. Maldanado claimed a nine hundred pound cow had been "mutilated" on his ranch three-miles east of San Luis, near the Sanchez ranch, site of several previous recent cases.

Pat Sanchez called the sheriff on November 19, to report finding two of his cows "mutilated." Deputy Marquez investigated and wrote, "I noticed the cut around the rectal area was *not so perfect* as was determined in other mutilations . . . The cutting area around the area of the place the utters were removed was a *sloppy job* according to the owner of the cows. . . The man (Pat Sanchez) has stated that he has seen a cow dead and *then returned to find it had been mutilated* on one occasion." (my italics)

I have italicized indications of misidentified unusual scavenger action in the above reports. Ragged incision areas are often an indication of a mundane explanation or, as Marquez observed, perpetration by hoaxers, or pranksters. Although, as I've previously established, "appearances are misleading," Marquez's sense of unprofessional "mutilators" at work could have merit. The

195

possibility of predators, or even peculiarly-motivated humans, is obviously valid. Two years before, Emilio Lobato, Jr. had suffered through a similar scenario that suggests at least some of the UADs and missing animals resulted from very terrestrial human agendas. The day before, on November 18, 1977, neighboring rancher Mike Maldanado called the sheriff's office to report another UAD case on his ranch. To my knowledge almost none of these official Costilla County cases in 1977 and 1978 were covered in the local papers. The rest of the valley, strangely enough, had no official reports of UADs in 1977 through 1978, and I wondered if the lack of press coverage had anything to do with the lack of perceived and/or real UADs.

The last local article pertaining to the UAD flap of 1975 through 1978 appeared in the Valley *Courier* on Tuesday, December 6, 1977. It stated that Sheriff Sandoval was investigating "three cattle mutilations in the San Luis area." A possible helicopter sighting the night of December 1, was also mentioned.

The next local newspaper article I can find regarding SLV claims of UADs was written by the Valley *Courier*'s Ruth Heide, reporting the Manuel Sanchez case, thirteen years later! It is also interesting to note that Sanches experienced yet another mutilated head of livestock in June 2006.

No other reports were filed by ranchers after December, 1977, until the third week of August, 1978. A rather routine report was written by investigating deputy Arnold Valdez

On Thursday, August 17, 1978, at 1:58 p.m., Mike Maldanado called the sheriff's office to report that some of his cows had been mutilated or so it appeared. On August 19, 1978, at 12:00 p.m., deputies Steve Benavidez and Arnold Valdez went out to the incident scene. This incident was the same as all the rest of the possible mutilations that have happened in this area. No evidence was found in the immediate area. Pending further investigation."

This report shows a change in perception. For the first time, we see indications that the rancher and investigating officers view these latest UADs as "mutilations, or so they appeared to be." The two animals, a cow and a bull, were not found for over a week and the photographs show bird-droppings on the carcasses and the uneven incisions.

On August 28, 1978, Eban Smith again called to report a "mutilation" of a cow the previous night on his ranch. Deputy Valdez was again dispatched to the crime-scene and noted at the end of his report, "My opinion is that it was unprofessional due to the fact that it was very sloppy compared to some of the previous mutilations."

Again there is evidence of doubt. Was it a true mutilation? The

196

last official Costilla report from the decade of the 1970s stated:

September 16, 1978, at 9:30 a.m. the sheriff's office received a call from Mike Maldanado from San Luis reporting that another one of his cows had been mutilated . . . Mr. Maldanado said that he would not be there today because he was going to take them (his cows) to the auction because he could not afford to lose anymore.

Another mystery is why so many UFO sightings during the mid-1970s were not reported. I have uncovered accounts from the time period, but unfortunately, only a handful can be corroborated. Witnesses have come forward regarding an incident in the fall of 1975 when a large cordoned off area was set up by "troops," just north of the Taylor Ranch, while rumors circulated of a possible crash retrieval operation. One account mentions a "UFO dogfight" with one combatant ship evidently shot down by another. There seems to have been a press blackout regarding this alleged event and many other anomalous aerial craft and light sightings. The late fall of 1975, in particular, had many sightings of unexplained, non-ballistic craft but they were downplayed as being "helicopters."

So ended the official UAD wave of the 1970s. We will never know how many animals were truly "mutilated" in the United States and how many had mundane explanations for their demise and subsequent disfigurement. It is impossible to ascertain the true extent, or quality of any anomalous event based on the perception of the principle witness(es), or with simple research and hindsight (or wishful thinking.) We will examine the UAD conundrum in more detail later on in the book.

Sinister hands seemed to be hard at work during the 1970s, in the pastures of Costilla County, and in countless other pastures around the United States, Canada and elswhere. The guilty party(ies) may never even be identified, let alone be brought to justice. In my estimation, unusual scavenger action can be assumed as the causal factor in many of the San Luis Valley cases, but, by no means all cases. There were, and still are, numerous cases that defy rational explanation and warrant scientific attention and further scrutiny.

197

Snippy the Horse 1967

Berle and Nellie Lewis

Cochetopa Pass Case—note the downside excision

Palomino w/ scorched rear-end, LaGarita 1975

Maybe it's just a cow thing—let them work it out amongst themselves?

199

The Business 1993

With John Altshuler and Tom Adams, Crestone 1993

CHAPTER SEVEN:
The Plot Thickens

Manhunt

Spring had finally returned to the valley, and the shrill, buzzing sound of the newly-arrived broadtailed hummingbirds filled the still mountain air. Things seemed to have blissfully quieted and I was looking forward to our six months of warm weather. It had been a fairly mild winter and it sure felt good to be outside in the warm spring sunshine.

My new band, The Business, was getting down to business as we prepared for back-to-back weekends at a local Alamosa biker-bar called, The Eastside. The gigs went well but I found out in the paper the following Monday, April 24, 1993, that quite a drama had occurred, right next door to the bar that previous Saturday night, as we rocked.

Evidently, two illegal Mexican immigrants had been stopped for a defective taillight. A cooler on their front seat contained a couple of ounces of marijuana. The cop handcuffed one of them, leaving the other man uncuffed because he was missing one of his arms below the elbow.

According to the article, the officer was then hit in the face with the top of the cooler, and both men escaped across the bar's parking lot, disappearing into new moon night.

I was returning from Alamosa, up 17, with my brother Brendon. As we approached Road T, we noticed bright lights and a knot of cars parked at the intersection. I made the turn with bright spotlights shining in my face and a police officer motioned me to stop. I rolled down my window. "What's going on?" I asked.

"Do you both live here?" the cop inquired.

"Yes, officer. . . what's all the commotion?"

"We're looking for two escapees that may be up here," he answered with a frown, jotting something down on a clip-board.

"You mean those two guys in Alamosa I read about in the paper?"

"That's them," he said, backing away from the car. He waved me through. As I drove slowly by all the official looking cars, I noticed the monograms of several Federal agencies. Brendon asked, "Did you see that guy with the FBI hat on? There was a guy with a DEA jacket." Why were almost every law enforcement arm of the Federal Government, Colorado State Police and local county sheriffs manning a roadblock for two unarmed Mexicans, one cuffed, the other with one arm? For a couple of ounces of pot? And I saw bluish white flashes when they had the spotlights in my eyes. Had we been photographed?

As we approached the Baptist church, just outside of Crestone, we noticed the parking lot filled with squad-cars, four-wheel drives, and unmarked sedans with whip antennas and small hubcaps. There must have been twenty – twenty five of them. Many of these vehicles stayed around town for nearly a week, presumably searching for the two scared men, even when it was announced that one of the fugitives had been captured. The thought ran through my mind that this activity could be hiding other objectives.

Two weeks before military trucks had been seen coming and going from the Baca Ranch. And this was just after it appeared I'd been followed by a car with no lights. My level of paranoia rose another notch. I had to take a deep breath and remind myself that all this activity was just circumstantial, it's just a coincidence! Right? Then the strange symbols appeared on Road T and Camerno Baca Grande — the main road into the Baca Development

John Altshuler and Timothy Good

I had received a letter from English ufologist Timothy Good. His new book had just been released and he was coming to the United States to see Denver resident, hematologist Dr. John Altshuler. They planned to fly down to the SLV in Altshuler's plane and Good wondered if I was up for a visit. The first thing the flashed through my mind upon hearing this was, 'wow, Altshuler is finally coming back to the SLV.' He had made a promise never to return after his last visit and I was surprised he had agreed to the trip.

Pilot Altshuler, Good, my brother Brendon, and myself, were winding up our flight around the San Luis Valley. As we flew over the old King Ranch and headed toward the Alamosa Airport, I casually asked John to fly over the Dry Lakes. "It's where compasses have been known to spin for no apparent reason." He banked the plane and we flew directly over the glittering ponds that mirror the San Luis Lakes to the north.

Altshuler called the Alamosa tower to obtain clearance for landing. There was no response on any of his three radios. He called again, still nothing. Someone joked, "He must be in the bathroom." After a third call, he continued south, lining up his final approach.

We touched down and taxied toward the terminal and I noticed someone running toward us waving his hand. It was the furious tower operator. "Why didn't you answer me?" he shouted. "What's the matter with you? I had cleared another plane for a landing, they had to break off!"

The four of us looked at each other, as the other plane landed and taxied toward the terminal. John explained, "I called three times, and there was no answer." The three of us backed him up, we had heard him. John radioed the plane that had just landed and received an immediate reply. We were lucky the other pilot was able to spot us in time. We could have easily collided in mid-air! Altshuler was shaken by the episode. "Nothing like this has ever happened to me in over five-thousand hours of flying!"

Tim Good interviewed me about our recent reports, over lunch. I was surprised to learn that this was Altshuler's first trip back to the SLV since his "abduction," as he called it, in the Sand Dunes and his subsequent examination of Snippy the following day. Altshuler remained quiet during the rest of our visit. Good promised to send me some photographs he had taken during the flight and Brendon and I drove them back to the airport.

Another unusual aerial episode over Alamosa was brought to my attention. I received an interesting letter from a pilot who was referred to me by psychologist, Dr. Leo Sprinkle:

> I had an experience that might be related to a UFO. I am a retired Marine Corps pilot and, after I retired in 1965, I started to fly corporate aircraft... After forty years of flying for a living I decided to be a free-spirit and get away from structured life.
>
> I have about 15,750 hours of flight time and this experience was the only time an unusual thing happened to me... I was captain on a Learjet 24 and we were flying our boss and his wife from Palm Springs to Denver where we were based. We were at 41,000 feet near Alamosa, it was between 2200 and 2300 (hours,) or very close to that time, and according to my log book, it was November 15th, or 26th of November 1988. The cockpit lights were out, instrument lights were on and we were not talking. As well as I can remember, it was a clear night. All of a sudden the cockpit and outside the aircraft turned to daylight for about one second, maybe one and a half seconds... We looked at each other and one of us said, "What the hell was that?" We were really perplexed because it was such a strange event. I called Denver Center

and explained what we experienced and asked if they had any reports of a similar event. There was a pause, I assumed he asked other controllers, and then came back and said, "Negative on any reports."

A moment after this, a United pilot came on the frequency and said, "Where was that aircraft that saw the light?" The controller said, "He is about 20 miles ahead of you." The United pilot said, "We saw that light." The controller said, "Do you know what it was?" The United pilot said, "Negative" or "No I don't." That was it. To this day I regret that I didn't try to contact the United pilot and ask him to describe what he saw. . . I wish I knew what I saw.

In September, 1967, Dr. Altshuler, straight out of residency, had come to the San Luis Valley for a camping trip in the Great Sand Dunes. While in the dune field after dark, Altshuler observed four unusual lights approaching from the north. "They came down, stopped, and then they turned ninety degrees or hundred degrees and came toward me. There were four of them. One of them came right in front of me. You know, maybe fifty feet away. It was big."

Years later, Altshuler underwent hypnosis to help him recall more details of the encounter . "I saw two things in front of me. . . They were not the typical gray kind of creatures. They were different. I don't know if that's simply a figment of my imagination or not. I don't know. They have huge heads. Huge. With a very small body. The head had four definite wrinkles on the forehead. The eyes were wide open, literally."

Early the following morning, after stumbling out of the dunes, he met a ranger who, upon hearing he was a doctor, asked him to accompany him to the "Snippy" site. He anonymously conducted the now famous examination "within three of four days" of the horse's death. As a result of this sighting and visitation experience over twenty-five years ago, Altshuler never went 'camping' again. After going back to school to get a degree in pathology, he died in a bicycle accident in 2004.

Boomerang

May 31, 1993, 7:20 p.m., Road T, Saguache County:
Isadora and I are returning from a soak at Cottonwood Hot Springs and approaching the last "S" turn, eight miles east of the Baca. "What's that, over there?" Isadora slows the car and points straight ahead toward the Sangres looming toward the northeast.

A wedge-shaped, boomerang-looking object, skims north toward San Isabelle Creek and we catch a clear view of it. It is about thirty to forty feet across and appears to be about five miles away. As I watch, for about three or four seconds, it suddenly slows and performs a rapid falling-leaf decent toward the ground. I see the orange glow of the setting sun glint off the bottom, then the top, then the bottom, before it rocks downward out of sight. "Wow, it landed! Quick, let's drive over to Camper Village and see if we can spot it!" I excitedly tell Isadora, who because she's driving, has not seen it descend.

We race the five miles to the RV park and try to find a dirt-road to the location where the object has landed. We can't find access. It went down in a depression which was invisible from the dirt roads, crisscrossing the area of open prairie.

"It may have been even further away than I thought," I say. "If that's the case, that thing could have been pretty big." Darkness ends our search.

The following afternoon, I talked with a woman rancher, who lives several miles west of Moffat, about a construction project at their ranch. I mentioned my sighting the day before and she countered with this story.

"I was approaching 17, on Saturday and I saw an army truck heading south on the highway with a small old-looking yellow helicopter flying above it. Then, a while later, I saw them again, going back north."

Whoa! I asked her to describe the chopper. It fit the description of the yellow Sutherland UH-1 chopper I'd seen, perfectly. She also told me her husband and his partner had seen a whole formation of "Apaches," on May 28, headed south from Bonanza.

June 29, 6:00 a.m., the Baca:
A loud boom echoes through the mountains. Startled piñon jays take flight in a raucous chorus as the last remnants of the sound dies away. "Honey, what was that?" I ask Isadora, rubbing the sleep from my eyes. I sit up and listen. I hear no sound of jet engines, just the laughter-like cries of the jays. Isadora, who had already been up for a while, had also not heard any plane go over. The boom came out of nowhere. Oh, no, not this morning. There'd been a late rehearsal the night before. I yawn, roll over, and go back to sleep for another hour.

Later that day, I ask a few people if they had heard the early morning boom. About half had. The boom seemed localized. I quickly forget about it, and continued about my day. The following morning, three Huey helicopters were reported, flying down the Sangres toward the Dunes at 10:30 a.m., and I watched two smaller choppers head the same way at 2:30 p.m.

Izzy's Evolutionary Imperative

June 19, 1993, Libre 25th Anniversary Party, Farisita, CO:
Tom Adams, who had been quietly assisting me over the phone for six months, bringing me up to speed concerning this region's shadowy past, had mentioned several times, there's someone in your area you've got to meet, "as soon as he gets back from Australia."

David Perkins, "Izzy Zane" to his researcher friends, had been fascinated with the UFO and UAD questions since 1975, when he found a UAD in a pasture, just down the hill from his home. Tom Adams had known Perkins since 1978. Perkins, a Yale graduate, had arrived in Colorado in 1970 to study non-traditional communities. He was so fascinated by the people and the idyllic setting of the Libre commune, that he moved to the alternative community. Twenty years later, he still calls Libre, in the Wet Mountain Valley, his home.

During the first week in June, Adams informed me that Perkins had finally returned from his trip to the South Pacific, so I gave him a call. I found that he hadn't spent much time actively investigating unusual animal deaths (UADs) during the past there years due to the illness and death of his wife, Carri.

David has become a good friend, mentor and he has influenced my thinking more than any other investigator/researcher. It is with great honor and pleasure that his literate, witty introductions have prefaced all three of my Mysterious Valley books

My investigation and enthusiasm was well-received by Perkins and he during that first phone conversation he told me several interesting Huerfano Valley accounts. We had something else in common. We were both musicians. Perkins and his band, The Roids, had played the Colorado/New Mexico circuit for years. He mentioned a twenty-fifth Anniversary party Libre was having on June 19 and 20 1993 and suggested my band The Business come over and rock!

What a day! Several hundred people converged on the commune and enjoyed good music, sunshine and each other. Adams had told me he couldn't make it but his research associate, Gary Massey, was headed up from Texas. I stayed for three days, much of it around a campfire engaged in philosophic debate with Perkins and Massey, over (and over) the more salient points surrounding UFOs and UADs. I learned that these many subsequent get-togethers would be fun, with good-natured razor-sharp, deadly earnest, repartee. These two guys had obviously been arguing for years.

206

Some of Perkins' early investigative UAD work in the 1970s hypothezed that the cattle death phenomenon might be a form of environmental monitoring program. Perkins is the acknowledged formulator of this theory. He noticed that areas of high incidence were downstream and downwind of nuclear plants, weapons labs, uranium mines, nuclear missile deployment areas and nuclear test sites. He speculated that someone was appraently monitoring the environmental effects of radiation in cattle in these areas of high incidence.

Perkins has been working on a unified theory which attempts to explain all paranormal phenomena and has developed a "big-picture" theory he calls The Evolutionary Imperative. He defines it for me:

In looking for an answer to the conundrum posed by the paranormal, I'm basically turning everything upside down. I'm starting from an end point and working backwards. I know this is not "good" science where hypotheses are developed, tested and verified. In this instance, that just hasn't worked. Everyone who has tried the traditional approach seems to have eventually hit a brick wall, mostly because they were forced to exclude data which didn't fit neatly into their hypotheses. I'm beginning from a Darwinian bottom line that individual and species survival is at the core of virtually all human behavior. It is a biology-driven approach. If in doubt, try to figure out how phenomena, or the perception of phenomena, contribute to human survival strategies. The new sciences of sociobiology and evolutionary psychology are helpful because they give compelling evidence that our "modern" psychological traits and behaviors are shaped by our evolutionary past. As humans, we have reached the point in our evolutionary trajectory where it is generally agreed that we can't last here on Earth forever. Something will eventually do us in. Any way you look at it the sun is going to burn out and the earth will be reduced to a cold floating cinder. And that's the best case scenario. As the scientists who study comets and asteriods tell us, we've been awfully lucky in dodging the cosmic bullet and "it's not if, but when." As a species we have been unusually successful in developing survival stategies. I'm suggesting that this is both a conscious and unconscious process. If our conscious progress falters or is insufficient, then the unconscious will find ways to kick it up a notch. Who knows what a Jungian-style collective unconscious is capable of? The writing is on the wall. We simply must become a space-faring civilization. We are risking it ALL if continue to keep all of our DNA eggs in one basket. As a so-called "keystone species" there is a lot more riding on our success than the survival of our own species. What could be a greater imperative with any more potential energy behind it?

Perkins speculates that paranormal phenomena like UFOs and UADs are somehow being "manifested" by us as a species to pull us off-planet. The net effect of this process is to condition us gradually to the inevitability of space travel and the possibility of extraterrestrial encounters.

The UFO mythology is pulling us into the future. The melding of popular culture, science fiction and ufology has created a new belief system which has many (if not all) of the classic elements of religion. Mutilations are the stigmata of a space-age religion. They are the "miracles" or spontaneous manifestations of faith that we need to give the belief system its dynamic transformative power.

This creative, out-of-the-box insight makes sense to me and I suspect that Perkins has identified what may turn out to be an important clue that may be a hidden-in-plain sight clue that neatly links most, if not all, paranormal phenomena together.

Traditionally, during extended flap periods, UFO and UAD reports in the valley, take a nose-dive during the June-July summer months. At the start of August, 1993, I carefully looked through my sighting-log and found only a handful of publicized reports during the summer months. The steady trickle of calls reporting helicopter activity, and my intuition, told me something was afoot.

I've Been Chasing Them For Years

August 1, 1993, 10:00 p.m., Five-miles SE of the Great Sand Dunes:

Rocky arrives from Denver and we find ourselves traveling north toward the Sand Dunes Road intersection. I see a flare just below the horizon. Rocky slows. A single bright-white light appears at the western edge of the dunes at the eastern border of the Medano Ranch. There are no roads in this sand-swept area.

"Let me roll some tape!" I call, as I quickly power up the camera and shot eight or nine seconds before we pulled over at the intersection. I scramble out of the truck and begin to set up the camera and tripod in the middle of the road. The light fizzles out.

"Damn, I was ready to start shooting again," I say. We both stand there to see if the light returns. A loud humming sound punctuates the still August night. We walk toward the side of the road in the direction of the sound. The corner utility-pole, on the line that stretches to the dunes, is vibrating so loudly, we heard it thirty-five to fifty feet away. I carefully approach the barely-visible pole. It is unquestionably vibrating. A loose insulator covering, at the top of the pole, rattles randomly but there is no transformer on it.

I put my ear against the pole and hear a complex mixture of hums, rattles, clicks, whooshings, and a deep rumbling. I ask Rocky to grab a flashlight which reveals nothing out of the ordinary, just a visibly vibrating utility-pole. I crouch near the base and listen. The sound seems louder the closer I get to the ground.

The next day I get a call from the Medano-Zapata Ranch foreman. "They were back last night!"

"What time?" I ask.

"Between 9:30 (p.m.) and 10:00 (p.m.).

"You're kidding," I say. "We saw a weird light around ten, right out on the edge of the Medano!"

"The dogs started barking pretty good around 9:30. My ranch hand called me and said they surrounded his house and lit it up real good. I could see the lights from here."

"How many were there?"

"Five of six, at least," he says, adding "I've been chasing them for years but that's the most I've ever seen at once."

The timing of our sighting was perfect, the right place at the right time. There was a good chance that we had witnessed and partially-video taped one of the mystery bigfoot-truck lights the ranch foreman had been chasing at night on his motorcycle over the past two-years.

Gary Hart, an investigator from Illinois, had previously managed to record an SLV vibrating utility pole with sophisticated recording equipment. The electric company suggested that it was simply the wind vibrating the wires but, as in my own experiences, Gary's recording suggests a much more complex phenomenon.

August 5, 1993, 8:30 a.m., the Baca:
Brisa slithers down the stairs and I say, "Good morning," although I hardly look up from my work.

"Did you see the helicopters outside last night?" she asks.

"What helicopters?" She has my full attention.

"The quiet ones that were outside my window."

"What are you talking about, sweety?" Isadora asks.

"I got up to go to the bathroom, around two or three o'clock, and on my way back to bed, I noticed a beam of light outside. It was going from one helicopter to the other. They were right over the tree, right outside. I never would have seen them if I hadn't noticed the red light. I pinched myself to make sure I was awake, even!"

We ask her what else she noticed, and she tells us that the tree underneath the craft was swirling around. She didn't remember going back to sleep. Brisa, is a bright, well-adjusted child, not at all prone to flights of fantasy. I observe her earnest body language and listen her account.

Later on that day, Perkins phones. He has just got off the phone with a rancher who had found a "mutilated bull under a power line, on the other side of Medano Pass, the day before. The rancher had noticed a dark, military-style chopper making low-level passes over the rented pasture and later discovered the slain animal. My hunch was right. There appeared to be a surge of rare, mid-summer activity underway.

August 14, 1993, the Baca:

The second week of August was quiet, with no reported activity. I received a call from Sherry Adamiak, head of the Center for the Study of Extraterrestrial Intelligence's (CSETI) Rapid Mobilization Team (RMIT) called to introduce herself. She had heard about our on-going activity from Jim Nelson, head of Colorado Mutual UFO Network (MUFON) who suggested she "give Christopher a call."

Sherry, a paralegal, was interested in driving down to the valley with three other CSETI members to do some "vectoring" (The CSETI system for calling in crafts using an elaborate attraction system utilizing powerful spotlights, "coherent thought sequencing" and amplified sounds that had been recorded in an English crop-circle formation. She spoke about attempts to attract a UFO, climbing aboard, and establishing "contact." Sure, I had nothing better going on.

Evidently, each CSETI team member has a specific role in their "protocols." They have step-by-step instructions from Steven Greer (head and founder of CESETI] of what to do, in case a ship lands and they interact with an extraterrestrial intelligence. I told them I'd be happy to meet with them, and take them to a good skywatching location.

They arrived and we set off toward the switch backing Radio Tower Road, and ascended the side of the Blanca Massif. The weather was perfect for a skywatching exercise. I showed them the basic airline routes and bid them "Good hunting."

The following day, they arrived back at the Baca. Sherry was pretty nonchalant about their sighting. "We saw an amber light appear right over town (Crestone) at about 3:30-4:00 (a.m.). Then two smaller white lights came on, one just to the east and one to the west. They didn't stay on very long. We all watched the larger amber light hover for quite a while before it finally went out." CSETI would make several trips back to the valley, organize a local CSETI group, conduct trainings, and "vector" out into the infinite sky.

The Shadow Visitors

August 18, 1993, 1:00 a.m., Baca Chalets:
A strange howling sound filled the house high up in the Chalets. Hetty, a visiting Englishwoman sat bolt-upright in the bed. No one else was in the large house but the owner's dog. She peered through the darkened room at the German shepherd who was mournfully howling out the window.

"What's this? Shhh," she told the dog. The dog appeared to be reacting to something outside. Hetty left her bed and looked out the window facing the mountains that loomed three-miles away.

Two "red orbs" hung motionlessly below the tops of the Sangres. Suddenly, as if on cue, they both "moved sideways, really fast," and sailed out of sight, down the range to the southeast. She mentioned the incident to a local, who told me of her experience the following week.

August 19, 11:00 p.m., the Baca:
Isadora and I had just climbed into bed. The cool breeze of the late-August night oozes under the slightly open window. Fall arrives early in these here hills. As I reached up to turn out the light, I noticed faint movements streaming into the room through the wall from the outside. Blinking several times, I checked if I was somehow seeing things. I wasn't. Whatever it is, it had entered our bedroom and stopped at the foot of our bed. My eyes grew accustomed to the dark.

I blurted out, "Honey, do you see that?"

"What?"

"I swear something just came in the room, and now it's standing at the foot of the bed!" The only way I could describe what I was seeing is like reflections bouncing off shadows, like a faint, localized shimmering, or rippling of energy hanging in the dark.

211

"Its moving. . . it's coming around to your side."

"I don't see a thing," Isadora answered, sitting up in bed.

"It's really faint, but it's definitely there!" I said slowly, carefully watching the faint shimmer in the dark. I had never observed this type of phenomenon before. I looked around to see if an external light source was somehow reflecting into the room. I couldn't locate any light that could account for this effect I perceived in the room.

"I don't feel anything from it," I said. "It feels kind of... neutral."

I lay there for several minutes just observing, running through my mind various possible mundane explanations to rationalize the visual oddity I was sure I was perceiving. At one point it felt like whatever-it-was came up to my side of the bed and bent over right in my face which then began to tingle. This was too weird! I don't remember how long I lay there observing this phenomenon, but finally, I fell into a deep sleep.

August 19, 1993, 12:45 to 1:00 am

About two hours later the widow of a famous author fluffed her pillow and settled into bed. Her house sat a couple hundred feet away from our house, it's the next house up the hill. She hadn't been able to sleep and had watched some late-night TV. As she turned out the light, she heard a noise coming from the kitchen. Several neighbors had reported bears rummaging through garbage cans lately and she worried that a bruin feast is in progress. She called out, "Who's there?" but there was no reply. The kitchen was intact but she still felt a little spooked.

A few seconds after the light went out, just as her eyes were getting accustomed to the dark, ". . . thru the wall, ten or twelve creatures, about three-and-a-half to four feet tall" glided into the room in a "tight group," less than three feet from where she lay.

"When they were coming in, I could see right through them," she related later. "They looked like the color of water. As they got into the room, they became solid and I couldn't see through them." They clustered around the foot of her bed, looking at her.

"At first, I wasn't afraid. They were cold. They seemed completely indifferent, well, maybe a little curious. It was hard to tell. . . they were small and slight and had huge almond-eyes."

Sleeping next to her in a trundle bed was her five-year old son, Charlie. Charlie had been waking up occasionally over the past year, telling his mother about the "earth shaking." She had made notes of his comments and was surprised to find that he was apparently "predicting earthquakes." She hadn't told many people about her son's apparent abilities; she wanted to make sure she wasn't just

212

attaching significance to her small boy's curious pronouncements. Several more times his predictions proved correct. Each time he would mention these dreams, she told me, "Sure enough, I'd read about a large earthquake somewhere." Well, earthquakes happen every day, but I can agree that little Charlie appeared to be a gifted child.

She suddenly thought of Charlie and became afraid. She remembered thinking, 'They're here because of him!' She "banished them," forcefully stating, "If you're not of the light, leave, and don't come back." They silently glided out through the wall, the way they came in.

The woman claimed she had no interest in UFOs, never read any books nor saw movies about them. For a couple of days she had fought the urge to tell anyone about her shared experience but finally confided in a friend, who urged her to contact me. Three weeks later, my next door neighbor and I sat down to talk.. She had written down the night and time of her experience but, at this point, I was unaware that her experience coincided with mine. I remember the shiver up my spine when I checked at my calendar and realized the timing.

The revelation that my neighbor's and my experiences were minutes apart completely convinced me that something very strange was going on around me, and somehow I was right in the middle of a perplexing, unfolding process of manifestation. It was around this late summer 1993 time-period that I began to have a suspicion that the demarcation line between the observer, and what is being observed, had become blurred and I would need to re-double my efforts to document this process as carefully as possible.

September, 1993 arrived. I figured after six-months of intense excitement, the SLV was in for an active Fall. Nothing. Abruptly, no activity worthy of note was reported to me for over five weeks. I devoted this off-time whipping my musical self and the band into shape and continuing my research into the valley. During this early Fall period, I began fielding dozens of requests from around the country for information about our region's activity. These requests slowly began to overwhelm my time and my energy. I found myself writing a generic form-letter, listing the various reports, then just typing in the person's name.

This helped, but it didn't provide a very viable format. I began to kick around the idea of a time-line, formatted newsletter, documenting my on-going investigation. I figured, if I could write down all the information in one place, I could publish it, charge folks a nominal fee, to cover printing and postage, and send it out bimonthly. The *Mysterious Valley Report*, for over two years, had

213

reached investigators the world over.

October 14, 10:40 p.m., the Baca Chalets:
As is my usual custom after the late local news, I usually step outside to light a cigarette and take a few minutes to look around. This night found me preparing for the next day's trip to Boulder, to conduct a short seminar for the Colorado MUFON organization pertaining to my investigations.

As I stood outside the door, marveling at the still, partly cloudy sky, a large white, oblong blob of light slowly curved silently overhead, headed south. As it disappeared behind the trees, it left a ghost-image behind that slowly faded. I estimated its visible duration at about 3 or 4 seconds. The blob of light looked like a giant glowing kidney-bean. The curved-shape mirrored the curve of its flight through the air. I had just seen another "cheap firework." It looked like it was less than a-half-a-mile away.

These puzzling orbs of light still baffle me to this day. Some have a liquid appearance as they undulate like a blob of water flying through the air in slow motion. At various times I've seen them under complete uniform cloud cover, light up the tops of trees, make right angle turns and hover. They give me the impression of balls of plasma, in all variety of sizes and colors.

The Quickening

August 15, 1993, Boulder, CO:
I was looking forward to meeting State Director, Jim Nelson, second in command, Ken Spencer, and several other MUFON members to whom I'd spoken over the past few months. They seemed genuinely excited to have me come and address one of their monthly MUFON meetings, and finally, we were able to work out a good afternoon for me to travel up to Boulder.

My first out-of-town talk was underway. The video camera across the room did nothing to alleviate my nervousness. I calmly introduced myself and gave the thirty or so attendees a brief personal background. Then I asked the audience:

"Why are we all in this room right now? There's something going on. I think everybody who has an interest in this subject-matter has a gut feeling that there's something going on in the world. There probably always has been. We seem to be witnessing a quickening. We have more and more activity worldwide, and researchers, who really keep their fingers on the pulse of 'what's going on' in the paranormal, I think, would all agree that we're seeing a flowering of activity right now, and we have been for the past year." The rest of the hour-and-a-half was spent relating the results of my investigation and research.

I was pleased with the ease in which I accessed my data. I had a feeling that this would not be the last public lecture I would give concerning my investigation into the mysterious valley.

In the thirteen years since that first invitation to speak to groups about my San Luis Valley investigation and research, I have traveled all over the country offering my insight and data to thousands of people. Since my call to the Rocky Mountain News, early on in my investigation, I have never once made a call to the media or to any organization to promote myself or my work. I have chosen the less lucrative path of allowing the "work" to speak for itself and if people hear about me and my efforts and want me to speak or appear in a TV segment, fine, but I somehow felt it was important NOT to promote myself.

The following three nights, lights were reported over the Baca Ranch by multiple witnesses. These lights were described as "rapidly blinking dots of white light," similar to reports that surfaced the previous December. No one I interviewed was able to positively identify them and two sighting reports awaited us on the answering machine when we returned from Boulder. Those same three nights, strange glowing lights were reported one hundred miles east, just south of La Junta, CO, out on the Front Range. Jacob Magdelano, Brisa's father, had heard about these La Junta sightings from his sister, who had witnessed the unexplained lights. The timing and descriptions of the concurrent reports, as usual, were too coincidental.

October 31, 1993, Halloween, 6:00 p.m., the Baca:
Dusk was gathering over the valley and Arnette Cookerly was talking long-distance with her daughter. Arnette and her husband Jack had moved to the Baca the previous summer and bought a house way out in the Grants with a breathtaking view of the Sangres. Arnette had sold her advertising company, and Jack, a world-class composer and inventor, had moved his sound recording studio to their new house.

Jack played on many of the golden-age of television series including: The Twilight Zone, The Untouchables, (the original) Star Trek and The Fugitive. His list of television and movie soundtrack credits is endless, over six hundred in all.

Arnette claims her daughter's voice on the line slowly faded, as Poet, their dog began barking furiously at the sky. Half-mile away, their neighbor's two dogs also barked and whined at the sky. Jack stepped outside to see what all the ruckus was about but saw nothing.

The next day, Poet fell "sick and lethargic." Jack called his

215

neighbor to see if they had seen or heard anything that previous evening, which they hadn't. He mentioned Poet's unusual behavior and found his neighbors dogs suffered the same symptoms after barking madly "around dusk." He called me to report the the incident later that afternoon.

November 3, 1993, Libre, Huerfano County:
Tom Adams, Gary Massey, and David Perkins had organized a meeting of ufologists and investigators in 1987 and dubbed it "Crestone I." Adams had wanted to conduct "Crestone II" for several years. Notables like Linda Moulton Howe, John Lear and screenwriter Tracy Tormé had attended the first three-day confab, and all in attendance agreed that future meetings should be organized. This was where John Lear first revealed his now infamous "Lear Hypothesis." Several years went by, then low and behold! They heard that someone at the Baca was willing to investigate the SLV's strange activity, which gave them the perfect impetus for a second Crestone conference.

Tom had kicked the idea around with me that previous summer and had suggested the first week of November. His hope was that our activity would provide the attendees with a well-timed flurry of activity.

Two days before "Crestone II," Brendon and I drove around the Sangres to meet Adams and Massey at Perkins' house at Libre, high on the side of Greenhorn Mountain. I was eager to meet Tom before the conference. I had talked with Tom for hours on the phone but now we would meet. I had already met Gary and David, that previous June during Gary's trip to the Libre Anniversary party.

Over the course of the next night and the following day we tossed around many questions concerning UADs and UFOs. The lively arguments rose and fell in intensity, with Perkins baiting Massey with zingers well-honed over the many years of repartee between the two.

Adams, a usually quiet man with dark hair and medium build, occupied a strategic corner and provided detailed information upon request, to bolster everyone's arguments. His computer-like memory amazed me. Very few people, incidents or details escaped his steel-trap mind and recall ability. The evening ended with a rousing dice-game named "Farkle." I was cajoled into participating, much to their misfortune.

This weekend was instrumental in my development as an investigative team player. I felt acknowledged and appreciated by these veterans of the field and this inspired me to really dig and probe into the true nature of the phenomena being reported. I

216

remember the realization that it is only by a concerted team effort that these secrets would ever be revealed and I felt ready to do my small part.

November 4 through 7, 1993 the Baca Grande Townhouses:
"Crestone II" was on. What had started out to be an "invitation only affair" had blossomed into a full-blown conference. Tom had asked all invites to keep word of the conference "low-key." Of course, word of an event like this has a way of leaking, and the week before the conference I received several inquiring calls.

A whole contingent from New Mexico MUFON attended including: Gail Staehlin, and Debbie Stark. They arrived early and eager. The Denver contingent of John and Barbara Altshuler, Kalani and Katuiska Hanohano, and Candice Powers arrived shortly after. Hollywood screenwriter and producer, Tracy Tormé and a friend, Marc Friedlander, flew in, arrived at the conference and tossed around a football outside. Steven Greer and Sherry Adamiak brought a no-nonsense contingent of CSETI members. Other attendees included, from Dallas, The *Eclectic Viewpoint's* (magazine) Cheyenne Turner, and researcher Bill LaParl from Hopkington, MA.

Linda Moulton Howe had been invited but was unable to attend. Author and abductee Travis Walton had also wanted to attend but at the last minute had to cancel. He sent along a friend to attend in his stead.

Pointed debate was to be expected from this assortment of investigators and researchers with such divergent views. I kept fairly quite and took notes with the aid of a small microcassette recorder. A recorded exchange between Greer and Tormé concerning Greer's enthusiastic claim that official disclosure of the existence of extraterrestrials to the public was imminent is memorable. As Shari grimaced Greer enthusiastically-stated "ninety days, I guarantee it, ninety days."

David Perkins' friend, videographer Tom Vail recorded Perkins' interviews with Greer, and with hematologist Dr. John Altshuler.

November 7, 1:45 a.m., Road T:
Perhaps drawn by the excitement, or the convocation of seekers, the activity continued the following evening. Three members of CSETI were leaving Crestone to head back to Denver. As they headed east and approached the first set of "S" turns, six miles west of town, someone in the back seat saw something pacing the car, off to their left. Next to them, about "thirty-five feet from the road," zipped a "twelve foot craft." They all got a glimpse of the object before it disappeared into the gloomy night. As if on

217

cue, a smaller reddish globe was also seen for an instant as they entered the "S" turn. They called me the next morning with a good description of their sighting.

The next week found my band "The Business" taking care of business and replacing one of our guitar players. On-stage antics and a bad attitude found the band in agreement, he had to go. We all knew about guitar-wiz George Oringdulph. He could play anything, country, bluegrass, metal. He had attended the Guitar Institute and could shred it up! We arranged a "live" audition, in front of a local audience at a small bar in Saguache. George showed up and dazzled everyone with his one-shot renditions of a dozen rock classics. Then, he came up with a smoking, off-the-cuff lick for one of our originals. It felt good to play with such a talented professional plus he had a good singing-voice. The band had enjoyed a brief hiatus that early Fall, mulling over who to call, but it was time for the band to get back to business.

November 17, 1993, 9:30 p.m., Moffat - Baca Ranch:
I'm traveling home from Alamosa after the first rehearsal with George. I left, elated about the new addition and I scanned the horizon and surrounding terrain for any unusual lights, as is my usual custom, driving on the twenty-five-mile straight-as-an-arrow Highway 17. As I got to the halfway mark between Hooper and Moffat, I noticed an orange-amber light out in the middle of the Baca Ranch, in an area that has no roads. I pulled over to have a look with my night vision binoculars. It appeared to be moving toward me. I estimated its distance at about five-miles away. I watched for several minutes before I watched the light move straight up in the air, maybe one-hundred feet, simultaneously as it appeared to extinguish.

Six miles up the road, Al, Donna and Alta Koon were outside with two friends for their nightly skywatch. It was a foggy night with intermittent cloud cover scudding by at low altitude. Al noticed an orange light flare, low to the ground, directly east. They watched for several minutes before the light appears to go out. A scant five minutes later, I passed by Light Reflections, their crystal shop, and noticed the Koons standing outside in the cold, looking toward the Baca Ranch. They had evidently seen the same light I had observed just minutes before. It gratifies me when I have sighting experiences with other alert witnesses who are willing to go on-the-record.

November 18, 1:00 a.m., the Baca Chalet II:
Healer, Kimmy Martin, awoke with a start. She looked into the gloomy night outside her window and wondered why it felt

218

like someone was watching her. Something moved on the porch outside. She reported that a "large group of grays" had peered through the window at her. She was not sure if they were physically manifest, or just on the other side in "the etheric" but she had no doubt that they were definitely out there, outside her house, watching her. She told me she hadn't felt the least bit threatened or frightened, and that she watched them "for almost an hour" while they silently watched her. Finally, wanting to go to bed, but feeling uncomfortable about her "twenty to twenty visitors," she silently told them to "go away, and let me sleep." She claimed, they trooped away obediently and a nonplused Kimmy rolled over and went to sleep.

Fireball

One of the more compelling types of aerial phenomena reported in the Southwestern United States involve objects described as "fireballs." First documented in the early nineteen-fifties, fireballs – especially the huge green variety, have been witnessed by thousands sailing over the Four-Corners region of Colorado, New Mexico and Arizona.

I suspect that these so-called fireballs may have a natural explanation. Obviously there are many misidentified "fireballs" that surely have a mundane explanation They do not appear to be celestial objects entering the atmosphere, such as a bolides or meteors. The smallest are most often bluish-white and observed close to the witness – sometimes within feet. They tend to be somewhat short-lived and sometimes, if descending steeply, leave a faint smoke trail. The medium-sized versions are orangish and are most often seen within ten-miles from the witness. Often these types move in a smooth, steady trajectory, although somewhat smaller versions are an intense ruby-red color; are seen within two-miles of the witness and tend to move quickly with purpose. The largest fireballs are most often a majestic roiling green color and are usually seen a considerable distance away from the observer traveling in a straight trajectory.

I again stress; these are not mundane celestial objects. I have seen examples of all these types and I am convinced they constitute versions of as-yet undefined phenomena. After dozens of personal sightings of "cheap fireworks," and a few of the larger versions, I contend that this is a fruitful area of investigation and research by earth-scientists interested in as-yet undefined phenomena.

November 30, 1993, 6:07 p.m., the Baca Grants:
Composer Jack Cookerly, a trained observer who was a naval

aviation navigator in the late-forties, arrived home in the Baca Grants and had just stepped out of his Blazer when he realized that he was casting a shadow on his driveway.

"It was bright-white as it streaked [east-to-west] for three of so seconds, directly over my head, and I instantly thought it was a meteor. But as it approached the horizon, it flared up about ten times its original size, turned into an oval shape and stopped. It was HUGE!" Then to Cookerly's amazement, "It changed from its original white color to a bluish -white and started to descend slowly like a parachute flare, for five or so seconds. I looked for an object like a parachute above the oval, but I didn't see anything."

Unlike a parachute flare which fizzles out, Cookerly observed the object instantly disappear. "It couldn't have been a meteor because, whatever it was, it made a ninety-degree, right-angled turn, and changed its color, shape, size and velocity."

I asked him how far away the object appeared to be. Cookerly stated, "I'm absolutely sure it came down in the valley. I thought I could run right out and find it. It seemed so close that I actually waited for an explosion to blow me off my feet!" Cookerly ran inside the house and immediately called to inform me of the incredible celestial sight he had just witnessed. He wasn't the only one who witnessed the sky-borne phenomenon.

The same night, 6:07 p.m., Moffat, CO:

Al Koon, also a trained ex-military observer, was sitting with his family in their living room with its panoramic view to the south and west, seven miles west of Cookerly. The Al Koon described what they saw.

"It was a little bigger than a full-moon and visible below the horizon before it blinked out." Al, along with his wife, Donna, and daughter Alta, was convinced that what they saw was not a meteor. "It appeared to break apart into several pieces just before it blinked out."

Three other locals also reported the object's arrival into the SLV. It streaked in from the northeast "through the clouds," directly over the development, and appeared to descend on the western side of the valley. Fort Garland residents, forty miles to the southeast, also reported seeing the object, as was reported in the following day's Pueblo Chieftain.

After some digging, I found that SLV residents weren't the only folks who saw something strange flash through the darkening sky on November 30, 1993. Something evidently flew along the border between New Mexico and Colorado. Bill Papich, of the Farmington, NM, *Daily Times* wrote on Thursday, December 2, 1993:

A bright light seen Tuesday evening in skies over San Juan County remains a mystery, although a federal agency says it probably wasn't space debris.

The light was reported by numerous people who saw it streak across the sky between 6:00 and 6:30 p.m., traveling from east to west. Some strange stories about the light were being told Wednesday.

Pilots flying over the Four Corners area Tuesday evening radioed air traffic controllers in Farmington (NM) about a bright light traveling from east to west.

Sgt. John Harrison of Kirtland Air Force Base in Albuquerque (NM) said he's not aware of any Air Force operations that could have caused the light.

Professor Mark Price of the observatory at the University of New Mexico in Albuquerque said the light could have been a meteor or space debris burning up as it entered the atmosphere. "They are very bright," Price said of burning space debris.

However, the North American Air Defense Command (NORAD) in Colorado Springs, CO, had no reports of satellite debris burning up in the earth's atmosphere Tuesday evening. The agency monitors objects entering the Earth's atmosphere.

In a follow-up article Papich interviewed two witnesses of an unusual celestial object that traveled overhead, on Monday, November 29, 1993, the night before the fireball.

Rig workers who read newspaper accounts of a strange light over San Juan County Tuesday night say they saw something in the sky Monday night that may have been even stranger. "I've never seen anything like it before," said Pete Corey of Farmington. Corey said he and four other men were at a drilling rig four miles southwest of Aztec (NM) at 8:00 p.m. Monday when they all saw what appeared to be a mysterious object with lights pass overhead. "What we saw was big. That thing was low enough where you could almost see the whole body of the thing," Corey said. "To me it was square looking with four lights. There seemed to be a light on each corner of this thing. There was no sound. We couldn't hear a thing." Corey said the object drifted across the sky for fifteen to twenty seconds before it was out of sight.

Gabe Montano of Bloomfield (NM) was among the five men and said the lights didn't blink like airplane lights. He said

221

the object looked rectangular. "It was kind of gliding across the sky. It wasn't going very fast," Montano said. "It wasn't very high at all. It was right there." He said the drilling rig was one hundred and ten feet high and the object appeared to be only about four hundred feet above the top of the rig.

Several points come to mind when looking at the eyewitness accounts. First off, the fireball was seen over a very large area. The Crestone-Moffat sighting was about one hundred-thirty-five miles from Farmington, NM, the furthest point west the object was reported. Both Koon and Cookerly, ex-military trained observers, were sure the object, or a piece of it, had gone down in the San Luis Valley. If the accounts from New Mexico are accurate, the main body of the object continued on past the SLV headed southwest, passing over Del Norte and Pagosa Springs, before crossing the Colorado/New Mexico border near Arboles.

Koon's description of the aerial display breaking apart over the SLV may be significant, not to mention the synchronicity with a similar event that would occur fifty-four weeks later.

Perhaps an initial piece did fall off and descend in the SLV, while a second piece crashed to earth — just north of Cuba (NM) as during the 1993 NORAD event, which we'll cover later in the book. Both events produced witnesses that described a large flare, trailing smoke, descend toward the ground with a trajectory of north-to-southwest; and all described a phenomenon that appeared to occur in fairly close-proximity to their vantage point.

Ethel Baca, of Cuba described it as "a big firework," that apparently landed on Cuba Mesa, just to the northeast. Could this have been a second piece? One of two, or three pieces may have separated off the main body of the unidentified object and veered south, slowing as they fell. Reports of a boom indicate the main object slowed through the sound barrier near the Bloomington-Farmington area.

NORAD claimed they observed nothing unusual in the region the night of November 30th. How could they have possibly missed such an obvious event? If this had been a routine, mundane celestial object, like a meteor, wouldn't NORAD be forthcoming about the reports? One would think so as they must have seen it on their scopes as it entered the atmosphere. The sighting was noteworthy – over a dozen ground observers reported the object's arrival over a one-hundred-thirty mile corridor.

What exactly is happening over the San Luis Valley and other Hot-Spot regions? Several synchronistic elements are obviously present. I have stopped trying to prove that something high-strange occurs in the sky high above the San Luis Valley, it should be obvious by now. However, back in the day, I had started to interpret these perceived synchronistic correlations as a head's-up signal.

After researching the timing of fire-balls; especially during the fifties and sixties, I asked myself; could it be that these spectacular events "not-so-cheap fireworks" portend the onset of increased levels of unusual regional activity? At the time, I assumed that this was the case. With the onset of the activity that occurred during the ensuing two month's flurry, looking back, I think my suspicions were confirmed and, as the next night attests, I have video to prove it!

December 1, 1993, 8:45 p.m., The Baca Ranch:

Rocky had called me Tuesday night, and I related the sighting reports of the fireball earlier that evening. He immediately made plans to drive down to the valley from Denver the following day.

It was 8:30 p.m. and we were sitting in his Ford Explorer, four-miles south of Road T, out on the Baca Ranch. We both felt a sense of relaxed anticipation. Rocky had brought along his latest toys, a scanner which he had "tweaked" to extend its capability for receiving bandwidths, a new pair of third-generation night vision goggles and a video camera night vision lens. Unfortunately, the lens didn't attach properly to the camera, but we managed to make it work. It was well below zero outside his SUV, but we looked forward to any excuse to get out into the cold.

As we sat out toward the middle of the Baca ranch, one of a handful of times I've parked out there to skywatch, we listened for any unusual activity on the scanner. Then, out of no where, we both witnessed directly south — toward the Dry Lakes and Alamosa, an unusual-looking flare that fizzled out a couple of thousand feet above us, about five miles south of our location. The two of us clamored out of the truck into the minus-10-degree cold. Rocky fired up the night vision-equipped video camera, ready to capture anything we saw. I put on the goggles and looked south where the flare had vanished and immediately picked up movement. The footage of the following event has never been aired.

With the night-vision equipped camera rolling, four bright, unblinking objects approached from the southwest. Right behind them came three, possibly four more.

"That's military," I said. "Film that!" Although this may not have been an accurate assessment on my part, it was my recorded, first-impression.

Over the next fifteen-to-twenty minutes Rocky and I videotaped seven or eight lights milling around in the area to the south where a piece of the previous night's object may have landed. Several of the night-vision shots of the swarming objects are spectacular as they flew behind a large silo in the foreground. I took off the night-vision goggles at one point and was surprised that the objects we were filming (and their occasional blinking lights were totally invisible to the naked eye. How many citizens are out with light-aided technology skywatching on any given night? How many nocturnal flights are undoubtedly taking place routinely around US airspace without notice? What are they up to? We could not tell if they were helicopters with close-formation infrared strobes, although several times two or three of them reversed course and/or hovered in place. Could they have been searching for something?

At the beginning of the event, the objects appeared to head up from the south — in our direction. They traveled fairly close to our vantage point and with the wind in our faces, we didn't hear a thing; no sound of engines or props. At their closest approach, about five or six miles away, a group of the objects peeled off and headed southeast – toward Blanca Peak. Several of them stopped, reversed course and began to hover – directly south of our location. There didn't seem to be any purpose behind their flight activities. Although there did not seem to be any particular pattern to their aerial coverage of the sky above the southern Baca Ranch, at one point the area was swarming with aerial objects. At the time we assumed they were helicopters, but, I'm not so sure. Looking back at the footage – thirteen years later, there is something wrong about what we filmed. Invisible to the naked eye, we filmed eight silent aerial objects, flying in loose formation for over twenty minutes over an area where a sizeable object was seen to descend to the earth. After stopping the camera, we hustled out of the minus ten-degree SLV freezer back into Rocky's warm SUV and watched for any additional craft or objects from the south where the other objects had appeared. We were positive there would be some sort of a finale.

About 10:15 p.m., Rocky suggested that we head toward Del Norte for a closer perspective. As we were driving north to hit Road T, I put on the goggles and caught sight of a large unblinking orb that appeared from behind the mountains, north of Villa Grove. Rocky pulled off the ranch road.

"Quick, fire up the camera," I called as we got out and started filming the large, slow-moving orb. The unidentified object skimmed the tops of the mountains moving west. It appeared to go behind some peaks and in front others. Later, I would determine that it was traveling around forty miles away from us.

The object would have been invisible to anyone close enough to have observed it with their unaided vision as it was low, and just far enough into the mountains, to be invisible to a casual observer.

Only with night vision, and our proximity so far to the south, were we able to see them skimming the tops of the peaks.

Another interesting aspect of this second sighting were three smaller blinking lights which flew below and to the south of the larger, unblinking orb. It was as if they were riding interference between the object and any observers in the northern part of the valley. All four appeared to be traveling slowly, less than one-hundred miles per hour. We filmed their entire transit for about fifteen-minutes until they disappeared off to the west – toward Gunnison, Colorado.

Rocky and I gave each high-fives in the cold darkness. Yes! I had acted upon my intuitive sense that the prior night's activities indicated I should be ready for something the following night. It's one thing to "claim" sightings of unusual aerial activity, it's another to figure out the right time to whip out a video camera and document your suspicions! Over the course of the prior nine-months; hours and hours spent chasing elusive aerial phantoms, I finally wound up in the right place at the right time with the right gear. Rocky and I had captured something important on tape. Viewing the footage today, I am disinclined to believe what we captured on video were helicopters, but, quite honestly, I don't know what they were. But what we captured were real craft — we didn't invent them. Today, in 2007, this sighting event nightvision footage has yet to be broadcast.

The following night, December 2, 1993, After sunset, Antonito, Colorado: Ray and Lucy Jaramillo reported the following event to the Conejos County Sheriff's Office. Apparently the Jaramillos, along with some friends and relatives, were watching through binoculars what they described as a "large fire" on the hillside, west of Antonito. They gave the dispatcher directions which placed the fire near the (narrow gauge) Cumbres-Toltec train stop, halfway up the mountainside.

The witnesses said they had "such a good view [of the fire] they could see thirty-foot-high flames." The sheriff's office dispatched deputies and, together with four of the initial witnesses, they rushed toward the site.

They found absolutely no trace of a fire or explosion! After a couple of hours scouring the hillside, they found no evidence to back up the Jaramillo's report. The sheriff's party finally called the search off.

Now, what's wrong with this picture? Or what is right with this scenario? Three straight nights of unexplained reports along with videotape evidence of unexplained interest. Was there a connection between these supposedly unrelated events?

Secrets of the Mysterious Valley

December 5, 5:30 p.m., the Baca Grants:

I was on my way to visit Jack Cookerly, to conduct a follow interview concerning the November 30th event, the glow of sunset lighting up the western horizon, heavy clouds approaching from the east. Two lights slowly appear ed together, about five degrees apart, over the distant silhouetted mountains. I quickly pulled over to watch. They just hung there, possibly reflecting the still-setting sun. They diverged from one another, one appearing to descend westward, the other heading directly north, toward me. As it apparently collides with the Earth's shadow, the object fades into the darkening sky. I scratch my head and wonder.

OK, things began to get more perplexing. Four days later I received several reports of an inexplicable, localized boom . . . .

December 9, 12:08 p.m., the Baca Grants:

Arnette Cookerly was working at her desk when the whole house rocked, walls shook, shelves rattled. My phone rang. "Did you just hear a huge boom a few seconds ago?" Arnette asked innocently. I hadn't. "I know this may sound weird but it sounded like a cow just landed on my roof!" In the background I heard Jack's voice. Arnette asked him if he just heard the boom.

He took the phone and said "I was out in the studio and I felt a huge boom, not like a sonic-boom, but more like a huge fist hitting the ground. I didn't really hear it as much as I felt it. I did hear the garage door rattle from the shockwave, though."

A half-mile away, musician Barry Monroe and two house mates also felt the shockwave rattle the house around them. I called Barry several minutes later to check if anyone else near the Cookerly's had heard the localized shockwave. He described it in a similar fashion, "like something really big hitting the ground."

Nobody else I called in an ever-increasing circle around the apparent epicenter had heard the boom. Five people, in two houses, in a two-square mile area had experienced something huge and powerful, but what was the cause of the localized boom? This was the same area where the barking dogs fell ill a few weeks before. Was this a coincidental occurrence? Was it somehow connected to the previous three day's activities?

December 13, New Moon, 9:35 p.m., the Baca Chalets:

Rocky called from Denver and I filled him in about the activity that had taken place since he was down the prior week. He set up a time to meet me in the late morning of the following day. I kidded with him and told him that he must want to "come back down for more punishment." Rocky and I, by this time, have spent at least one-hundred, mostly uneventful, hours skywatching here since his

226

first trip to the San Luis Valley, that previous April, 1993. Our prior excursion, two-weeks earlier had proved rewarding and we were both ready for an encore.

An hour, or so later, a few friends were gathered for a weekly American exercise of Monday Night Football-style male-bonding. Several local football fans are friends of mine, and we gathered ritualistically every Monday night during football season. Yes, even in a spiritualized, New-Age community, some of the guys still watch football. I've been an avid football fan since the famous Ice-bowl game between the Dallas Cowboys and the Green Bay Packers in sixty-five.

Halfway through the first quarter, Brendon's girlfriend, Faye, called and asked for me. "What's up?" I asked.

She told me, "I just now saw a dime-sized glowing white orb fall *into* the ground south of the Baca. It was three or so stories off the ground when I first saw it and when it disappeared it was like it went underground this side of Hooper."

I cover the phone and told the guys about Faye's sighting. Dr. John Short chimed in, "Earlier, right around sunset while I was on the phone, I saw a streak outside and the phone faded out for a couple of seconds . . ."

I thanked Faye for the report and we started talking about the "cheap fireworks." We only forgot the game momentarily, but I remembered the fireball and the next night's aerial footage we obtained two-weeks prior. Rocky arrived the following morning.

The following morning, December 14th at 7:00 a.m., The Vigil Ranch, Chama Canyon, Costilla County:

It had been a bitterly cold night. A sharp wind had cut through Chama Canyon, gusting down from the Sangres just a mile east of Clarence and Dale Vigil's secluded ranch. A snowstorm had dumped two inches two days earlier.

According to both brothers their prize Limousine seed-bull had appeared healthy and normal the day before. When Dale went out for his routine check of the herd, he felt uneasy. He drove around the frozen pasture, and looked for the bull where they had last seen him, off by himself. Nothing. Vigil climbed into his pickup and drove back to the house to get help to locate the bull. Clarence and his young son accompanied Dale back out to the snow-covered pasture to look.

"There he is," Clarence's son called out. They looked toward a row of scrub willow, and sure enough, there was their bull. The red-colored animal lay on his left side and they could see a faint trace of steam rising from the carcass in the frigid air. They climbed out of the truck to check him. He had been "mutilated." The animal's rear-end had been cut out and his genitalia was removed. Both

227

brothers were angry as they carefully examined the area around the animal looking for signs of predators. This was getting out of hand. They couldn't find a single track.

"Over here," Dale, examined the scrub willow bushes twenty feet to the east of the animal, and called out to his brother. They looked at the branches carefully. Small clumps of red hair adorned the tips of branches that looked like they'd been bent over and snapped off. One clump of hair even had a small drop of blood on it.

I received a worried call from Dale that morning. "I had another one," he told me. "I can't take this! I'm going to sell my herd, I can't afford this!" He asked me to make the long trip down to his Costilla ranch to help investigate the animal death.

Perfect timing, as luck would have it, Rocky was due to arrive momentarily, so I gathered up my field investigation equipment for the trip to Costilla . Rocky arrived and quickly agreed that we should go. We were both quiet, lost in our thoughts as we headed south.

We arrived at the Vigil's and headed out into the frozen pasture. The brothers were gathered around the dead bull.

"Thanks for coming down, you just missed the vet," [Ben Kanoshi] Dale told me as we unloaded the video camera and my doctor's bag of gear. The veterinarian had done a necropsy on the animal and found that the bull's lungs were riddled with pneumonia. The animal had been laid open during the necropsy, and his examination determined that the animal had died of pneumonia and scavengers had inflicted the suspicious wounds.

The Vigil brothers were pretty confused by the vet's findings. "The vet said he died of pneumonia but I don't know about that," Dale said. "He seemed to be perfectly healthy, he didn't appear sick at all. We looked everywhere for predator tracks but there aren't any." He then led me over to the scrub willow thicket, just a few feet to the east of the animal. "Look at this." He pointed to the broken branches with bits of red hair sticking to the tips. "It looks like they crashed him into the bushes here," he concluded.

I examined the six-foot high branches. There are clumps of red hair, the exact shade of the bull's hair. "I didn't know cattle could high jump," I said, trying to lighten up the distraught brothers who shook their heads and muttered in Spanish.

We returned to the bull. I studied the immediate area. The animal lay under overhanging scrub willow branches, and about six feet above the carcass, the tips of the branches had also been broken off. I bent one downward to snap it off. Freshly broken branch tips littered the ground below it. "These branches were broken-off too, and it really looks like they were broken off from above, in a downwards motion," I told the Vigils. It looks to me as if the animal had been dropped. I suggested, "I'll bet they tried to sling him in under the branches and missed on their first try. They must have snapped off the branches when they initially tried to drop him."

We began taping. I noticed Vigil's dogs stayed twenty-or so feet from the carcass. They seemed wary and hesitant to venture close.

I sent forensic samples to Dr. John Altshuler in Denver. He reported to me a couple of weeks later, "Evidence of high-heat was found around the incision areas."

December 29, 1993 10:10 p.m., Moffat:

As was my usual routine, I was traveling north after rehearsal on Highway 17 during my sixty-mile commute. We had realigned the band, adding a new drummer to replace my drummer of the past three years and added a new name. Laffing Buddha was now the moniker, and the addition of new blood found us writing original songs, rehearsing two-days per week, and honing our stage skills. My weekly routine found me traveling one-hundred plus miles round trip to rehearsal, twice — sometime three times per week for the next three years.

As I headed north and approached Moffat, I noticed a bluish-green light appear directly north over the Alfred Weiss Ranch in town. I quickly grabbed the camcorder from the seat beside me and attempted to focus on the light. It blinked off. I took stock of what I'd just seen. The light had appeared to be less than four miles away and hovering around one-hundred feet above the ground. I slowed the truck and put the camcorder down.

Flash! As soon as I let go of the camcorder — there it was again. But it had moved west about a mile. Again, I fumbled with the camera and managed to get two, or three seconds of footage before it went out for a second time. I slowly made the turn onto Road T scanning the pasture for the evasive light.

The following morning, Brendon mentioned seeing a Bell jet-ranger flying low up Burnt Gulch at around 2:30 p.m. the day before. He thought he would mention it because, "It sounded strange, like a jet airplane."

Bigfoot

Late December—Early January, 1993, the New Mexico-Colorado Border:

During a seven-day period, from the last week of December, into the first week of January, the equation became more complicated when seven "Bigfoot" encounters were reported to local authorities in Costilla County. The encounters were all reported within a seven-mile area – along the CO/NM border, south into New Mexico. Because of the locals reluctance to go on record, I've not pinpointed the exact location of these events. These locals seem very protective of the occasionally seen "Bigfoot," not to mention their own privacy. The following events were related to me by a undersheriff Joe Taylor, Jr., who is now the current Conejos County Sheriff.

Several days before, a niece of Joe Taylor, Sr., called to tell him that "she had found some tracks that he'd better come look at." She described them as being huge, human-looking, barefoot tracks. Not taking it too seriously, both he and his son didn't immediately investigate. On the morning of December 31st, the Taylors followed up on her call and went out to the remote location with a video camera to document the scene. They wished they had gone out the day she called, for what she showed them was incredible.

Out in the middle of nowhere, descending for hundreds of yards down a cow trail toward the stream bed were two sets of human-looking tracks. One measured twenty-inches, the other 18 inches long. They were documented traveling downhill over a variety of terrain: rocks, snow and bare ground. To the two veteran outdoorsmen, they were unmistakably human and impressive to behold. One of the larger prints was so pristine that I was told "you could see toe-nail marks!" I have seen the footage of these tracks, visited the site and there is no mistaking the classic evidence of Bigfoot tracks. Shaquile O'Neal would be the smaller one's baby brother. Shaq has a size twenty foot, the smaller of the two tracks were a size thirty-five to 40!

The woman, an avid amateur photographer, also related a strange story worthy of note. On the eve of discovering the tracks, she had heard her trained guard dog bark furiously. She went out to see what he was barking at, seeing nothing, she went back inside. A short time later, she heard huge "footsteps go running by the house." Going back outside, she found her dog cowering inside the fenced yard. The dog had been locked outside of the yard. Puzzled, she put him back outside the fence, thinking this a bit strange. A short time later, he started barking again, and once more she heard the huge running footsteps running outside the house and "a twang of something hitting the barb wire fence." She went back outside and found her dog shaking. Again, inside the fence! She was very confused having just put the dog outside of the fence.

The following morning, while stalking a herd of deer to take photos, she happened to stumble on the giant barefoot tracks. She called her uncle to report the possible encounter and the tracks.

Taylor related several other recent reports to me the following week: One report found a mother and son driving back from the mountains just after sunset. As they rounded a curve, their headlights revealed a creature covered in hair with large glowing eyes and pointed ears in the middle of the road. The mother slammed on her brakes. Not knowing what to do, the thing was blocking their way, she put the car in reverse and backed up. This evidently scared the thing, for "it dropped down on all fours and ran away like a dog!"

They proceeded directly to the sheriff's office to report what they had seen. "They were real upset about it," he told me. Their insistence impressed the authorities enough for them to mount a search for the creature. They combed the hills but found no sign of the it.

One interesting correlation to the above, during this same two-day period, a Washington State man reported seeing a Bigfoot with large pointed ears and wings near Mount Rainer. What's up with this? How could an observant researcher ignore such a blatant correlation?

Two additional reports were subsequently filed by motorists who had spotted large hairy humanoid creatures, at night, next to the highway. One report was made by a trucker who claimed the one he saw was "all white."

Yet another event featured a man who claimed he witnessed a pair of Bigfoot "stalking a herd of elk" on the side of San Antonio mountain. He was close enough to see them "signaling to each other" while watching them through his binoculars.

I had heard about alleged Bigfoot sightings during my research of the SLV but could find no hard evidence in the form of names of witnesses, dates, locations, etc., so I had naturally figured that these few "legendary" sightings were nothing more than local folklore. As a result of these Conejos reports, I have learned that these creatures have been historically sighted in several valley locations and I began to research. What I discovered confirmed my suspicions,

When the Independence Mine first began operations around the turn-of-the-century, seven miles south of Crestone, large human-looking footprints were said to have been found by area miners near the entrance. A lifelong valley resident and local tracker was told by his grandfather that he had seen a Bigfoot one night in the late 1920s. According to the tracker, the locals had named the elusive creature "Boji." Sightings of this ilk have appeared to be rare in the southern Rocky Mountains but the hesitance of locals to come forward, during our recent flurry of encounters, illustrates why it may be so difficult to investigate.

A New Mexico Cattle Inspector who lives in Rancho de Taos, NM, told me he watched with binoculars, "a white Bigfoot" clamor up a rocky slope during the late fall of 1993. It ascended the seemingly-impossible slope in minutes. He became impressed with the creature's agility when he tried to make the same climb the following day. It took him over two hours.

December 30, 1993, The Valley *Courier* Office, Alamosa:
I called the *Courier* to see if they would allow me to again peruse their newspaper morgue of back issues. They said it would not be a problem, "Come on in."

I arrived and introduced myself to Ruth Heide, the reporter who had written the "mutilation" story in November, 1992, concerning the Manuel Sanchez's unusual livestock death case. I had talked to Ruth over the phone a couple of times but had never actually met her. She seemed very interested in my research and investigation and asked if she could "interview me, and take some notes." I agreed, so we spent an hour going over some of the stranger cases that had been reported in the area. She seemed fascinated with the amount of information I had managed to compile concerning these unexplained events. Most of these reports were news to her and, as I later found out, the subject was not well received by her boss, Keith Cerny. I whipped through back issues, looking for additional stories to bolster some of the more vaporous cases I was interested in while she snapped some photographs of me at work.

The following day, Ruth's article appeared as the main front page story! I assumed that she would write a story, but not the front page story. Oh boy, I was stopped by complete strangers who wanted to comment on what they had read, I received time-wasting phone-calls that started to show me I was becoming part of the story and that I was possibly getting in the way of my investigation. Since this article, many stories have appeared in local, regional and state publications concerning my efforts.

As I've said, I have never made a single call to the press to promote myself, or my investigation since my experience with the *Rocky Mountain News* stringer in January 1993. Somehow, the press invariably finds me when things are popping around here and to date, I have appeared in over twenty television and film segments covering the region's unusual activity. This high-visibility factor would prove highly cumbersome to the my investigative efforts in the late nineties.

Because of the local, regional and national articles covering my investigative efforts; and the many television show appearances, I gained a weird sort of celebrity status around the valley. At first it was flattering, but became cumbersome in that I had to deal with complete strangers who stopped me, called me, showed up at the house to pick my brain, or relate some unusual experience that "grandpa told us about."

Other people simply averted their gaze when I approached. There is a fine line between getting enough exposure to let people know you're there on the case, and too much coverage that clutters the investigative environment. Not to mention the inevitable perception by some skeptics, oh *that* guy – he must be nuts!

Two years had passed since that fateful New Year's Eve party when Baca witnesses described their peculiar experiences. Since that fateful evening, time had somehow elongated and my life re-defined 'high-gear.' Every moment seemed important. I had managed to conduct a real-time investigation into dozens of reports of the unusual and yet I was also able to bring myself up-to-speed concerning the vast historical record of ufological events and data. I'd come a long way since that night when I began my amateur investigation. By 1994, and with a lot of help, I'd managed to compile an impressive collection of legends, reports, stories, photos-videos and my own personal experiences of the high-strange, yet I was no closer to figuring out what was going on than when I began. In some respects, it felt like I was traveling further away from clarity and understanding.

It is inconceivable to even contemplate the process a single individual would have to undergo to effectively analyze the proverbial mountains of data that has been accumulated by ufo investigators and researchers since 1947. My intentions have never been to solve mankind's last remaining mysteries but rather put forth simple intuitive insights garnered in a pristine investigative environment — based on my own experiences, for others to interpret. In true Thoreauean-style, I contend that the San Luis Valley is a microcosm of an as-yet undefined macrocosmic whole. For what that is worth. Think about it; document a small part of the micro and you may have a glimpse of the whole. This approach may be too ahead of its time, or I might just be crazy, as this road of inquiry is fraught with major obstacles and conundrums.

Because the ufological database is not yet standardized, there are no steadfast, adhered-to systems of classification. As a result, the mind reels from the kaleidoscopic effect of dealing with misinformation from possibly unreliable sources. My microcosmic approach decreases, but does not eliminate having to question everything

As I've stated, I feel that the individual and his or her perception of an unusual experience, may be as important as the actual experiences themselves. Taken as a whole, these perceptions melt into a cauldron of mythos and although they may retain elements of their original character, they invariably become part of the greater, mythological whole. This fact is impossible to ignore and may be a crucial factor when attempting to examine the true nature of the phenomena.

January 5, 1994, 5:30 a.m., Highway 160, Alamosa County:
Yet another impressive fireball descended through the clouds and dazzled witnesses in the San Luis Valley. How many witnesses? We will never know. However, the LaBord's were headed out of the valley for a day trip, headed east on 160, about ten-miles outside of Alamosa, when the sleepy foursome witnessed a spectacular "large, green fireball" descend straight down into the Blanca Massif. (The Indians, viewing similar phenomena since ancient times, regarded these celestial phenomena as portents. I can identify with this attributional thinking.) I think back fondly in appreciation on their report. They were convinced that their sighting was not of the usual mundane celestial variety. "It was really big," Pam told me later. Evidently, Roger, Pam, and their two daughters, Angela and Jennifer, all got a good look at the display. I asked Angela how long the green-colored object was visible. She estimated the duration of the sighting at "about three seconds." Pam agreed, "We saw it for about two to three seconds." Jennifer said it looked like "a big green golf ball." I love the glowing golf ball description!

January 7, 6:45 p.m., Highway 17, south of Moffat:
One of my "skeptics," the former guitar player of The Business, Scott Olson (at the time, the music teacher at Moffat School), called excitedly from Hooper. "I just had a sighting. I don't know what it was, but I just saw something." He exclaimed on the phone in a rather low-key but breathless voice. "Sighting of what?" I asked.

"It looked like a swarm of bees. They were all lit up."

"Bees? What do you mean, bees? How many of them were there?" I asked, enjoying that one of my "skeptics" had obviously seen something unusual and wasn't too afraid to report it.

"It was a large, tight formation. There were oh, maybe twenty-five or thirty lights. They were all blinking rapidly . . . but at random."

"What color were they?"

"White."

"Which way were they going?"

"They were coming from the Dunes. From the east — headed west, I saw them right at the sand piles (seven miles south of Moffat, on Highway 17). He paused. Has anyone ever reported seeing something like this?" I was reminded of Berle's "old-time switchboard" sighting from his cabin porch.

"Well, I figured you'd want to know about it, so raced down to Hooper and called you right away so maybe you could spot them. I've got to get down to Alamosa, so I've got to go. You know, I never thought I'd ever see something so out-of-the-ordinary."

I thanked Oly for calling me right away, grabbed my night vision binoculars and raced up to the porch. I scanned the far side of the valley – toward Highway 17 for fifteen minutes and, seeing nothing, retreated inside from the frigid night.

Our unusual activity had hit high gear and everyone wanted to get involved. Get a little publicity, people start really looking, and presto! If things are truly occurring, you'll get more reports than you could possibly investigate.

Chasing down another report 1996

Chopper-born magnetometer survey, Baca Grande 1993

With Tim Good and Brendon before flying w/ John Altshuler

Donna, Al and Alta Koon, Mofatt, CO

Are you ready to rock? Laffing Buddha 1994

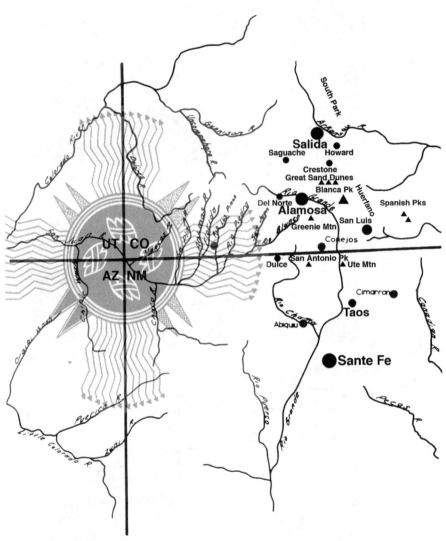

Key Locations in the Greater San Luis Valley

PRINCIPAL RIVERS OF THE AREAS

CHAPTER EIGHT:
Into High-Gear

One of 1994's most important, albeit dark-horse UFO events occurred in the SLV on January 12th. Exactly eleven years before an eerily similar sequence happened in Northern New Mexico. Both unexplained series of events feature green fireballs, mysterious fires, unexplained explosions and unusual attendant military activity. Obviously, no two Ufological events are exactly alike but the parallels between these two cases are striking and the possible big-picture connection may be crucially important to our microcosmic examination of the "mysterious valley."

The following is a detailed look ay the San Luis Valley's NORAD Event of January 12, 1994, and New Mexico's Gallup Incident, January 12, 1983. I've mentioned the uncanny parallel between the November 30, 1993 fireball reports with an event that occurred fifteen months later, as you will see, for good reason!

The most comprehensive look at 1983's Gallup Incident can be found in the *Project Stigma* publication, *Pardon the Intrusion* or *UFOs Over, On & Under (?) The State of New Mexico*, written and compiled by Tom Adams in 1992. Adams had immediately noticed the similarity between the two events after a phone call I made to inform him of the NORAD Event. The following are excerpts from Tom's publication.

The Gallup Incident:

The Farmington, New Mexico *Daily Times* article on January 13, 1983 headlined: "Goodness Gracious - Great Ball of Fire." Written by reporter Rex Graham it stated;

What investigators believe was a meteor smashed into the side of a mountain about fifteen miles east of Gallup Wednesday night about 5:50 p.m., starting a fire and causing a deluge of calls to the McKinley County Sheriff's Office. The incident is believed to be part of a broad "meteor shower" that caused sonic booms in Gallup, Farmington, Aztec, Bloomfield and north to at least Durango, Colorado. McKinley County Sheriff Benny Padilla said today that his office had received one hundred and twenty-six calls after as many as seven "booms" were heard by area residents beginning at 5:50 p.m. and continuing until about 8:00 p.m.

Undersheriff Jack Graham quickly drove east of Gallup to investigate a fire burning on a hillside in the Springstead area, thought to be connected with the "explosion-like noises." Padilla and Graham initially feared an airplane had crashed. Graham walked through an empty crater about five feet across and six inches deep. There was no sign of plane wreckage.

Then, about 10:00 p.m., Padilla and Gallup Police Chief Frank Gonzales were driving in the area when they saw a "green-object" traveling toward the ground. "It looked like a fireball," Padilla said today, "and it disintegrated before it hit the ground; it was kinda scary."

Reporter Chip Hinds wrote in an article for the Durango, CO, *Herald*, on January 13, 1983: Durango police dispatcher Ruth Mastin reported that her office was told by Federal Aviation Agency officials in Grand Junction that the noise was created by classified military aircraft and that they had been instructed not to answer any further questions. McKinley County Sheriff Benny Padilla in Gallup said that a "green object" which "slowed, struck the ground and went out" was spotted near there. . .

A Farmington man, Rick Wilkie, reported seeing hunks of a "meteor falling off" as the meteor came in from the western sky as he was watching from a point about twenty-five miles from Farmington. Research associate Norman Thomas of the Lowell Observatory in Flagstaff, Arizona said authorities should be "skeptical of any meteor theory unless a full investigation is made."

The *United Press International* release of January 13th reported, in part:[McKinley County Undersheriff Jack] Graham said he and other officers trying to get to the fire site Wednesday night "saw a falling star or meteorite fall, and it burned longer than it should. I saw three or four falling stars, lasting longer than usual, about fifteen or twenty seconds."

One other report written by Rex Graham on Sunday, January 16, 1983 in the Farmington *Daily Times* stated in part:

McKinley County Sheriff Benny Padilla said the noises around Gallup ceased about 8:00 p.m. At about 10:00 p.m., Graham, Padilla and other law e.n.forcement officials saw a "green fireball' swing across the sky for about fifteen seconds, then disappear. This time there was no sound as the meteor vanished. Residents in the Farmington area reported seeing a similar glowing object in the sky. To many, the booms, meteor sighting and explosion and fire seemed part of the same phenomenon.

Reporter Lynn Bartels wrote the front page story in the Gallup *Daily* on Friday, January 14, 1983, which contained the following:

Continental Divide resident Cheryl Meyers said today there have been numerous military helicopters and vehicles in the area (just east of Gallup) since the investigation began Wednesday . . . And Chip Hines, a reporter with the Durango Herald, said today that the Federal Aviation Authority (FAA) in Grand Junction, Colorado, still denies someone from its office commented on the booms Wednesday. Hinds said a spokesman on Wednesday (the 13th) said there was a classified military aircraft in the area, but not to ask any more questions as "it was over...

On Thursday morning (the 14th), FAA authorities said no one from their office issued any statements about the noises.

When Tom Adams contacted Lynn Bartles he found that Chip Hinds had unfortunately been killed in a "mountaineering accident" shortly after covering the Gallup-Farmington events for the *Herald*. Other peripheral events and reports accompanied the events in the Four-Corners area (northern NM) on January 12, 1983. These included, evidence of dynamite and blasting caps at the (possibly diversionary) burn-site crater, noxious gases fifteen miles south of the burn-site, and rumors of some sort of crash-retrieval operation near Chaco Canyon.

Were the rumors heard by Tom Adams during and after his immediate investigation an indication of what actually transpired that cold January evening and during the following several days? He shares some of his information from his insider sources about the Gallup Incident:

241

Then we began to hear rumors, from sources previously reliable. Some of the bits and pieces were said to be 'the word' making the rounds among the military-intelligence scientific community in New Mexico: Some of the confusion resulted from the deliberate injection of mis or dis-information. This was necessary to obscure the highly sensitive 'truth' to what actually happened. A 'Top Secret' operation was in progress that night, and a classified aircraft crashed or exploded. The aircraft was indeed a highly sensitive experimental military device or …An extraterrestrial craft crashed or crash-landed. One account says that it sort of skip-crashed, bouncing into or along one site before finally coming to rest at another site. The primary crash site was somewhere near Chaco Canyon. A 'retrieval' operation ensued, while attention was diverted to Gallup and Farmington and Durango. 'Something' (be it terrestrial or otherwise) was removed from the side of the canyon or ravine into which it crashed. It was transported by air to Kirtland Air Force Base. It was set down and a protective structure was built around it. There were reports unconfirmed, of 'silver spheres' descending and ascending somewhere in the Gallup area. There were also reports of independent investigators in the technical community in Albuquerque (civilian scientists and technicians working at Kirtland AFB or Sandia National Laboratory) who were threatened and/ or harassed or otherwise warned to stay away from the Gallup area, after they had expressed interest in pursuing their own investigations of the event(s).

Was this entire collection of reported events more than a synchronistic array of mundane coincidences? Compare the above to the following. The (on-going) NORAD Event investigation was initially covered by Mark Hunter for the Valley *Courier* and my article in the Crestone *Eagle*.

The NORAD Event

The NORAD Event was actually a series of events over a six-week period (including reports of two green, two blue, one white and two orange fireballs, two orange orbs, two mystery fires, mysterious booms, a flurry of Bigfoot reports, a documented unusual cattle death and many reports of accompanying military-esque activity) that began on the night of November 30, 1993, at

6:05 p.m., and continued until the early evening of January 17, 1994.

The height of these events occurred during the afternoon of January 12th, when a NORAD official contacted the Rio Grande Sheriff's office at 3:40 p.m., and reported "a significant explosion" logged at 2:55 p.m., in the Greenie Mountain-Rock Creek Canyon area by a NORAD satellite scope operator in Cheyenne Mountain.

Exactly two hours later, at 4:55 p.m., Florence, CO, resident Lt. Col. Jimmy Lloyd (ret.), a thirty-year veteran fighter pilot and self-professed UFO skeptic reported seeing "a battleship-sized," glowing green group of "six or seven objects in close (crescent) formation" streak overhead just south of him that appeared to "go down into the San Luis Valley."

According to Lloyd, the objects were not mundane celestial objects, i.e., meteors, or any type of conventional craft, or missile and were completely silent. This effect-first, fireball-later aspect appears to have had the same two-hour time lag characteristic of the explosions and fireballs heard and seen in the Gallup Incident.

Going with the questionable assumption that all these objects were under intelligent control, (no aspect of the newspaper accounts or witness reports from either event suggests that they were) maybe in this January 12th event, for the sake of argument, the fireballs decided to arrive together, more inconspicuously, instead of separately over several hours as in 1983. Could the significant explosion which NORAD detected have been the heat signature of the tight formation of objects as they swept into the Mysterious Valley two hours later?

The fireball jockeys must have figured out how to silence the boom part. The NORAD Event made no apparent noise. There were several curious reports of "booms" but they did not occur as the primary focus as in the Gallup case.

At noon on December 9, 1993, five witnesses in two houses about a mile apart reported a localized sound like "something huge hitting the ground." Unsubstantiated reports of explosions were reported between January 13th and 15th in the Rock Creek Canyon area, on the northern side of the Greenie Ridge portion of Greenie Mountain. These booms did not appear to occur in conjunction with any of the other "fireballs" that were reported in the six-week period.

Portions of north-central Texas heard several loud boom-like noises on the afternoon of January 20th. Could these reports be significant, or were they just another bunch of noisy Texans?

Aerial craft or helicopter sightings and rumors about ground activity were present at both the Gallup Incident and the NORAD Event, combined with probable misdirection by the government. Maj. McCouch, FEMA supervisor of the NORAD scope operator, may have given Rio Grande County undersheriff Brian Norton mis-directions to search a rugged area nearly twenty-five miles from the probable impact site.

Was this to allow a military search of Greenie Ridge with the B-52s and helicopters reported the following four days? Heavy-equipment and snowshoe tracks were reported by two UFO Institute members near the same area — around the northside of Cat Creek.who also claim to have stumbled on huge "metal doors" in the ground a week after the NORAD story broke. The area is dotted with closed up, abandoned mine shafts.

To my knowledge, there is no verifiable evidence of a retrieval operation in either the Gallup Incident or the NORAD Events. Perhaps some other agenda was at work. Eyewitness accounts, eleven years apart, are similar. Sheriff Padilla's description of a "green object" breaking into pieces just before it appeared to crash echoes Al Koon's description of a "green fireball" breaking apart before appearing to strike the valley floor. Both relate the unusual flights as slowing, making a forty-five degree turn and then descended straight down towards the ground.

Most witnesses of the NORAD fireballs mentioned the long duration of the sighting. This was repeated by Padilla and undersheriff Jack Graham in their observation of the objects near Gallup.

As usual, more questions are raised than answers. What are these fireballs? Are these the same type of fireballs that have been seen periodically in the southwest since the late 1940s? Starting in late 1948, New Mexico was the epicenter for the green fireball phenomenon. De-classified government documents show that the military was quite concerned because the enigmatic fireballs had a high selectivity to for New NMexico's nuclear installations.

Who, i.e., what agences or group is conducting flights in and around the sites of these unexplainsed occurrences? How many unknown witnesses are there to the known events and do these known events represent the full-scope of the localized phenomena? Were the preceding booms and the two-hour later fireballs related? Were the Bigfoot sightings related?

Attendant Activity

January 15, 1994 6:30 p.m., Capulin:
As the glow of the setting sun faded, three Capulin residents: Jonas Archuleta, Clint Valdez and Randall Trujillo, were walking

244

downtown. One looked up to see, hovering above, two bright orange globes.

"They hovered for two to three minutes over 'Cap' (Capulin, Colorado) and at first they were pretty high and they looked just like two orange streetlights. Then they seemed to get closer. Man, when they took off it was like a streak! They went across the valley and disappeared over Romeo," Archuleta told me. "It was pretty freaky, one of the guys was pretty scared about it and swore he would go to church every day!"

Several minutes later, Chama, Colorado rancher, Dale Vigil observed "a very bright orange light," west of San Luis. According to Vigil, who was on his way to watch the local high-school basketball team, the light hovered for several minutes. It was then joined by a second "bright orange light," and both lights "shot straight up and out of sight. There is no way those were planes or helicopters, they moved too fast."

Vigil claims he and a friend had observed a similar light two weeks before, "around New Year's" over the San Luis Hills, which are located in the south-central valley, between San Luis, and Capulin.

Who Done It?

A source close to the NORAD Event told me in March, 1994, that a newly-promoted captain, in her third trimester of pregnancy, was found dead in her garage of carbon-monoxide poisoning, two-weeks after the NORAD phone-call to Undersheriff Norton. A note was allegedly left but no death notice was carried by local papers. I hit a brick-wall trying to corroborate the source's claim until a chance encounter a year later in Colorado Springs when an unexpected source turned up. I was asked by Timothy Green Beckley to speak at the first annual Pikes Peak UFO Conference. Abduction investigator, Budd Hopkins, one of ufology's most eloquent speakers was to give the keynote address and I was scheduled to follow.

I overcame my nervousness and championed the coordinated teamwork approach to field investigation. My twenty-minute talk was very well-received by the standing-room-only audience of two-hundred and fifty and I was included in a UFO talk show called UFOAZ, hosted by Ted Loman, from the conference.

During my workshop the next day, after fielding several questions about UADs I quipped, "The Ancient Mariner had an albatross around his neck, I guess I have a dead cow around mine!"

So, I was enjoying the conference when a NORAD employee introduced himself. I mentioned the NORAD captain's alleged suicide, hoping he could confirm it. "One death?" he asked. "There were three!" He went on to tell me of two additional suspicious base suicides. He hinted that the three deaths might be related. My initial NORAD source, out-of-the-blue insinuated had that a certain pregnant captain's death at NORAD might have been directly related to the call made to the sheriff's office. He thought it strange that a newly promoted pregnant captain would allegedly kilkl herself with a hose in the exhaust pipe. Talk about overkill! I have been unable to verify these claims.

When "Varied Directions," a film production company contracted by Ted Turner's TNT network to produce a UFO documentary, told me they were planning a trip to NORAD to cover the NORAD Event, I told the producer the rumors about the suspicious deaths. NORAD had initially granted permission for the film crew to visit the secret base at Cheyenne Mountain. When it was revealed that they were interested in the NORAD Event, their visit was promptly canceled without explanation.

Varied Directions was the first film crew allowed aboard a Trident submarine when they produced a documentary for the PBS program Nova. They had also worked with NASA on a documented history of the space-race, called *Moon Shot*. This is obviously a well-connected production company. But even with these impressive credentials, permission to film inside Cheyenne Mountain was still rescinded .

The Wheat From the Chaff

Many longtime residents of the SLV profess to be able to differentiate between the usual and the unusual. Newcomers, not fully accustomed to our glorious night sky. This place is a skywatchers' paradise at almost eight thousand feet above sea-level, and sometimes mundane celestial objects are reported as UFOs.

On February 11 and 12, 1994, I received a total of four reports of a "light hovering over the mountains." After rushing to my roof, within seconds of their calls, I realized that these earnest folks were probably viewing the star Sirius that happened to be rising in the east, above the mountains. Although spectacular, these sightings of the heavens' brightest star did not make it into my sighting log.

How many reports of stars, planets, satellites and space debris litter ufologists sighting logs? Another call came within minutes and, the following night, I had two more. At least folks here are keeping their eyes open. These reports underscore the importance of careful separation between the wheat and the chaff.

March 2, 1994, just after 10:00 p.m., the Baca Chalets:
A visitor to our area possibly experienced "the real thing." The witness, a professional photographer from Seattle was photographing the vivid night sky four days after the full moon. After venturing outside she found herself facing the Great Sand Dunes, fifteen-miles south, where she noticed a group of red lights pulsing and flashing.

She had the conscious thought to raise her camera and take pictures but was so mesmerized by the display that she felt paralyzed. Excited by her sighting, she was puzzled why she was unable to photograph the lights. I can't count the number of times I've heard a similar story. This woman was a professional photographer, the camera was loaded and set up for nighttime exposure, yet, over the course of this alleged ten-minute sighting, no pictures were taken. I've done it myself.

Four nights later around 9:15 p.m., yet another 'cheap fireworks' display was observed traveling SE to NW over the Sangres where it flared out over Crestone. I wonder how many of these displays go unnoticed by our sparse population. (If a fireball falls in the valley with no one to see it . . .)

The rest of March was quiet, with no other logged reports until the morning of March 30, at 10:45 a.m. I was four miles south of Moffat, heading south on Highway 17 traveling to the Ozark UFO Conference (Eureka Springs AR). A bright silver reflection directly ahead of me, forty-five degrees above the horizon, caught my attention and I watched an apparent silver sphere hover about three thousand feet above Hooper for about fifteen seconds. Denver UFO researcher, Candice Powers, and Baca resident Richard Copeland, who were driving in a second car directly behind me, also saw the brightly reflecting object.

As I fumbled with the thirty-five mm camera on the front seat, the reflection flashed off. The object could not have been a fixed-wing airplane simply reflecting the sun. which was approximately twelve degrees east of it, on the same horizontal plane. I slowed my truck and fixed my eyes on the spot where I had observed the object's reflection, not having to watch the road which continues south, straight as an arrow, for twenty miles.

After five or six seconds, the reflection was back and it had moved fifteen or so degrees to the right and away from me, directly south. It hovered for another ten or so seconds before disappearing south. Because the reflection was so bright, I could not discern structure but it had to be round (or spherical) to be able to reflect structure but it had to be round (or spherical) to be able to reflect sunlight at the angle we observed.

I have seen many conventional aircraft reflect the sun (I grew up near McCord AFB in Washington State and currently see military and private aircraft constantly) but I have never seen this reflection-effect in such close proximity to the sun, nor the hovering action we observed. The sky, that morning was crisscrossed with contrails. The sphere left no trail.

This was near the location of the bell-shaped object sightings of December '92, and the "swarm of lights" the night of January 7, 1994.

That night, after a long drive across Oklahoma and Texas, we arrived in Eureka Springs. Multiple sightings of our cheap fireworks were made by area residents over the western slopes of the Sangres the same night. Four low-altitude displays were seen sporadically over the next three nights. All were described later as being at tree-top level before, as one witness described, "They flared. Like, poofed out."

During this three-day period at the Eureka Conference, a calf was discovered "mutilated" sixty miles south of the Eureka Springs, and a cow was discovered with "classic mutilation" incisions right in Taos, NM.

The day I returned from Arkansas, I met with Bob Weiss, a director for *Unsolved Mysteries*. Janet Jones, a researcher for the program had heard about our activity and my investigation. I discussed with Weiss some of our most spectacular reports, including the NORAD Events. Weiss agreed that there were many stories here.

April and May are traditionally two of the most active months (in the greater SLV region) during years of heightened activity, and 1994 was no exception. From April 1 through May 31, there were nineteen sightings of anomalous objects and/or lights, three reported UADs (and a reliable unreported case of two, possibly three cattle deaths complete with a twelve inch by twelve inch square burn-mark nearby) and numerous sightings of helicopters and military vehicles. The usually subtle presence of "the watchers" became less translucent that spring of 1994. Local law enforcement officials professed to be as mystified as ever by the incredible amount of reports that were generated that spring.

SLV residents were becoming more aware of our unexplained activity due to increased sightings and all of the newspaper coverage. Specific areas (where activity continues today) were buzzing with rumors. It appeared the locals were gaining the courage to report these sightings to police and reporters.

My daylight sighting of the sphere on March 30 was followed by three reports of cheap fireworks on April 1, and 2, at just after 10:00 p.m. These displays were bluish-white and appeared to be just above tree-top level. They are only reported in a ten-mile wide corridor extending from the Blanca Massif, north to Valley View Hot Springs on the western facing slopes of the Sangre de Cristos. This eastern area where I live, has traditionally had more reports of anomalous aerial objects than the remaining valley.

The pattern abruptly broke in December of 1994. The western valley now has its share of sightings. The epicenter moved northward in April and May.

On Thursday, April 7 at 10:00 p.m., an orange light was seen by three witnesses, rising above the La Garita Mountains in the west, toward Creede, Colorado. The light hovered thirty degrees above the horizon for almost ten minutes before "blinking out." It was described by witnesses as brilliantly lit and "much larger than a planet."

April 9, 9:30 p.m., Moffat, Colorado:
Several lights hovering "low in the western sky" were seen by (trained observers) the Koon family in Moffat. The remote unpopulated area near Creede, where they estimated these two lights were hovering, is a large minimum-intensity aeromagnetic anomaly area that's rumored to have a possible underground facility. Later, I will cover my theory concerning a possible correlation between areas of continual reports of paranormal events; like UFOs, the location of which, seem to be tied directly to the areas where minimum and maximum intensity field-strength closely interact in close proximity to one another. This area of speculation, in my estimation, has not been adequately addressed by researchers and investigators.

April 21, 1994 around 6:00 a.m., Monte Vista, Colorado:
Two complaints of a "large jet flying low over Monte Vista" were forwarded to me. At the time, the military was attempting to expand the La Veta Military Operations Area, and according to public relations officer Maj. Tom Schultz of the Colorado Air National Guard, "We have more pilots than planes." As a result, pilots are "careful to fly according to regulations to keep themselves from being grounded." Regulations include remaining subsonic and well-above five-hundred feet to avoid noise complaints by area residents. According to witnesses, the "huge jet" lumbered "less than two-hundred feet above the trees."

The Sphere Returns

April 30, 1994, at 10:00 p.m., Crestone:

Lifelong Crestone resident and local historian, Jack Harlan, witnessed something he'd "never seen before" in his seventy-plus years. "It was large and round, like a sphere," he told me the next day. "There were red and green lights blinking (in sequence) around the underside."

Another witness, a neighbor thinks he also saw the strange craft. "I had just stepped outside when I saw a large bright light going straight up and out, [to the southeast] with sparks shooting off it!" According to this second witness, "Jack [Harlan] said it was so close he could see two raised ridges on the underside that were lit up by the bright blinking lights." Harlan told his neighbor that he felt unusually fatigued the entire following day.

Dr. Steven Greer, founder and head of CSETI conducted a Rapid Mobilization Investigation Team (RMIT) training May 5 through 9, 1994, here in the valley. Greer arrived in the late morning of May 4th, after flying into Denver, and observed "two large camo'ed dropped-bellied semi's" near Villa Grove, Colorado at the north end of the valley. "We saw similar (military-esque) activity when we were in England," he told me.

The next morning, Greer observed "a silver sphere hovering silently over the mountains" while jogging in the Baca. The sphere did not leave any vapor trail (unlike the aerial traffic observed at the time). According to his description, the sphere hovered silently for several minutes before heading east [over the Sangres] and out of sight. Greer was unaware at the time that a similar sphere had been reported five days before by Jack Harlan and Harlan's neighbor. He was also unaware that similar objects had been seen during the same time period near Blanca and Ft. Garland, or my March 30, sighting.

RMIT-head Sherry Adamiak and Dr. Greer instructed over a dozen CSETI-ites in the system of protocols that Dr. Greer has devised to elicit contact with extraterrestrial craft and their occupants. Aspiring RMIT team members included "Bootsy" Galhbreth (wife of a United States Ambassador) and George Lamb, who was Laurance Rockefeller's right-hand-man until his retirement several years later.

The morning of my presentation to the group, a nasty grass-fire had erupted out in the Baca Grants, driven by a stiff breeze out of the west. The fire raced toward Spanish Creek as the siren blared. Brendon and I, hearing siren and seeing the smoke, raced to the location and headed out with shovels and slappers to head the blaze off. We battled the hot-spots with other early responders for ten, or so frenzied tense minutes until we were joined by members of our crack volunteer Fire-Department. I had joined the Baca department when I moved to the area but had resigned after an fire-related injury in 1992, but I was still ready to dash to a fire-scene. Two hours later, a team of thirty or forty residents and fire-personnel had headed off a disaster and, after a few minutes of oxygen, I headed late to my mini-workshop with Greer's people, coughing and reeking of smoke. I gave the group a quick apology and an overview of my research, and during a question an answer period, I was asked what I thought of the CSETI approach to UFOlogy. I remember looking directly at Steven and reminding him, "your message is more important than you are, Steven." Shari gave me a small, but knowing smile.

Uncle Larry

At this point, I must further digress in the interest of full-disclosure. For years I kept the following events low-key. I'll continue the time-line of my investigative process in a moment, but I should note that this first major CSETI training in Crestone was my first, real introduction to a group of top-echelon movers and shakers that have come to the Baca over the years to experience the roaring silence of the Baca Grande, or the "Big Cow" if you prefer. Religious, political, business and social elites have ebbed and flowed through this community for years and more than a few leave the area professing to have had profound experiences, or insights while visiting the valley

It was around this late summer 1994 time period I began to get to know my neighbors, Hanne Strong, her sister Marianne Marstand and her interesting family. Over the years, I have come to know Hanne's daughters, Christine and Suzanne, as well. Isadora and I also began to be included in gatherings at the Strong's and I found myself trotted out to help supply an unspoken process of educating to influential visitors she had invited to visit our unique community. Three and one-half years after this afternoon meeting w/ Greer and his trainees, in late July, 1997, I was fortunate enough to spend a one-on-one weekend with Laurance Rockefeller during what may have been his last visit to *Tsissnajiini* before his death at age ninety-four in 2004.

One morning Hanne called and asked "Are you busy right now?" Rhetorical question, of course. Upon hearing that my time could be made fluid, she suggested I quickly put together a package of information relating to my investigative work and head over to her house immediately – saying: "there is someone here I

251

think you should meet." This was the first time Hanne had made such a spontaneous request. I spent an hour or so putting together a folder of data and then headed out the backdoor -- south toward South Crestone Creek.

The Strong's gorgeous house sat two houses away, across the creek, several hundred yards from where I lived. I arrived at the front door just as two men exited the house. It was Harvard's Pulitzer Prize Winner, Dr. John Mack and a friend, "Sequoia Trueblood," an ex-special forces operative. Hanne introduced us and, much to my dismay, the two of them left. Hanne waved goodbye and nonchalantly motioned me to go inside. I silently chastised myself for taking so long before coming over. I was bummed that I had missed the chance to meet Dr. Mack.

I entered Hanne's house and standing there in the entrance foyer was a smiling Laurance Rockefeller. I immediately recognized the eighty-seven year-old billionaire and something came clearly into focus. Hanne introduced us and we sat down. Hanne fussed over us for a few minutes and then left us alone while Rockefeller and I talked for over three hours. We covered a whirlwind of subjects and I was impressed by Laurance's wide-ranging interests and his insider knowledge of crop-circles, UFOs and other so-called paranormal phenomena.

While Hanne's grandkids played around the house, Rockefeller and I quickly established a conversational rapport. He was a cut-to-the chase kind of guy. After some pleasantries he quizzed me concerning several researchers he had been funding, including Colin Andrews, John Mack and Steven Greer. I carefully acknowledged the many positive aspects of their work but also shared with him my subtle reservations concerning potential inconsistencies in their "ET" based thinking. He seemed upbeat and impressed at my out-of-the-box thinking and the conversation never seemed to lag.

Toward the end of our meeting, I mentioned what I felt was a correlation between the complexity in the Great Britain crop-circle phenomenon and the coincidental spread of mad-cow disease through the England between 1986 to 1996. I then mentioned my further suspicion that random macro-burst blow-down events, documented along the Continental Divide, in the Rocky Mountains, may be connected, somehow, to the recent outbreak of chronic-wasting disease in Colorado. My of-the-cuff thinking struck a cord in both of us. As I was leaving, he asked Hanne if it was alright to have me back to speak further about my theories the following day. You bet I would! I returned home my head reeling from all the rarified air I had been breathing.

After an evening of further preparation, I arrived back at Hanne's the following morning with no lust result and found out

I had been granted an entire day.; a one-on-one audience with Uncle Larry. His Gulfstream jet crew was gassed up and ready to depart, but he had decided to stay an extra day in the valley. I was the agenda.

I immediately picked up where we had left off and our conversation ebbed and flowed through a variety of subjects. I felt relaxed and confident and a bit playful. It was a beautiful late summer day and we both reclined on comfortable lawn furniture in Hanne's back yard discussing philosophy, (Rockefeller earned a degree in philosophy from Princeton University) Heisenberg and quantum-physics, and several other cutting-edge topics before lunch.

After lunch, about halfway through the afternoon, I sensed an opportunity and brought up my suspicion concerning the ancient practice of ritual sacrifice and the possible connection to the unusual livestock death phenomenon. He looked at me and gave me a thin-lipped smile. I quickly gave him an overview of the data I had accumulated related to this blood-based mystery and, in a low-key manner, suggested that this was an important area of potential research and investigation. He expressed somewhat of an interest, but, like most of us, he seemed uncomfortable with the subject of humankind's relationship to cattle.

He really lit up, however, when I then brought up more user-friendly phenomena. We spoke about undefined natural phenomena that I felt were being reported. I mentioned Tesla's rumored trip to the area in the late nineteenth-century and recounted several reports of what may be quartz generated, static electrical discharges that have been reported to shoot up out of the Sangres on extremely cold, dry winter nights. Tesla was renown around Colorado because of the electrical systems built in Telluride and Cripple Creek Colorado.

The subject would invariably be brought back to the cereal glyph phenomenon. Rockefeller obviously had an intense fascination with crop-circles. I gently reminded him that many of these formations could be hoaxed, but this didn't seem to be an issue with him. The entire unfolding phenomenon was important – it didn't seem to matter to him who was authoring the message. We talked at length about crop-circles and I argued that human performance art was different from ET activity. He acknowledged my time-line correlation methodology when he gifted me with a first-edition copy of Michael Glickman's seminal 1996 work *Corn Circles* that had just been published by Wooden Books. This unassuming fifty-page masterpiece is a time-line, formatted presentation of the unfolding crop-circle phenomenon during the eighties and early-to-mid nineties. The little book ends with the 1995 cereal glyph

253

season – at the height of the Mad-Cow epidemic in England and it perfectly illustrates my theory concerning the unfolding patterning of complexity of crop-circles and their possible correlation with the spread of *prion* disease. I will address this theory later.

The beautiful scenic splendor of that July afternoon on Spanish Creek sticks like epoxy in my process. I remember thinking how lucky I was to be briefing a billionaire concerning recent reports of weird, documented UFO sightings and huge blow-down events in the Rockies. I observed the apparent synchronicity between the most recent "blow-down" near Fort Collins, Colorado and the subsequent outbreak of chronic-wasting disease in deer-and elk herds from the north-central Colorado mountains. An outbreak that ten-years later has spread across the United States. He became a bit animated. I told him that one of the primary goals of any investigation into these occurrences should be a detailed aerial survey of the affected forest and he enthusiastically agreed.

At one point he asked me about scientists who were willing to officially study unusual phenomenal events. I asked him if he was aware of the work of W.C. Levengood and BLT Research. He wasn't aware of their work. I provided him with a quick overview of Levengood's work and suggested that he meet with BLT's Nancy Talbot; the T in BLT, to obtain more detailed information about their work. He took me up on this suggestion and, after being urged by David Perkins, Nancy followed up on this advise and contacted his office. Uncle Larry met with Nancy several months later. I'm happy to report that this connection helped generate a sizeable amount of Rockefeller funding to help BLT Research to further their scientific process.

By the end of the afternoon, the conversation began to meander away from ufology and related topics. I felt relaxed and at home with Laurence. Hanne called the kids in and we began to talk about the perception the masses had about the "Rockellers." I was curious how such an intelligent, curious individual could have such a suspect reputation with the "fringe" crowd. At one point I coyly, but jokingly asked him, "Laurence, I keep reading about the Rockefellers on the Internet. How come there are some people out there on the 'net that think your brother David is 'The Antichrist?'" His eyes grew large as he began to slowly guffaw – then laugh. His laughter became deeper, more hacking and intense. I'm not making this up. His initial reaction ceased being a laughing response and it became a deep unstoppable cough that slowly began to get more and more severe. I started to get a little worried and gently patted him on the back. It didn't help.

I had only been kidding, but by that point, it didn't matter. He evidently was so amused by my mock question he was laughing himself into an apoplectic fit. He had to excuse himself and leave.

A concerned Hanne appeared—gave me a withering look, and quickly took him upstairs. At this point, I felt a bit concerned and very uncomfortable. What had I done?! The scenario of Laurence Rockefeller choking himself to death with laughter over a joke about his brother being thought of as "The Antichrist" flashed through my head.

After awhile, Hanne still hadn't come downstairs and I was starting to get real concerned. Then, she finally tip-toed down the stairs and told me quietly, but brusquely that my meeting with Laurence was over. Yikes! I gathered my data and sheepishly left. A local massage therapist, Diane Skye arrived and hustled upstairs to attend to Rockefeller evidently laid out in the guest bedroom, recovering. I arrived back home shaking my head.

Needless to say I was very relieved to find out from Hanne the next day, that Rockefeller was OK, it had been scary and his handlers weren't happy, but he had had left that morning and flown out on his private jet from Bergman Field in Alamosa. Hanne, was obviously not pleased with me and how my prior afternoon with Laurence had ended. I explained to her that Laurence had only been laughing at my casual joke but that didn't seem to make any difference, she definitely wasn't pleased that he left after recovering from his laughing fit and, evidently he had not finalized his commitment to Hanne's latest project. Rockefeller, over the years, had been kind to Hanne's foundation.

Imagine my surprise a week, or so, later when I opened a personal letter from Laurence to find a nice, fatty check with my name on it. As I type this, that letter is framed proudly on the wall behind me. In retrospect, I suspect that Rockefeller was genuinely intrigued by my observations and analysis regarding a number of topics —some having to do with paranormal subjects, others not. Surprisingly, at no time during our many hours of conversation, did I ever feel that he considered me to be anything but an equal. I'm a fairly bright guy and he was a good listener, but I couldn't get out of my mind the question: why was this man devoting two days to listening to me and my theories? You billionaires, take notes! Some of us great, unwashed masses may actually be objective, critical thinkers—whether you like it or not, there are some of us who deserve to be heard! Laurence poked and prodded me and my humble, tenuous theories, but much to my surprise, he never flat-out corrected me or refuted my thinking. I was impressed by his many insightful, probing questions during our conversation, and, at times, I felt like I was the teacher and he was the enthusiastic student. I know that might sound grandiose, but I am serious; Laurence Rockefeller was on a mission of understanding concerning the many mysteries that you and I are also intrigued by and he felt what I had to say may help him on his journey. Wow!

Thinking back, I never really paid much attention to what the UFO conspiracy buffs had to said about Laurance Rockefeller. I found that the man had a healthy air of open-minded innocence as I would be proud to have when I'm eighty-seven years old. He did not seemed attached to any specific agenda other than the pursuit of personal understanding and increased awareness. Not having to be encumbered with cash-flow and income concerns sure must be nice. There were several touchy areas that I brought up – including his early support of Eugenics, I asked him about the controversial subject and he responded openly, candidly. I was impressed, he obviously maintained a close connection with his innate, childlike wonder—born out of an ageless sense of curiosity and a thirst for knowledge. That "sense of wonder," when lost, means we have succumbed to growing old.

His energy was timeless, refreshing and it showed through as I watched his interaction with me and Hanne's offspring. All during the afternoon, Hanne's many grandkids buzzed about the place, they were well-behaved and exuberant, they only interrupted a couple of times and I recognized Uncle Larry's natural ease when focusing on the children. They didn't know who he was, and it didn't matter. He glowed and seemed uplifted to be around such exuberant, non-judgmental, youthful energy.

I feel blessed to have experienced feedback about my work from an influential legend. Rockefeller earned a degree in philosophy from Princeton and he still had a mind like a steel-trap. Rumors of his eccentricities are well founded, but these are not ungrounded, "eccentric" interests. We all know a true "seeker" when we spend quality time with one of them and I suspect that he was part of the solution, not a part of the problem. I still wonder how someone of his social and political stature could devote enough time to educate themselves about fringe subjects and be as up-to-speed as he appeared to be.

Laurance Rockefeller has become somewhat of a mythical character in ufology, His low-key philanthropic interest in the field helped drive research forward in the eighties and nineties. Rockefeller publicly funded the Sturrock Report on UFOs, Marie "Bootsy" Galbraith the wife of Evan Galbraith, one-time US ambassador to France and BSW's Best Available Evidence (of UFOs) document, written by Don Berliner and Antonio Huneuus), crop-circle researcher/investigator Colin Andrews, abduction investigator Dr. John Mack, Steven Greer and CSETI and others. Rockefeller's efforts were welcomed by the field as a potential benefactor. Having said this, I stress that at no time did I ever mention money, or funding etc. As with the media, I have never asked any individual or group for funding. I have always thought that the data should do the talking and asking. I enjoyed spending casual time with Rockefeller. My fond recollections of that long afternoon are centered around the wonderful, blissful feeling I was experiencing. Never in a million years had I every thought I'd be spending quality time with a billionaire.

The following is taken from the *New York Sun* in 2004:

> Together with his famous brothers, [Laurance Rockefeller] used his petroleum-fueled patrimony to tremendous advantage, accumulating vast sums in business while disbursing immense amounts as charity, leading philanthropic organizations, and serving in a number of public administrative positions . . . . After graduating from Princeton with a major in philosophy, he attended Harvard Law School for two years . . . .
>
> "In 1935 he began working at Rockefeller Center, where he concentrated on his family's philanthropic activities. Already a self-described "gadgeteer" with a strong interest in flight, he provided financial backing for Eastern Air Lines when the World War I ace Eddie Rickenbacker became its president, in 1938. In 1941, Rockefeller became chairman of the aeronautical committee of the Commerce and Industry Association of New York, which formulated plans for airports. He served in various organizations fostering private flight, and in 1946 Mayor William O'Dwyer appointed him to the newly formed New York City Airport Authority.
>
> The third of five sons of John D Rockefeller, Jr., he seems to have inherited his grandfather's business acumen. Having emerged from Princeton with a philosophy degree, he co-founded Eastern Airlines (1938), quickly becoming the firm's largest shareholder. After serving in the U.S. Navy in World War II, [and administrating the occupation of Japan] he invested in a variety of enterprises, including computers, nuclear technologies, and resort hotels. His principal philanthropic interests focus[ed] on the environment, having donated some thirty-three thousand acres to the Grand Teton National Park. He was the head of the Citizens Advisory Committee on Environmental Quality (1969–73), and [was] on the executive committee of the Jackson Hole Wildlife Park. Quoted from,http://infoplease.com/ipa/A0771997.html

257

The following facts have been an Internet staple for years and sums up conspiratorial thinking:
An Alien Conspiracy? by Dr. M. Sabeheddi http://www. mt.net/~watcher/uforocke.html

Late last year, the *New York Daily News* ran a curious story on eighty-five year old billionaire philanthropist Laurance Rockefeller who is funding a special report on UFOs to be sent to President Clinton and other world leaders.

Michael Luckman, director of the New York Center for UFO Research, says the Rockefeller report entitled '*The Best Available Evidence*,' "features testimony from former military officials andastronauts that contradicts Air Force denials of an alien landing."

The billionaire's name again pops up as a VIP attendee at Bill Clinton's birthday party held on a Rockefeller estate in August last year. The *New York Daily News* of August 24 reported that while President Clinton was on the prowl for campaign cash, Laurence was on the look out for ETs.

Rockefeller has been pressing the Clinton administration to open the government's UFO files," the *Daily News* notes. Apparently, Laurence thinks it's time the government came clean on the subject of UFOs, particularly the rumored crash of a spacecraft in Roswell, New Mexico in 1947.

Is Laurance just another 'truth seeker', or could there be a more sinister motivation behind his devotion to this obscure quest? certainly there is no doubt that the Rockefellers constitute one of the world's wealthiest and most influential dynasties.

Laurence's brotherD avid, a longtime chairman of Chase Manhattan Bank, heads the family's global corporate empire. The Rockefeller family played instrumental roles in establishing powerful supranational bodies like the Trilateral Commission, the Council on Foriegn Relations and the Bilderberg Society

If anyone doubts the global power of the Rockefeller dynasty and their active behind-the-scenes involvement in international affairs, just consider these remarks by investigative author Malachi Martin in *The Keys of This Blood*. He states:

Television commentator Bill Moyers found out during a fifteen-day, globe spanning trip in the company of David Rockefeller that 'just about a dozen or fifteen individuals made day-to-day decisions that regulated the flow of capital and goods throughout the entire world.'"

As Bill Moyers himself said:

> "David Rockefeller is the most conspicuous representative today of the ruling class, a multinational fraternity of men who shape the global economy and manage the flow of its capital. Rockefeller was born to it, and he has made the most of it. But what some critics see as a vast international conspiracy, he considers a circumstance of life and just another day's work... In the world of David Rockefeller it's hard to tell where business ends and politics begins.

The open-minded philanthropist backed up his professed interest in my "photographic work on tree-circles." After returning to New York Laurance immediately wrote out a sizable personal check, declared as "a gift" with no strings attached and sent to me. " . . . I share your enthusiasm and am pleased to send along the enclosed gift . . . . to help you in your photographic work on 'tree-circles.'"

CSETI

The CSETI agenda appeared to me, at the time, to be a logical step forward out of the morass in which ufology finds itself. An investigative presence in flap areas of heightened activity made a lot more sense to this investigator than yet another rehashing of the Roswell case (NM, 1947).

CSETI has had some alleged success in attracting "craft" to specific locations in the United States, Mexico and England but no boardings have occurred. CSETI's expedition into the mysterious valley couldn't have been timed more perfectly. On May 7th and 8th, the group had several additional sightings of unknown lights and objects. Their sighting reports pointedly coincide with Blanca and Ft. Garland residents reports of unknown lights in the sky on the same nights, thirty miles southeast of Crestone, and the flurry of reports forty miles to the west, near Monte Vista.

At 10:30 p.m., (as reported by Mark Hunter in the *Valley Courier*) six Monte Vista residents reported, to undersheriff Brian Norton, a fast moving brilliant "white strobe-light" low to the ground in the area of Rio Grande County roads 4N and 3W, known as "Maxiville" to the locals. Norton himself saw the light, which he said was "just above the trees and really moving! It had to have been traveling at least as fast as two hundred to two hundred-fifty miles per hour." Norton added that his office had received two calls Saturday night and four calls Sunday night officially reporting

259

the unusual low flying strobe-light.

Valley Courier editor Mark Hunter told me "cars were lined up along 285 watching it." Norton said those present "refused to go on-the-record" about the sighting. The Undersheriff said the light seemed to mirror his actions when he and others tried to get close enough to identify it. "I would chase it north, and it would head south. I would stop, and it would stop. Then I made a U-turn and headed back south, and the light immediately headed north."

Could the objects reported over that weekend have been attracted by Greer to the valley the weekend of May 7th and 8th? I mentioned to Greer and Adamiak that, when CSETI was vectoring-in craft that weekend, maybe they gave bad directions because none of the craft showed up in the Baca area.

Norton also mentioned seeing a "dark unmarked helicopter" the next morning (Monday the 9th) while investigating. "The chopper appeared to be buzzing the area where the light was seen" during the previous two nights.

He called me because he knew, back on January 21st, I was videotaping over Greenie Ridge in a dark purple chopper, which was reported in the *Rocky Mountain News* as a "black unmarked helicopter." Evidently two Rio Grande County sheriffs had chased my craft all the way across the county. I assured him it was not me this time, and I would inform him before flying in his jurisdiction again.

Several reliable sources told me of a rumor that a Maxiville-area farmer had two, possibly three, cows "mutilated" on Monday night, May 9th. These sources also mentioned a landing by some sort of craft on the farmer's property. The landing traces allegedly consisted of "a twelve foot by twelve foot burn mark" in the farmer's freshly-irrigated field. According to his neighbors, the farmer didn't want to officially report these cattle deaths and landing because "he doesn't want to scare folks." Evidently the farmer quickly disposed of the carcasses and possibly covered the evidence of a landing. Overflights of the area by a local pilot revealed nothing worthy of note.

This possible example of a witnesses' reluctance to acknowledge the high-strange is probably the norm, not the exception. Again, it may be the fear of ridicule. And the human mind has built-in mechanisms to help to deal with that which it cannot comprehend and very often the result is denial. If they close their eyes, maybe it will go away…

Laurance Rockefeller

Hanne and monks at the Ziggeraut

Sheri Adamiak and Steven Greer of CSETI

ROOM 5600
30 ROCKEFELLER PLAZA
NEW YORK, N.Y. 10112

August 7, 1997

Dear Mr. O'Brien:

Thank you for your letter of July 30 and for your update on the "tree circles". I share in your enthusiasm and am pleased to send along the enclosed gift in the amount of $10,000 to help you in your photographic work on "tree circles."

Since I am very much interested in your findings I would like you keep me fully informed on how the work is proceeding and of any developments in the field in general.

With best wishes,

Sincerely,

Laurance S. Rockefeller

Mr. Christopher O'Brien
Christopher O'Brien Investigations
P.O. Box 223
Crestone, Colorado 81131

enclosure

CHAPTER NINE:
The Curse of Mutology

Eagle, to the Eagle Nest

The study of mutilations. Or "mutology" (as coined by long-time Gardner mutilation researcher David Perkins in 1979) seems to have a propensity for name-game synchronicity. The father of mutology, Tom Adams, observed that three recent UAD cases in Eagle, Colorado, in November and December and the two new cases that occurred the following May in Eagle Nest, New Mexico, have that tantalizing name connection.

In the fall of 1993 there were reported UAD cases in Adams and Perkins Counties in North and South Dakota. Is someone (or something) sending blatantly subtle messages to Tom Adams and David Perkins? When investigating this unsolved serial crime spree of the century, one must scrutinize the evidence from as many angles as possible. Clues, dear Watson, clues.

Two cows were found by rancher Eli Hronich on May 10, 1994, next to a lake, in Eagle Nest. The UADs were found with "classic mutilation" incisions, rear end cored out, (ad nauseum) and may represent an historic first. New Mexico paranormal investigator Gail Staehlin, New Mexico cattle inspector Philip Cantu, veterinarian Tim Johnson and hematologist Dr. John Altshuler, were all on scene together within ten hours of discovery. To my knowledge, there has never been such expertise on-site so quickly, in the history of the UAD phenomenon. Initial results derived from preliminary forensic testing indicated cooked hemoglobin and cauterization of the incisions.

Doctors Altshuler and Johnson also noticed that both animals' lungs were riddled with pneumonia. Altshuler remembered the Vigil bull, and the finding of pneumonia in that animal's lungs, and thinks the affliction may prove significant. Very few animals, that appear to be true UADs, are examined as carefully as the two Hronich cows.

The area just beyond the southern end of the SLV (near Taos, NM) has quietly undergone a wave of unusual cattle deaths since

263

the fall of 1993. By this time, Hronich has "lost (and reported) ten head since September." He is only one of several ranchers in the area that have been plagued by the mysterious cattle surgeons of late.

These cases (and the cow found last March, right in Taos) were a prelude (publicity campaign?) to the "Animal Mutilation Conference" presented by Gail Staehlin, on May 21, 1994 in Taos. The conference was publicized in the area for three weeks and "somebody" may have seen the ads and flyers. Proper forensic, postmortem photographic and general investigative techniques were presented to a dozen ranchers, two state cattle inspectors and a local veterinarian over the course of the five-hour gathering.

This type of networking with ranchers and local officials is crucial. Expediency is of paramount importance when investigating UADs. In the words of investigator Gail Staehlin, "Somebody's got to help these folks!"

I Heard What I Heard

As reported by Mark Hunter in the *Valley Courier* on Tuesday night, May 17, 1994, at 9:30 p.m., Monte Vista residents Stephanie Malouff and Debbie Jiron reported seeing a "huge bright light with lots of little bright lights around it." Malouff and Jiron saw the far too large to be a conventional craft, flying in a northerly direction south of the town. They also observed that this larger object was being "chased by a second smaller object at high speed." As the smaller object closed in on the larger one, the larger one appeared to turn from bright-white to red, as it "all of a sudden made a fort-five degree turn to the west and disappeared over the mountains near Greenie."

Hunter reported that the two witnesses were excited about their sighting and said, "You couldn't miss it. It was bright and it was huge." As a strange twist to this story, Malouff told Hunter that, although the objects were silent, she heard a "pinging sound" like bullets ricocheting off metal. Was the smaller object shooting and hitting the larger one? Malouff didn't care to speculate about this but she insisted, "I heard what I heard."

Malouff said she called several relatives to see if anyone else had seen the strange objects and one woman told her she had seen a similar object the previous night at around 2:00 a.m. On that same Monday, 7:00 a.m., a Colorado Springs radio station KKFM apparently broadcast a "Live" UFO sighting report of a strange silver object hovering over Colorado Springs. According to a friend who told me of the broadcast, a similar object had apparently been spotted the night before over Trinidad, CO. I have heard an official version, that the object was a "six hundred foot long weather balloon flying at one hundred thousand feet."

My sources said that it was launched by the National Weather Service "out of New Mexico." Supposedly, it was launched on the 15th, in "northern New Mexico" and it drifted east, towards Trinidad, then it went north towards Colorado Springs. Knowing a little about our weather patterns and factoring in our activity during the following two nights left me with some doubts. A six hundred foot-long weather balloon?

The following week, Undersheriff Norton received a report from a South Fork, Colorado resident of a twenty to thirty minute sighting on May 24th, from 9:30 to 10:00 p.m., of a large silver sphere (the one with the multi-colored lights blinking around the underside) flying south down the Rio Grande between South Fork and Creede. This sphere certainly gets around. That made five sightings since March 30, of what appears to be the same (or same type) object.

May 25, 1994 at 9:35 p.m., the Baca Chalets:
As May progressed I wondered if our activity would wane as usual in June and July. So, naturally, I immediately witnessed the most bizarre cheap firework display out of the dozens I have seen to date.

Our house sits two hundred feet above the valley floor and I was standing on our 2nd story deck. It was completely overcast with uniform cloud cover seven thousand feet above the entire central and northern valley floor. I was looking directly south, out over the southern part of the Baca Ranch when I saw a bright blue light appear (thirty degrees below the horizon) that appeared to be flying in a slight arc, parallel to the ground, fifty to one hundred feet above the tree-tops. It was about a mile or so away, at a lower elevation than my vantage point! I was actually looking down at it as it flared for almost a mile over the piñon trees one hundred to one hundred fifty feet below me.

These objects are real, and I only have a couple of theories. We could be witnessing an as yet undefined natural phenomenon like a form of static, or plasma discharge. Or, they could they be an effect caused by an unknown aerial craft, much like a jet produces a contrail. They come in all sizes, the smaller ones tend to be bluish the larger, midsized models are orangish and the huge fireballs are green. The comical tiny ones (that are only reported as occurring very close to the observer) are especially puzzling.

May 30, early a.m., North of Questa, NM:

Ranch foreman, Tom Reed found a three-month old heifer "mutilated," and reported it to cattle inspector, Jerry Valario. Valario drove out to the ranch to investigate the death.

Cutting the animal open, Valario was startled to find that the meat looked like it had been boiled, or cooked in a microwave. It was gray and flaky. He probed inside the calf's mouth, inadvertently getting the animal's saliva on his hand. "My hand started getting irritated," he later told me. "It started itching and turning red. It was like an acid burn, or something." He had noticed the burning sensation several minutes after examining the calf, as Nellie Lewis had twenty-seven years earlier.

11:15 p.m.-11:30 p.m., Moffat:

At 6:00 that evening, Isadora dropped me at our rehearsal studio for our four-hour-plus rehearsal. Later, George Oringdulph, guitarist with Laffing Buddha, offered to drive me home. George and I found ourselves headed north on 17 toward Road T and the fourteen mile jaunt east toward the Baca.

As we approached the sand piles, halfway between Hooper and Moffat, I noticed a picket line of four faint blinking lights over the Sangres, near Crestone. I pointed them out to George, and we watched them hover for almost five minutes.

Three of the lights (about three, or four miles apart) proceeded west, across the valley, where they stopped in a line, between Highways 17 and 285, just hanging there, blinking. George pointed out a large, unblinking, orangish-white light appear just south of where the fourth light was still hovering.

George asked me as the light slowly brightened, "Is that a planet?"

"No way. There's no planet in the northern sky." The bigger fifth light began to drift west toward the first three lights. We estimated its speed at around fifty to sixty miles per hour. The larger light did not resemble airplane landing lights. The smaller, fourth blinking light appeared to escort the larger light toward the three blinking lights now hovering over the center of the valley.

George stepped on the gas toward Moffat (where my night vision binoculars were sitting on the front seat of my truck) trying to get underneath the two lights, as they crossed the highway, just south of Moffat. Realizing we couldn't get there in time, I suggested we stop the car, get out and take a good look at them.

George turned his headlights off but left on his rather large, orange, Ford Tempo parking lights. We stood in front of the parking lights for better night vision. As soon as we obscured the parking lights, the large unblinking orange light slowly started going out, as if in slow motion. It took almost ten seconds for the light to totally

266

extinguish. The smaller fourth light that had been accompanying it kept flying west at the same apparent speed, toward the other three blinking lights, still waiting. They all vanished to the west.

Around 2:30 a.m., George, back at home in Alamosa, was awakened by a large helicopter hovering "right over my house." After several minutes, he realized it wasn't passing over. As he ran outside, the chopper bolted. However, a second one hung low in the air at the end of his street for several minutes before leaving.

I received reports of unusual aerial activity on (almost) every thirtieth of each month since November 1993. Although February has no 30th of the month, there was a sighting on the thirtieth day, March 2.

The first week of June featured an increase in reports of unexplained military (-esque) activity. According to Rio Grande County undersheriff, Brian Norton, the local National Guard unit was shipped out to Kansas on March 27th, for two weeks of maneuvers. Then who was driving the eastbound thirteen-truck convoy on June 4th, on Highway 160? The convoy consisted of ten, green-camoflaged one-ton trucks, two identical unmarked white-semis, and two brand-new Dodge scout-type trucks at the head and tail of the two-mile long convoy. Our National Guard unit has surplus vehicles that are at least ten-years-old. All the vehicles in this convey appeared to be new. Could this convoy be related to the many helicopter sightings reported between June 1st and June 8th?

Or, might they be related to the convoys with UN equipment on flat cars sighted on Interstate 25 during the first week of June near Ft. Carson, south of Denver, and in Montana and Wyoming? Over fourteen different helicopters sightings were reported during the first week of June, 1994 (1st, 3rd and 8th) in the central SLV. Most of this aerial activity was reportedly traveling north and south, up and down the Sangres.

One rather unusual chopper seen by several people, including myself, was a immense white, single prop-type with a flat rectangular box attached directly underneath. Two antennas appeared to be sticking out the front of the box. Just below the tail rotor were two black objects which looked like large tires but obviously weren't. It flew over the valley about seven thousand feet up and I studied it with binoculars as it traveled towards Greenie Mountain.

There had been numerous reports of a fast-moving strobe light seen north of Monte Vista, during the first weekend of May. The skeptics claim everyone was just observing a strobe light on a center-pivot sprinkler and, curiously, no additional reports were noted until Sunday, June 5, 1994 at 2:30 a.m., when three Saguache residents on 285 observed a rapidly blinking strobe light pacing them a half-mile west of the road, "going over the tree-tops."

They stopped and watched it continue northwest until it disappeared. When I told one puzzled witness that this light had been reported in May and was dismissed as a strobe on a center-pivit sprinkler, he remarked, "I've never heard of a fifty foot high sprinkler that can travel at sixty-five miles per hour."

10:00 p.m., Crestone:

That same evening, a sizable cheap firework display was observed over Crestone, traveling west. It was brilliant white and left a glow behind.

June 9, between 10:00 and 10:30 p.m., Rio Grande County:

A large reddish light was observed by several witnesses zig-zagging over the South Fork area and reported to the sheriff's office.

Does the Right Hand Know?

June 21, 1994, the Medano Ranch:

Three A-10 Warthogs flew less that two hundred feet high, as part of the Air National Guard's noise-level study for their "Air Space Initiative" (their attempt to expand the La Veta Military Operations Area into the SLV). The Air Force brass met with the foreman of the Medano Ranch, to monitor his bison calves' reaction to the low-flying jets.

The foreman was concerned about low-flying military aircraft scaring his herds. The A-10s (quietest of the military jets used here) appeared out of the north, passed over and . . . the herd didn't even look up. As the brass patted themselves on the back for their successful demonstration, three jets screamed out of the south at less than one hundred feet, making all those present "jump out of their skins!" The embarrassed brass professed no knowledge of the identity of the mystery pilots or their planes. The bison nonchalantly looked up at the roaring jets, then returned to grazing.

It would appear the right hand doesn't know what the left one is up to. Could this innocent-sounding example of professed ignorance be an indicator that our military is genuinely not aware of other agendas at work here in the valley and elsewhere around the planet?

June 27, 11:00 p.m., Moffat:

Six witnesses were skywatching when one of them noticed a large shadow moving slowly overhead. There were no clouds over the valley but something huge was blocking out a sizeable portion of the brilliant Milky Way. The first witness to notice the anomaly alerted the others' attention to the object. They all claimed later that they saw a "triangular ship, with no lights," slowly fly eastward over the Sangres. "It was so big it blotted out the stars!" observed one witness. Based on their descriptions, the craft was "the length of three hand-widths (at arm's length) or, about fifteen degrees. They attempted to shine a million candlepower spotlight up toward the object in an effort to illuminate it as it passed overhead, but had no success. Whatever it was appeared to be over one thousand feet above the valley floor.

The witnesses also reported a smaller triangular craft following the first. Sightings of triangular craft have been reported during the past four fall seasons by hunters before dawn in the mountains surrounding the SLV but I have no other report of a summer sighting of this type.

The following morning I was writing on my computer when the phone rang. Probably another report I thought. I answered the call and the voice stated: "Christopher, Mark Vertullo, *Sightings*, we spoke last winter." I had already been contacted by *Unsolved Mysteries* and *Encounters* about my investigation but nothing had panned out. Vertullo assured me that *Sightings* wanted to produce a segment on the Unusual Animal Deaths our area was experiencing. I was impressed by his up-to-speed demeanor and, after evaluating his interest, I offered to field-produce the *Sightings* segment. This would entail location scouting, case selection and witness selection and scheduling. He agreed to my conditions and we set-up a shoot date for the third week in July. Okay, an international TV segment. I reminded myself, this is 'the big-time' I better have my "proverbials" together.

June 30, 10:00 p.m., the Baca Chalets:
Dan and Joanie Retuda and two visiting friends were skywatching when six small orange objects, traveling east, shot across the sky with a pulsing, zig-zag motion.

"They were really high and at first, we thought they were just satellites. But I've never seen satellites jerk like that. Two of the lights even did the same moves in tandem," said Dan Retuda. "They sure weren't regular satellites." They appeared to blink out as they moved east into the Earth's shadow.

That same evening, investigator Gary Hart, visiting our mysterious valley from Illinois, recorded a vibrating utility pole five miles south of the Moffat sighting location. There are several poles in our area that sporadically vibrate during sighting periods. Gary is the first investigator, to my knowledge, that has successfully recorded a vibrating utility pole. The tape indicates a complex, multi-source group of sounds that together, reveal a low vibration. There was no wind that night and the sound seemed to emanate from the ground. The closer to the ground, the louder it grew. The vibrating poles I had monitored near the Dunes never seemed to vibrate when the area was not experiencing sightings.

From July 3rd through July 7th, there were seven sightings of anomalous craft by sixteen witnesses in the north central valley. These sightings include: more "jerky satellites" on the 4th and 5th, the before-mentioned Dunes area sighting on the 3rd, a daylight sighting of a "bell-shaped" sphere seen near Hooper by two witnesses on the 6th and a fireball that dazzled witnesses on the 7th.

Four witnesses in the Baca claimed to see a "large, fluorescent orange fireball" descend through the clouds over the Baca Ranch. They called again, seventeen minutes later, to report two white, unblinking dots flying over the area where the fireball supposedly went down. The eight to ten second fireball traveled from west to east. They have usually been observed going in the opposite direction.

July 13, 8:42 a.m., CO-NM:
A loud boom echoed across most of central Colorado from Wyoming to New Mexico. Windows were reportedly broken in Denver. According to a FEMA spokesperson, the boom was caused by a SR-71 Blackbird on a "classified mission for NASA." This boom was heard for hundreds of miles, and I didn't believe that a conventional sonic-boom could be heard over so vast an area. When the FEMA worker returned my call, trying hard to convince me, he was unable to answer any questions concerning the supposed flight. Even if the plane made a sweeping turn over the state, and the atmospheric conditions were right, I had serious doubts that the resulting boom could be heard over such a large area.

MUFON State Section Director, Jim Nelson, told me that afternoon he had read that all six NASA Blackbirds had been grounded two weeks before! The article mentioned cracks in the plane's tires.

More and More Sightings

July 18 through 21, 1994:
We were in the midst of three days of hectic shooting of the "Sightings investigation team's" scrutiny of the UAD phenomenon. Director Keith Fialkowitz planned a hard-hitting segment. Ernest Sandoval, Emilio Lobato and Clarence Vigil met us in San Luis. We caught up with Eli Hronich in Eagle Nest.

Fialkowitz jumped at my comment that the UAD phenomenon

may be "the greatest unsolved serial crime spree of the twentieth century." (I repeated it for all fifteen camera takes.) The segment aired in September of 1994.

A follow-up segment on UADs was filmed in August for broadcast that Fall. It featured myself, Gail Staehlin and the Eli Hronich cases.

July 19, around 9:30 p.m., La Veta, CO:
A red, pulsing light seen near the town of La Veta, and the Spanish Peaks, was reported to investigator Barbara Atkins. The next morning choppers were spotted over the same area.

July 24, Moreno Valley, NM:
Eagle Nest, NM, rancher Eli Hronich found another steer "mutilated." He also reported that a gray unmarked helicopter hovered over him as he examined the animal. This happened five days after being interviewed by Sightings.

July 30, Ft. Garland, CO
Barbara Adkins reported that on July 30th, just after midnight, witnesses saw a large orange light "with a tail" moving "real fast" from south-to-north, again, near La Veta.

Three dark, military-type choppers were seen in formation flying south down the Sangres and a Huey was seen landing at Alamosa airport at 2:15 pm.

There was apparently a flurry of unpublicized activity in the La Veta area, just east of the SLV that spring and summer. Although I haven't received verifications for most, including several sightings during the spring of 1994, and a possible landing, there is evidence to suggest that the La Veta area has experienced UADs which were hushed by the locals. An insurance agent claimed that three ranchers lost twenty-one head of cattle in a short time to supposed lightning strikes.

Another case featured an isolated farmer who found three dead pigs, mutilated (by literal definition) in their pen. He said they had been "slashed-up with a machete-type knife." There was no blood, tracks or evidence of a struggle. After calling the sheriff, who came out with a deputy to investigate the case, and burying the bodies, the farmer occupied a trailer on-site to guard his remaining animals.

In the middle of the night, he heard digging. With shotgun in hand, he approached a dark figure who was attempting to dig up the pigs. The surprised digger apologized and swore he was retrieving the carcasses for the Colorado Bureau of Investigation, for analysis. The farmer helped him dig and load the bodies into a pickup. When the farmer called CBI several days later to see what they had found, they denied someone from their office had picked up the carcasses!

For The Ripley File

In a continuing case. A Baca couple since October 1993 had been seen a two to three foot long creature darting around their yard. It appears to be partially translucent and tapered at both ends while opaque in the middle. It moves quickly, the couple's dog responds to it, it leaves no tracks and seems to disappear into thin air.

They made the decision to report it to me after an unexpected indoor sighting. Around 9:45 one evening, "it" was seen entering the living-room through the closed stereo cabinet doors, scampering silently across the floor to the other side of the room and out a spot in the wall six to eight inches above the floor, within inches of the couple's feet!

The next morning, when they let out their dog, he "immediately ran to the outside wall [where whatever-it-was disappeared], dug up his bone" and went to bury it somewhere else. The amazed witnesses (who requested not to be named) said they both have seen the thing move through the dining room and out through the wall twice since January. To my knowledge, this was the first encounter with such a creature in the area, a distinction they would rather not have.

August 8, 8:55 a.m., the Baca:
I was refinishing the same couple's floors while they were away. As I walked out their front door, less that fifteen feet away, there one went! It reminded me of a two to three foot-long lizard gliding quickly across the gate opening in the low picket fence that surrounds their house. I heard a trilling sound in my head as I saw it. I immediately ran to the spot. It had only been visible in the gate opening, appeared to be eight to ten inches off the ground, (I didn't see any legs) and left no tracks in the treeless desert sand. This one will have to go in the Ripley file

August 17, 1994, Moreno Valley:
Eli Hronich found another "mutilated" steer near Eagle Nest, NM, and the following day, three UADs were found twenty miles south, near Truchas, NM, on the Max Cordova ranch. Cordova was sure the cows were pregnant but no fetuses were found. According to Albuquerque investigator, Gail Staehlin, who has spent a considerable time investigating New Mexico cattle death

cases, "These latest ones seem to decompose abnormally fast." Could they have been killed, brought somewhere else, and kept for a day or two before being dumped where they were discovered.

Two members of the Cordova family reported that they received chemical-like burns after touching one of the animals and the entire family said they had suffered "flu-like symptoms" the following day. Hronich claimed his hand "burnt like hell for two weeks" after touching one of his dead cows, just as Inspector Jerry Valario had a burn-type rash on his hand after touching Tom Reed's dead calf. I've never heard of this being reported anywhere since Nellie Lewis burnt her hand on the piece of Snippy's mane-hair.

I left to visit my parents for a week in Washington State, starting on August 19, 1994. Two nights later at 9:15 p.m., witnesses driving up Highway 17 claim they saw a "low flying flashing light move parallel to the highway." Later, outside their house in Moffat, they also saw an orange light that moved east toward Crestone, then disappeared.

Around midnight, twenty witnesses in Del Norte, saw a formation of twelve lights hovering over "D" Mountain (a painted-stone "D" signifies Del Norte). According to Mark Hunter of the *Valley Courier*, who interviewed five of the witnesses, the objects created the capital letter "G," then a circle, then a triangle as they hung silently in the sky. Then one of the objects descended through the clouds and flew close enough for them to see a sphere-shape and "red and blue lights" that reminded them of sequencing "Christmas lights." The show went on for almost an hour.

I find it interesting that witnesses in Del Norte mentioned to lights forming the shapes that suggested the word GOD. However, witnesses further east observed the light show from a more flattened angle and the G was flattened to become a D, thus spelling DOD. I find this detail highly intriguing and possibly revealing.

Over the years I have pointed out the apparent "reflectivity" that seems to accompany ufological events. Often the witness(ess) are convinced that the object is "beaming them" or that the anomaly they observed directly responded to their thoughts or wishes. Witnesses will invariably attempt to use familiar terms and symbols to describe their experience to others and this fact of human nature may help us understand paranormal phenomena manifestations. Parapsychologist George Hanson insightfully refines this concept and suggests there is a more complicated process at work. The following is from his seminal work: The Trickster and the Paranormal:

> The ideas of reflexivity, mirroring, reflection. self-reference, and projection are interrelated. Though some

of these terms are often used interchangeably, it can be helpful to make distinctions. Self-reference is the source of a number of paradoxes. One of the best known is: "This statement is false" (Epimenides paradox); the sentence refers to itself, and, if it is false, then [the statement is] true. On the surface, this seems trivial or even silly, but the consequences are profound. This paradox confuses subject and object; it explodes that distinction. Reflection is a slightly different idea; when one is reflective, one is aware on one's awareness. Reflexivity is the turning of some function back upon itself, as in using awareness to learn to be aware or using logic to study logic.

Other Del Norte witnesses claim lights were seen nightly the entire third week of August. More sightings were confirmed on the nights of August 24th and August 28th.

On August 29th, a second *Sightings* film-crew arrived in the SLV for a segment on the previous winter's NORAD Event. I again field-produced for Director Keith Fialkowitz and was extensively interviewed. As we arrived at the *Valley Courier* office to interview Mark Hunter, he was on the phone fielding a previous night's sighting report. Resident Mary Jones claimed that she and two other witnesses observed a "honeycomb shaped object" west of "D" Mountain for an hour between 11:00 p.m. and midnight on the 28th. (The phone call was reenacted for the camera after it was revealed to be a sighting. Jung would chuckle at yet another example of synchronicity.)

This segment aired on November 10, 1995 and featured interviews with Jack Cookerly, the Koons, Brian Norton and Mark Hunter in addition to myself.

On August 30th, Eli Hronich found yet another dead steer. Exasperated and almost embarrassed, cocked his hat and asked me "I wish I knew why they're picking on me," he e me during a conversation the first week of September. The steer had been grazing on rented pasture at the T.V. Gorman ranch south of Eagle Nest. By now Hronich had suffered a substantial financial loss at the hands of the mystery cattle dudes who seem to have singled out his herd of twenty-five hundred. "This whole thing just doesn't make sense," he added, perplexed and worried. "We've got to get some help from somebody." That fall Eli moved his herd downhill to winter pasture and hoped for the best.

A wave of UAD cases were then reported to the west, to the east, and southeast of Taos. The Raton, NM, area had generated several reports and Sandoval County rancher Ray Trujillo reported twenty of his cattle had been mysteriously slain on his

Jemez Mountain ranch since April 1993. One of the animals allegedly had its spinal cord excised. An April 1994 case in Arroyo Seco, north of Taos, said a nine-day old bull was found with its jaw mandible hide excised.

September 2, 1994, Highway 160, east of Del Norte:
While driving between Monte Vista and Del Norte, the South Fork ambulance crew had an unusual experience. The vehicle went dead for three or four seconds. Rio Grande County Undersheriff Brian Norton was told, "Even their pac-set went dead," ruling out electrical system failure in the ambulance. The crew didn't see anything unusual and the vehicle quickly resumed power, the pac-set came on and everything returned to normal.

One reviewer of my first book mentioned how disconcerting the San Luis Valley activity appeared to him. He used the previous three reports as an example of his bewilderment. He was unable to comprehend why I jumped from one incident to the next without drawing any conclusions. Another reviewer echoed his frustration by calling my approach as akin to writer's attention deficit disorder. I'm smiling as I write this. I guess some readers don't understand my time-line formatted approach. In case you haven't noticed, these events are presented chronologically and as close to the original, primary data as possible. I don't apologize for this approach, rather I remind you the reader that when weird events happen in such quick succession, it is similar to looking backwards through a kaleidoscope. I'm simply relating these events as accurately and as contextually as these perplexing reports allow.

Weird And Weirder

Friday September 9, 1994, Huerfano County:
And just when I thought the activity couldn't become any stranger, investigator David Perkins called. "This one's real bizarre," he prefaced his account. According to search and rescue personnel and local residents, it seemed that two hunters, the prior week period, ended up reported as missing. When the first showed up a day later, the frightened man, "raced away in his truck without saying a word."

The second, Mark (not his real name) wandered into the Libre community and approached the ornate house of a local artist. Hays told the artist an incredible story of an ordeal he claimed he'd suffered over the past four days. He didn't seem hungry or thirsty, appeared to be rational, "remarkably calm," and "didn't seem traumatized." The artist told Perkins, "He looked like a cop with a four-day growth of beard."

275

The hunter claimed he had arrived at a rented cabin on Dry Creek, on Greenhorn Mountain, high above the Libre on September 2nd, for a weekend hunting trip.

Hays claimed that a large group of "aliens dressed in camo appeared," at his campsite and before he could react, he was gassed, captured and tied up. They never spoke to him and never fed him. He said he survived by eating grasshoppers. The camo-clad, human-looking aliens appeared to Hays to be conducting "some sort of maneuvers." He said that at one point the group started to get aboard a small ship. Hays was astonished when the "ship expanded" to accommodate them all. The ship allegedly took off, morphed into the shape of a bear, then morphed into "a three-headed wolf," then turned into a cloud! (Could it have been Amanita mushroom season, or another flashback from the 1960s?)

Perkins also didn't know what to make of Hays' claim. "This is so weird!" he said several times, with a light-hearted laugh. These events supposedly occurred on the mountain right behind Perkins' house, so that may have explained the hint of nervousness. When law enforcement officials went up to the cabin they found his vehicle trashed, with the passenger-side door open and the remains of a campfire, just outside the open door. His "half-burnt clothes" were scattered around the area.

September 5, El Paso County:
Pikes Peak Cattlemen's Association board member Clyde Chess found one of his cows missing its genitalia, tongue, lips, ear, and udder. The heart had been removed from an incision behind the leg. The cow's unborn fetus was also reported missing. The hide around the incisions was "curled, as if they was cut with something hot." Chess also noted that rigor mortis never set in, the bones were bleached clean of meat and all the hair fell off the face within days.

September 7, at 8:25 p.m., the Baca Chalets:
Six witnesses observed another one of those unexplained satellite-like lights, zig-zagging and pulsing across the heavens, from west-to-east. "When the kids ran in to tell us to come look, I thought they were just seeing a satellite," observed Al Koon (based on the description). "But it sure wasn't any type of satellite I've ever seen. I wonder what we have up there?" The diligent skywatcher ran out with three other witnesses and verified the kids' sighting.

September 12, El Paso County:
Rancher Mary Liss found "a 1,200 lb. cow mutilated" on her

ranch, northeast of Colorado Springs. The animal's reproductive organs had been removed with what she described as "a technology that's not readily available to just anybody. This was a cow that you don't just walk up to. We had a hard time getting her in for a vaccination," said Liss. She had seen the cow alive the evening before. She also mentioned, in an article in the *Rocky Mountain News*, that a nearby rancher had found another "mutilation" about a month prior.

September 13, 4:30 p.m., Chacon, NM:
Investigator Linda Moulton Howe investigated this highly unusual case, one of the most bizarre ever reported. Evidently, Larry Gardea was bear hunting on the ranch where he worked when he heard a loud humming sound. As it began, a group of cattle nearby were startled and ran from the noise. According to a Las Vegas, NM, newspaper, Gardea claimed that a cow was dragged by the sound backwards, up the hill, into the underbrush. He said it appeared to be struggling to get away but was unable to escape. Gardea said the animal sounded as if it was being tortured. Being understandably spooked, he said he fired several shots from his 30.06 towards the sound, and it stopped.

Gardea headed to the sheriff's office and returned to the site with a deputy. They found one cow had been "mutilated," a second cow crippled, and the third cow, which had been dragged uphill, was missing. Gardea also mentioned the humming sound being heard by locals several times before the incident he reported. (My repeated calls to Gardea went unanswered.)

7:30 p.m., Highway 160:
Three hours later, a Del Norte woman called to say she and her teenage son had just seen "two fluorescent orange lights that looked like streamers moving in tandem." She said the two lights were between four and six feet in length and flew right across the front of the van she was driving. The location was the exact stretch of road where the South Fork Ambulance went dead on September, 2.

They rushed home and called me. I immediately fired a call to one of my watchers, an amateur astronomer who lives within two miles of the alleged sighting, which revealed that his satellite-TV had inexplicably ceased functioning for several minutes during the approximate time when the fluorescent orange streamers were sighted.

September 24, Highway 285, North of Antonito:
Laffing Buddha was rocking "The Office," an Alamosa hot

spot. As we wound up our first set, my *Sightings* segment flashed on the bar's TV. The last chord was still ringing as I dashed to the bar to watch. An attractive blonde woman was glued to the set, sipping beer between takes of dead cows. Her mouth hung open and she nodded as the Christopher O'Brien on the set intoned, "I believe this to be the greatest unsolved serial crime spree of the Twentieth Century."

I sat next to her. She glanced over and let out a shriek, looking back at the TV, then at me. "That's you! On TV," she squealed. I had even worn the same shirt I wore for the shoot that night at the gig. I simply smiled at her, but honestly it was pretty exhilarating watching myself on network television.

.

September 26, Clayton, NM:
That same Monday night, at 9:50 p.m., I was visiting with Texas investigator Gary Massey (who declares that wherever he goes, he scares the phenomena away) when we watched a sizable cheap-firework display streak from west-to-east and descend straight down into the foothills between the Baca and the mountains. It was bluish-white and had a duration of about three seconds. It appeared to descend about two to three miles east of our vantage point. It wasn't a meteor, even Massey agreed.

September 29, 10:30 p.m., Great Sand Dunes Campground:
A bus load of Del Norte Middle School students were bushed after a day of dune climbing and, after some good-natured rambunctiousness, settled down in their tents to sleep. One fifth-grade student, Kodi Whitehead, felt restless. He couldn't sleep. He and his two tent-mates, Michael Richardson and Justin Kerr had stopped talking and goofing-around and lay quietly looking out the tent flap at the partly-cloudy sky facing the Dunes a mile away. Suddenly, a "large whitish-red ball of light" sailed over the dunes headed north. Kodi shook Michael and pointed it out. They promptly roused Justin, and dashed outside to watch. After ten, or so seconds, it disappeared behind the trees.

About a minute later, the "oval-looking" ball of light returned. It seemed brighter as it streaked by their campsite. By now, six or seven other kids, scattered in tents around the campsite, had been alerted by the boy's shouts. They all watched in wonder as the circular light suddenly flared-up many times it's original size and "lit up the whole valley." And, it was gone.

Two teachers stumbled out of their tents amid the chaos of excited, pointing kids. They had missed the spectacle.

September 30, around 10:00 p.m., Highway 17, Saguache

County:

Three Pagosa Springs, Colorado residents, traveling north just outside Hooper, observed what they described as a pulsing red light, north of Center, about twenty miles west of the Dunes. They also noted the red airport beacon south of the larger pulsing red light. The unusual light appeared to be a floodlight, above the ground, shining downward and was estimated at less than five miles away. I heard them talking about their sighting while visiting Al and Donna Koon in Moffat. This happens a lot to me around here.

Salida, rancher James Neppl reported to the Saguache County sheriff's office finding a dead cow and (forty yards away) its dead calf. The site was rented SLV pasture on the former Triple L Boy's Ranch. Neppl thinks they were both killed the night of September 30th. This is the exact area where the three women claimed to have seen the red pulsing light that night.

It was the first official UAD report in Saguache County (to my knowledge) since June 1, 1980. Both animals were missing udders, rear-end, and ears. Neppl said, "I do most of my own vet work. I've never seen anything like those two animals. The cuts were so clean and precise, there was no blood anywhere. . . the hair quickly fell off the faces." He also noticed that they were untouched by scavengers until human scent had been introduced to the crime scene. The calf had the entire left side of it's skull "peeled and cleaned" of tissue, and all hoof material had been removed with the underneath foot bones bleached white. "The joints were cut as smooth as could be," he observed.

Neppl said that the animals had not been hit by lightning and the calf was cut from chin to rear end with what can only be described as pinking shears. A front foreleg had been completely excised of tissue and hide. I obtained video footage for the Sightings' UAD update segment. This case was reported by Michelle Le Blanc Hynden in the *Center Post Dispatch* on October 14th and in the November issue of the *Crestone Eagle*.

As per the norm, the entire crime scene was gone over with a "fine-toothed comb" by investigating officers and no tracks, footprints, or additional physical evidence was uncovered. Saguache County asked the Colorado Bureau of Investigation for help with the case. "You hear about them [UADs], but you don't think they'll ever happen in your county. Then when they do, you really don't know what to think. There was something real strange about those cattle!" commented then-Saguache county sheriff Dan Pacheco.

October 7, Conejos County:

Rancher Mack Crowthers reported to the sheriff a "mutilated" steer had been found on his ranch in Sanford. The ears and testicles had been removed and a "leg had been boned-out," (all the tissue and hide excised from a leg-bone). The steer was found in dense scrub-willow, suggesting it may have been dropped. The boned-out leg is very similar to the Jim Neppl case from the previous week.

A neighbor, Mrs. Warren Reed, claims to have seen "weird green floodlights" in the Crowther's pasture the night this steer had apparently been killed. Investigating deputy Steven Gottlieb and undersheriff Joe Taylor Jr. found fresh tire tracks heading into the pasture near where the animal was found. These tracks stopped cold and there was no indication that the vehicle turned around nor that the tracks had been obscured. "It was like it (the vehicle) had been picked up from the air and whisked away," Gottlieb said.

Crowthers reportedly lost three more cattle the following week. Two of the animals were found dead on their stomachs, with their legs splayed out to the sides. There was no evidence of bullet holes nor obvious signs of cause of death. The animals with "classic mutilation" wounds seemed to decompose unusually fast and "did not bloat," similar to the last five Hronick cows in Eagle Nest. Complete photographic evidence was obtained.

According to Gottlieb, another Conejos County rancher had "found a bunch of dead cows" on his ranch in a similar condition. They happened during the last week of September and the first week of October.

Alamosa County, having escaped any official UAD reports for over a decade, may have had three unusual cattle deaths during October and two more in November. During a lecture I gave at Adams State College on November 4, I was approached by an Alamosa Wildlife Refuge worker named Donna Knowles who had attended my first lecture at the college two years before. Evidently she had been trying to locate me since the first week of October and learned I was going to speak again that Thursday night.

She said she'd been patrolling, late in the day during the first week of October, when she found three "mutilated" cattle in a remote part of the refuge. There were many locked gates and fence lines between the cattle and any nearby pastures.

She returned early the next morning with a thirty-five mm camera and a co-worker and found only one cow. The other two had vanished without a trace. She told me emphatically, "There is no way cows could get in and out of there without being dropped and then picked back up!" As she and her co-worker examined the animal, according to Knowles, they both heard a "high-pitched whirring sound."

She took four pictures at the end of a roll and dropped the film later that afternoon at an Alamosa one-hour photo shop. She later picked up the pictures, slipped the negatives in her purse and put the packet of photos on the dashboard (including the four shots of the dead cow, which she looked at immediately to make sure they had come out) and went into a store.

When she returned to her vehicle, she discovered "the four pictures of the cow were gone!" Because she had separated the negatives from the prints she was able to provide me with reprints. The animal was missing the hide and tissue from the left-side of its face and the rear end appeared to be cored out. Knowles says the animal's wounds appeared to be caused by a laser-type instrument.

October 9, 11:15 p.m., Casita Park:
A massage therapist, visiting the Baca from Colorado Springs, and several Casita Park residents observed a glowing ball of bluish-white light slowly arcing over the Sangres, above Mt. Adams. It made a slow seventy degree arc over the mountains with a duration of about fifteen seconds. It appeared to two of the witnesses to be slowly moving away to the southeast.

Five hours later, at 4:00 a.m., eighty miles south in Questa, NM, rancher Tom Reed observed a "a bright blue floodlight lighting up the forest in the [Sangre] mountains . . . around the [CO-NM] border." Reed saw the light while traveling north on highway 159 on his way to La Junta with a load of sale cattle.

Then we were blessed with a three-week lull. When I began investigating these mysterious events, I never thought that there would be times when I would actually welcome the quiet periods of no reports. There was time to catch-up on my sightings log, my band, Laffing Buddha, was offered a recording contract and I even overcame my aversion to industrialized beef protein and pondered a stop at Arby's for a roast beef sandwich. Just kidding.

October 18, 10:00 p.m., Hooper:
George Oringdulph, Chris Medina (the two guitarists in Laffing Buddha) and myself observed an orange light flying over the north central valley. The unblinking light made a slow turn to the northeast and disappeared over the Sangres. Minutes later, two smaller unblinking white lights were seen heading on the same flight path.

The phantom cattle surgeons returned to the eastern Colorado plains that same night. But this time they were playing a different game. A bison was discovered the following morning "mutilated," on the Denver Buffalo Company ranch

281

near Simla. Linda Moulton Howe was fortunately in Colorado and investigated the case. (A second bison was found in similar condition later on the same ranch, November 8th). According to Howe, the necropsy of the first bison showed two perforations between the ribs, but oddly no break in the hide above them. Tissue around the incision areas on the cored-out rear end were hard and the spleen was an abnormal pinkish-white. Lab results revealed no virus or bacteria and yet the vet said the animal had "died of illness four days before."

This was impossible, for the bison was seen inside its pen with twenty other animals at 6:30 p.m. the previous night when the rancher was medicating his herd. The genital incision area had an unusual characteristic. One side of the incised oval was hard, the other side soft. There were holes in the muscle tissue.

Linda told me, "I couldn't believe that this buffalo death was just a few hours old." She noted that fresh liquid feces were present and that the blood present was not congealed. The lab called her back two days later with the observation that the tissue was already rotten.

I finally confirmed rumors of an additional UAD case south of Alamosa in October. My bass player, Lyman Bushkovsky's uncle-in-law, rancher John Harr, told him of a strange occurrence. Harr and his family were awakened the night of October 20th, by what Harr described as a terrible noise. It sounded like a "huge helicopter hovering right over the top of the house." Harr, also the Del Norte Postmaster, said. "I went outside and all I could hear was the downdraft from the propeller, there were no engine-sounds. I didn't hear anything mechanical!"

Two days later, October 22nd, Harr's two sons discovered two cows and two calves one-half mile away from the house to the east, dead for "no apparent reason." According to the rancher, the oldest cow, who "would've died soon anyway," was discovered missing the flesh off her jaw, and the tongue and rear end were "cut out." He also noticed that, "It looked like she'd floundered around a bit before she died."

The other cow and two calves "looked like they had just died in their sleep." These three animals displayed no incision-like marks and scavengers made short work of two of them. The second cow was untouched, even by birds. No additional clues appeared to be present at the site. No tire-tracks, footprints, scavenger tracks or any blood was discovered at the scene. No vet examined these animals, and Harr never bothered to roll the "mutilated" cow over to ascertain if the downside had been butchered.

Alamosa County K-9 deputy Jim McCloskey investigated the Harr report. For some reason, he left his animal partner in the car while at the site and no animal reactions were noted.

The Alamosa River snakes through a corner of the ranch where the animals were discovered. This river is polluted with heavy metals forty miles upstream in the mountains, for seventeen miles, by the Summitville Mine superfund site. It is one of the only known sources of pollution in the pristine Greater SLV. This appears to give more ammunition for "the UAD as environmental monitoring" theorists.

Harr "stewed for a couple of days" and then started making phone-calls. He called Senator Ben Nighthorse Campbell's office about the matter and was referred to the governor's office. The governor's office told him to talk with State's Veterinarian advocate, Dr. John Maulsby. The vet spoke knowledgeably about the phenomenon. "He [Maulsb]y told me he was going to put an article in our local paper requesting ranchers provide him with fresh samples for testing," said Harr. "But if he ever put one in, I never saw it."

Dr. Maulsby has offered to help in any way he can with any future cases that are found in a timely manner. Not many people are aware of the intense activity the La Veta-Spanish Peaks region has been experiencing over the years. This area was home to several reports that summer. A multitude of interesting rumors had been circulating the area but confirmation of these stories proved difficult.

I received a call from David Perkins concerning a new series of UAD cases that had just come to his attention. It seems that rancher Ermenio Andreatta, about three miles west of the town of La Veta had discovered a crippled cow on Sunday, October 23rd, with in sight—just a quarter mile away from his house. Returning to the same area the following day, he found a "mutilated" cow; the rear end, reproductive tract and left-side teats were removed, and the animal was half submerged in a small creek. Nearby were several nine-foot wide circular discolorations in the grass. "They look like giant tractor-tire marks," Andreatta later told Perkins. Two more mutilated cows were found over the next three days.

The La Veta *Signature*, article of November 3, stated, "a fist-sized dark spot was visible on the chest of each of the dead cows." District Wildlife Manager Lonnie Brown investigated the site, and according to the *Signature*, "Brown just shook his head in amazement and perplexity as he examined the cattle for bullet holes or other causes of death."

A carload of Huerfano residents told Perkins that they witnessed an unusual aerial craft hovering over the Yellowstone Road shortly after the Andrietta's lost their livestock. The craft was silent and was seen shining a powerful spotlight down toward the ground.

The witnesses were "pretty freaked-out" by their sighting.

The Andreattas experienced a fourth case later in November. Linda Moulton Howe, who had arrived in the San Luis Valley at my invitation for a sheriff's UAD training seminar, went to the Andreatta's Middle Creek Road Ranch and conducted a thorough investigation of these four cases. They were included in her Research Grant Report of UAD Cases in 1994.

Howe even obtained plant samples from the scene for analysis. She has begun carefully collecting flora from the head and rear end of UADs, along with a control sample some distance away from the carcass. Preliminary results from other UAD cases have shown changes in the plant's respiratory process. According to Howe, this result is similar to findings from plants affected in crop-circles.

The La Veta-Blanca-Forbes Trinchera reports continued. They were all found within The La Veta Military Operations Area, previously associated with UFO activity. Now the same areas were handing out UADs. Locals are used to seeing military flights over their area on a daily basis. Some of the UFO reports could be misidentified conventional military flights but several reports remain unexplained.

October 26, 1:00 p.m., Blanca:

A Blanca resident observed what she described as a "large silver oval" hanging for about five minutes in the cloudless sky above Mt Lindsey, just east of Blanca Peak. She claims she has seen the object before in the same location and a third time in 1987 over the Sand Dunes. It "was completely silent" when it flew out of sight and left no vapor trail.

October 28, the Baca Chalets:

I received a call from Joe Taylor, Sr., who works at the Conejos County Sheriff's Office. He told me of several recent sighting reports and then casually mentioned that there was a man there who wished to speak with me.

A man named Alan got on the phone and related several wild stories. He lives with his extended family near the New Mexican border, near the mouth of the Rio Grande Canyon. He told me, rather matter-of-factly, that all during the previous spring, he and his family had been watching "every kind of ship you could imagine," flying around the desolate semi-arid desert near where he and his family live.

"Some are discs. Some are triangles. Big ones and small ones. Some of them even give off red and blue flashes like a laser disc." He added, "My mother found out that they would come closer if you called to them in your mind." (A self-styled, CSETI approach.)

"One night, toward the end of May, a friend (who didn't believe they had been seeing the craft) and I went out a couple miles north of the ranch to watch. It was around 9:00 to 9:30 p.m. We were sitting in his pickup truck, out in the middle of nowhere, when a strange bank of fog rolled in and surrounded us. We saw a light straight ahead shining out of the fog and a craft appeared and hovered in front of us, about two hundred yards away. I started to call it closer and it approached and just sat there about fifty feet away. Well, my friend kind of freaked out, grabbed his rifle from the rack and popped off a couple of shots at it. It went above us and somehow it lifted up the truck and put it in the bar ditch!"

Evidently, the family has tried to photograph the ships but the objects have other ideas, zipping away out of camera range. Alan's mother had recently seen "three blue balls of light bouncing over the prairie" near their ranch.

One investigator told me that, over the border in New Mexico, somewhere in the Rio Grande Canyon, a secret underground base entrance was located. "I watched a large door open and a concrete pad extend out from the opening. A helicopter was sitting on the pad and it flew off. The pad went back in and the doors closed."

I have not confirmed this particular claim but it has been suspected that one, or possibly more secret bases are located in the CO/NM border area. NM Representative Bill Richardson, did some checking and speculated in early 1993 that the so-called Taos Hum could be defense-related. A few weeks later NM Senator Pete Domenici said he was given assurances from the Pentagon that there was no military involvement. The Taos Hum has been described as an extremely low frequency sound or vibration that has been recorded and measured to be around thirty to eighty Hertz. An extensive survey by University of NM, The US Air Force's Phillips Laboratory and both Sandia and Los Alamosa National Labs found that twenty percent of those surveyed claimed they could hear the hum. Interesting to note, according an archaeologist I interviewed, to de Anza reported in his diary hearing a similarly described hum while chasing Comanche Chief Cuerno Verde up through the San Luis Valley.

Helicopters were reported over La Veta Pass on the next three days October 27-28 and 29. On Friday, the 28th, around 10:00 p.m., a large disc-shaped craft was spotted by a Forbes Trinchera resident that appeared to be shining a spotlight at the ground. A short time later helicopters were seen "buzzing" the area where the disc was seen.

Four hours later, The Koon family was arriving at their home in Moffat, (forty miles to the northwest) when they observed "three bluish balls of light" descend separately in a four or five second period with a zig-zag motion, just south and west of Moffat.

On October 29th, at around 10:00 a.m., two Crestone residents, on their way to Gunnison, spotted a military convoy on Highway 50, headed west. According to their description, the convoy consisted of seven humvees, two of them were "large ones;" the other five were the standard smaller versions. What immediately impressed them was the fact that none of the vehicles had license plates or insignias. All vehicles had "desert-style cammo." I was under the impression that any vehicles, private or otherwise, were required to have license plates and identifying markings.

Any relationship between this activity and the unusual aerial craft reports could be anybody's guess but my suspicion is that there is a link. These reports of government activity have a tendency to ebb and flow in concert with the reports of unusual craft.

The Mother Ships

November 4, 1994, 7:00 p.m., Greenie Mountain:
According to undersheriff Brian Norton, Sharon Compton reported to the Rio Grande County sheriff's office seeing "something glowing, landing near Greenie," and drew a picture of the object for sheriff's deputies. Compton and other witnesses watched the object for several minutes before it disappeared behind the mountains.

Also, according to Norton, November 5th, at around 1:00 p.m., an ex-sheriff was working in his front yard when he heard a roar overhead. He saw helicopters escorting a triangle-shaped craft. As he was watching the aircraft, someone pulled into his driveway and, as he turned to see who it was, the sound above him stopped. He looked up and saw nothing! He had only looked down for "a couple of seconds" before all the craft "just plain disappeared."

November 6, 1994at 11:15 p.m., CO-NM border:
While returning from a seminar I had conducted in Madrid, NM, Isadora and I saw an unusual light across the valley, just above the eastern horizon (over the La Veta area). We were traveling north on highway 285, near Antonito.

Ten minutes later we noticed that the light began increasing in velocity, towards our location. Isadora pulled over and I grabbed my 3.5 magnification nightvision binoculars (never leave home without 'em) and viewed a tight wedge-shaped configuration of three unblinking orange lights fly directly overhead. It silently moved almost twice as fast as a conventional airliner.

It may have been an F-117 stealth fighter (which I have never seen here). The fact that it flew right over us and was silent is puzzling. It did not appear to be more than a couple of thousand feet up and we should have heard something.

Several hours earlier on Sunday, November 6th, at dusk, two Crestone residents had seen "Two large iridescent lights over the western horizon," near La Garita. Both witnesses (independently) reported the sighting, which were on my answering machine when I arrived home that night. Each viewed the lights for several minutes before they appeared to blink out.

The following two weeks in the SLV must have constituted a UFO rush hour. Multiple reports of numerous aerial craft were reported by valley residents, with some claiming the lights were chasing each other and "in a dogfight." Two of these reports claim as many as twenty craft were observed at one time. Could these be reports of military maneuvers?

On Sunday, November 6th, a hand on the Crowthers ranch reported to the sheriff seeing ten or twelve jets flying in formation around Antonito. Deputy Steven Gottlieb of the sheriff's office told me that three families had called to report a "two hundred yard long saucer flying over Antonito," on November 7th, accompanied by as many as a dozen jets. Gottlieb hurried out and claims he saw the craft himself.

In another probable example of the fear of ridicule (and of the unknown), reliable independent sources have told me that several firemen saw as many as thirty UFOs flying over Greenie Mountain on November 7th. All second-hand versions of the alleged event were similar. Law enforcement and reporters in the area have obtained off-the-record confirmation of the event from several of the firemen but cannot get anyone to go on-the-record about it or (heaven forbid) call me. I have received several suspicious-sounding denials concerning the alleged event, leading me to believe the incident was genuine. Sometimes all I can do is grind my teeth in frustration. Aarrgghh!

November 8, 1994 at 10:00 p.m., Alamosa:
I received a call from Adams State college student, John Finehart, who claimed he and several friends were watching five bright lights, (four blinking white lights and one unblinking red light) wheeling around in the sky over Alamosa. He said they appeared to be in a dogfight with each other and that the white lights were chasing the red light, which was "outmaneuvering the other lights."

Five minutes later I received a second call reporting the aerial display. All witnesses mentioned that the white lights were chasing the red one which, to one witness, appeared to be "playing with the other (white) lights." A Rio Grande County Captain also observed "a bright light" over the Greenie area that same night.

November 9, 1994 11:00 p.m. Five miles north of Villa Grove, Highway 17:

Chris Medina, George Oringdulph and myself, were returning from a mix-down session in Salida, when we observed a picket-line of eight small blinking white lights in the west, stretched from Saguache to La Garita. There were approximately three-to-four miles between each light and they did not appear to be in motion.

As we watched the line of lights with our night vision binoculars, we noticed a ninth light appear low on the horizon. This light was much larger and reddish-orange colored. It never blinked. The new light appeared to be moving in front of the picket-line from Greenie to the northwest. It moved slowly past the other lights and disappeared toward Gunnison. George asked, "How come whenever I drive somewhere at night with you, I see something weird?"

November 9, 1994 Del Norte Peak:

A Rio Grande County deputy and two hunting partners reported seeing a group of helicopters over Del Norte Peak. The following night, the same three hunters saw what they described as a "huge craft" which they thought might be a "sky-crane" chopper accompanied by another group of helicopters in the same area. They could not see structure, and assumed it to be a gigantic helicopter.

On his job at the Del Norte Post Office, rancher John Harr hears a lot of local scuttlebutt concerning unreported sightings in the Greenie Mountain area. According to one account (which he verified by finding two other witnesses who claimed they were present), "Cars were parked along State Highway 160 near the Comnet tower, watching a house-sized ship" glide silently across the highway in the middle of the afternoon, during the second week of November.

One of those who confirmed the details of this sighting was the son of a local astronomer. He claimed the object had a "thruster-type propulsion system." The object appeared to be under one thousand feet in altitude.

An SLV law enforcement official told me he was called in to the sheriff's office to respond to a peculiar request late Thursday night, November 10th. It seemed an ex-sheriff had called for an officer to "come out to his home and arrest him." The undersheriff went to the man's home and found him sober, dressed and ready to go. He, however, could not remember why he should be arrested but was adamant that he should be. "It took a while" for his family and the officer to convince him to stay home. The undersheriff and the family had no idea why he made such a bizarre request!

Curiously, that same Thursday night, the Mineral County sheriff was murdered near Lake City, CO. The resulting hunt for the man and woman suspects went on for several days before their bodies were found near where they had abandoned their truck in the snow. Their deaths were attributed to suicide.

Also, that same night, a group of investigators met between Taos and Eagle Nest to pool data and discuss the on-going activity in the southern Colorado-Northern New Mexico region. Gail Staehlin, Carolyn Duce-Ashe, Becky Minshall and Debbie Stark made the trip from Albuquerque. Tom Adams and Gary Massey arrived from Texas. David Perkins arrived on Friday. My brother Brendon and a friend, Richard Copeland, went with me.

At one point during the chaotic get-together, Gail brought up an alleged incident where an Eagle Nest rancher, named Mutz (pronounced mutes!) in broad daylight, watched his cattle form into a group out in the pasture. When the cows moved apart, there was a mutilated calf lying there. David "Izzy Zane" Perkins drolly observed that mysterious cattle mutilation phenomenon must just be "a cow thing" and all in attendance agreed that we should get out of the way and let them work it out amongst themselves.

Training The Cops and Inspectors

The following Monday, November 14th, Linda Moulton Howe, Tom Adams, David Perkins, Gary Massey, investigator Chip Knight and myself met with sheriffs and deputies from six Colorado counties. I had been asked by several law enforcement officials if I could put together a UAD training seminar for law enforcement. With all the recent publicity surrounding the latest wave of animal deaths, the officers wanted to become more up-to-speed.

Law enforcement turn-out was less than expected. Due to the murder of the Mineral County sheriff, all the adjoining counties plus others were involved in an extensive manhunt and could not send anyone to the training. Officials who attended included: Brian Norton (Rio Grande), Steven Gottlieb (Conejos), Martin Dominguez and John Luther, from the Alamosa County Sheriff's Office, Bill Mistretta and Tom Davis from the El Paso County Sheriff's Office, and Kevin McClellan and Steve England from the New Mexico Livestock Board.

289

Tom Adams started the session by giving the attendees a quick overview of the history of the UAD phenomenon. He also detailed the helicopters sightings he had documented around "mutilation" sites. David Perkins covered some of the most prevalent theories about who or what was behind the mutilations, and why. I covered some of our regions most recent cases, and then Linda began the training session.

Armed with videotape and her business-like manner, Linda took the officials step-by-step through the UAD investigative process. The burly lawmen sat politely and listened, seemingly a little bored. A couple of them seemed to be almost dozing. Then, while showing video of one of the recent bison mutilations, Linda pointed at the screen showing a veterinarian excising a bison penis. Someone coughed as I took a quick glance around the room. Everyone was wide awake.

The lawmen watched, riveted, as the vet expertly removed parts of the organ with a scalpel. Several eyes grew wide, postures stiffened, and a couple pairs of legs were crossed. You could hear a pin drop as Linda, with her back to the audience, described the process in detail. David Perkins and I had to stifle chuckles. Here was an attractive woman, surrounded by burly lawmen, innocently describing most male's darkest fear, oblivious to the subtle responses in the room. You could have cut the air with that scalpel.

November 14, 1994 8:00 p.m., Road T:
Linda, David and I were returning from Alamosa after the training, when I observed an orange light over the south central portion of the valley. I first noticed it flying over what appeared to be the San Luis Hills, southeast of Alamosa, and I pointed out the light to Perkins. We watched it travel directly north towards our location. As we continued towards Crestone, Linda, in the car behind us, and I noticed two smaller blinking white lights headed north from Rio Grande County out of the southwest. They were about two miles apart and flying in formation. They seemed to join with the first orange light (which now appeared to be faintly pulsing) over the Sangres behind Crestone.

As we arrived in town, I mentioned the sighting and its possible importance to the others. My day was finished, although Linda was all set to drive to Greenie. We should have.

According to Brian Norton, that night, between 8-9 p.m., a group of lights were reported circling the Greenie Mountain-San Francisco Creek area. Two lights peeled off the main group and headed north. It was these two lights we saw as they headed north over the Sangres into the La Veta MOA.

At around 10:00 p.m., an Alamosa student named Robbie

290

Trujillo left a message with Isadora that he and friends were watching "ten to fifteen planes chasing three or four rapidly flashing strobe lights, west of town."

November 18th, 19th, and 20th were intense. Multiple fires, auto accidents, fights, unusual numbers of animal kills on the roads and the sheriff's murder were covered extensively by local and regional press. And top it off, the maid-of-honor at her sister's wedding, knifed the bride.

Friday, November 18, 9:45 p.m., seven helicopters were spotted circling Greenie. A deputy saw them himself. Two of the choppers were shining spotlights at the ground and witnesses watched them for almost forty-five minutes. I wondered at the time if the military could be pulsing microwave frequencies around the valley, similar to microwave radiation beamed at the US Embassy in Moscow (in the 1960s) to either debilitate embassy personnel or disrupt communications, or both. During the 1970s and 80s the Soviets beamed a shortwave signal dubbed "The Woodpecker Signal" at the continental US which disrupted communications. Depending on who you believe, the Woodpecker Signal was either an "over-the-horizon" radar system or an attempt at psychotronic mind-control.

November 22, 9:09 p.m., La Veta:

A family in the La Veta Pass area called to report a flying triangle had just flown over their house. They insisted that it was not a stealth aircraft. It was silent and much bigger. The following night, just after 10:00 p.m., a Conejos County deputy saw two "weird looking planes fly over." He described them as having rows of lights, and said they were "odd-shaped and real quiet."

November 23, Conejos County:

Joe Taylor, Sr., father of the current Conejos County sheriff, reported seeing "two planes with lots of unusual blinking lights" flying over the northern part of the county. The craft made no apparent sound and were flying below five hundred feet. Taylor mentioned that he had never seen planes with lights like that before.

November 29, 12:40 p.m., 1:10 p.m., and 1:39 p.m., the Baca:

A series of low frequency rumbles were heard by workers at a job site three miles south of the Baca in the foothills. One of the three workers, Creede deAvenzar, noted that the rumbles had an eight to ten second duration, sounded as if they were "coming from deep underground" and appeared to be centered "just north" of where they were working.

December 2, 1994 around midnight, Moffat:

Baca musician Barry Monroe was driving north on 17, near Moffat, when he observed a large ball of light northwest of town. "It appeared and moved parallel to the ground. It had almost a tumbling effect and lasted for almost four seconds. The colors were different from something just on fire." He noted that the object was below the clouds and that it didn't look anything like a shooting star; it was "way too big."

December 6, 6:45 p.m., the Baca Chalets:

Two reports were logged of a reddish-orange light hovering over the Sangres, just east of the Great Sand Dunes. From 10:45 p.m. until 11:00 p.m., I was traveling north on 17, returning home after a rehearsal in Alamosa, and I noticed a bright reddish light hovering over the mountains to the east. The light I saw was two to three times the size and brightness of Mars. After repeated sightings over fifteen minutes, I looked up from the road and it was gone.

The following morning, two winter campers, three miles east of Crestone in Burnt Gulch, told friends that around 11:00 p.m., a large formation of jets flew over and, seconds later, a blue spotlight shown down on their site, illuminating the entire area. They claimed that they "heard eight to ten thumps" emanating out of the ground under them. There was about an eight second interval between the extremely low frequency sounds that they could "hear in the ground."

December 7, 5:00 p.m., Highway 160:

Valley Courier editor Mark Hunter reported seeing a green cheap firework with a duration of around two seconds over Greenie Mountain while traveling on 160.

That evening at 10:12 p.m., an Alamosa resident standing on his front porch looking west observed "an orange light over Greenie." The light moved in fits and starts for several minutes, before it flew off to the north.

December 27, 4:00 a.m., Osier Park, Conejos County:

While on a holiday snowmobiling trip with his family in the mountains west of Antonito, UPS driver Dave Jaramillo shot more than just family footage. He woke in the middle of the night and looked out the south-facing window of the remote cabin. A light appeared to be hovering under a mile away. He grabbed his camcorder. Over the course of the next hour, he shot twenty minutes of video. At several points, the bright oblong light appeared to tilt backwards, revealing a large black spot on the underside. A light beam then snaked out of the bottom with a second light at the end of the beam.

The twenty minutes of footage of the unexplained object shows some electromagnetic interference. Jaramillo never took the tape out of the camcorder and the footage of the family's activities from the previous and next day were crystal clear. There were, fortunately, ten to twelve seconds of jitter-free footage. I watched this footage of the unknown craft on a thirteen inch TV screen and could see details like what appeared to be an appendage that snaked out of the main light and hung like a crooked arm.

January 16, 10:10 p.m., South of Alamosa:
On January 16th, Adams State College student Amy Mascarenas had just turned onto Highway 368 to go a quarter-mile home. She was startled by a craft resembling "the top half of a slightly oblong bubble," hovering over some trees less than one thousand feet directly northwest of her. "It was glowing a yellowish color" and had "randomly blinking yellowish-orange, and bluish-green lights around the rim and underside," she said.

"It was the size of a small house, or large garage." She called me from her home. "When I first saw it, it was hovering just over some trees. It looked like it was about seventy feet up. The bottom was flat, like a pancake. I think it knew I was there, because when I stopped in our neighbor's driveway to get a better look at it, it went and hid behind the trees!"

Mascarenas reported the incident in a calm manner but was obviously excited. "I kept glancing at my watch to make sure I wasn't missing some time." She said her car never experienced any problems and that she heard or felt nothing unusual after rolling down her window and watched it light up the trees for several minutes.

January 17, 6:15 p.m., Highway 160:
According to a report filed with Brian Norton, a man was driving west toward Del Norte on 160, just northwest of Greenie, when he noticed "a large triangle-shaped" craft hovering near the Comnet tower, east of Del Norte. He told Norton it was about two-hundred feet in the air and between forty and fifty feet in length, silent, and exhibited a bright bluish-white strobe light. The amazed witness pulled over and, for about twelve minutes watched the object hover and then slowly move southeast. Then the object "suddenly disappeared at great speed." This was the exact location of the triangular object sighting during the second week of November.

I called back to verify some details of Amy Mascarenas' sighting two days later and talked with Amy's father, Pat, to leave a message for her. The elder Mascarenas told me, "Amy is a very down-to-earth person and there's no question in my mind that she saw something all right. It's funny you should call, I just saw something pretty strange fly over the house about five minutes ago!" (9:35 p.m.)

I got a detailed description of a "line of brilliant strobe lights, flashing in exact sequence with one another, flying west toward Greenie." Mascarenas, an ex-Air Force officer, said, "They were flying real low, with a yawing motion, at great speed. I've never seen these types of lights on an aircraft. And it was flat cookin'!" He heard a roaring "that almost sounded like a Pratt-Whitney J-67." He has seen unusual craft in the area before. "Who knows what the government's flying around here."

Less than five minutes later, I received an excited call from Georgia Van Iwaarden who lives less than two miles from the Mascarenas. "Something really weird just flew over, and is flying around over by Greenie. My husband is outside watching it," Georgia told me excitedly while her husband, Steve, yelled descriptions from outside in the yard.

"It's blinking, moving up and down. Now it's going sideways," Steve called. "Now it's taking off over the mountains!"

I asked Georgia to give me a description of the lights. "They are bluish-white, and blinking randomly, there is no pattern to the flashes. The lights are really bright, brighter than anything I've seen fly around here!" I asked her how big and how close it had come to them. "It was pretty big, about the size and shape of a horse pill. (at arm's length) I'm not very good at estimating distances at night but it seemed pretty close, maybe a mile or so away."

1:09 p.m., Alamosa:

That same night, I received a call from my bass player, Lyman Bushkovski. He told me, "I thought maybe you'd like to know that six green camouflaged helicopters just landed at the Alamosa Airport." He described three of the craft as large and the other three smaller two-man choppers. A call to the airport revealed that it was a shuttle flight, headed south into New Mexico. I never did figure out to which agency they belonged, nobody would claim them.

January 19, 10:15 a.m., the Baca:

Four witnesses saw four more helicopters flying north in the SLV executing some unusual maneuvers. The lead choppers, three Cobras, would dive to below one hundred feet and then climb to around one thousand feet, then dive again, roller-coasting up and down. The other scout chopper followed along behind.

I spent that afternoon making phone calls to every military branch and government agency that is known to fly around the valley. A call to Buckley AFB came up empty. I then left a message on the Colorado Air National Guard Hotline. A call detailing the morning's sightings was made to Ft. Carson. No one could speak with me but they promised someone would call back.

Less than fifteen minutes later the Ft. Carson Community Relations Officer, Liz Kalish called. She seemed very accommodating and helpful, "Yes, those four you saw today were ours. I just talked with the flight commander but he denied his group made any unusual maneuvers while flying in the valley." She claimed that she had "no idea who else had been flying around the previous three days" and said that "if they came from another installation, we wouldn't necessarily know about it, we have our own fly zones."

I then called FEMA. I spoke with a man named Fletcher. "If it was a classified mission, I couldn't divulge anything... but I have no knowledge of any activity, classified or otherwise, going on in your area." I proceeded to tell him about some of the unexplained aerial activity that had been reported over the course of the last year. He seemed interested but didn't really comment about the hundreds of sighting claims.

At the end of the conversation I made the light comment, "What am I telling you for? I'm just barking up the wrong tree."

"How do you know it's a tree?" he quipped. Now what was that supposed to mean?

The following morning, I received a call from Lt. Col. "Buck" Buckingham. He claimed to have no knowledge of any nocturnal flights in the valley. He was very interested in the sighting reports and mentioned he had been reading my *Crestone Eagle* articles. He also said he would very much like to read my newsletter, the Mysterious Valley Report! He said, "If I was aware of classified flights in your area, I would tell you I knew about them."

January 23,1995 10:00 p.m. and 10:15 p.m., Highway 17:

While driving north on 17, near Mosca, I saw a rapidly sequencing series of strobe lights flashing around five to ten miles away, directly west. I slowed and watched the low-flying light show travel up the entire west side of the SLV and disappear near the town of Saguache. The five or six-light strobe had a duration of less than a second. It would repeat the series every two seconds with machine-gun-like precision. It appeared to be under one thousand feet above the valley floor and traveling around one hundred and fifty mph.

Fifteen minutes later, as I turned onto the T-Road, I saw that pesky orangish light hanging just over the mountains. About three to four times brighter than Mars, it disappeared north behind the mountains after I watched it for about four or five minutes. It wasn't a star or planet and it moved to the north.

The Creeps

On March 7, 1995 I received a call from Brian Norton. He had attended the UAD training seminar in November, and up until now, he had never investigated a UAD case. He told me of a report filed that morning by a rancher a mile south of Del Norte.

Bob Kernan had been driving past his pasture when he noticed his herd circling around something on the ground. At the time, he thought this unusual but didn't check. Later, he noticed the herd had drifted away from the area and saw a calf laying on the ground. Thinking the animal was sick, he went out , and made a grisly find.

Of the hundreds of UAD cases I had personally investigated or researched, this is the one that physically gave me the creeps. When I arrived on-site and viewed the unfortunate calf, the hair literally stood up on the back of my neck, and I got a severe case of goose-bumps.

The month-old female was missing its spine from the hips to the skull, the brain was gone. Also missing were the right front leg, all but two ribs, both eyes plus a two-inch circle of hide around the upside socket, both ears, the intestines, reproductive track, lungs, and a small two-inch diameter coring out of the rectum. The heart and liver, scavenger favorites, were left intact. The spine appeared to have been savagely torn out.

The rancher's dogs had never barked, there was no blood, tracks or signs of scavengers, and a strange cloying smell emanated from the body cavity. Kernan had put the calf in his garage on a piece of plastic and after five days there wasn't even a hint of decay. The closest description I can think of to describe the unusual odor would be "a sweet, pungent, earthy smell." Not everyone agreed. Visiting Colorado Springs, investigator, Ed Burke described the smell as "just like a bathroom disinfectant."

Bob Kernan, initially, didn't want the animal death publicized. He told me "I don't want to alarm people." This reaction made sense after seeing the carcass. Kernan was overwhelmed by the response to the death of his calf, "If I had it to do over again, I wouldn't even have called the sheriff." Because an official report was filed by Kernan, Sam Adams, of the SLV Publishing Company, caught wind of the case and called him. Kernan granted Adams an interview which resulted in a front-page article in the *South Fork Times*, March 16, 1995.

Another rancher, half-a-mile away, reported to the sheriff's office, that he had watched a strange beam of light shining straight up in the air, just north of his ranch, at 3:00 a.m., around the night the calf was killed. A motorist driving on Highway 160, west of Del Norte, also reported a strange light coming out of the pasture, near where the calf was found. Kernan also lost another calf during these two days. "It just plumb disappeared," he told me. "We never did find any trace of it."

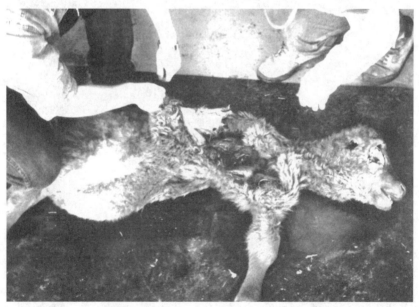

The Del Norte calf gets my Spookiest Case Award.

Eli Hronich and Tom Reed Why were their ranches singled out?

Area 51? Is the San Luis Valley "Area 52"?

Gary Massey explaining the finer points of the ET Hypothesis.

Lt. Col. "Buck" Buckingham Colorado Air National Guard.

299

Prone on the Range by Wes Crum.

CHAPTER TEN:
Can I Get A Witness

June 24, 1995:

The beautiful high-mountain summer was in full-swing. Outside the window, Broadtail and Rufus hummingbirds angrily buzzed each other, like little rocket-powered dive-bombers in the brilliant sunshine. Underneath their feeder, several of our little town's thousand resident deer browsed quietly—always alert to any danger.

That fresh lovely morning, I had finished my customary morning coffee and decided to go to the post office to pick up the mail. After many months of investigating flap-levels of unusual activity, the countless reports I had been fielding, sometimes several per day, had inexplicably ceased. The San Luis Valley had been "officially," and I might add blissfully, quiet for two whole months without a single report.

I've always wondered about the down-times with no reports. To me this is an indication of the absolute reality of unexplained events. If folks here in the SLV (and elsewhere) were reporting simply misidentified mundane occurrences, then why no reports for weeks and months at a time? If people are truly reporting misidentified phenomena, you would think that there would always be at least a trickle of reports, not a complete cessation of apparent activity. This fact alone has convinced me that these waves of unexplained reports contain real cause and effect events.

I darted into Crestone that morning in my little Toyota truck. "Town" was in full-swing, and I noticed cars from several different states parked in front of The Road Kill Café. As I made the turn to head up the small hill to the post office. The following letter, one of hundreds I've received since I began my investigative efforts, awaited me in my mail-box:

Dear Christopher:
    I have been interested in the phenomenon [sic] since I had read the newspaper reports about NORAD picking up an object on radar which reportedly crashed near Greenie Mountain. In April I attended your lecture on

301

the Mysterious Valley during the convention in Colorado Springs. I subscribed to your newsletter as a result.

This past weekend, (June 15-18, 1995) six of my friends and I camped out in the North Crestone Creek campground. All of us were anxious to view the night sky in hopes of seeing something out of the ordinary. Over the course of three evenings, we all saw a host of satellites, airplanes, and shooting stars.

On the evening of June 17, we all were watching the sky from the area just west of the bridge at the entrance of the North Crestone Creek campground. As you no doubt know, this area provides an excellent view of the Valley. At exactly 10:58 PM, just as we were ready to head back, all seven of us saw an aerial phenomenon, the like of which none of us had ever seen before in our lives. We were looking north, when a sizable, bright, yellowish-orange oval-shaped light appeared out of nowhere and blazed across the sky from west to east. It was traveling parallel with, but thirty-five to forty degrees above the northern horizon. It was hurtling through the sky at a high rate of speed (faster than any commercial aircraft, but slower than a shooting star). It was silent, and had no "tail." We watched it for approximately seven to ten seconds (enough time for all of us to see it and make comments about it). It disappeared behind some cloud cover over the mountains.

Those present during the sighting were two criminal prosecuting attorneys, a computer programmer, two employees of the rape assistance and awareness organization, a realtor and a crime-victim advocate. All are from Denver, except the computer programmer, who is from San Francisco.

We were all fascinated and knew that we had seen something "mysterious". Our question is did anyone else report this same phenomenon to you. Can you rule out that it was a simple meteor. I am looking forward to the next issue of the Mysterious Valley [Report].

Sincerely,
Chris Ramsay

One of the seven witnesses, Dave Brase, is now working as a law enforcement officer. He confirmed details of the group's sighting by phone and remarked, "I've worked outdoors all my life and I have never, ever seen anything remotely like it."

Before Chris Ramsay's letter, I had not received a report of an unusual aerial object in two-months, and two more months went by without receiving another, not even a report of our "cheap fireworks." These dazzling orbs of bluish-white light I've dubbed "cheap fireworks," are not mundane celestial objects and I invariably receive reports of these perplexing objects during our many active UFO sighting periods. I have seen them below me in altitude with a completely uniform overcast sky, I have seen them flash within a hundred feet of my vantage point. In 1993, one man called to report a very small one that he had just seen and described the event as like ". . .watching Tinkerbelle crashing."

No UFO or "mute" reports were logged between March and June 1995, yet undoubtedly during this stretch of time, cows had died naturally, were scavenged and found; meteors had flashed innocently through the thin mountain sky and dazzled witnesses. I find it curious that not one unexplained event was reported to officials (or myself) during this time period. Your average true-wanna-believer would probably ask where do the ships and meteors go when they're not flying around this particular neck-of-the-woods? Or, are they flying around but no one is reporting them? This question has dogged ufologists for decades. It reminds me of the old saying, "If a tree falls in the forest, and no one is there to hear it, does it make any noise?" If the group of seven skywatchers accompanying Chris Ramsey had left just the vantage point *one minute or two minutes earlier,* would that same object have soared across the sky? The object they did witness could have been a meteor, but then again, it may have been something unusual, something out-of-the-ordinary – worthy of report. I received no other confirmation of this event.

I'm not complaining about those down-times. The past two-years had been such a whirlwind that this unexpected three month lull allowed me the time to begin to attempt to put this current activity into some kind of historical context. I had actively researched the past thirty years but I was convinced clues existed in the more distant past. It allows me the time to dig even deeper into the history of the wondrous Southwest.

I have a curious, inquiring mind. What some find tedious, I find compelling —like rooting around in old newspaper archives or dusty library shelves. The research aspect of my investigative endeavors is a constant source of enjoyment, for you'll never know what you'll find with the simple turn of a page. My "microcosmic approach" dictates that the interested investigator/researcher must cover his defined geographic area like a soaked asbestos blanket. I am convinced that any particular "location" has unique indicators, in the form of unexplained phenomena, that may contribute to our further understanding of all paranormal phenomena. In my mind, UFOs and unusual animal deaths are inexorably linked to religion and belief; haunted house and spook lights are related to sub-cultural interpretations found in local legends and myths; and secret military activity and underground bases are entwined in the perception of Identified Flying Objects (IFOs) as UFOs.

Mother Mary Made Me Do It

Early on in my investigation of the San Luis Valley, I had a hunch that there were some notable characters to be found. Because of the hundreds of reports of real-time reports that I found myself investigating, it wasn't until the spring of 1995 that I made a concerted effort to dig into the region's nineteenth-century past. Sweeping through SLV libraries and data bases revealed a treasure trove of interesting characters and historical events that deserve mention. My second book, *Enter The Valley*, features some of these historical figures, but one little-known figure is most intriguing.

Two books I discovered during my down time in June 1995, deserve mention. Jack Kutz's *Mysteries & Miracles of Colorado* and *Mysteries & Miracles of New Mexico*. Both books are filled with wonderful, little-known stories.

The concept of a "serial-killer," primarily an urban phenomenon, was unheard of in 1863. Few documented historical criminal cases of note can be called "serial-killings" until London's infamous "Jack-the-Ripper" and his killing of seven women in 1888.

The following story is the saga of an unforgettable San Luis Valley trio. They are truly characters from anyone's worst nightmare and may be America's first documented serial killers.

Felipe Nerio Espinoza was born in Veracruz, Mexico in the late 1830s to parents of average means, and in 1846, when Felipe was still a boy, the Mexican-American War commenced. In March 1847, General Winfield Scott was ordered to lead the United States Army, by sea, and capture the vital seaport of Veracruz. During the ensuing three-week siege, a massive American naval bombardment rained thirteen hundred shells down on the city and, in many instances, took out whole sections of the city's residential neighborhoods. Prior to the furious bombardment, young Felipe Espinoza was sent away from home by his family, probably for safety's-sake. When he returned to his grandparent's home he was horrified to discover that his entire family had been decimated by a shell blast from a US warship that had completely taken out their small house in the *barrio*. He was forced to identify the mangled bodies of his parents, his grandparents, and his brother and sister, as they lay on the floor in the convent of Santo Domingo, along with scores of other civilian casualties. Felipe was sent to the U.S.

Territory of New Mexico to live with his only surviving relatives, including his two cousins, Vivian and Julian.

Nothing much is known of Felipe's teenage years, but as he grew up in the San Luis Valley it is thought that he became more and more disillusioned with his unfortunate life in the cold and remoteness of *del norté*. Chaffing under the oppressive poverty and austere environment we don't really know why Felipe and his cousins rebelled, but in 1855 —led by Felipe —they struck out on their own and became aspiring Northern New Mexico horse-thieves. Stealing horses and mules from white ranchers they sold them to miners in the upstart mining camps to the north in Southern Colorado. Felipe probably had developed a life long, deep hatred for "gringos," as they poured into the mountainous region. After two or so years, the Espinoza cousins moved their base of operations back to Conejos County, in the San Luis Valley, and began selling stolen beef to the mining camps. Espinoza's motivation for his soon to erupt rampage remains an enigmatic mystery, but history does mention a curious claim that may provide us with insight into the state of his twisted mind. The local Conejos Catholic priest who ministered the local flock is on the record as stating that he was told by Felipe the details of a strange vision Felipe experienced during a particularly vivid dream.

> TheVirginMaryhadcometohimandcommandedhimto killonehundredAmericansforeachof his(six)slainrelatives. He wished to kneel at the altar and make a vow to do so....

The startled padre of Colorado's oldest Christian Church absolutely refused his request to make his vow and the horrified priest tried in vain to convince Felipe that his interpretation of the dream was wrong. The priest later told Conejos County Sheriff Harding how he had tried to dissuade Espinoza,

> I tried to explain to him that it could not have been the Virgin Mary who came to him in his dream. It was the devil, tricking him. But he would not listen. Or perhaps he could not listen. If you had seen the unholy gleam in his eyes, you would understand. He went away, and I have not seen him since.

In May, 1863, the unprecedented serial-killing-style carnage began. The first victim was found between Parksdale and Cotopaxi, (just east of Salida,) CO along the windy fifty-mile route that follows the course of the Arkansas River down to Canon City. The young male had been shot between the eyes; his heart violently removed from his chest. The second victim was found a few short days later. "Judge" William Bruce was discovered shot between the eyes and was also missing his heart, which had evidently been removed from his chest with an ax. A cursory examination of the crime scene revealed that three perpetrators were involved. Posses were hastily formed and dispatched, but before the month ended, another victim, Henry Hawkins was discovered on the banks of Fountain Creek in the same grisly condition.

The next central-Colorado victims were two young cowboys, Nelson Shoup and Tom Brinkley. Shoup was killed instantly during the ambush, about seventy-miles north of the first killings. Wounded in the initial volley, Brinkley had luckily managed to crawl away and tried to hide himself between some rocks. His luck quickly ran out. The Espinozas found him; Felipe shot him point-blank between the eyes, and commenced his divinely-inspired ax-work.

Figuring they had found an ideal ambush location on the road to Leadville, the cousins waited for their next victim. George Carter never knew what hit him as he became corpse number five. Before the murderers could dispose of his body, a teamster named Henry Metcalf happened along and narrowly avoided a furious torrent of bullets. He was the first person to escape the Espinozas diabolical ambushes and gave authorities their first description of the three marauders with their soot-blackened faces.

The trio of murderers lurked around the Upper Arkansas River Valley —just over Poncha Pass in a canyon still renown for its beauty. The sparse population of Fremont County recoiled. They had real serial-killers on their hands and panic gripped the entire region during that 1863 summer of fear. Miners, cowboys and travelers only ventured out in heavily-armed groups and many volunteered to be deputized as the man-hunt for Espinoza moved into high-gear. But the elusive Espinoza gang managed to stay one-step ahead of their many pursuers. By August over twenty men had been bushwacked, and their hearts had been hacked out in the same horrific manner. Area residents had no choice but to take the law into their own hands and at least one account of a mistaken killing can be attributed to revenge-minded posses, who were hell-bent on annihilating the sordid threesome. The Espinozas finally "'fessed up" to their rampage in a letter written by Felipe in August 1863 and sent to Territory of Colorado Governor Evans.

We have cut the hearts out of twenty-six American dogs so far but we are willing to forgo further slaughter if you will grant me and my followers full pardons and permit us to retain five thousand acres we now claim in Conejos

County with the free use of all adjacent grazing lands and that you will appoint me and any of my followers whom I designate as captains in the Colorado Volunteers. For these things we will desist from further molestation of your subjects. I will give you until the end of September to do these things and if it is not done, five hundred and seventy-four more gringos will die. Among them will be yourself. (signed)
Felipe Nerio Espinoza.

Governor Evans, quite taken aback, the rumors of their identity were confirmed, immediately sent a cable to Conejos County Sheriff Harding who started an official Territorial investigation into the killings. Evans announced that the Territory of Colorado was posting a dead-or-alive reward of twenty-five hundred dollars for Felipe Espinoza. The Territory needed help, and there was one man who some thought could get the job done quickly and cleanly. After the twenty-eigth victim had been discovered, an exasperated Colonel S.B. Tappan, commander of the Colorado Volunteers, dispatched Lieutenant Harold Baldwin to enlist the famous mountain man and scout, Thomas Tobin.

I found the following biographical information in *Colorado Magazine* article from 1943.

Thomas Tate Tobin was born in 1823 at St. Louis, Missouri. His father was Irish, his mother, Nova Scotian. He came West in 1837, living for some years at trading posts. He settled on the Trinchea near Fort Garland in 1858, and spent the remainder of his life there when not on the trial. Tobin gained his great reputation as a trail man by his uncanny ability to detect and follow 'sign.' Those who had seen him trailing told me that he always took the most likely starting point, swung round and round in ever widening circles until he 'cut sign,' then clung to his 'sign' until his quarry was overtaken. This technique in trailing Tobin probably learned from the Indians.... . Those who had seen him on the trail told me the he often went on all fours with his face close to the ground, following 'sign,' that was imperceptible to less acute eyes. He 'could track a grasshopper through sagebrush'.... asked if he knew Kit Carson [Colorado's most famous scout and mountain man]: 'I et [sick] many a beaver tail with him.'

The twenty-five hundred dollar reward had motivated dozens of amateur man-hunters to go out and blanket the south-central

Colorado mountains in an attempt to track-down the Espinozas, but Tappan knew he needed a true professional to get the job done. Tobin had been a scout for the Colorado Volunteers for several years before retiring to his farm. He was considered *the* best man-hunter in Colorado.

After a long conversation with the lieutenant, Baldwin and Tobin set out to track the desperados, and they left to ride to South Park to meet Col. Tappan in Fairplay. Tappan immediately offered the help of his whole volunteer corps, which Tobin politely declined. He asked for six, well-provisioned, experienced soldiers, and a Mexican boy to take care of his horse, who accompanied him and Lieut. Baldwin.

The men immediately departed and headed toward the latest crime-scene on the South Platte. Tobin without much trouble was able to pick up the trail. They rode upstream and began the arduous task of following the careful killer's tracks. For three-days the posse slowly followed the Espinoza's trail, pausing every so often when the prints became harder to locate. Finally, Tobin silently signaled for the men to stop near La Veta Pass.

We'll let Thomas Tobin himself, finish the story as quoted in *El Palacio Magazine* in 1946:

> .... I watched carefully and soon located their camp. I told the soldiers not to speak, it I raised my hand to squat down and cock their guns but not to fire unless I told them to. I took a step or two in front and saw the head of one of the assassins. At this time I stepped on a stick and broke it; he heard it crack, he looked and saw me, he jumped and grabbed his gun. Before he turned around fairly I fired and hit him in the side; he bellowed like a bull and cried out, 'Jesus favor me,' and cried to his companion, 'Escape, I am killed.' I gave a whoop and sung out, 'Yell, boys, I've got him, so if there are any more of them they will make their appearance.' I tipped my powder horn in my rifle, dropped a bullet from my mouth into the muzzle of my gun while I was capping it. A fellow came out of the ravine, running to an undergrowth of quaking aspen. I sung out, 'Shoot boys.' The three fired and missed him. I drew my gun up and fired at the first sight and broke his back above his hips. I sent the Mexican boy off on a run to tell Baldwin what had happened. The four soldiers who were with Baldwin came to where I was. Espinoza had started to crawl away. He did not go very far. He braced himself up against some fallen trees, with a pistol in hand waving it over his face, using a

word in Mexican that means *base brutes*. I had run down to where he was; I spoke to him and asked him if he knew me. I told him who I was; his reply was '*base brutes.*' A soldier went to lay his hand on him. I said look out, he will shoot you. He fired but missed the soldier. I then caught him by the hair, drew his head back over a fallen tree and cut it off. I sent the Mexican boy to cut off the head of the other fellow; he cut it off and brought it to me. I put their heads in a sack and camped on the Sangre de Cristo that night... I rolled up in front of the commanding officers-quarters and called for Col. Tappan. I rolled the assassin's heads out of the sack at Col. Tappan's feet. I said, 'Here Col., I have accomplished what you wished. This head is Espinoza's. This other is his companion's, there is no mistake, for we have this diary and letters and papers to show they are the assassin's.'

Jack Kutz asserts that the governor reneged on the reward claiming to Tobin "the Territory had no money available" to back up the reward. (Other sources claim Tobin was eventually paid five hundred dollars.) But, noticing that Tobin was wearing an old tattered coat, Evans offered to buy him a new coat, so he'd look good for the photographers covering the conclusion of the Territory's most sensational manhunt.

Evidently Felipe Espinoza's head was kept in a jar of alcohol at Fort Garland and was finally sold to a traveling carnival. Imagine growing up in the 1870-80s and seeing that side-show face in a jar in some penny-arcade, glaring out into oblivion. No one knows what finally became of the head of Felipe Nerio Espinoza.

Another one of the many stories told about legendary Thomas Tobin comes from the San Luis Valley. Although a little out of context to his before-mentioned involvement in the man-hunt for the Espinozas, I just couldn't resist including it here. Life in the San Luis Valley, in the mid-nineteenth-century, could be a bit distasteful, and I found an unusual story in *El Palacio*, called by author Edgar Hewitt, "Indian Cakes."

It was late evening when Tom Tobin arrived at an Indian camp near the mouth of Mosca Creek [at the Great Sand Dunes]. Tobin upon entering the camp became aware of a feeling of uneasiness among the Indians. After the usual formality of greetings were completed, Tom asked the chief if he might have some food. The chief ordered his squaw to prepare Tom some supper. At first, she refused, but after a stern command by her husband, she reluctantly began fixing batter for corn cakes into which she blew her nose. Tobin was emphatically ordered to eat the cakes. Tom later related that he never had such a hard time swallowing. After eating, he excused himself and traveled on home. The following day Tobin learned that some whites had killed an Indian.

But, back to the Espinozas. I was taken aback by their unholy rampage. Felipe's motivation and subsequent deeds easily surpass the stories surrounding the handful of serial-killers in this country's history. I mused, after reading several riveting accounts from various sources, why I hadn't heard of the Espinoza's "reign of terror" before? Tabloid mass-murderers have always captured the American imagination. I admit, they've captured mine. Jeffrey Dahlmer, Wayne Gacy, Ed Gein, David Berkowitz, and his demonic voices: these societal aberrations have periodically and unquestionably stunned our culture. I went ahead and checked "the record" to ascertain Felipe Espinoza's impact in nineteenth century media in an effort to place his deviant actions into a broader cultural context. This search revealed that his story is not generally known, even in Colorado's San Luis Valley where the trio was headquartered.

Why did Felipe's confederate cousins allowed themselves to get involved? How had they become swayed by Felipe to assist him on his murderous crime-spree? There is no evidence to suggest they had shared their cousin's "vision" so why did they embrace his pathos and embark on such an ill-conceived mission? Did they really think they could extort the Territory for the lush Conejos ranch lands Felipe coveted? And what about Felipe's vision? Did he really believe the "Blessed Virgin Mary" had commanded him to exact such retribution on so many unsuspecting gringos? Going with the assumption that he had experienced a vision of some sort, could he have misinterpreted the message? Or, more realistically, was the message simply delusional? In a more sinister vein, did an outside influence diabolically design the visitation and vision to trick the psychologically-fragile Espinoza into enacting his reign of terror? For what purpose? Even the pious local padre had a sense that Felipe was being manipulated and tried to argue with him concerning the reality of his proclaimed "vision."

The Conejos area, where Espinoza lived, contains many interesting legends and stories pertaining to the supernatural and extraordinary. In *The Mysterious Valley*, I noted several rare legendary appearances of "old scratch," the devil, who it is said visits north-central New Mexico and south-central Colorado, and, as I've learned, other rural areas of the great Southwestern United States.

310

There is a local perception that the Conejos towns of Sanford, Antonito and Manassas may have hosted alleged appearances of this "devil" at dances and/or social events. It is interesting to note that I've never been able to find an actual witness to mister devil's urbane antics, but I've interviewed many people who claim solemnly they "knew someone who was there."

Is there a connection between Felipe's vision of the Mother Mary and these local Conejos County devil legends? It's difficult not to leap to the conclusion that Felipe's "vision" was something akin to demonic in nature. What well-meaning benign spirit like our "Blessed Virgin Mary" would demand such retribution? Appearances by the historically angelic Mother of Christ have usually been just a bit more benevolent and light-hearted in nature. Children have channeled Marian messages as a result of her visits; the sun has zig-zagged and spiraled playfully for thousands at her arrival; and fresh-water springs have joyfully emerged and bubbled-forth at her behest. To my knowledge, no one has ever been instructed by Our Lady to slaughter six-hundred innocent people!

They Took My Pet Black Bear

I suspect that a certain percentage of any group of people are bound to act abnormally when faced with the unknown. I wonder why certain people are compelled to do certain things in certain situations? Does one's perceptions of his "local" environment somehow affect how a person responds to elements of reality not normally experienced? Can unusual circumstances, combined with a traditional local history of "the unusual" drive certain people to do things a normal person might not even contemplate? I pondered these questions and looked for more examples of little-known social aberrations in the historical record.

Meanwhile, back here in the late twentieth-century, unusual events in the San Luis Valley began to quietly escalate during the summer of 1995.

I don't quite know what to think of the following events but they are worthy of note. Running in a straight northwest to southeast line for over two-hundred and thirty miles, the rugged Sangre De Cristo Mountains, longest continuous mountain range in the United States, border the eastern side of the San Luis Valley. I have traveled the mountainous region stretching from Alaska to Mexico, and the Sangres are truly one of North America's most breathtaking scenic wonders. Ten peaks soar to over fourteen-thousand feet in altitude and scrape the thin Colorado sky. A perfect natural barrier, the imposing rock wall soars over a dozen high-altitude lakes found nestled in vales located between the mountains. Most of the San Luis Valley's population is located in the center of the Valley, and I'm blessed to be able to look out my window and see, four "14'ers," less than three-miles away.

In a high, remote area twenty-five miles north of Crestone, just over the Sangres and the Rio Grande National Forest and Wilderness area, a small trailer sits in a clearing surrounded by the quiet piñon forest. There are no houses, stores or residents, just miles of quiet dense forest in the area. The trailer belongs to Larry Williams (not his real name), a mountain-man, ex-Vietnam vet who prefers the company of his pet black bear over people.

A mutual friend called me about Williams and told me I should contact him because he claimed some very unusual events were occurring at his property. "Almost nightly" during June and July, 1995, Larry noticed strange lights buzzing low over the forest that clings to the steep eastern side of the Sangres. During several days in late July, he noticed increased military helicopter activity over his high-mountain property and he began to notice odd things around his place. A stream that flowed down from the mountains through his land would inexplicably raise and lower its water level for no apparent reason. Then something happened that he was really not expecting.

Williams arrived home from town August 15, 1995 at 8:45 p.m., and noticed a bright light off to the north. Checking to make sure he had his camera with him, he sat in his truck and watched the light carefully. It appeared to either get brighter or, to head south toward his location. The man allegedly took a series of sixteen still photos that show the light as it apparently flew toward him. The final photo was taken shooting straight up at an "enormous boomerang craft" as it hovered above him. Then, quite inexplicably, he found himself sitting in his truck, looking out over a dark, quiet Wet Mountain Valley.

He checked his watch, and was startled to find out that thirty-five minutes had elapsed since he last remembered checking the time right when the boomerang craft began to approach. Confused, he got out of his truck and looked around with a flashlight. He was amazed to find his truck sitting "six-inches away from its tracks." Like something had moved his truck up and over a half-foot. He ran to the house to check on his pet black-bear and was again startled to find whatever-it-was had moved his trailer "six-inches off it's foundation" and picked up his bulldozer and set it down, "six-inches from where its tracks ended!" Fresh branches, up to sixty feet off the ground, appeared to have been sheared off nearby trees, and William's pet black bear had vanished.

This was the last straw. A couple of days earlier, he had discovered quite a number of animal skeletons scattered around his property. He could not venture a guess concerning why so many unexplained animal carcasses littered his land. "I've found elk, deer, fox, raccoon, and a lot of cattle skeletons have been found. They're just laying around. Nothing touched 'em and tore 'em up.... I've seen at least fifteen to twenty cattle carcasses and skeletons alone since last year. I don't know who they belonged to." Coincidentally, a rancher, directly over the Sangres in the San Luis Valley has reported losing several dozen cattle without a trace since 1992.

Williams told me, "I've been waking up at exactly 2:00 a.m. and seeing lights pretty near every night since June... We've found little tiny four-toed tracks walking around the perimeter of my place. I've seen some pretty odd things in my life, but nothing like I'm seeing in those Sangre de Cristo's." Much to his dismay, he couldn't help but notice that he now had a "thumb-sized rectal wart" after his thirty-five minutes of missing time. It required medical attention.

The same evening, as Willaim's encounter, at 10:00 p.m., a family of four was returning to Blanca, Colorado after watching a movie in Alamosa with a family friend. This is about forty-minutes after Williams claimed he was returned to his mountaintop home. As the family headed east on State Highway 160, about five-miles out of Alamosa, a large bright light caught their attention. Surrounding the brilliant light were "lots of helicopters" traveling along with the single light in a southwest to northeast direction. They pulled over to the side of the highway and got out. The huge light never varied in intensity, and at one point the adults got so excited, that two little boys in the back seat became very scared and started to cry. One of the excited witnesses, guitar-player George Oringdulph, called me the following day to make a report. "It was huge, whatever it was, and it was pretty strange the way all those other blinking lights seemed to be flying with it."

The day after William's close- proximity sighting he claimed ten or twelve choppers had been "buzzing all over his place." His house had also been broken into and all his photographic equipment rifled through. "Thank God, I had my camera with me. Whoever they were, I'm positive they were looking for those pictures I took the night before!" Several months later I had the opportunity to see one of the photos which just looked like a blob of light in the night sky.

Williams reported the strange events to the local sheriff who

313

Secrets of the Mysterious Valley

conducted a brief investigation. Williams was frustrated. "I showed 'em how my truck, trailer, and bulldozer had been moved, but what could they do?!" He is very protective of his property, and his privacy and, was not pleased when he found large boot tracks and cigarette butts at the edge of the clearing where his trailer sat. He was also perturbed when a large mirror outside his trailer was repeatedly moved from it's secure position. Someone was snooping around his place, and with all the other weird events, Willliams was starting to get pretty paranoid about the whole situation. I called the local sheriff and found that investigating officers were skeptical of these alleged high-strange events, but did acknowledge to me receiving reports of unidentified lights in the same vicinity. Williams also mentioned to me that images of a "large post" kept appearing on freshly developed rolls of film. He could not identify the location of these photos, and doesn't recall taking the pictures. If something like this only happens once, not a big deal. . . but after a fourth time, one would really start to wonder. Members of two investigative organizations visited Williams and according to the witness, "someone used my name publicly even after being asked not to." This incensed him to the point where he was absolutely unwilling to talk about his experiences with investigators, or the press. "I don't care if you weren't the one who used my name. . .you can all GO TO HELL!" he told me angrily during our last conversation. It was hard not to remember my *Suggested Rule of Investigation #3 —Always credit your sources and respect requests for anonymity.*

Like other residents scattered sporadically in this sparsely populated corner of south-central Colorado, Williams has heard stories of "troops" on maneuvers, seen many helicopters and heard stories of black-uniformed soldiers chasing people off of Methodist Mountain a few miles to the northwest. Sitting innocently on the top of Methodist are two groups of high-tech-looking antenna arrays — several, obviously cellular phone towers and microwave relays, but there are other arrays nestled on the ridge. Unreported sightings of chopper activity in the area had reached me several times over the past couple of years, but I had not actively investigated this forgotten, little traveled region, where the reports originated.

One night in 1993, during a visit with a computer scientist who worked for a major defense contractor for a number of years, on classified military projects, I was told of an odd sight he and his family had witnessed sporadically since their move to the area in 1991.

"I've only noticed it late at night during wintertime. I look out at the mountains, and I see this small light just sitting there, way

314

above tree-line. It's not always there, but when it is, it's plainly visible. I've pointed it out to my wife, and we can't figure out what it could possible be." We were sitting in his office located on the second floor of his new home at the base of the northern Sangres.

"Where exactly do you see it?" I asked, hoping to get a more precise idea of its location. "Just right up there," he said pointing casually out the window at the Sangres rearing their majestic tops into the sky. I looked and obtained an accurate fix on the exact spot.

Now who could have a light above tree line at around thirteen thousand feet? That following summer, I was talking with a frequent visitor to the San Luis Valley, who loves to visit the "clothing optional" Valley View Hot Springs, located southeast of the scientist's home. He told me a rather interesting story of a conversation he overheard while soaking in one of the several natural pools that adorn the foothills, east of Villa Grove. It seems our nature-buff was told by "a local" that ten-to-twelve miles north of the Hot Springs, above tree-line, a secret underground base exists inside the Sangres; its main purpose was to send out fighter planes to "chase UFOs." Normally, when I hear such sci-fi sounding information, I don't pay much attention, but this particular claim intrigued me.

"Where exactly did he say the base entrance was?" I asked him. The visitor replied that he had asked, but the view from the pool did not afford a sight line up the range. He did say the man was "…emphatic" about his claim. The "local" claimed on several occasions he personally had seen jets flying out of the mountain.

This rang a major bell. It was the same approximate location of the scientist's sighting of an infrequent light, above tree-line, and, it seriously reminded me of a rancher, named Harry King's claim of seeing little jets flying *into* Middle Creek Hill, about thirty-miles south in the Blanca Massif, back in the 1960s. Harry King was the brother of Nellie Lewis, owner of "Snippy" the Horse, considered the first publicized animal "mutilation". I had heard continual rumors of "underground bases" or staging areas during the eight years I'd lived here, so, I figured, maybe there was something to this latest rumored information. Interestingly Tom Clancy mentions a facility in one of his novels, which features a scene with a helicopter flying to a secret mountain base. Located where? In the Sangre de Cristo Mountains in southern Colorado, of course.

Other strange sightings began to occur in the Northern Sangres. On August 25, 1995, at dusk, a local electric company owner reported triangular-shaped objects over Methodist

Mountain. The witness claimed the objects were red and blue in color and that "there was a field of energy around them." The following morning, on August 26th, a triangular-shaped object was seen from the Salida sales barn, a mile east of town. Later that night, at 10:20 p.m., campers on Silver Creek, near Poncha Pass, witnessed a red and green streak of light moving south-to-north just west of the Continental Divide, again, near Poncha Pass. The two witnesses were interviewed by Colorado MUFON. That same night, also at 10:30 p.m., a very large white globe with red, green and blue colored lights was seen hovering over Poncha Pass and reported by a former Naval officer. The object was viewed from the McCoy trailer park in Salida. The Sophia Institute investigated this claim.

The following morning, August 27th at 8:30 a.m., the beginning of a flurry of sightings that Sunday began innocently outside of Grand Junction, Colorado, a hundred-fifty miles north of the San Luis Valley. Two men, one a disc-jockey from a popular local country-and-western radio station, were out for their usual Sunday morning jog in the Colorado Monument. As they rounded a bend in the trail, they were startled to see a large pencil-shaped craft darting low near the mountain range. As it darted about, it expelled two smaller objects, and all three flew at fantastic speed, and then, a "FLASH," and they disappeared *into* the mountain without a sound. The DJ was so taken with his sighting he broadcast the details to his Grand Junction radio audience requesting that anyone else who may have witnessed the objects call the station.

That same morning, in the Collegiate Mountains just northwest of Salida, a jeep load of tourists reported a cigar-shaped object similar in description to the object seen by the DJ and his friend.

I had a speaking engagement in Denver that weekend and missed all the excitement. The events of August 27, 1995 would become international news. It appeared we had another potential "flap" of UFO activity cranking up.

UFOs Over Salida

Photographic evidence of the many unidentified flying objects reported in Southern Colorado is at best, extremely rare, and daytime film or video footage until now was virtually non-existent. As I mentioned in *The Mysterious Valley* the only south-central Colorado sighting film footage I had heard about was taken in the late summer of 1948 on the Conejoes River. In 1993, Paris, TX researcher Tom Adams had sent me a small article from a San Francisco newspaper that told of a Center, Colorado resident named Grant Edwards, Sr., and the eight-millimeter film he was screening to local San Luis Valley civic groups. The film allegedly featured several flying saucers flying in broad daylight – less than one-half-mile from the witnesses. I looked in the local phone-book and remembered Saquache County Commissioner Keith Edwards, who lived in Center, Colorado. I thought he may know and *voilá* he said yes, his father was film-buff Grant Edwards, and his dad had been the one that filmed the objects. He had never actually seen the film but confirmed the story. At the time, the possibility that this little-known footage could be the earliest civilian film of UFOs never entered my mind, and I redoubled my efforts to find out more about this obscure 1948 film. I looked for clues, wherever I could find them. No luck.

I called Keith back, and he referred me to Marianne Jones-Brown, a Crestone resident and Valley native, who Edwards claimed had been their neighbor and that she had seen the film many times and was quite taken by it. She was right here in Crestone? I called. She remembered the film as if she had seen it recently.

"Grant brought it over to our house right after he filmed them [UFO], and my dad and I saw it four-or-five times in a row, right there in our living room."

"When was this, do you remember?"

"Well, yes. It was in the late summer of 1948. When was that crash in Roswell, New Mexico?"

"July, '47"

"It was the next summer in August, 1948

"How old were you at the time?" I asked.

"I was ten, or so. . . in fourth or fifth grade."

"Well… what did you think? What was on the film? Keith told me he remembered hearing it was daylight footage of a couple of round spheres hanging over the Forbes Trinchera."

"Oh no, he [Grant] filmed them down by the (New Mexico) border on the Conejos River, west of Antonito. And it wasn't two objects, it was five!"

"Really? Five?!"

"Yes, he had just bought a new camera, it was brand new. He'd just loaded it for the first time when his wife looked up and saw them and pointed them out. He shot the whole roll. It seemed like twenty minutes."

"I think those little eight-millimeter film rolls were only about two and half to three minutes long." I used to have one.

"It sure seemed a lot longer than that, I couldn't believe it. The UFOs would come down right over the trees and hover, then go off real fast, then the others would come down. They even flew in formation, with two together in front and the other three behind. At one point they hovered and turned on end like frisbees. The

When they hovered low over the trees, you could even see his wife and daughter standing in the foreground watching them."

"You mean, there were shots of the objects with people in the shot?"

"Yes, when they were low over the trees. I've watched all of the films they show on TV, and nothing compares with Grant's film. It was the best footage I've ever seen! I was really mad when I heard they took it." This perked my curiosity.

"Who took it? You mean the film…?"

"Yes, I remember hearing that the government sent two men and they confiscated it. I think they may have been FBI, or something. Two men just showed up at his house one day and took it. I guess they didn't like him showing it at the Chamber of Commerce or something."

"How long after he shot the film did they show up?"

"Oh, I don't know, maybe six-months after…"

Marianne sounded animated. Her recall seemed superb and it was obvious that seeing the Edwards film at a young age had made a lasting impression on her. She noted, "I've been fascinated with UFOs ever since. Too bad you didn't talk with my dad. He died three-years ago. He was really into it and knew a lot about the sightings around the Valley. I bet there's some old farmers around who could tell you some stories. Back before they had the circles [center-pivot sprinklers], they irrigated by hand and the farmers would spend hours at night just sitting in their trucks. And what would they do? Why, they looked up at the sky."

I asked her, "As a Valley native who grew up here, you must have heard a lot of stories about UFOs people were seeing around here. What do you make of these events; I mean, what do you think, or, who do you think is flying them?"

"Well, when Grant Edwards came over and showed us his film, I just knew what he filmed was not of this earth." She added wistfully, "I just wished you could have talked with my dad. . . he didn't talk about it [UFOs] unless he knew the person believed him. Then he'd talk about it. I think most folks around here are like that. Back when I was a kid, you just didn't talk about them because people would think you were a kook, or something."

She adds, "I've seen a few objects around the Valley. One night in 1965, when my husband and two friends were coming back from Valley View Hot Springs, we were on Highway 17, north of town [Alamosa] when we saw a real bright light over La Garita. It would come up and stay in one spot, then go straight down real fast. We pulled over and watched it for at least twenty-minutes. A couple I know were at the Sky-Hi Drive-In [in Alamosa] and they saw it too."

318

Marianne was on a roll. She continued with another incident. "Back right after we got married, in fifty-seven, we were driving in the canyon over Poncha Pass when the whole canyon lit up. Something flew over. My husband is a civilian-worker for the Air Force, and is familiar with most of the aircraft they fly today. What we saw that night sure wasn't what the Air Force was flying in 1957. He was real impressed with this incident because he knew 'it wasn't one of ours.'" Later when I talked to him, Mr. Brown did not offer any further speculation.

I thanked Marianne and reviewed my notes. I racked my brain trying to remember the earliest civilian UFO footage I could recall. My mind drew a blank. I was sure that the earliest films were from the early fifties. If that was the case, the government confiscated what may have been the first corroborated and publicly acknowledged, multiple-object, UFO footage ever taken by an amateur film-maker. Where? Why, right here in the mysterious San Luis Valley, of course!

"Daddy, there's something up in the sky!"

August 27, 1995, 9:25 a.m.

The sound of hammering roofers, and gunshots at a rifle-range, filled the bright August morning. The nearby Arkansas River flowed serenely in the morning sunshine as a pair of workers busily put the finishing touches on a gutter that adorned a brand new house just northwest of Salida, Colorado. A cacophony of gunshots punctuated the hammering, as members of a gun-club practiced skeet shooting, just down a short, steep hill from the house. The Edwards family lived in the large, tastefully designed and decorated house located several blocks from the Fairview cemetery, and owner, Tim Edwards, forty-two, was preparing to go outside and check on the carpenter's progress. Tim is an unassuming, local restaurant-owner and outdoor enthusiast. A big screen TV and a quality high-fidelity stereo set-up adorned the living room, The father and daughter headed for the kitchen door. The etched-glass kitchen cabinets reflected the bright, slanting morning sun as a little puppy yapped in the yard.

Tim's blonde, bright and inquisitive, six-year-old daughter Brandy walked out the back door into the lovely late-summer Sunday morning. On the surface, just another lovely, typical Colorado high-mountain morning. Brandy looked up....

319

SLV *Lifestyles*

St. Patrick was Medieval hero

THE SOUTH FORK TIMES

Gateway to the Silver Thread

Volume 14, Number 11   South Fork, Colo. 81154   Thursday, March 16, 1995

Another calf found mutilated

Rio Grande Sheriff tracking grisly mystery

Mysterious lights, then a strange harvest

Del Norte rancher Robert Kernen found one calf mutilated on March 4, two days after he noticed his cattle acting strangely. A nearby rancher claims to have seen an unusually bright blue light shining down toward Kernen's pasture the night before the calf was found.

(Staff photo by Samuel Adams)

By Samuel Adams
Staff Writer

A short, short film called "Godzilla versus Bambi" was released years ago that had one scene.

Bambi is feeding peacefully. Suddenly a giant dinosaur foot comes down and smashes the deer, a puddle of blood seeping from under the foot. The End.

In much the same way, but leaving no blood puddle, Del Norte Rancher Robert Kernen found his calf had been destroyed.

This time it wasn't fiction.

Whoever or whatever was responsible had neatly removed the spinal cord, brain, heart, lungs and ribs in such a manner not currently known to science, according to experts consulted about the incident.

"The one out there, the nervous

and circulatory systems, that was a bizarre one," said Chris O'Brien, a researcher who lives in Crestone.

O'Brien has investigated about 150 "unusual animal deaths" in the valley.

"I'm not a starry-eyed believer or a hard-boiled skeptic," he said.

He expects a book he is writing, "Mysterious Valley," to go to the printer this spring.

The book is a history of unexplained occurrences in the San Luis Valley that includes "unusual animal deaths" in the valley.

"I don't call them mutilations, I call them unusual animal deaths," he said "It's very methodical and purposeful."

Usually, the parts cut out of cattle or other animals found mutilated are the genitals. The rectum is also cored out and the head is missing an ear and an eye.

Kernen, a cattle rancher about two miles west of Del Norte, found his calf missing eyes and an ear but the genitals and butt were left untouched.

Kernen's calf was the "weirdest" animal death O'Brien said he'd seen.

"I find it inconceivable that the ribs and brain were removed in that fashion," he said.

The rancher discovered the calf Saturday, March 4, but believes the incident occurred Thursday night, March 2, because his cows acted strangely Friday morning.

Lights in the night

O'Brien said the same night, a rancher to the south saw a strong blue light come from the sky for an hour in a spot to the north, just about where Kernen raises cattle. The light became elongated and then disappeared.

The rancher, who did not want to be named, reported the sighting the next morning to the sheriff.

After finding the calf, Kernen said he saw his cows gather around its carcass and hold a wake.

"I saw 50 cows standing around looking at the calf," he said. "Boy, if those cows could talk."

Kernen said he could tell his cows are stressed by the occurrence.

O'Brien said other incidents he's investigated involved strange animal behavior afterward.

"It's fairly common," he said. "In Costilla County, cows did a clockwise dance around a carcass."

The behavior and incident has not shaken Kernen.

"I just accept it as something that can't be explained," he said.

"I've been ranching all my life and I've never seen this before," Kernen said. "This always happens to the other guy, but this time it happened to me."

The cattleman said his initial reac-

tion was to keep the incident out of the newspaper because he didn't want a bunch of sightseers driving by.

"There's nothing to see now anyway," he said.

The calf's remains are stored out of sight.

Kernen was also concerned for an older man who lives next to him.

"I talked to a couple of ranchers before I went to the sheriff," he said. "They told me to take it to the sheriff. Undersheriff (Brian) Norton said he wouldn't say anything to the newspaper."

Norton made good his promise, saying he wouldn't comment specifically about the incident other than to say specimens were taken and sent to three different laboratories.

He went out to investigate the scene, about 50 yards south of County Road 14A near two cottonwood trees.

See Cattle on Page 10A

Tim's blonde, bright and inquisitive, six-year-old daughter Brandy walked out the back door into the lovely late-summer Sunday morning. On the surface, just another lovely, typical Colorado high-mountain morning. Brandy looked up....

Meanwhile, at that same moment, my partner Isadora and I were pulling into the parking lot of Boulder, Colorado's Broker Inn. I'd been invited by the Denver-based Sophia Institute to speak at an inaugural conference Sophia founder Jack Steinhauser had organized. Experiencer/author Leah Haley and her ufologist/author-husband Marc Davenport greeted us as we arrived. The two-day affair is in its second day and I am the first speaker that morning. Marc has formulated an intriguing theory that UFOs are somehow time-travelers appearing in our space-time continuum. We had a good, enthusiastic turnout and I was impressed by the attendee's breadth of knowledge related to UFOs. I also appreciated seeing true pioneers like Marc and Leah again. Little did we know of the real-time drama unfolding one-hundred miles south of us....

Tim Edwards promised his youngest daughter Brandy that they could go hiking that day if the weather was nice, so naturally, the first thing little Brandy did, upon going outside, was look up to see if it was going to rain. She immediately noticed something dancing high in the air. She smiled. "Daddy, there's something up in the sky!" Tim, busy checking on the carpenters' progress, initially paid her no mind. She repeated her observation. Edwards, legally blind in his left eye, obediently looked up in the direction Brandy was pointing. The new gutter blocked out the disc of the sun, and the sun's corona blazed out into the brilliant sky. Movement near the sun caught his attention. What he saw high in the sky, forever changed his life.

Edwards stood there for several seconds, dumbfounded, watching a sight the likes of which few have ever seen before. A bright object was darting playfully to the northeast of the sun. Were his eyes playing tricks on him? He watched for a couple of minutes in amazement, then ran inside and frantically started making phone-calls to anyone he could think of. Wasting precious time, he finally ran and grabbed his video camera and managed to shoot six and-a-half minutes of videotape, over the next hour and fifteen minutes, of an enormous cigar-shaped object, hovering and darting silently, high in the sky to the northeast.

The audio portion of the tape recorded these comments between the initial witnesses: Tim, Brandy and Tim's father, George Edwards.

322

Brandy asks, "Daddy, can spaceships grow bigger like that? Can they?" Tim answers, "Uh-huh."

"It could?"

"Uh-huh," Tim answers again, obviously concentrating on following the object with the video camera. You can hear him breathing and understandably not paying full attention to his little girl. A small-plane noisily flies low over their heads; amid the pop-popping of the skeet shooter's guns. Brandy is more insistent and comments rhetorically, "If a spaceship can grow bigger like that. . . then it *is* a spaceship!" Tim asks her to "Go get the binoculars." He is joined by his father George, and the two men watch for several seconds in silence while Tim films. Then Tim's dad chimes in, "Oh my god… Geez it stops like that. . . man, it's erratic!" Tim agrees. "It's erratic as hell… it ain't no kind of aircraft, I'll tell you that."

"Ahh-h no," George agrees, and Tim turns off the video tape for the first of nine different shot sequences.

The tape comes back on with Tim's father noting, "[If] you keep looking at it and you can see, like a,…a ball going around it —I mean, way off around it, you know. . . like it's shooting things off it." Something appears to be flying out of the object.

Tim observes, "Well. . .the more you look at it. . . it's just amazing! Where's your spotting scope at Dad? In the fifth-wheel?"

"I don't think you'll get it on that spotting scope."

"You might be able to; it's stationary a lot."

Brandy, who has returned, observes, "Gosh, it's looking orange. There's something orange going around it." Several more seconds go by with the skeet-shooters obliviously firing away, and Brandy, in the background, continues an unintelligible dialog with no one in particular. The three are joined by Tim's oldest daughter, fifteen-year-old Laray, who also is spellbound by the enigmatic object high in the sky.

"I'm going to get under the edge of the house so the sun's not in our eyes." Tim moves the camera. He inadvertently discovers the resulting technique he will use for hundreds of subsequent hours of "solar corona" filming. The object darts impossibly around the sky with the roof edge providing a perfect point of reference in the foreground for analysts to later study and ponder. "It's going all over the sky," Tim's dad says. Tim observes, "There ain't no little

323

airplane that goes five-miles in two seconds."

"I know it, that's what I mean..." George answers emphatically.

". . . It's moving more than five-miles. It moved over to that part of the sky. . . it probably moved a hundred miles in the matter of a second, or two!" Tim sounds genuinely amazed and baffled. Then something unexpected happens.

The elder Edwards is awestruck, "What are those up there now? Do you see that now? See the big one? See it going? Did YA SEE IT?!"

"I can't see it with this," Tim responds while looking through the camera's tiny viewfinder. Another plane flies low over the house. Several more seconds go by with Brandy asking indecipherable questions, then the footage ends.

As soon as Edwards was convinced that the object is real, and not a trick of light or a conventional aircraft, he called his restaurant, the local radio station, the sheriff, The National UFO Reporting Center in Seattle, *Channel Four* news in Denver and Salida *Mountain Mail* editor Chris Hunt. Hunt was instantly interested and immediately went to the Edwards' home.

Hunt told me later, "Edwards thinks the object was extremely high up in the sky because routine airline traffic appeared to fly under it." He actually thinks it could have even been higher. Edwards said, "It could have been twenty or thirty or one hundred miles up for all we know."

Edwards has consistently told everyone "It was kind of eerie. . . I know it wasn't from this world. I know I sound crazy, but I really believe it was from another world." Evidently, Edwards was not initially frightened by the unusual craft. "I was really excited just to get to see it. . . I don't think there was any reason to be scared. Actually, I wish it had landed. If it had landed, it would have covered the whole town of Salida; it was that big."

Tim noted, "The object's north and south movements could be described as darting, but east to west, the craft appeared to step, or walk across the sky —almost like it was projecting itself to the next frame and location." He also claims that with his binoculars he and his father could make out two distinct rows of individual light panels on the object. Hunt, who watched the footage within minutes after it was shot, commented, "At one point the camera zooms in and you can actually see red and green lights sequencing around the rim of the craft." Later, while watching the footage, I couldn't help but wonder what the heck the enigmatic object was! It looks unlike anything one would expect to see flying around conventional airspace. I could clearly see the object's two rows of sequencing lights. Both adult witnesses' noticed that the object, at times, appeared to be boomerang, or V-shaped.

Alerted by Edwards, portions of the footage were sent to news stations, and immediately broadcast on several Front Range Colorado TV stations. The full footage was provided to *Channel Three* in Denver when they visited the Edwards, the following day. Within a month, I was interviewed by the Paramount TV program *Sightings, CBS News, Extra* ,and *Inside Edition* about Tim's footage, and the many sightings of unusual objects that have been reported here in Southern Colorado.

Eventually, over twenty-three witnesses came forward and related seeing a mysterious darting craft, high in the sky. A couple traveling over Cochetopa Pass, about thirty-five miles southwest of Salida, saw what they later told the Saquache County Sheriff's Department, was a "bright cigarette-shaped object," and another couple traveling over Poncha Pass reported a "cigar-shaped" craft the following day, Monday August 28, 1995. Seven witnesses reported a similar object to the Colorado University astronomy department and a maintenance man at the Crestone/Baca Grande Los Cumbres Golf Course, later reported to me he had witnessed a "cigar-shaped object hovering between Kit Carson Peak and Mount Adams" —just east of Crestone—at 4:00 p.m., on August 27th. He didn't immediately report it because, ". . . when it left, it disappeared right into the mountain! I didn't think anyone would believe me, so I didn't tell anyone. Then I read about that guy in Salida filming something the same day that sounds like exactly what I saw. So, I figured I should tell you."

From no activity to a blizzard of reports scattered across all of central Colorado. My vacation was over; I had a lot of work to do. I found out about Edwards's sighting the following day, but something told me to hold my enthusiastic-self back and carefully watch how the information was disseminated. I had worked tirelessly for two-and-a-half years trying to prove to myself that something very strange and wonderful was going on here in the San Luis Valley, and, just two towns away, was validation of a lot of hard work. I decided to not call Tim, just sit back and watch the drama unfold. And drama, indeed, unfolded.

Michael Curta, Colorado State Director for MUFON, stated for television cameras what I've proposed for quite awhile. "Could it be otherworldly technology? Yes, it could. Could it be military aircraft? Yes, it could. Could it be some unexplained weather phenomenon? That's also possible. There's an awful lot of strange things that occur in the mysterious valley of Colorado, and this is racking up to be one of them." Thanks for the plug, Michael.

The sighting immediately became sensational national news. Phone-calls and requests for interviews and tapes poured into the Edwards' household, overwhelming the unprepared family. Tim immediately tried to find professional video labs and analysts to examine the footage. Of course, with all the media publicity he unleashed, every UFO investigative group in the state immediately descended upon him and his family. The MUFON, The UFO Institute, the Fund for UFO Research, the Denver UFO Society, The Sophia Institute; you name 'em; they showed up. I kept a low-key but close eye on developments, and, unbeknownst to Edwards, I combed the southern Colorado countryside for additional witnesses to corroborate his sighting.

Since that fateful Sunday in August, I have become quite friendly with Tim and his family and was stunned by the incredible amount of energy that Tim has devoted to getting attention for his video. Edwards started networking with investigators all over the world trying to "get the word out" about UFOs in general, and his footage in particular.

An Arlene Shovald article in the *Mountain Mail*, September 7, 1995, dealt exclusively with the UFO sighting's effect on Tim. The headline read:

UFO Sighting Changes Edwards' Life

.... Since he videotaped an object in the sky that morning, he has been in demand by newspapers, radio, and television sources and the demands are taking time from his [former] business, the Patio Pancake restaurant on U.S. 50.

Edwards isn't sure he likes the idea of being a celebrity, but he doesn't have much of a choice. Copies of Edwards' original video were aired on *Channels 7, 4* and *Channel 9* in Denver, which includes the ABC, CBS and NBC Networks.... Edwards remains a bit uncomfortable with the whole thing, stating he is putting his whole family's credibility and reputation on the line with his report of the sighting, but fortunately, he has the video to back up his statements along with information from the National UFO Observatory [sic] in Seattle which was flooded with calls from Montana and Pennsylvania from people who had seen the same thing I'd seen."

Another article in the *Mountain Mail* celebrated the seventy-eighth anniversary of another curious Salida sighting. Arlene Shovald did a excellent job researching and came up with the following compelling stories, one of which occurred the same week of the year as Edwards' sighting. The headline read:

Edwards' UFO Sighting Not Salida's First

...The Salida Record of September 7, 1917, tells of Salida residents seeing mysterious 'vehicles of the air' flying about the night sky during the previous week.
"Nearly every night some kind of light was observed in various positions in the 'blue depths.' The lights were described as very far away. They would disappear for an instant, only to reappear stronger that ever, and then vanish. Among those observing the strange phenomenon were some of the pillars of Salida society - Rev. and Mrs. Oakley... . Rev. Oakley examined the object with a telescope one night and could discern what appeared to be a wheel... . While the wheel seemed to revolve, vari-colored lights appeared. Without the telescope, the light appeared to be about the size of a croquet ball as compared with the stars....What the objects were remained a question. According to the article, it was surely not an 'aeroplane' because an aeroplane does not have a wheel, which revolves slowly. The same might be said of a dirigible balloon. And besides, there was no known aviation field in Colorado....' The article concluded, 'is it then some genius who has discovered some new principle of flight, and is trying out his invention? It's your guess. What is it?'"

Twenty years earlier, in 1896-7, strange floating craft were seen across the United States. I had never heard of any sightings of these enigmatic "airships" in Colorado until Arlene sent along this curious three-line article:

April 30, 1897 Buena Vista *Republican*:

The mysterious air ship about what so much has been heard lately seem to have passed over BV and made it's appearance at GJ. [Grand Junction] If anyone here saw it, they have not the hardihood to make the fact known.

As various paranormal television programs have pointed out,

the word *salida* means "gateway" in Spanish. Tim White, the host of the Paramount television program *Sightings* stated the following before broadcasting Edward's Salida footage the following November, "It takes a lot to impress the *Sightings* Investigative Team, and what you're about to see is among the most intriguing footage we've ever broadcast."

Since his infamous tape was shot, Edwards has become a local clearinghouse for reporting UFO reports in the Upper Arkansas River Valley. When sightings are occurring, calls pour in from all over the region, and Tim has managed to interview quite a number of witnesses about their experiences.

That pesky name-game synchronistic connection between the two only-known daylight UFO films from south-central Colorado is undeniable. The fact that the unrelated filmmakers shared the same last name "Edwards" is compelling, and so is the time proximity; late August, when both the 1948 and 1995 films were taken. I am convinced these connections are somehow important.

The Salida UFO sightings, over the course of the next six-months, became sensational front-page news in the *Mountain Mail* with over ten stories published about the area's many on-going UFO reports. According to Edwards: "Dozens of people in Colorado and other states looked my name up and called to talk about sightings they witnessed through the fall. I only wish I had documented some of them better."

Intriguing peripheral events began to unfold around the Edwards property. He started to notice strange brand new sedans with "government plates" lurking around his home, and during episodes of the area's sightings, he videotaped many military-style choppers buzzing overhead.

During two days of UFO activity in September, eagles showed up and wheeled on thermal currents over his house, while UFOs cavorted high above them in the sky. Edwards felt intuitively this synchronicity was an important sign, "... I have said since day one, the main craft was sending a message to the world; it was aware of our presence and *wanted* to be filmed. It [Edwards' sighting] was science and history at the top of the technological ladder, a two-thousand-year history was transpiring, and it was very important for the world to know the truth. It was almost as if it [the main craft] was showing us where to look in the sky for our subsequent filming. The bald eagles are a key part of the spiritualism and message conveyed through our sightings."

Three days after the first sighting he noted in his diary, "Smoke-alarm goes off in the master bedroom. Throughout the fall of 1995, our smoke alarms in numerous rooms went off independently of each other, even though they're all wired together." On September

328

15, 1995, he wrote in his diary: "I'm still trying to get myself calmed down. Still couldn't eat or sleep. I have lost twenty-five pounds." The strain of the pressure prompted him to think later, "I feared for my family's safety at first. We didn't have the luxury of a long term conditioning process." The arrival of the unmarked sedans and choppers during subsequent sighting periods didn't alleviate the feelings of fear either.

Although I had decided initially NOT to attach my name publicly to the Salida sightings, I did quietly begin a process of investigation of the primary witness. According to several people who knew Tim, he had become obsessed with his sighting experience. Owning and operating a successful restaurant is time-consuming, hard work, yet Tim still found time to completely immerse himself into the politicized, kaleidoscopic world of ufology. Tim's innocent exuberance and riveting videotape were immediately embraced by several "name" researchers including Whitley Strieber.

Edwards started feeling something harder to explain: Feelings of pre-destiny, the compulsion of some kind of purpose. He felt he'd been chosen to see and videotape the "main craft," as he referred to the object he had filmed. At first he had tried to attribute these feelings to the excitement of the event itself, but this didn't explain the rising obsession with UFOs and the unexplained. One would think that the effects of any experience would gradually fade, but in Tim's case, the experience increased and reverberated around inside of him, seeking a way out.

Tim continued to lose weight and spent countless sleepless nights, tossing and squirming in bed, not knowing what to do with himself. He had a check-up with his family doctor, but nothing lessened the underlying imperative to find out as much as he could about UFOs, and why he was "chosen" to view them.

It was in this period I met Tim. During the second week of September, I did some serious checking around for additional witnesses, and after talking with Saguache County Sheriff Al King, I had learned of the Cochetopa and Poncha Pass reports. Then, in the middle of a rousing round of golf with a couple of duffer-buddies, a Los Cumbres Golf Club-worker walked over while we were on the fourth-tee box and casually mentioned an object that he had watched disappear into Kit Carson Peak around 4:00 p.m. that same day Edwards' filmed the "main craft." This unsolicited report from a fifth witness left no doubt in my mind; It was time to give Mr. Tim Edwards a call.

I went ahead and called Tim. He seemed to know who I was. He was puzzled, even a bit miffed, as to why it had taken me so long to contact him. I listened carefully as he described his sighting and the subsequent ufological media circus that had erupted around him. I told him, this was exactly why I didn't contact him. I wanted to observe the process of dissemination he'd set in motion, from as objective a perspective as possible. Since I hadn't found out about the case before the press ran with the story, I opted not to get publicly involved right away.

He was very excited while describing the whirlwind events to me. Even though he had become an instant celebrity, I didn't get the sense that his excitement was at all ego-motivated, or that he had dollar signs in his eyes. He seemed genuine and matter-of-fact, but he was convinced *he* had been chosen to tell the world "I'm one-hundred percent convinced this is a craft from another world....There's no doubt in my mind.... The time has come. THEY are here." Edwards feels that he was personally allowed to videotape his sighting by the pilots of the craft. It was now his duty to spread the word far and wide. And spread it he did.

Tim has given away dozens of videotape copies of his footage and TV news shows covering the event, press releases, newspaper and magazine articles and video analysis reports. He has been interviewed on countless media programs: made trips back east to syndicated TV talk-shows; spoke and and a video presentation at the International UFO Congress in Mesquite, Nevada. Even the king of tabloid TV, *Inside Edition* produced a show on his experience.

He told me he had had hired "an entertainment agent" to handle all the media inquiries concerning his remarkable footage. The agent, Michael Tanner, was also involved with a video analysis firm, Village Labs, in Tempe, Arizona, founded by video analyst Jim Dilettoso. Both men were very excited about the footage. According to a Tanner press release, Dilettoso is "a recognized authority on film and video image analysis technologies and their applications to purported UFO evidence," and has even done analytical work for the Jet Propulsion Laboratory (JPL).

I found out that Tim and Cheryl were getting ready to drive to Arizona and hand deliver the master-tape of his footage to Village Labs the following week. Edwards was very concerned about sending the tape and was extremely hesitant about conventional mail delivery services. To ease his fears, he had opted for the hand delivery method.

His new agent, Michael Tanner, released the following information in a press-release dated September 19, 1996.

> The Village Labs of Tempe, Arizona has just completed today its preliminary analysis on the extraordinary UFO videotape recently recorded by Tim Edwards of a large

object in the skies over Salida, Colorado. Jim Dilettoso, the president-founder of Village Labs who is personally conducting what is planned to be an exhaustive analysis of the unique video footage, has concluded thus far that, "… it is certainly not lens flare, a reflection of some kind or any type of 'over the shoulder' optic aberration… it is definitely a very large, solid and three-dimensional, possibly cylindrical, object at high altitude. We don't know how large it is as yet, but the object clearly is emitting brilliant white and colored lights, is demonstrating unusually rapid, darting movements in the sky, and we have confirmed on the tape the presence of smaller objects coming from it which confirms the witnesses' visual accounts. Further testing of the Edwards UFO footage at the Village Labs will include in-depth thermal and motion studies, image enhancement and enlargement as well as computer graphics simulations of the UFO event based on the spectrum of data collected and the results of analysis.

After he performed further video analysis, Dilettoso was interviewed by UPN Network's television show *Paranormal Borderline* where he stated:

When analyzing video, we have to take this low-resolution image, transfer it to the computer, and begin to study whatever we can. First thing, remove the noise —take out the video noise; take out the lines, and then look for data.… We believe that the object is about a half-a-mile long, about two-to three-thousand feet long and about seventy-five thousand feet in the air. What does that compare to? Seventy-five thousand feet, fifteen-miles. Fifteen miles in the air. Half-a-mile long, two Sears Towers stacked end-to-end. A huge object! This analysis reveals to us that there are definitely structures to the light. The data seems to support the concept that these are moving lights —moving with the pattern —moving with some intention —they move one direction, move back the other direction and the brightness of the lights tends to support what the witnesses said.…The fact that in 1917, and 1995, in Salida, Colorado, two people viewed. . . eighty-years apart.… the same thing. I think that's a remarkable coincidence. What if the method of transportation for these large objects to come to our planet involved, a coordinate, with very specific physical properties; Polarity, resonance, magnetism, and they lock on to it, and that's where they arrive. There could be some interstellar homing-beacon —either purposefully, or naturally located high in the Rocky Mountains.

Dilettoso told *Channel Four News* in Denver: "At a technical and visual level, I believe this to be a real object — not a mistake — a large object a great distance from the camera because it has the optical characteristics of a large object, and most importantly, it fits identical criteria of objects like this that have been seen all over the world. . . I think this is a very large craft, piloted by people from another world, visiting earth."

Dilettoso was referring to objects filmed in Krasnador, Russia in 1990, the footage captured in San Francisco by John Bro and videographer Tom King's Phoenix film of what appears to be similar to the craft witnessed over Salida.

Chip Peterson, an aerospace engineer specializing in computer-enhancement and stabilization, was contacted by the Paramount Television program *Sightings* and asked to take a look at Edwards' video. He was interviewed for a segment on the Salida footage and came to a more cautious conclusion:

> When you look at moving video, what you're actually seeing is thirty frames-per-second flipping on the screen very quickly, and that's what we've got right here. What you're seeing is the edge of each frame I had to stabilize by hand in the center of the screen." Peterson points to the object on the screen which shows a completely stabilized gutter edge and the impressively darting craft, which appears to move great distances effortlessly in the blink of an eye. After you stabilize the image, you can see the motion much more clearly. Based on what I know of atmospheric flight, it doesn't look like any conventional aircraft.

It sure doesn't. Once the wobbly, hand-held movement is factored out of the image, the object's movements look virtually impossible to perform based on our understanding of conventional propulsion and inertia.

Another analyst was enlisted to scrutinize the footage for the television news-magazine *Inside Edition*. John Deturo is a video analyst working at the United States Military Academy in West Point, NY, who has actively debunked supposed UFO footage.

Deturo was also convinced that the image on the video was a real, three-dimensional object flying at an extremely high altitude.

I coincidentally received a report the same day as Edwards'

sighting, August 27, 1995, of "fifteen military planes flying in formation" low over the town of Blanca, Colorado. The day after the Edwards' sighting, I received an interesting report of an "underground boom" called in by June Walkley, an Alamosa resident, who was convinced the deep sound was not a sonic-boom.

Since his initial sighting, Tim Edwards claims he has captured "thousands" of small, fleeting aerial objects, flitting in the sky over Salida. In just one thirty-second clip, Edwards has taped literally hundreds of these anomalies zipping merrily about. Local skeptics have scoffed at the claim saying he's just filming cottonwood particles and insects floating in the air, but this investigator is not thoroughly convinced of this explanation. Sure, during daytime skywatch session I've noticed some particulate matter floating by, but what about the spheres Edwards videoed that hover, reverse course, dash away, *against the wind?* Or the ones that break into several objects, then reform? Or the larger spheres that climb high in the sky and disappear behind high-altitude clouds?

A week later, September 3, 1995, at 11:00 a.m., one of my former skeptics reported seeing a silver-disc while driving south on State Highway 17 into Alamosa. Much to his surprise, on his return trip two-and-one-half hours later, he saw a "silver pencil-shaped object" high in the sky to the west. He called and rather sheepishly reported his two sightings.

Monday, September 25th proved to be an exciting day around the Edwards' household. Tim's mother saw them first. He told me, "She looked up in the sky and observed a tiny silver object near the sun." Tim immediately called the Chaffee County Sheriff's Office and Officer Chester Price drove out to the house. Tim's mom, Jean Edwards, had been alerted by her husband to go outside and look up in the sky for anything unusual because the local FM radio-station KVRH transmitter had inexplicably shut down. As Price arrived at the Edwards house, he noticed that a small group had gathered in the yard and were watching several objects scooting around in the sky near the sun.

Price later was interviewed by KVRH and was quoted elsewhere as describing the objects as "bright and shiny silver objects traveling from north to south around the sun." He estimated he witnessed up to ten objects. KVRH received four other calls reporting the objects. The *Mountain Mail* article the following day mentioned that the transmitter went off at 9:00 a.m., and came back on at about 9:45 a.m., and the station had no idea why the it went down. When Edwards called the radio station to report the sighting, several curious station employees went outside to have a look. Joann Gleason and Pidge Cribari observed something shiny moving quickly across the sky. The radio tower just happens to be right next to the Cellular One tower on Methodist Mountain. The *Mail* called Cellular One manager Nedra Swope to see if anything unusual happened to their tower. "'Swope said their signal went out at about 1:00 p.m. and was still out at 4:45 p.m.'"

Tim managed to get three hours of taped footage of the unknown objects cavorting around the sun. In the foreground, distracting insects, ragweed and cottonwood fluff flit by the camera, but sure enough, way in the background, high in the sky, you can plainly see the silver objects traveling high above the clouds. There is no bit of fluff or insect that can be visible so far from the camera.

The time proximity of the object's apparent arrival and the inexplicable crash of the radio tower is highly suggestive of a connection. Were the objects responsible for the shut downs, or was it just another coincidence? Officer Price, while watching the mesmerizing objects in the sky, told bystanders he was reluctant to leave the Edwards' house because he might get into a wreck while driving because he'd be so busy looking up at the sky!

It would be quite the understatement to say that Tim was surprised that he was able to witness and videotape even more objects after his celebrated sighting on August 27th. He told the *Mountain Mail*, "…To see similar objects a second time was more than I ever expected." It would not be the last time he and his family would witness unusual aerial objects.

Tim summed up the impact of his experiences during an interview on my *Mysterious Valley Report*, National Public Radio Show on KRZA-FM, and in an interview with D'Arcy Fallon, a reporter for the Colorado *Gazette-Telegraph.*

> Back during the first sighting when we got the binoculars on the 'main craft,' I had a very overwhelming feeling come over me. 'It' was aware of our presence and wanted to be filmed and photographed. 'It' was sending a message to the world, and it was very important for the world to know the truth. I think this goes all the way back into history. You've got your sun-gods and apparitions by the sun; weird things have happened by the sun throughout history, and it's interesting that 'the main craft' was also up by the rays of the sun, flying around for an hour and fifteen minutes, and then a month later, all the other solar corona activity begins…
>
> The first two months after my filming was a very emotional time for me. I didn't understand anything about ufology, and the whole thing was a kind of a

spiritual awakening for me. People that have had major sightings, close encounters, abductions, this and that, don't have the luxury of a long-term conditioning process; they're conditioned in a matter of seconds. One second, you've never even thought about the subject [UFOs] the next second, there's the knowledge of higher things, the knowledge that reality is much more than we ever imagined." He told Fallon, "They put some feelings in me I've never had before. When I was looking through the binoculars at the main craft, I got, like, an electric impulse though my body.... . Now, I'm convinced we're not alone. Not since Jesus was here has something so major come down. Most people are terrified that something could be out there.

Edwards thinks there's a purpose behind these sightings. "The UFOs are buzzing the earth because they're concerned about its inhabitants, much like humans are curious about whales and dolphins." And how should we respond? "Brotherhood, universal love, and get rid of the nuclear stuff."

Tim admits he's undergone a undeniable life-change. "Since August 1995, all my free time is spent researching and trying to get the truth out to the public, and since I've become so involved, I've lost my privacy, but I've gained a lot of good people, the new friends I've met." He adds, "I guess I needed a hobby, or something. I've put a lot of money out of my pocket into this, and I'll continue to try and get my story out and make more people aware that there's a lot more things going on in the world. Most of us don't have a clue what's really going on out there."

Salida's reluctantly famous videographer/witness thinks networking is the key. "The Internet is the best thing that's ever happened to UFOlogy. When there's a sighting in Japan, for instance, we can hear about it in a matter of a few seconds. This information can't be covered up anymore. . . The people in the Salida area —the majority of them take this subject matter real seriously, and my belief is that something very profound is happening....Cosmic awareness is going to help put the world in a better direction."

The Tim Edwards saga continues. His hours of raw video footage awaits a patient expert with the time to wade through the hours of tape he has recorded. Much of his subsequent footage is inundated with airborne debris; however, there are strange objects present in much of the additional footage. Several other visual oddities can be seen in some of his later footage from the spring of 1996. Beautiful sheets of spider-web-like material waft

335

hypnotically through the frame in several shots. These sheets of material have no known origin, to my knowledge, nor do the bizarre segmented shapes and my personal favorite, the Rocky Mountain flying-fish. In two sequences, the viewer is treated to an undulating fish-shape that wiggles quickly through the frame, above the house against the sky and clouds. Tim freeze-framed the image on the second-generation tape he gave me, and the unmistakable image of a fish is a big hit at my various speaking engagements. I suggest to audiences that the best way to catch one of these rare Rocky Mountain flying-fishes is to use a sky-blue Rapalla lure. That usually gets a chuckle or two.

Jose Escamilla, formerly from Midway, New Mexico, (just up the road from Roswell) captured the imagination of ufology in March of 1994, when he announced that he and his sister Becky had been filming strange "rods" and other shapes and craft flying over their home. Some of the tape they've shot reminds me of the later Edwards' solar footage. Peculiar, almost alive, the aerial creatures seem to dance and dart around the screen, and as far as I know, no one has adequately explained what these images are. Tim's tapes contain many of these perplexing images.

Could we be seeing simple video camera focus distortion of airborne debris? Are they as yet undefined atmospheric life forms? Thought forms? Could they be astral, or spirit-creatures? Until now, no expert has even ventured a guess that can be proven. There are many mysteries whirling around us that we have yet to define, let alone comprehend, and as is usually the case, the help of genuine experts could be a great help.

Another Edwards' video clip of an unusual sighting deserves mention. On September 10, 2001, less than eight hours before the attack on New York's World Trade Center, Tim was driving home at around 10:00 PM when he spotted a strange triangle formation of lights flying low — north of Salida, headed west. He stopped his car, hopped out with his camcorder and captured about one minute of footage of an unexplained triangle array of lights. They appeared to be at less than five-hundred feet. The object appeared to be less than a mile from his vantage point, had three brilliant lights and was completely silent. Several elements about the footage are especially intriguing. First of all, the triangle array was flying with the point light in the back, headed away from the direction of travel. Also, during a two to three second portion of the footage, after Edwards was able to zoom in on the object, you can see structure just above the lighting array. The lights do not conform to any known conventional craft.

As the chill fall air oozed into the high-mountain valleys in late September, 1995, I felt a tension in the air. Something seemed ready to bust loose. I re-doubled my efforts to keep informed and up-to-speed, and as I found out, I didn't have to wait long for more reports and cases to further occupy my investigative curiosity.

The Sangres: Is a doorway to another dimension located here?

Rare winter UAD case, Hooper, Colorado

Volume 5   **April through May 1998**   Number 3

The *Mysterious* Valley Report

A LISTING OF REPORTED ANOMALOUS ACTIVITY IN THE GREATER SAN LUIS VALLEY CO-NM

Written and Compiled by Christopher O'Brien © 1998

MUTES, LIGHTBEAMS, AND HIGH HEAT

Next Month: "A Study of Bovine Excision Sites"

UFO's and UAD discovery times and dates in **BOLD**, suspected military activity in *ITALICS*, (Investigator) EVIDENCE, <u>Media</u>

A Quiet, Windy Springtime

This is turning out to be an uneventful spring. Since 1993, we have had 5-6 years that featured impressive spring-time activity. In early 1998, we find reports of anomalous San Luis Valley events at lower than usual levels.

There could be several different causes for our event downturn. This investigator has noticed that real-time reports of activity seem to have subsided, yet anecdotal reports from "last week or month" seem to be on the rise. Perhaps our activity is becoming more mundane and "not a big deal" in the region. I'm getting a lot of those, "I was going to call, but I didn't want to bother you"-type stories or the, "oh geez, I forgot to tell you . . ." scenarios. The 50%-50%, it-could-go-either-way-status of the Colorado Airspace Initiative/MOA expansion finds the "military" stepping lightly. A trickle of conventional aerial reports indicate a more subtle AF presense--possibly to not further jeopardize the delicate expansion process at the State and Federal levels. We shall see . . . I always assumed expansion was a foregone conclusion, and let's face it, up to 70% or more of our "ufo" reports could be "military" night flight activity.

Five UFO Photos Taken in NM

April 3, 1998, 11:00 am, AN1 20 miles south of Las Vegas, NM on Highway 84-near Apache Springs. Duration: 10 minutes.

Five daylight photos were taken of an anomalous object south of Las Vegas NM, by scientist Nick Schmidt and a friend. Schmidt contacted me and asked me to help with analysis of the photos. He visited me the following week after he snapped the intriguing photos (which can be seen X400 in the Photo Archive section of my web-site under "Visual Evidence.") We scanned the images into my computer using imaging software.

More Photographic Anomalies

The five photos show a bright, reflective object that seems to pulse, or elongate into two, then three segments. Atmosphere distortion appears around the object which seemed to Schmidt to just hover around "5-miles away" from the two witnesses. Additional photo analysis is underway.

The Fosbury Flopping Cow

May 2, 1998, Rd 10, Possible MUTE Junne and Virgil Walkley were returning home from a friend's house when they happened upon a "mutilated bull" that appeared to be "dropped on a fence line." The animal, which turned out to be a cow, had apparently been dead for three or four days. It was lying on its back directly ON an old fenceline that extends north-to-south, on the western edge of the San Luis Valley Ranch Estates, 12 miles east of Alamosa, CO., where the Walkley's property is located. The Walkleys are subscribers to the Mysterious Valley Report, and avid skywatchers.

The mandible flesh and hide had been removed cleanly from around the lower teeth, up and around the jaw, and back under the lower jaw around to the lower teeth. The rear end and lower internal organs had been reamed by coyotes and scavenging birds. At this time, the owner of the animal has not been established and no report has been made to Alamosa or Costilla County authorities.

This investigator conducted a thorough investigation of the crime scene and was unable to locate any further clues as to why the animal died, or what "mutilated" it. Because of the untimely nature of the report, no forensic or soil samples were obtained.

G.M. Scallion WATCH out!

This latest case extends the defined line of "mute" cases east from the Alamosa Rio Grande River confluence where a number of cases have occurred. This makes seven cases in a perfect crescent-line along the Alamosa River that have been reported and investigated since 1994. This investigator jokingly predicted the location of this latest possible mute (last March) to within 1/2 mile of where it was discovered! I can hear it now . . . Oh Boy, get the blue-turban-call the cops-heaven forbid--he's prophesying!

CHAPTER ELEVEN:
We Keep Our Eyes to the Sky

Just over La Veta Pass; directly east of the middle of the San Luis Valley, is the Huerfano Valley (orphan in Spanish). This beautiful diamond-shaped county is truly an undiscovered Southern Colorado gem. This area extends from the eastern side of the Blanca Massif and the Great Sand Dune area, southeast down the eastern side of the Sangres almost to the New Mexico border, where it jogs straight east out onto the Front Range — past Walsenburg, then north to Colorado City.

Little-known, even to many Coloradans, the Huerfano is steeped in traditional mystery. One of the earliest Spanish treasure legends in the region is centered around the two imposing Spanish Peaks, (West Spanish Peak 13,626 feet and East Spanish Peak 12,683 feet) ancient volcanoes sitting side-by-side; apart from the Sangres, dominating the southern Colorado Front Range landscape like two giant sentinels. Because of the close geographical connection between the San Luis Valley and four bio-regions that surround the valley, (the Upper Arkansas River Valley, The Espanola Valley/North Central New Mexico hill country, the Upper Rio Grande River Valley, and the Huerfano). I decided early on in my investigation, to examine the Greater San Luis Valley region closely and identify any elements that link these neighboring areas together with the San Luis Valley.

The Huerfano

Many reports of the sublime and unexplained, from this forgotten corner of Colorado, just to the east of the San Luis Valley would've been lost to the murky seas of time had it not been for the dogged efforts of resident journalist/theorist David Perkins, a thirty-year veteran investigator of the "cattle mutilation" and UFO phenomena. "Izzy Zane," as he's known to his many friends, has lived in and explored the Huerfano since 1970. One of the original independent "mute" investigators from the mid-1970s, Izzy has wrestled toe-to-toe for years with the tar-baby called

"The Cattle Mutilation Phenomenon." In my estimation, Izzy has applied *the* most original thinking concerning the true nature of this much ignored, high-strange phenomenon which we will cover more in-depth a bit later. It is not by accident that he has set the stage with his forewords for all three *Mysterious Valley* books. Many of his stickiest most perplexing cases have occurred right where he lives, in the heart of Colorado's Huerfano. One puzzling series of Huerfano events illustrate the complexity inherent in the "UFO" reports investigators log from this forgotten region of south-central Colorado.

The third week in September, 1995, I received a call from Huerfano resident Barbara Adkins. A woman with a life-long interest in the paranormal, in 1993, she had heard through the local grapevine about my investigative work, and has subsequently supplied me with leads concerning periodic Huerfano County sightings. She called with a sense of urgency, which I sensed right away. She said, "I'm here with someone who really needs to talk with you." A friend of Barbara's, named Jeannie Shaw got on the phone.

Friday, September 22, 1995, at 8:45 p.m.

Shaw began to tell me of an impressive sighting experience over the Navajo Estates subdivision where she lives that sits on a small ridge east of Silver Mountain, just over La Veta Pass, in the middle of Huerfano County. The group of houses have a commanding view of the long sloping plain that stretches toward Walsenburg.

Resident Jeannie Shaw, her fifty-two-year-old sister Loni Smith, and Jeannie's two grown children in their twenties were finishing dinner. It was a beautiful regular evening in the Colorado mountains. The few clouds in the sky to the west drifted majestically over the nearby Sangre De Cristo's, which were silhouetted in a lean alpine glow. Almost imperceptibly, Jeannie began to feel a "deep, low humming sound" over the house, which sits on a ridge just to the east of La Veta Pass. After several seconds, her sister Loni, who was visiting, looked toward the window. She turned and the sisters looked at each other in quizzical silence. Someone asked rhetorically, "What *is* that sound?" The "sound" seemed to be growing louder, and appeared to be headed toward them from the east, right in their direction. Jeannie's two kids bolted from the dinner table and headed to the window as dogs in the subdivision began to howl and bark. Now joined by the two sisters, together the four of them peered out into the darkening sky. The vibration grew steadily louder, and they could feel the sound reverberating inside their bodies more than they could actually hear it. Then, out the window, movement. They couldn't believe their eyes! A huge lumbering craft was rumbling slowly past their location at tree-top level "sixty-to-seventy feet" above their gaping mouths. The four incredulous witnesses rushed out onto the porch, which afforded them a picturesque view of their new temporary sky-borne neighbor, the "one-hundred-yard wide rectangle" slowly flying west-to-east, over the Shaw's vibrating house.

Almost instinctively Robert, Jeannie's son, dashed down the porch stairs. He stopped momentarily, and before better judgment set in, he ran down the arroyo that stretches down the hill attempting to keep up with, and get better look at, the underside of the "monstrous" craft flying overhead. Loni began waving her arms theatrically from the porch and shouted at the slowly departing ship, "Here we are, here we are!" In horror, a very serious Jeannie punched her in the arm and told her to, "Shut up,… or they'll beam us up!"

Over the next "eight-to-twelve minutes" the witnesses watched the craft fly slowly east, then loop around to the west where it disappeared behind a ridge. A bright white light then rose up over the ridge, flared and blinked out. In a few short moments, eight to ten blinking lights appeared over the ridge and begin flying in a criss-crossing pattern over the area.

"My legs buckled; I screamed. It was in our face's. . . I just couldn't believe it," said Shaw later. "There were yellow and white lights oscillating around the front; which was rounded, and my son ran down the driveway underneath the object and kept up with it. . . that's how slow it was flying." She added, "…. as it moved away from us, we could see red lights on the rear. They looked just like giant Cadillac tail-lights." Loni added, "I never thought about UFOs before, but I'll tell you, we keep our eyes to the sky now…"

Shaw estimated the object sighting at about "eight-to-twelve," maybe as long as "fifteen-minutes" before they lost sight of it. "We were so amazed, we really didn't time how long we watched it."

After an immediate call from Shaw, a neighbor corroborated their observations. Shaw continued making calls. Next, she called the Huerfano County Sheriff's Office. According to Shaw, a bored-sounding deputy fielded her excited call. She was told, rather bluntly, that the officers on-duty had also heard the low, rumbling sound (it had apparently rattled the sheriff's office windows), but not to worry about it. It was only "'a helicopter.'" A bit perturbed, Shaw also contacted the Huerfano *World* newspaper and was told the paper had called the Walsenburg, Colorado police department about the excited reports and they were told "'it was *two* helicopters.'" Shaw had a very hard time believing this explanation. "This thing looked like *the* mothership," she told me. "How could they say it was only a 'helicopter?!'""

The Shaws live underneath the La Veta low-level Military Flight Operations Area. If this object is an example of what our military is testing over civilian areas of the country, I don't wonder at all why the "Cold War" is over. If we have technology that can propel a "three-hundred foot long rectangle" at single-digit speeds, it's no wonder the Soviet Union and the Eastern Bloc countries opted out of the "super-power" game and are now playing catch-up; wrestling with establishing "free-market" economies, instead of investing in trillion-dollar defense budgets.

The Shaws were apparently not the only area residents who witnessed the large barge-like craft lumbering over the verdant Huerfano. Jeannie rattled off the names and numbers of other witnesses who saw the strange, giant-rectangle. One woman, who lives about two-miles away from Shaw, told reporter D'Arcy Fallon, of the Colorado *Gazette—Telegraph*, she was "just getting ready for bed. She heard a low humming noise and figured it was a helicopter. But the sound persisted, and her dogs were going wild. She looked out the window and gasped. Like Shaw, her knees buckled. 'It was huge. I saw it going over the trees. It was a shock to see something that big. I thought, holy-shit what is that?'"

Shaw, (and this investigator) have located additional area residents who saw and/or heard the giant craft that moonless Friday night, and in the process, found out about other recent sightings in the La Veta, Colorado area.

Fly-Boys With Toys

With a population of just over six-thousand, most of the northwestern portion of the Huerfano lies in the shadow of the La Veta Military Operations Area. The end of the Cold War with the former "evil" Soviet Empire finds our Air Force fly-boys with billions of dollars worth of aeronautical toys and no defined enemy to use them against. Granted, we've spent many billions of dollars on hardware and our pilots need to train, but who (or what) are we training our pilots to do battle with? Iran? China? Osama bin Hidin? Use/fly 'em, or lose 'em seems to be the rationale. Either we give our fighter pilots flight time, or we lose them to the airlines. With thousands of sorties costing millions of dollars, the Air Force is conducting business as usual in the skies over the Huerfano. So

342

are the multi-national arms developers who supply the toys. The F-22 has now officially joins our arsenal of state-of-the art aerial weapons systems as our most advanced "conventional" fighter plane.

There are legitimate arguments against so much aerial activity. Accidents do happen, and during a seven-day period in September 1997, six United States military aircraft crashed, including an F-117A stealth fighter, which narrowly missed taking out spectators at an air show in Virginia. Except for "air show" appearances and other exhibition flying, our fly-boys scream around in designated flight areas where training and simulated aerial war games are conducted.

As mentioned in *The Mysterious Valley*, the La Veta Military Operations Area (MOA) covers the low-level airspace over a parts of Huerfano, Custer, Saguache, Alamosa, Costilla, Chaffee and Pueblo Counties. Air Force and National Guard flight operations are conducted here almost daily.

For reasons not clearly stated, the government wants to expand our countries MOAs. Why? Aren't our pilots getting their ya-yaas out in Mesopotamia and elsewhere(?)

The Front Range of Colorado reaps the rewards of an annual influx of billions of dollars, and the citizens of the SLV and the Huerfano, who gain nothing, have to tolerate the many ear-splitting over-flights. Some flights even conducted by foreign air forces!

It is apparent, that the military is conducting undisclosed flights and aerial maneuvers in and around Colorado. With the second-largest source of State income being utilized and spent by the intelligence agencies and military for projects here in Colorado, you would think they would concentrate their activities in the remotest areas of the State. That may mean here in the San Luis Valley, and possibly elsewhere in the state.

I find it ironic that my assertions in *The Mysterious Valley* suggesting a high percentage of the SLV "so-called" nocturnal UFO sightings may be due to secret military activity was ignored by the media and opponents of the MOA. It can be frustrating investigating the realm of the unknown, people automatically assume you are "a UFO crazy," running around sensationally claiming "the Martians have landed." Nothing could be further from my thinking. My hunch has always been that the government is utilizing the San Luis Valley high-ground (and other specific hot-spot regions) for "secret" projects. I've stated this suspicion publicly many times, but the media and critics tend to hear only what they want to hear.

It would stand to reason that certain cutting-edge military technologies may be so fantastic in appearance, witnesses might think they were witnessing something "other worldly." The operators of these exotic technologies would want to examine their secret toy's impact on unsuspecting witnesses as they would undoubtedly want to use this potential for misdirection through misperception. It makes sense: why not trot out new technology in a remote region and gauge the resulting perceptions as they filter into culture through the media? The military would want to know; what was reported, and by whom? How was their technology perceived? How does the media and law enforcement view the claims of puzzled witnesses? Are these claims publicized? Do the reporters put a spin on their reports? This obvious rationale explaining some (but not all) of our UFO sightings may have more than passing relevance to the UFO field in general.

Regardless of this mode of thinking, one underlying probability needs to always be factored into the equation. Something else has apparently been flying around in our airspace for hundreds, perhaps thousands of years. No matter how hard the skeptic in me might try, the above hypothetical government/military scenario can only explain a sizeable percentage of our sightings—not all of them.

I have testimony that the military has conducted all kinds of San Luis Valley-based operations in the past. Ex-superintendent of Rio Grande National Forest, Buddy Whitlock told me in 1993, that he knew of secret military maneuvers, back in the early 1980s in the inaccessible Upper Sand Creek Lake region of the Sangre de Cristos. He was asked to "clean-up" their mess, strewn around the fragile environment, after the troops departed. He saddled up and headed out with a pack-horse and barely escaped disaster when an early Fall blizzard bludgeoned the mountains. He was "lucky to make it out."

Other accounts tell of the CIA training "Tibetan Nationals" up on the Blanca Massif back in the mid-1960s, and ex-County undersheriff Lynn Bogle confided to me that "Aryan Groups" were known to train in remote inaccessible areas in the Sangres. I've often wondered if some of these clandestine mid-sixties activities might have somehow been tied to the Snippy incident.

My incidental sighting on January 23rd, 1995, of what appeared to be three military planes flying side-by-side, traveling west; flashing synchronized strobe lights sequentially down the leading edge of all three aircraft, may be tied to these "secret" nighttime operations. The reports I have fielded of helicopters, or other craft, shining intense spotlights at civilian cars on the ground in an unusually provocative and aggressive manner may also be tied to these maneuvers.

Reports of large unconventional objects in broad daylight – in one instance, accompanied by fighter aircraft suggest a terrestrial explanation to at least a portion of "UFO" sightings. The area's close-proximity to a dozen military facilities, combined with an isolated rural population could be considered a perfect laboratory for so-called psychotronic weapons testing. If you examine key cases/reports from the historical SLV database, you must factor in the possibility of human involvement. From the Edwards UFO footage on the Conejos River, in late 1948, through Snippy in 1967, the history of unusual events in the SLV might indicate something less than otherwordly. There may be a program of government experimentation going on here. It may have began in the late 1940s and continues today.

If you attempt to examine all the elements that may be at work and play here in the SLV and other hot-spot regions, there is circumstantial evidence to suspect direct, covert government/ military involvement in perpetrating and manipulating manifestations of inexplicable events. However, I sense something ancient and primordial appears to be lurking beneath mundane human agendas and this element lies at the core of our equation.

I realize that my data log of aerial phenomena reports, for the sake of argument, could be saturated and adulterated with misidentified conventional and unconventional terrestrial craft sightings. Nevertheless within these reports are relevant, important high-strange, occurrences that undoubtedly contain important clues. For what it is worth, I suspect that a sizable percentage of these so-called anomalous events are being choreographed by human players alongside truly high-strange, non-human phenomena that have been witnessed by humans for hundreds, perhaps thousands of years. Having said this, I remind the reader that no one (to my knowledge) can supply quality data to definitively prove or disprove any hypothesis to explain or define events of the high-strange, or paranormal. For instance: the potential for misidentification tempers all analysis of anomalous light reports from the eastern side of the Sangres—over the La Veta MOA, and for that matter, all of Southern Colorado and Northern New Mexico. This illustrates my point that the Real Thing is nestled within the data. It appears to be ancient, omnipresent, but, in the twenty first century the Real Thing is surrounded and layered over by high-strange *appearing* events. There also appears to be a program of subterfuge at work.

To sum up my thinking; there's no question in my mind that the "boys with toys," have been utilizing the SLV's airspace for decades. There is also the likelihood that someone or something has been manipulating perceptional of regional events, perceived as unexplained, in this isolated subcultural petri dish.

I visited Roger and Pam LaBorde, two of my more diligent skywatchers, at their newly acquired dream house at the base of the south side of the Blanca Massif, with it's stunning front-row seat view of Little Bear and Blanca Peak, on August 15, 1997. I arrived with Brisa, who was spending the night with her friends the LaBorde girls. Roger was showing a Colorado State Forest worker an area he and Pam were considering turning into a small wetland. As I waited for Roger, I leaned against my truck and scanned the breathtaking view of the Blanca Massif with my binoculars while Brisa visited with her friends.

Low, droning airplane engines caught my attention and I looked up to see what appeared to be a bright silver C-131 flying over the mountain about thirty-five thousand to forty thousand feet up. I brought the binoculars up to my eyes and located the plane. At that instant, it shimmered and disappeared! I quickly looked around the cloudless sky as a couple of seconds went by and the sound abruptly ceased. Nothing! I realized it was strange to see a bright aluminum-colored C-131. And it was very weird the way the plane vanished into thin air. Roger came walking up the driveway. I told him what I had just witnessed, and he said, "Oh, I've seen that [planes disappear into thin air] a couple, three times since we moved here." We went inside and sat down at the kitchen table, with me scratching my head, still trying to figure of what I had just seen.

Could it be that Native American stories of a "doorway" in the Sangres are not merely legends, but a true entrance to another world or dimension? Could this doorway be some kind of portal, or opening that is a direct route to ...somewhere? Is this someplace potentially being used by the military? For what purpose? Of course, the first question that comes to mind is: where does the doorway go? And how do we ascertain the physics of this doorway? There have been dozens of reports of these types of disappearance sightings, and looking back through my data involving objects disappearing into the Sangres, I noticed one connecting fact. All the objects described are silver or aluminum-colored in appearance. I cannot find a single report of an object with a paint-job being observed disappearing into the mountainside. I'm not sure if this is important, but it is worthy of note.

The Slippery (Eastern) Slope

After almost an eight-month lull in cattle mutilation reports, our mystery perpetrators appeared to have returned to the Huerfano

346

and the Greater San Luis Valley. But, did they ever leave? Our intrepid Huerfano investigator David Perkins related to me the following report and we both wondered if these reports were just the proverbial tip of a bloody iceberg:

On Tuesday, September 26, 1995, Gardner, Colorado rancher Larry Chacon found his old horse "Whiskey" dead with a six inch diameter perfect circle rectum coring; half the tongue had been removed with a clean diagonal slice; the upper eye was "sucked out;" the hair and hide was "blackened and stiff" as if heat had been applied. As per the usual, no additional tracks, footprints, signs of predators, or a struggle, were noted. Just another one of those inexplicable animal deaths, I suppose.

The Huerfano County sheriff's office investigated the report, which occurred about fifteen-miles north from where the one-hundred-yard rectangle had been seen by Huerfano residents earlier on September 22nd.

Incidentally, the horse was found in the same area where San Luis Valley Publishing Company reporter, Barry Tobin, and I happened to find an unclaimed dead and cut-up horse in March of 1995.

Chacon had been renting grazing pasture from an old "hermit" who had told him of strange activities on the remote ranch land on the eastern slope of the Sangre de Cristos. The old man told investigator David Perkins he had also "seen ships in the sky" over the ranch, and even claimed one had landed near his cabin a couple of years ago. He said "two bearded human-looking" beings had appeared from the craft and "floated" toward his cabin shining a very bright spotlight. The man claimed that when they pointed the light at his cabin, "the light went through the wall." Holding a gun, he says he was blinded and paralyzed as the light illuminated the inside of his cabin. The hermit noted that the two beings were "not from around here."

To the northeast, during this same end of September time period, Douglas County officials are investigating a two-year livestock-killing spree on the Mike and Kandy Toll ranch. The Tolls then claimed thirty sheep and a bull-calf had been killed on their Franktown, Colorado, champion sheep spread. "The animals have been brutalized, led astray and possibly poisoned."

According to a *Denver Post* article, Douglas County Sgt, Attila Denes said "The Tolls hadn't reported the incidents in the past because they had hoped they would just go away, but it looks like she had several incidents this week that made her think it over." A seventy pound lamb that drowned Wednesday would have had to be lifted and placed in the three-foot tank with its head held down in only three and one-half inches of water."

A neighbor claimed to have found all her turkeys locked in a hot enclosure with no food or water. She said, "I hope it's not people just killing for the shear meanness of it." Good point. Why on earth were these animals killed? I bring up this recent Colorado Front-Range report to illustrate the probable involvement of *human* vandals in some cases involving the mysterious killing of animals. I wonder where human culpability ends and *non*-human culpability begins?

In these Douglas County cases outside of my Petri dish, law enforcement (and the ranchers) suspect someone in the rapidly growing suburban community around the Toll's ranch. These cases may be examples of potential, albeit occasional, human culprits at work.

Good Morning!

The third weekend in September, when Huerfano residents were dazzled by the flying monster-barge, I was in Denver proudly finishing recording a recording for the first the first Laffing Buddha album. Living in the "boonies" and recording an album up in the big-city was a grueling process, traveling ten-hours per session; I'd drive from Crestone down to Alamosa to meet the band, and then we would car-pool the long four-hour journey up to the studio in Denver. We tried to book consecutive days in the studio, but a popular facility like Time Capsule had very little block-time available, so we found ourselves having to put in long hours commuting two-hundred miles one-way to Denver for a few hours of recording. We figured that for one-hundred-and-forty hours of recording and mixing time, we spent almost *two*-hundred hours driving back-and-forth to the studio. It's only rock and roll... but, at the time, I still liked it.

That particular four-day period, during the third weekend in September, 1995, we were finishing lead-guitar tracks over the course of an all-day, ten-hour recording session that lasted late into Sunday night. We were able to book an eight-hour session the next day, and we were staying at guitarist Chris Medina's Uncle Frank's house, about five-miles south of the studio. A veteran Denver firefighter, Uncle Frank had given us a standing invitation for the band to stay at his house whenever we were in town. So, that night, we finished recording and headed back to his house to re-charge for the following day's session.

Frank Archuleta lives in a rambling ranch-style house with a guest bedroom at one end of the house, a spare bedroom used for storage at the other end of the house, with his master bedroom located in the finished basement. Three of us made this particular trip, Frank's nephew Chris Medina, guitarist George Oringdulph, and myself. As producer, I was there for every session. After settling in and joking around a bit, we bid Uncle Frank goodnight and arranged ourselves unceremoniously on the floor in the guest bedroom; with me on the futon in my mummy-bag; George on the floor at the end of the futon in his sleeping bag, and Chris to my right, in front of the bedroom door. He completely blocked the door in his sleeping bag as we drowsily watched a trashy movie on a big screen TV at the foot of the futon and cracked the usual cynical musician jokes. I suggested we change the channel and we began to watch a "live" performance clip of a Texas alternative band named the Toadies. They thrashed away on a local access show, as I quickly faded into slumber after the intense day of recording. The last thing I recalled was Chris asking George "how can a band like THAT get a record deal?"

The next thing I knew, I awoke shivering. I blinked and looked around in the pre-dawn light hesitantly glowing in the window, confused as to why was I out of my mummy-bag — lying on a bare mattress. Where was I? I got up and immediately fell off the bed and stumbled on some packing boxes. I was REAL confused. I remembered falling asleep on a futon located on the floor in the guest bedroom. I awoke a foot and a half off the ground. I gingerly tip-toed my way out of the storage bedroom; around boxes, file cabinets, weight sets and bicycles and headed out into the hall. I had awoken in the wrong friggin room. What the hell was going on? I shook the remaining vestiges of sleep out of my befuddled head, and shuffled down the hall back to the guest bedroom. Now, fully awake, I tried to enter, but Chris was snoring and his prone form blocked the door from opening. I gave the door a couple of knocks and Chris had to get up to let me in. My mummy bag was lying undisturbed on the futon and Chris iasked me ". . . why are you banging on the door so early." I noticed an itching behind my left ear and started to scratch it, when I felt a large, rather painful bump. I mumbled some kind of excuse to Chris, apologized for waking him up so early, and headed into the bathroom to look behind my ear. In the mirror, I could barely see a hard, red bump and I peeled off a small scab just behind my ear. It was a dried clot of blood; about the size of the head of a pin. Was it a bug bite? I headed back to the guys, who were both starting to wake up. "Chris, do you remember me getting up and leaving the room last night?"

"No, I never had to move all night, that I can remember."

"George, how about you?"

"I don't remember anyone leaving, I slept like a log," he answered. "Then how did I end up down the hall in the storage room?" What was wrong with this picture? Chris would've had to have woken up and moved in order to let me out of the room. He completely blocked the door all night.

"Guys, this is really weird. Are you sure, both of you don't remember me leaving the room? Chris sleepily looked at me with his customary dirt-eating grin and said, "Maybe you were abducted, or something. . ." He laughed. I told myself NOT to jump to that conclusion.

I ran the whole late-evening scenario through my brain a second time. We'd all been pretty tired and I faintly remember the movie and a song or two from the Toadies before I drifted off to sleep, but how had I managed to exit the room without disturbing my two band mates? Maybe, it was possible, but, at the time, I felt it was highly doubtful. Now that I thought about it, I didn't remember having to get up at all during the night to go to the bathroom, or get a drink of water, which is very unusual. I usually wake up at least a time or two at night, especially when I'm not at home. The tight-fitting mummy-bag, on the futon, was still zipped all the way up, which made it impossible to get out. In the morning, I usually end up twisted around in the tight-fitting bondage-bag. I admit, I'm convinced something strange transpired, but we had an important session all day and I refused to make a big deal out of the experience. I can't stand it when I lose my focus when I'm paying thirty-five dollars an hour and that was a half-price rate. I casually quizzed both George and Chris later that day during a break. Neither of them remembered any one of us getting up, and they laughed the episode off.

Three-weeks later and we were back in Denver. Laffing Buddha was pumped. We had two ten-hour sessions back-to-back, October 18th, and 19th at Time Capsule. It was mix-down time, when the result of all the hard work is realized in sonic form. The Wednesday session went well. Three songs down — seven to go!

The mixes had really started to click, and I looked forward to celebrating later that night with Littleton, resident, Shari Adamiak, Associate Director of the Center for the Study of Extraterrestrial Intelligence (CSETI). Shari and I had become good friends since our initial meeting in Ft. Collins, Colorado in the late summer of 1993. Soon after, Shari told Dr. Steven Greer, Director of CSETI, about the San Luis Valley mini-conference in 1993. CSETI conducted the first of their yearly training intensives in Crestone in 1994. Both Steven and Shari were very taken by our magical Valley, and visit often. Shari had dropped by the studio a couple of times over the course of the three-month recording sessions, and seemed to like the band and our tunes. I looked forward to playing a cassette of our newly mastered songs on her nice high-fidelity home stereo.

During our visit to her tasteful top-floor apartment, with its panoramic view, Shari introduced me to the Internet and showed me several paranormal-related sites. I had my first international "chat" with a friend of Shari's in Australia, and an "experiencer" in Canada. At one point, I mentioned the strange incident during the band's previous Denver trip, three weeks prior and showed her the still visible hard lump. She noticed that there was still swelling around the wound. I joked that a spider bite usually doesn't last three weeks. She didn't know what to make of the incident either, and offered no theories.

The slight swelling lasted over two-months. The "bump" slowly reduced in size and ended up becoming a small, hard scar behind my ear. It's still there. I sometimes wonder if my Denver experience was somehow connected to the eventful circumstances that occurred just east of the San Luis Valley, that same weekend. But, of course, I must assume mundane explanations...

Chasing Cows in UFO Central

I've attempted to convey to the reader the on-the-ground intensity of our waves of UFO-type phenomenon and unusual cattle deaths and the resulting effect these events have on the many witnesses and ranchers. When things were really popping around here, I was run ragged trying to keep up with all the interviews, phone-calls, site visits, and subsequent investigative work. I'm sorry to say, without working at it full-time during flap periods, there's just no way for one investigator to keep up in the San Luis Valley. I know there are countless reports and cases sliding off into the ghostly realm of undocumented history. I try not to think about all the cases that go by without proper attention. In a perfect world....

The fall of 1995 found the greater San Luis Valley experiencing twenty "UFO" reports that included: silvery objects, full-moon-sized green orbs, swarms of small blinking lights, pencil-shaped craft, along with the usual variety of fireballs and streaking night time phenomena. As my Report Log shows, some of these UFO reports occurred the night animals were supposedly mutilated. There were five unusual animal death cases investigated during this time period — all with a regional correlation to attendant UFO, and in one case military helicopter sightings.

One fall 1995 UAD deserves mention. I investigated this

covered-up case that probably occurred October 8th. The following day, October 9th, I received a call from a Blanca, Colorado skywatcher who told me of a fresh case that may have been discovered the previous morning. As I re-arranged my schedule for the day and then headed out the door for the two hundred-mile round trip drive, I hoped that this call was legitimate. I've been burned on more than a few and with the immense distances one must travel, a false alarm can trash a whole day. The amazing distances locals travel here every day are mind-boggling to most folks from outside of the Valley. Sixty-miles to the nearest hospital, super-market, movie theater etc., is the norm in many locales in the Valley, and a two-hour drive to investigate a report is routine. The call came in, and I responded. Evidently, the rancher had discovered a cow "missing her rear-end and bag" on his ranch the morning of the eighth and thought it had been killed Sunday night. I learned of the case from the rancher's sister the following day and she arranged for us to go to the ranch that afternoon. I made the two-hour drive with my brother Brendon and a mutual friend of ours.

The fall colors of the verdant aspen groves blazed up the mountains' sides like wide swaths of brilliant golden patchwork as we headed around the huge Blanca Massif. The air had a cold bite to it, and it was obvious that winter's chill embrace was lurking around the frigid mountain tops, waiting for the opportunity to cover the low-lying areas with a furry blanket of frost.

Upon arriving at the remote, idyllic ranch, it quickly became apparent that the rancher was a no-show. The rancher's sister introduced us to his wife, who claimed she hadn't gone out to see the animal since her first look at it that morning. I noticed a large beautiful horse across the driveway in a small pasture limping badly. I asked the sturdy Hispanic woman what had happened to the animal. She told me they weren't sure what was wrong, but it happened the same night the cow had been killed. We noticed the corral area where the cow was supposedly found was empty. No sign of a carcass. We found large tire-tracks indicating a tractor had been used in the area recently. We decided to cover the front part of the ranch and look for a bone-pile while waiting for the rancher to show up. The rancher inexplicably ducked our meeting. He never showed.

His wife was pretty puzzled by his absence, claiming "If he told you he'd be here, he should be here." We easily found where the animal had lain, less than one hundred feet from the house; found the drag marks and tractor tracks, but no dead cow. She described the condition of the vanished cow for us, but claimed she didn't know who had moved it, or what had happened to it.

Another mystery.

I called the rancher that evening, and he claimed "the government" had told him to bury it. He was told it was an 'environmental hazard.'" According to the rather brusque Hispanic man, local officials had told him to keep the animal death quiet. He had reluctantly admitted to the animal's death and subsequent discovery, and mumbled an excuse for not showing up for our meeting. He had told me during our initial conversation, "We found her right behind the corral, just a few feet away from the house. My dogs never even barked." I could tell he was nervous talking with me about his mysteriously-slain cow.

It's interesting to note that it's a common practice in the San Luis Valley to leave your dead livestock on a bone-pile or leave it where it dies. Carcasses from the two to three percent of all grazing animals that routinely die every year can be found laying in repose in the vast pastures of the San Luis Valley. It can literally take years for some carcasses to finally melt into the ground.

This is a perfect example of local authorities secretive way of dealing with "mutes" and illustrates the fear and uncertainty that are pervasive in many North American rural ranching communities where these types of unusual animal death cases occur. I have found local officials, while in office, can be extremely reluctant to even acknowledge the existence of these reports. I found the ex-sheriff of Costilla county next to impossible to work with, unlike many sheriff's departments in the San Luis Valley who welcome any assistance they can get. This southeast Colorado corner of the Valley is a world unto itself. And, does it have a history.

The quiet little ranch where this October 8th case allegedly occurred lay just below the Taylor Ranch; about two-miles to the west. Several ranches away to the east were rancher-neighbors Clarence and Dale Vigil. The Vigils lost two cows to the cattle hackers; one in April 1993, and another in December 1993. The small isolated Chama Canyon area, in my estimation, could be the epicenter of the cattle-mutilation phenomenon as it occurs in the SLV. I can find nowhere else that can rival the ferocity this little picturesque region suffered through, during two wild and woolly months in the fall of 1975, when as many as one-hundred head of cattle were "mutilated". These cases may reflect the full force and fury of the 1970's most intense wave of activity with the injection of the human element ignored by all, but a few investigators like myself.

Prior to my book, *The Mysterious Valley*, evidence of possible Taylor Ranch involvement has never fully been made public, but

353

ex-Costilla County Sheriffs, Ernest Sandoval and Pete Espinoza went on-the-record claiming that at least some of the helicopter crews responsible for many of the mutilations in the area were "taking off and landing at the Taylor Ranch." This is the first time (to my knowledge) that ANY law enforcement officials, anywhere, at any time, have publicly offered up the names of suspect parties they feel were directly involved in the mysterious mutilation of thousands of cattle across North America and elsewhere. When my first book was published in September 1996, I confess, I felt rather proud that I was the first investigator (to my knowledge) to convince law enforcement officials to go on-the-record with an actual name to associate with any of these thousands of puzzling cases. Espinoza and Sandoval's insistence was compelling, and the fact that they allowed me to quote them convinced me they weren't out to simply slag John Taylor's name. They were serious and felt they had acquired enough circumstantial evidence to feel confident enough to point their accuser's finger at him. I am surprised that hardly anyone commented about this on-the-record naming of our first suspect in the history of the "cattle mutilation" phenomenon. No reviews of *The Mysterious Valley* mention this groundbreaking fact. Nor does the revelation that the first "wave" of animal deaths in the early fall of 1975, in the SLV, featured mutilated cattle *that had been shot* with firearms.

Other interesting events occurred all through the Fall into Winter 1996. Normally, when readers of my books arrive in town wanting to speak with me, they have somehow obtained my number beforehand and call ahead to make an appointment. Even though it's is unlisted, folks manage to obtain my phone-number, and I have met with quite a few interesting readers who have visited the valley. The one's who arrive and aren't successful, often go to considerable lengths to find me. I've had folks with out-of-state plates drive up in front of my house; hop out in the middle of our cul-de-sac and snap a couple of quick photographs, then zip away. I've even had people track me down at job sites, gigs, and one time, I was followed around the Baca by suspicious-looking white unmarked van. I was looking for my brother at several locations and couldn't shake them, believe me, I tried. Finally, I pulled over and confronted them. Turns out, it was a "retired Air Force major" from Boulder, and his son, and someone told them I drive a little yellow Toyota pick-up, and I happened to drive by. The chase was on. Talking with them, they were really nice; had interesting comments to offer and I signed their books while they asked a storm of questions — apologizing for interrupting my day. I suppose this notoriety comes with the territory.

Let's Throw Rocks At It

A couple of weeks later, my band Laffing Buddha, had finally finished our album at Time Capsule Studio. It had been a long, time-consuming, expensive, tedious process, but we had done it! We couldn't wait to get back to Alamosa and play the tape for the two band-mates who hadn't made that final trip to master the album.

As we were headed west over La Veta Pass, returning from our final mix-down and mastering session, October 19, 1995, at 6:00 p.m., I was sitting in the front passenger seat looking to the northwest when I noticed seven blinking lights in close proximity to one another, ten or so miles to the north. I pointed this out to my two band mates, Lyman and George, and told them it was highly unusual to see so many lights within five degrees of one another, even over the La Veta MOA. I commented that "we should keep our eyes open; something may be going on."

Two or three minutes later, bass player Lyman asked me quietly "what is that?" He pointed to a small, fast-moving orangish-red dot moving quickly from east-to-west across the sky. It was traveling very fast and seemed fairly low above the winding road headed west down La Veta Pass. An eighth slowly blinking white light hung tantalizingly low over Blanca Peak.

Lyman was excited by his sighting of something unusual in the sky. "I never see anything… you guys are always seeing something, and I miss out. Alright! I finally got to see one!

We watched the unusual unblinking orangish-red light disappear over the eastern horizon. These red globes baffle me. They seem fairly small, yet move with purpose, and, at the time I felt excited. I was sure something was going on. We all kept an extra vigilant watch the remaining forty-five minutes into Alamosa to the band's headquarters. As we pulled up to our rehearsal space, band member Chris Medina, who hadn't made the trip to Denver with us came running out.

An hour earlier, just minutes before our "sighting," Chris and his cousin Roy had been returning from Capulin, CO, about twenty-five miles south of Alamosa, where Chris and his world-famous weaver-grandmother, Eppy Archuleta, have a large wool carding and spinning mill.

As they headed east toward Highway 285, they both noticed four bright glowing lights against the western side of Saddleback Mountain, located a couple of miles east of Sanford CO; about fifteen miles from their vantage point. This center-of-the-valley region, north of the Colorado border; in the center of the Valley, is a jumbled mass of brooding volcanic hills, some of which are capped by remnants of flat-lying lava flows. Here turquoise is mined, a product of hydrothermal alteration of copper minerals in the volcanic rock. One of North America's oldest Paleolithic mines is the King Mountain mine – a few miles south of Saddleback Mountain.

This mineral composition gives the "Brownies" as they're collectively known locally, their ruddy brown complexion. This grouping of hills, including the Piñon Hills, The South Piñon Hills, known collectively as the San Luis Hills, is a barren, dry, no-man's land, with very few houses or roads. But the middle of the southern valley region has an old tradition of witches and *brujos* and the center of the Valley around the border is not actively settled. Having explored the area extensively, and knowing the locale well, Chris and Roy knew there was no possible light source anywhere close to the area, so, naturally, they hot-footed it over to investigate. They quickly located a four-wheel drive trail, just east of town, and were able to wind up Saddleback Mountain to "within a quarter-mile" of the lights. The dark mass of the volcanic mesa loomed in the twilight, and the pulsing large bright array of lights stabbed beams into the surrounding hillside. They were the first ones on the scene.

"It looked like a football stadium, or like some big ships had landed" Chris excitedly told us. "I was pretty scared, I have no idea what it could have been, there's nothing up there." Chris's younger cousin Roy was feeling brave. "Roy wanted me to drive closer so he could throw a rock at it to see if they could hear it hit metal." Chris said the light sources were several hundred yards apart; roughly in a square pattern, and all four were blinking sequentially with each other. Several other witnesses evidently witnessed the lights which were highly visible for miles.

Chris noted, "There was something really weird about them, and I wasn't about to find out what was going on. You always think you'll be brave and walk right up to the mothership, until you're standing right there up close and personal. I wasn't about to get any closer, I was fine right where I was!"

Chris finally convinced Roy that they should leave, and they drove back down the hill toward town. On the way down, a line of cars streamed up to the area to investigate. No reports were filed with authorities, and the "sighting" did not make the papers. Later I learned that a nearby mountain, where the local high-school had outlined a big "S" out of whitewashed rocks had hosted a homecoming bonfire the prior weekend, but this did not explain the strange sequencing lights, Chris and Roy observed, the following week.

The Cloud Ships

Winter arrived like a lamb and the area experienced a rather mild winter. This season finds most folks indoors, so naturally, the number of reports tends to drop. But during this mild winter, one report deserves mention.

Since Salida, CO resident Tim Edwards riveting footage of an enigmatic pencil-shaped object on August 27, 1995, numerous anomalous objects have been sighted by Greater San Luis Valley residents. One sighting on Tuesday, January 25, 1996, at 4:30 p.m., was partially videotaped by one of the witnesses, Center, CO resident, James Armijo. With all those camcorders around it's inevitable that more quality footage will be obtained. Courier editor Mark Hunter and I visited with Armijo and his wife in Center, February 7, 1996. Armijo, a gregarious man of thirty-one, told us he had been at his cousin's house, six-miles north of Alamosa. When, while standing in the yard, he noticed a bright silvery object "floating low over Greenie" Mountain to the west. He alerted his cousin Soccoro Guitierez and they watched for about thirty minutes. Armijo claims he then remembered he had his new video camera on the front seat of his truck. He ran and grabbed it and immediately focused on the object that seemed to be disappearing just over the mountains. Much to his surprise, he noticed two more objects hovering five to 10 degrees above the mountains, just to the south. He focused in the northern-most object and then zoomed in on the second object, to the south, which appeared disc-shaped.

Armijo seemed matter-of-fact while watching the unusual objects hovering on histwenty-five inch TV set. "I was born and raised here and I've seen them all my life." He added, pointing at the screen "If you really look at it, when I zoom in, you can see it's spinning!" After pulling the camera's zoom back to show both objects, he then zoomed in on the third object. The footage ends with another shot of both objects. "This is noth'in bud, you wait and see what I get, I always look to the sky."

Rewinding the footage, I scrutinized the close-up image of the second object. It was translucent and roughly disc-shaped and had the appearance of spinning, and/or rippling. It reminded me of several Ed Walters photos from Gulf Breeze, FL. There is an almost holographic sense to their appearance. . . like they're not completely solid objects. The wide-angled shots show glowing objects, but up close, they become translucent looking and ill

357

defined.

Armijo is convinced that he will capture additional objects with his new video camera. More than ten-years later – he is still waiting. He went on to describe two other sightings he and his wife had had in the prior two-weeks that he had been unable to videotape. Now he takes his camera everywhere. What does his wife think of the sightings? "I don't want to believe, but I have to, I've seen them too!"

Previously that same day, (Armijo's video was shot) found your gum-shoe heading into Alamosa south on Highway 17. The sky was partly cloudy with a thin, multi-tiered layer of impressive linticulated clouds hugging the tops of the Sangres.

Often times during similar weather conditions, disc-shaped clouds hover over this huge valley like fleets of arriving ships. January 25, 1996, at 10:30 a.m., was no exception. My brother Brendan commented on the array of "saucer-clouds" in the sky that morning.

As we approached Hooper, I looked east across the valley toward the Great Sand Dunes. A perfect disc-shaped cloud appeared above the dune field eighteen-miles away. I immediately brought Brendan's attention to the saucer-shaped cloud and we marveled at how quickly it was building.

After watching five or so minutes we were sidetracked by conversation for a minute or two, before I glanced back over toward the dunes to check on our rapidly forming cloud-ship. The five mile-long cloud had vanished without a trace! All the other nearby clouds hung innocently in the sky, unchanged, and were still right where we had last seen them, but the real striking one had vanished. We were convinced that we had witnessed something highly peculiar. I made note of it at home, but something struck me about the unusual sighting. As is my usual custom, I immediately sought a mundane explanation for the "saucer" cloud. Could the famous disappearing Medano Creek have had something to do with the rapid formation? Medano Creek, which disappears into the southern edge of the dune field must pump a lot of moisture into the air when the hot ultraviolet rays of the sun heat the sand of the dune field. I wondered, could the cloud have been moisture rising up from the warm, creek-soaked sand into the frigid January air, where it condensed, forming the cloud? If this event had occurred in the spring, or fall, I would have conveniently jumped toward this conclusion. But the cold, sub-twenty-degree morning may not have been conducive for this effect. The event is still puzzling, and in my mind, remains unexplained. Coincidentally, six hours later,

James Armijo shot his video,

I sent Armijo's footage (certified, United States Postal priority mail) to be analyzed by the Paramount Television program *Sightings*. I also sent along a second "viewing tape" I had taken of several of our recent "mute" cases. Much to *Sightings* and my surprise, the package never arrived. I had been sending tapes back and forth to the program for almost three-years, and this was the first time anything like this had happened. When I asked our postmaster, Monte Collins, if I could start a trace on the package, he had a hard time even finding a form for me to fill out a claim. Certified mail doesn't normally disappear. According to *Sightings* producer David Green, a package did arrive a month later, with only the viewing tape inside. There was no trace of Armijo's master tape. I must say, this made me angry. Since 1993, twenty-four photographs, three cameras, and now a videotape had disappeared without a trace. When people ask me, "Do you think the government is keeping tabs on you?" I just smile through grinding teeth.

I address what I call "local mythos" extensively in my first two books. I contend that this area of research and investigation should be an integral part of *all* paranormal investigator's efforts. I suspect that the perceptions of an experiencer of "the unknown" is probably subtly shaded by his or hers personal/ regional mythological bias that ties them to their particular locale. The reason I bring this up is simple. In the San Luis Valley, I am occasionally reminded by residents that "If there are disc-shaped clouds around, there are ships around." I can't remember how many times I've heard this. I have noticed over the course of my investigation, that disc-shaped clouds do sometimes occur in close time proximity to sightings. Jacques Vallee and Aime Michel mentioned the French cloudships of the '50's in this context, but I've not heard of this phenomenon (and/or perception) recently. There are many types of craft reported in the San Luis Valley, but a new kind of report began to surface.

What ARE Those Things?

At this point in the investigation I began to field a number of reports of huge craft reported as being unlit, but blocking out the stars, over the greater San Luis Valley. I feel these craft may have a terrestrial explanation. They are often reported flying in the La Veta MOA, and from time to time, usually during mid-fall, large triangle-shaped objects are occasionally reported in South Central Colorado. Sometimes the reports mention "hypnotic" lighting displays, and the craft are usually reported as flying along in a leisurely manner. The John Browning sighting from November

1992, comes to mind.

Recently, an even newer type of report has surfaced. During the past two and one half years, reports have been logged describing "darker than dark" triangle-shaped shadows "blocking out the stars" as they sail slowly over the valley. Most reports are from diligent skywatchers, not from motorists or casual observers.

Granted, some clouds at night can assume almost any perceived shape, but several of these reports have come from very credible witnesses who, you would think, are not prone to misidentification. These large craft invariably instill awe and wonder in the witnesses who observe them, and the reports are often accompanied by awed descriptions of "The Mothership."

I wonder if these sharp-eyed witnesses may actually be observing secret military craft that *give the impression* of something otherwordly. Could our military be utilizing such fantastically advanced aeronautic technologies? Several recent sightings of these craft feature estimated airspeeds as low as in the single digits! Now correct me if I'm wrong. . . wouldn't you need a gravitational-based propulsion system to enable you to fly such a large craft (some have been estimated as being at least two miles in length)? Or are these craft lighter-than-air stealth blimps? And, if you are trying to keep this technology "secret," why occasionally light them up like a Christmas tree and send them sailing over populated areas? It's obvious to me that this is by design, and maybe our government is trying to fool, or condition us all into believeing we are seeing something from off-planet.

However, if these are ships from "off-planet," it is inconceivable to me that an ET mothership would fly so brazenly around one of the most strategically sensitive areas of North America and not be challenged by defensive-minded pilots under orders from on high. Or maybe those reports we saw in the San Luis Valley, in the spring of '93, concerning "dogfights" between UFO-type lights and conventional-looking fixed-wing aircraft were our military standing tall and trying to chase off unwelcome "ET" spacecraft from the high ground here in the Rockies. This following report was experienced up close and personal, and if it belongs to "us," I know why the Cold War is over...

The Ojo Caliente Encounter

February 16, 1996, at 10:05 p.m., Nick Archuleta, his wife Lorraine, and the couple's two-year-old daughter, were driving north on State Highway 285, two or three miles south of Ojo

360

Caliente, NM. They were on their way to Capulin, CO to attend Nick's brother Tobias' wedding. Nick, who was driving, needed to make a pit stop. Climbing outside and walking around their pickup truck, Nick commenced to relieve himself. All of a sudden, while looking down at the ground, he noticed his shadow. Realizing there was no moon out that night, he immediately looked up to see what was causing the light.

Much to his amazement, "a huge ship" hovered "less than fifty feet overhead" with "a circle of fifty to seventy-five lights blinking in a clockwise pattern." He felt, or heard a low vibrating sound, like a rumble. He yelled for his wife and sister-in-law to look, which turned out to be a bad idea. The two women immediately "started screaming and getting all hysterical." Evidently, Nick was pretty calm about the sighting, but he was pretty amazed. "It covered the whole sky it was so big and close. I couldn't stop looking at it and get back in the truck." Then, without any sound, "it went straight up, maybe a mile, or so, until it was the size of a quarter." Then to the witnesses' consternation, "It zoomed at the speed of light back down" and again, hovered fifty feet over them. Then it flew out about a quarter-mile or so out over the small valley over the Rio Chama River (which runs parallel to Highway 285) and then it started to leisurely head north.

Archuleta was excited. "I got back into the truck and went after it." He took off in the truck and continued heading north on 285. After driving "about four, or five miles" with his wife looking up and out the passenger window to report on the craft's progress and they caught up to it. Again, it hovered directly over their truck. "My wife threatened to divorce me if I stopped, but I really wanted to get another good look at it, so I stopped anyway."

Nick climbed out and the object "turned off the lights." The three of them watched in wonder as it headed majestically out east over the mesa and out of sight.

The Archuletas estimated the event lasted "over twenty minutes," and they heard a "low vibration" which they immediately associated with the craft. They continued on their way and it took the women "the rest of the trip" to calm down after the close encounter.

§§§

I talked with another witness who lived twenty miles away, to the west, and she claimed several area residents had seen the craft, off to the east in the distance that same night.

Later that Spring, the day Timothy Leary died, another

361

mysterious cattle death and fiendish disfigurement was reported west of Saguache. For some reason I haven't figured out yet, I suspect, somehow psychedelics and psycho-active substances are synchronistically tied to the "cattle mutilation" phenomenon. For example; Where do hallucinogenic pysilocybin mushrooms grow in nature? In cow-pies, of course!

They're Both Lumberjacks and They're OK

May 13, 1996, at 8:00 a.m., Two loggers were headed up State Highway 114 toward the Cannero Pass Road which turns to the south eight miles west of Saguache. As they traveled up the dirt road after making the turn, they noticed "a cow lying near the road." One of the loggers (who has been avidly following my livestock death investigation) blurted out, "That's a mute!"

They stopped and climbed over the fence to investigate, immediately noticing that the rest of the herd seemed "trapped in the corner of the pasture." They appeared to be agitated. "There were about thirty to forty head, maybe twenty cows with calves, milling around moo-ing like the dead one was blocking their path... There's a stream that runs through the pasture with only about twenty-five feet between the fence-line and the stream. The dead one was in the path and they wouldn't go around it."

The other logger took up the story. "I started to walk over to the dead one and the biggest cow in the herd charged over and stopped about twenty feet away and let out a moooo. . . You know how a herd moves like water, one goes and they all start to go? Well, when that cow moo-ed, a momma and a baby ran past the dead cow. I moo-ed again and me and that cow kept moo-ing until the rest of 'em made it past. . . I used to ride bulls and it was pretty weird the way they were acting. I don't know, it was almost like us being there gave them courage to go around it (the dead cow)."

The two loggers described the "mute" as missing its rear-end; "It was definitely cut in a circle," and "its udder and an upside eye and ear were gone.... There were what looked like strap burns behind the front legs.... We luckily had a camera with us and took a bunch of good pictures."

"Did you get any good close-ups of the incisions?" I asked, "Yes. The jaw cut went up around the eye and a stain that discolored the ground spread out from its face. We didn't see it when we were there, but you can see it in the pictures." They had visited a one-hour photo shop and had the film developed. "It was

362

really fresh. We could see that a little blood was still uncoagulated and oozing. It looked like it happened maybe two or three hours before, around dawn."

They quickly scoured the scene for clues. "There were no unusual tracks or footprints that we could see. No bear or cat did that… We didn't spend much time because we had to get to work." Their untrained eyes revealed no additional clues. No drops of blood, cigarette butts or clues to what or who did the unfortunate animal in were found. "When we came back about four hours later to cut samples and check around again, it was gone! Somebody must have hauled it away; there was no sign of it." The two loggers were convinced that their discovery was no accident. "I couldn't help but think that this was done for *us* to find. Like, somebody knew *we* would be on *that* road *that* morning!"

I did some checking and found out the name of the owner of the pasture. He was not very helpful. In fact, he seemed nervous that the local busy-body, me, had found out about it. "I rent out that pasture and I'll tell him to call you." He wouldn't tell me where the cow ended up, and I could tell it would take quite a bit of hounding to get anywhere with him. If they bury it; in their mind, it goes away. Permanently.

The area where the animal was found was within five-miles of Hoagland Hill where the cops were supposedly chasing "lights" on the night of May 4, 1996 and it's the western end of the area that had the first cases in the SLV back in the fall wave of 1975.

We Need MORE Hard Scientific Investigation

During the late summer and early Fall of 1996, *Taos News* reporter Phaedra Greenwood, and long-time *Spirit Magazine* reporter/investigator David Perkins covered a half a dozen "mutilation" reports from the Tao, New Mexico region of the southern San Luis Valley. While researching one of several articles concerning on-going "mutilation" wave, Greenwood contacted Dale Spall, an analytical chemist at the Life Sciences Division in the Los Alamos National Laboratories. Spall, who had conducted testing of animal mutilations to look for evidence of carcinogens and radiation back in 1978, at the behest of the infamous Rommel Investigation, is very interested in the phenomenon. He told Greenwood: "'We looked at the liver, the spleen, did gross observation and a number of other studies. The problem with cattle mutilations is that a lot of information tends to be anecdotal in nature. There is a certain natural death rate among cattle.'(2%) He said he thought most cattle mutilations were natural deaths and

363

scavengers. 'There is a distinct possibility some people are playing copy cat,' he said. 'Cattle mutilations follow a fifteen to tweny-year cycle,' he added. 'They've been reported in England, Brazil, Argentina, Venezuela.'" [Also in Puerto Rico, Canada, Ireland, Australia, Canary Islands and probably other countries as well].

Greenwood told me that "Spall said he experimented with one of his own animals; when he slaughtered it, he also did a mimic mutilation. 'I cored the anus, took out the sexual organs, cut off an ear, cut out the tongue.' He said he did the whole thing in about half an hour with a skinning knife. 'If you leave it lying out for about six hours, it does the same thing. The edges of the wound curl and stretch as they dry and look like precision laser cuts,' he said. He admitted he had never seen the 'cookie cutter' kind of edges mentioned by pathologists. He also said he had never heard of a mutilation that took place in the winter and thought this was because ranchers kept a closer eye on their cows in the winter... He said he enjoyed his volunteer research and had actually brought a whole cow into the lab to do an autopsy which included an analysis of urine, blood and tissue. He also scanned the animal for radiation and took bacteriological samples. Unfortunately, all his reports disappeared from the lab, he said, and nobody knows where they are. 'The deeper you get into it, the more mysterious it gets,' he said.

What Spall didn't mention to Greenwood is that, on a whim, he had pulled the files out and left them on his desk one afternoon in 1994. He went to lunch, and when he returned, the files had vanished!

I had spoken with Spall back during the so-called New Mexico Wave of 1993-1994 about "cattle mutilations," and Spall had related the mysterious disappearance of the 1978-1979 mutilation files from his desk. "I have no idea why someone would have just taken them."

Draft Horses Don't Jump

August 6, 1996 Estrella, Colorado
Not all "unusual animal deaths" involved bloodless incisions and missing soft-tissue organs. The following report comes from a August 7, 1996 *Valley Courier* article written by former editor Greg Johnson.

> ... A large Morgan draft horse was found wedged in the fork of a large tree in Estrella, (Colorado) about seven miles south of Alamosa near Highway 285, apparently dead

from suffocation... Gary Haddock, land-use administrator for Alamosa County, said the horse... may have eaten some loco weed, or may have been trying to jump through the fork of the tree for some unknown reason, but fell short. Haddock said he is treating the incident as a freak accident, and that he didn't know what would motivate a (twelve to fourteen hundred pound) horse to jump in a tree.

Reading this strange account, and looking at the photograph of the huge horse with all four feet off the ground, I searched my research for a similar event. I found one from Arizona.

Tom Dongo has been investigating reports of the unusual around Sedona, Arizona for over twelve years. He has seen many unusual events and described the following incident involving terrified horses in *Alien Tide* (co-written with rancher Linda Bradshaw).

During an eight month period at the end of the summer, 1994, I was investigating a number of reports from a ranch outside of Sedona. Several bigfoot sightings occurred around this time, and the owner of the ranch told me of an ordeal involving one of their horses. Well, I went and saw the spot where this happened, and it was pretty strange. The rancher told me that one of his horses became wedged between two large branches on a good-sized tree near the house. It had evidently been trying to escape from something and became wedged while on a dead run. It was so stuck, they had to cut the two branches to get it out. Fortunately, it lived....

Just prior to the horse getting stuck, we had a near encounter with a Bigfoot. It was dark, and we were staking out the property. We heard something grunt real loud on the other side of the apple orchard opposite the house. It wasn't a lion or a bear.. Well, when it grunted, six horses in a nearby corral went wild. They were racing around and literally screaming. The next morning we found bigfoot tracks near where we had heard the grunt, and they had a thirty-five to forty inch spread between strides! Whenever the Bigfoot was around, their horses were literally terrified.

Now, I'm not suggesting that the SLV draft horse was being chased by a Bigfoot, but in light of the time proximity with "mutilations" to the south, I wonder, what could have terrified the animal enough to prompt it jump off the ground into the crotch of a tree?! Unusual cattle death cases began to arrive with a new wrinkle. This following case is an example.

Landing Traces?

United Parcel Service driver David Jaramillo and his family were spending quality-time relaxing up at their Osier Park cabin, Sunday September 22, 1995, directly west-by-southwest from Antonito, CO, just above the New Mexico border, when they discovered a "mutilated cow" near their cabin. The animal, laying on its left side, was missing its udder, rear-end and tongue. There was a large circular portion around the right ear that was missing and the tip of the animal's tail appeared to have boned-out. About one hundred feet away from the carcass, much to Jaramillo's surprise, he found three, four foot swirled circles flattening the lush meadow grass. Each circle was about twelve feet from the others arrayed in a triangle pattern. Around each three foot circle were three small four inch holes in a triangle configuration, punched into the ground. In the middle of the triangle patterns of circles, Jaramillo's brother found long tail hairs that appeared to be the missing hair from the unfortunate cow.

Jaramillo happened to have his video camera with him and documented the entire scene. He tracked me down the following day while delivering in Crestone, and told me of his find. We watched his video tape, and I cringed at Dave's relative standing in the middle of one of the twelve-foot circles — perfect physical evidence, now rendered not-so-perfect. The animal had no brand or ear tag, and Jaramillo was unable to ascertain who was the animal's owner. His remote cabin was occasionally visited by the local's herds that meander around the La Magna Pass area during every summer and early fall, before they're herded together and taken down to winter pastures. As luck would have it, an early fall snow storm that very night made the site inaccessible to me, much to my annoyance. Yet another chance to try and conduct "good science" was thwarted by this remote, high-mountain environment.

Jaramillo's footage was broadcast in a *Strange Universe* television segment later that fall. I directed and field-produced the segment produced by Scott Catamas.

Approximately the same week, a rancher later reported to undersheriff Brian Norton at the Rio Grande Sheriff's Office, who told the rancher had discovered a "mutilated cow" in the center of a thirty-foot swirled circle in the grass. The area was only fifteen to twenty miles north of the Jaramillo site. The rancher's horse would evidently not approach the grass circle, and upon examination, the rancher reported to Norton that there was a fine dusting of what appeared to be similar to "baby-powder" on the carcass and on the swirled circle. To my knowledge, there were no UFO sightings associated with this unofficial mute report, however, upon while they were examining the carcass, a "military helicopter" allegedly flew low over the site, obviously watching the rancher. The chopper swooped in, then left at tree top level.

The rancher, unfortunately, reported the case some time later, hence no exact date, but the same late September time-frame is interesting in light of the Jaramillo find during the same time period. Norton told me of the report early the following spring.

The BBC In The Wild, Wild West

The winter of 1996-1997 passed by like a whisper. The uncharacteristic mild weather and record snow falls relieved 1996's dry conditions, the regions ski areas profited handsomely. The spring arrived and the cattle death cases began in earnest, first just north of Taos, then in the heart of the San Luis Valley.

It was early in the morning when the rancher discovered his prized breeding cow dead in the pasture, about five-hundred yards from the front door of his ranch house. He couldn't believe the animal's condition; left eye carved out, and the left-side mandible neatly "sliced off." He muttered to himself when he realized her young calf would probably die as a result of losing it's mother. The rancher had been hearing about area "mutilations," and had watched a video tape taken by a nearby neighbor, of another strangely slain cow, less than a mile from his spread, in southern Alamosa County. He had not been convinced by the video that the animal had killed and mutilated. He told his neighbor that it very well may have been a "cat" [mountain lions are rare out in the valley, over twenty miles from the foothills]. He couldn't explain the lack of any tracks or the slightest indication of a struggle which is usually present after a predator kill or another death by attrition. Like all ranchers, death in the pasture is a part of life and his neighbor's loss seemed unusual but he blew it off, not aware that in a few short days, he'd lose a cow under similar circumstances. Angry, he placed a call to the sheriff's office to report the unusual livestock death. The investigating deputy aware of my on-going investigation, sensed something very strange about the crime scene and the animal's demise. He attempted to obtain my phone number from Richard Gottlieb at the Narrow Gauge Bookstore in Alamosa. Richard immediately called me and told me of the deputy's request and told me to call the sheriff's office right away.

A fresh one, less than eight hours old! I set up a rendezvous at the crime-scene with the deputy and rushed down with a musician-friend, Barry Monroe. The three of us examined the grim scene in a diminishing light. It was deathly still but cold out and to my amateur eye, it looked "The Real Thing," a true high-strange case. I made arrangements to return the following morning, meet the rancher and conduct a full investigation of the crime scene. The temperature would be just above thirty-five degrees, and the animal carcass would stay in pristine condition overnight.

Meanwhile, two weeks prior, your media-magnet San Luis Valley investigator had finished up a television shoot with England's British Broadcasting Company (BBC) with an extracted promise to let Louis Theroux's *Wild Weekends* BBC crew know if we had any "fresh cases." The day they were finishing their shoot in Arizona, I called with the grim news. They rushed back to the San Luis Valley to film the investigation. They arrived early the following day and we rushed the several short miles to the scene.

Louis, the urbanized correspondent, begins the questioning as we drive the several miles south toward he site, "So, what's the story Chris?"

"I received an interesting call yesterday. It seems the [Alamosa County] Sheriff's Office received a couple of reports, over the last four days, of 'cattle mutilations.' The investigating deputy asked me to come down and check one of the cases out."

"Have you already been to see it?"

"Yes. I wouldn't have called you out, Louis, unless I suspected a report worthy of gathering forensic samples and conducting an investigation."

"What kind of animal is it?"

"It's a four year-old cow with a calf, about three-and-a-half months old. It was part of a large herd of about one hundred and ten animals. Fifty-five cows and their calves. The rancher came out yesterday morning at five in the morning and found it 'mutilated.' It's mandible's been excised and an eye was carved out"

"NO way!"

"Way. You'll see."

"Is it the real deal?"

"Based on my amateur eye, it definitely looks bizarre, Louis. Strange"

"Has it got a name?" I grimaced and tightened my hands on the steering wheel, "I don't know Louis, I just call them all 'Bessie.'" He chuckled. A fierce wind ripped across the bleak pasture, within sight of the south end of the Alamosa Airport, as we arrived at the site, cameras and investigative tools in hand. We approached the tarp-covered animal and I pulled the tarp off. Louis took his first look at the animal and I comment, "That is not natural!"

"Oh check it out!... the eye socket! Chris, the eye socket is bubbling!" Simon, behind the camera muttered "Oh my God...

"Chris, how come the eye-socket is bubbling?" Louis asked,

"Well it's pressure from the fluids in the body going to the lowest point [of the carcass]. You'll have a certain amount of activity [and settling] until all the blood coagulates. The fact that the blood isn't coagulated is interesting." Louis' cavalier demeanor had rapidly faded. He stared at the carcass with a rather grim look on his face as I walked back to get my tool-bag and gloves. Louis asked, "You're putting gloves on so you don't get gunk on your hands?"

"Several cases in the last two years have had people getting their hands really burned after touching one of these."

"No!" Louis wrinkles his nose as the wind changes. "It smells a bit. . ."

"Louis, you wanted to help? Here put this tape measure as close to the head as you dare. That's right, right on the nose."

"On the nose? Do you want me to actually tuck it in the mouth." I began the process of measuring out a five foot, ten foot, twenty-five foot, and fifty foot marks for gathering soil and plant samples." Louis, the glib reporter, had lost a bit of his normal light-hearted demeanor.

"How does this figure as far as mutilations go, or mutes, as you call them? How does this rate? Is this an extreme one, an average one. . .?"

"I'd say it's average for this part of the San Luis Valley. Over the last three years, we've had a number of intact rear-ends."

"Rectums?"

"Yeah Louis, as you can tell, the rectum hasn't been cored out. Further south in New Mexico, in all their recent cases, the rear-end has been taken. I don't know if that's a trend, but this appears to be a typically average case." Louis momentarily rediscovered his English-style humor and opined, "Maybe rectums aren't a hot commodity anymore. . . ?"

"Uhh right Louis, maybe now it's lip and eye stew, instead of udder-rectum soufflé. So Louis, what do you think, now that you've seen one?" I clapped him on the shoulder in a cold manly embrace.

"Well-l-l, it's pretty repulsive seeing the eye-socket bubbling like that!" We took the rest of the tarp off, revealing the intact rear-end. Louis almost loses his cookies. "Oh, oh-oh-oh MAN! Is-is-is that normal?!" He starts to cough and retch. "It's rectum... is. . . bubbling!" I started laughing and patted him on the back, "I know it's tough Louis, but you can handle it."

"Is that normal?! Why is it bubbling?!"

"Well, it's natural. The animal had probably eaten a lot. When it died, the vegetable matter all fermented and created gas. So what you're seeing is the process of that gas bulging out and bloating the animal."

"But why is it bubbling out of that little hole right there?"

"There is so much pressure, it split the animal's uhh, soft-tissues."

Louis tells Simon the cameraman, "Get in close on that bubbling rectum."

"Oh-h, man! YOU get the close-up!" Simon, the cameraman is not having fun. Louis looked down at the animal's missing mandible flesh and comments, "Well, at least it died with a smile on its face." I laughed, "You're pretty sick, man." I started to videotape down wind, "Oooo wee, geez Louise. That's the problem with these things. . ."

"What's the problem?"

"The problem is the smell downwind. You just don't want to get downwind." Even though the animal had lay in a pristine, refrigerated environment, my well-exposed nose caught a whiff of cadaverine.

Louis coyly suggests, "Let's go downwind and get a good sniff! Come on Chris, let's do it! It's good TV, come on-n-n. Come on Chris, as a favor to me." He pulled at me insistently, trying to get me to move downwind for a video shot. I declined, just as the rancher arrived bouncing over the pasture to the site. Sternly, he slowly climbed out of his truck accompanied by his son and a couple of their alert blue-heeler ranch dogs.

Louis regained his journalistic composure and asked, "Chris, what are the characteristics of this animal carcass that mark it as a possible mutilation, and make it mysterious?"

"Well, first of all, Louis, the cut around the jaw and snout area is peculiar. The cut obviously starts here and goes around in this direction. And the eye was apparently carved out. It wasn't plucked out, like from a bird, the whole socket has been reamed out. You can see the fluids bubbling in there from the pressure. It is kind of gross!"

OK, I told myself, enough of this. It was getting colder and the wind had picked up. It echoed the stone face of the rancher who stood surveying the scene. The dogs darted purposefully around the perimeter, their alert senses on high alert and the sun sunk below the line of clouds on the western horizon.

"Let's go gentleman, I'm going to get some samples here." After the rancher and I gave a quick analysis of the unusual cuts for the camera the Brit's eyes bulged as I started the forensic sample gathering procedure. I carefully cut into the animal's flesh. Louis lost it completely and started making strange gagging noises. His hands were steepled in front of his face and his face was screwed up and turning a cold purple. He almost upchucked his lunch. "Oh God! I don't think viewers can watch this, it's-it's too disgusting!... Don't you think?"

"I can't *believe* I'm doing this, Louis. It does take a little bit of getting used to." Louis regained his composure and tries his lighthearted approach

"Chris, shouldn't you get a sample of the eye juice?"

"No, I'll let the vet do that, I can't have all the fun." I looked at the mandible cut closely and noticed hair follicles that appear to have been cut during the original excision as Louis turned away. I cut into the mandible flesh for the second sample and told him, "you get used to it after a few dozen of them." I finished the tissue excising and began gathering the final plant and soil samples tested later by Dr. W.C. Levengood at the Pinelandia Biophysical Laboratory in Michigan.

It had really gotten windy and the wind sucked the moisture out of the thin, freezing air. I started gathering plant and soil samples ten feet from the carcass in the rock-hard ground. I was busy digging away with my back to the carcass when just behind me I heard Louis gag and moan, " OOHHHH!!!"

I turned just in time to see the rancher's dog furtively licking the quietly oozing blood and fluid from the upside, excised eye-socket. The rancher gave the pooch a casual kick and put his hands back in his pockets. "Oh, OOHHH, Ohhhhhh, Ohh, the-the-the dog is licking the juice from its eye-socket!" The rancher scratched his head — he didn't know what to make of these BBC boys. I did; welcome to the wild-wild west, blokes.

I looked at the rancher and said "they do that. They're dogs. You should see what a pack of coyotes would do to this thing. . ." I asked the rancher, "right?" He didn't answer. Louis kept repeating, ". . . the dog was licking the juice from the eye-socket of a mutilated cow. . ."

"Louis, you are really funny, man! So you almost lost your cookies again, huh?"

He repeated, "the dog was licking the eye-socket of a mutilated cow!"

"It's a natural thing."

"I'm never going to forget that image." He turned and stepped away from the carcass. "You've got a FUN job." I pointed to the rancher, "Owning a cow that's had this done to it is no fun. What do you think?" I asked the rancher for his opinion again. He stood and looked down at the cow. "It's very suspicious.... I've never seen one like this, in over thirty years of ranching. I see dead cows

371

all the time, but I've never seen one that's cut up like this. Or been cut at all!... I've never seen an animal that's been cut on like this!" Louis was still amazed by the dog. "Have you ever seen a dog licking an eye-socket before?"

"Yeah probably, and other parts too." He turned away from the BBC boys, "this is very strange, Chris. This animal has been cut on by a sharp knife or high-heat, or something. Normally, if a cow just dies that cheek patch wouldn't be missing and the eye-socket would still be there."

"So what do you think did this?" Louis asked. The rancher paused a second before he answered, "I wish I knew. . . That's why Chris is here, maybe these samples will enlighten us."

Louis asked, "Do you think it's UFOs and aliens?"

"I guess it's possible. Either that, or we have some real strange individuals in this country that would get a sick thrill out of this. This is our livelihood. There's been too much of this going on. It's not happened to me previously, but [this] one's quite enough. . . It's happened to my neighbors."

Louis, again re-discovering his journalistic demeanor quips, "I've read accounts that say this is just predator damage. Vultures, maggots and what-not. . ." The rancher looked off and his jaw tightened before he disagreed, "totally impossible. Vultures, predators, varmits; they did not do this. This was done by some. . . it may have been a varmit, but it's of a two-legged kind. It's not animals. This is not an animal kill at all, if it was, they'd be around the backside of the animal. That's where they always start. I've hunted all my life, I butcher my own beef. To do that kind of work up there on the jaw-bone where the skin's extremely tight, you'd have to have a lot of experience, or a very good instrument. They did this in the dark. We live less than five-hundred yards away; the dogs never barked. It's very unusual! That cow was healthy prior to her death and there's no visible indication of how the animal was killed. There's no sign of a struggle, or anything else. . . This cow never did anything to anybody! Why her? Why me?! Why my neighbors? We need answers to who, what, and why this is happening. I don't care to have any more."

The mood turned more somber, I felt uneasy. The rancher was actually a bit choked up over the loss of his cow, and I could tell Louis and Simon were uncomfortable at the rancher's anguish. I know I was uncomfortable. We covered the animal with the whipping tarp as the cold San Luis Valley wind tore fiendishly at our clothing and further chilled the darkening scene.

Before leaving I thanked the rancher for coming forward and reporting the case. The BBC boys were quiet and lost in their thoughts as we drove the few miles to the Alamosa airport. Gone was the lighthearted banter and glib attitude. I dropped them off at the airport, bid them *adieu* and headed home mulling over several explanations for these perplexing animal deaths.

A couple of months passed before the BBC sent me a copy of the show. I cringed as I watched Louis tear into a Nevada militia group that has been formed to protect the aliens after they land and poke fun at the two owners of competing crash sites in Roswell. Then my segment came on. Louis treated my investigative efforts as a straight, serious news story.

John Harr with Jane's Defence Weekly's Nick Cook shooting *Billion $ Secret*

The BBC Cow: Welcome to Louis Theroux's Wild Weekend in Colorado

UFO SIGHTINGS

'Mysterious Valley' sheds light on a litany of anomalous events

By Zack Van Eyck
Deseret News staff writer

THE MYSTERIOUS VALLEY, by Christopher O'Brien; St. Martin's Press; 300 pages; $6.99 (paperback).

Skeptics who dismiss UFOs and other paranormal phenomena say flatly that you just can't trust eyewitness testimony.

There's no escaping that many claims of the unusual are actually mundane events mistaken for something more profound. Many sightings these days are captured on videotape, which skeptics say can be faked. They're right, of course. And still photographs are just as easily manipulated.

But what about mass sightings in which several, if not dozens, of sober adult witnesses see the same orange fireball streak across the sky, change direction, split into several pieces, reunite as one object and then vanish? What about cattle mutilations, in which physical evidence of a bizarre encounter is left behind?

The skeptics are forgetting, of course, that our entire judicial system is based on eyewitness accounts. If three ranchers in rural Colorado say they saw a man shoot another, their claims are taken seriously. If they say they saw a giant triangle-shaped craft glide across a field, shine a beam of bluish light on the ground, then fly silently away with six helicopters in pursuit, they are ridiculed and second-guessed.

Chris O'Brien's biggest accomplishment in "The Mysterious Valley" — aside from his appropriate choice to focus on a current UFO hotspot rather than add to a growing collection of diatribes about the Roswell incident and alleged alien abductions — is his refusal to cast judgment on the people of the San Luis Valley.

O'Brien's first foray into paranormal journalism reads like a novel but is in fact a true story of high strangeness on the high plateau nestled between the San Juan and Sangre de Cristo mountains of south-central Colorado and northern New Mexico.

The story actually begins in south-central Utah in 1989, where O'Brien, a thirtysomething musician and fossil hunter raised in Seattle, experienced several hours of "missing time" while camping in the desert. His travels take him to Crestone, Colo., where he settles in — unaware of the strange occurrences he is about to observe and document. At a New Year's Eve Party in December 1992, O'Brien overhears friends talking about unusual lights and glowing objects in the sky.

"My full-time investigation liter-

ally began that night, and I can't help but look back at that pivotal evening and view my naive excitement with a smile," O'Brien writes. "If I had known what I was getting into, my excitement would have undoubtedly been tempered with the realization that years of frustrating and unrewarding hard work lay ahead with no promise of any firm answers."

Indeed, "The Mysterious Valley" raises more questions than it ever attempts to answer. But that is its value and charm. O'Brien, with a healthy amount of objectivity, reports in great detail through first, second and thirdhand accounts of an incredible litany of anomalous events. Included in the mix: bigfoot, abductions, shapeshifters, triangular ships, orange and green fireballs, 6-foot-long orange "streamers," a partially translucent lizard-like creature, unmarked helicopters, unusual animal deaths, UFOs that come closer if you "call them in your mind" and a mysterious "glass skull" artifact.

One of the more bizarre cases he comes across is the story of a hunter missing for several days in Huerfano County in 1994. He claimed that "a large group of 'aliens dressed in camo appeared' at his campsite and before he could react, he was gassed, captured and tied up. They never spoke to him and never fed him. . . . He said at one point the group started to get aboard a small ship. (The hunter) was astonished when the 'ship expanded' to accommodate them all.

"The ship allegedly took off, morphed into the shape of a bear, then morphed into a 'three-headed wolf,' then turned into a cloud!"

Many of the tales and sightings are more down to earth and, O'Brien concedes, could be linked to a growing military presence in the San Luis Valley. But it's hard to tell from simply watching the night skies whether the UFOs are really secret military operations or if the military is secretly observing otherworldly exercises.

"As I look back on my past years of investigation, I see that this has not been merely a quest to explain unusual lights in the sky nor to explain the unusual deaths of (mostly domesticated) animals," O'Brien confesses in the final chapter. "It has been a quest to learn more about humanity's perceptions, about the origins of human consciousness, about myself."

For Utahns, O'Brien's work offers a greater understanding of events similar to those that have allegedly taken place in the state's own paranormal wonderland, the Uintah Basin.

CHAPTER TWELVE:
Up Close and Personal

In late July, 1997, while I was diligently finishing up the manuscript for my second book, *Enter the Valley* (ETV), I had a hunch there were other witnesses out there who were going to be included in my second installment of the Mysterious Valley trilogy, but from where in the woodwork would they emerge? I talked with *Valley Courier* editor, Mark Hunter, pumped him for any leads and told him of my suspicion that there were stories out there to be included in ETV. After talking with me, he published a short update article that prompted valley witnesses, who had experienced an unusual event, to file a report. I received responses from three credible-sounding "experiencers" who, as it turned out, had been unsuccessfully trying to contact me for several months. Since 1995, my notoriety had escalated dramatically as a result of all the media coverage, so I had attempted to keep a rather low-key profile locally. Because of my unlisted number, local folks sometimes had a difficult time reaching me. As an aside, I will always wonder how many experiences are out there waiting to be shared from those who were unable to contact me?

On July 28, 1997, I received a call from a thirty-something-year-old woman named "Dorothy" (not her real name). She had been referred to me by a county sheriff's dispatcher. Dorothy began to tell me her life story that featured visitation/abduction experiences with at least three different types of "aliens." She told me her family had a three-generation history of contact now that her daughter was having visitations.

Interestingly enough, I had received few, if any, credible abduction claims over the course of my then five-year investigation, and Dorothy's matter-of-fact accounts were, even for me, an open-minded individual, quite unbelievable. I recalled an abduction claim from the early 1980s and the story surrounding Nelly Lewis' "diary" but only two or three individuals during my then four and one half year investigation had approached me concerning these types of experiences. Dorothy conveyed her wish to remain anonymous, stating: "I'm a very private person." She insisted she was not interested in making money or gaining fame and notoriety. Having to live in the San Luis Valley, she did not want the locals to

375

know who she was and what her family had experienced, and as I quickly learned, she had good reason for being publicity-shy.

After listening to her for twenty minutes on the phone, while furiously scribbling page after page of notes, an interview with her in person was in the cards and we set up a meeting at her ranch on July 30, 1997.

I remember the day I conducted her interview clearly. The entire valley region was ringed with majestic towering thunderheads that had blossomed dramatically over the mountains surrounding the Valley. Little puffs of clouds floating in the morning had grown into towering columns that rumbled and grumbled, brilliantly lit at and above twenty thousand feet. I made a mental note of the lightning that flashed to the north, right as I arrived at her humble farm in south-central Saguache County, near the Russell Lakes. As I climbed out of my Jeep, I was immediately confronted by her highly alert Doberman pinscher. Dorothy's eleven year-old daughter skated merrily around the yard on roller-blades while I made quick friends with the wary dog. I love Dobies. In high-school, my girlfriend's family, the Wardens owned a championship Doberman kennel that was home to Gunga Din and their expert dog training lessons.

Dorothy emerged from the house and introduced herself. An attractive but demure strawberry blond, she looked me in the eye and gave me a firm handshake. I was invited in and we sat down at her kitchen table. I quickly scanned her bookshelves for books about UFOs, aliens and the paranormal. There were none. I pulled out my cassette recorder, placed it on the table in front of her and double-checked with her if it was alright to record our interview. She wasted no time beginning her story. I noticed she had a low-key but bubbly, hyper personality. She talked with a rapid-fire delivery; one sentence tumbling into the next, but she never strayed too far from her point.

She launched into her story and for forty-five non-stop minutes she related her "over two-hundred" conscious encounters/ visitations/abductions by "aliens." Toward the end of her account, I reached over to check the tape-recorder. It was off. I had put the tape in on the wrong side so it hadn't recorded a minute of her story. Being a recording musician who, at the time, had a professional eight-track studio set-up, I'm very good at getting everything down on tape, and I was not pleased with myself. Embarrassed, I asked Dorothy to tell me the whole story again. She sighed, and immediately launched a complete second 'take.' I had listened carefully to her accounts, and I was impressed when, upon concluding her second go around, I discerned no factual variation between version one and version two. The information related in both accounts was identical.

376

I felt it was important that she told her own story, without judgment or embellishment. You decide whether you believe her or not. To me, sitting across the table from her, she certainly seemed sincere and I had reason to suspect that her rare, fully-conscious experiences were real to her, but were they real to me and you? Dorothy was just getting warmed up and she began re-relating her fascinating accounts:

"The earliest recollections that I can remember happened when I was about eight or nine, in Denver growing up. We'd see lights in the night and I'd tell my older brother, 'look, there's Santa.' He'd say, 'Santa doesn't come in May, or October,' whatever. . . We'd watch these lights, and they'd play tag with each other… We had an old Rambler, and the back seat could face backwards, so you could see where you'd been. I'd say, 'that star is following us,' and my father would say, 'oh no, it's just us moving.' Then the star would start getting closer, and brighter…

"As kids, we'd play games outside. One time the ball went behind a tree, and I remember telling my friends, 'the bogey man is right there,' and there was this figure; a horrible brown shriveled thing wearing a black cloak."

"How tall?" I queried.

"He was taller than me at age eight or nine. Probably, about four feet tall. I told my brother and he went back there. We had another friend, and we all went back there. . .we left the ball there! I remember little bits and pieces [from childhood]… like something now will trigger it." She exclaimed in wonder. "I remember that from when I was young. I would always watch. I'd leave the window open at night sometimes and my mother would shut it. I wanted 'them' to come in. She'd lock the doors, and I'd think, how can they come in? I'd open the window again. There were times when I'd hide in the closet. "

Having gone through a similar childhood encounter of my own, I was curious how her family; especially her parents, had responded to her claims.

"Have you told your folks about all of your experiences?"

"Well, my Dad's dead, but he knew about all of this stuff. He and his mother experienced some things. My mother knew, I told her about it. She would say, 'why don't they just leave you alone?' When I was up there [Denver] last summer, one night they were at the bottom of her [Mother's] bed making sure she didn't move when they checked on me. She saw them. She didn't believe in any of this, until she saw them at the bottom of her bed. She couldn't move. She said she tried and tried."

This was interesting information. Dorothy's assertion that her *grand*mother had also had visitation experiences suggested a rare, multi-generational history of visitations. I wondered if this casual remark was to be believed. I tried to get a handle on the frequency of these claimed childhood events.

"So, how many times as a child did you have visitation experiences?"

"From my teenage years? I really don't remember a lot of it. Maybe they were around, maybe they weren't. I've always had paranormal things going on around me; like ghosts and things... My sister had some strange things happen to her too. My brother has never had anything happen to him. She, [pointing to her teenage daughter] had a few things, my son had one instance." Did she have any physical proof? I wondered, then asked, "Any physical marks? Any scoop marks or lasting scars?"

"I have them all over the place. Triangular ones, scoops, I don't know if it's because I'm getting older and my skin is sagging more, but I'm noticing these things. I can't remember where they're from. I've got barb-wire scars, dog-bite scars, all kinds of scars. Most of them are accounted for. But there are several I know that aren't. One on the bottom of the foot, and on my thigh, I have this strange laser-type burn thing... here..." She shows me her leg. "There's a lump on the roof of my mouth that swells during full-moons. Believe it or not! There's a lump in my nose. I've had MRI's and x-rays of it. I've had sinus problems ever since 'they' put it [the implant] there. I've gone though my stack of medical records and compared them to some notes I have" [of her many abduction experiences]. This lady certainly had an unusual health history!

Down in The Valley

I really wanted to find out more about her experiences as a Valley resident.

"How long did you live up in Denver?" I asked. "Well, until I moved down here in August or September 1982."

"What happened when you moved to the Valley?"

"We moved to the Bonanza area, on Kerber Creek. It really escalated. We saw all kinds of ships and lights. We would hear this low vibration at times, like a big old diesel truck idling. There's nothing up there."

"At that time there were maybe what, twelve people living there?" I queried.

"Not even!"

This revelation was interesting. Huge low frequency vibrations have been reported for decades, across the Valley in the Sangre de Cristos, but this was the first time someone claimed to have heard these noises in the mountains around Bonanza, Colorado. I looked forward to hearing about her SLV encounters.

"So, what other kinds of things happened when you moved here to the Valley?"

"Coming to the Valley, I experienced not only close-encounters of the first, second, third and fourth-kind, then abductions; medical experiments. And 'they' showed me things. It tapered of in '88. After that there was no more physical probing."

"How many experiences did you have in that five-year time period?"

"Ohh, I couldn't begin to count them. I have no idea. I'd say at least two-hundred or more! ..."

"Wow...are you serious?" This was an unbelievable figure. "...and they were all with beings. Beings of all types."

"Describe the different types."

"There's the short, little, dark leathery-brown types. They're not lizards. They're definitely little aliens, and they're all wrinkly, and I think they come up from South America. They're three-and-a-half, to four feet tall. The dark greys, are about four feet tall. The light greys, about four and-a-half feet tall. The tall greys are about six feet tall."

"Just Like Elvis, But Not So Tacky"

"Then there's this one leader, I'm sure he's a hybrid--he has emotions--and he's about six and-a-half to seven feet tall. He has emotions, so I know he has to be a hybrid. None of the others have emotions. He will explain things a little bit to me. He won't let the others mess around with me."

"When you say 'others,' you're referring to the little ones?" I probed.

"Yes, the little ones that do the experimenting. If he doesn't want them visiting you, he will make them leave, and he'll just stay and visit. Or he'll take [me] and leave them there. There's a bond between him and I. I'm not exactly sure this sounds sane! But it's like a boyfriend, girlfriend-type relationship." This is not an uncommon impression felt by female "abductees." Sometimes, a woman experiencer will find kinship, even a form of relationship with a single being that often is perceived as being in charge of other more drone-like entities. I found her accounts and perceptions quite matter-of-fact, and I dug deeper for more detailed information.

"What happens during a typical event?" I asked. She quickly launched into an overview. "You could be lying in bed or sitting on the couch, it doesn't really matter. You're sitting, or lying there and you're paralyzed--totally immobilized. You get the feeling that something is there, and then you see the lights. There's a very bright white light, or sometimes a yellow one. And then they're there! Then they take you up to the ship, and inside, it's totally white and very, very bright. Probably… twenty times brighter than a big florescent light, and there's no fixtures. You know 'central-heating?' Well it was central lighting. Just like the sun. It was right there. No switches, no lamps, no nothing. You couldn't tell where the light was coming from; it was just everywhere.

"The room was totally round inside. I never saw square corners of any type. There is always a fog when you're up in there. There is always fog. I never went up and didn't see [fog]. It's associated with a sweet and sour type smell."

"What's the closest smell that you can compare it to?" This was a new sensory wrinkle.

"Kind of like burning rubber in molasses. At first you're nauseated, then there's a little pleasant smell, then you're nauseated again. Then they touch your forehead right there…" She touched her third-eye "…then you're not nauseated by anything, the heights, the smell. I'm [a person] who's very afraid of heights, VERY afraid. I'd be up there looking down on several things. I was high above the earth several times. I'd think to myself, wow, I could be an astronaut! This description reminded me of "Michael's" claims of being shown "gold" from an altitude of around one-thousand feet.

"OK, then you're on a table, you're always laid in a prone position. You're laid on your back, I've never seen anybody laid any other way. They don't experiment on you when you're standing. I never saw any restraints of any kind, but nobody's moving."

"So there were other humans there?"

"Right, but they're not necessarily next to you on another table. I saw them in other rooms. I was taken to the other rooms; just in the doorway, I wasn't allowed to go in. I'd hear them screaming, you'd hear their cries, and you'd want to help them, but you're not allowed to say anything. You just can't." She looked at me with a look of sadness.

"Who was usually with you when you saw this type of scene?"

"Always the tall guy and a few of the little grey ones. They're only there because 'he' says so.

"So they follow his instructions?"

"I think they're there to make sure I don't bolt, or something, because I don't think he has the total physical capability to do what they do. The mental stuff… because he is a hybrid. They're there for backup in case something gets out of hand." I wanted to find out more about the "hybrid," tag so I asked, "What is the tall one dressed like?"

"Several times I've seen him in gold lamé. He has a long cape. Like something Elvis would've worn, but no so tacky. He doesn't have that scarf." She and I both begin to laugh. "The outfit is tight around his legs. His body is thin--he's got the alien-type body. He doesn't have a human form. Absolutely no hair."

"What do his eyes look like?" I stifled another chuckle. This was wild.

"They're almond-shapcd. Up and down almond-shaped. He has five fingers, and they're all the same length, and he's light-ish grey and translucent, but he has emotion! His emotions are conveyed every time he visits me. Every time. Quite overpowering."

"It sounds like you had formed a relationship with him."

"Oh we did. We still do... As far as being connected with the tall-one, I'd ask him 'why me?' He [said] I was different from other people and he said, 'You could belong up here. I said, 'I could live here?' And he said 'yes'. One time I said 'I don't want to go back,' and he said, 'you have to.' I've always been sent back, sometimes against my will. I thought, after being up there a couple of times, and there was no probing and prodding on me, I thought this is nice, I'd like to stay here." Again, this was a fairly common perception. Often, after undergoing a number of these "abductions," abductees feel a kinship, or connection, with their abductors, and several have publicly said at times, they wished they could have stayed with their abductors. She continued after I asked rhetorically, "You mentioned they also took you for rides."

"Oh yes, I did some excursions, if you will. Those were the times when I really wanted to stay up there. Being with 'Him...' I bonded with him. I don't know why, but I think he bonded with me. Having to say goodbye was kind of awful! Then having to come back down here with all the dumb earthlings polluting the planet... it is really exasperating!" She rolled her eyes, "...I've always kind of felt that I didn't belong here. Always on the outside--looking in. They never came out and said, 'Ya, you're a two-point-four percent alien.'"

"It sounds like they are very coy with information."

"They only let you know what they want you to know. Like the government. They are a little more honest than the government though. They show you with action. Our government will hide it to the very end." We talked for a bit and I asked her to give me a quick recap.

Alien Mining in The Sangres

" So, there's the little grey ones, the little brown one, the light grey ones. I've never seen the Nordics, or…what do they call them? The Plaeidians? I've never seen the reptile ones. I'm not saying they don't exist, I've just never seen them."

"I've seen the motherships, I've seen the regular disc-shaped craft, I've seen the triangle-shaped ones, with red and green lights. Those are dark grey, they're not shiny. The dark-leathery ones seem to be on the triangles, more than anything else. I've never seen the dark brown ones on the ships with the grey one. The usually are on their own ships, the triangles. Or they're down here—doing whatever."

"You mentioned when we first talked on the phone something about the aliens "mining in the Sangre de Cristos." What's that all about?" She had tweaked my curiosity when she mentioned this particular detail.

"Yes…the lithium crystals. We went over there and they had a couple of those little guys, they were wearing overalls, they were white plastic, with hoods. I have a drawing of one of those types. We went in there, and they [the crystals] were all dirty. You can't tell what the crystals are; they just look like rocks, but then they'd clean them off. I was allowed to carry of few of them out, but I wasn't allowed to keep them. I got to feel them, but had to put them in the pile in the middle of the ship for them to use as power. He said this is where they've been getting them."

In the original Star Trek TV series, the ships were powered by dilithium crystals. A connection? Mineral Hot Springs—now named "Joyful Journey" is a natural lithium hot-spring and this was the location of the 1991 landing circle and snake in the blast-hole. I asked for more specific information. "Where in the Sangres is this mining activity taking place?"

"Well, there was a four-wheel drive road over a pass, that's all I know. It's down here in this part of the range," she said pointing toward the Great Sand Dunes glistening across the Valley. "It was down here somewhere. When they took me, I looked down and could see the area here [northwest of Center, CO] that I'm familiar with."

"Well, there's only two four-wheel drive pass roads over the Sangres; Medano and Hayden Pass." Hayden Pass is about ten miles east of the lithium hot-springs and this correlation is noteworthy.

"Well I do make a point of remembering landmarks and feeling things, and smelling things to help me remember."

"Well, you certainly have kept quite an extensive log!" I looked through her spiral notebooks with pages and pages of drawings, dates and times of "visits," and descriptions of her alleged encounters. Many o her entries dovetailed with other sightings around the valley. She continued, "You know, 'they' cloak a lot of these visits with owls and other things, but I've noticed a lot of owls. They're always around me. Even in the day. Have you ever seen owls in the day? She asked. "No, not usually, sometimes at dusk… " I answered…

"I've been out around here, and heard 'hovering,' but you don't see a thing. But you know what it is! There have been nights that I've been terrified to go outside. Still [even today]. On those nights, I feel the energy, and I know they're there. And it's like, I'm NOT going outside. Then there's other times when I think, I'd like to see them and a couple days later, they'll be by.

"A few nights after the Hale-Bopp comet, [the family] saw something. We looked through the binoculars and we saw something up there shining. We saw little ones going around it. Right over there." She points to the west, over La Garita. "That was probably near the end of March [1997]. That was the last time I had a sighting. I don't think they've been by since then, but I can't be sure…"

Dorothy had mentioned some terrestrial oddities that had occurred, so I changed tack and asked her about other peripheral events to her on-going contact with "aliens," Especially the phone calls and strange mail delivery problems she had told me about during our first conversation on the phone.

The Evil Blues Brothers

She continued her story and familiar …"I did have a strange phone-call a couple of weeks ago. It was this metal screeching in the phone. I called the sheriff's office and asked them 'what IS this?' It wasn't a fax machine. I've called the phone company so many times because there's beeping, like I'm being recorded, there's so much noise. I get calls and somebody just hangs up…. So many things."

"You mentioned before on the phone two strange men out at your mailbox. . ."

"Oh yeah, the men-in-black. They look like the Blues Brothers, but evil. Basically that's what they look like. One time, they were just standing there at my mail box going through my mail. The Post Office sent somebody down here from Denver to check it out. Then they had a guy from Colorado Springs come out."

"So, It sounds like you've had problems with your mail. . ." I asked innocently.

"Constantly! I got a Post Office box because these men-in-black were constantly going through my mail. That one time, I ran down to the end of the driveway and they took off in a vehicle with no plates or tags. So, I got a box in Center, [Colorado] and I was still having problems. I quit getting my mail there…we moved back up to Denver for awhile, and I was having problems with my mail there! We moved back, and I now have a box in Monte [Vista, Colorado], and I haven't really had any problems there. It was like I would never get my mail, or it would be opened on my end, or opened on the receiving end. I've received several items addressed to my name, and the address of either Center, or Saguache, U.S.A. With no postmark at all. It went to the sheriff's office. They called me, I picked it up, and it was UFO-related! I thought that was really quite strange." Intrigued by her claims, later I called and confirmed this with a long time sheriff's office worker.

Dorothy had also mentioned some bizarre health problems and medical anomalies she had been dealing with and I was curious if she thought there was a connection between these health issues and her "abductions." "Describe some of the medical problems you told me about on the phone."

"I'm highly allergic to any food preservatives of any type, I digest no protein of any kind, I have anti-nuclear DNA; they don't know why. I have a lump in the roof of my mouth. My nasal cavity has been x-rayed because I have sinus problems. There's a lump in there, and they don't know what it is.

"I've had several [false] pregnancies, which I have nothing to show, I've probably been pregnant ten times or more, including two sets of twins. No one knows what happened. I've always used contraceptives…that's not a good plug for them… I [had] one miscarriage. All of a sudden it was just gushing everywhere. There was no tissue at all to scrape clean when they went in there. They tried to get tissue to see what sex the baby was, and they told me 'Hon, there's nothing there. There's nothing in there at all.' It was scraped clean. I can't have general anesthesia, I go into shock. For my heart surgery, I had local anesthesia! Because, I will die. I have gone into shock so many times… ever since I was young and had my tonsils out, I cannot handle anesthesia. I've been diagnosed with Lupis. "

"My goodness!" This lady really had gone through some health challenges. I decided to change the subject. Just hearing about these many health problems was making me feel uncomfortable. She showed me a pile of documentation to back her claims and I knew I had my investigative work cut out for me.

Hell Fire and Brimstone

"Ah, let's move on to something else. What sort of information have you been given by the 'visitors?'" I changed tack back to our "aliens."

"They had this screen. It was like a TV monitor. Flat." She outlined a long flat surface on the kitchen table with her hands, about three feet by one foot. "They showed me these scenes of fires, devastation, humans starving, the older people being wiped out, and unfortunately there will be no more animals left."

"Did they tell you why they were showing you this?"

"Yes, this is something they want us to try and avoid because it's happened in the past. Maybe on their planet, because these things haven't happened here before. Maybe it has and we just don't know about it."

"Did they tell you where they were from?"

"Some are Martians. Some are from a wormhole in another solar system, I can't remember where it is, but they're from there--I saw it on their map. I've seen their 'cryptoid' writing all over the ship."

"Cryptoid, what do you mean?"

"It's basically like letters, but they're not our letters. Well, they called it 'Cryptoid.' "

I scratched my head. "I've never heard that term before. . ."

"There's letters and they use some that are like hieroglyphs. They use mainly their alphabet. There was a piece of paper [with writing on it] that I wanted to take, but they wouldn't let me have it."

Invariably, many contactees/abductees try to bring back a physical artifact to prove to themselves and others, that their experiences are real. I asked, "Good point, have you ever tried to grab something. . . ?" She interrupted:

"...constantly! I constantly tried to sneak stuff out. But you just can't! There was one time I found two discs on the ground, like hubcaps. They had some kind of writing on them. They let me have them for awhile, but then they took them away when they left."

"You know, I've contacted Budd Hopkins, MUFON, Whitley Strieber... I contacted just about everybody. They were like 'yeah, we want to see this, we want to see that.'"

"What prompted you to contact them?" I am always curious as to witness' motivations to call well-known researchers, and/or the media. She didn't hesitate a second and told me earnestly, "I wanted to figure out why this is happening to me! And why I was the unlucky one being picked on all the time. I was being bombarded with this stuff. In a twenty-four hour day, if I wasn't questioning what just happened the night before, I was questioning when it was going to happen again. I wanted to sort out what was happening...Lately more things have been coming to me. Bits and pieces."

"You mentioned you'd never gone through any [hypnotic] regression and these are all conscious memories?" This interesting non-element is the exception, not the rule. A majority of "abduction" cases feature hypnotic-regression and retrieved information.

She said matter-of-factly, "I've never been regressed. I'm not going to. I don't believe hypnotism is your best bet. I've been thinking that finally, they [the aliens] are letting loose of the reins on me."

I wondered if the alleged entities … had told her anything about their motivations so I asked, "Did they ever tell you why they picked you? Why they are doing this?"

"No, they would never answer any of those questions. I kept asking them 'you can cure this, you can cure that, why aren't you helping us down here? Why are you picking on me? Why do you need to do this?' They'd never answer. Usually, they'd totally act like they never heard you ask, of course when they speak to me, it's through telepathy. I wouldn't even get a blank thought out of them. Nothing. I was totally ignored.

"A lot of time when they were doing experiments on me, and I'd keep asking, and they'd get quite angry with me. I could tell because they'd get, how would I say? A little bit rough? I've come down with bruises, even a dislocated shoulder. I was running from one and fell down eleven stairs and broke a rib and my tailbone, and still have those to deal with. You can't get away."

"You said 'that's what the little guys are for. To make sure you don't get away…" She added: "…and be a cooperative human."

The Valley Is A Hot-Spot

At this point in the interview, I was reeling from the accounts I was hearing. I didn't know what to think. On one hand, Dorothy seemed very believable, and I was captivated by her matter-of-fact delivery, but her story was *too* fantastic. It was difficult for me to accept the information she was relating at face value, and I wanted her to talk further about the San Luis Valley, so I asked, "What do you think about this place?"

"The Valley has so much activity, and honest to God, with all the stuff that's happened to me here, I don't know why I've always stayed, but every time I try to leave, I can't make it out of here, I get homesick. I have to be here. I don't know what it is, but I have to be here. This is going to be one of the safe places. When all the stuff starts breaking loose, this will be one of the safe places. I do know that. Now if you're a 'Doubting Thomas', you still have a chance. But if you are an evil person, if you've been evil a lot in your life, and don't care about correcting any of it, this will be a Sodom and Gomorrah for you! This is information I was told, not stuff that I saw. They told me this. Most of my family should be safe."

At one point during our initial phone call she had hinted that her daughter was an experiencer: "How about your daughter? Has anything happened to her?"

"When she was small; she was probably about a year-and-a half, to two years old, I was reading *Communion*, [by Whitley Strieber] up at my Mom's. I was staying up in Denver. It was too thick and heavy for me down here, and I really had to get away. Why I thought I could get away, I don't know, they'd follow me to Denver, anyway."

"Why were you reading *Communion?*"

"I wanted to see if Strieber had some explanations. Something I could relate to. I admit, I was grasping at straws at that point, to make myself say, 'you're NOT crazy!' My daughter saw the book on the couch and she said, I know that lady, she comes to me. Unless you've read the book, you don't know that picture [on the cover] is of a female-form. It's a female. She knew! Go ahead, tell your latest one. Go ahead honey" She prompted her eleven year-old daughter, who had been sitting and listening with her roller-blade skates on. The girl looked at me and appeared a little uncomfortable. Her mother insisted: "Go ahead! Don't be shy...when you were in your room, remember? " Her daughter rolled her eyes. "Oh, that was a dream..."

Her mother jumped in, "Well, it may have been, or maybe not..." The young girl shyly started to describe her 'dream.' "Well, there was this big... kind of like a hybrid." Echoing one of her mother's often used term, 'hybrid' raised a red flag in my skeptical mind. Her daughter continued, "He had kind of long hair. His hair was curly and he was standing at the bottom of my bed. He had kind of tight—loose clothes on, [an interesting contradiction] and there were reporters in my window... They would look at me, then write stuff down. I couldn't move, I just looked straight up. My cat was by me and I levitated about that high off my bed..." she indicates about a foot-high, and continued, "...I kept looking at my cat and he was just a statue. He wouldn't look at me, or anything!"

"When did this happen?" I asked. "Oh, about four months or so." Her mother interjects, "...probably right around the time the comet was here." She reminded her daughter, "You said he looked like he was in armor, or something?"

"It looked like shiny-dull armor." This second contradictory description was even more interesting. Her mother turned and looked at me and chimed in, "That night I was also visited. That was the night… Oh God, what happened that night? Oh, they just came by to check on me. To see how I was doing. It was after the brown-colored medicine they gave me."

During her original call, she had mentioned that during her last visitation, the beings had given her a brown colored liquid that she was told was some kind of medicine. For what particular affliction; she has several, she didn't know. She had told me, "It didn't taste very good…"

Dorothy continued, "…they were just checking to see how things were going. I was scared, I saw the light coming in, she [her daughter] was sound asleep. I went to her room—nothing! This light was big, and it was coming, so I laid down and heard this noise. A throbbing, a pulsating… I knew what it was, and went, 'Oh God, not again!' I was scared for some reason, probably because it had been awhile. I was really terrified, and I thought to myself, should I crawl under the bed, or should I just lay here and cuss them out when they came in? I decided to just cuss them out. When they came, I couldn't cuss them out, of course. I was just probed over, basically. They just kind of checked everything…"

"What process do they use when they do that?" I asked Dorothy.

"They just run their hands over me like this." She ran her hands lengthwise across the top of the table, about a foot above the tabletop."…there are electrical points in your body they just 'feel.' That's what they told me."

"And which beings were those?"

"The little grey ones. Darker grey. Which was probably why I was kind of scared. The big tall guy was nowhere around. When he's there, I know everything's going to be OK. With them [the little dark greys] they can try to get away with something if they want to. They're always thinking of other things they can pull. You're 'on your toes' when they're around because you never know, if they will decide to take me up to the lab again…That was the same night my daughter had something happen, because she told me the next day."

The girl was uncomfortable talking about it, so I let her mother take over the story.

Ships and MORE Ships

I decided to shift gears again. I suspected that there were more database correlations within her unfolding testimony, so I asked about specific San Luis Valley aerial craft descriptions. "What kind of ships have you seen around here?" She thought for a moment then said, "There [aren't] too many motherships down here [in the SLV]. Mostly I've seen them up around Denver. Big flying pancakes, dark grey--they're not shiny at all. They're like a dull, dull, grey primer color. There's all these metal squares on them that makes them look like they're patched together. Sometimes they have the little pod-ship saucers come off of them. When they land these arms come out, with little pod-things on the bottom of the feet, and they're huge. Really, really huge!"

"How big?" I asked. "They're like a giant spider when the legs come down. They have to be at least two, or three football fields long. That's when I see them—it's dark at night, and they have no lights, I can feel their presence before they come. My hair all stands on end. The electrical field in me is going crazy, and I know they're around. I often wonder why people in the city don't see them. They cover a couple of city blocks! "

"And this is up in Denver where you see these?"

"Yes, I see them sometimes down here, but I usually see them up in Denver."

"How about the ones down here, what are the predominant ones you…"

"…usually the disc-shaped ones. There have been a few triangle ones, but usually it's the disc-shaped ones." I was trying to factor in or out data she had collected concerning her alleged Valley sightings and find how her data dovetailed with my existing database, so I asked "Was there a time-period down here when you saw these craft more often than other time(s) [periods]?"

"1987 through about 1990. It seemed like every other day. At least once a week. I was doing chores one day and saw two of them playing around to the north of me. They were going from west-to-east, right over from the La Garita area. Across the Valley, right over the Sangre de Cristos."

"This was during the day?"

"Yes, broad daylight, around four o'clock, I was doing chores. The horses were running around the corral; the rabbits were scared to death. I went between the rabbit cages and the building to hide. Like the rabbits would really protect me…" She chuckled, "Two days later, one of the rabbits died. Probably had a heart-attack. Anyway, the horses were going crazy and that's the only reason why I noticed them—they were acting up, and I thought, what the heck? They would usually come in for their grain, and the sheep were going crazy, the chickens… We have a lot of animals, and you can tell [when something is not right]. The animals won't go outside if there's one of 'them' around. My daughter was walking one of the dogs once (when we lived to the north of here) and there was a big craft over the house. The dogs were scared to death and wanted to come in, and she could hardly keep them on the leash."

I didn't tell her, but animal reactions to ships and entities is an area of research that, in my estimation, deserves more investigation. It would seem that animals, in general, tend to be highly sensitive to high-strange events; sometimes before the event actually occurs. I have received many reports from San Luis Valley witnesses that include mention of unusual animal reactions to objects as they fly over. I realized that a cursory examination of reported animal reactions would probably reveal evidence of an instinctual awareness of strangeness, possibly tied to the ability of animals to become agitated by impending earthquakes before they actually occur in real-time.

So, What Do The Neighbors Think?

I was curious if Dorothy had revealed her contacts with her neighbors, or heard from her neighbors about sighting episodes they may have also experienced.

"How about other people…have you ever had folks around your neighborhood mention seeing these craft?"

"A friend of mine in Center, was looking for her son one night. He'd run away, and the police were there, and there was a UFO above the ditch in Center. She asked me if I had seen it. I had not seen it."

"What do you think about people around here, generally. Do you think they believe this kind of thing is going on here?"

"I think there are believers and I'm sure most of them have seen stuff. I think there are a lot of people that have had things happen to them. I did see one mutilation when I lived north of here. I never really knew, or thought about who is doing this, but I know it isn't 'devil worshippers.' After seeing the light above the field that night. There was no one in the field that night…"

"When was that?"

"1993. Right before we moved from there. The cow was out there the next morning, right below where the lights had been."

I mention, "There was another possible case in September, or October 1994; very near there."

"The owner never reported it, and didn't want to." She remembered.

"It seems a lot of ranchers around here are like that." I commented.

"He hauled it off to the ditch. I remember some time later I said, 'what happened to that cow you put in the ditch, did the coyotes eat it?' He said, 'No, they wouldn't touch it.' Nothing would touch it. We had cinnamon bears that would come down, and they wouldn't even touch it!

"Bears come all the way out this far?"

"They did over there. There's a wolf over there too. I don't know how many people know that, but he's a big gray one. He was over there, and he wouldn't touch that cow." Interesting, there were no wolves officially anywhere near the SLV.

" When we talked on the phone you mentioned seeing owls."

"It's usually great horned owls. You see them during the daylight, I think they are a cloaking device, or something. It's usually a memory cloak. It's for your benefit, to keep you from remembering. I don't know why they use an owl, I haven't figured that out yet. I've heard that they [the aliens] will use something you like, but I like horses and they've never used one like that. I don't know why they use owls."

The Conditioning Process

Up to this point, my interview with Dorothy had gone well. However, I wanted to get a sense of how her experiences had colored her world-view and her vision of the future. "A lot of people are going to read this. What would you like to convey to them? What would you tell someone who hasn't had these types of experiences?" I asked.

She quickly stated, "It could happen to them. And if it does, you don't have to think you're crazy. This kind of thing really does happen. Just try to make the best of it. In a way you're blessed, in a way you're cursed. And if it never happens to you, just think of yourself as lucky." She chuckled nervously. "One thing is for sure. They're out there! One day everyone's going to know it."

"Do you think that day is soon?"

"Yes, I do. I do. The government's conditioning all of us now, trying to get us used to the idea. There's all that 'alien' propaganda, with all this merchandise, shows. . ."

"AT&T commercials." I add.

"Oh God, yes. And car commercials. That one where the alien family comes down, and then they drive away in the new car. I think it's all in bad taste myself. . ."

"With the ugliest dog and kids in the galaxy in the backseat. . .Do you think 'they' are going to show up and say, 'here we are?' What do you think the government knows?"

"The government knows. Jimmy Carter knows, Ronald Reagan knows, Clinton knows. I know there are several hybrids around, you can feel that. I can walk around in a crowd of people and I can feel who's been on a ship and who hasn't."

"What sense do you get from me?" I asked, curious to hear her impression of your gum-shoe investigator.

"I know you've seen some things."

What is Going On With The Abduction Phenomenon?

I honestly don't know what to make of Dorothy and Michael's incredible claims. Both experiencers claim they were fully conscious when they interacted with the strange beings, and have not needed to undergo hypnotic regression therapy to reclaim details of the events. They are matter-of-fact and very convincing.

Looking at Dorothy's medical records, her "scoop" marks and the other "proof" supporting her story, I still must objectively question the true nature of her perceived experiences. She seemed genuine and truthful, but whom, or more accurately what, are the causal factors behind her perceptions? Was she tricked? If so, to what extent? By who, or more accurately, what?

I later contacted a woman Dorothy mentioned during her interview. The woman, a "devout Christian," (and that's putting it mildly) admitted that she was convinced that Dorothy had undergone some really strange paranormal events in her life. Then the woman's religious interpretation overshadowed our conversation. The woman stated flatly that she "knew" all of Dorothy's experiences were "demonic in nature." She preached: "Only through atonement and acceptance of Christ," could Dorothy "banish her fallen angels" Sounds great on paper but a bit naïve. It appears to me that there is a more complex scenario at work.

There seems to be something truly extraordinary at the core of Dorothy's story, but how much of her story is real is difficult, perhaps impossible, to accurately determine. I sense innocent psychological front-loaded influences [*Communion, Star Trek, ET*] may be influential elements, but to what extent, I don't know. It doesn't matter what kind of front-loading is at work, misperception, miscommunication, confabulation or wishful thinking all could be present. It doesn't necessarily mean that all of her experiences were delusional, something extraordinary appeared to be occurring. whether her interpretation was accurate or not was beside the point, something was real to her and she claimed she had evidence to back this assertion up.

The Abduction Investigation Wheel Is Broken

Michael's claim of being shown gold is even more puzzling. At last word he had spent the intervening years diligently searching for the location of the four lost gold caches he was shown while aboard the "saucer." Michael is a highly intelligent, sober individual who, one would think, would not go wasting his time running about the countryside on such a quixotic chase. The fact that he claims to have located the exact locations is even more compelling. He also claims that he is in the process of either buying out-right one location, or acquiring Colorado Treasure Rights for the locations for other sites he has identified. Remember, he did not contact me to tell me about his "abduction," rather, he contacted me to help him locate electronic, aerial gold-seeking gear. Only with the help of his son, I was able to pull the story out of the reluctant man.

What do we make of these sincere-appearing witnesses' claims? Are their experiences real? Both of them are one-hundred percent convinced they lived real events, but are their perceptions and recollections accurate? These questions lie at the center of this important, experientially-based, aspect of all so-called manifestations of paranormal events. I have always suspected that the effects of these "experiences" were more important than the actual events themselves and there are several reasons why I have publicly shied away from the so-called "abduction," or "visitation" phenomenon. I admit, as a result of my own personal experiences, I have maintained an interest in this puzzling phenomenon and I feel it's safe to say, there does appear to be an outside casual element at the core of these encounters. But, perhaps not to the extent that media coverage of these claims leads us to believe.

Having said this, I do not buy into the conclusions that all, so-called negative-appearing abductions are perpetrated by operators enacting a military/government-based agenda, or, that all benevolent appearing CE-V encounters are truly extraterrestrial in nature. Unfortunately for true-believers there is little if any demonstrative evidence to support either of these conclusions. You could say this is the realm of Occam's shaving cream. The place where the overly-simplistic inside-the-box explanations fall apart for lack of data.

This is very complex territory fraught with quantum peril, or something like that... To me a vast majority of abduction investigators appear to be flying off on oblique investigative tangents; attracting experiencers drawn by their investigative model.

I'm convinced that hypnotic regression is not an accurate tool to ascertain the "Truth." For instance, I suspect that most, if not all, abductees' hypnotically obtained recollections only reflect a portion of their perceptions. There is a strong probability that *fully-conscious* human impressions do not accurately represent the totality of fully-conscious experience. Reality can sometimes fool all of us from time-to-time, so how can we hang our hats on hypnoregression as a totally effective investigative tool? In my estimation, these uncovered perceptions cannot all be attributed to encounters with "ETs." So-called retrieved information by investigators is problematic, first off, there is the problem of subjective bias by the investigator. It is likely that anecdotal data is not being interpreted correctly by the experiencers themselves, let alone the hypno-regressionists who mostly seem intent on gathering supportive data to bolster their foregone conclusions. We need to get creative, folks; re-examine the abduction meme and re-think the equation already.

It is safe to say that ETs, as a cultural meme, are real, but there is a veneer of trickery and subterfuge around their perceived agenda(s). Granted, rarely are witnesses supposedly shown "gold" or "lithium crystals, " as in the San Luis Valley cases I've covered, but so what? Where does the investigator place the relative importance of one case against another? What rating system do we use? Is this supposed to be done based on intuition alone? If not, then what? Is a Mensa member with a photographic memory more relevant than a rancher woman with a stack of medical evidence and a three-generation history of contact? If so why? If not why? I suspect it's likely most "abductions" are impeccably micro-designed for particular individuals by the manipulators, for what overall, macro-purpose, we may never be in a position to know.

On the surface, these potential examples of individualized, mythological programming exercises, or experiments—by unknown agents, alien or otherwise don't make sense. If they are truly off-planet "aliens," messing around with us, why come all the freaking way here to this backwater planet out an arm from *hunab ku* as some Maya still refer to the balanced creator at the galactic core. Slipping into *ad homonym* mode: Hey, you big-headed grey little buggers, why come here from somewhere else, light years away, and enact what appears to be a systematic program of deception and trickery? Because we dumb humans have "da bomb?" Or is it because we have an emotional body/mind and you don't? Or that we have the coveted genetic material that you little dudes need? Uhh, this investigator doesn't think so...

Whether we like it or not, space-fans, I think it is obvious that we are pondering a much more complicated formula. It appears to me as if the abduction scenario could be equated to the moving bump twitching under the blanket of culture; pretending to be a mouse for the cat's amusement. I think we need to define who or what the cat and mouse are instead of being mesmerized by the bump move around under the covers.

It is apparent to me that individual human front-loading has coalesced into a belief structure that has been programmed into experiencers by their environment. It has probably always been this way. This 'wanting to believe' inclination that humans possess potentially becomes a causal factor behind the individualized manifestations of many paranormal occurrences. Why certain individuals are selected, and why cliché medical experiments continue to be reported will always be puzzling. Something about the entire subject of abductions is askew. It makes sense that we should rethink our approach to the conundrum and use an Occam's Razor to shave away all closed-system, earth-bound explanations before jumping toward more high-strange off-planet conclusions.

Patients who have been diagnosed with temporal lobe epilepsy have produced interesting experiential data that suggests certain manifestations of their affliction could be interpreted as alien-like abduction experiences. New Mexico researchers Richard Rowland and Carolyn-Duce-Ash's work in the mid-1990s comes to mind.

I hate to be the one to tell you, but Jacques Vallee (and other more progressive thinkers in the field, like David Perkins) may be right after all: it appears we may be pondering an ancient methodical process far beyond our comprehension. Whatever this process might be, this manipulation of our overall, cultural reality view may be responsible for many important aspects of basic human belief. Many researchers have pointed out that abductions and other encounters with "ETs" may be a modern version of a form of misunderstood contact with "the gods" or other forms of divine so-called "higher beings." This makes sense as these countless encounters appear to have been experienced by humans for thousands of years. Manifestations of this gradual layering of experience may provide potential clues to what we are attempting to define. Something that lies beyond religion and belief?

It makes sense to me that hot-spot regions, haunted sites and what some call portal areas could be the wisest investment of our investigative resources. There are apparently targeted individuals who appear to have been marked for other-worldly-style interest and they are obviously perfect experimental subjects for gathering valid empirical data. For instance, W. C. Levengood proposed an idea in the late 1990s that I feel has merit; why not conduct controlled experiments and suspend ungerminated seeds on select "abductees." It would take time and the entire effort would should be stringently monitored and results replicated to be taken seriously. We need to get creative, folks!

The so-called abduction phenomenon appears to exist in a netherworld of select, front-loaded experiences of "special destiny" individuals in our culture. A certain portion of modern culture appears to be in the thrall of these disseminated experiences and this may be impacting the rest of us. Since the eighties we have seen the advent and spread of the North-American description of the almond-eyed, "grey" alien archetype. These descriptions of "greys" were virtually unheard of outside of the United States until the late-eighties release of Whitley Strieber's *Communion* and the striking alien face that graced the cover.

Now most parts of the world have reports of these beings, where as, twenty five years ago, A subtle programmed version of abduction reality appears to be manifesting, under different guises of cultural interpretation of, what we assume is otherworldly, or divine.

Has the spread of these archetypes in the past been dictated by the church and now, in the modern age, by the media? There is no doubt to me that that this cultural meme of the *Communion*-style alien has established its ugly, bald head into Culture. We would be advised, this alien image focuses on a stylized interpretative view of these perceived "aliens," it does not define their true nature or any agenda behind the image.

For the record, I've never come to grips with my own strange visitation-style experiences beginning at age six that I suspect had a modicum of paranormal reality and I have politely refused offers from several (over?)qualified hypno-therapists to be "regressed."

Careful Where You Dig

The Fall of 1998 and the winter of 1999 found the SLV's activity tanking dramatically. Looking back through my data base I immediately notice what appears to be a complete cessation of unexplained aerial object sightings and unusual livestock deaths.

So, I began an in-depth look into alleged underground bases said to exist along the Colorado—New Mexico border. In 1991 I became involved with a group of SLV businessmen who enlisted my help to launch a local SLV television station. Unfortunately, we were never able to pry start-up capital out of the rich potato farmers that we approached. After six months and hundreds of unpaid hours, we finally shelved the project. I kept in loose touch with the group and in the Fall of 1998, one of them called with a peculiar story. It seemed that a childhood friend of his was moving out of the valley the following day and wanted to talk with me. He got on the phone and told me a rather intense account of a local "militia" group that had somehow stumbled on/discovered an underground base in the valley. They allegedly spent weeks documenting the comings and goings; compromised a worker and compiled a dossier that they presented to the authorities. The information was immediately sent up the food chain and an investigator was sent a to meet with the group. The agent allegedly turned up mysteriously dead—his body "thrown down a well." My solitary source was convinced that this death was a warning and he was was moving his family out of the valley the following day.

Now I realize this is an uncorroborated story, but several details of his account came from a reputable local source and it also confirmed several other snippets and clues I had uncovered concerning the subject of "underground bases." I began to dig into the subject in earnest. Several weeks later, in November 1998 our house as apparently visited by person(s) unknown who rifled through my files. They didn't attempt to hide the fact that they had been there. I found pictures off the wall, maps unrolled and left on the floor of my office, I ended up missing more photographs and most of my official law enforcement documentations from the Great Sand Dunes Rangers and several Sheriffs' reports from the mid-seventies disappeared around this time period. I never made an "official" report but quietly communicated my displeasure.

After several years of high-visibility in the Valley and in the media I began to occasionally wonder whether I had attracted any close attention to my activities besides collegues and fans. I never gave it much thought really, I just assumed that this was so. Except for the strange event of the car following me witnessed by my brother out on Highway 17 and a couple of suspicious visitors I had never been given any reason to think anyone was watching me, or, for that matter cared at all about my investigative work. But after our uninvited visitors, I knew I could not subject Isadora and Brisa to spooky attention, so I suggested it would be prudent if I moved out. Although Isadora didn't say this, I could sense that the prior six years of craziness was getting old and she wasn't having fun living with a extremely motivated and busy investigator who was hardly ever home. I quickly found a place to relocate and Isadora and I casually parted on friendly terms.

After a brief stint out at the White Eagle Inn I moved out to a rental house in the Baca Grants that conveniently sat on the western edge of a zone that featured the strange localized boom reports and portal-type activity i.e., "prairie dragons," and strange orbs. My nearest neighbor a quarter-mile away lived in the house where groups of diminutive beings wearing "keystone cop" type hats and dozens of prairie dragons were routinely reported during the several years prior. Soon after moving to this spectacular lookout site, I began to experience strange inexplicable events. One of the first events featured a rapid loud rapping sound that made a cumnambulation of the house in mere seconds, then November 10, 1999 at dusk, 6:20 p.m., I observed a six foot tall form move from left-to-right across the front of a large plate glass window facing west. The form appeared to be about ten feet away as it glided across my field of view and I thought I saw deer-like antlers on its head. Later that same evening at 11:30 p.m., a friend and I observed a prairie dragon-like form enter the porch through the dog door. A third witness simultaneously saw a "beige form enter" through the dog door, which was only two feet away from us, and rheard what sounded like a "whine."

The St. Martin's publicity machine was in full swing for my second book *Enter The Valley* and I was slated to appear on a big Colorado Springs heavy metal radio station for an early morning, drive time interview. Later that same day I was featured across town at a major book store chain book signing. Because of the three hour drive, I had to get up at the ungoldy time of three in the morning. The alarm clock rang and I grabbed my already packed bags and headed down the stairs into the dark first floor living room. As I hit the bottom of the stairs I felt a pecular presence outside. It is hard to describe it know, but it was like a huge slow breathing, and a large slow envelope opening and closing. Puzzled, I groped in the dark for my trusty one million candlepower spotlight I kept at the door. I quietly wntered through the sun-porch door and stepped out to the back door. Slowly opening the door I clicked the spotlight on and illuminated hundreds of pairs of fiery orange pin-points of light that extended as far as I could see. As my eyes focused, in a single motion the entire Baca Ranch elk herd stood up and as I swept the light around the lush meadowland that surrounded the house, the herd thundered away across the grants toward the Ranch. I'll never forget the sound of hunderds of elk booming away, snorting their displeasue at being so rudely rousted.

I was wide awake and forgot about Mr. Coffee. I headed to the Springs for my book signing with the Sangres, to the east— back lit by the emerging day. While I was away that day, a Del Norte, resident called to ask me if "anything unusual has been going on?" He nonchalantly mentioned on my answering machine watching a "...table rising two feet off the living room floor for several seconds." He also mentioned seeing "strange shadows going across the wall." The witness seemed almost embarrassed but was sincere and I have no reason to disbelieve this report in light of the day's activities.

That same day at approximately the same time, 3:00 p.m. A large silent unmarked white aerial craft was reported "gliding" south-to-north up the Northern San Luis Valley. "There was something weird about it, I should have heard something." the witness remarked. It was really low--maybe three thousand feet above the valley floor and I couldn't see any wings, just the vertical tail." At 3:15 p.m., I was returning from Colorado Springs on Highway 285, near Johnson's Village when I observed an unusual-looking silent, white craft that did not appear to have wings. It was headed north by northwest, up the upper Arkansas River Valley headed toward Antero Reservoir in South Park. I estimated its altitude at twenty-five hundred feet. I was intrigued enough to pull over and get out of the car to observe it with binoculars. I thought it was strange and was greeted by the additional high-strangness report on my answering machine as I arrived home at 4:30. That same night between 6:15 —7:30 p.m., Bonanza, residents Mary and Roger Osmond reported watching a very bright pulsating light hovering just south of Salida. They described it as being like a "brilliant strobe light, pulsing red, white and blue." The Osmonds contacted a neighbor who also observed the patriotic object(s). Mary estimated the large light's size as "three times as bright as Venus." They also observed the light "going up and down," when it was joined by "three smaller blinking white lights that almost looked like satellites." They were 'milling around the larger light" before they accompanied the larger light slowly off to the northeast at around 7:15 p.m.

Naia

It was during this fall 1999 time period that I researched and wrote a proposal for *Stalking The Herd* which I envisioned as being the first definitive text book on the cattle mutilation phenomenon and how human's ancient relationship with cattle may be directly involved in what was responsible for the scourge of mutilations that have plagued the pastures of the Christian world. My agent in NYC was pumped and had already recieved some verbal interest in the proposal. She sent it off to twenty-three of the largest publishing houses and assured me it would be picked up. She was on a 13 and 0 placement winning streak for her past thirteen submissions and was extremely surprised, even baffled when the proposal was promptly rejected by every one of them. I noticed that almost all of the rejection letters used the word "fear" or "afraid" in their pass letters, as in "I'm afraid we'll have to pass as this title is not right for our list..." Hmm. Both Janet and I knew the subject matter was compelling and was well presented but perhaps humankind's relationship with cattle is *too* compelling and scary. Evidently the editors decided that this is a closet subject that most beef-eaters should not know about. Oh well, someday, someone will see the importance of this title and offer to publish it. Or, I'll end up self-publishing it myself.

Immediately after the rejection of the cattle mutilation book proposal, I changed tack, drafted a proposal for a video documentary that focuses on a wide-reaching expose of cattle and their role in culture Everywhere, Spain, Argentina, India. Made a couple of calls. It is inevitable; this documantary will made—if not by me by somebody else. As fate would have it, my idea caught the attention of a wealthy woman in NYC. She was referred to me by two members of a well-connected family in the Baca.

At the time, it all seemed so concedental and in the flow but I wonder now what that was all about. I was headed to NYC for a book signing and a multi-tasked whirlwind visit with family and old friends. so a last-minute meeting was conveniently arranged. She was described as wealthy insider; a mover and shaker in-the-know. Sounded good to me—perfect timing, several birds with one stone. I was slated for gig back in Colorado on December 20th so I had just enough time to pull the it all off.

I traveled to NY to meet with this casually referred contact. The city had a hard clean Guilliani smile and I saw a store owner scraping bubblegum off the sidewalk in front of his Fifth Avenue sidewalk. I was impressed. Instead of flop houses and questionable impressions I found Disney and Red Lobster in Times Square. Just up Seventh Avenue I had a book-sgning and family and friends I was scheduled to visit in Manhatten, New Jersey and the Bronx.

The day before I returned I met the mystery woman at the St. Regis Hotel. Our mutual friends had a glow about them as well and the snifters and flambe further illuminated the reparte. We talked and quipped about everything but unusual livestock deaths and video projects. At one point "people of color" and soon after the term "useless eaters" loomed as descriptive terms. I looked over at Chris who had many friends of color and she blanched. The atmosphere plunged a couple degrees and woman then urged me to "boost my immune system" and make sure I left Manhatten before the Y2K celebration to take place in less than two weeks in Times Square. Before I left, she gave me two bottles of an immune system booster. I still have the unopened bottles and the label is mostly in Chinese but the front reads:

> Aquamax is a remarkable mineral ion product made from totally natural resourses (sic) such as prunes, peaches, walnuts and eggshells. Aquamax would sure help (sic) any firm to step ahead of the competitives (sic) in certain industries.

The subject of next year's election came up with the woman assuring me that "Bush will be elected next year." She scoffed at any aside I made to the contrary. Her insider manner seemed subtle but *wink* in the know. OK. I chose not to comment or argue and her ethnocentric asides dashed any lust for result I may have imagined before meeting her. But the glass should be full.I left a copy of my proposal with her assistant and flew back to my empty pantry unsure of what had happened the night before in New Rome. The woman whined and dined me but never did officially respond to my expose proposal.

I arrived back just in time to dash back to the Baca to engineer a live recording of the Crestone Community Choir live Christmas program from the Colorado College Annex I tried to make time to stock up inpreparation to Y2K but decided it wasn't important. The third week of Dccmeber 1999 found Y2K hysteria at its height. Several months earlier I had been nominated as Head of Security. I knew instantly, at the time that this would be the only Y2k Preparedness Group meeting I would ever attend.

As I recoverd the following day after a blessed night's sleep with no rest for almost three days, a nondescript white car turned off the exposed dirt road and bounced down the driveway of my crow's nest vantage point—looking across the Baca Ranch to the northern San Luis Lakes. Virginia plates "HAPPY2BE. I cringed, who is this? My first thought was "wow, those agency guys work fast!"

Naw.

Out of the car stepped the latest Baca arrival "Naia." She had arrived in town that day and had been invited by my absentee-roommate, Barry Monroe to crash on my couch until her rental property came available the following day. Seven years later I smile when I think back on that bleary-eyed afternoon; Naia and I have been together for seven-plus years.

Grandfather Martin of the Hopi and Naia Sept 2001

The Carmalite Monastary, at the Baca Grande

Prairie Dragon Curve, Road T, Baca Grande

Looking over the Baca Grants "portal" area toward the Sangres

Rare view of the Great Sand Dunes from the Baca Ranch

CHAPTER THIRTEEN:
Analyzing the Mystery

"Everything you believe is wrong…but I like your enthusiasm," stated David Perkins with his over thirty years of first hand experience investigating and researching cattle mutilations. "Izzy Zane," as his investigator buddies call him, spoke with me at length during a visit to his mountain top home in the third week of June, 1994. He stated emphatically (much to his chagrin now), "We're dealing with a reflective phenomenon that has no answers; we won't ever figure it out!"

After almost fifteen years of bull dogging the "cattle mutilation" phenomenon, I must reluctantly agree that Perkins' assertion may be true; however, today, I can say that I feel somewhat less confused about the mystery. Instead of giving up the quest, I'm even more motivated to prove him wrong. Izzy and I have spent the past thirteen-plus years headin' and heelin' the data and formulating potential answers for this perplexing, misunderstood mystery that defies conventional wisdom. His steady determination and creative thinking have been invaluable to my analytical thinking process over the years. In my estimation, his unsung-hero insight stands head, horns and shoulders above that of the rest of the research community herd.

Post modern manifestations of paranormal events and the resulting effect these events have on the culture within which they occur is a highly controversial subject. Culturally, these events are socially deconstructive and/or antistructural in nature and are the bane of academia and bureaucratic control systems. Culturally-taboo, low-status subjects such as manifestations of psi energy i.e., psychokinesis, clairvoyance, spontaneous healings, religious miracles, ghosts, phantasmal/spectral manifestations, and other unexplained "paranormal" subjects such as mutes and UFOs could be called "Trickster" elements within postmodern society. For thousands of years shamans and healers held exalted status within their social systems, but they have been relegated to the fringe element on the edge the "great unwashed masses." This "low-status" designation defines not only the social peril that goes along with expressing even the slightest interest in these subjects, but it perfectly illustrates the many difficulties toward making any sort of demonstrable headway toward a definition of meaning. George P. Hanson, in his seminal work *The Trickster and the Paranormal,* insightfully points out:

> The problem of meaning is central to deconstructivism and other strands of postmodernism. These movements challenge the notions of rationality and objective reality. The resulting reaction of the establishment is instructive. The furious denunciation of postmodernism in academe by status-conscious, high-verbal, aging white males are exceeded in intensity only by their frantic utterings of rationalistic incantations to ward off the paranormal... Both deconstructivism and psi subvert the rational, and there are similar, important consequences to both.

Oh well, I suppose it goes with the territory out there on the range. This "low-status" element has been somewhat problematic for this investigator, but not overly so, for if an open-minded billionaire, albeit an elite-class black sheep, recognized the importance of this work, maybe the scenario is changing and there is hope.

So where do we begin, space fanz? When analyzing any series of events, it makes sense to first look for patterns. Sometimes perceived patterns will indicate potential trends, but, even though paranormal researchers and investigators invariably uncover patterns that help to confirm their various theories, the UAD phenomenon seems to counter all attempts to analyze and pattern it, supplying data to both affirm and negate all possible scenarios. Recognizing a pattern seems to doom it to failure. For instance: I noticed a strange correlation of events occurring on the thirtieth of every month for almost an entire year. Boy was I excited! A couple of weeks later, the thirtieth rolled around and ... nothing! Not only was the pattern broken but from that point on the thirtieth was devoid of reports for the next six months. It would appear that one theory only works as well as another theory, which only works as well as yet another. What does this self-negating aspect of the subject suggest? Is it scientifically possible for a measurable, physical manifestation not to have a "cause" to account for the "effect?" This slippery, self-negating factor is one of the main stumbling blocks to UAD, UFO and paranormal research/ investigation. This calibrated trickster element also appears woven in and around interest in these phenomena, and this anti structural component appears to reside at the bloody heart of the so-called "cattle mutilation" phenomenon.

406

Some Probables in the UAD Phenomenon

OK, let's begin our analysis with our friend the cow. Here is your typical "cattle mutilation" scenario:

When a UAD occurs and is subsequently discovered by the owner, the first phone call is usually placed by the distraught rancher to his local sheriff, who is, and always has been, rendered impotent by the parameters of the phenomenon. The sheriff then calls a government agency that claims no knowledge of the phenomenon, and offers no answers or recourse to explain the unexplained physical event. This non-response further solidifies the local law enforcement official's feeling of societal impotence. Importantly, this lack of help or interest effectively negates his law enforcement "protector" role in the rural community where the death occurs. The sheriff can then do nothing but go into denial and downplay the report.

Often, mystery helicopters are seen in and around UAD sites, further frustrating law officers and ranchers, reinforcing the impression that "the government" *must* be involved in the death. The rancher then calls friends, neighbors and relatives, starting a chain reaction of disclosure and response by dozens of people: second; third; and fourth-hand accounts are generated.

The local media only hears of and reports a portion of these animal deaths. The regional media only reports a series or outbreak of deaths. The national media only carries ongoing waves of UAD reports across wide swathes of the countryside.

It is hard to feel the subtle undercurrent of fear experienced by mostly poor, subsistence ranchers and their families day-to-day, and it's no wonder a sizable percentage of UFO sightings and UADs probably go unreported. It has become obvious to me that we are witnessing what appears to be a systematic mythologic conditioning program with the lid of disclosure—media coverage, bouncing on and off the phenomenon. This self-negating feedback loop of inaction is conditioning most of our law enforcement system (and our perception of it) to feel helpless in the face of "the unknown." This may be a crucially important fact. The phenomenon (and the agenda behind it) seems to be toying with our social protective structure leaving our law enforcement officials with a feeling of vulnerability and without recourse, a fact which most in the top rungs of society refuse to acknowledge. As a direct result of this impotence, these protectors are helping perpetuate the mystery by simply deying the validity of its existence.

One could easily envision some frightening scenarios as to why someone or something is programming a perception of impotence into our protection structure, staging the phenomena in select rural areas and letting the subliminal impact of the inexplicable events filter into mainstream cultural consciousness through the media.

But why in select rural areas? That's where the cattle live but many rural ranching areas escape the scourge. Why the SLV? As I mentioned in my first two books, this wondrous locale could be described as a perfect laboratory, one of the only pristine areas left in the continental United States. This hidden valley at the top of North America is the perfect location for a monitored control group of experimental subjects—bovine and otherwise. Another possible explanation could be that the inhabitants of remote areas—like the SLV—and the inherent isolation that rural residents experience may indicate that they are potentially more susceptible to mythologic and/or psychotronic programming agendas. But, is this isolation a sufficient rationale for the SLV to be targeted? I personally intuit that the SLV, whether area residents like it or not, has been targeted by someone or something; I've said for years that this particular region is a perfect sociological "Petri dish."

Let's continue the analytical process and attempt to define what we can surmise are the givens within the mute phenomenon.

• A true Unusual Animal Death is a real, measurable, blood-based phenomenal event.
  • There are true inexplicable UAD cases that defy the known laws of science and are, by definition, impossible to perpetrate, yet they are reported.
• A percentage of UADs are occurring with the aid of high-technology such as high heat.
  • Soft-tissue body parts are excised.
  • The number of UAD reports increases in areas where the media has publicized other UAD reports.
  • A sizable percentage of these subsequent UAD reports are misidentified scavenger action or other mundane phenomena.
  • The government, or a faction thereof, has not disclosed the full extent of its knowledge concerning the UAD phenomenon and appears to be actively engaged in undisclosed aspects of the phenomena.
  • There are very few, if any, additional clues ever present at a UAD site and as a result, no one has ever been officially charged or convicted with perpetrating a UAD.
  • Helicopters or UFOs are sometimes seen around UAD sites.
• Certain specific, well-defined (rural) areas are more prone to be hit than others.

408

• Certain ranches are hit repeatedly.
• There appears to me to be more than one group and/or agenda involved.

Even assuming that a majority of UAD and UFO reports have natural explanations, i.e., predators and lightning, we are still left with a sizable percentage which are unexplained. First off, there are several historic elements that may be important that need to be addressed. Paranormal phenomena have always existed alongside humankind. Angels, demons, ghosts, spirits, jinn, fairies and trolls have always been with us, couched in the technology and culture of the times, as pointed out insightfully by astrophysicist/computer scientist Jacques Valleé in his book *Dimensions*. (Valleé, a preeminent ufologist was the real-life model for the French scientist "Lacome" in Steven Spielberg's film *Close Encounters of the Third Kind*.)

The UAD phenomenon appears to be a new face (high technology) on an age-old mystery that could be, in part, responsible for man's ancient practice of animal sacrifice. It stands to reason that an ancient rancher would rather sacrifice an old or sick animal than wake up in the morning to find his prized breeding stock or seed bull dead.

The UFO phenomenon should be linked to Ezekiel's Wheel, the descent of the Blessed Virgin Mary at Lourdes, and countless other reported historical examples of the descent of superior beings. If this is so, various groups today in the twenty-first century appear to be capitalizing on (mis)perception of what may be ancient anomalies. Pursuing their own current agendas, they could be called masters of deception.

There is a small percentage of true UADs and true UFO sightings that I describe as The Real Thing. They are the UADs and sightings that are, by definition, physically unsolvable and may tie in to the ancient history of the paranormal. The vast majority of UADs, however, seem to be perpetrated for different sociological, political and scientific reasons by human groups who I believe became directly involved in fostering deception in 1947, with the advent of the modern UFO era, and in 1973, with the introduction of the "cattle mutilation" meme into our cultural mythos.

Probable human involvement in perpetrating these mysteries has deflected serious investigation and disclosure of the phenomenon by dedicated investigators. It's probable that the very belief that "the government knows more than it's admitting" is being manipulated cleverly by these so-called "masters of deception."

There is circumstantial evidence to support the conclusion that our government, or a faction thereof, may be actively engaged in a program involving a multi-level process of societal, political, scientific and/or mythologic manipulation of an unsuspecting public. It is conceivable that the government is capitalizing on the true nature of the Real Thing while pursuing its own agenda. It is also highly probable that this group or groups within the government is simultaneously hiding the Real Thing by imitating it. But, no matter how convenient, it is disingenuous to suggest that the government is unilaterally responsible for UADs and UFOs.

A Blood-Based Mystery

As I have suggested, the ultimate core truth behind the UAD phenomenon may have been first experienced by social groups in ancient times. In our scrutiny of the core of the phenomenon, it appeared some sort of as-yet-undefined predatory presence decided to begin the modern, publicized era of the UAD phenomenon on the King Ranch in 1967. Could this predator have existed alongside humankind for thousands of years, mocking our attempts at proving its existence and agenda by hiding its true nature and purpose behind a veil of religion, magic, superstition and manipulation of this veil of plausible deniability? David Perkins has spent over thirty years chasing this preditory presence and he has come to the conclusion the "Gaia" may be directly involved in perpetrating the phenomenon. Perhaps he is on the right track. Gaia may be triggering a collective human subconscious warning that is manifesting as cattle mutilations. Perhaps Gaia is using us to warn ourselves about cattle and their detrimental impact on Gaia's delicate ecosystems. If this Gaia-based scenario is true, one would hope we haven't passed a point of no return.

By definition, UADs are a blood-based phenomenon and modern day blood-based belief systems can still be found in many primitive cultures that exist in remote areas of the planet. Sorcerers in South Africa still create powerful "muti" out of animal blood and glandular tissue, as a ritualistic receptacles of will, that are used against perceived enemies. In the US alone, there are around 800,000 followers of Santaria, a Christianized form of pantheistic worship with its roots in the west African Yoruba Tribe, who use chickens and goats for ritual religious animal sacrifice. Santaria's numbers are growing. Voodoo and Macumba are other ritualistic belief systems are also attracting more and more followers here and in South America.

The United States Supreme Court overturned a Hialeah, FL, ban on animal sacrifice, which opened the door to the legal sacrificing of animals for religious purposes by the estimated one million people who have been involved in doing so in the United States. Santaria also has a curious feature that involves the drawing down of various deities (through rhythmic drumming and blood sacrifice) to "mount" special participants. The god (one of twelve different orishas) then controls the motor functions of a specific person who has abandoned him or herself to the deity in ecstatic frenzy. The roots of this occult form of belief system are ancient and primitive but what happens when you bring high-technology into the equation? A researcher passed along the following "what if" speculation to researcher Tom Adams in 1978.

What if there existed an organization which dabbled in the headier realms of 'Black Magic?' What if they succeeded in creating a 'thought form', a very powerful entity brought into being by sheer force of will, couched in ritual and agreement among these occultists, who were impressively powerful and proficient themselves. Perhaps things got a little out of hand when the 'thought form' became too powerful to control and began demanding 'blood sacrifice' and, again, life essence. Both magic and technology, a powerful combination, might be employed to obtain the life force of animal victims to be fed to an increasingly powerful 'thought form.' Undoubtedly the hope would be that this 'thought form' would remain satisfied with the life force of lower animals, without developing a 'taste' for it's creators.

As I've mentioned in my other books, the virtual match between cattle and human hemoglobin may be a crucial clue toward understanding the puzzle-box. I will return to this subject in a minute, but first lets look at ritual blood as it has been venerated for thousands of years. Blood has always been used and recognized as a powerful, mystical substance and the Western esoteric tradition contains oft-overlooked blood-based elements and several belief systems that still use blood in an occult manner. The transubstantiation of wine into "The Blood of Christ" in the Catholic Mass could have even deeper, more hidden significance if looked at in this hypothetical "pagan" context. The Hebraic tradition of Passover, with the story of "The Angel of Death" passing over houses of the Jews who put lamb's blood over their doors, sparing the families first-born, also has a curious "blood-based" tradition.

It appears that our theoretical "thought form" mentioned above may have attempted to manifest itself into culture at key historical moments as an alien/divine presence. This alien or divine-appearing presence seems to have its own peculiar hidden objective; it is highly selective; adapts to the times and has always had what could be described as an arrogant veneer of impunity. But what form does this hidden objective take on today and what is the real agenda?

Linda Moulton Howe, the most visible of all UAD "experts," put forward an argument for the extraterrestrial hypothesis to explain cattle mutilations in her 1988 book *An Alien Harvest*. Many paranormal researchers share her suspicion that extraterrestrials are directly responsible for true UADs. Pop culture theories have been suggested that ETs require cattle blood and glandular material for a variety of reasons: as a food source and/or for medicinal use and/or genetic engineering. Sounds more believable than New Mexico crashed aliens craving "strawberry ice-cream" while being held captive by Uncle Sam's agents. But something about this anthropomorphic line of hypothetical thinking doesn't make sense to me. For instance, if the animal tissue is being gathered for food, why would they usually harvest only one eye or one ear? This question also holds for tissue supposedly gathered for medicinal/genetic use. If ETs are conducting genetic engineering, why are they so grossly indiscreet? Certainly, animals could be more easily harvested in Third-World countries with less media attention and official capability for humans to investigate. If it is blood and bodily fluids they are after why don't they gather the liquid refuse found at your local slaughterhouse? If, as some suspect, our government is involved in genetic experimentation, for reasons unknown, why would they use your tax dollars employ all that high-tech equipment to steal animal parts from private ranchers instead of buying its own herds and graze them out at Area 51 or some other classified area, out of sight, out of mind? The bottom line is that every single theory you can propose gives rise to more and more questions that negate all possible theories, regardless of their possible validity.

A vast majority of my two-hundred or so UAD cases feature incisions that appear to be caused by a sharp cutting instrument—like a scalpel or knife—not high heat. Contrary to popular belief, although there are more than a handful of cases on-record that appear to have been caused by some sort of lasing instrument, these are the exceptions not the norm. This may be a critical clue. It is also important to note that most cases have not been drained of blood as popularly thought. There are also a surprising number of cases that feature bullet wounds found in the carcasses.

You probably notice that my thinking flies in the face of more conventional, unconventional thinking. In case you haven't figured this out by now, there is a much more complicated scenario at work at the heart of the mutilation mystery that involves some

412

sort of as-yet unknown agenda. There appears to be a subtle conditioning process at work. I know this might be disturbing to some readers, but, for the sake of argument, could ritual blood sacrifice be somehow involved in some of these unusual animal deaths? As I've mentioned, for years I have strongly suspected that a portion of these cattle death cases involve human perpetrators. If this is so, what could possibly be their less than holy motivation? If ritual is somehow involved, can we surmise that aspects of this process, with its roots in prehistory, are being enacted to supplicate or appease my hypothetical, supernatural predatory presence; a presence that may be responsible for the most high-strange cases? Are human agents reacting to a shadowy predatory form that appears extraterrestrial in nature but may be *as terrestrial as we are?* Occam's Razor suggests we eliminate all terrestrial scenarios before looking off-planet.

Serial Crime Spree of the Century

Tom Reed manages a large cattle spread, north of Questa, NM just below the border with Colorado. His mundane ranching job continues to expose him to this high-strange, Western legend most cowboys in New Mexico, and elsewhere, have heard about but never directly experienced. The few that will talk about "cattle mutilations" shrug their shoulders and scratch their heads before declaring "it's the government," or maybe "cults," or (privately) some ranchers who have experienced high-strange cases mention "aliens" but most ranchers think it's "a bunch of BS." Reed's sprawling remote workplace—the five thousand acre Tres Ritos Ranch, has been the targeted site of upwards of fifty unexplained cattle death reports since 1993, and what makes this ranch's saga most intriguing are several early 1990s reports that featured attendant occult-based ritual signs in and around the mutilation site. So-called "devil-worship" devices were discovered in conjunction with carcass of the first "mutilated" animals as it lay in the glowering shadow of 10,093 foot Ute Mountain. The first three mutilated cattle exhibited no apparent cause of death. They were discovered missing various soft tissue organs, and investigating New Mexico State Patrol officers and forensic scientists are still at a loss to explain these (and many other) unusual livestock death reports. Reed, on the front line of this mystery, has became so frightened by what he describes as "satanic" elements in these early cases, he has become a devout born-again Christian.

Discovery of occult evidence at a cattle mutilation site is extremely rare. Reeds' Tres Ritos conundrum represents one of just a handful of cases justifying the popular and widespread

413

1970's media speculation unexplained cattle deaths to occult or "satanic" cult activity. This fact may be crucial as no other official US reports in the 1990s, to my knowledge, feature occult-based ritual evidence tied by law enforcement and ranchers to a crime-scene. For perspective, in recent years, a miniscule percentage of the estimated fifty thousand ranching operations in the United States have reported (an estimated) 2,000 suspected cases of unexplained animal deaths per year. No one knows how many real cases actually occur and the actual numbers are probably higher than official numbers suggest.

Long-time researchers of the UAD phenomenon have come up with several theories concerning possible culpable parties and their agendas. There are several manuscripts gathering dust, completed years ago, pertaining to the UAD question that will probably remained unpublished. Jacques Valleé spent two years investigating UADs in the 1970s yet he is unwilling to release his findings. He states in his book *Confrontations*:

> Another domain I have explored concerns cattle mutilations. Over a two-year period I interviewed ranchers, veterinarians, and law enforcement officials in Arkansas, Missouri, and Kansas. Today a number of the episodes I investigated are still unexplained. They may have a direct relationship to the UFO phenomenon. Because I cannot yet prove this relationship, I have decided not to burden the reader with what may be irrelevant data. But the entire subject remains very much open in my own mind, even if the UFO research community, except for a few courageous investigators, prefers to sweep it under the rug and keep it there.

Perhaps the ever-mounting circumstantial evidence connecting the government, or a faction thereof, to a sizable percentage of these animal deaths is discouraging investigators from disclosing the connection. Valleé goes on to state his suspicions concerning the potential for abuse in the UFO controversy:

> Like many of my colleagues in the field, I have become convinced that the US Government, as well as other governments, are very involved in the UFO business …The belief in extra-terrestrials, like any other strong belief, is an attractive vehicle for some sort of mind control and psychological warfare activities.

A sobering thought. Is it too fantastic to suggest the possibility

414

of the government's role going even further, into the realm of societal or military control mechanisms being engineered and administered through beef, a primary food source?

Now let's examine cattle's ecological impact on the planet. Without question, the livestock sector is one of the top two or three most significant contributors to our most serious global environmental problems. In December 2006, the United Nations published a report on the effect of livestock on the environment with the following startling conclusion: Livestock production accounts for more greenhouse gases than automobiles. For every calorie of meat we consume, at least ten calories of fossil fuels were needed to produce that meat. Animal grazing takes up seventy percent of all agricultural land, and thirty percent of the land surface of the planet. Today, seventy percent of "slash and burned" Amazon rainforest is used for expanding pasturelands, and feed crops for livestock cover much of the remainder. The ultimate ramifications of the report suggest that the average American can do more to reduce global warming emissions by changing their beef-eating habits than by driving the most fuel efficient hybrid vehicle available today. Negative environmental impacts can be greatly reduced by reducing (or eliminating) beef consumption and/or buying locally grown and sustainably-produced meats, dairy and other animal products.

A Worldwide Phenomenon

We need to somehow convince top-level science to get involved in investigating the mutilation mystery. This mystery is apparently found throughout the Christian world and not in the middle or far East. Veterinarian pathologist Dr. George Onet, D.V.D, National Institute of Discovery Science (NIDS), made a rather sobering assessment in the NIDS abstract when he stated:.

> The incidence of animal mutilation cases is variable. They have been reported in different parts of the world, such as: Mexico, Panama, Puerto Rico, Brazil, England, Ireland, France, Germany, Sweden, Australia, Japan, the Canary Islands, Canada, and the United States...It is estimated that nationwide, [USA] there are at least two thousand a year.

After two decades of apparent disinterest and public denial, scientists are finally becoming directly involved in the process of investigation and analysis. But to what end? In the early 1990s

415

NIDS took an important first step and acknowledged there is a real "problem" out there on the range. NIDS founder, Las Vegas, NV real-estate tycoon Robert Bigelow, assembled a world-class team of scientists and investigators who contacted every ranching operation in the United States and conducted field and lab studies across the country to determine the true nature and extent of the unexplained livestock death phenomenon.

One thing is for certain: *If even a handful* of truly unexplained, high-strange animal deaths are being perpetrated, then the phenomenon is a tangibly real, blood-based phenomenon worthy of further investigation.

One NIDS mutilation study focused on the perplexing rampage experienced by Montana ranchers in the mid to late 1970s. Working with ex-Montana sheriff Keith Wolverton, NIDS attempted to analyze the outbreak of cattle deaths. David Perkins and I are puzzled why the study refused to address "over sixty other anomalies that were not included…" including Bigfoot lurking around in the neighborhood where mutilated cattle were discovered. One would think that this wrinkle would be important, but apparently is wasn't considered to the noteworthy to the NIDS team. Why is this? And for that matter, what the heck are Bigfoot doing around mutilation sites? Bigfoot have been reported to be associated with UADs in other locales, a spate of mutes and Bigfoot sightings in Missouri comes to mind. Bigfoot are a perfect illustration of a tricksterish factor that supplies a decontructive, self-negating element that may be attempting to render theses particular mute scenarios null and void.

Back to our in-depth analysis of ancient human belief systems centered around cattle. I have shown how the symbolic image of cattle has evolved, and it could immeasurably aid our current understanding of the cattle mutilation mystery as it blisters the modern age.

Cattle statistically account for a vast majority of reported unexplained animal death cases but a bewildering array of animal species, including humans, have been found in a similar mutilated manner. Why mostly cattle?

From Egypt to India, Africa to Spain, bovines have played an important role in cultural religious belief. The term "sacred cow" comes from India, where there are no Big Macs and cows are venerated—not eaten. White colored Brahma cows for a thousand years have been allowed to meander through cities and towns unencumbered, and the act of reverently hand feeding them as they obliviously wander by, is considered to bring a person good luck. This culturally sanctioned bovine-worship is unique to the Indian subcontinent. Brahma cows in India are rarely killed, instead they are milked and their dung patties are collected, dried and burned for fuel. By contrast, in today's America, Brahma bull's hindquarters are cinched-up tightly while courageous cowboys attempt to stay on their backs for eight seconds before being bucked off. It is interesting to note that I cannot find a single case of cattle mutilation from the Indian subcontinent.

In Africa and elsewhere cattle are an important symbol of wealth for all that the animals provide the particular tribe and its owners. Hathor, the ancient Egyptian cattle god, was revered for thousands of years in Egyptian culture and was considered the ancient mother goddess. Some images show her in her cow aspect, others show her with a human body and a bovine head. She was often depicted with an airborne disc between her horns. It was said Hathor is "the great celestial cow" responsible for creation of the world and all it contains; her milk, it was believed, "nourished all creation." The Minoan civilization worshipped the bull above all other god-forms, and the cattle cult of Mithra was the radical new belief system Christianity muscled aside to gain prominence in first century Rome.

Today, in Spain and Latin American countries, selectively pure bred bulls are raised to be ritualistically teased and then publicly slain in the arena by famous matadors wielding bloody swords, worshipped and revered by thousands of adoring fanatics. With its roots in pre-history, the role of cattle in humankind's ancient cultural belief systems and how these beliefs endure even today is worthy of note.

Our twenty-first century examination of our historical connection with cattle reveals important roots established before the dawn of civilization in ritual magic. There is the undeniable evidence that cattle and (other warm-blooded mammals) have, for thousands of years, been ritualistically slaughtered by priests, prophets and heroes and offered up to the gods. Predictably, cattle, which are considered the first species of domesticated livestock, play a prominent, pivotal role in the evolution of the ancient practice of animal sacrifice.

Sacred Cow: It's Not for Dinner

The role of the cow and bull as important religious symbols in the first known urban centers in early Near-Eastern and Mesopotamian civilizations, show how these god-forms and traditions continue to evolve today.

In the Caananite tradition, Ba'al (bull) and his sister Anat (cow) were both important god-forms, and (curiously) they were also incestuous lovers. And they were both (according to tradition) able to fly. Sumerian scholar Zecharia Sitchen points this out in his seminal work, *Stairway to Heaven:*

> The ability of the gods to fly about is accepted as a matter of course; and their haven [is] in "The Crest of Zaphon"...Ba'al's epithet is "The Rider of the Clouds.

Oh how the mighty have fallen. In today's global village, cattle's sacred, revered image and ancient symbolic preeminence has devolved to the point where these creatures are now kept in feed lots reminiscent of concentration camps. Thousands of years ago they flew, were revered, worshipped and honored in the East, but today in Western culture (except in the Judaic tradition), cattle and other livestock are mechanically slaughtered and processed *unceremoniously*, out of sight, behind bloody doors.

As the role of cattle in the practice of animal sacrifice is examined, the reader is reminded that the ancient urban cultures in the Americas (Olmec, Mayan, Toltec, Aztec, etc.) developed and practiced blood-based ritual sacrifice *without* warm-blooded livestock in their environment. They produced a viable, culturally excepted sacrificial alternative—each other.

The Americas today are the epicenter of the animal death mystery and these non-indigenous "unusual cattle deaths" represent a vast majority of reported cases worldwide. Since 2000, well over fifteen hundred cattle mutilations have been reported in the Americas, Argentina, in particular being hard hit. Several cases are worthy of note including a 60,000 gallon water tank being drained, and a mutilated cow (from the nearby herd) found inside the empty   container.

McEarth: You Are What You Eat

Today, who or what is behind the vast majority of millions of routine livestock deaths?   Carnivorous, beef-as-protein eating Western culture. At this point in our narrative the average hurried customer at Burger King would surely comment, "Huh? cattle mutilations?   Yeah right, so what's the big deal? ...they're just cows."   It's a valid argument and our whopper-eatin', protein consumer would be correct. Even with a well-versed understanding of our culture's relative codependence with cattle-as-a-protein source, a few thousand mysterious cattle deaths are certainly no big deal. But if its your cow, or your neighbor's cow, it would be an immediate problem.

Have you ever wondered how many burgers are fried at MacDonalds and other industrialized beef-based protein outlets each day? Or how many "ham" burgers are really being sold? Or how they keep the price so low? Or how a "hamburger" got its name? Do you know what constitutes Kosher meat? Do you know how veal is grown? Or how many pounds of grain or gallons of water it takes to raise a single pound of beef? Do you know how many head of cattle are physically slain each day on our planet? And slain under what circumstances? Do you know how many cows are co-existing with us here on the planet? The average person will never stop to ask themselves these questions while standing in line waiting for his Biggie Meal at Wendy's.

As we enter the twenty-first century we find millions of cattle butchered in the United States (and elsewhere) every year to help feed a growing, hungry population in need of protein. The piles of livestock carcasses are growing and the beef industry of slaughter, for the foreseeable future, will provide this expensive food source for western humankind. And the Third World is demanding more beef—the numbers of cattle being consumed are climbing as fast as subsidized beef prices in the United States plummeting. Huge United States-owned herds in South America andare Australia now number in the millions and, not surprisingly, there is a looming ecological downside to the insidious growth of beef consumption.

It has been determined by some scientists and environmentalists that cattle represent (one of) the most detrimental forces impacting the health of the earth's biosphere. Ozone-depleting, cattle produced methane gas, in its various forms, may be one of the most destructive natural elements impacting the Earth's protective ozone layer, and many square miles of rain forest are being razed every single day to produce more grazing land for the world's growing cattle herds.

Amid the clouds of cattle flatulence, a new health problem has been discovered lurking in bovine brain and nerve tissue. The outbreak of bovine spongiform encephalopathy (BSE), better known as "Mad Cow Disease," and chronic wasting disease (CWD) is an emerging medical concern. Self-replicating *prions*—a thousand times smaller than the smallest life form yet detected by man—are thought to be responsible for BSE. Other transmissible spongiform encephalopathies (TSEs), can survive in bone ash made from cremated livestock. The human form is known as Ctuetzfeld-Jacob's disease (CJD) and new variants of vCJD are fatal, wasting diseases in humans that make AIDS look like a mild cold.

As I have noted above, cattle hemoglobin, out of all the various types of blood in the animal kingdom, is the closest genetic match to human hemoglobin. Because of our reliance on beef as a viable protein source, we may literally be becoming what we have eaten for thousands of years. This incestuous symbiotic relationship is an important fact, and the implications of this crucial clue could be important when examining the cattle mutilation phenomenon.

Before That Horse was Snipped

Animal mutilations and the unfolding phenomenon of unusual warm-blooded animal deaths may be an important connecting element between humans and their ancient relationship with their livestock. There is evidence to suggest unexplained animal mutilations have been occurring around the world for hundreds, perhaps thousands of years. Worried Egyptian ranchers in the Middle Kingdom period, around 3000 BC, reportedly petitioned the sitting pharaoh to implore the priests to attempt to somehow stop (through rituals and prayer) the unwanted slaughter of cattle by the gods. In the sixteenth century, England's King James was said to have been asked to investigate unnatural rural English livestock slayings. And there are more examples down through history.

Some early to mid twentieth-century reports prior to Snippy include the report I received that described a close proximity sighting of an unusual disc-shaped object in 1949. The hunter, then a teenager, along with several adult hunters found a mutilated elk the following morning; right where the disc had seemed to descend and land in a clearing in the forest.

This case is from the 1930s. A Missouri farmer named Leon J. Sale wrote in a 1978 letter to Thomas Adams' *Stigma* (magazine):

> I don't remember the exact year, but it was either 1934 or '35 soon after I went to Missouri to live with my grandparents. We found a hog slaughtered in a mysterious way in a pasture after we had seen a shiny object flying over the farm at about tree-top level, and we thought it went down in the pasture across the creek from the house. By the time my grandfather and I walked over there it was gone, but there was a ring about twenty-five feet in radius burned in the grass and the hog was laying in the middle of it. At that time we had never heard of UFOs and I don't think my grandfather ever said anything to anyone about it.

Curiously, the storyline of the first Australian movie, *Haunt of the Billabong*— shot in 1902, featured a wave of mysterious sheep mutilations in New Zealand, currently the location of the world's largest sheep herds.

420

Wile E. Coyote's Debunker Friends

Early scientific involvement investigating the mystery occurred in several state diagnostic crime labs. What do results of testing in these early 1970s cases tell us? What did science postulate was responsible for a vast majority of mutilation claims? Who, or what , were crime lab directors singling out as the culpable parties? Meet Wile E. Coyote and his fine-feathered friends; crow and magpies and multi-legged varmits of every breed. As we will see, in most cases, the debunkers may be right, this phenomenon does contain much misidentification and misunderstanding. Importantly, however, this does not explain away all cases, but proves the total number of true, high-strange cases may be smaller than popularly thought.

Knowledgeable skeptics refute the true high-strange nature of a majority of unusual animal deaths and immediately cite Dr. Carl Whiteside, current head of the Colorado Bureau of Investigation, and former head of the CBI crime lab: "...out of eighty or so cases analyzed, only five showed signs of unusual cuts." They naysayers also quickly cite the 1980 Rommel Report, and James Stewart's paper "*Cattle Mutilations: An Episode of Collective Delusion*," that analyzed the rapid rise and rapid decrease in public interest measured by newspaper coverage ofthe mutilation flap in South Dakota and Nebraska. The author argued that these reports (and how they were generated by media coverage) were "classic examples of mild mass hysteria." According to the author, the damage to cattle carcasses was due to small "predatory animals," case closed.

How accurate is this conservative but highly effective scavenger-as-villain argument? There is hard- vidence supporting and in some cases, but I would refute the debunkers assertions that *all* cattle mutilations are due solely to miss-identified (unusual) scavenger action and media hype. Granted, in this author's estimation, a high percentage of animal "mutilations" are due to misperception of natural predation and/or catastrophic death and targeted scavenging, but, again, not *all* cases are so easily explained away.

The introduction of early hard-science testing in the mid-1970s quickly polarized law enforcement and rancher opinion across the west. One frustrated Colorado sheriff, after being officially told repeatedly that tested cattle from his county were being scavenged, actually resorted to grossly mutilating forensic hide samples with his own knife. The state crime lab returned results indicating a fox had caused the wounds and incisions. There hadn't been a fox seen in the county in "over one hundred years."

One study that was funded and conducted under "official"

421

auspices was the Rommel Investigation 1979-1980. Named after retired FBI investigator and Santa Fe' County district attorney Kenneth Rommel, who headed the probe, the investigation was allocated fifty thousand dollars to, once and for all, get to the bottom of the mutilation mystery that gripped the state in the late 1970s and baffled New Mexico State Police investigators. The results of Rommel's probe brought forth howls of indignation from civilian investigators and State Police investigators on the front line of the mystery. Rommel concluded that ninety-six cattle they exhaustively tested post mortem revealed only several that seemed to have been mutilated due to anything else but scavenging by Wile E. Coyote and friends. And Rommel didn't stop there. He blasted State Police investigation techniques and their resulting conclusions, and he pointed out a lack of understanding in the ranching communities that reported strange livestock deaths. He also cited irresponsible media coverage as a culprit.

The field of veterinarian pathology consistently shown a low key interest in these claims of mutilations, but why the reluctance by mainstream science to get publicly involved? There are difficulties applying the scientific method when investigating claims of unusual animal deaths and the doubly difficult task of getting ranchers to report cases in, a timely fashion. Depending on weather conditions, carcasses only stay pristine enough for collecting forensic samples for twenty-four to thirty-six hours. Typically a missing animal isn't located for two to three days and in most cases an official report is never even lodged. If, luckily, a report is filed, but samples are not acquired in time, the necrotic, rotting sample's arrival at the lab creates problems for post-mortem analysis, the most important being, nothing unequivocal can be ascertained. Due to the untimely nature of the few mutilation report filings, science has shown an understandable reluctance to get involved with unqualified civilian field investigators and smelly tissue samples.

Because the cow is already dead, ranchers most often don't report cases and/or, have a vet out to perform an onsite examination because, why spend more money on a lost investment? Add to this a serious lack of official interest and funding from the government, and the easiest way for all involved to "get rid of the problem" is to claim it doesn't exist in the first place. This appears to me to be an ingenious formula that attains cultural wave-cancellation. The role of local veterinarians presents another problem. Over the years, a few rural vets have shown interest in quietly investigating high-strange cases, but until recently, there has been no officially funded effort to pay for qualified field work and the establishment of rigorous scientific protocols.

As noted earlier, in the early to mid 1990s, a new well-funded scientific organization appeared on the ufology/mutology scene, The National Institute of Discovery Sciences (NIDS) was comprised of some of the best and brightest scientists in the country willing to study paranormal subjects such as exotic propulsion systems, life after death, UFOs and our irksome livestock deaths. With board members such as Dr. Jacques Vallee and Dr. Harold Puthof, NIDS publicly commenced a serious investigation of mutilation claims by North American ranchers and law enforcement.

Coordinated initially by veterinarian pathologist Dr. George Onet, NIDS' teams fanned out across the country following up on a mass mailing sent by the organization to every ranching operation in America. Finally, a well-funded, serious effort seemed to be underway staffed by reputable scientists and lab technicians. The small "mutology" community was abuzz over what appeared to be a major step forward toward legitimacy and credibility. But soon it became apparent to some that there were troubling circumstances looming under darkening skies.

NIDS founder Robert Bigelow is low key to the point of appearing secretive. Although many have looked, no known photographs of him have surfaced, and stories began to emerge concerning his fanatical avoidance of any and all publicity. One episode found the television program, *Strange Universe* sending a photographer to the dedication of a new science wing at UNLV—which was funded by Bigelow. The day following the public ceremony, *SU* called the photographer who told them, "'He made me an offer I couldn't refuse.'" Bigelow had bought his film and his silence— there were no photos or film for the TV segment. Several ex-intelligence operatives are said to be associated with NIDS and there are indications that the NIDS agenda is not exactly what it publicly appears to be.

However, their groundbreaking scientific paper *Unexplained Cattle Deaths and the Emergence of a Transmissible Spongiform Encephalopathy (TSE) Epidemic in North America* published in 2003 raises disturbing questions. The paper's abstract they state the following:

> Overall, the evidence suggests that animal mutilations are a long-term, covert, prion disease sampling operation by unknown perpetrators who are aware of a substantial contamination of the beef and venison food supply. Although this paper presents evidence in favor of a motive for animal mutilations, there is still insufficient evidence to identify the perpetrators.
>
> We present evidence that a correlation exists between reports of animal mutilation and the emergence of a Transmissible Spongiform Encephalopathy (TSE) epidemic

in North America.

We show that sharp instruments are used in animal mutilations. Our data contradict the conclusions of the 1980 Rommel Report that claimed predators and scavengers could explain reports of cattle mutilations.

Using data obtained from a NIDS nationwide survey of bovine veterinarian practitioners, we show that certain organs are preferentially removed during animal mutilations.

We focus attention on the temporal and geographical overlaps between the animal mutilation and TSE epidemics in NE Colorado. The most highly publicized TSE epidemic in North America, chronic wasting disease (CWD), emerged in NE Colorado in the late 1960s.

We show evidence in support of an epidemic of *prion* disease that is both subclinical in cattle and clinical in deer/ elk in North America.

We describe evidence from two laboratories that a number of *prion* diseases in humans are misdiagnosed as Alzheimer's disease and therefore currently escape detection.

The historical record shows that high levels of infectious TSEs were imported from New Guinea into research facilities at Fort Detrick and Bethesda, Maryland after 1958 and were used for intensive cross-species infectivity experiments.

We hypothesize that animal mutilations represent both a TSE-disease sampling operation on domestic animals AND a graphic warning that the beef and venison in the food chain is compromised...

The hypotheses described in this paper yield a number of testable predictions. Examining these predictions in the coming months and years is increasingly urgent because they have considerable public health implications ...[and] ...brought the issue of the contamination of the human food chain into sharper focus.

Former NIDS director Colm Kelleher is a biochemist with a twenty-year research career in cell and molecular biology. His work coordinating the NIDS study inspired him to dig even deeper into the possible link between the mutilations and the possible monitoring of Mad Cow Disease in the food chain. The results of his in-depth investigation can be found in his excellent but disturbing book, *Brain Trust*, which is a sobering medical detective story that traces the origin and spread of the deadly infectious prions that cause Mad Cow Disease as they jumped species and ended up in America's food supply. The book also shows how human Mad Cow Disease is hidden in the current epidemic of Alzheimer's Disease. He convincingly exposed the devastating truth about Mad Cow Disease, including his coverage of a second prion epidemic in the nation's deer, elk and other wildlife. *Brain Trust* attempts to inoculate Americans with an effective cure: The Truth.

Back in the 1997, I remember bouncing the possible linkage between Mad Cow with ex-Fyffe, Alabama police chief Ted Oliphant who has gone on to explore this frightening link for the past ten years. This subject is very troubling and echoes David Perkins discovery of what he recognized a potential "environmental monitoring" link he noticed thirty-years ago. Without question this avenue of thinking deserves much more investigation, research and media attention.

NIDS decided to abruptly close its doors in 2005 after eight years monitoring the enigmatic Sherman Ranch in Utah's Uintah Basin and ten years of investigating cattle mutilations. Izzy reminded me recently that they "got their butts kicked" by the mysteries they attempted to investigate for ten years. The apparent cessation of North American mutilation reports, combined with Bigelow Aerospace's interest in launching the world's first space hotel, found the NIDS effort relegated back to the bullpen by coach Bigelow.

Mad Cows and Angry Ranchers

There have been various law enforcement approaches to ascertain who or what was responsible for these many unexplained animal deaths. Mounting frustration and a complete lack of help from the Federal government back in the mid-to-late 1970s prompted many sheriffs departments to mount highly unusual county-wide stakeouts in an effort to apprehend the perpetrators. Several northeastern Colorado Counties actually hired pilots to fly round-the-clock to monitor areas continually targeted by the cattle surgeons. Several exciting cases include pilots chasing mystery helicopters in the air, and county authorities vainly trying to keep the mystery craft in sight from the ground. Law enforcement officials had several motivating factors driving their investigations. The mounting furor in the ranching community combined with sizable rewards prompted sheriffs to devote sizable amounts of manpower and resources to investigating the problem; to no avail.

By 1979 Colorado reward money reached thirty thousand

dollars and lawmen began devoting their free time to solve the problem. The chapter ends with several short interviews with long-time sheriffs who spent years wrestling with the mystery deaths and several who still do.

As I've stated previously the role of the press and media covering the mutilation mystery should be considered a crucial sociological element in our equation. In regional areas where cases are often reported, media coverage of these reports, without question will (depending on the slant of the article or show segment) help formulate or negate public opinion. As Stewert pointed out in his paper: often, media coverage appears to generate more and more reports to law enforcement officials. Why is this?

Maybe Its All True?

At this point, what can we surmise? There is no single prosaic answer to this bovine death mystery for several theories may be simultaneously valid. As I have stated, there are many possibilities (1.) some group within the military has publicly undisclosed knowledge about (and shows a continuing interest in) the "cattle mutilation" phenomenon. (2.) There are real, unexplained high-strange cases that have no mundane explanation and (3.) there appears to be an effective disinformation campaign in place to render the totality and validity of the mystery null and void to the vast majority of the beef-eating population who are unaware or completely in denial. These apparent elements do not necessarily mean that we can absolutely factor out more exotic theories. David Perkins and others have long entertained the possibility that western culture may be somehow collectively manifesting these cattle deaths from the realm of the collective unconscious as mentioned earlier. This would suggest that mutilations could be likened to "cultural stigmata," that for some reason, is manifesting instantaneously as these peculiar cattle deaths and disfigurements. On the surface this theory sounds a bit fantastic, however, there is something to be said for this line of thinking. Perhaps the "collective" unconsciously realizes how detrimental bovines are on the eco-system and perhaps these deaths are being instantaneously manifested as a warning to ourselves.

Thomas Bearden has further suggested that "tulpoids," (as he calls theoretical, collectively manifested thought-forms) may somehow be responsible. While not mainstream theories, Perkins' and Bearden's out-of-the-box theorizing deserve as much scrutiny as the mundane theories which haven't been able to explain the mystery up until now.

As we have seen, until now these animal deaths cannot been

explained by a *single* simple answer due partly to an ingeniously conceived, well executed smoke-screen quietly in place for decades. This subtle program of obfuscation has masterfully manipulated public opinion; negated law enforcement efforts and confounded independent investigator's efforts. Until the pivotal NIDS paper was published in 2003, this "program" has even managed to nullify scientific acceptance of the validity of the mystery, which has mostly rendered the phenomenon into the shadows of pseudo-science, myth and rumor. The programmers of this program of sleight-of-hand could well be called the masters of deception.

Now that we have defined the ingeniousness of whoever (or whatever) is behind the on-going "mutilation" scenario, we need to identify the parties with the necessary resources to conduct a seamless program of subterfuge. What are the capabilities needed to conduct such a wide reaching, well thought out program of deception?

First of all, resource capabilities and access to technology are paramount. Second, a motive or rationale to justify such a risky and difficult program. Third, a fool proof and methodical approach is needed to accomplish the task. An obvious question would be why would a well-funded, highly competent group with access to military technology sneak around in pastures killing livestock and removing soft-tissue organs? Perhaps if someone, or something, has identified a real pressing need to take such drastic steps, it stands to reason the results would have to undoubtedly outweigh the risks. It seems, on the surface whatever group is hypothetically doing this evidently has no choice but to operate in this fashion. It stands to reason if we can establish their motive, then an urgent need has been established and a covert operation is still in motion effectively meeting this need. An obvious question would be how could something so nefarious be kept secret for so long?

There is doubt that certain well-kept government secrets have effectively been in place for many years. Look at the Manhattan Project, or the Tuskegee experiments (conducted on prison inmates), or any number of revealed, secret programs and operations enacted by the United States and other governments. It is safe to say, it has been proven that the government can, and still does keep secrets.

Logically, our next question should be who then is doing these animal mutilations, and why? What rationale could possibly create such a risk-filled program involving such bloody deception? Wayne Holland says he knows from personal experience. While a member of US Army Intelligence he claims he was involved in perpetrating animal mutilations in Indiana and Illinois between 1973-1975. His fascinating account involves secret United States military operations conducted in Midwest pastures to attempt to ascertain why something or someone else is mutilating cattle. Utilizing "saucer-shaped aerial platforms," Holland claims he accompanied "mutilation teams" out into the field and was responsible for logging data on computer punch cards while covert surgical teams clandestinely removed bovine cattle parts in an effort to ascertain *why other unexplained animal deaths were occurring.*

To this day Holland is haunted by the troubling task he claims he helped perform but his fantastic claims and disturbing story, unfortunately, are not unique. After years of secrecy and silence, other disgruntled members of covert government mutilation teams are beginning to cautiously come forward.

Now that we have identified the possibility of an ongoing program of direct government involvement in perpetrating (at least a portion of) these gruesome animal deaths, what is the purpose behind such improbable risk-taking? David Perkins' environmental monitoring theory may explain many of these cases. In an exposé published in *Westword* Magazine, the story of Environmental Protection Agency (EPA) scientist, Brian Rimar's study of sheep herds grazing on the Alamosa River; downstream of the Summittville Mine Superfund site casts new light on the government's interest in grazing animal's soft-tissue organs. Especially when they are located in close proximity to adverse environmental conditions. Rimar in 1995, at the EPA's request, placed sheep in pastures downstream of the heavily polluted upper seventeen-miles Alamosa River for one hundred and twenty days to ascertain levels of heavy metals in the grazing grasses— supported by the river; and ingested by the sheep.

Researchers analyzed tissue from all over the lambs' bodies, but especially the livers, which tend to rust away if the animals eat to much copper …the results were alarming. "What we finally found was that at the exposed site, the amount of copper in the forage plants was twenty-seven times greater that at our control site. The livers of sheep in the exposed area held twice as much copper than those from the uncontaminated site— a concentration that could have been fatal …Why weren't the sheep dropping dead in the field?"

This brings to mind yet another insightful observation David Perkins has made: The cattle mutilations seem to be a last frost to first frost phenomenon. Few cases occur after the onset of below freezing weather and this would indicate to Perkins that there may a some reason that cattle are targeted mostly when they are grazing on pasture grass—not during the winter time period when they are being fed hay or silage from elsewhere. This may be an important clue.

428

What makes the above EPA study even more intriguing is that eight out of the last fourteen unexplained mutilation reports from the hard-hit San Luis Valley also occurred downstream of the Summittville superfund site on the Alamosa River, between 1995 and 1998! Also worthy of note is the fact that Alamosa County features the highest per-capita rate of diabetes and thyroid cancer in the United States.

Because the San Luis Valley is the only locale in North America with no measurable pollution, in this chapter, it is proposed that grazing animals in this pristine high mountain valley are being considered a control group representing baseline data. It is now evident to me that a certain percentage of mutilation cases in the hard-hit San Luis Valley are perpetrated scientifically to adjust this baseline data, against which all other North American environmental monitoring cases may/are being measured. This program of environmental monitoring also represents an ingenious program of plausible deniability when viewed in this context for these cases help obscure the totality of government involvement in the mutilation phenomenon; in the San Luis Valley, or elsewhere. To further complicate matters, some cases in North America may be perpetrated as red herrings—just to throw of investigators.

Another recently revealed pollution study was a seventeen year examination of the effects of radiation from ninety above ground nuclear tests on the North American environment conducted by the National Cancer Institute (NCI). In 1997, investigator David Perkins immediately noticed a tantalizing correlation between the NCI map of regions most impacted by radiation and regions suffering continual reports of "cattle mutilations." In Perkins' words, "both maps are almost an exact match!" Perkins' "environmental monitoring" theory has tangible evidence supporting the theory that at least some livestock deaths are an experimental program to determine pollution levels in the environment. As with all theories ventured to explain the animal deaths, this theory even if true, again does not explain all cases. What other rationale can we find to help explain the rest of the cases?

So after factoring out mundane misidentified reports; cases due to environmental monitoring, red-herring cases and a few cases that may be perpetrated by pranksters and copycats, we are still left with a small percentage of unexplained cases that cannot be explained away by conventional theories. Linda Howe may be, in part, correct. Are these high-strange cases due solely to "extraterrestrial biological entities" harvesting "genetic material" for the purpose of improving alien genetic stock, or to make alien/human hybrids? Although this explanation sounds highly improbable when attempting to explain cases, skepticism aside, it appears there actually may be a grain of truth to this improbable line of reasoning.

If this is so, we need a unifying theory that makes sense, looking at the totality of the phenomenon and Howes' theory, if true, would certainly explain a few highly improbable cases. There is a disturbing theory that no "mutilation" investigator has been willing to entertain, for it is highly troubling and not as glamorous as the popular ET visiting McEarth or government conspiracy scenarios.

Recently, I was jolted when I received a call from a former San Luis Valley deputy sheriff (now an investigator for a District Attorney's Office) with the following incredible story. The officer was recently asked by his county to attend a special seminar for training in "reading gang-sign" and differentiating between occult sign/evidence and mundane youth gang sign and these different group's secret written inscriptions. The course was taught by a well-known law-enforcement expert from Los Angeles, California whose investigative work was dramatized in a Hollywood film in the early 1980s and who now specializes in training cops to investigate occult crime and ritualized homicides. Upon hearing the deputy was from the San Luis Valley, where "all the cattle mutilations occur," the expert, over lunch, told the officer he had recently testified before "a secret congressional committee" in Washington DC that had been quietly tasked with investigating the unexplained livestock death problem. According to the deputy, he was told by his trainer that the committee "...has smoking-gun evidence tying a ritual group with access to military hardware" to the mutilations. He was also told that livestock— mainly cattle were being targeted because so many "human sacrifices would eventually be noticed," although human sacrifice is allegedly "preferable to the group."

Obviously a majority of disappearances have mundane explanations, but does not explain what has happened to countless thousands of missing persons who simply vanish without a trace, year-after-year. Where are these people and where are all the bodies? This is a very troubling subject that deserves more scrutiny.

The Sacrificial Altar

A small band of Diné (Navaho) elders slowly wind their way up Zapata Creek on the western side of the Blanca Massif, or Sisnajini— Sacred Mountain of the East, "the place where all thought originates," in the San Luis Valley. The year is 1963 and for millennia, the Native American elders have traveled over five hundred miles to perform the blessing of the holy mountain, *Sisnajini*. Due to a breakdown of traditional ceremonies that have been performed by the Diné and other tribes for hundreds of years, four years later, in 1967, out in the valley—near the mouth of Zapata Creek, a horrific event occurs. The Snippy Case. Curiously, within weeks of Snippy's strange demise the first-ever outbreak of *prion* related chronic wasting disease blooms in Colorado deer herds.

I have always wondered about this synchronistic fact. And I have also wondered why the Snippy case is considered to be the first publicized *cattle* mutilation. Snippy was a horse and the unusual condition of the animal has *never been duplicated in any other case.*

Here is an intriguing theory: It is a known fact that Native Americans dislike non-indigenous cattle and cattle ranching because of the adverse effect the animals have on the environment. The land, and all it contains, is considered sacred to most indigenous peoples. Granted, Indians weren't above occasionally stealing and eating beef when the opportunity arose, but Native Americans, for the most part, have not engaged in cattle ranching. But they did revere horses. Introduced by the Spanish, horses gave them a wonderful newfound mobility never seen in North America prior to the fourteenth-century. Perhaps the Snippy Case was due to an angry response at the cessation of the traditional blessings by something mighty and powerful that was not pleased with the indigenous population. Also of note were the two *bison* allegedly found mutilated during the same period when Snippy met her untimely demise in September. 1967. Bison were the most important animal utilized and were worshipped by mid-west and western Indians and there may be a direct connection. There may even be a cultural connection to the 1967 mass "turning on" to psychedelics and to the Snippy case, as well, as we will see.

Could North America's most pristine environment (in the San Luis Valley) be called America's sacrificial altar? Like the altars atop hundreds of Meso-American pyramids and the high peaks of the Andes where humans were sacrificed for a thousand or more years, the San Luis Valley sits like an altar at the apex of the North American continent. The fact that this region may represent the hardest hit mutilation locale in the world, in my estimation, is no coincidence.

Without question, there has always been something awesome and powerful happening in the world's largest alpine valley and other so-called sacred-site hot spots in the Western Hemisphere. And it appears our government; *your* tax-dollars, has at least a limited knowledge of this predatory "presence" and may be actively engaged in appeasing, emulating and studying something revered in awe by the indigenous peoples the world over for thousands of years.

431

The Only Alternative?

As we have seen, for thousands of years sacrificial blood has been utilized as an important elixir of cultural belief by symbolizing an important religious connection between humans and a deity (or deities) that demand ritual blood sacrifice. Perhaps the power elite, the hidden control structure on our planet, has made a *Faustian* bargain with this ancient presence and is placating it and/or holding it at bay by conducting ritual blood sacrifice. Humans have violently shed the blood of millions of individuals in countless wars for millennia and perhaps the only viable blood alternative is the closest hemoglobin alternative cattle. The nightmare years at the start of the cattle mutilation waves of the early 1970s coincided with the end of the Vietnam War. This is an important clue that will shed light on the rationale behind perpetrating these unusual animal deaths.

I am convinced that the UAD and UFO phenomena represent two distinct aspects that merge in the valley and may have far-reaching ramifications. UADs and UFOs at the core of the phenomena are "real," physical manifestations. But it is important to remember that these phenomena, even in the modern age, also exist within the framework of cultural symbolism, or shared psyche. In our culture, the very perception of the San Luis Valley as the "birthplace" of the UAD phenomenon is important.

Here in the valley we find the case of truck driver Henry Ozawa who saw strange lights around 1945, two years before the term "flying saucer" was coined. "The lights were floating around. It looked like an automobile, they were blue, you know, like headlights. They were floating all over the place. You'd think it was a car coming and, before you knew it, it floats away."

Ozawa said he was not frightened by the spectacle and returned to the site, five miles north of Antonito, with many of his friends. "I wasn't married, I was single back then, so I'd take a girlfriend out there. I and another guy, we'd go out there in pairs." He even took one of his sons out to see the lights.

Years later, the same son who had viewed the lights with his father, returned to the site with his high school buddies. They were not disappointed, although some found the strange phenomenon disturbing.

The modern era of the "classic cattle mutilation" began when the media discovered the phenomena and began disseminating awareness of it to the public in 1967. But there are documented cases from the Midwest that have been uncovered by researchers that lend credence to the proposition that the programmers have

432

been at work for far longer.

A case in point:

Oklahoma City, OK, from Leon J. Sale in a 1978 letter to Tom Adam's *Stigma*:

> "I don't remember the exact year, but it was either 1934 or '35 soon after I went to Missouri to live with my grandparents. We found a hog slaughtered in a mysterious way in a pasture after we had seen a shiny object flying over the farm at about tree-top level, and we thought it went down in the pasture across the creek from the house. By the time my grandfather and I walked over there it was gone, but there was a ring about 25 feet in radius burned in the grass and the hog was laying in the middle of it. At that time we had never heard of UFOs and I don't think my grandfather ever said anything to anyone about it."

This is but one of many incidents that has been uncovered by researchers looking for clues in the historical record, hoping to uncover the definitive case that will enable us to finally solve this enduring mystery. How many other residents of remote regions of the world have had similar experiences?

There are literally thousands of stories from rural areas of the world that attest to strange beings, objects, lights and other unexplained phenomena. If the complete history and tradition of the San Luis Valley's original part time inhabitants is taken into account, we discover a very important clue. The ancient legends of many Indian tribes who used the valley, are rife with alien-like references and the valley is one of several holy, revered locations in the Southwest with unusual electromagnetic and gravitational anomalies.

George C. Andrews, in his recently-published book Extraterrestrials, Friends and Foes, excerpted in The Leading Edge writes:

After purchasing maps from the United States Geological Survey, it became evident that there was indeed a valid connection between these areas and UFOs to Mr. Lew Tery, who gave a public lecture about this relationship in Arizona. He was subsequently harassed by the FBI and ceased to give public lectures on this subject.

Both the Aeromagnetic and Gravitational (Bougier Gravity) maps indicate basic field strength, as well as areas of high and low field strength. Interestingly enough, the areas of maximum and minimum field strength have the following:

-All have frequent UFO sightings.

-All are on Indian reservations, (sacred sites) government land, or land the   government is trying to buy. (or restrict usage)

-Many of them, especially where several are clustered together, are suspected base areas and/or where mutilations and abductions have taken place.

The SLV contains all the elements stated above. The Aeromagnetic and Gravitational qualities mentioned above are readings of basic field strength, gravitational or magnetic fluctuations attributed to various areas on the Earth's surface. The valley contains both minimum and maximum intensity zones in close proximity to each other. The interaction or seam between these zones, the Dunes area for example, is often a repeated location of our unusual activity.

The field of UFOlogy has several systems of classification including the Hynek "Close Encounter I through IV" and the Valleé addition of the effects of "Anomaly, Fly-By, and Maneuver" classes of UFO sightings and encounters. As the number of UAD reports continues to climb, isn't it about time that a standardized system for classifying these on-going mysterious deaths and the potpourri of other unexplained mysteries is adopted by field investigators and researchers?   Standardization and education of the public are all essential. These so-called paranormal phenomena are no longer "closet" subjects. There is something going on in the world around and above us. It seems there always has been.

Works in Progress

How does one sum up fifteen years of head scratching? The easy way out is to not attempt to propose any definitive answers, just present the data and explain what this body of information suggests. This is what I have hoped to do by re-presenting my investigative work along with my concerted attempt at analysis. I sincerely hope that I have sparked your creative process with this work. I don't know what's behind these many mysterious events, they often appear to take place in a vacuum, of sorts. Most of the events I've documented make no apparent sense, but added up into their entirety, as I've pointed out, certain elements seem to be at work in the San Luis Valley and elsewhere.

In the meantime, this investigator has completed a manuscript on the ufological work of Ray Stanford, who gets my vote as the most important figure in the field's fifty-plus year history. The work is written entirely in Stanford's own words that I obtained over a two-year period and over twenty-five hours of taped conversations. The book's tongue-in-cheek working title is ...*and my dog sings*

434

Chopin. When Ray gives the OK, I plan to publish this work and hopefully blow the lid off this broken-wheel field. Stanford has quietly worked for decades analyzing his "forty-nine films" of UFOs he has taken since 1956—including the famous opening sequence of the 1970s TV series *In Search of.* The information he has patiently gleaned from these films is breathtaking and deserves acknowledgment in the form of scientific attention. I can't wait to be given the OK by Ray to publish this important work.

I have also been working recently with members of the Indiana Ghost Trackers and electronic voice phenomenon expert Michael Esposito. Location-specific haunted sites, in my estimation, may be our most direct investigative path to determine the true nature of paranormal energies. I have co-produced an on-going series of DVDs with Ronald James Television titled: *Dead Whisper.* More information on this project can be found at http://deadwhisper. com.

In closing, I would like to thank you the reader for your interest in my investigative work and research. These subjects are crucial to human's understanding of the last remaining mysteries of the twentieth-century. Your interest and support will further the scientific process needed to roll back the mystery and solve these enigmatic riddles inside a hall of mirrors with a quicksand floor. Good hunting space-fans!

Christopher O'Brien can be reached at cob@tmv.us. His websites are: http://tmv.us and http://ourstrangeplanet.com

Suggested Rules of Investigation

1. Controversial subjects generate polarized responses.
2. Record or write down everything as soon as possible, no matter how inconsequential or insignificant it seems at the time.
3. Always credit your sources and respect requests for anonymity.
4. Always be ready for anything, anytime. Look for coincidences when investigating claims of the unusual. Often there may be a synchronistic element at work.
5. It is impossible to be too objective when scientifically investigating claims of the unusual.
6. Always assume a mundane explanation until proven extraordinary.
7. Appearances can be deceiving. There may be more happening than meets the eye.
8. If you publicize claims of the unusual, choose your words wisely, for your spin may have tremendous influence.
9. Media coverage of the unusual, because of its sensational nature, is often inaccurate and cannot be accepted as totally accurate by the investigator.
10. The human mind, when faced with the unknown, reverts to basic, primal symbols to rationalize its experience.
11. When investigating claims of the unusual, one cannot reach conclusions based on intuition alone.
12. There is a possibility that we may cocreate manifestations of unexplained, individually perceived phenomena.
13. No leading questions.

Credits:

San Luis Valley Map: Myrna Schrader
Foreword:
David Perkins: David Perkins Collection
Chapter 1
Author pictures from the TMV Archives
Snippy picture: Pueblo Chieftain
Chris and Peter: Debra Floyd
Chris & Debra: Jonathan Goldman
Sangres: Author
Chapter 2
Filming Dead Whisper: Ron Busbee
Juan Anza an Onate: David Childress
Carson & Fremont: SLV Historical Society
Pike: SLVDweller.com
Sniders Store: Katie Snider
Manitou Map: Manitou Foundation/Institute
Hanne Strong: Manitou Institute
Maurice Strong: Email to author, from the Internet
Crestone Peak: TMV Archive
Grandfather Martin & Tibetans: Crestone Eagle
Sierra Blanca: SLV Historical Society
Miners: SLV Historical Society
Aca Innn: TMV Archive
Haunted House: Kay Thompson
Chapter 3
Taos Pueblo: www.taos-history.org
Ute Indians: pbs.org
Dig Here: Adventures Unlimited Press
Gold Panner: David Childress
Disappearing Cloud: Brendon O'Brien
Chapter 4
Baca Beehives: TMV Archive
Shaman's Cave: Jonathan Goldman
Isadore: TMV Archive
Catherine O'Brien: TMV Archive
Rainbow/Hawks: TMV Archive
Mutilated Bull: Virginia Sutherland
Cow Skull: TMV Archive
Toyota: TMV Archive
MOA Map: COANG
Chapter 5
San Luis Lakes Map: sangres.com
Pricilla Wolf: Pricilla Wolf

Petroglyphs: travel.com
Isleta Casino: Isletacasino.com
Devil: Google search image
Lobo Light: Pricilla Wold
Marie Jesus Agreda: Javier Sierra/ Ana Cero Magazine
Mineral Hot Springs: joyfuljourney.com
Auther/Perkins?Adams: Kizzen Laki
Palamino mutilation: Deputy Gene Gray
Chapter 6
Snippy the Horse: Don Anderson/David Perkins
Berle and Nellie Lewis: Don Hand Collection
Mutilation Photos: Saguache County Sheriff
Cattle shot: TMV Archives
The Business: Scott Alexander
Author/Altshuler/Adams: Kizzen Laki
Chapter 7
Chasing a report: TMV Archive
The Thing: TMV Archive
Author w/ Tim Good: John Altshuler
The Koons: TMV Archive
Laffing Buddha: Roy Archuleta
Chapter 8
Laurance Rockefeller: www.mega.nu
Hanne and the Monks: Manitou Institute
Shari and Steven: Shari Adamiak
Chapter 9
Del Norte Calf: Edward Burke
Hronich and Reed: TMV Archive
Open Range: TMV Archive
Gary Massey: TMV Archive
Col. Buck Buckingham: Kizzen Laki
Chapter 10
Sangres: TMV Archive
Hooper mute: TMV Archives
Chapter 11
John Harr/Nick Cook: TMV Archive
BBC Mute Case: TMV Archive
Chapter 12
Martin and Naia: TMV Archive/Naia
Camelite Monastary: TMV Archive
Prairie Dragons: TMV Archive
Sangres/Portal Area: TMV Archive
Chapter 13
Author Mt Shasta: TMV Archive

438

BIBLIOGRAPHY

Adams, Thomas R., *Project Stigma Reports*, 1974-1978 Paris, TX

Adams, Thomas R., *Crux*, 1974-1987, Paris, TX

Adams, Thomas R., *The Choppers and The Choppers*, Paris, TX 1991

Altshuler, Dr. John, *Tissue Changes in Unexplained Animal Mutilations*, MUFON

Bond, Janet, *Flying Saucer Review*, FSR Publishing, Kent, England. 1970

Brandon, Jim, *Weird America*, Millenium Press, 1976

Brandon, Jim, *The Rebirth of Pan*, Firebird Press, Dunlap, IL. 1983

Bryant, Alice, *The Message of the Crystal Skull*, Llewwllyn, St. Paul, MN 1989

Childress, David, *Lost Cities of North & Central America*, Adventures Unlimited, 1994

Childress, David, *Lost Continents & the Hollow Earth*, Adventures Unlimited, 1999

Dongo, Tom, *The Mysteries of Sedona*, Hummingbird Pub. Sedona, AZ. 1988

Dongo, Tom, *Unseen Beings, Unseen Worlds*, Hummingbird Sedona, AZ. 1994

Eker, Anne, *Shedding Some Coherent Light on Mutilations*, UFOlogist 1993

Elliott, Mark, *Bloodless Valley*, Gatesgarth Productions, Crestone, CO. 1988

Fagan, Brian M., *Journey From Eden*, Thames and Hudson, NYC NY 1990

Fell, Barry, *America B.C.*, Wallaby Books, NYC, NY. 1976

Foor, Mel, *Kansas City Star*, November, KC. MO.1967

Fort, Charles, *New Lands*, Ace Books, NYC, NY orig/pub 1923

Fort, Charles, *Wild Talents*, Ace Books

Fort, Charles, *The Book of the Damned*, Ace Books

Foster, Dick, *Rocky Mountain News*, various articles, Denver, CO. 1993-4

Gaddis, Vincent, *Mysterious Fires and Lights*, Dell Books, NYC, NY. 1970

Good, Timothy, *Alien Contact*, William Morrow, NYC, NY 1993

Green, John, *Sasquatch*, Hancock House, Seattle WA. 1978

Greer, Dr. Steven, *Foundations of Interplanetary Unity*, position paper, 1993

Greer, Dr, Steven, *CE-5: A Proposal for an Important New Research Category*, 1993

Harlan, Jack, *Post Marks, and Places*, Golden Bell Press, Denver, CO. 1976

Howe, Linda M., *An Alien Harvest*, LMH Prod. Huntingdon Valley, PA. 1988

Howe, Linda M., *Glimpses of Other Realities*, LMH Productions, PA. 1994

Howe, Linda M., *1994 Animal Mutilation Research Grant*, LMH PA. 1994

Hynek, J. Allen, *The UFO Experience*, H. Regency Co. Chicago, IL. 1972

Iler, David, *Up The Creek*, Crestone article, Denver, CO. 1992

Jung, Carl G., *Flying Saucers*, Dell Books, NYC, NY 1969

Jung, Carl G., *Man and His Symbols*, Dell Books, NYC, NY. 1968

Kagan, Daniel, *Mute Evidence*, Bantam Books NYC, NY. 1983

Kaku, Michio, *Parallel Universes,* Kurzweil AI.net 2003

Keel, John, *Operation Trojan Horse,* Putnam NYC, NY. 1970

Keel, John, *Guide to Mysterious Beings,* Tor Books NYC 2002

Keel, John, *Why UFOs?* Manor Books, NYC, NY. 1970

Kelleher/Knapp, *Hunt fot the Skinwalker,* Paraview NYC 2005

Le Pour Trench, B., *The Sky People,* Neville Spearman, England, 1960ß

Levesque, Tal, *The Call of the Four-Corners*, Atzlan Journal 1978

Lewis, Berle, Interview with author, February, 1993

Secrets of the Mysterious Valley

Lewis, Nellie, Interviews with East Texas State University, 1967
Lorenzen, C.E., *The Appaloosa*, Fate Llewellyn Pub. MN. 1967
Lorenzen, C.E,. *Flying Saucer Occupants*, Signet, NYC, NY. 1967
Lorenzen, C.E. & L., *Encounters With Flying Saucer Occupants*, 1976
O'Brien, Christopher, *The Mysterious Valley,* St Martins NYC 1996
O'Brien, Christopher, *Enter the Valley,* St Martins, NYC 1999
Olsen, Gail, *Rio Grande Sun*, articles, Sante Fe, NM. 1984
Lovelock, James, *Gaia,* Oxford University Press UK 1979
McKenna, Terence, *The Archaic Revival,* Harper/Collins Canada 1992
McKenna, Terence, *Chaos, Creativity, and Cosmic Consciousness,* 2001
Onet, Dr. George, *Animal Mutilations: What We Know,* nidsci.org 1997
O'Sullivan, J.J., *Deep Underground Construction,* Rand Pjct 1959
Parsons, John, *Freedom is a Two-Edged Sword,* Falcon Press NV 1989
Perkins, David, *Altered Steaks,* 1979
Perkins, David, *Boulder Monthly*, Fall 1979
Perkins, David, *Spirit Magazine*, Fall/Winter 1994-1995
Porter III, Miles, *Valley Courier*, articles 1975-1978, Alamosa, CO
Randles, Jenny, *UFO Reality*, Robert Hale London, England 1983
S Acharya, *Suns of God,* Adventures Unlimited Press, IL 2004
Salisbury, Frank, *The Utah UFO Display,* Old Greenwich 1974
Sanderson, Ivan, *Invisible Residents,* Adventures Unlimited Press, 1970
Simmons, Virginia, *The San Luis Valley* Pruett , Boulder, CO.
Sitchin, Zecharia, *The 12th Planet,* Avon Books, NYC, NY. 1976
Steiger, Brad, *The Rainbow Conspiracy*, Windsor, NYC, 1994
Strieber, Whitley, *Communion,* William Morrow, NYC, NY. 1987
Talbot, Michael, *The Holographic Universe,* Harper NYC 1991
Temple, Robert, *The Sirius Mystery,* Destiny, Rochester, NY. 1976
Thomas, Kenn, *Parapolitics,* Adventures Unlimited Press, 2006
US DOT, FAA Report on Mystery Helicopters, 1993
Valarian, Val, The Leading Edge, LERG, Yelm, WA. 1990-1995
Vallee, Dr. Jacques, *The Invisible College*, E.P. Dutton NYC 1975
Vallee, Dr. Jacques, *Messengers of Deception*, Bantam , NYC, 1979
Vallee, Dr. Jacques, *Dimensions,* Ballentine Books, NYC, NY. 1988
Vallee, Dr. Jacques, *Confrontations*, Ballentine Books, NYC, NY. 1990
Vallee, Dr. Jacques, *Revelations*, Ballentine Books, NYC, NY. 1990
Vallee, Dr. Jacques, *Forbidden Science,* Ballentine Books NYC, 1991
Waters, Frank, *Book of the Hopi,* Viking Press, NYC 1963
Watkins, Leslie, *Alternative 3,* Sphere Books, London, 1978
Watson, Lyall, *Supernature,* Hodder & Stoughton, UK 1974
Watson, Lyall, *Secret Life of Inanimate Objects,* 10 Speed UK 2000
Wilson, Colin, *Alien Dawn,* Fromm NYC 1998
Wilson, Colin, *Beyond the Occult,* Carrol and Graf 1989
Wilson, Colin, *Mind Parasites,* Oneiric Publishing 1990
Wilson, Robert A., *Cosmic Trigger 1* and *2,* New Falcon Press 1979-1991
Wood, Ryan, Agenda "NORAD Incident," S.F. CA. 1994

440

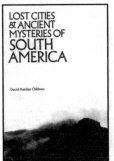

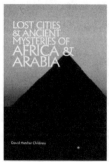

LOST CITIES & ANCIENT MYSTERIES OF AFRICA & ARABIA
by David Hatcher Childress

Childress continues his world-wide quest for lost cities and ancient mysteries. Join him as he discovers forbidden cities in the Empty Quarter of Arabia; "Atlantean" ruins in Egypt and the Kalahari desert; a mysterious, ancient empire in the Sahara; and more. This is the tale of an extraordinary life on the road: across war-torn countries, Childress searches for King Solomon's Mines, living dinosaurs, the Ark of the Covenant and the solutions to some of the fantastic mysteries of the past.

423 PAGES. 6x9 PAPERBACK. ILLUSTRATED. $14.95. CODE: AFA

LOST CITIES OF ATLANTIS, ANCIENT EUROPE & THE MEDITERRANEAN
by David Hatcher Childress

Childress takes the reader in search of sunken cities in the Mediterranean; across the Atlas Mountains in search of Atlantean ruins; to remote islands in search of megalithic ruins; to meet living legends and secret societies. From Ireland to Turkey, Morocco to Eastern Europe, and around the remote islands of the Mediterranean and Atlantic, Childress takes the reader on an astonishing quest for mankind's past. Ancient technology, cataclysms, megalithic construction, lost civilizations and devastating wars of the past are all explored in this book.

524 PAGES. 6x9 PAPERBACK. ILLUSTRATED. $16.95. CODE: MED

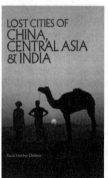

LOST CITIES OF CHINA, CENTRAL INDIA & ASIA
by David Hatcher Childress

Like a real life "Indiana Jones," maverick archaeologist David Childress takes the reader on an incredible adventure across some of the world's oldest and most remote countries in search of lost cities and ancient mysteries. Discover ancient cities in the Gobi Desert; hear fantastic tales of lost continents, vanished civilizations and secret societies bent on ruling the world; visit forgotten monasteries in forbidding snow-capped mountains with strange tunnels to mysterious subterranean cities! A unique combination of far-out exploration and practical travel advice, it will astound and delight the experienced traveler or the armchair voyager.

429 PAGES. 6x9 PAPERBACK. ILLUSTRATED. FOOTNOTES & BIBLIOGRAPHY. $14.95. CODE: CHI

LOST CITIES OF ANCIENT LEMURIA & THE PACIFIC
by David Hatcher Childress

Was there once a continent in the Pacific? Called Lemuria or Pacifica by geologists, Mu or Pan by the mystics, there is now ample mythological, geological and archaeological evidence to "prove" that an advanced and ancient civilization once lived in the central Pacific. Maverick archaeologist and explorer David Hatcher Childress combs the Indian Ocean, Australia and the Pacific in search of the surprising truth about mankind's past. Contains photos of the underwater city on Pohnpei; explanations on how the statues were levitated around Easter Island in a clockwise vortex movement; tales of disappearing islands; Egyptians in Australia; and more.

379 PAGES. 6x9 PAPERBACK. ILLUSTRATED. FOOTNOTES & BIBLIOGRAPHY. $14.95. CODE: LEM

A HITCHHIKER'S GUIDE TO ARMAGEDDON
by David Hatcher Childress

With wit and humor, popular Lost Cities author David Hatcher Childress takes us around the world and back in his trippy finalé to the Lost Cities series. He's off on an adventure in search of the apocalypse and end times. Childress hits the road from the fortress of Megiddo, the legendary citadel in northern Israel where Armageddon is prophesied to start. Hitchhiking around the world, Childress takes us from one adventure to another, to ancient cities in the deserts and the legends of worlds before our own. In the meantime, he becomes a cargo cult god on a remote island off New Guinea, gets dragged into the Kennedy Assassination by one of the "conspirators," investigates a strange power operating out of the Altai Mountains of Mongolia, and discovers how the Knights Templar and their off-shoots have driven the world toward an epic battle centered around Jerusalem and the Middle East.

320 PAGES. 6x9 PAPERBACK. ILLUSTRATED. BIBLIOGRAPHY. INDEX. $16.95. CODE: HGA

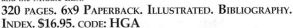

TECHNOLOGY OF THE GODS
The Incredible Sciences of the Ancients
by David Hatcher Childress

Childress looks at the technology that was allegedly used in Atlantis and the theory that the Great Pyramid of Egypt was originally a gigantic power station. He examines tales of ancient flight and the technology that it involved; how the ancients used electricity; megalithic building techniques; the use of crystal lenses and the fire from the gods; evidence of various high tech weapons in the past, including atomic weapons; ancient metallurgy and heavy machinery; the role of modern inventors such as Nikola Tesla in bringing ancient technology back into modern use; impossible artifacts; and more.

356 PAGES. 6x9 PAPERBACK. ILLUSTRATED. BIBLIOGRAPHY. $16.95. CODE: TGOD

VIMANA AIRCRAFT OF ANCIENT INDIA & ATLANTIS
by David Hatcher Childress, introduction by Ivan T. Sanderson

In this incredible volume on ancient India, authentic Indian texts such as the *Ramayana* and the *Mahabharata* are used to prove that ancient aircraft were in use more than four thousand years ago. Included in this book is the entire Fourth Century BC manuscript *Vimaanika Shastra* by the ancient author Maharishi Bharadwaaja. Also included are chapters on Atlantean technology, the incredible Rama Empire of India and the devastating wars that destroyed it.

334 PAGES. 6x9 PAPERBACK. ILLUSTRATED. $15.95. CODE: VAA

LOST CONTINENTS & THE HOLLOW EARTH
I Remember Lemuria and the Shaver Mystery
by David Hatcher Childress & Richard Shaver

Shaver's rare 1948 book *I Remember Lemuria* is reprinted in its entirety, and the book is packed with illustrations from Ray Palmer's *Amazing Stories* magazine of the 1940s. Palmer and Shaver told of tunnels running through the earth—tunnels inhabited by the Deros and Teros, humanoids from an ancient spacefaring race that had inhabited the earth, eventually going underground, hundreds of thousands of years ago. Childress discusses the famous hollow earth books and delves deep into whatever reality may be behind the stories of tunnels in the earth. Operation High Jump to Antarctica in 1947 and Admiral Byrd's bizarre statements, tunnel systems in South America and Tibet, the underground world of Agartha, the belief of UFOs coming from the South Pole, more.

344 PAGES. 6x9 PAPERBACK. ILLUSTRATED. $16.95. CODE: LCHE

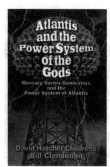

ATLANTIS & THE POWER SYSTEM OF THE GODS
Mercury Vortex Generators & the Power System of Atlantis
by David Hatcher Childress and Bill Clendenon

Childress' fascinating analysis of Nikola Tesla's broadcast system in light of Edgar Cayce's "Terrible Crystal" and the obelisks of ancient Egypt and Ethiopia. Includes: Atlantis and its crystal power towers that broadcast energy; how these incredible power stations may still exist today; inventor Nikola Tesla's nearly identical system of power transmission; Mercury Proton Gyros and mercury vortex propulsion; more. Richly illustrated, and packed with evidence that Atlantis not only existed—it had a world-wide energy system more sophisticated than ours today.
246 PAGES. 6x9 PAPERBACK. ILLUSTRATED. $15.95. CODE: APSG

THE ANTI-GRAVITY HANDBOOK
edited by David Hatcher Childress, with Nikola Tesla, T.B. Paulicki, Bruce Cathie, Albert Einstein and others

The new expanded compilation of material on Anti-Gravity, Free Energy, Flying Saucer Propulsion, UFOs, Suppressed Technology, NASA Cover-ups and more. Highly illustrated with patents, technical illustrations and photos. This revised and expanded edition has more material, including photos of Area 51, Nevada, the government's secret testing facility. This classic on weird science is back in a new format!
230 PAGES. 7x10 PAPERBACK. ILLUSTRATED. $16.95. CODE: AGH

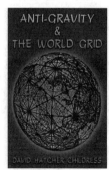

ANTI–GRAVITY & THE WORLD GRID

Is the earth surrounded by an intricate electromagnetic grid network offering free energy? This compilation of material on ley lines and world power points contains chapters on the geography, mathematics, and light harmonics of the earth grid. Learn the purpose of ley lines and ancient megalithic structures located on the grid. Discover how the grid made the Philadelphia Experiment possible. Explore the Coral Castle and many other mysteries, including acoustic levitation, Tesla Shields and scalar wave weaponry. Browse through the section on anti-gravity patents, and research resources.
274 PAGES. 7x10 PAPERBACK. ILLUSTRATED. $14.95. CODE: AGW

ANTI–GRAVITY & THE UNIFIED FIELD
edited by David Hatcher Childress

Is Einstein's Unified Field Theory the answer to all of our energy problems? Explored in this compilation of material is how gravity, electricity and magnetism manifest from a unified field around us. Why artificial gravity is possible; secrets of UFO propulsion; free energy; Nikola Tesla and anti-gravity airships of the 20s and 30s; flying saucers as superconducting whirls of plasma; anti-mass generators; vortex propulsion; suppressed technology; government cover-ups; gravitational pulse drive; spacecraft & more.
240 PAGES. 7x10 PAPERBACK. ILLUSTRATED. $14.95. CODE: AGU

MAPS OF THE ANCIENT SEA KINGS
Evidence of Advanced Civilization in the Ice Age
by Charles H. Hapgood

Charles Hapgood has found the evidence in the Piri Reis Map that shows Antarctica, the Hadji Ahmed map, the Oronteus Finaeus and other amazing maps. Hapgood concluded that these maps were made from more ancient maps from the various ancient archives around the world, now lost. Not only were these unknown people more advanced in mapmaking than any people prior to the 18th century, it appears they mapped all the continents. The Americas were mapped thousands of years before Columbus. Antarctica was mapped when its coasts were free of ice!

316 PAGES. 7x10 PAPERBACK. ILLUSTRATED. BIBLIOGRAPHY & INDEX. $19.95. CODE: MASK

PATH OF THE POLE
Cataclysmic Pole Shift Geology
by Charles H. Hapgood

Maps of the Ancient Sea Kings author Hapgood's classic book *Path of the Pole* is back in print! Hapgood researched Antarctica, ancient maps and the geological record to conclude that the Earth's crust has slipped on the inner core many times in the past, changing the position of the pole. *Path of the Pole* discusses the various "pole shifts" in Earth's past, giving evidence for each one, and moves on to possible future pole shifts.

356 PAGES. 6x9 PAPERBACK. ILLUSTRATED. $16.95. CODE: POP

SUNS OF GOD
Krishna, Buddha and Christ Unveiled
by Acharya S

Over the past several centuries, the Big Three spiritual leaders have been the Lords Christ, Krishna and Buddha, whose stories and teachings are so remarkably similar as to confound and amaze those who encounter them. As classically educated archaeologist, historian, mythologist and linguist Acharya S thoroughly reveals, these striking parallels exist not because these godmen were "historical" personages who "walked the earth" but because they are personifications of the central focus of the famous and scandalous "mysteries." These mysteries date back thousands of years and are found globally, reflecting an ancient tradition steeped in awe and intrigue. In unveiling the reasons for this highly significant development, the author presents an in-depth analysis that includes fascinating and original research based on evidence both modern and ancient—captivating information kept secret and hidden for ages.

428 PAGES. 6x9 PAPERBACK. ILLUSTRATED. BIBLIOGRAPHY. INDEX. $18.95. CODE: SUNG

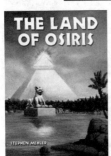

THE LAND OF OSIRIS
An Introduction to Khemitology
by Stephen S. Mehler

Was there an advanced prehistoric civilization in ancient Egypt who built the great pyramids and carved the Great Sphinx? Did the pyramids serve as energy devices and not as tombs for kings? Mehler has uncovered an indigenous oral tradition that still exists in Egypt, and has been fortunate to have studied with a living master of this tradition, Abd'El Hakim Awyan. Mehler has also been given permission to present these teachings to the Western world, teachings that unfold a whole new understanding of ancient Egypt . Chapters include: Egyptology and Its Paradigms; Asgat Nefer—The Harmony of Water; Khemit and the Myth of Atlantis; The Extraterrestrial Question; more.

272 PAGES. 6x9 PAPERBACK. ILLUSTRATED. COLOR SECTION. BIBLIOGRAPHY. $18.00 CODE: LOOS

SECRETS OF THE HOLY LANCE
The Spear of Destiny in History & Legend
by Jerry E. Smith

Secrets of the Holy Lance traces the Spear from its possession by Constantine, Rome's first Christian Caesar, to Charlemagne's claim that with it he ruled the Holy Roman Empire by Divine Right, and on through two thousand years of kings and emperors, until it came within Hitler's grasp—and beyond! Did it rest for a while in Antarctic ice? Is it now hidden in Europe, awaiting the next person to claim its awesome power? Neither debunking nor worshiping, *Secrets of the Holy Lance* seeks to pierce the veil of myth and mystery around the Spear. Mere belief that it was infused with magic by virtue of its shedding the Savior's blood has made men kings. But what if it's more? What are "the powers it serves"?

312 PAGES. 6x9 PAPERBACK. ILLUSTRATED. BIBLIOGRAPHY. $16.95. CODE: SOHL

REICH OF THE BLACK SUN
Nazi Secret Weapons & the Cold War Allied Legend
by Joseph P. Farrell

Why were the Allies worried about an atom bomb attack by the Germans in 1944? Why did the Soviets threaten to use poison gas against the Germans? Why did Hitler in 1945 insist that holding Prague could win the war for the Third Reich? Why did US General George Patton's Third Army race for the Skoda works at Pilsen in Czechoslovakia instead of Berlin? Why did the US Army not test the uranium atom bomb it dropped on Hiroshima? Why did the Luftwaffe fly a non-stop round trip mission to within twenty miles of New York City in 1944? *Reich of the Black Sun* takes the reader on a scientific-historical journey in order to answer these questions. Arguing that Nazi Germany actually won the race for the atom bomb in late 1944,

352 PAGES. 6x9 PAPERBACK. ILLUSTRATED. BIBLIOGRAPHY. $16.95. CODE: ROBS

THE GIZA DEATH STAR
The Paleophysics of the Great Pyramid & the Military Complex at Giza
by Joseph P. Farrell

Was the Giza complex part of a military installation over 10,000 years ago? Chapters include: An Archaeology of Mass Destruction, Thoth and Theories; The Machine Hypothesis; Pythagoras, Plato, Planck, and the Pyramid; The Weapon Hypothesis; Encoded Harmonics of the Planck Units in the Great Pyramid; High Freqquency Direct Current "Impulse" Technology; The Grand Gallery and its Crystals: Gravito-acoustic Resonators; The Other Two Large Pyramids; the "Causeways," and the "Temples"; A Phase Conjugate Howitzer; Evidence of the Use of Weapons of Mass Destruction in Ancient Times; more.

290 PAGES. 6x9 PAPERBACK. ILLUSTRATED. $16.95. CODE: GDS

THE GIZA DEATH STAR DEPLOYED
The Physics & Engineering of the Great Pyramid
by Joseph P. Farrell

Farrell expands on his thesis that the Great Pyramid was a maser, designed as a weapon and eventually deployed—with disastrous results to the solar system. Includes: Exploding Planets: A Brief History of the Exoteric and Esoteric Investigations of the Great Pyramid; No Machines, Please!; The Stargate Conspiracy; The Scalar Weapons; Message or Machine?; A Tesla Analysis of the Putative Physics and Engineering of the Giza Death Star; Cohering the Zero Point, Vacuum Energy, Flux: Feedback Loops and Tetrahedral Physics; and more.

290 PAGES. 6x9 PAPERBACK. ILLUSTRATED. $16.95. CODE: GDSD

THE FANTASTIC INVENTIONS OF NIKOLA TESLA
by Nikola Tesla with additional material by David Hatcher Childress
This book is a readable compendium of patents, diagrams, photos and explanations of the many incredible inventions of the originator of the modern era of electrification. In Tesla's own words are such topics as wireless transmission of power, death rays, and radio-controlled airships. In addition, rare material on a secret city built at a remote jungle site in South America by one of Tesla's students, Guglielmo Marconi. Marconi's secret group claims to have built flying saucers in the 1940s and to have gone to Mars in the early 1950s! Incredible photos of these Tesla craft are included. •His plan to transmit free electricity into the atmosphere. •How electrical devices would work using only small antennas. •Why unlimited power could be utilized anywhere on earth. •How radio and radar technology can be used as death-ray weapons in Star Wars.
342 PAGES. 6x9 PAPERBACK. ILLUSTRATED. $16.95. CODE: FINT

THE TESLA PAPERS
Nikola Tesla on Free Energy & Wireless Transmission of Power
by Nikola Tesla, edited by David Hatcher Childress
David Hatcher Childress takes us into the incredible world of Nikola Tesla and his amazing inventions. Tesla's fantastic vision of the future, including wireless power, anti-gravity, free energy and highly advanced solar power. Also included are some of the papers, patents and material collected on Tesla at the Colorado Springs Tesla Symposiums, including papers on: •The Secret History of Wireless Transmission •Tesla and the Magnifying Transmitter •Design and Construction of a Half-Wave Tesla Coil •Electrostatics: A Key to Free Energy •Progress in Zero-Point Energy Research •Electromagnetic Energy from Antennas to Atoms •Tesla's Particle Beam Technology •Fundamental Excitatory Modes of the Earth-Ionosphere Cavity
325 PAGES. 8x10 PAPERBACK. ILLUSTRATED. $16.95. CODE: TTP

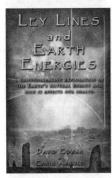

LEY LINE & EARTH ENERGIES
An Extraordinary Journey into the Earth's Natural Energy System
by David Cowan & Chris Arnold
The mysterious standing stones, burial grounds and stone circles that lace Europe, the British Isles and other areas have intrigued scientists, writers, artists and travellers through the centuries. How do ley lines work? How did our ancestors use Earth energy to map their sacred sites and burial grounds? How do ghosts and poltergeists interact with Earth energy? How can Earth spirals and black spots affect our health? This exploration shows how natural forces affect our behavior, how they can be used to enhance our health and well being. A fascinating and visual book about subtle Earth energies and how they affect us and the world around them.
368 PAGES. 6x9 PAPERBACK. ILLUSTRATED. BIBLIOGRAPHY. INDEX. $18.95. CODE: LLEE

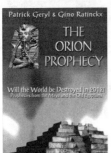

THE ORION PROPHECY
Egyptian and Mayan Prophecies on the Cataclysm of 2012
by Patrick Geryl and Gino Ratinckx
In the year 2012 the Earth awaits a super catastrophe: its magnetic field will reverse in one go. Phenomenal earthquakes and tidal waves will completely destroy our civilization. These dire predictions stem from the Mayans and Egyptians—descendants of the legendary Atlantis. The Atlanteans were able to exactly predict the previous world-wide flood in 9792 BC. They built tens of thousands of boats and escaped to South America and Egypt. In the year 2012 Venus, Orion and several others stars will take the same 'code-positions' as in 9792 BC!
324 PAGES. 6x9 PAPERBACK. ILLUSTRATED. $16.95. CODE: ORP

TAPPING THE ZERO POINT ENERGY
Free Energy & Anti-Gravity in Today's Physics
by Moray B. King

King explains how free energy and anti-gravity are possible. The theories of the zero point energy maintain there are tremendous fluctuations of electrical field energy imbedded within the fabric of space. This book tells how, in the 1930s, inventor T. Henry Moray could produce a fifty kilowatt "free energy" machine; how an electrified plasma vortex creates anti-gravity; how the Pons/Fleischmann "cold fusion" experiment could produce tremendous heat without fusion; and how certain experiments might produce a gravitational anomaly.

180 PAGES. 5x8 PAPERBACK. ILLUSTRATED. $12.95. CODE: TAP

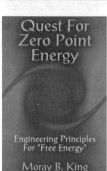

QUEST FOR ZERO-POINT ENERGY
Engineering Principles for "Free Energy"
by Moray B. King

King expands, with diagrams, on how free energy and anti-gravity are possible. The theories of zero point energy maintain there are tremendous fluctuations of electrical field energy embedded within the fabric of space. King explains the following topics: Tapping the Zero-Point Energy as an Energy Source; Fundamentals of a Zero-Point Energy Technology; Vacuum Energy Vortices; The Super Tube; Charge Clusters: The Basis of Zero-Point Energy Inventions; Vortex Filaments, Torsion Fields and the Zero-Point Energy; Transforming the Planet with a Zero-Point Energy Experiment; Dual Vortex Forms: The Key to a Large Zero-Point Energy Coherence. Packed with diagrams, patents and photos. With power shortages now a daily reality in many parts of the world, this book offers a fresh approach very rarely mentioned in the mainstream media.

224 PAGES. 6x9 PAPERBACK. ILLUSTRATED. $14.95. CODE: QZPE

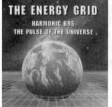

THE ENERGY GRID
Harmonic 695, The Pulse of the Universe
by Captain Bruce Cathie.

This is the breakthrough book that explores the incredible potential of the Energy Grid and the Earth's Unified Field all around us. Cathie's first book, *Harmonic 33*, was published in 1968 when he was a commercial pilot in New Zealand. Since then, Captain Bruce Cathie has been the premier investigator into the amazing potential of the infinite energy that surrounds our planet every microsecond. Cathie investigates the Harmonics of Light and how the Energy Grid is created. In this amazing book are chapters on UFO Propulsion, Nikola Tesla, Unified Equations, the Mysterious Aerials, Pythagoras & the Grid, Nuclear Detonation and the Grid, Maps of the Ancients, an Australian Stonehenge examined, more.

255 PAGES. 6x9 TRADEPAPER. ILLUSTRATED. $15.95. CODE: TEG

THE BRIDGE TO INFINITY
Harmonic 371244
by Captain Bruce Cathie

Cathie has popularized the concept that the earth is crisscrossed by an electromagnetic grid system that can be used for anti-gravity, free energy, levitation and more. The book includes a new analysis of the harmonic nature of reality, acoustic levitation, pyramid power, harmonic receiver towers and UFO propulsion. It concludes that today's scientists have at their command a fantastic store of knowledge with which to advance the welfare of the human race.

204 PAGES. 6x9 TRADEPAPER. ILLUSTRATED. $14.95. CODE: BTF

One Adventure Place
P.O. Box 74
Kempton, Illinois 60946
United States of America
Tel.: 815-253-6390 • Fax: 815-253-6300
Email: auphq@frontiernet.net
http://www.adventuresunlimitedpress.com
or www.adventuresunlimited.nl

ORDERING INSTRUCTIONS

✓ Remit by USD$ Check, Money Order or Credit Card

✓ Visa, Master Card, Discover & AmEx Accepted

✓ Prices May Change Without Notice

✓ 10% Discount for 3 or more Items

SHIPPING CHARGES

United States

✓ Postal Book Rate { $3.00 First Item / 50¢ Each Additional Item

✓ Priority Mail { $4.50 First Item / $2.00 Each Additional Item

✓ UPS { $5.00 First Item / $1.50 Each Additional Item
NOTE: UPS Delivery Available to Mainland USA Only

Canada

✓ Postal Book Rate { $6.00 First Item / $2.00 Each Additional Item

✓ Postal Air Mail { $8.00 First Item / $2.50 Each Additional Item

✓ Personal Checks or Bank Drafts MUST BE
USD$ and Drawn on a US Bank

✓ Canadian Postal Money Orders OK

✓ Payment MUST BE USD$

All Other Countries

✓ Surface Delivery { $10.00 First Item / $4.00 Each Additional Item

✓ Postal Air Mail { $14.00 First Item / $5.00 Each Additional Item

✓ Payment MUST BE USD$

✓ Checks and Money Orders MUST BE USD$
and Drawn on a US Bank or branch.

✓ Add $5.00 for Air Mail Subscription to
Future *Adventures Unlimited* Catalogs

SPECIAL NOTES

✓ RETAILERS: Standard Discounts Available

✓ BACKORDERS: We Backorder all Out-of-
Stock Items Unless Otherwise Requested

✓ PRO FORMA INVOICES: Available on Request

Please check: ✓

☐ This is my first order   ☐ I have ordered before

Name

Address

City

State/Province   Postal Code

Country

Phone day   Evening

Fax

Item Code	Item Description	Qty	Total

Please check: ✓

	Subtotal ▶	
	Less Discount-10% for 3 or more items ▶	
☐ Postal-Surface	Balance ▶	
☐ Postal-Air Mail	Illinois Residents 6.25% Sales Tax ▶	
(Priority in USA)	Previous Credit ▶	
	Shipping ▶	
☐ UPS		
(Mainland USA only)	Total (check/MO in USD$ only) ▶	

☐ Visa/MasterCard/Discover/Amex

Card Number

Expiration Date

10% Discount When You Order 3 or More Items!